THE THEORY OF
THE ARTS

Francis Sparshott

PRINCETON UNIVERSITY PRESS
PRINCETON, NEW JERSEY

Copyright © 1982 by Princeton University Press
Published by Princeton University Press,
41 William Street, Princeton, New Jersey
In the United Kingdom: Princeton University Press, Guildford, Surrey

ALL RIGHTS RESERVED
Library of Congress Cataloging in Publication Data will be
found on the last printed page of this book

Publication of this book has been aided by a grant from
The Canadian Federation for the Humanities, using funds provided by The
Social Sciences and Humanities Research Council of Canada

This book has been composed in Linotron Baskerville

Clothbound editions of Princeton University Press books
are printed on acid-free paper, and binding materials are
chosen for strength and durability

Printed in the United States of America by
Princeton University Press, Princeton, New Jersey

DIS MANIBVS
EDVARDI FRAENKEL
VIRI HVMANISSIMI
FAVTORIS BENEVOLI
DISCIPVLVS OLIM
QVIA MELIVS NEQVEO
HAEC INDIGNA
GRATO ANIMO
DICAVI

PREFACE

This book is the last of three surveys of parts of the field roughly designated as "aesthetics." The first, *The Structure of Aesthetics* (abbreviated herein to *SA*), sought to make the variety of aesthetic theories less bewildering by assigning them definite places within a schematic framework of all the kinds of questions that could be plausibly raised in aesthetics and all the answers of which they were logically susceptible. The second, *The Concept of Criticism* (hereafter cited as *CC*), sought to explain the various things critics of art and literature do by relating them to an everyday notion of what it is to criticize someone for doing something, or to criticize what he does, and showing how this commonplace activity can be expected to take special forms when it is done professionally or when it is applied to special objects. The third, part of which you are now reading, expounds what has to be said if one is to talk in very general terms about what art is and make some sort of sense while doing so. Its underlying contention is that general theories of art can only be understood when they are related to an old-fashioned kind of theory that we are all familiar with and in effect take for granted, though we mostly assume that it is so obsolete that the question of its relevance to our present concerns cannot even arise.

The present book, then, expounds a general theory of art. More precisely, it expounds a theory about theories of art. The main text presents, rather austerely, the main line of the explanation; side issues, however important in themselves, are relegated to notes and appendixes. The notes comment on the text in various tones from various angles. In reading to follow the argument of the book, it is better to ignore them; a more ruminative reading should take account of them. The extent of this annotation, its segregation at the end of the text, and on occasion the placing of the numbers that refer to it are matters on which I have insisted against the best advice.

I would like to think that my book assigns a suitable place, if only by implication, to most of what people have said about my subject at the appropriate level of generality. But I have not considered alternative views when to do so would not have furthered my argument. I have used three writers in ways that call for comment. One of them is Plato, whom I have used for four reasons, one of which is personal predilection. The other reasons are, first, that since he stands at the beginning of our philosophical tradition his positions are less elaborated and mystified than those of modern writers; second, that he still holds a privileged place in the intellectual traditions of our civilization, serving as a point of common reference in a way that no other author does; and third, that Western philosophy of art does in fact unfold from his work, developing out of, or reacting against, his specific doctrines. The second writer of whom I have made special use is Professor Joseph Margolis of Temple University. As will be explained in due course, chapters 6 to 8 appropriate a definition from one of his books (Margolis 1965) and develop it in a way its author seemed to use without being fully aware of it. Professor Margolis has now developed his argument in a book of his own (Margolis 1980a). Readers of his book and mine will find that even in the parts where we coincide we have very different styles and emphases; but his concerns and mine have much in common, and the reader should assume that in whatever we share he is the creditor and I the debtor. The third writer of whom I have made special use is myself. The frequency of reference to my own writings reflects a hope that they combine to form a corpus whose parts sustain and explain each other.

For the most part, I have not debated the views of others: my reasons for differing from them should appear sufficiently from the statement of my own position. My concern is to develop a coherent line of thought, and little of what other people have written proves to be of actual use when one's own direction has become specific. To accept the duty of responding to other writers is to commit oneself to their preoccupations and their formulations of the issues, which from one's own point of view appear merely as what one used to think before one started working. In fact, if one did not disagree with their starting point, one would be writing little articles and not a big book. I console myself with the thought that an article in a journal, even a learned journal, is journalism. What we value in Kant or Hegel is not their shrewd replies to Jacobi or Mendelssohn but what they found to say for themselves. It troubles some writers that the practice of writing before one has read everything must lead to a babel of mutually independent voices;[1] but it does not worry me. The proper time for order is in the past. The present is the storm front. And the tumult rectifies itself. No one reads everything, it is true, but everyone reads something and everything is read by someone. In time, everything is diffused in a sort of intellectual gene pool, and nothing is wholly lost.

Should one be writing a big book, anyway? At about the time when I was putting this one into its first shape, Cyril Barrett alluded to "a view, which has been prevalent in the English-speaking world for some time, that aestheticians, and, for that matter, philosophers generally, should declare a moratorium on all-embracing systems, and tackle particular problems" (Barrett 1966, vii). Actually, that phase has pretty well passed, but even in its heyday the answer was often voiced: a "particular problem" makes sense only within the framework of agreement within which it is raised. No such framework has ever been established for philosophy, and no such agreement reached.[2] Consequently, no such moratorium could be observed.

The basic idea for this book was formulated in 1965, and a first draft completed by 1970. So the book that took this final shape at the end of 1979 was ended at a different time of my life, in a different state of the academic world, and in a different state of the philosophy of art (a state that has known both Goodman and Dickie) from the innocent days of its inception. I trust that the result of all these internal transformations will be richness rather than confusion.

Thanks are due to Professor Geoffrey Payzant, who read the second draft and made helpful comments, and to three anonymous readers, who strove to save me from myself and sometimes succeeded. My work was assisted by a leave fellowship from the Canada Council in 1970–1971, and a research fellowship from that Council's Killam Programme in 1977–1978. Funds for typing the final version were provided by Victoria University and the University of Toronto, and the labor was expertly and cheerfully performed by June Hewitt, Margaret Imrie, Elizabeth MacGregor, Laurie Wallace, and Rea Wilmshurst. To all of these, my thanks.

Victoria College, Toronto

CONTENTS

LIST OF ABBREVIATIONS

APQ *American Philosophical Quarterly*
BJA *British Journal of Aesthetics*
CC F. E. Sparshott, *The Concept of Criticism* (Oxford: Clarendon Press, 1967)
JAAC *Journal of Aesthetics and Art Criticism*
JAE *Journal of Aesthetic Education*
JP *Journal of Philosophy*
PAS *Proceedings of the Aristotelian Society*
PG J. P. Migne, ed., *Patrologiae Cursus Completus, Series Graeca* (Paris: Migne, 1857–1887)
PQ *Philosophical Quarterly*
PR *Philosophical Review*
SA F. E. Sparshott, *The Structure of Aesthetics* (Toronto: University of Toronto Press, 1963)

The Theory of the Arts

I

INTRODUCTION

Art and Its Theory

Art is a simple matter. Consider five objects, all familiar at least by proxy: Leonardo's *Mona Lisa*, Shakespeare's *Hamlet*, Beethoven's *Eroica*, Dante's *Divine Comedy*, Michelangelo's *David*. Each of these is a work of art, if anything is; we would be more surprised if a history of the relevant art left them out than if it included them.[1] Suppose now that you found the experience of looking at, listening to, or reading one of these neither enjoyable nor interesting. You would then feel entitled to say that either you were not up to it (it was beyond you, or was not your kind of thing, or you were not in the mood) or it was no good. That is, you would have no doubt as to what standard should be applied in deciding if it was any good, although you yourself might be in no position to apply it. And the standard in each case would be essentially the same. There is really no doubt about what these things *are for*. If they were not made for that (something we might not know), at least that is what they are produced and promulgated, preserved and prized for; they are expected to provide worthwhile experiences merely in being listened to, looked at, or read. The less doubt we have that that is what a thing is for, the more confidently we take it to be a work of art. All that part of life which consists of the production, enjoyment, study, and other activity in relation to such objects we refer to in a loose and vague way as "art"; the practices of producing different sorts of them are the arts, and the people who produce them are artists.

There is, then, really no problem about what art is and what art is for. Nor is there anything that cries out for explanation in the practice of art. It is plainly something that people find engrossing and enjoyable in all its aspects. We see everywhere people intensely absorbed in the production of works of art for themselves and others, and other people hardly less intent on the enjoyment of scrutinizing them. How could anything so evidently found to be of such direct value be considered problematic, or be thought to stand in need of theory?[2] Of course, art might distract one from other valuable or necessary occupations, but that is only because one cannot do two things at once, and every good is a potential rival of every other good. One might indeed say that art is put to many uses, and claimed to serve many purposes, and that these uses and purposes call urgently for examination. But why should they? They will be extraneous to the value for which art is evidently prized and practiced; why should we concern ourselves with such incidental advantages? May there be many such! It is not in this sense that a good stands in the way of another good. Art theory seems to be much more of a problem than art is, because the purport of art theory is to place restrictions on the manifold good of art, or to impose extraneous demands on what is already found sufficiently good.

All sorts of problems lurk beneath the surface of what I have just written. These problems are what books like this one deal with. But the surface itself is clear, and it is important not to lose sight of this superficial clarity. One can too easily be tricked or shamed—by fancy arguments or by blatant appeals to one's humility—into making a mystery of art. And one may then come to suppose that art is somehow suspect, in need of justification before the bar of reason, its evident worth insufficient without some further values that a profound theorist might find in or behind it. But it is not so. Art needs nothing from theory.

If art is a simple matter, why should it become a problem? A man who paints pictures or writes poems is doing something that is of absorbing interest to himself and may give harmless pleasure to others. Even if it seems strange that this should be so, we might as well accept it. Not everything about people can be explained or need be. Yet art has become problematic. This seems to have happened in three ways. First, it has come to be supposed that poets and painters are in some sense doing the same sort of thing, and it is not easy to say in what sense this is so. Second, it is claimed that the class of activities to which both poetry and painting belong may also include the most diverse forms of behavior, such as leading cows through a maze or proposing to wrap a countryside in cellophane. Some such claims are hotly disputed, and it is not easy to see how they are to be assessed. Finally, it is claimed that all such activities are *important*, and that their importance has nothing to do with any simple pleasure they may give. People who have to do with works of art only for the pleasure and interest they find in them can find this claim very unsettling.

These three ways in which art has become problematic add up to a sort of imperialism. The various arts form an alliance, annex neighboring states, and proclaim themselves an empire with a historic mission. What art theory does is mostly to scrutinize the credentials of this empire.

Some people say that such scrutinizing of credentials is a waste of time. Art being the simple matter it always was, such complexities are a matter of power politics and may be left for history and sociology to disentangle. Nor are theorists required to define the word "art," which is used in such different ways in different contexts that one cannot suppose that there is any systematic connection to be found between the various uses. But it is too late for such heroic measures. Art theory already exists. It is too plentiful and too popular to be ignored. In fact, the very arguments I used to show that art theory was gratuitous may be turned around and used in its defense. People do theorize about art freely, and with gusto, and it is natural that they should.[3] Since art is of absorbing interest, it would be absurd not to talk about it; and talk that rises above gossip enters the domain of theory. Besides, though art as a whole may need nothing from theory, an artist and his supporters may feel a very practical need to give reasons why attention should be turned their way, or to explain how an excellence not evident here and now will become clear when rightly viewed. The problematic moves in art and its theory often come from the inertia of practice, as an artist takes what seems to him the natural or inevitable next step along a road on which he inevitably becomes more and more lonely. The resulting diversity of lonelinesses is such as already to cast doubt on our initial simplicities. But the exigencies of isolation fall far short of explaining the tangled mess of inchoate theorizing that accompanies the creation of art. The arts seem always to have been the sort of activity one explains and argues about as one engages in it.[4] Perhaps the fact that art is felt to call for a lot of explanation is one of the things about art that most needs explaining.

People theorize incessantly about the arts, and will go on doing so. Since many of those people will be better at art than at theory, it can hardly be out of place for a professed theorist to bring a little order and clarity into the theorizing.[5] What are the alternatives? To leave people to get on as best they can? But unless all theories are equally clear, equally defensible, and of equal scope, there is no special merit in such renunciation. One might certainly turn away from all such theorizing in disgust at its abstaction, its inadequacy to the subtlety and richness of our more specific engagements with art. But to do so might be rather like rejecting all maps because they fail to reveal the concrete experience of the terrain. That might be a foolish thing to do. Certainly, all actual maps are full of errors. No useful road map, however free from errors, can be detailed enough to tell one much about the countryside, and no map whatever can indicate what it is like to live in the place it maps. But that is no reason for giving up maps altogether or for using maps only of places one cannot visit. Even a close and intimate knowledge of a place is no more a substitute for a map than the map is a substitute for it, nor does such knowledge make even a bad map useless. Maps provide a supplementary orientation, a kind of summary overview that fills its own place. So too one might think that a highly general theory would provide an orientation for reflection at a level on which we often reflect and are surely not wrong to do so. Why should we not try to frame reasonable notions about the general purport and interrelations of the main sorts of things people do with their lives? One might concede that point and still wonder what such a general theory could possibly contain. Obviously it could not say everything about every issue. On what principles could one decide what to put in, what to leave out?[6] But a general theory of art is not one that purports to tell the whole truth about art. It is rather one that seeks to indicate what art is all about, where art fits into the general scheme of social life, what we are asking ourselves when we wonder what art is, and so on. And such questions, though general in the sense that their scope is broad, are as specific as any others.

Someone might concede that the spinning of general theories about art is humanly and practically justifiable, as I have argued, but objectionable in principle: the very notion of a general theory of art is an absurdity, so that what passes for such, if it contrives to make sense, would more properly go under another name. One such objection formed a basic principle of *SA*, in which I urged that a theory could not be defined by a subject matter (such as art) but only by a problem to which it essayed a solution. But that objection, if it has any force at all, fails to rule out such a theory as we are here considering. In the first place, as I have just suggested, it is not obvious that "What is Art?" is not a specific problem in the required sense. In the second place, the objection will not hold if the concept that forms the subject matter is one developed, as the concept of art was, in response to a theoretical demand rather than to the pressures of everyday discourse, for such a subject matter embodies the specific concerns that led to its formulation. In the third place, the objection would not hold if the subject matter was not a mass of phenomena but a set of activities defined by a function or complex of functions in relation to other human activities,[7] for the general theory would then have the clear task of establishing what that function (if any) was, how it was determined, and so on.[8] Nor will the objection hold if art is not a kind of thing but a way of thinking about things.

Another objection to the very idea of a general theory of art purports to derive from the thought of Ludwig Wittgenstein. A word like "art," one argues, takes definite meaning only from the exact way it is used in this or that context of life. In general philosophical theories, such a context is lacking: the language idles, the verbal machinery is not connected to anything. This objection certainly has weight, as a warning that whatever a philosopher may say can have no authority over the serious and complex engagements of life. But the precise measure of that weight is hard to assess; indeed, the objection almost defeats itself. Not only is it itself a theory of a very general sort, but it invites the rejoinder that theorizing is an activity like any other, a language game with familiar rules, a part (however sluggish) of the stream of life. The theorizer uses the word "art," not without any context, but with a theoretical context: the only question is just *what* machinery the spinning wheels are meshed with. Wittgenstein wrote as if he thought philosophers would stop doing philosophy as soon as they realized that what they were doing was not identical with some other, reputable activity. They continued to philosophize, perceiving correctly that philosophy was itself a reputable and long established activity, to the nature of which Wittgenstein never paid serious attention. The appropriate response to this sort of objection would therefore seem to be caution in theorizing rather than abstention from theory.

Though one may insist that the idea of a general theory of art makes some sense, and that one might produce a theory to which such a description would be apt, and that such a theory would have some use in ordering one's reflections on a matter of general interest, actually to propose such a theory requires some hardihood. The project of bringing new order and clarity into theorizing about art is presumptuous and foolish. Existing theories of art were framed by people most of whom were at least as intelligent and well informed as we are; a new theory is accordingly unlikely to annihilate them, and if it exists alongside them it will only add to the mess. Nor can we expect that future theorists, equally bright and knowledgeable, will be reduced to silence because we have spoken. Order and clarity, it seems, cannot be introduced by superseding or preempting alternative theories. They could only come from a framework within which the relations of various theories could be discerned and their justifications and limitations mapped in such a way that the choice of a limited theory remained a live option but was not imposed as a necessity. And the same framework could provide a schema for justifying or deploring any practices in the arts that depended on such theories for their justification.

Theorizing about art has involved radical disagreements both about what art is and about what is art, about how to describe the phenomena and about what phenomena are to be described. It is hard to see how theories that differ not only in what they assert but also in what they assert it about can be regarded as alternatives to each other. There are three likely explanations of all such strange rivalries. One is that rival groups are trying to take over a social institution with its associated roles and privileges. Another is that tendencies and processes stemming from a common root have taken divergent directions and are claiming legitimacy against each other. The third is that practitioners of rival practices are each claiming for their own doings a certain kind of esteem. If, as I suspect, all three explanations apply to the present case, a reconciling frame of reference might take the form of a schematized and rationalized history tracing the dynamic relations of the concepts and institutions (together with their associated practices and values) around which the ideological battles rage.

Present Purposes

What this book attempts is fundamentally a dehistoricized history of the kind I have just mentioned: a rational reconstruction of the logical relationships whose half-systematic exploration has formed the history of the philosophy of art. But it is in no sense a history. The ideas are systematically set out, as permanently possible ways of thinking, in an attempt to provide a coherent way of thinking about art for the future rather than to recount how it has been thought of in the past.[9]

If one could find an approach to art that not only evidently suited its subject but had some claim to be the only proper one, and if one could develop that approach from a natural beginning to an inevitable conclusion, and in doing so could combine a single coherent way of organizing all one's thought about art with a demonstration that all other approaches are partly justified but ultimately limited, one could claim to have produced not one theory of art among others but *the* theory of art. Such would have been the aspiration of this book. But it seems only an idle dream. There will always be other ways of doing things, and even on the way one has chosen one cannot rid oneself entirely of discontinuities and arbitrary decisions. Nonetheless, such preemptive inclusiveness has been my ideal. Accordingly, I have accepted the duty of dullness. Grand speculations and breathtaking challenges are certainly not out of place in discussing art or anything else. They are almost always interesting and exciting rather than true, but truth is not everything—we need truth only where our livelihoods are concerned, but we like excitement whenever we can get it. Unfortunately, systematic inclusiveness demands a plodding sobriety. It may well be a philosophical virtue to do as little philosophy as possible. In any case, the following account aims to be serious, plain, and useful to the perplexed.

It is not only philosophical sobriety that gives this book the kind of dullness it has.[10] A contributing cause is the level of generality it works on. A theory that aims at general orientations cannot discuss all problems or affirm all the possibilities it envisages. Rather, it assigns a place to the former and describes the latter, reducing to a dismissive phrase what suitable rhetoric and exemplification could have (and often has) filled a wise book with. But there is also a more specific reason for my aridity.

The most exciting theories about art, the ones most quoted and debated, are those that affirm or deny an interesting relation between art and some pressing concern of one's contemporaries or of humanity at large. That is no accident. To ask what art is all about must be to ask how it is related to the necessary concerns of mankind, and that would certainly be interesting to know. But such theories operate at a lower level of generality than that which concerns me.[11] Most of them seek to establish a relation between some kind of human interest that is independently established, or, more often, independently conjectured or stipulated,[12] and art as a going concern whose general nature is supposed to be already understood. It is that going concern, supposedly understood but never fully accounted for, that is my affair. In most cases, the relation between art and its assigned function turns out to be contingent. The theorist points out a purpose that art can and no doubt often does serve, but does little to show that art has no other purpose to serve or that only art could serve that purpose. The relation may be interesting and striking, but the claim that such a theory holds for all art would be absurd:[13] the claim could be upheld only by stipulating that nothing that fails to serve the alleged purpose is art, or *real* art. No one in his senses would make such a stipulation.[14] One can hardly expect to intimidate those whose main artistic interest lies in what is thus excluded, much less those who have made similar stipulations in favor of some different function.

It is not quite so silly as it might have been to hope that a rational reconstruction of an ideal history might come close to providing a unique theory of art. Until recently all thought about art shared a common tradition, whose single source lay in ancient philosophy and ultimately in the thought of one man. That man was Plato, who made the concept of an art one of the key terms in his system. The argument of this book therefore begins by exploring the implications of this classical concept of an art (Latin *ars*, Greek *technê*), the neglected foundation of all later speculation. Since this concept has to do with the relation of intelligence to action, our topic is thus anchored in the philosophy of action and hence in the philosophy of mind.

The Platonic concept of an art has nothing specifically to do with what we nowadays call art in the sense of "the fine arts," but includes (what are indeed Plato's own prime examples) medicine and statecraft no less than music. Our next task is therefore to consider how, if at all, a set of "fine" arts can be distinguished from all others. There are two accepted ways of doing this, and it turns out that each leads to the other. In terms of the resulting concept of a fine art we then develop notions of what it is to be a work of art and what it is to be an artist. (One might have expected the notions of an art, a work of art, and an artist to be simply interdefinable. Most theorists take it for granted that they are. But they are not.)

The development of the notions of a fine art, a work of art, and an artist from the general concept of an art constitutes what I take to be the normal theory of art. But it has a fatal weakness. It has no place for the general notion of art itself in the sense in which that term has come to play a key part in our thinking about the arts; yet it leads inevitably to the formulation of that notion. That normal theory of art has accordingly to be supplemented by alternative notions of what art is and does, each with its associated concept of an art, of a work of art, and of an artist. Much confusion in thinking about art is a result of slipping unawares from one of these sets of notions to another. My inquiry follows an examination of the general idea of art by examining three of these rival sets of notions, and explains them as reacting against some one aspect of my "normal" theory and emphasizing others. I argue that they are as one-sided and incomplete as this explanation of them would suggest. But I also argue that we need them. The line of thought represented by the "normal" theory will be called the *classical line*. Rejection of its emphasis on skill yields the *poetic line*, according to which art is the creation of new realities. When the poetic line is fully articulated it becomes the *expressive line*, for which art is the expression of unanalyzable intuitions. Rejection of the aestheticism of the classical line, its emphasis on "contemplation," yields the *mystic line*, according to which art relates us to the underlying realities of the universe. Rejection of its elitism and consumerism yields the *purist line*, for which art is activity eminent in its uselessness. If it could be shown that no other lines of thinking about art in general were viable, and that these four—or five, if the poetic line be granted an individuality separate from that of the expressive line—could be systematically interrelated in no other way than the one essayed here, the claim to have given an account (however lame) of *the* theory of art, rather than to have developed (however brilliantly) one theory of art among others, would receive some support. It does not seem that anything of the kind could be established, even if it were true, for only a logically exhaustive classification can be shown to be complete, and such a classification must in the end cheat by setting up a classification for "everything else." But I hope that the book makes out a good enough case to sustain interest.

Philosophy of Art: Three Hard Words

The present inquiry falls within the scope of the philosophy of art. What, then, is the philosophy of art? The question is as debatable as any of the questions within its scope. But some preliminary remarks will help to indicate the general orientation of this book.

The phrase "philosophy of art" is made up of three hard words. With regard to the first of these, although there is not much argument about what is included in philosophy and what is not, there is a lot of argument about what the proper task of philosophy is, how that task should be carried out, and how it may be fittingly described. That question cannot be settled here, and probably cannot be settled at all.[15] The view assumed in this book equates philosophy with deliberative discourse about meanings. A philosopher tries by argument to reach and guide decisions about what it would be best to say and how it would be best to think. It is not his business to establish what is definitely the case, a task that when formalized belongs to science. His discourse is thus deliberative and in this sense belongs to the realm of practice rather than to that of theory. Philosophy is for making up minds. The subject matter of this deliberative discourse is meanings, in whatever sense may be given to that word. There are different views about what may properly be said to be or to have a meaning, and these different notions answer to different views about what philosophy is and does.[16] Thinkers who maintain that only words and their combinations can have meaning hold that philosophy has to do with language and nothing else. Thinkers who insist that life and the world can be meaningful hold accordingly that philosophy must try to make sense of the world and of man's place in it. Thinkers who hold that, although it really makes no sense to ascribe (or deny) meaning to the world at large, human activities may be meaningful and hence proper objects for interpretation will conclude that nothing human is alien to philosophy. Since art is certainly a human activity, I do not have to choose between the second and third of these positions. But one would expect a philosophy of art to go somewhat beyond the first: if any nonlinguistic activities have meanings that lend themselves to deliberative discourse, art is surely among them. For this very reason if for no other, however, many philosophers of art would hold that art is itself a linguistic activity, even if they have to redefine "language" to make it one.

"Art" is another hard word, and the whole of this inquiry is devoted to softening it up. In the context of such a phrase as "philosophy of art," it can mean any of at least five distinct things—in other contexts it can mean many other things, but the context of serious general discussion confines it for the most part to these five.[17] First, "art" can stand for a level of spiritual accomplishment or intellectual insight. Second, it sometimes means the products of the arts of painting and drawing and other related arts, perhaps including sculpture. Third, it may refer to the products of all the activities loosely grouped together as the fine arts. Fourth, it might mean the practice of producing such objects together with such production. Finally, it might (but nowadays seldom does) mean that human faculty or class of human activities which has to do with the production of anything. The present inquiry does not opt for one of these at the expense of the others, but proceeds from the last to the first, following the precedent of the classical authors who drew attention to the importance of art in the last sense but did not go on to relate it to any of the other four. Among the moderns, Etienne Gilson (1957 and 1963) has insisted on the importance of giving priority to the fourth sense over the first three, but has rather perversely denied the others any independent status. In getting from the fourth sense to the third, I have borrowed a train of thought from Joseph Margolis (1965). The second sense, though most common in other contexts, has no special relevance to inquiries of the present genre, so I ignore it.[18] Finally, how we get from the third sense to the first is a long story, and the second half of the book tells it.

Over and above these five, everyone uses the word "art" in the way I mentioned at the start of this chapter—as a vague general gesture toward the whole area of our life that is marked out by the scope of all five of the senses specified and a good many others as well. Often, in the course even of this book on the theory of art, I shall say "art" and mean by it nothing in particular: "all *that* sort of thing." Art, we might say, like politics or religion, is a *Lebensform*—if only one knew just what that meant.[19]

There is a very special sort of vagueness in the way we sort out our activities into these grand domains, and a very special and quite necessary vagueness in this gestural use of language to refer to them. We say "art" and mean: "over *there*." And we do not necessarily mean thereby to refer to the whole of that shadowy-edged domain, only to something in that direction, perhaps all or part of what some more special sense of "art" would designate, that is uppermost in our minds at the time; and we may not know at all what it is. It follows that someone who makes a general statement about "art," since he may not even have decided just what he is referring to, is unlikely to be clear in his own mind as to whether what he is saying is to hold universally of all that he himself would identify as art, or for the most part, or only occasionally; and, consequently, it is unlikely to be clear even to himself whether he could be confuted by a single counterexample or only by a statistical survey or a religious conversion. In everyday life we often use words in this way, varying both the point of their use and the range of phenomena they cover almost from sentence to sentence as the flow of discourse suggests ever new problems and relationships. Such flexibility represents, perhaps, the kind of intelligence suitable to a brain, a machine that consists of millions of semiinsulated units rather than the few perfectly insulated switches of a computer and is called upon not to solve complex but specifiable problems so much as simultaneously to create and respond to indefinitely many situations for action. But terms cannot be used in this way in formal arguments, in which we demand consistency, for consistency rests on the use of terms with constant and identifiable (and hence definable) meanings. Logicians must think like computers, not like people. In serious discussions one tends to use terms as nearly as may be in the way that formal argument requires, and hence to avoid such terms as "art" in its generic sense; but it is arguable that it is foolish to deprive ourselves of the resources of flexible intelligence, and that the logical intractability of such language is rather a reason to refrain from pushing statements that use it to logical or metaphysical conclusions. And in fact such assertions of quite indeterminate scope abound not only in casual conversation but even in the writings of theorists, especially of those whose theorizing flows as naturally as talk.[20] Although no argument can be based on them, and no argument can be effectively directed against them, they play an essential part in the thinking and talking through which we find our bearings in the world and form our strategies for living. Epigrams and proverbs have something of the same character. This book will no doubt abound in them, though I trust that no inferences will be drawn from any of them. They are addressed "as man to man," relying on the tact of mutual adjustment that forms a basis of all communication; if you get what I am driving at, there's no more to be got.

People talk about "art," then, and we know what they mean. If a philosopher says, as many do, that he *does not know* what they mean by the term, he should mean only that it is impossible to give a single consistent account of how the term functions. He should not mean (though sometimes he does) that what they say is gibberish; but they for their part should not suppose (though often they do) that their usage is really somehow consistent, if only they could hit on the right explanation.

In any dictionary, it is the shortest words that take up the most room, and of the three words in "philosophy of art," the word "of" could be the hardest. It might be genitive. Philosophy of art would then consist of all those problems and considerations suggested to philosophy by reflecting on art, the status of which would be that of a source of enlightenment for philosophers (which is how Schelling took it). Conversely, the "of" could be possessive, in which case the philosophy of art would be an attempt by philosophy to explain something about art: instead of art serving philosophy as a resource, philosophy would use all its resources in the service of art. This view too has been taken.[21] But the "of" could be simply connective, in which case philosophy of art would consist of an assortment of problems that happened to be connected with art and to require philosophical techniques or concerns for their solution; that is how most textbooks take it. The most ambitious philosophers, such as Hegel, try to combine all three relations. They start with a set of large notions about the world and use these notions to explain the significance of art, but they pretend that this explanation is forced on them by the nature of art itself and thus affords an independent support for the large notions from which it was in fact derived. The argument is made to look weightier than it is by using the same terminology to discuss as many incidental questions as possible, thus producing the illusion that the system is all-embracing when all that has really happened is that the philosopher has failed to vary his vocabulary to suit the subject matter.

The present inquiry takes the word "of" in the second way. It presumes the reader's prior interest to be in art rather than in the universe at large. It seeks to provide a way of thinking consistently about art, one that will neither impose nor obstruct any set of critical judgments and will not pretend to determine what new products and practices are to win a place in the disputed domain of art.

Philosophy of Art and Its Neighbors and Rivals

Several current words and phrases pick out disciplines or areas of concern that may be thought either to be identical with the philosophy of art or to take over its territory. Chief among these words is "aesthetics," which I initially used to pick out the general area to which my inquiry belongs.

"Aesthetics," even when confined to philosophical inquiries,[22] is an ambiguous term. For simplicity's sake, we can distinguish a broad sense and a narrow sense. In the broad sense, it includes all philosophical questions having to do with art or beauty.[23] To equate aesthetics with the philosophy of art, as is often done,[24] is therefore to make one of two implausible assumptions: either that no one finds beauty in anything other than a work of art or that the beauty found in things other than works of art cannot possibly be a matter for philosophical concern. The former of these needs no argument for its refutation. The latter is rendered implausible by the fact that eminent philosophers from Plato on have written about beauty without confining it to art. Perhaps all those philosophers were foolish, but that would have to be shown, not assumed. One could certainly argue that aesthetics and philosophy of art were for all practical purposes the same on the grounds that the beauties of art do not differ in any significant way from those of nature (cf. Collingwood 1925). But that too would need to be shown and is hard to believe. For example, works of art are usually thought to be proper objects for critical evaluation and exegesis, and the works of nature are not.

One might agree that the equation of aesthetics with philosophy of art is implausible and still insist that the philosophy of art is a *branch* of aesthetics. Aesthetics would be a general study of the human concern with beautiful things; the philosophy of art would be that branch of aesthetics which dealt with the special forms this concern took when it was directed toward things made by men. But this view is open to two related objections. First, to make the interest in art a special case of the love of beauty denies the status of the arts as forms of communication and cultural expression (cf. Gadamer 1960). It both reflects and fosters that degradation of the arts which Tolstoy deplored, in which they are thought of as (and thus actually become) mere amusements and decorations. The second objection to the inclusion of philosophy of art within aesthetics is that it tends to treat works of art as *found objects*. But works of art are made before they are enjoyed. Not only does their status as things made by people radically affect the way we perceive them and think about them, but the making itself is a human activity that one would expect to be more rather than less an expression of human intelligence than the appreciation and criticism of them. Surely the natural order of proceeding for a philosophy of art would be to start with a study of artistic creation. But to treat philosophy of art as a division of aesthetics casts doubt on the legitimacy of this procedure. There may be an end in which it comes to the same thing: it may be that the productive activity is adequately defined by the character evident in the product and by the interest that product serves, and that the beauties of art are so evidently and intimately related to their human origin that aesthetics inevitably goes on to consider the creative activity. But it is as well to get things in their right order.

The word "aesthetics" was originally coined to mean something much more specific than the philosophy of art and beauty. It was to form a sort of counterpart of logic. What logic did for analyzable symbols aesthetics was to do for unanalyzable symbols: logic is to ratiocination as aesthetics is to intuition.[25] If such symbols are identified with art, aesthetics and the philosophy of art turn out to be the same. But this equation rests on a special and highly controversial interpretation of the data with which it deals, so it is unwise to commit oneself to it at the outset of one's inquiries.[26]

The classical writers to whom all writers on aesthetics look back were concerned with a question subtly different from those that preoccupy their successors. What interested them was the fact that men find some things immediately attractive without regard for their use, and this attraction is a powerful motivating force. What, they asked, is the nature of this attraction, and what does it show about men and the world they live in? The foundation work of this study, sometimes called "callology," is Plato's *Symposium*, in which works of art play only a minor part.[27] But in the eighteenth century, when the study was once more ardently pursued, works of art took the center of the stage. The reason for this change of emphasis was that the beauties of such works are the objects of an acquired taste—a taste that is manifestly molded by education and cultural convention, yet can be made the object of rational discussion and appears in some form to be universal among men. The phenomena of artistic taste therefore lent support to those moralists of the day who liked to think that morality could vary according to social circumstance and training without being wholly a matter of arbitrary convention or directly explicable in terms of social utility.[28] Such thinkers postulated a moral sense, malleable yet innate, on the supposed analogy of a sense of beauty that education could modify but neither create nor annihilate. In the context of their concerns, works of art figured as *objets d'art*, which the connoisseur relished without needing to consider either their origins or their human significance. Whether as the theory of taste or as the classical study of idealism in general, such callology seems to be suitably equated neither with the philosophy of art nor with aesthetics in either of the two senses we have outlined: neither its scope nor its motivation is the same as theirs.

Some recent philosophers have equated philosophy with logic. What the word "logic" means when it enters into this equation is by no means clear, but it has to be some sort of inquiry into the meaning of language. Such philosophers have to deny that philosophy can deal with art otherwise than by discussing what already has been or might be said about it. Consequently, since criticism comprises all that is characteristic in the discussion of art, they take both aesthetics and the philosophy of art to be identical with the philosophy of criticism.[29] Philosophers who do not equate philosophy with logic will wish to maintain that the philosophy of art and that of criticism must overlap but need not coincide.

Certain fashionable disciplines, primarily concerned with the theory of literature and language, bid fair to replace or subsume aesthetics and therewith the philosophy of art. Of these, the most general in scope is semiotics. Theoretically, this would be the discipline that studied all forms of symbol-using behavior, including art, gesture, speech, and every sort of animal communication, providing an integrated terminology and an overriding theory together, perhaps, with a common set of axioms or models.[30] Linguistics and the philosophy of art would figure, if at all, as special sciences within this larger unity much as zoology and botany figure within biology.[31]

The idea of semiotics derives from Saussure's rather narrower notion of a semiology, which would be confined to signs that operate within such cultural communication systems as languages.[32] And it is as a development from linguistics that this type of theory has had most influence. Strong claims for its relevance to art are based on R. Jakobson's subsumption of poetics within structural linguistics.[33] But the claimants have not noticed that Jakobson's takeover bid was not supported by enough theoretical resources to buy up many of the shares. At present, the prospect of effective subsumption seems remote, and the terms "semiotics" and "semiology" stand for little more than the conviction that these ranges of phenomena must somehow inevitably admit of a unified treatment and the decision to talk about them all at once. But the program remains an attractive one and certainly provides one of the contexts within which art and works of art must be considered.[34]

Akin to semiotics and even more closely related to semiology are the ways of thinking, mostly French, that go by the name of structuralism. As with some other French intellectual movements, such as the *politique des auteurs* in the criticism of film, it is not clear whether structuralism should be thought of primarily as a discipline, as a methodology, or as a doctrine in that its practitioners do not always distinguish between the field they investigate, the way they investigate that field, and the results of their investigation.[35] But that is our problem, not theirs, and they might well retort that the distinctions we say they ignore are unreal: the method is what determines the field and dictates the results, the required results demand the method and identify the field, the field yields only to the one method and its characterization is completed by the results.

Not all books with the word "structuralism" in the title and dealing with art or literature turn out to be concerned with the same topic. In fact, the word sometimes means little more than "whatever the French have been saying about literary theory lately." To speak roughly—and to speak otherwise would require an extensive survey of writing in the fields of linguistics and criticism—three different sorts of things have been called structuralism. One of them is of little interest to us: it is that type of literary criticism which, like the American New Criticism, treats the literary work as a self-contained entity but, unlike that movement, seeks to relate works to a typology of rhetorical and narrative structures.[36] More interesting to us is a movement in speculative anthropology, associated with the name of Claude Lévi-Strauss, that seeks to interpret all cultural phenomena within a given society in terms of a fixed set of relations (normally reducible to binary relations) that will be found embodied in, for example, its kinship system and its dietary habits as well as in its mythology. The society transforms its world into culture by consistently describing it in terms of this mythical pattern; and, since the mythology is projected onto the world, culture in turn becomes nature. For the people of such a society, and for the anthropologist who understands it, everything becomes a text: the trail to the well is a piece of "writing" to be deciphered no less than a dedicatory statue or a folk tale. To this way of thinking a work of art, if that concept retains any distinctive meaning, is distinguished from other objects, not by its patterning or its meaningfulness, since everything is patterned and meaningful in much the same way, but by the fact that it does nothing else or does it conspicuously: it not only manifests but in one way or another celebrates cultural form. It is obvious that if that is what art and its works are and do, there is no place for a philosophy of art: it will be swallowed up in a philosophy of culture, which in turn will be little more than an abstract anthropology. Before welcoming that prospect, one should bear in mind that it apparently entails that no work of art can have any meaning or any real interest outside the culture to which it belongs.[37] One should also note that it assigns a merely marginal significance to the specific content of representational works and to the aesthetic aspects of any works.[38]

19

The third thing that goes by the name of structuralism is a doctrine promoted by Roland Barthes (1970) and to some extent by Jacques Derrida (1967). Jonathan Culler has in fact urged that the word be used in this sense alone, on the ground that no other precisely stated doctrine can be found for the word to mean (1975, 4). Barthes essentially uses notions derived from structural linguistics and information theory to effect a destructuring of works of art—specifically, of literary texts. Whereas the notion of a work of art requires that a text or artifact be interpreted as a single organized entity in which the various strands and shades of meaning are integrated in a strict hierarchy supposedly determined by the author's intention,[39] what a text actually contains is an indeterminate multiplicity of interplaying meanings,[40] a skein of expectations aroused and deferred and at last partially satisfied in terms of many cultural codes of reference.[41] The critic can unravel these, but has no warrant for imposing on them any hierarchy or any determinate pattern of interrelation.[42] The defining unity of the work of art is denied, or, more significantly, demoted in favor of textural qualities in the work.[43]

It is easy to object to Barthes' thesis that his own practice in *S/Z* demonstrates that his principles are bogus, since the significance of every point he makes about the reading of Balzac's *Sarrasine* depends on his and our knowledge of the determinate structure of that work; the fact remains that Barthes appears as a champion of the reader's rights to enjoy any literary work, and by extension any work of art, in his own way.

It will be seen that the kind of thought I have attributed to Barthes is the very opposite of structuralism in the first sense I identified. Like that, it develops some themes of structuralism in the second sense, but in the opposite direction. Does this third kind of structuralism, like the second, constitute a possible rival or successor to the philosophy of art, or is it, like the first, just another theory of criticism? The latter seems to be the case. Its pantextuality, its conversion of everything into writing, has no revolutionary consequences. Its attitude to its objects remains aesthetic and interpretive in exactly the way that traditional theories of the aesthetic have laid down. In extending the approach (insofar as it does so) to phenomena other than paradigmatic works of art, it assimilates them to art rather than assimilating art to them. And its denial of unique structure and of hierarchy and concomitant insistence on textures lie well within the scope of normal philosophy of art.[44]

The term "hermeneutics" does the same job for German thought that "structuralism" does for French thought, namely, serving as a blanket term for whatever is modish in the critical theory of that national tradition. But, like "structuralism," the word has a history and a core of definite meaning. Originally, the word meant the methodology of interpreting sacred texts. Its original impetus is thus quite the opposite of that of structuralism: interpreting a sacred text may indeed be like seeing pictures in the fire, but one cannot admit that it is, and the Author's meaning remains authoritative and (in principle) recoverable across whatever distance of space, time, or cultural change. Taken out of its theological context, hermeneutics accordingly becomes the general study of the interpretation of texts, with special reference to problems arising from the double relation of a text's inherent meaning to the context of its origin and to the context of its enjoyment. As such, it is a subsidiary inquiry within the theory of criticism and in that capacity will concern us later on. I mention it here because it has been given a more general application. Originally, hermeneutics deals only with texts, which it treats as messages whose meaning cannot but be transformed but must somehow be preserved from one context to the other. But anyone's dealing with any historical, cultural, or personal phenomenon requires that he understand it, and this effectively transforms it into a message: it had its original meaning, and it has its meaning for him. Hermeneutics thus becomes a general philosophy of cultural meanings and transactions. As such, it overlaps the philosophy of art and indeed dissolves it. In hermeneutic inquiries, it is possible for the fine arts and their works to lose their differentiating characteristics and become just part of the general *Gestalt* of the culture or the individual mentality to which they relate. One may then think of hermeneutics either as superseding the philosophy of art, by destroying the distinctness of its subject matter, or as providing an alternative to the philosophy of art by treating the appropriate material of the latter from a point of view no more and no less valid than its own. Our present enterprise commits us to the latter possibility, for which there are in any case two good reasons. The first is that works of art are not merely messages, if they are messages at all. They are also monuments, to be considered as achievements in their own right. The second reason for not abandoning the field to hermeneutics is that the latter typically presupposes that its objects have unique and ascertainable meanings for originator and recipient. The philosopher of art should not start by supposing this, though he may conclude it. In fact, hermeneutics tends to retain certain peculiarities stemming from

21

its origin: the demands a believer makes on a sacred text are so special that a study designed to satisfy them can hardly be extended to deal with other kinds of interest without awkwardness.

In any case, what this book contains is not callology, not strictly aesthetics, not all philosophy of criticism, not hermeneutics, not structuralism or semiology, and only accidentally semiotics. It is the philosophy of art, in the form to which that phrase seems most appropriate. The starting point that defines my approach is the classical definition of art, to which I now turn.

PART I

ARTS

II

THE CLASSICAL LINE
1: ARTS

The Concept of an Art

Our study takes its start from some obvious truths about people. Among those truths are these:

—that people spend their lives making things and doing things;
—that they can reflect on what they make and do;
—that they can tell what other people make and do;
—that things can be made and done well or badly;
—that people can tell when something made or done is the same sort of thing, or the very same thing, that was made or done before;
—that conscious skill and knowledge can be brought to the making and doing of things;
—and that such skill and knowledge can themselves be reflected on and developed.

Nothing is more characteristic of people than that they think about what they do and try to do better. More specifically, they think about what they have done and try to *do the same* thing better. Learning in animals is a matter of repeating successes and not repeating failures. Human beings reflect on the causes of success and failure and so discover natural laws; these laws, being unobvious systems of likeness and difference between situations and events, enable them to extend the range of their successes.[1] Unlike other animals, men learn beyond the range of their experience, and can expect to succeed at things they have never tried. As knowledge and skill thus become generalized beyond that element in experience which is evidently repeated, they develop into concatenations of reliable and applicable practical principles. These concatenations are the organizations that early philosophers called arts.

In reflecting on the skill and knowledge whereby things are well made or done, men come to formulate standards by which making and doing are judged. In developing that skill and knowledge, men come to found institutions in which making and doing are taught and skill and knowledge are preserved and enhanced. To be thus preserved and enhanced and judged by standards is what gives a concatenation of practical principles the character we recognize as that of an art. It is from this notion of an art that our inquiry begins. Recent philosophy of art has made little use of it. But knowledge and skills are still organized to make changes in the world, and it is a weakness in recent philosophy that it has paid little attention to this traditional notion.

An art in the traditional sense may be defined as a corpus of knowledge and skills organized for the production of changes of a specific kind in matter of a specific kind.[2] Our first task is to look at the various components of this definition.

The corpus that constitutes an art is one of knowledge and skills. It is because knowledge and skill can be transferred from an operation to other similar operations (defined as similar by this transferability itself) that arts exist. The different things that are made and done are the body of the art, but it is the skill embodied in this practice that works as a soul to make the body a single organism. If, for example, musicians no longer shared any agreed technique, the unity of the art of music would be merely extrinsic, an outcome of the circumstances of its production by accepted promoters in accepted halls in the presence of invited accredited reviewers and with the other trappings associated with music in the eyes of the musical profession and public. And it is hard to imagine that this exoskeleton of sustaining institutions could have formed itself around a body of practice that had not originally been sustained by some intrinsic unity.

The corpus that constitutes an art is organized. Primarily, the organization must depend on the interconnection of techniques necessary to achieve ends that are inherently or functionally conjoined.[3] Medicine consists of all that doctors need to know in order to heal or comfort anyone whose condition is thought of as a sickness or an injury. But usually a secondary kind of organization supervenes. The corpus must be maintained in existence and transmitted. So far as our definition goes, the organized knowledge and skill could be that of one person, sole practitioner of his art; and Aristotle, for one, located arts within individuals. But it is normal for many practitioners to share an art and for no one of them to be master of all the knowledge and skill that constitutes it. And an organization of the knowledge and skill of many persons cannot well rely on its inherent dynamics. A practitioner learns from his own experience in a quite natural way, but the transference of techniques from one person to another and the accumulation of knowledge beyond what any one person's memory can retain call for the deliberate development of institutions devoted to storing and transmitting information. There must be accessible repositories of lore, training and teaching organizations, guilds of accredited practitioners. And, once such an organization exists, it is certain to affect the internal structure of the practice and doctrine it exists to maintain.[4]

The corpus that constitutes an art is organized to produce changes of a specific kind in a matter of a specific kind. The formulation is Plato's and fits best the sort of art he had most in mind—doctors produce health in bodies, cobblers make leather and thread into sandals.[5] It does not seem to fit the fine arts so well. Painters do change the arrangements of pigmented materials, but one thinks of them rather as creating forms—creating, not rearranging, and working with such timeless entities as color and form rather than paint and canvas.[6] Our definition, however, does not require us to equate "matter" with material in the sense of stuff to be manipulated. The word is to be taken more generally: whenever anything is done or made, there is always something that the agent or artisan accepts at the beginning of his work as that to which, or with which, or about which, something has to be done, whether this something be a lump of rock, a fictional theme, or an awkward situation.[7] And one of the first things that has to be said in distinguishing what authors do from what physicians do is that the former work with words and the latter work on people's bodies. One might go on from there to reflect on the difference between working *on* things and working *with* things and on how a doctor's relation to a patient's body (or bodily condition) differs from a writer's relation to words (or his theme), but such reflection would not make the crude initial distinction less important.[8] Complexities and ambiguities in what constitutes the matter proper to any given art will answer to complexities in the practice and theory of the art itself. Do doctors treat patients, or diseases, or communities? Different answers to that question reflect different ways of practicing medicine and different views of what medicine is.

The second apparent misfit between the general notion of an art and the way we think of the fine arts, that alteration is not creation, is easily disposed of. Whoever makes or does anything is applying his skill and experience in a situation that is in some respects like others and in other ways unlike any other. It is when we think of the unique aspects that we speak of "creation."[9] In the fine arts, for reasons that will appear later, the unique aspects of works are especially important. And it is possible, as we shall see later, to think about art in a way that refuses to countenance any other aspects. However, though there is such a thing as beginner's luck, it almost never happens that an artist does his best work, or even his most original work, at the very start of his career. Objections that art cannot be thought of in terms of arts (in our sense) tend to founder on this fact. In any case, we can and do speak of "an art" only where knowledge and skill are organized, or where an institution that once organized them has acquired its own inertia. For the rest, the concept of creation threatens to introduce metaphysical and theological ideas that are out of place at this stage in our discussion.

The definition of an art in terms of production in accordance with knowledge and skill does not require that the producers or anyone else must be able to find words to explain everything they do. It does require that the changes produced should be controlled and continuously corrected and criticized by whoever is responsible for them.[10] Such control, correction, and criticism must obviously be exercised in the light of some end or ends: that is, an art, as a corpus of knowledge and skills, provides a context within which the changes to be made are thought of as improvements. An art cannot exist without some agreement as to what, in a given field and from a given perspective, would be a change for the better and hence as to what is worth doing. But the changes need not be improvements from any other point of view than that which the art itself defines: the standards, values, ideals, and objectives involved are internal to the art. It is not a doctor's professional business to wonder whether his patients might not be better off sick or dead. In reality, arts come into being to serve ends that already exist. Doctors exist because in fact many people want long and healthy lives. But the notion of art as such does not require that the standards operative in an art coincide with the values current in society at large. Insofar as such coincidence holds, it does so as a consequence of the natural dynamics of social pressures.

There is a certain oddness in the position just laid down. That people in general want long and healthy lives is not a mere fact that might have been otherwise. A world in which it was not a fact would not be our world at all: it makes no sense to treat as arbitrary the major ends and orientations that govern our lives. The position taken in the preceding paragraph, in which the values of art are held strictly separate from those of life as a whole, is Aristotle's.[11] It is not Plato's. Plato held that an art must be directed to some objective good, for no merely arbitrary system of preferences could provide the stability that an art requires.[12] And in later antiquity the most widely accepted definition of an art was not the Platonic one I have used, but one formulated by the Stoic Zeno: "An art is a system, made up of insights that have been exercised together in the interest of some advantageous objective selected from the objectives of everyday life."[13] If one adopted this definition (as I will not), one would have to say that an art whose end did not conduce to the well-being of mankind in the world was art run wild, a perverted art, not an art at all but something nameless. One who rejected the definition might do so on the grounds that it explained not so much what an art is in itself as how an art should function in the economy of a world wholly explicable as the manifestation of reason in material form.

Plato argued that the improvements that an art exists to bring about must be thought of as perfections: because the art of medicine consists neither of error nor of ignorance but of knowledge, it must be infallible, so a doctor in error errs as a man and not as a doctor.[14] It is tempting to dismiss this contention as an absurd consequence of an obsolete, perfectionist theory of knowledge. But at worst it is an illuminating exaggeration of what the notion of expertness involves and of how technical criticism (whether of practice in the light of theory or of theory in the light of more advanced theory) has to proceed. A medical textbook describes not what doctors actually do, much of which is wrong or indifferent, but what they do right, and when a textbook errs it fails to expound medicine and expounds error. There can be an art only where, and only insofar as, there can be a definitely right and a definitely wrong way of doing things. Whatever lies beyond that point lies outside the range of knowledge and skill. Yet to make art coextensive with the definitely right or wrong seems paradoxical or perverse. It is precisely where not everything is cut and dried that we speak of "an art" as opposed to "a science." When someone has followed the rule book and come a cropper, we explain his failure by saying "Ah, there's an art to it." Such cases, however, do not really tell against the Platonic thesis, for to speak of "failure" and "coming a cropper" is to postulate that what was done was definitely wrong. The "art to it" that the man lacked was not something other than skill but something other than book learning—the inarticulate manual skill, or know-how, that cannot be spelled out into "knowing *that*." There is nothing here to suggest that arts are arbitrary either in their ends or in their means. But, as Plato failed to explain and may not have realized, it is only ideally that the improvements of art amount to perfections. In practice, we do not criticize in the light of perfection but in the light of the best knowledge we have. The idea of perfection functions regulatively, as an acknowledgment that technical criticism habitually operates with standards for which it can afford no operational warrant.[15]

The organization of an art shows itself in the development and application of a set of standards specific to the art, by which one measures how closely the relevant perfection has been approximated. But any knowledge and skill, once developed into a body of accepted practice, can be judged in abstraction from whatever ends the technique was devised to serve. Thus a secondary set of standards may be generated for any art, one that does not measure how closely the relevant perfection has been approximated but how fully the relevant expertise has been shown. A surgeon may brilliantly perform an unnecessary operation. In the fine arts, it is a judgment in accordance with such secondary standards that is generally condemned as academicism.[16]

The distinction between primary and secondary standards, as stated, begs an important question. To speak of the end that a technique "was devised to serve" is to imply that its original end is its only proper end. Our argument does not need this implication. It requires only that we distinguish between the employment and assessment of skills as mere exercises and their use for an end. Sometimes an originally subsidiary end comes to predominate, and sometimes a developed technique is put to the service of an end that was not envisaged at the time of its development.[17] So long as an end remains distinguishable from the expert handling of the means to that end, the standards associated with it are primary standards. But because of this variability of ends, the distinction between primary and secondary standards may be blurred. This is likely to happen where the end to be attained is akin to the manifestation of expertise in attaining it.[18] In playing the violin, for example, agility and tonal purity are technical accomplishments any display of which will have something in common with a successful musical performance, and it is not easy to decide at what point the cadenza of a concerto becomes a mere showpiece. Primary and secondary standards are likely to be more sharply distinguished in crafts whose products are meant for use.

Knowledge and Skill

The phrase "knowledge and skill," which I used in defining an art, glosses over a possible source of embarrassment. The original sponsors of the classical line insisted that an art must consist of knowledge strictly defined as a system of general propositions supported by reasoning.[19] The restriction sounds unrealistic and remote, but it makes sense. One learns from experience by remembering what worked last time and finding that it works this time too. But it will only work if "this time" and "last time" are really the same, in the relevant respects, and if one manages to identify and repeat the relevant features of whatever it was that worked. And to make these identifications with justified confidence requires that one understand why one's procedures work, that is, that one grasp the causal principles involved. Thus, the reliability of one's procedures, and hence one's art, is coextensive with one's ability to formulate general principles. Aristotle makes it quite clear that this is why arts are important to epistemologists. They represent the first appearance of true rationality, the transition from a mere reliance on uncriticized experience (differing in no essential way from the conditioned responses of brutes) to the intellectual self-consciousness of humanity.[20] In arts, the universal element latent in all experience (that is, in all the recognitions one has learned to make) becomes fully conscious, hence both subject to correction and susceptible of systematic transmission to others. Besides, when one has grasped the causal principles involved in one's technical successes one can systematically extend one's art to include new applications of the same principles, whereas a mere knack can lead to nothing beyond its own repetition.

Whatever its appeal in its original theoretical context, the plausible classical doctrine that an art is a system of general propositions is too remote from our ways of thinking to call for close inspection here. I merely observe that the propositions in question would presumably include truths about the effects of procedures and the properties of materials, recommendations specifying intermediate objectives, and imperatives prescribing means to acknowledged ends. But however widely the net is spread, we will want to insist that no system of propositions suffices for an art without the actual ability to put knowledge into effect—in a word, without skill. A system of apprehended truths is not the same as the ability to turn out a product, and it is by his ability actually to make things that a craftsman is judged.[21] It is useless to urge that, in theory, manual dexterity can be equated with the correct application of some set of general laws; what is called for is the ability actually to provide what the job in hand specifically requires. Nor can one relegate skill to a merely extrinsic position by saying that it is only a matter of muscular coordination, acquiring which is no more to be reckoned a part of the art than the purchase of a lathe would be. A violinist smitten by arthritis can no longer play, but there is an important sense in which his skill, like his ear, is unaffected. Reading a new piece of music, he will still know how it should sound and how he would make it sound like that if only he still had the use of his fingers. And this would not be something that he could put into words, but something he could hear and feel. The artist's skill, then, is neither verbalizable nor mechanical, and hence neither reducible nor subordinated to propositional knowledge.[22] Nor is it unreliable, as the Aristotelian argument would persuade us; even the archintellectualist Plato began with the recognition that artists regularly achieve successes they are powerless to explain.[23] Conversely, verbalization is no guarantee of reliability. It is the novice, and not the skilled practitioner, whose knowledge is contained in the precepts he can recite, and many of his failures come about because his skill does not run beyond his grasp of general truths.

The doublet "knowledge and skill" serves to acknowledge that intelligence may be shown no less in manual than in verbal operations, and that the intellect has no privilege in the practical world,[24] although Aristotle's point about the importance of universalizability and explicability loses none of its force. We would not want to go so far as Gilson, who is seduced by the fact that all that is ultimately required of a painter is the successful movement of his hand into saying that it is in his hand that all his skill is located, and infers that nothing useful can be said about the art of painting or about paintings considered strictly as products of that art. In the first place, different arts differ greatly in the extent to which they involve explicitly formulated principles.[25] In the second place, Gilson ignores all that can be verbalized in the art of painting: experts may have forgotten all they know, but there is a tremendous amount that a beginner needs to be *told* about how to use his paints if he is not to waste time. In the third place, Gilson excludes from attention all the institutional aspects of an artist's life, his relations with dealers and so on. In that exclusion many will concur. But by concentrating exclusively on the moment when an experienced painter sets brush to canvas, and even then allowing himself to think of nothing except the arrangement of pigments on the prepared surface, Gilson throws some things into a relief that is sharp only because the background is left dark.

It is not easy to decide just how seriously one should take the doublet "knowledge and skill." One might, for instance, begin by saying that most arts consist of two interacting but contrasting components, verbalizable knowledge and inarticulate skill. But it is possible to make too much of that contrast. One cannot, for example, hold that knowledge can be taught but skill cannot. Up to a point, skills can be taught by demonstration, supervised practice, and correction; and it is only up to a point that knowledge can be taught, for the learner must somehow find within himself both the logical connections and the vital context that convert learning by rote into understanding.[26] It might be thought that knowledge could, and skill could not, be communicated in the absence of the occasions for its use or of the objects on which it is to be used; but the distinction here is rather that a verbal principle can be learned through a wider range of exemplifications than is required for imparting a skill. Similarly, one cannot hold that knowledge is the same for everyone, whereas a skill is a personal matter. Plato seems to have held that view, on the reasonable ground that physics and geometry, the paradigms of knowledge as he conceived it, are not only interpersonal but cross-cultural. But the sense in which two men can know the same thing is hardly stronger than the sense in which two men can have the same skill (so that, for instance, it might make little difference which of two glass blowers was working a given shift)—H. S. M. Coxeter and I both know Pythagoras' Theorem, but what he knows in knowing it is something I cannot even imagine. But the two cases are by no means the same. When two men know the same thing, the difference between them lies in the vital and theoretical contexts to which the propositions they both know are related; when they have the same skill, the difference lies in such things as the distinctive manner in which each executes what one would call the same movements.

Fundamentally, the distinction between knowledge and skill lies in this: that what a man believes counts as knowledge only if he believes it for the right reasons, and what he does counts as the exercise of a skill only if he does it in the right circumstances. The validating context for the one lies in logic, for the other in practice. It might be thought that even this contrast is made to appear only by illegitimately contrasting the *disposition* of belief with the *exercise* of skill. But then it turns out that the contrast can hardly be made in "legitimate" terms: the belief that may count as knowledge can be thought of and assessed in abstraction from the occasions on which it is uttered, but a skill cannot be thought of in abstraction from the occasions on which it is or may be exercised. There are powerful arguments to suggest, however, that the abstraction by which we think of a belief as something existing apart from its manifestations is itself illegitimate, a mere bad habit of mind that might equally well have clung to the concept of a skill. So perhaps in the end we must concede that the distinction between knowledge and skill as components of art is by no means a sharp one. There is rather a continuous spread from what can be verbally formulated without loss to what cannot be formulated at all. "Bake for 45 minutes at the bottom of the oven at 450°'" comes near one end of the spectrum; near the other end are the occasions when one says "No, not like that—that's more like it—*now* you've got it."[27]

Making and Doing

The traditional version of the classical line has it that art is a matter of making things, as opposed to doing things. One sees why. If an art is to be defined by what changes it produces in what, the existence of a thing on which skill has been exercised and in which changes have been wrought is the best testimony to the operation of an art; and the paradigm of such an object is an artifact, a thing that has been made out of something. But there are arts of which it is at least not obvious that they are essentially arts of making things. A doctor who cures a patient is not usually said to be making anything (except money). Consequently, my definition avoided the word "make," even going so far as to speak of "producing" changes rather than making them.

What is the difference between doing something and making something? Such a distinction is made in most familiar Indo-European languages (*faire* and *agir*, *facere* and *agere*, *machen* and *thun*, *poiein* and *prattein*), but not always in the same place and not always in ways that are easily reduced to system.[28] The distinctions made in some of these other languages might well suit our theoretical purposes better than the ones made in English. But if we are thinking in English, the difference between doing and making can hardly be one between different sorts of proceeding or operation. For example, it is not the difference between activities that issue in separate artifacts and those that do not, for one speaks of *making* a mistake or a scene and of *doing* a film. Rather, it is a distinction between aspects of activities, for to make a birdbath may be to do one's own thing. Every activity has both aspects. To make something is always to do something, namely, to make it. The converse holds, though less obviously: if I am strolling, I seem to be making nothing, except possibly an arabesque in air. But there is at least one thing I am sure to be making. I am making a difference. To do something is always to make a difference; if I made no difference to anything, I have done nothing.[29] One should note, however, that one cannot give "A difference" as an answer to "What are you making?" That question can only be properly answered by a noun or a noun phrase that names an artifact; otherwise one must say "Nothing." Such answers as "A difference," "A fool of myself," "$10,000 a year," or even "A lot of sawdust" are not proper answers but only bad jokes. It looks, then, as if there is one sense of "make" in which only artifacts can be made, a sense too narrow to cover what we mean by an art, and a lot of other senses, which are too various and too broad. But the point that was to be made by introducing the concept of making might be preserved by saying that the arts have to do with the differences that actions make in specific fields.

In Chapter 7 of his *Poetics*, Aristotle makes it a necessary condition of a complete action that it have a beginning, a middle, and an end. That is, we identify an action by picking out from the world's confusion what we isolate as an initial state of affairs, conceived as answering to a specific description; by identifying a process or processes that change this state of affairs in some or all of the aspects described; and by deciding on a later state of affairs, which we define as terminal because we do not look beyond it, and which we identify as that which the changes in question have brought about. And to speak of such a change as an action is to imply that some agent was responsible for these changes, which in turn implies that the agent should have defined the action in the same way that we do, making the same selections of phenomena for initial and terminal phases and for the connecting processes. It is characteristic end states of actions, rather than characteristic artifacts, that arts in general exist to produce. These considerations suggest an analysis of the operations of art into three terms: an artist's intention; the processes he intentionally initiates; and the result he intentionally achieves.[30]

The analysis just arrived at affords a sort of paradigm of action and of the operations of an art, replacing in the latter capacity the traditional paradigm of artifact making.[31] But there are important complications.

The question what a person is doing at any particular time does not always (perhaps ever) admit of only one answer. One can say "Go and see," but what one sees when one goes can always be described and explained in more than one way. Different answers cover wider or narrower temporal spans and take in greater and smaller ranges of effects, depending on the interests of the observer and on how he interprets the intentions of the agent. The man who crooks his finger is also, in performing that one action, firing the gun, killing the emperor, starting a war, imperiling his immortal soul, and setting an example of self-abnegating heroism. But if one points out that he is at the same time scratching his ear with his other hand, one is referring to a different action.[32] It is not quite clear what the conditions are in which one is entitled to say that one has to do with the same action under different descriptions rather than with different actions, but it seems to be when there is a common core of identifiable physical movement, or when there is a nesting of intentions or of effects such that one can say that *in* doing one thing he was doing another, and not merely *while* doing it.[33] If that is so, movements and intentions afford independent criteria for identifying actions. The independence would reflect a difference in the ways in which people identify their own actions and those of other people, for I am an authority on my own intentions and on the movements I observe in others. When there is a difference of opinion about what has been done, in the sense of which of several descriptions of "the same" action is the most appropriate or the only admissible one, we allow the agent's point of view a certain limited privilege. Up to a point, we allow a person to be the best judge of what he is doing, as he is of his intentions. But only up to a point, for he may abuse the privilege so as to disavow responsibility for the natural consequences of his actions. "You summoned the fire brigade," we say. "I only put out my hand to keep myself from falling," he replies. We may believe him. But for all that, his hand did land on the button, so that he did in fact summon the fire brigade, whether he meant to or not and whether he cares to admit it or not.[34] People should watch where they are putting their hands.

What we say a person is doing may not be what he meant to do. But it is always the kind of thing we think he could have meant to do. What we accept as an action depends on what our notions are about the possible range of human purposes—we construe the physical movements so that they make some kind of human sense. Without such prior understanding of what it is to be human and more generally to be a living thing, we would have nothing to go on in deciding which of a person's or an animal's movements constituted something he or it was doing, much less what was being done. In all our interpretations, a sort of ghost of an intention lurks. But not all actions can be made to fit our paradigm in which actual intention leads to its objective through an intended process. The pattern must be generalized so that the three terms become conceivable intention, meaningful process, and significant outcome. That is the first of our complications.

The second of our complications arises from the presence in our paradigm of a time element. Not all actions are temporally patterned in that simple way. In the first place, though people do sometimes make plans and then carry them out, not all actions are planned. A person's "intentions" are what he plans *to do*: we identify them by the state of affairs his actions are meant to bring about, not by his state of mind at any given moment. To specify his intentions, one gives the whole rationale of his action, what makes it intelligible in terms of the strategy of his life.[35] This is a crucial point in the theory of art criticism, in which it is often wrongly held that to report an artist's intentions must be to introduce irrelevant data from his life. In fact, it is more like explaining how what he has done makes sense. In the second place, and at the other end, one cannot always distinguish between the process of an action and its outcome. In some contexts at least, the distinction becomes that between the thing done and the doing of it. Every activity can be viewed in either of two ways: as an episode in, or a slice out of, the history of a continuously active mind, or as an action in or on the world, making a difference to it. In relation to one's own activity, one may be aware of the fact of one's being active, or one may think about what one is doing, what one is accomplishing. Two distinctions seem to be combined here. One is that between the continuous stream of change, in the mind or history, and the episodes into which we divide that continuity by describing, planning, and criticizing; the other is that between experience as it is lived and events as they are observed. The distinctions tend to go together, but are not identical. Continuity seems more appropriate to the experience of living, the subjective or "existential" viewpoint, and discontinuity seems to belong to the objective viewpoint from which actions are observed. But that is a complex and much debated question and need not concern us now.[36] What does concern us is that it is possible to distinguish the doing of anything from what is done, and that is not necessarily the distinction between a process and its outcome: it may be that between the dancing of a dance and the dance that is danced.[37] To dance the dance, not to take the final bow, is the object of a dancer's art. Besides, though a person who is riding from Aix to Ghent has not finished what he is doing until he reaches Ghent, so long as he stays in the saddle there is something that he is already succeeding in doing, namely, riding.[38] And in riding he is manifesting a skill that may be the object of an art.

Arts exist to make differences, and every operation of art is undertaken to make a difference. This difference may be embodied in an artifact, or it may be the situation brought about. But it may also be the operation itself conceived either as a sample or as a slice of a certain kind of activity of which expert performance is prized. And it may also be the whole operation from beginning to end, conceived as having a certain kind of pattern. A dance seen and remembered may be a possession for ever, something added to and enhancing the world. What is primary in art is not skill in making; it is a thing done, as opposed to the doing of it, as the object of skilled performance. Whether this done thing is (or is construed to be) an artifact, or an end result, or a sample of accomplishment, or an entire performance, we can in each case regard it as the object of the activity or process of doing it and that in turn as answering to an agent's intention. If we criticize a man's style in horsemanship, we refer the motions his body makes to controlled activity and to the skill that controls activity. But in criticizing a style, an artifact, an achievement, a performance, an accomplishment, we are not so much observing or inferring as *postulating* the corresponding action and intention. The way we talk implies that what is criticized was deliberately produced. Any activity conceived from this point of view, not as process nor as intention, but as what got done and hence as the proper object for criticism, I shall call a *performance*. In the version of the classical line I am offering, it is a performance that stands in the place allocated to the "thing made" in the traditional version. This artificial concept of performance plays a key role in what follows, and our next task is to reintroduce the concept somewhat more formally and to take a closer look at it.

The Concept of a Performance

Every operation of art involves three terms: a changer, the changes he makes, and the changing he does. These three must be strictly interdefined and abstracted from three more familiar sorts of entity not so defined. The change made must not be identified with any physical object or situation, complete with all the characteristics it may happen to have, but must be taken strictly as all and only that in an object or situation which is the outcome or product of the appropriate changings. The producer of the changes must not be conceived as the actual human being with his own personal life history and complex social relationships, but solely as the intelligent agency to which the changes in question are imputed. And the process of changing is not to be taken as a slice of history, including all that takes place within a given stretch of the time-space continuum, but takes in only those movements made and transformations started by the producer that are directed to the effecting of the change or the formation of the product in question.[39] In describing a surgical operation, one can do either of two different things. One can give the "human interest" story of what sort of people do what things in what surroundings, or one can say how the operation as such was carried out, specifying numbers of stitches but omitting the color of the nurse's hair. The former account might appear in a biography, the latter in a medical bulletin, and it is the latter that describes an operation of art.[40] In such a description we talk only about the proper exercise of knowledge and skill in an appropriate context and are concerned only with what constitutes such exercise or manifests its failure. In theory, then, technical discussions are governed by stringent canons of relevance. But such stringency is possible only when the technique in question is quite cut and dried. In practice, it is sometimes doubtful what the relevant abstraction would be, or how far it can be carried out. In the fine arts, especially, as we shall see later, the relevant skills may be thought of as expressive, and hence as involving the artist's personality in a manner and to an extent that cannot be precisely determined. Similar questions may arise as to what aspects of an artifact are to be viewed as the artist's work rather than his good fortune and as to just what movements have contributed to the outcome in the relevant way. If Wagner can only compose when wearing a smoking cap, that does not make his donning his cap part of the act of composing *Tristan und Isolde*, presumably, because no particular feature of the score can be analyzed in terms of cap wearing. But if he had been forced to work bareheaded, might he not have written a different work? Well, he might, but we cannot say just how it would have differed. So we exclude such preparatory and peripheral matters as irrelevant, but at the risk of making irrelevance a function of our ignorance.[41]

Besides the changer/producer/maker/artist with his changes/ products/artifacts/works and his changing/production/manufac- ture/creation, a fourth term is involved in the operations of art. Where there is art there are standards, and where there are stand- ards there must be people to formulate, impose, and imply them. An art would hardly get organized if there were no one whose purposes it served, and it is unlikely (if not impossible) that it could become established without an organized group of people having an avowed common interest in its products. In the case of the fine arts at least, such a social group is what is called their public. As the maker must be distinguished from the man who makes, so the public for an art must be distinguished from the whole society within which the art operates, is used or enjoyed. And, as with the other three terms, the public is best considered as an abstraction, constituted strictly by the interests of those actually or potentially interested.

Standards as such do not need social groups to formulate and impose them; they require no more than a certain constancy in judgment. In the limiting case this constancy may be that of one person for quite a short time. An artist can be his own public, and the art need endure no longer than is necessary for skills to be developed and standards conceived—a time that could be shorter than it takes to produce a work. Without going to such fanciful lengths, we insist so much nowadays on the autonomy of the in- dividual practitioner of the fine arts that we have grown used to the idea that in those arts the artist is normally his own first, and often his only, public. But except to the extent that skillful pro- duction requires constant critical scrutiny of the work by the worker, and that this scrutiny necessarily precedes any judgment that any mere observer can bring to bear, such artistic solitude is not the norm for all arts. Ordinarily, the constancy in judgment is that of a group of people exchanging information with each other and influencing each other's attitudes. Arts can exist without societies, but cannot be recognized and hardly survive.

The close relation between producer, production, product, and public is not peculiar to the arts. The same relation is found, or may be imputed, whenever something done is singled out for at- tention from a specific point of view. Such singling out is the specific operation of teleological intelligence, whether on the part of agents or of observers. It is what is thus singled out that I am here calling a *performance*, in my special sense of that term. A performance in this sense is whatever is performed by a performer as such in and by the performing of it, and can be defined as the imputed end of any action conceived as intelligently intended to achieve just that end. More briefly, a performance is anything made or done, as one conceives it when one attends strictly to the making and doing.[42] A performance is conceived in abstraction from its moral and social context and in isolation from the stream of life in which from another point of view it would form an eddy. Such conceptual isolation has often been thought appropriate only to works of fine art, but it is in fact the counterpart of any abstractive teleological judgment, the judgment that considers things made or done as the objects of makings and doings.[43] The fact that a performance as such is conceived in abstraction from its moral context does not mean that moral considerations cannot be relevant, for moral considerations are not necessarily contextual. Any action may be such that it can only be defined in moral terms and may consist essentially in the fulfillment of a moral requirement. Nor does the isolation and identification of a performance mean that it will never be appropriate to consider it in relation to the context from which it was abstracted. It is, in fact, only if its identity is maintained that it can be definitely related to something else, rather than merged with it.

To be a performance is to be the object of an isolating act of attention. And attention may be focused in many ways on the same occasion. Watching a dancer, I may attend to the choreographer's composition, or to the dancer's interpretation of his role, or to his execution of certain routine movements, or to all of these in turn or at once. More subtly, there may be variations in my interpretation of what he is intending or attempting to do.[44] What I take to be success in performing a graceless movement someone else might take to be failure in performing a graceful one.[45] In any case, though, whatever I regard as a performance I regard as meant to achieve some end, and hence potentially as well or ill done, as successful or unsuccessful.[46] And this is so even if, as is very often the case, I cannot specify what was intended otherwise than by pointing to what was in fact done. It is when we cannot name or describe the supposed task that we say things like "It didn't quite come off."

To pick out a performance is to isolate and join bits of activity that taken together might constitute a single success or failure. As *CC* argued at length, the terms "performance" and "criticism" are correlative. To criticize anything done or made is to discuss it precisely as a performance, and a performance could alternatively be defined as any object of criticism as such. It follows that an act of criticism may make what is criticized into a performance of a certain kind, by describing something it could be succeeding or failing in and interpreting it as succeeding or failing accordingly. Since the standards by which something is adjudged well or ill done are properly those of a public, they need not be those envisaged by any agent or performer,[47] but may be those of a consumer or a critical consortium or an interested bystander.[47] The extreme case here is that in which what is criticized is not something done or made at all but something that just happened: the boy was not dancing but stumbling; it was not a sculpture but a piece of driftwood. If a critic then says it was a clumsy dance or a fine sculpture, he is surely making a mistake, for in treating something as a performance he assumes intelligent agency. But the intelligent application of standards for performance does not depend on the correctness of this assumption; his mistake is not a mistake in criticism unless he is mistaken in judging that the lad would have been dancing clumsily if he had been dancing at all, or that if it had been a sculpture it would have been a fine one. One might, indeed, go further. Such a critic could be making a mistake—celebrated hoaxes have exploited the possibility. But need he be mistaken? Could his judgment that it was a clumsy dance, or a fine sculpture, not be made in full knowledge that in historical fact what he was judging was a stumble, or a piece of driftwood? If so, there is nothing that the ingenuity of critical interpretation could not conceive as the performance of some unknown performer or as its product, and the term "performance" stands rather for a possible way of regarding anything than for any particular kind of thing. In my view, this would go too far: where nothing is done, there is no performance, hence no particular kind of performance; and the critic's judgment would be perverse unless it were put hypothetically. But however that may be, to criticize something as a performance of a certain kind may be more or less appropriate, on various grounds. One thing that makes for appropriateness is that the criticism manifestly fits—other suitably placed observers recognize the criticized performance. Another is that what is criticized was in fact deliberately done by someone. Another is that the agent meant it for the kind of performance the critic takes it to be. Another is that the kind of performance in question is publicly recognized as an appropriate object for human endeavor. All these factors converge, and the locus of their convergence is an art. Arts, with their public recognition, their determinate standards, and their organization of skills and practices, furnish exactly those conditions that make the most appropriate criticism possible. Operations of art, things artisans do in accordance with their art, are thus paradigm cases of performances and preeminently objects of criticism.

The existence of an artifact, a solid and lasting product, symbolizes in a satisfying way the separateness of a performance from its context. Here is something we feel we can point to without fear of being misunderstood.[48] But a performance need not leave any permanent relic, and need not exist otherwise than as the perceptible or intelligible aspect of an action. And where the outcome of an action is an artifact, the physically separate and durable object is not to be identified with the performance itself, the actual changes that the performer as such effected. In a thing, such as a pot, that someone has made, we can distinguish three aspects. First, there is the actual pot, conceived as an object with its own physical properties and history and without emphasis on its status as outcome of intelligent agency. Next, there is the product or artifact, the actual pot considered as a thing turned out by a man of skill, its properties viewed in the light of their history as outcomes of deliberate changes. Finally, there is the performance, the changes themselves wrought in the pot, that which the potter has effected in his potting.[49] What the critic talks about is the performance, but what he sees is the pot, which he takes to be an artifact. But, since the potter takes into account all that he knows of the properties of the material he works in, the distinction between performance and artifact tends to vanish. Only a beginner finds his material intractable; it is the mark of the artist that he incorporates its given properties into his design.[50]

Arts

The concept of an art as an organized corpus has a deceptively simple look. In actuality, though arts certainly exist, we have no criteria for what constitutes a corpus. Knowledge and skills do not come in neat packages whose precise boundaries and contents can be established, either in society as a whole or within the capacities and operations of an individual. Nor are knowledge and skills ever organized in any determinate way. In reality, there are individuals and groups of colleagues, each of whom has an idiosyncratic set of preferences among things to do and ways to do them.

Even in those cases where knowledge and skill are most clearly organized, we have no set rules as to what should constitute an art rather than a branch or specialism within an art or a categorization embracing many arts. Painting is an art; but there is nothing strange in saying that oil painting or portrait painting is an art, though each is contained in the art of painting. Sculpture is an art, although stone carving, woodcarving, and clay modeling for bronze casting are very different kinds of operation, and many sculptors practice only one of them. Drawing is an art, but most of the artists who practice it are also painters or sculptors and do their drawing in intimate conjunction with their sculpting and painting.

The conceptual and practical fluidity to which we have just referred was best described by Denis Diderot.[51] Human skills are indeterminate in number and scope, he observed, but tend to cluster around certain foci of practical concern. We refer skills to an art when we identify them as relatable to some focus; but there are no boundaries between arts, and there is no definite way of determining what skills *constitute* an art. What Diderot says fits well with the Stoic definition according to which items of skill or knowledge form an art by being exercised together to a common end, identified by a common interest. But ends and interests can be broadly or narrowly defined (a person who wants filet mignon, rare, is a person who wants steak, wants meat, wants food . . .) and may generate arts of varying scope.[52] And a particular skill may join various sets of other skills to form a variety of practices some or all of which may count as arts.

The particular areas of vagueness suggested by our examples of variously identifiable arts answer to different terms in our original definition. Oil painting and watercolor painting effect comparable changes in different matters (i.e. media); portrait painting and landscape painting effect different changes in the same set of matters. But a wider classification reveals them all as effecting the same sort of change in the same sort of matter, viz. arrangements of pigmented materials on surfaces. Carver and modeler among sculptors have quite different manual skills, but the skill that lies in their feeling for arrangements in three-dimensional space is what they share and what makes them sculptors.[53] And because this spatial sensibility may in different individuals have more or less in common with the analogous sense of surface space that a painter must have, we allow that sculptor and painter are in a sense practicing a single art (which we call simply "art"), the practitioner of which, like Picasso, may turn his hand (or his assistants' hands) to painting, drawing, sculpture, ceramics, etching, engraving, furniture design, and architecture.

Intrinsically, then, arts are nebulous constructs, and we assign a practice or a practitioner to different arts depending on which other persons or practices we wish at the moment to combine or contrast them with.[54] Extrinsically, however, arts may become sharply differentiated. This happens when the organization of the corpus of knowledge and skills is not left to the inherent dynamics of practice, but is reinforced or imposed by an organizing institution. The layman, for example, never thinks of a dentist as a kind of surgeon, although dental and other surgeons both produce health by mechanical intervention in the body. Dentists go to dental school, surgeons go to medical school. It may be no coincidence that such sharp differentiations arise in arts where the proportion of knowledge to skill is high. If we use the word "knowledge" to stand for what can be communicated verbally and away from practical situations, it seems likely that the communication of knowledge will give rise to classrooms that are not studios, teachers who are not practitioners, and the like, whose connection with the art must be emphasized formally because it cannot be shown practically, and that practitioners will have certificates to testify that they have acquired a nameable and describable knowledge whose presence or absence does not reveal itself in practice to the uninitiated.

The extrinsic unity imposed on an art by its organizing institutions is matched by one imposed by the organized demand of a public. It is not only the extensibility of his space-organizing skill that turns a painter into a sculptor. There is also the fact that people with money to spend on ornamenting their quarters are not always sure whether they want something to hang on a wall or something to put on a table, and that the range over which their desires wander is transmitted in a very concentrated way by the galleries through which painters deal.[55]

We have seen already that an art such as painting can be variously defined by picking out various matters and correspondingly various changes in those matters. These differences reflect various possible opinions about the point of what the artist is up to and broader or narrower views about its scope. From one point of view, rearranging pigment is what painting is: why pigments should be rearranged, and how, is consciously or unconsciously excluded from consideration. From another point of view, the painter introduces order into visible space: to mention that this is done by manipulating pigments would be bathetic. Such redefinition is always possible for at least three reasons. First, all description must be selective: the initial situation or datum that constitutes the matter of the art must be described and identified in this or that fashion. Second, a practical grasp of a situation and what to do about it need not be conceptualized, and what one says about it (if anything) may be far from representing the whole of one's practical understanding. And third, one is generally clearer about one's immediate objectives than one is about the ultimate or even the middle-range goals of one's action, which often serve only a programmatic or ideological purpose.

A Platonizing philosopher might argue that in theory one could give a uniquely correct definition of a stable practice in a static society by working out the whole system of purposes within which it moved: such a procedure would doubtless yield abstract definitions of arts very generally conceived, and specific systems of changes introduced into specific matters would figure within this framework as subsidiary arts or practices. But this theoretical possibility has no practical application, and conditions in which it might be worthwhile trying to approximate to it are not likely ever to obtain.

The possibility of redefining an art increases wherever the unity of the art is chiefly extrinsic and institutional, so that the way in which the art is carried on is more evident than the purposes it serves and its secondary standards are clearer than the primary standards. Alternative definitions of arts are even easier when the social role of a practitioner clearly exists but neither the extrinsic nor the intrinsic unity of an art can be easily established. This possibility gave Plato the opportunity for the *jeu d'esprit* in his *Sophist*, in which a number of satirical definitions of the sophist's "art" are posed as equally valid alternatives. Social roles and social identifications need follow no system, and Plato's immediate point is that sophistry is not an art at all but a miscellaneous box of tricks; but the debate between Socrates and Thrasymachus in the *Republic* suggests that only the less important and interesting arts admit readily of a single description.

The redefinability of arts is important, because the shift in viewpoint it represents may answer to practical realignments, to inclusions in and exclusions from this or that body of practitioners. If sculpture comes to be thought of as exploring the experience of space, sculptors may become environmental critics, and vice versa; if architects think of themselves as environmental engineers, they may come to number among their ranks social commentators and publicists.

It seems, then, that there are at least six factors, all identifiable in terms of our original definition and its explication, that unify and differentiate arts: shared matters; shared changes; transferable skills; to a lesser extent, transferable knowledge; organizing institutions; and organized publics. These factors do not operate independently, but they represent different emphases and stand for tendencies that may diverge. It is therefore not surprising that we have no set way of deciding what is or what is not to be dignified with the name of art. And it is of no consequence. Provided that we understand the ways in which arts are united and divided, nothing of any theoretical significance depends on how many lines we draw or where we draw them.[56] Techniques and their products are very variously grouped for various purposes and from various standpoints. To differentiate arts, and to elucidate the principles of their differentiation, are fully rational procedures, but to try to compile complete and definitive lists of *the* arts, or of all arts of a certain kind, is not.

Arts and Art

Because there are many different ways of grouping skills together to constitute an art, and because such groupings are neither determinate nor mutually exclusive, we cannot form a single collective out of them and call it "the arts." For that to be possible, we would need a single basis of classification, so that we could draw up one definitive list. It makes a bit more sense to talk about "the useful arts" or "the industrial arts," where the epithet we choose suggests a single consistent principle of classification, but the phrase "the arts" in general is altogether too vague. In a particular context we might talk about "the arts," much as we can talk about "the cat" where the context shows which cat we are talking about, and we often say "the arts" when we mean what at other times we call the fine arts; but in general the principle holds. The generic or collective term that corresponds to arts in general is not "the arts" but "art" in one of its significations to which we have not yet given any special attention.

The word "art" in this generic sense stands for the human propensity to form arts, the habit of organizing practical knowledge; or it stands for the type of knowledge that goes to make up an art, viz. knowledge and skill in general insofar as they are organized for production. In this use, the word functions as we saw it does in the phrase "philosophy of art," not designating or describing a type of organization or a collective of organizations, but vaguely pointing toward an area of concern—a *Lebensform*. It was this sense of the word that scholastic philosophers captured in their deceptively simple looking phrase *recta ratio factibilium*, "the right use of the mind in relation to production." The simplicity is deceptive because it seems to suggest that there is one such right use, known or knowable and describable, but all it actually commits one to is that *some* uses of the mind in relation to production are right uses, even though life might be too short to specify what they were or even what their rightness consisted in.

Arts and Artists

Abstract structures exist in concrete embodiments. Such an abstract structure as an art, being an organization of the skills of men, can exist only in organizing and organized men. Partly, then, art is embodied in the institutions that form the exoskeleton of arts, but its primary embodiment is in the individuals who have the skills.[57] Knowledge and skills are abstracted from what cognizers and agents know and do, and the cognizers and agents of arts are human individuals.[58] Arts exist in artists and are what artists know how to do.[59]

If the reality of art lies in the knowledge of individual artists, it may after all not be possible to distinguish, in practice or even in principle, between an artist's knowlege of his art and his knowledge of other things. Since anything he is or knows may affect anything he actually does, it may be harder than we have made out to sort out a professional and a personal component in what he knows. The distinction in question certainly seems a familiar one: we are accustomed to discriminate between a man's technical competence and his social character and between "the man who suffers and the artist who creates." One person can be a brilliant surgeon and a moral reprobate; another may cheerfully write a heart-rending lament. But these familiar distinctions purport to differentiate between all skills and what is not skill at all, rather than to separate one sort of skill from another. And the question of whether or not the latter separation is possible has some theoretical importance. If it cannot be done, we shall have to redefine an art, perhaps as the sum of those skills possessed by persons who skillfully produce changes of a certain sort, or such skills as they may from time to

48

time exercise in making such changes. And any such redefinition must sadly aggravate the indeterminacy that we have already found infesting the concept of an art.

A distinction that promises to be the one we are looking for is that between the skills that a man shares with his fellow artists, what he formally learns in his apprenticeship and so on, and the unique component in his skill that he develops for himself. On that showing, only what is transmitted and maintained by the organizing institutions (or, if there are none, could be so transmitted and maintained) belongs to the art. But what if the art itself demands the personal component? Are we to say that a surgeon's unique touch forms no part of his technical equipment? Certainly it is not irrelevant to his technical prowess. And the teaching of an art may emphasize the importance of developing such personal competences, to which instruction can contribute only by providing opportunities for the supervised practice in which they may grow. In some arts, notably the fine arts, stress may be laid from the very beginning on the importance of erecting on the shared basis an original superstructure of individual skill. In such cases especially, it is absurd to recognize as belonging to the art only what is actually shared: the personal contribution belongs to the organized corpus of the art because the organization depends on it and is built around it.

We cannot after all equate those of a man's skills that form part of his art with those that he shares with his fellow artists. One obvious alternative is to say that all that part of an artist's total available knowledge and skill which analysis reveals as having contributed to the perfection of his product forms part of his art; another is to say that all and only that part of his knowledge and skill which he consciously applies to his product is part of his art. But both these alternatives fail in the same way. A novelist may apply to his writing his specialized knowledge of bell ringing, or a painter exploit in his paintings his architectural or archaeological expertise; and such knowledge, whether consciously applied or not, is not rendered part of his art by its contribution to a successful work.[60] It is something he uses, part of the matter rather than of the method of his art. At most, it is part of his professional skill to be able to use such knowledge in his work.

The failure of the proposed distinctions suggests that what is needed is to discriminate, within those of a man's skills that he does not share with others, a component that is connected in a direct and functional way to the body of skill common to his trade or profession. One such component has already been suggested: those personal skills that an artist is professionally encouraged and required to foster. Another way of identifying such a component (which for all we can say might prove after all to be the same one) is to apply a distinction like the traditional one between law and equity, the law of a case and the case itself, general principles and their specific applications. However fully a body of skills may be codified, in applying it to situations as they arise each individual needs a skill that cannot be codified, because situations are infinitely variable. If that skill could after all be codified, its codification would only show the need for a new uncodified skill in applying this new code to cases (see Sparshott 1970b). An uncodifiable skill of this kind is common to all artists, in the sense that each has a common need to apply his knowledge, but the skill itself is not common, for each will apply his knowledge in his own individual style and will be skillful in his own way. Being both personal and inseparable from the common core of the art, these individual versions of their skill that practitioners develop have just the character we are seeking.[61] And it is tempting to equate them with those individual skills that institutions foster, to which I referred before. Painters are taught to be original and judges are not, but each judge has his own style just as each painter does.

Because of Aristotle's classical discussion of "equity," the relationship between a general law and its application to a particular case often serves as a paradigm for the relation between a general skill or knowledge and its application. But the relation is hardly typical of that which obtains in most arts. In the legal case, the law comes first: logically if not temporally, a principle is first enunciated and then applied. But in most arts, as the very strangeness of the expression "a skill and its application" attests, laws and principles merely codify practice that has proved acceptable. This generally holds even for the secondary standards that evaluate technique: though academic or unimaginative critics may treat accepted rules as shibboleths, and teachers may insist for pedagogic reasons on a rigid and unargued conformity, most appeals to secondary standards are concerned, not with whether or not a rule has been violated, but with whether or not a work comes off technically, a happy condition of which compliance with rules is no certain index. The atypicality of the legal case, however, is not very important and may be only apparent. Law itself for the most part codifies what judges have decided in particular cases—openly in common law; indirectly in civil law. And it makes no difference that in most arts rules remain rules of thumb, as they do not in law. Neither priority nor the rigidity of principles is the issue here; all that matters is the looseness in the relation between a generalization and a case that exemplifies it. For there to be an art, cases must be enough alike for learning to be possible, so that generalization must be possible; for the art to be practiced, the generalization must be exemplified in particular cases. The distinction between an artist's doing what all his fellow artists do and his doing it in his own way remains.

The foregoing attempt to identify among an individual's unshared skills those that belong to his art, though it rests on real and important facts, will not do. First, one cannot equate the personal component in skill with the uncodifiable. If it is indeed skill, and especially if it has enough consistent character to be called a style, it must be codifiable in the same way as a shared skill. What one has learned in the past will be helpful in the future only if one has correctly picked out those common elements in old and new situations and practices that explain one's success. Second, the personal component in professional skill need not have the subsumptive role I have assigned it. The proposed account implied that the principles that could be thus extracted from an individual's skillful practice must either fall outside the domain of his art or else have the status of mere subsidiary rules for applying the principles and rules he shares with others. But I gave no solid reason for that: I merely argued that certain suggested alternatives were unsatisfactory. But surely the salient fact to be considered in characterizing the personal component in professional skill is that different practitioners of the same art do work in different areas, and each practitioner of a complex art will contribute unique skills to his practice, not as external adjuncts and materials, but as his way of practicing the art itself. Our question should be, Which of an artist's skills are thus to be counted as part of the art itself and which are to be held extraneous? A clue is to be found in the Stoic definition of an art as a set of insights *exercised together* in the pursuit of some utility. There is an element of metaphor here that cannot be entirely eliminated, but the point seems clear and valid: any personal skill forms part of an art if it is functionally integrated with those skills that the artist shares with his colleagues and by which the art is defined. The skills that can fitly be described as skills of application ("his own way of doing things") will belong to this class, but they will not necessarily exhaust it.

There may be nothing more to say about which of a man's personal skills form part of his art. But there may still be a question about how one discriminates a man's skills from his personal endowments. An artist's temperament may affect his performance, so that he does everything in a melancholy way. Might not someone claim that such melancholy is knowledge or at least "a cognitive phenomenon," a system of interpreting events? One might respond to this claim by inviting the claimant to examine the work in which Sartre (1939a) takes the same view of moods: such a mood is interpretive, not by adding a layer of meaning or contributing to detailed knowledge and understanding of events, but by interposing as it were a reductive and simplifying filter that works against such knowledge and understanding. Such an "interpretation" can hardly count as a system or as part of an organization of skills. An artist's melancholy is part of his art, we should say, only insofar as he makes it so by its subtle manipulation, deployment, and exercise. But perhaps it is enough to say that *if* and *insofar as* melancholy is a system of interpretation, its application to production is indeed a form of skill—really, one has to use one's common sense, a large part of which (as Aristotle remarked about equity) lies in repudiating spurious counterexamples. A more serious difficulty may be raised in specific connection with the fine arts, which are those that will concern us. These are often called arts of expression, and their expressive character associated with the demand for originality. But if such an art lies in expressing one's unique self or one's private vision, it seems impossible to differentiate artistic skill from personal temperament. If we take that view of the matter, there are at least three different things we can say. First, if we take art in the sense of the mode of operation that characterizes the fine arts to be entirely a matter of expression, and define expression in such a way that it excludes any kind of generalizable skill, we are thinking of art in a way that completely excludes the notion of *an* art, as developed here or anywhere else. Most of those who have understood art in this way have intended that exclusion, and I have accordingly identified their views as an expressive line quite separate from the classical line I am expounding here. Second, if all we mean is that the fine arts have an expressive aspect that exploits the artist's temperamental endowment, and that this exploitation can itself be done skillfully, we will not be differentiating the fine arts from any other arts in which personal endowments make a contribution, and the temperament of the artist becomes comparable with the cool head of the airport flight controller or the muscular coordination of the mechanic. But there is a third position that lies between these two. We may say that success in poetry or painting is not entirely a matter of skill, but requires (as Plato said of poetry) inspiration as well. In arts as we have defined and discussed them, a skilled practitioner should be able to predict success or failure, with an allowance for error. If his technique is adequate and a thing is technically feasible, he will succeed in doing it unless he suffers an accident or makes a mistake. But a poet in full possession of his craft cannot guarantee that he will write a good poem. He may indeed be sure that, unless his mind suddenly goes, he will be able to turn out a competent set of verses, with such point, eloquence, elegance, or forcefulness as his métier may command. But beyond that success there is a success of which he can never be sure, in which his controllable skills find themselves at the service of an unpredictable and unrepeatable insight. On this third way of looking at the matter, the "art" of the fine arts exceeds the limits of the fine arts as we understand them: the artist needs his art, but he needs something else as well. It might be objected that this elusive, uncontrollable factor is not to be equated with that personal temperament the expression of which was the element whose integration with the corpus of an art we originally called into question. But it may well be the aspect of such temperament that cannot be made the object of skilled exploitation; for the "personality" to be expressed functioned in our argument precisely as whatever in a person's endowment could systematically affect the quality of his work but could not be reduced to skill, and "expression" has not here been given any meaning more definite than "utterance not governed by skill."

The common strategy of our solutions to the problem of differentiating skills from other personal endowments in arts of which the successful exercise depends on personal expression concedes that to the extent of that dependence such practices are not strictly arts at all. If one prefers to insist that the fine arts are arts and a poet is a practitioner of an art, one can reinstate the difference between skill and temperament by saying that *whatever* passions, experiences, insights, inspirations, and inklings he puts into his work are part of the material he exploits as an artist. An artist cultivates himself as an experiencing-machine to provide himself with things to show or say. Of course, a man is not two men, a personal self and an artistic self that exploits the former and is assumed when he starts to paint or write. But our question was a logical rather than an existential one, and the validity of an analysis is not affected by the substantive unity of what is analyzed. Even if some of the things a man does, or his ways of doing them, or what he does them with, are to be counted both as parts of his personal life and as parts of his artistic equipment, we may still distinguish between their aspects as members of these two complexes. As students of his product, we are concerned with his life only as it issues in his work, not with its personal significance to him.[62] If someone writes poems of orphanhood, the fact that he is really an orphan and writing from his personal experience rather than imagining that status (and perhaps using it as a metaphor for some other aspect or chance of the human condition) will concern us only insofar as that fact enters into the poems themselves: that is, insofar as we judge that it was not only causally but logically (or even ontologically) necessary that the author of such poems should have been an orphan. And that would be a strange way to think about poems, though it is one in which many people do think.[63]

It seems, then, that if such practices as poetry involve the practitioner's personal experience in a way in which such arts as medicine do not, we can pursue either of two lines: either we can exclude poetry from the arts, or we can say that the personal experience is involved only as instrument or subject matter. A sensibility is not skill, but it can be skillfully cultivated and exploited.[64] These two alternative ways of understanding the matter are not only options for the theorist but correspond to familiar live options for the artist. Insofar as a writer regards himself as a professional, he will regard his personal life as material to be mined; it is the writer who makes a mystique of his art who will treat his personal experience as holy.

The sense in which, and the extent to which, the fine arts actually are, or morally should be, or aesthetically had better be, arts of personal expression are open and complex questions. Ernst Kris, for instance, claims clinical support for the distinction between masturbatory fantasy, solitary daydream, and original narrative and for the identification of artistic success with the last of these, in which the creative power has become detached from whatever personal conflict may have given it its initial force (Kris 1952, 29). But he excludes fairy tales and popular fiction from the domain of art, and not all will accept that exclusion, far less allow it the clinical warrant that Kris's argument must vindicate for it (ibid., 42).

The classical line takes it for granted (and so, in its own way, does the expressive line) that a work of fine art as such is autonomous: a thing done or made, certainly, but construed as a performance. And a work of art surely is that and can properly be considered so. But it is obviously also possible to refer each work essentially to its origins, to consider it as the work of an actual artist or artists located in the real world, or to refer it to the world of artistry of which it seems eloquent. That option can never be closed off, and any reasons we give for not taking it represent a willed adherence to the values of aesthetic autonomy. One may argue, as Radford does (1978), that what is wrong with a fake is not that in the end it may prove disappointing (as Goodman argued), or that it lacks association value. Those explanations would not account for the sudden and radical revulsion of feeling that follows the exposure of fake or forgery. Such revulsion suggests rather that a work of art *as such* is experienced as the expression of an actual sensibility that it embodies, the real outcome of "a particular man's inspiration and skill" (Radford 1978, 76). It seems that we can choose where to fix our interest and whether or not we shall accept all such fixings as equally legitimate. But if we rule out as illegitimate either of the two approaches mentioned, we will have a hard time justifying our exclusion, for we will not be able to name any other equally appropriate target for either interest. It may be that it is right and necessary for the classical line to isolate an aesthetic domain of performances, but that this interest may often and with perfect right be supplemented or overridden by a more generally human interest. Art is not everything, and to identify an interest is not to assign it exclusive rights over us.[65]

Conclusion by Way of a Simplified Summary

An art is a recognized concatenation of skills. As soon as such a concatenation is recognized by its practitioners, it comes to be practiced as an end in itself and not merely as a means. "All men by nature desire to know" and take pride in doing things well: culture as anthropologists understand it consists largely in transforming necessary practices into ceremonies, like the escaped circus bear in Couturier's poem who danced for glory though he had lost his chains.

Not every man can practice every art: a consequence of the concatenation of skills into methodical systems is that it takes much of a man's time to master one. Thus, the wielder of such skill finds himself exercising it for other people who have not mastered it. These others form his public, whose views about the ways their interests interact impose on the art a second kind of organization.

As skills ramify beyond what one person can hold in his head or show with his hand, they become dispersed systematically among many people who collaborate in practice, share stores of information, and initiate successors. Thus organized, the practitioners of an art form institutions whose rules of procedure become independent of the wishes of their members. The same institutions serve the necessarily ignorant public as guarantors that its demands will be properly met by their duly qualified members. Once it recognizably exists, the social structure of such an institution becomes an end in itself. Membership in it is valued, if not enjoyed.

Individual practitioners of an art have roles in their institutions and specialisms within the art. These roles and specialisms are themselves institutionalized. In addition, most practitioners have their own private specialisms (things they are good at, or go in for), and each, being an individual human being, has his own personal way of doing what his art requires. Specialized skill shades into personal accomplishment, personal life into institutional life: skills and roles function as gravitational fields rather than as compartments. Much of what a man does may be purely personal, much purely professional, but there is likely to be a large area in which he is not sure how his activity and interest are to be classified.

The general human tendency to take dodges that have worked and develop them into productive systems with their related sustaining, teaching, and marketing organizations is what is vaguely designated by the Greek and Latin words we translate as "art."

One of the bases of art is the notion of success. Continuously, and under many aspects, things turn out well or badly. We try to do things and succeed or fail; we aim at consequences that are achieved in full, in part, or not at all. At any time there may be a large number of things we can truthfully be said to be trying to do, to be succeeding or failing in, and the division and classification of these things need not correlate at all with the observable movements of parts of our bodies or with things we actually say to ourselves or others. When other people judge us to have succeeded or failed, the task they have in mind may be one we never set ourselves. Any person at any time is likely to be simultaneously engaged in an indefinite number of enterprises, which give manifold meaning to what he does. He will accordingly *make sense of* the doings of other men by ceaselessly relating them to what might be meant. In other words, insofar as what I or others do is not disregarded as meaningless, it is construed as one or another kind of performance. Sometimes, especially in simple cases where only a gross description is offered, a spectator's interpretation of what performance an agent is engaged in coincides with one that the agent himself would offer or at least acquiesce in; often, especially in complex cases, and almost always where a very detailed account is attempted, it does not. The process of analyzing the ceaseless stream of an intelligent being's activity into performances and discussing whether, to what extent, and in what way they have been successfully performed goes by the generic name of criticism. Such discourse is peculiarly applicable to the arts, whose organization already imposes an analysis and provides standards by which success and failure may be assessed. In the fine arts, where the simplifying and facilitating effect of this institutional framework is nullified by the peculiar manner in which standards are complied with, criticism becomes both obviously appropriate and exceedingly difficult, and itself becomes an art.

III

THE CLASSICAL LINE
2: ARTS OF DISENGAGED
COMMUNICATION

Imitative Play

Our business is not with arts in general but with the fine arts—painting, music, and the like. But what is "the like"? It certainly seems simple enough—did we not say at the start that art is a simple matter? We began by singling out works of art as artifacts whose function was to provide worthwhile experiences simply by being cognized. Accordingly, we can define the fine arts as all those arts that produce such objects, differentiating the particular arts by the different methods or different media they use. But there is one thing wrong with this simple solution: for most of the time that people have spoken of "fine arts" a quite different definition has prevailed. And with reason. One can get a worthwhile cognitive experience by peeping through the right keyhole; there must be more to art than that. Pyrotechny and cosmetics are arts devoted to producing occasions for enjoyable experiences, but are usually thought too trivial to be classed with epic poetry. Theorists have accordingly preferred an alternative way of characterizing the fine arts, one that relates them to more profound human concerns.

Like the definition of art itself, the attempt to delimit a class of arts that lie between the skills needed to sustain life and the mere tricks and knacks of adornment and entertainment goes back to Plato, and its history is colored by his special concerns. Besides being interested in arts of all kinds, as prime instances of knowledge controlled by organization and confirmation, Plato had two reasons for being interested in arts whose products are useless but not trivial. First, while any art controlled by ideal standards affords a paradigm for the relation between the intelligible and visible worlds, and hence holds the clue to the structure of the world as a whole, the typical products of such arts as poetry and painting seem to be intended to represent the properties of other objects that are their archetypes. To say (as Plato wanted to say) that a doctor produces in his patient a replica of the idea of health that he has before his mind is an interpretive statement, and to say that that is what a doctor intends to do is simply false; but to say that a portraitist paints either a real model or a model that he has in his mind's eye, and that at least part of what he intends is to produce a likeness, is a mere truism.[1] Second, arts of gratuitous production, such as poetry and painting, afford possible clues to the origin of the visible world. If one thinks, as Plato was inclined to, that the visible world somehow emerges from a higher and more real spiritual world, the emergence seems a sad come down. One may well wonder what that inferior world is for. The observable human propensity for producing objects that are both useless and less real than their makers might offer a clue.[2] Plato's interest in representation combines with his interest in useless production to pick out a set of arts roughly coextensive with our fine arts, to be defined as *arts of imitative play*, the word "play" being used generically to cover useless activities. This definition was actually formulated in Plato's circle, and its variants long dominated the history of philosophical reflection on the fine arts.[3]

In picking out and characterizing a set of arts as "arts of imitative play," Plato and his associates were not, as modern writers often suppose (e.g. Danto 1964, 22-23), perversely or mistakenly describing the fine arts or claiming that "all art is imitative." That supposition is a grave anachronism. Neither art in the modern sense nor the fine arts could have been Plato's target, for no one had as yet formulated any such notion. What we call the fine arts had in his day no bond of conceptual or institutional unity.[4] Nor is it appropriate to say, as George Dickie does (1974, 50), that the Platonic definition rests on the mistaken idea that only representations could be candidates for appreciation; there is no reason to think that Plato or any of his contemporaries had any interest in such candidacy, much less that they were concerned to isolate and characterize a set of arts devoted to it.[5] Plato in *Republic* X, which is the passage on which these criticisms rely, is not describing a group of arts or art as such but using the art of representational painting as an analogy for the art of dramatic poetry.[6] And the point of the analogy is that these arts make presentational or fictional use of the main cognitive modes. From that point of view, the idea of arts of imitative play has a strong and immediate attraction, regardless of whether or not the idea can be so stretched as to apply to such other arts as music and architecture.

Social life is almost entirely a matter of communicating thoughts and feelings and concerting actions accordingly, and nothing is more distinctive of human beings than their ability to formulate and convey information. If there is something I want to communicate to you, I can tell you (in words) or show you (by gesture or mime) or both: these are alternative ways of conveying or representing something.[7] Skills obviously can be and are developed in doing these things, and their importance in our lives makes it certain that such skills will be intensively cultivated. Equally obviously, the development and exercise of such skills are independent of the truth or importance of the ideas conveyed. The skills thus can be (and typically are) used fictionally, that is, with regard to the interest of what is conveyed, whether it is true or not.[8] Moreover, even if there is nothing of interest in the substance of what is to be said or shown, there will be a skill of saying or showing it in an interesting way. It is thus inevitable that there will be arts of communication or quasi communication in which the interest is purely fictional or formal, and these are the arts of "imitative play" or *disengaged communication*.[9]

Saying and showing as I described them are not the same as writing and drawing or painting, which may come to mind first as arts of disengaged communication. Writing and drawing (in Plato's Greek these are the same word, *graphein*) can be thought of as intermediate between saying and showing: in some ways, drawing is closer to writing than it is to mimicry, and writing is closer to drawing than it is to saying (one is getting something down on paper, not acting out or speaking out). But if we assimilate these graphic modes to our original pair, as it seems natural to do, making a picture of a thing or a person or a scene or an event and telling a story or giving a description of it or him form a natural pair, in both of which the development of skill and the transfer of interest take place with equal inevitability and in the same sort of way (cf. Sparshott 1975b).[10]

The point of calling poetry and painting arts of imitative play or disengaged communication, we now see, is, not that in these arts the function of the play is to imitate, but that the function of the imitation (the use of the means of communication) is to please (as Aristotle put it) or is nonserious (as Plato had it). To think of those arts in this way may be obsolete and will not apply without special pleading to all the fine arts as we know them or to the full range of any fine art as we know it; but the defect of thinking of them in this way is not that it imposes heteronomy on arts that were born free. Rather, the development of communicative skills into arts of the fictional and formal use of means of communication is a great liberation of the mind, surely one of the decisive episodes in the making of mankind.

The considerations I have just brought forward explain why the notion of arts of imitative play retains some force; but Plato's own use of the notion was pejorative, and its application to any of the fine arts has an air of paradox. It dates from an age when those arts were neither socially problematic nor theoretically controversial, so that one could characterize them easily by their relation to moral and economic life and their distinct character as uses of symbolic and mimetic devices. What the notion omits is something that would explain the importance we have come to attribute to the fine arts and the power we think we feel in them, an importance and power to which the word "play" is inappropriate. One might get round that difficulty by redefining play (in the appropriate sense) as a higher seriousness; but the word "imitation" remains to suggest derivativeness rather than original power. That difficulty can be got round, too, for, if what I said was right, the imitation in question has the value that attaches to all our means of formulating and conveying meanings, and that value can hardly be overestimated. It is not much of an exaggeration to say that it constitutes our humanity—from which we may infer that the values of such arts are likely to be multifarious indeed. We will see shortly that there are yet other ways of finding importance in imitation. Nonetheless, the word "imitation" retains its derogatory ring, and one is tempted to say that, even if the classical line that employs it is true to the actualities of the fine arts, it is false to their aspirations.

This chapter and the next will explore the two alternative accounts of what distinguishes the fine arts from other arts: that they are playful uses of imitation, and that they yield worthwhile cognitive experiences.[11] Whatever the merit or demerit of these styles of definition, it is noteworthy that both of them are not only possible but have achieved currency. Philosophers nowadays habitually deplore the practice of defining art; instead of deploring its prevalence, they might have noted how extraordinary it was and sought to explain it. Few terms are subjected to such continuous attention. There is evidently something about these arts that many people find peculiarly inexplicable and important. One wonders what and why. The obvious answer may be the right one: claiming a value for useless activities immediately raises the question of how what is useless can be valuable.

In much of the foregoing I have been writing, as most people do, as if the alternative views about how to define the fine arts testify to their problematic character, offering alternative further characterizations of a set of practices that everyone nowadays recognizes as sharing a certain common bond.[12] That might not be so. The definitions seem to pick out two different but overlapping sets of arts.[13] There could be other reasons for playful imitation than to provide worthwhile experiences, and an art of producing such experiences could well be nonrepresentational. In practice, however, the rival theorists seem to want to talk about the same arts and are prepared to deform their concepts and add riders to their theories to achieve this conformity. Nowadays, part of the reason for this is that the fine arts are institutionally definable as those supported by certain foundations, taught in certain curricula, and so on. One is tempted to argue (as many have argued) that the institutional unity is imposed and factitious, but that seems not to be so. The notion of the fine arts is the outgrowth, not of inarticulate wisdom, but of sophisticated endeavor: early attempts to characterize the fine arts did not explain a factitious unity, but were the grounds on which the unity was postulated. The institutions in which the notion of the fine arts found formal expression were set up in the belief that an affinity existed. In any case, the institutional unity is a reality now, and as many will urge as will deny that it reflects a unity of nature or function.[14] But however close that unity may be, art as the classical line conceives it consists of the fine arts with their artists, institutions, and publics, which constitute a practice or a set of practices rather than a "form of life" or *Lebensform.* The concept of art in general, as conceived in part 2 of this book, goes beyond a set of practices and does seem apt to generate a *Lebensform.* So that, if we have independent reason for thinking of art as a *Lebensform,* we thereby have reason to think the classical line inadequate or downright wrong.

Because the fine arts are institutionalized, a work may be assigned to them (on either definition) in one of two ways. A work may be called a work of fine art because it has whatever we decide are the defining characteristics of such a work. But it may also be so called because it is, for instance, a painting, and the art of painting has as its general aim the production of objects having those defining characteristics even though this particular painting does not have them.[15] Thus, if we equate a work of art with a "work of fine art," we will have different ways of deciding whether or not something is a work of art. And so we do. The question will occupy us considerably in chapter 6.

Play

Although calling the fine arts arts of imitative play makes most sense as a recognition that the disengaged uses of communicative skills form an important and natural group of arts, it has been most widely current as the conjunction of two separate contentions: that the fine arts as we know them have a character that is best captured by the word "play," or by the word "imitation," in somewhat special uses of those words. The term "play" as used or implied in defining the fine arts refers primarily to two supposed characteristics of playing, one negative and one positive.[16] Negatively, play is non-directed, not engaged in for the sake of any biological, economical, moral, or prudential advantage. It may in fact further some such purpose, but that is not what it is done for. Positively, play is activity carried on for its own sake, because it is enjoyed, or simply because it is preferred; it has a definite value, but the value lies in its own worthwhile nature. Positive and negative attributes come to the same thing, namely, that the only value that players recognize in play is inherent; but emphasis on the positive side exalts play, whereas emphasis on the negative side trivializes it. Thus, to classify the fine arts as play is to suggest, or to recognize, that their status is controversial or equivocal.[17]

The fine arts issue not in formless stretches of activity but in works of art: if art is playlike, it is not just like playing but like playing games, activities that are not merely undertaken for their own sakes but have an internal structure that makes success or failure possible in them without reference to any external objective. I have already remarked that whatever is done for a purpose comes to be done for its own sake, that culture consists in men conspiring to cram their necessities with value. Activities thus tend to divide themselves into episodes that have some of the quality of games. A large part of what makes this possible is that men come to observe recurrent situations and enjoy the recurrence: they "enter into the spirit of the thing" and thus make a game of it. These games are essentially imitative games, for the fun lies in finding interesting ways of making what now happens like and unlike what happened last time. It can thus be argued, and many writers have argued, that the skills that go to make culture are fine arts.[18]

Although the value of each game is in the playing of it, playing in general has (and may deliberately be undertaken for) a recreative function: however one plays, and whatever one's business, one is expected to return from one's play to one's business refreshed. Insofar as art is playlike, it should share this recreative function. Some theorists have urged that art fulfills this function in an un-usually intensive way by providing a moral holiday, a detachment from all moral, social, and economic concerns in which these serious matters are made the object of a sort of spiritual game. In playing that game we recover our mental freedom and return more effec-tively and more humanly to the workaday world.[19] An art that could serve this purpose would have to be imitative in some sense, for its games would need to be in some fashion disengaged or "playful" versions of serious activities.

Art is not really a game, and the operations of the fine arts are only gamelike to some extent and in some respects. A game is typically an activity not merely regulated but constituted by the rules that govern it (cf. Rawls 1955); and though an artistic genre or form may be defined by rules, it is not conceptually necessary to a work of fine art that it belong to any such genre or form. C. J. Ducasse made the same point by contrasting playfulness with the "endotelicity" of art: play is "the systematic pursuit of an end set up or accepted expressly for the purpose" (1929, 99), whereas in endotelic art "the self-imposed end which it aims at is really wanted" (ibid., 110). Success and failure in art cannot be reduced to winning and losing. But the point is perhaps moot, for Wittgenstein has taught us to think of the concept of a game itself as an exceptionally elusive one.[20]

Whatever the intentions of its users, the term "play" as applied to the fine arts is derogatory in effect; mere play is contrasted with serious work, and the implication is that artists either are like chil-dren who have nothing to do but play because they are not serious persons,[21] or are engaged in a mere pastime. The view of human life implied by this derogation is one in which nothing matters but the care of the body, which is a strange view indeed (cf. Sparshott 1973b). It seems better to follow Aristotle in distinguishing between those arts that secure necessities and those that contribute to the quality of civilized life. Like politics and parties, religion and as-tronomy, the fine arts belong to what in man is distinctively human rather than generically animal. The concept of civilization itself, one might suggest, reflects a different estimate of what is serious and what is not, a different view of what it is to be human, from that which is enshrined in the notion of play.[22]

Imitation

The first way of distinguishing fine arts from others defines them as those that organize knowledge and skill to produce imitations for purposes of recreation or the enhancement of life. I have argued that this definition is best understood as one based on the identification of painting and poetry as disengaged uses of the principal cognitive modes,[23] followed by the recognition that such arts as sculpture, mime, and drama are doing the same sort of thing. Difficulties arise from the persistent use of the word "imitation," which hardly seems to fit anything these arts typically do. To imitate a thing or person is to mimic or copy its actions or movements or sounds, to "do an imitation"; and only comedians, and some kinds of mimetic dancers, do imitations. A painter who paints a flower is not imitating a flower or doing an imitation of one; but nor is he producing an imitation flower, which is a mimic flower designed to deceive by its likeness to the real thing, or to serve as a makeshift substitute for a real flower. But if we reject the word "imitate" on such grounds as these, we will not find any other word that suits better.[24] Nor are the difficulties merely verbal: it is not that we have no one word for what the fine arts do, but that it is hard to explain just what it is they are doing. The difficulties are greatly increased by the fact that the arts I have named have strong functional and traditional links with other arts that are even less obviously engaged in anything that could properly be called imitation. It is in coping with these difficulties that the "imitation" theory of the fine arts achieves profundity and subtlety but loses credibility.

It is a bit misleading to say that theorists of the fine arts have used the word "imitation," for want of a better, to stand for an obscure or subtle process that requires elucidation. It is rather that they use the word very broadly, to cover a multitude of different processes and relationships, so that one can give no single and consistent account of what the word means. Not that there is anything improper in this broad use: it may well be that all the processes and relationships such theorists elucidate share an important affinity that is what makes the notion of the fine arts meaningful. In what follows I try to disentangle a few of the more important relationships involved.

Let us begin with painting and sculpture. In such arts as these, one supposes that the artist imitates by making a thing that is like another thing, or, at least, that his doing so is a necessary condition of his imitating. But at once we meet the objection that this condition is vacuous: everything is like everything else in an infinite number of ways. The objection seems somewhat captious: all it comes down to is that one cannot lay down necessary and sufficient conditions of similarity in terms of the number of properties the similar things have in common, and there is no reason to suppose that likeness should be so defined.[25] The objectors themselves are perfectly able to tell what is like from what is unlike and to tell important likenesses from unimportant ones.[26] But what the objection does show is that it is meaningless to say that one thing is like another in all respects and in abstraction from all contexts and all interests. So our necessary condition must be made less vacuous.

The first thing to say, obviously, is that what the painter produces is not something like a flower—every flower is more like any other flower than it is like any painting, and every painting is more like any other painting than it is like any flower—but a *likeness of* a flower. What is it for a thing to be a *likeness of* another thing? In the first place, "being a likeness of" is a one-way relation: if a painted flower is a likeness of a flower, a flower is not a likeness of a painting. And the relation is one of dependence, in some sense (in what sense, I will consider later)—if there were no flowers, there could be no likenesses of flowers, but there were flowers before there were any likenesses of them.

If being a likeness is a matter of dependence or derivation as well as being like something, we have still to settle in what respect a likeness is like what it resembles. It could not be like it in *every* respect—we may take Leibniz's word for that. It is also evident that it is not a replica, not a copy, not a substitute, not a duplicate, though these are all familiar sorts of dependent likeness. By a "replica" of a thing I mean here something that differs from that thing (apart from its position in space and time) only in minute and negligible ways; and, as Eco observes (1976, 181), such replication can be secured only if one produces the replica by precisely the same procedures as were used to produce the original. The idea of a copy is close to that of a replica: a "true" copy of something is like its original in all relevant respects, conveys the same information that it does; and part of the notion of copying seems to be that true copies are possible—that one can know what all the relevant respects are and what counts as information. But for that to be possible, the original must already be a message or an artifact or a design or an action—something, that is, whose nature is exhausted by its intended properties.[27] For duplicates, the requirements are less stringent: a duplicate of a thing is something that will do as well for all practical purposes, because it has the same functional properties: a duplicate key opens the same doors as the original, however different it may look and feel. For substitutes, the requirements are weaker still. A substitute for something will do instead, but not necessarily as well: it is a makeshift, fulfilling the same essential function but not necessarily having all the functional properties of the original. Practitioners of painting, drawing, sculpture, and related arts have often found themselves using their skills in these four ways, and the use may have been "playful"; but such uses are not what their art is about. For one thing, things can be the object of these practices only if they are artificial, or messagelike, or functionally defined, as the case may be, and no such restriction holds of the things an artist takes for his subject or model. A painting may be a painting of anything whatever, provided that it is visible.

The proviso tells us in what respect a likeness is like what it resembles: it looks like it. That is, it presents an appearance similar to that of which it is the likeness. But again we have to ask: similar in what respect? It seems at first that we could now give the answer "in every respect," because it is a common experience that two things look so like each other that one cannot tell them apart—as like as two peas in a pod. From this point of view, however, painting and sculpture are differently placed. A sculptor can achieve something like replication: the likeness between a statue and a man can be specified by the identity of physical dimensions and local coloration, without direct reference to any observer; but a painter can only achieve depiction, and the likeness between a picture and a scene can be specified only by referring to what an observer would see from a particular angle.[28] In any case, even if it were practically possible for sculpture and painting to achieve perfect likenesses in their respective modes, the possibility is of no great importance.[29] The waxwork effigy, which comes as close to replication as anything a sculptor could do, is not a sculptural ideal.[30] And though trompe l'oeil painting is a possibility, trompe l'oeil drawing is not, and a drawing can be no less unmistakably *of* a particular thing than a painting.[31] On the other hand, if exact likeness of look is either too strict a requirement or quite inappropriate, it is not enough that a likeness should preserve the same relationships as are visible in that of which it is the likeness—should be a map of it. Mapping is systematically correlating the features of a surface with features of some other surface, either by some mechanical or quasi-mechanical means or by the "automatic" application of some equating formula. Ordinarily one uses some simple method of projection, as when one draws a building in accordance with the rules of classical perspective, or makes a photographic record with a system of lenses, or (of course) draws a map of the world on Mercator's projection. But I once heard someone say in a corridor that anything could be mapped on to anything by using a suitably complex or ad hoc means of projection, and so it can. It follows that, though the appearance of the map and that of the mapped are in one sense similar, a map need not look at all like what it maps.

What, then, do we mean when we say that one thing looks like another? Identity of appearance and identity of relations are not what we want; and we have already conceded that number and importance of points of likeness cannot be meaningfully specified. The fact is, one thing just does look like another. That is, likeness of look depends on a thing having a characteristic look that can be reproduced or caught. In yet other words, things are recognizable. But what makes them so?

Saying that one thing looks like another does not always mean the same thing. One may mean that, judging from its appearance, it probably *is* that thing ("That looks like my umbrella"); or that its visible characteristics are the same as, or very similar to, those of the other thing ("That umbrella looks just like mine"); or that its appearance is reminiscent of the characteristic appearance of another kind of thing ("That cloud looks like an umbrella"), or of a recognizable visible aspect of another particular thing ("That cloud looks like my umbrella"—a very different proposition from the one before). Presumably, the way things in pictures look like things in real life is more like the first two than the last two of these; but obviously one could not draw or paint "an elephant" unless one elephant looked enough like another elephant to be recognized. Anthony Quinton observes that general words could not be used unless the world presented their users with natural kinds—even twenty things can be arranged in 2^{20}-1 sets of from one to twenty members, so that a world with innumerable things presents innumerable options for classification, on which there must therefore be some antecedent limit (Quinton 1973, 262-263). It is already implicit in Aristotle's account of what an art is, and has often been pointed out since, that the survival of any but the simplest organism depends on learning and the generalization of conditioning, which is impossible unless there are ways in which things and situations really are like each other and appearances can be used as reliable guides to those likenesses. In short, real likenesses and real likenesses of look are a fundamental aspect of any world we can live in, whether we can explain the conditions of likeness or not.[32]

A dog that recognizes a rabbit on sight will not recognize a drawing of a rabbit; hence, if a drawing of a rabbit catches what for us is the characteristic look of a rabbit, what it catches cannot be identical with what makes rabbits recognizable to a dog. What else could it be? It could, first, be some convention of appearance. Such a convention would presumably be based in some fashion on what we and our dogs recognize, but not necessarily in any simple fashion. The convention might amount to a cultural definition of the essence or true nature of a kind of entity, to which the appearance of the likeness was expected to conform; but this would need to be coupled with a convention of depiction unless the essence were itself taken to be somehow visibly manifest.[33] And if it were thus manifest, it would turn into a special case of a visual stereotype, a cultural agreement as to what things of a certain sort look like.[34] Such a convention would be something like a learned habit of seeing and noticing, and is to be sharply distinguished from a language or convention of depiction, which, if really languagelike, would lead its users to *decode* a picture as depicting an elephant rather than to see the elephant in the picture (cf. Wollheim 1965, 25). But it is not so different from a convention of depiction (still doubtless based on what we and our dogs recognize) that would lead to an understanding, not that "this is what rabbits look like," but that "this is how we do rabbits."

Conventions governing how one does rabbits and so forth cannot form the basis of a practice of likeness making: for one thing, they would be conventions of what *stands for* what and not conventions of what *is like* what; for another thing, one would need a separate convention for each separate kind of thing one wanted to depict. Such conventions may govern how particular sorts of things are done *within* pictures, but not how pictures are done as a whole—though the skill involved in a way of doing rabbits might be extrapolated into a way of depicting other things, by the sort of development that we saw in chapter 2 was involved in the generation of arts of any kind.

The kind of convention of depiction we require must rather be a conventional *way of depicting* anything whatever, including things we have never seen before and can therefore have no separate convention for. The history of naturalistic painting, as Gombrich observes (1960, 326), is that of the discovery of schemes of equivalence that work. And what such a scheme requires, as Goodman's analysis shows, though he did not put it this way, is not so much a way of showing likenesses as a way of showing differences. If two real things can be told apart by looking, our way of depicting must have a way of registering the difference (Goodman 1968, 230).

A scheme of the kind mentioned obviates the need for separate conventions of how to do rabbits, elephants, and such, but it is still only a schema of standing for and not one of likeness making. It is a schema for what I referred to above as mapping, and (as I said before) a scheme of projection for a map need not result in anything that can be related to the characteristic look of anything without procedures of decoding and transformation. Not everything that has been mapped will serve as a map, for which one requires a simple system of projection from which the original can be read off immediately by reversing the system; and not every map that will serve in practice need do so by likeness, because simplicity and immediate availability are not similitude. The kind of schema we require is one in terms of which one can *see*.[35] And there are at least four distinguishable grades of recognizability that such a scheme can make available. First, one may be able to tell by looking at depiction X that it depicts a Y or an individual A; second, one may be able to recognize A, or the Y, in X; third, one may be able to tell from X what A or a Y looks like; and fourth, the depiction of A or of the Y in X may strike one as *looking just like A*, or a Y. "We are able to imagine," writes E. M. Zemach, "when we look at a realistic picture, that the observation conditions which prevail are such, that a real object of the kind depicted in that picture would look to us exactly as its depiction does in fact look to us" (1975, 574). The ability to imagine, to which Zemach appeals, is probably more labile than his argument requires; but it does seem to be the case that a cubist portrait of Kahnweiler would never lead anyone to imagine anything of the sort, though the passing decades have made cubist portraits thoroughly familiar and one can see immediately from the portrait just what Kahnweiler must have looked like (cf. ibid., 577).[36]

Conventions of depiction, then, include ways of depicting anything as well as agreed ways of depicting certain selected entities.

70

But by far the most important convention of depiction, and what really differentiates us from the dog who recognizes all rabbits,[37] but no pictures of rabbits, is that there is a practice of depicting, that we know there is such a practice, and that we can recognize likenesses as fruits of that practice. And how do we know that a likeness is a likeness, that is, that it is to be referred to that practice? Sometimes, or partly, by its context: it is labeled as a likeness, or is found where we look for likenesses. Failing such a context, it must have the character of a likeness. We know that an artifact is a likeness much as we know that a marked surface is an inscription. We know that either because we can read the inscription or because we recognize in it the kind of marks in the kind of order characteristic of the inscriptions we can read. Just so, we recognize likenesses by their consisting of the kind of marks in the kind of order characteristic of the likenesses we know. Likenesses no doubt use conventions, exploiting a repertoire of variables and variations to make their references and embody their resemblances. To know that a likeness is a likeness we need not know what those conventions are (need not be able to see the likeness) any more than we need understand a language to know that a language is being spoken, but we must be able to see that a convention is being used. The situation has not been changed at all by the practice of using likeness-making techniques for making paintings that are not likenesses—paintings of which Claude Lévi-Strauss has unfairly remarked that they are ultrarealistic demonstrations of the style in which the painter would paint pictures, "if by chance he were to paint any" (1962, 29n.). We scan such paintings for likeness as we scan them for formal principles, knowing for certain that they are potential likeness bearers.[38]

The factors I have named are not alternative explanations of what makes likenesses like, but may all be expected to be involved in any likeness, though to very different degrees. If identity of appearance were not possible in principle and could not be approximated to, things could not well have characteristic looks; without characteristic looks, conventions of appearance would be impossible and would reduce immediately to conventions of depiction; without conventions of appearance, conventions of depiction would have nothing to do with likeness. Recent writing on likeness, though brilliant, subtle, and learned, tends to suppose that one must choose between these as alternative explanations, and thus it is filled with useless controversies. This many dimensioned complexity of likeness making is only to be expected if depiction is a characteristic use of one of the two main communicative modes of beings whose energies are typically devoted to communication, and we would expect the complexity to be compounded in the "playful" or disengaged uses of those modes, in which complexity, remoteness, and obliqueness are deliberately tested and cultivated for their own sakes.

Likeness making, evidently, is a complex matter. Not only is likeness in appearance itself a matter of some intricacy, but to be a likeness involves also an element of dependence. That is not to say that there must be some original or model from which the likeness was taken, for there need be none; but that of which the likeness is a likeness is presumed to belong to an order of reality that in some way is antecedent to that to which the likeness itself belongs. The presumption is of a rather elusive sort, however. Pictures of unicorns are real things, and unicorns are not; but there can be unicorns-in-pictures only if we can make sense of the supposition that unicorns might have existed and, if they had existed, would have belonged to the same order of reality as the pigmented canvas or plaster and not to that of the unicorn-in-the-painting.[39] The asymmetry of the being-a-likeness-of-X relation depends, then, on there being a real world to which in general the practice of depiction refers, and not on there being for each likeness a real entity or kind of entity of which it is the likeness. But doubtless there could not be pictures of unicorns unless there were pictures of horses, rabbits, and such, and there could not be pictures of rabbits and such unless there could be a picture of a particular rabbit (or whatever) for which that particular rabbit served as model. In fact, as I said before, likeness making as we know it depends on there being a known practice of making likenesses, a practice that one can hardly believe would have become established unless there were real likenesses of look, some or some aspects of which some likenesses could be seen to capture.

The dependence of a likeness on an antecedent reality is not a causal or genetic relation. It is a matter of intention. To be a likeness of something is not just to be like it but to be meant to be like it and, since the practice of likeness making is an established one, to be accepted as being meant to be like it. Bare intention in the sense of empty wish is not enough: the meaning-to-be-like must amount to a purposeful and at least minimally skillful exploitation of perceptible likeness in appearance. And, on the other side, the acceptance that refers a perceived surface to the practice of likeness making may be erroneous. But such errors, and such empty wishes, could not occur without the true understanding and successful endeavors that they respectively emulate. And in the normal case there is a deep complicity of understanding between the painter and his public: the painter not only means his painting to be like but means it to be seen and accepted as like, and means it as well to be accepted as being meant to be like and as being meant to be so accepted; and the public accepts it on those terms.[40] It is for that reason, as Wollheim observes (1965, 24-26), that there is no conflict between seeing the rabbit in the painting as a rabbit and seeing it as the likeness of a rabbit, or between seeing a painting in configurational and in representational terms.

That casual and natural seeming use of the adjective "representational" reminds us that English-language discussions of depiction usually call it representation. The use of that term introduces fresh complications of a rather bothering sort, because it is primarily a political word: a person represents others if he acts on their behalf in certain limited respects for which they authorize him, either giving him a mandate to secure certain objectives or else assuming that his relevant interests are the same as theirs, or such as they would endorse. Richard Bernheimer argued (1961, 25-26 and passim) that being a picture of something really does have much in common with political representation: it is not to be a mere likeness but to stand for (stand in for) something that it is like in certain restricted functional respects. Political representatives are used where vicarious presence and efficacy are required; and the likeness of a place or person is more than a mere reminder, it is a vicarious presence. Even more obviously and notoriously, the icon of a deity renders the deity present, carries some of his power, and may receive communications on the deity's behalf (Bernheimer 1961).

We may agree with Bernheimer that such representational uses as he names are real and important; we may even agree further that artistically powerful and socially important representations stem from such uses, that mere likenesses of look are a vestigial form of representation and a trivialization of art (ibid., 209-211). But it is evident that pictures in which the representation is vicarious efficacy do not belong to the fine arts under the present definition, for they are straightforwardly utilitarian, not playful or disengaged uses of the communicative modes at all. They cannot, therefore, be discussed in terms of the classical line, but belong to a quite different way of thinking, which I treat of later under the rubric of the mystic line.

To say that a picture represents something is to say that it *stands for* it in the sense that we see the relevant part or aspect of the picture at one and the same time *as* what it stands for, as like what it stands for, and as referring to what it stands for.[41] I propose, however, to use the word in a more restricted way, to divide what I have been calling depiction into portrayal and representation.[42] Portrayal would be making something that will be recognized as a likeness of a given individual, whether or not it can be said to share any of the individual's spatial properties and whether or not any mechanical system of projection is used. And representation would be making something that will have the general appearance of a portrait of some thing of a certain kind, something that in suitable circumstances will be recognized as being a likeness of a thing of that kind rather than any other kind.[43] A picture X (or, more precisely, an X in a picture) would then represent a Y if and only if there could be an individual A such that if A existed X would portray A and A would be a Y. And what do I mean by saying there *could be* an A? I mean only that just as the scope of possible performances and actions depends on some individual, social, or generally human grasp of what could be intended, so what is acceptable as an object of portrayal or representation depends on an understanding as to what there is to be portrayed. As to what limits may be set to such understandings by human nature or culture, or even by physics or logic, I have nothing to say.

The distinction just sketched seems open to the objection that it is asymmetrical and combines two separate and unrelated distinctions: that between individual and kind and that between actual and possible existence. What is portrayed must be both actual and individual, what is represented is not individual and need not be actual. But that is not quite what I said: portrayal and representation as defined referred to real individuals and real kinds, respectively, though the sample of the kind chosen for representation need not be an extant individual. But, though the distinction as presented answers to one we make all the time and to what in general we mean by it, it is certainly clumsy and takes no account of the possibility of depicting imaginary individuals and mythical kinds. For this reason, one might reasonably prefer to adopt Nelson Goodman's much discussed account of representation, in which the issues of recognizability, reference, and individuation are kept distinct (Goodman 1968, 21ff.). On a view of this sort,[44] a portrait of Mackenzie King is such in the first instance because it is recognizable as a King picture, one of Pickwick because it is recognizable as a Pickwick picture, these being unanalyzable one-place predicates;

and horse pictures and unicorn pictures are recognizable in the same way. Since Mackenzie King existed, a King picture can refer to King, denote him, be a picture of him; since Pickwick never existed, no Pickwick picture is a picture of, refers to, denotes, portrays, or (in this sense) represents Pickwick. Since there are horses, a horse picture can (can be used to) represent a horse, denoting indifferently any horse; since there are no unicorns, there are no pictures, portrayals, or (in this sense) representations of unicorns. The point of this treatment of fictional entities, a good point, is that the reality behind Pickwick is the actual writing of Dickens and the reality behind unicorns is the actual stories, pictures, and so on in which they figure. But there are at least two troubles with this account. The first is that in treating "being a unicorn picture" as an unanalyzable one-place predicate, one is guilty of a transparent fiction: what unicorn pictures have in common is that they are recognizable pictures of unicorns. The second is that it slights the resemblance between pictures that denote and pictures that do not: a picture of Pickwick gestures toward a person whom it should denote, as a picture of King does toward a person whom it does denote. There is a sense in which each is a picture of a person in the same way; if there is a logical contrast between them, it is a contrast that it would be absurd to observe in our ways of talking and thinking when we have no occasion to. We might wish to say something more like the following: that there can only be a portrait of a real thing or person; but that there are pictures of persons both real and fictional or imaginary, only some of which (those that are of actual persons and are intended to denote and be understood as denoting those persons) are portraits.

The troubles just mentioned do not prevent Goodman's account of representation in terms of picture classifications, density and repletion of symbolism, and denotation from being the only account we have that is systematic and relatively clear. Its very strange look is largely due to its character of compromise: it is couched in terms of a modified nominalism, but presented with the implicit claims that, first, it could in principle be replaced by one in terms of the strict nominalism to which Goodman is committed and, second, though not answering to the way the word "representation" is ordinarily used, it could (together with other concepts introduced as part of the same system) serve all the theoretical purposes we should wish to retain from that use. Neither of these claims is at all plausible, because of factors I have already mentioned: the first, because nominalism postulates a featureless world; the second, because a symbol system is used by people for communicating with other people and cannot eliminate fictions functionally necessary for that communication.

Despite the title of his book, Goodman's account of representation in terms of denotation is singularly inappropriate to the fine arts, if those are defined as we are now defining them. We have remarked that since the communicative modes are used by the fine arts in a playful or disengaged way, their use will normally be fictional—that is, it is a matter of indifference whether what is purportedly referred to is real or not; and because what is used in a disengaged way is a mode of communication, the referential dimension inseparable from communication cannot be eliminated. Pictures have a referential character, whether there is anything for them to refer to or not, and it is to this character that we refer (not in error but necessarily) when we think of them as representational. In fact, they do not so much refer back to an antecedent reality (though we have seen that the antecedent status of *some* reality is essential to them) as project one. We see the horse in the painting, and we see it as a real horse in a real world, but without raising the question whether there ever was such a horse; and there is no difference between the way we see that horse and the way we see a unicorn in a painting, as a real unicorn in a real world, or the way we see (unless we are historians of bloodstock) Stubbs's painting of Gimcrack, which projects a horse and a world no more real than the unicorn and its world, even though it has a determinate denotation and they do not.

Discussions of referentiality have been bedeviled by a tendency to treat the issue as one of ontology, rather than as one of the functioning of symbol systems, and perhaps also by the supposition that questions of how such systems are understood belong to empirical psychology rather than forming an essential part of the study of the systems themselves. However that may be, the considerations that make me speak of projection rather than of reference are as follows. Let us suppose that I am listening to people talking about someone unknown to me. In the first place, I can make sense of what they say only insofar as their talk generates in me the notion of a person about whom they are talking—a notion that goes beyond the content of what they say partly by supplementing it with general knowledge of what is true of persons generally, partly by conjecture as to what a person so described must be (or would probably be) like. That is, their discourse generates a description that projects a person, the person about whom they would be talking if their talk was veridical. But, in the second place, it is not possible that anything in what they say could determine whether the person under discussion existed or not. Even if they spoke a language that employed different linguistic forms for fiction, no linguistic convention could prevent the misuse of such a convention: if language is possible, lying is possible. But also, in the third place, we cannot say that the person projected is simply the suppositious correlate of the sum of everything that is said about "him" or of any determinate part of that, because it is not only possible but highly likely that the sum of what is said of him will be not only vague but self-contradictory. On the basis of partial, partly erroneous, frequently conflicting reports, we form all those notions of the world we live in that do not depend on our personal direct observation. There not only is not, there cannot be, any feature of discourse itself that differentiates fictional projection from purported reference, any more than there can be any feature that differentiates truth from lies.

If I am to join in the conversation about the stranger, I must be able to talk about the person they are talking about, at least enough to ask intelligent questions about him and comment on the kind of person he must be. And I must be able to do this without any independent knowledge about him, without even knowing whether there is such a person. But if I am to be able to do that, I must also be able to talk about the person projected by a fictitious narrative, knowing that there is no such person. We cannot, therefore, as Nelson Goodman seems to do, say that the description of a person is a person description that denotes someone. Two more stages are needed. We have to say that the description projects a person. Then we have to say that the projection purports to be referential: that is, that the context is such that what is said purports to denote a real person. We then have to add something that does not even pertain, properly speaking, to the context of the discourse at all, namely, that the person purportedly referred to really existed or exists—that is, we as describing the whole situation add our own observation that the purported reference is veridical.

What I have just said about verbal discourse about things and people applies without significant alteration to pictures; the only difference is that nothing quite like joining in the conversation is now in question. If I can see the person in the painting, and it is a profile, I should be able to recognize the person the painting projects if I meet him head-on, provided it is well enough painted; and this capacity to envisage the projected person is quite independent of whether the painting purports to represent a real person and a fortiori of whether there is anyone whom the painting represents.

Nothing of what I have just been saying is novel, and it is hard to imagine that anyone would dissent from it or even find it interesting. But people have certainly written as though it were false, presumably from the baseless fear that it might be taken to imply the existence (or subsistence) of projected persons. But I do not know why it would be taken to imply that we are not conducting a census of imaginary worlds, but describing the conditions without which no effective communication would be possible.

The notion that reference back to an original is essential to realistic painting is no more than an eccentricity introduced into the topic to satisfy Plato's special interest in an ideal reality and the comparable interests of his Neoplatonic and Christian successors.[45] But our insistence on fictionality should not blind us to the fact that a reference back to actuality may be necessary to some particular disengaged use, because the "play" may consist in the manner of depiction of, and reference to, a known individual, the relation between what is projected and what is antecedently known or believed. One might contend that what is antecedently known or believed might or even must be absorbed into the fiction, so that a fictitious knowledge or belief would work as well as real knowledge or belief, which must in any case be taken up into the fictional mode before we can accept what is before us as truly a work of the fine arts. There is no doubt some sense in which that is true; but whatever sense that is, it remains true that a work may function by engaging our actual sense of the way certain matters are, so that one who lacks that sense can only imperfectly appreciate the work.

Projection is as complex as reference. We saw already that L. A. Reid argued that a picture may be thought of as "of" a thing in the sense that the thing was its model and is denoted by it; or in the sense that it shows the thing as the artist saw it aesthetically, with just those attributes that make it apt to be portrayed; or in the sense that the thing is recognizable in the painting. The third possibility is in a sense the limit of reference and, in the same sense, is the limit of projection. The picture also projects it in two further ways: as the thing-shown-by-the-painting, seen as real but with only those attributes and in those aspects that the picture shows, and as a real thing that might have a real nature and history of its own in the world that the picture creates and projects.

The foregoing are only some of the ambiguities and complexities that lurk in the notion of being a picture of something. To be a picture of a thing may be to be taken from that thing as a model, to be meant as a portrait of that thing, to be accepted as a portrait of that thing, to be accepted as or intended to refer back to a thing of that kind, or to project a thing of that kind, and so on without apparent limit. Some of the ambiguities are illustrated by the experience of the sculptor John Greenshields, who was commissioned in 1834 by Angus Macdonald of Glenaladale to execute a statue of Prince Charles. Greenshields sought to achieve the best possible likeness of the prince by examining an oil painting of him in a nearby castle; but, at the time of his visit, all the family were away, and he and the housekeeper hit on the wrong picture, a portrait of one George Lockhart. When he learned of his mistake, "he simply said 'It is much more fit than the Prince in pantaloons.' Apparently, Greenshields did not tell Glenaladale of his mistake, and so the statue was erected." The relater of this incident concludes that the statue is "not of Prince Charles" (Martin 1978, 654-656). The depth of the ambiguity may be appreciated if one asks oneself such questions as whether it would have made any difference if Greenshields had never discovered his mistake, or if both the oil portraits had been done from imagination, or had been misidentified by their owner, or (through the vicissitudes of copying from copies) if the final statue had actually turned out to be a better likeness of the prince than it was of Lockhart or than the pantalooned painting was of the prince.

The function of a portrait is certainly to refer back to an original, and the function of a representation of an imaginary person (an "imaginary portrait") is equally certainly not to refer back to but to project an entity. But, as I said of Stubbs's *Gimcrack*, we often do not know whether a picture was meant to be a portrait or not; and, if we know, we may not care, but may prefer to take it as projecting rather than as referring. The deep complicity whereby, I said, the makers and seers of pictures understand their common engagement in the business of likeness making may not extend to agreement as to what kind of likeness making is involved.[46]

The argument essential to this segment of the book is only that "imitation" in different arts must mean very different things, and that in sculpture, drawing, painting, and kindred arts it takes this or that form of likeness making. The convoluted (though still sketchy and crude) discussion of what likeness making could be was really something of a digression. I included it because it is vital, in discussing the equation of fine arts with arts of imitative play, to realize that the notion of likeness making is not a simple notion and the processes of likeness making are not simple processes, such that one could dismiss the definition as inevitably reducing the fine arts to heteronomy or to triviality.[47] The elaborations of my account are not complications of a fundamentally straightforward matter: in the fine arts, the convolutions *are* the matter, because the deft exploitation of the multiple possibilities and ambiguities is precisely the skill that is the disengaged use of the mode of communication. Comparable complexities could be introduced into the discussion of what imitation is in each of the arts: the complications could fill books, and often have. I omit them here, not because the relations involved are simple, but because to introduce them would not further my argument.

Whatever the complexities, the imitation in painting or sculpture is this or that kind of likeness making, producing a thing that is recognizably meant to be recognized as like another thing. But what of the imitation in drama? The actors' performances may refer back to actual persons, types, and historical eras and project characters as the action of the play as a whole projects a world, but the actors can hardly be said to make a thing that is the likeness of another thing. They use their bodies to furnish a mobile representation, but in acting out a scene they produce happenings that fail to be real only in the sense that they are not serious—outside the play they have neither motivation nor consequences of the sort they would have if they were not actions in a play.[48] To act a man telling a woman he loves her, a man tells a woman he loves her.[49] This mode of imitating seems to be less like likeness making than it is like presenting as a work of art a real soup can labeled "soup can."

In principle, as every theorist of acting has noted, an actor can work up his "imitation" in two ways: he can model his actions on those of someone seriously doing and saying the relevant things, or he can imagine himself into the character and situation required and just say and do them.[50] In the latter case, he is not so much imitating the actions of a person as imitating a person and doing what that person would do.[51] And that possibility gives rise to a whole other way of imitating or thinking about imitation, one that exploits a vocabulary I have not been using. Instead of thinking of the fine arts as arts of disengaged communication, we are now to think of them as "imitating nature" and to drop the qualification "playful" or "disengaged" as otiose. But now we encounter an equivocation: the word "nature" may mean the natural order of things as they are (*natura naturata*), or it may mean the system of causes that maintains that order in being (*natura naturans*). To imitate the order would be to take reality as in some sense one's model.[52] To imitate the causes would rather be to generate an order of one's own, much as the actor uses an imaginative version of his own personal agency to create the character he plays.

The imitation of nature by imitating the action of natural causes will hardly suffice to define the fine arts: it is a description applied by Aristotle to *any* art, which can bring about changes and produce artifacts only by exploiting the processes of nature, which already produces changes and substances.[53] If the fine arts do anything especially naturelike, they must create not substances but "worlds" ("heterocosms") having their own laws.[54]

The idea that the fine arts have a quasi-natural power to produce worlds of their own has often been applied to the visual arts, especially in ages whose faith made the analogy of divine and human creation attractive.[55] The idea is perfectly compatible with the notion that the artist's creative power is devoted to making likenesses of things. And the idea lingers on. Paul Klee, for instance, writes:

> He [the artist] does not attach such intense importance to natural form as do so many realist critics, because, for him, these final forms are not the real stuff of the process of natural creation. For he places more value on the powers which do the forming than on the final forms themselves.
>
> [He says of the world] "In its present shape it is not the only possible world." . . .
>
> The deeper he looks . . . the more deeply he is impressed by the one essential image of creation itself, as Genesis, rather than by the image of nature, the finished product (1924, 87).

But in this form the idea of *natura naturans* hardly fits in with the notion of the fine arts, because it is hard to reconcile with the idea of a corpus of knowledge and skill: it suggests, rather, a kind of natural creativity that is opposed to artifice and as such will be taken up in part 2 of this book. The idea in this form belongs to romantic and postromantic critical theory. The classical version of the view that the fine arts are arts of imitation remains the one established by Plato, in which the fine arts are alleged to produce likenesses that are differentiated from natural objects precisely by their lack of a "nature" or inherent organizing principle. Rather, they consist of mere accumulations of details. Their unity is extraneous, lying in the artist's intention or in their common property of resemblance to some object in the real world.

It is in literature rather than in the visual arts that the view that the artist imitates *naturam naturantem* and produces a heterocosm is most at home, because it seems natural to say that the author of a novel creates a world, though he does not do so by anything like likeness making.

Saying stands alongside showing as the other major mode of communication among human beings. Some things can be shown but not said, others said but not shown, and many things can be either said or shown, so it makes some sense to think of literature and painting as alternative ways of doing the same sort of thing and to say that anyone who knows the language a work is written in can recognize what it "portrays" or what sort of thing it "represents." But if a work of literature imitates, it does not do so by any sort of likeness making or acting out (though it may be associated with the latter, as the text of a play or the script of a film). A picture is *of* something, a literary work is *about* something and does not function by looking or sounding like the things it is about, which it describes, characterizes, and says things about rather than depicting. The structure of a literary work does not replicate and is not mapped or copied in any way from the structure of what it is about: its formal properties are systematically determined by the rules of grammar and the laws of rhetoric and not by any properties of its subject.

Because a work of literature imitates not by being *like* but by being *about* something, its scope is as wide as that of discourse itself. A literary work can unambiguously project whatever can be thought or envisaged: people, actions, events, things, scenes, thoughts, sayings, attitudes, feelings.[56] Alone of these, thoughts can be embodied in literary stuff, and a thought expressed in literature differs from one expressed in real life only (like the actor's speech) by not being seriously meant—or, rather, by its status of fictionality, by the question of its being seriously meant not arising. Everything else in the work is projected. The notion of projection is especially appropriate in literature, because all that the fullest description of narrative does for hearer or reader is to furnish clues, from which the audience constructs a world or whatever by filling in the gaps from his own knowledge of the way things are and can be.[57] We see the woman and the world in the painting, but we do not read the woman and the world in the book: we only read about them, and they themselves are reconstructed by us in the same way that we figure out from the sketchy narratives of everyday life what really happened and what it must have been like. The traditional analogy between painting and literature was made to seem closer than it is by the old fiction of the "mental image," according to which language worked by reproducing a sort of picture in the speaker's mind and evoking a corresponding picture in the hearer's "mind's eye." On that way of looking at things, all that separated literature from painting was that in the former the "pictures" were immaterial, and the writer's mental picture was not numerically identical with the hearer's. But that way of thinking is, fortunately, obsolete.

Fictional and make-believe characters are more at home in literature than in painting, which is more fertile of fictive species. When one talks about Mr. Pickwick, it is equally absurd to say that one is not talking about anyone and that one is talking only about the *Pickwick Papers*, though those absurdities are both perfectly true. One is referring back to Pickwick; and what one is referring back to is the personage projected by the book, a personage who is projected and remembered in the same way, in the same relation to the same sort of evidence, as anyone else known to us only by hearsay. Dickens himself, when he began to write, was not referring back to anything, only projecting; but when his work was far enough advanced for the characterization of Pickwick to be determinate, his continuations of his projection were at the same time references back to the projected figure that Dickens remembered from his own writing. It is just because Pickwick is not there to be seen in the writing as he is there to be seen in Robert Seymour's drawing that one cannot reduce him to the set of Pickwick texts as one might (on Goodman's principles) reduce him to a set of Pickwick pictures.

I have mentioned two ways in which literature may be thought of as an art of "imitative play" or disengaged communication: first, it produces alternative worlds in imitation of the genetic power of nature and, second, it projects worlds and entities that are simulacra of the real world and its denizens. But there is a third way that has been popular lately and is analogous to the way in which the action in a play is in fact an action, but not a serious one. For some purposes, at least, "the unit of linguistic communication is not . . . the symbol or word or sentence . . . but rather the production or issuance of the symbol or word or sentence in the performance of the speech act" (Searle 1969, 16). Such an act is performed in a context, for a purpose. But the work of literature is, as a work of fine art, free of context and purpose: its promulgation is a speech act of a special kind that works by simulating all the more ordinary kinds of speech act there are. One might try to construct a similar explanation of the disengagement of pictorial art, but it turns out not to work: a drawing is just a drawing, a likeness just a likeness. So this resurrection of imitation theory in the theory of literature has not as yet changed the way people think about the fine arts in general.

It makes a lot of sense to place literature and its associated practices alongside painting, drawing, and sculpture and their associated practices as the arts of disengaged uses of the two chief kinds of ways in which human beings explain themselves to themselves and each other, and any dramatic and mimetic arts there may be clearly belong in the same group. As we have partly seen, the characteristic differences in their ways of operating and in the range of effects open to them are as illuminating as what they have in common, and this fact is nicely captured by what otherwise seems the rather extravagant verbal conceit of saying that they all do the same thing (imitating) in different ways, or that they produce different species of a common genus (imitations). But this group of arts is not coextensive with what we call the fine arts. Specifically, music, architecture, and abstract dance have no place in the scheme. That might not matter, of course. It might well be that the notion of the fine arts is incoherent and should be replaced for theoretical purposes by a different scheme of classification, just as in the physical sciences we are accustomed to learn that common-sense groupings of organisms and stuffs are not quite right for scientific purposes.[58] But it is wrong to suggest, as was the fashion of a few decades ago, that the grouping of the fine arts is an artificial and fairly recent growth. Architecture, drawing, and sculpture were established as a unity (as *arti del disegno*) by the end of the fifteenth century (Panofsky 1954, 2, n. 3), and it is obvious that in the practice of such artists as Michelangelo they functioned as one. Music as song and as the accompaniment to song was thought of throughout classical antiquity as inseparable from lyric poetry and (though less intimately) from metrical language generally, and music divorced from song was thought of as marginal.[59] Hence, since the view that literature and painting are arts of imitative play in the sense we have indicated is one that it is merely stupid to deny, there is a strong temptation to show how architecture and music can somehow be construed as contributing to the communicative function. What happens when one yields to the temptation is what we shall see in the next two sections of this chapter.

Expression

Music owes its place among the arts of imitative play, and hence among the fine arts, to its association with literature. The question how music can be said to imitate, as well as what form this imitation takes, has a predetermined answer. Its imitation function must lie in whatever it does in closest association with literature. When I sing, what does the tune do that the words do not; what does it add to the words?

Imitation in vocal music might be finding a musical equivalent for the text set. But not much music sounds like, and even less functions by sounding like, anything except other music. The text might describe an event or a state of mind, but the musical setting can do no such thing. Music is not a language in which things can be said. Although its phrases can be, and often are, used as a vocabulary to stand for things and ideas, its syntax is determined by its own laws and does not permit even a full "vocabulary" to be used to make any but the crudest assertion. (Having the French national anthem drown out the Russian is a crude way of saying that France defeated Russia, but sheds little light on strategy.) Besides, the text set has already done all the saying that is necessary. What singing is, is a very special way of saying, a special use of the voice in delivering a verbal message. So presumably the difference between saying and singing is like the difference between saying and whispering or shouting, only much more subtle. It conveys what you feel or want others to feel about what you are saying, your attitude to it (or the attitude you wish to evoke to it), or how you want it to be taken (ironically, quizzically, seriously); it is an elaborate form of using a special tone of voice.

The music of a song, then, conveys not so much what the text means as what one means by the text or the way one means it. It does not say this, but shows it; and the word conventionally used for this kind of showing is "expression." But suppose there is no text? Music has, after all, been instrumental from the beginning. A person cannot say anything while he is playing a flute, but he can accompany someone else. And then he will be expressing the inner meaning of, the feeling implicit in, another person's saying or singing.[60] Now we at once see that there need be no text. What is accompanied could be a silent movie, in which the accompaniment expresses an ideal attitude to, or the emotion ideally inherent in, the story line. And if that is possible, it is clear (as we knew all along) that there could be an "absolute" music in which nothing is accompanied, in which the inner meanings expressed are not related to any events, but narrate or generate a pure subjective history of an imaginary mind. And if we permit ourselves to use the one word "emotion" or "feeling" to cover the subjective equivalents of attitudes to, feelings toward, ways-of-taking, that the tune of a song conveys,[61] we can point to the fact that a piece of music consists of a precise series of notes and no others,[62] and conclude that music gives precise expression to emotional states. Thus, we find Dubos writing in 1719 in a work whose very title announces the program of assimilating music to the "sister arts" of painting and poetry: "As the painter imitates the strokes and colours of nature, in like manner the musician imitates the tones, accents, sighs, and inflexions of the voice; and in short all those sounds, by which nature herself expresses her sentiments and passions" (Dubos 1719, I, 360), and "the richness and variety of concords, the charms, and novelty of modulations should be applied to no other use in music but that of drawing and imbellishing the imitation of the language and passions of nature" (ibid., 374). The second of these quotations, we note, is normative rather than descriptive and implies a warning: musical devices obviously can be put to other uses, but those other uses lie outside the proper domain of the art of music.

A slightly different way of putting the same matter would be to say that, whereas literature imitates (recounts and projects) events, music provides a second-order imitation of events: it projects *what it is like to be conscious* of events—not indeed of specific events, but such as may come one's way in a lifetime.[63] Such is in effect S. K. Langer's account of musical meaning, which has been as influential in our day as any (Langer 1942 and 1953), and, more explicitly and without the proviso, that of Lukács (1963). This way of putting the matter rests on one of those grand schematic simplicities that serve as scaffolds to build up our theories. According to Kant, we use spatial relations to articulate our knowledge of the objective world, temporal relations to articulate our subjective experience; music is articulated in time as painting is in space; thus painting represents the objective world and music the subjective world, which must in the last analysis be equated with consciousness of the objective world.

If one wishes to argue that music expresses emotion, one does not need to rely on association (at however many removes) with a verbal text. People spontaneously use vocal noises—snarls, moans, whoops, jeers—to make their feelings plain to themselves and others, and at least some music appears to echo and elaborate these sounds;

many people use music to celebrate or assuage a solitary mood.[64] That a professional musician, who must play to order, cannot always make this use of music is obviously true, but it is easy to defuse that truth by pointing out that a prostitute's simulated ecstasy tells us little about the nature of sexual passion. Again, music everywhere accompanies dancing, which it is plausible to think of as the most venerable of the arts and is itself a direct expression of personal or (more commonly) social emotions, aspirations, and attitudes. Other bodily exertions also have music that traditionally goes with them and facilitates them, by establishing their rhythm or simply taking the curse off them, and what the music does is express what it feels like to be turning a capstan or marching.

If there are arts of imitation, then, music (or part of what we nowadays call music) is one of them so long as the modes of expression we have alluded to can all be brought under that rubric. Music imitates nature in the sense that human nature is as much nature as anything else, and to express emotion in the broad sense we have sketched is to imitate human nature. But what about "play" and "disengaged communication"? Well, we will not allow music to be one of the fine arts unless, like literature and painting, it is cultivated and developed and elaborated for its own sake. And at this point we have to introduce a slight complication. In shouting, howling, cheering, and so on, one is expressing something one feels, and such expression seems to form the basis for an art of subjective expression in which one seeks to give such noises precision and force. But the setting of a text, as we observed, suggests rather an art of finding equivalents for the feeling implicit in it, and this feeling need not be one's own: one expresses rather, as Langer (1953) puts it, one's *knowledge* of feeling. No doubt it may come to the same thing in the end: if music is an art, the artist must know what he is doing, so that, if his work is an expression of feeling, his knowledge of his work must be a knowledge of feeling.[65] But could there not be an art, as indeed I suggested in chapter 2, the specific task of which was to transform one's own feelings (the only feelings accessible to one) into expressive entities? This would be an art of what Arthur Berndtson has called "transitive emotion," which he defines as "the passage of emotion from a primitive to a developed and adequate state through the mediation of form" (1969, 149). If music were such an art, one might urge that any music not related to a personal feeling in this way was a fake or inauthentic, not as a moral judgment, but because the artist had not fulfilled the necessary terms of his art.[66] But why should one adopt such a position? Its chief exponents have usually confused it with two quite different theses: first, that what we are really interested in is not the performance but the person, so that an inauthentic expression is a sort of lie; and, second, that finding articulate equivalents for feelings is a vital epistemological task that only sincerity can fulfill. But such considerations as these begin to take us out of the domain of the fine arts, and a careful consideration of the second proves it to be incompatible with any version of the classical line. It can only be accommodated by an "expressive line" of its own (see chapters 11 and 12, below).

If we take feeling in the most obvious way and equate it with nameable feelings like sadness, we can say that a piece of music expresses sadness by *sounding* sad and thus *being* sad. Just what that could mean is a much discussed topic, which I take up later (chapter 7) in dealing with the characterization of works of art. But it has nothing to do with what I am talking about here, which is the doctrine that it is the function of some or all of the works of some or all of the fine arts, not to have a character that may fitly be termed this or that, but to give expression to this or that aspect of human subjectivity. That being so, we may reflect that the fact that what one feels on a given occasion has a name (such as "sadness") is seldom a very important thing about it. Feelings don't all have names, and a fortiori the feeling expressed by a piece of music might have no name[67]—a fortiori, because the logic of my argument requires that a feeling expressed in a work of art need not be a feeling that anyone could actually have. On the other hand, it would be a mistake to say that music (rather than expressing joy, hope, fear, and other nameables) is simply expressive, for the word "expressiveness" is already in use to designate a special quality of some music that has nothing to do with the quality that is alleged to make music in general one of the imitative arts.[68] We do better to say that what a piece of music expresses is precisely what we hear expressed in it, not necessarily to be equated with anything more specific than the subjective aspect of experience at large. The task of explaining more precisely how music does this, if it can be heard to do so and, if not, how it can be known to do so, is a large one and has occupied much of the energy of the aestheticians of music.

Expression gets into the theory of the fine arts by way of music, but is not confined to music. A painting can be sad just as a song can. As with music, this could be a matter of the perceived character of the painting and as such would not be relevant to our present topic (see chapter 7 again). It could be a matter of the kind of scene, persons, objects, or events the painting represents and as such would not require special treatment. (Xenophon, in *Memorabilia* III. x. 1–8, makes Socrates remark that painters can represent [*ekmimeisthai*] qualities of soul as well as of body: that drawing [*graphikē*] is a likeness making [*eikasia*] of things seen, and *hence* of the expressions on people's faces, and *hence* of their characters. If Xenophon could see the point, it cannot be one that takes much subtlety to appreciate.) But it could also be a matter of the feeling implied in the act of painting. In fact, works of literature and painting cannot but convey personal attitudes, whether or not those attitudes were those of the persons who created them. Whatever is depicted must be shown as interesting and hence must express that interest. The artist must paint it in one way rather than another, and in doing so cannot but express an attitude to what he paints, even if what he expresses is one of that curiously subtle class of emotions we call objectivity.[69]

In any work of literary or visual art, there is a difference between the world of the work (the reality it projects by what it shows or tells of) and the sensibility the work reveals or projects by the way it is done, and between the particular things and events shown or described and the specific feelings or attitudes manifested in the showing and describing. We may thus discern a representative and an expressive aspect in any such work. But the difference is not absolute. The materials of the arts (colors, consonantal and vowel sounds) may have affective tendencies, be perceived as gay, somber, or what not; and the subject matter depicted or described will inevitably, like everything else we encounter, be experienced as having an affective character, which, though doubtless derived from associations, is as much a part of it as any other quality it has.[70] But whereas in natural things such qualities are perceived simply as inhering in the objects, in a work of fine art, which as such is taken to be a performance, the quality is that of something performed and hence imputable to the performer: if things can *be* perceptibly sad, things can be *made* perceptibly sad, and such making is a resource of the art. The two kinds of affective characteristics are part of what is shown or told of, but in the choice of a matter thus charged a sensibility becomes manifest or is at least implied. It thus appears that there may be harmony or discrepancy between the representational and expressive aspects of a work, wherever precisely we may choose to draw the line between them.[71] One might respond to this possibility by recalling the Stoic definition of an art and saying that the skillful painter or writer is one whose representational and expressive skills are so "exercised together" that they function as one, in a single creative act. Many theorists take that view.[72] But it might be criticized as simplistic, as arbitrarily singling out one possible relation between representation and expression: the artist's fusion of skills is shown rather in the acquired spontaneity with which he achieves whatever the relation between the two aspects of the work may be. It is in subtle variations on this relation that the effects of irony are achieved, and those effects are among the most precious resources of the fine arts.

Not only is expression of feeling, emotion, attitude, sensibility, or the inwardness of life generally a dimension of all imitative arts, it can easily be made out to be a predominant aspect of them. The argument might run as follows. The artist must imitate the world, since his repertoire of matters and forms cannot be generated from the pure and purely empty act of consciousness. He imitates the world, then, but necessarily the world as he sees and feels it: not only is it a sort of logical truth that what is seen must be seen from a specific standpoint, but one hardly sees why he would set up as an imitator unless he thought his own viewpoint on the world had (or could be made to seem to have) its own special interest. So he represents (let us exchange the words) the world as he sees it; but is this not to say that he represents, not the world, but his idea of the world?[73] But if what he represents is his idea of the world, do not the words "of the world" become a mere gloss, otiose or tendentious? What he is really doing is representing (but let us now change words again and say "expressing") his own ideas, feelings, and so forth. So one concludes that all art is in the first instance the expression of feeling.

That argument is a bit suspect. The idea that what one experiences is never an object but always something private to oneself saddles the logic of experience and perception with a groundless and useless solipsism. Setting up one's viewpoint as a separate entity from what one sees, an entity in which independent value could be found, needs explanation and defense; and one seems to be gratuitously importing the notions of self-expression and subjectivity into that aspect of a performance that answers to the way something is done rather than what is done. But one might grant the weakness of the case as presented and still insist that only the expression of a personal viewpoint can differentiate a work of fine art, of imitation that is at once playful and serious, from straightforward narration and depiction on the one hand—whether veracious or mendacious (for simply *failing to be* truthful cannot suffice to establish any high significance)—and mere decoration and doodling on the other.[74] It is the quality of the subjectivity expressed, or the perceived relation to an emotional urgency, that makes the difference. How one should continue after saying that is highly debatable, but the view that the function of fine art is in some way to express emotion has been as widely held as any.[75] John Hospers, in a penetrating critique of "the expression theory of art," has posed as a rhetorical question why this of all possible functions should be singled out (Hospers 1955). But the question is not unanswerable, and I have in fact just sketched the outline of one answer. What is missing is an argument to show that a single function of art, a single differentia of fine arts or arts of imitative play, is required.

I said that the emphasis on expression of subjectivity as essential to the fine arts originates with the need to acknowledge the integral unity of music with other arts already classified as arts of imitative play, and have accordingly treated expression as a kind of imitation. But the expressiveness of a painting does not depend on its representational aspect, and expression theories of art retain and even increase their attraction when the notion of arts of imitative play has been abandoned.[76] But as we gradually rid our thinking about the expressiveness of art of all traces of the idea of imitation, we move toward a kind of theory in which the difference between subjectivity and what expresses it vanishes. When that vanishes, the idea of an art vanishes too, and we find ourselves launched on what I shall be calling the expressive line of thought about art.

Form

Broadening imitation theory to include expression as well as likeness making and the rest is still not enough to give it the scope it requires. Neither kind of imitation has any obvious role in the products of architecture or of industrial design, whose form is determined by function and by considerations of good proportion. Traditionally, the values of architecture are the Vitruvian trinity of "commodity, firmness, and delight," charmingly vulgarized by Isidore of Seville as planning, construction, and decoration.[77] Yet we have already seen that a tradition no less firm and venerable linked architecture with the imitative arts of drawing and sculpture, and most people still want to include architecture among the fine arts and to discuss industrial design in the same terms as architecture.[78] Theorists have therefore felt the need to bring both under the rubric of imitation. They have done so by considering that proportions will only seem admirable if they meet formal requirements imposed on them by the beholder, that there is enough consensus about what proportions are admirable to support the contention that all normal beholders impose the same requirements, and that these requirements may then be said to be those of the mind itself, some aspect of whose nature they thus represent or express. Theorists tend to be vague about what mental structures are involved and about what "the mind" (as opposed to thinking people) may be.[79] But this extension of the notion of imitation is not so perverse and foolish as it seems. Why should the demand for formal beauty not be just as genuine an emotion, and need expression just as much, as any mood or passion whatever? And the theoretical justification for the extension is stronger than it looks: it is not merely a willful distortion of a concept in the interests of a dogma. If the attraction of fine proportions is not to be explained in some such way as this, there can be no art to achieve it: it will simply happen that some works find favor and others do not. In arts acknowledged to be representational and expressive, a task in which the artist may succeed can be intelligibly described: there can be organized and teachable skills of exploiting and developing communicative resources to project convincing likenesses and so forth. But in what must the artist of pure form succeed? At most he must be gratifying a cultural consensus. The cross-cultural or perennial appeal of a formal masterpiece becomes so inexplicable that it must be hailed as a miracle or dismissed as an illusion. The demand laid on the theorist seems stringent. He must either accept or deny that the acceptability of formal proportions crosses cultural boundaries. If he denies it, he has a formidable task explaining away the appearance of a measure of consensus. If he accepts it, he must admit either that some proportions are objectively good (in which case they are what the well-proportioned work exemplifies or "imitates" in a Platonic sense) or that there is a constant element in the formal hungers of human minds. And the last of these possibilities seems the least outrageous—as so often, to denounce the theory as perverse usually shows only that one has failed to consider the alternatives. As to the conundrum about whose mind "the mind" is, an obvious and quite adequate answer is that the phrase "the mind" has here the same typifying use as "the horse" in "the horse is a graminivorous ungulate." Metaphysicians are free to go further and perhaps fare worse, but they need not.

What are these "laws of the mind" that are to be conspicuously embodied and thus celebrated and, in a way, referred to? Because of the amount of measuring builders have to do anyway, the most popular answer has been a Pythagorean one, specifying certain proportions alleged to satisfy the intellect because they figure in important or intriguing ways in mathematical thought. Other supposed demands of the mind have been mooted—perceptual demands, to be satisfied by simple *Gestalten* (Arnheim 1954); adaptive demands, to be satisfied by the interplay of strict form and subtle variation (Ehrenzweig 1967)—but historically only the Pythagorean version has been important. And it is characteristic of Pythagoreanizing thought that the general principles it invokes, though immediately known by the part they play in intellectual constructs, are thought to be important only because they are the principles on which the world itself is constructed. And, since those principles must also be those in accordance with which the world of nature is generated, an architect who follows them is not only producing a plan that is like the world's plan but also imitating the formative processes of nature, *naturam naturantem*.[80]

Like theories of expression, formal theories of the sort I am discussing, though hatched and nurtured in the nest of imitation theory, take on a life of their own and are usually thought of as rivals of that theory. But what is distinctive in these theories is that they do not rest content with equating architectural values with formal values, much less with "aesthetic" values of the sort that my next chapter discusses, but insist on a specific kind of form that is valued because of its supposed relation to what nature embodies and mind demands. A theory of this sort has little in common with such theories as Clive Bell's postulation of "significant form," according to which a work of visual art is valued exclusively because it moves civilized observers to ecstasy by the way it looks (Bell 1914).

Buildings are not the only things that have shapes, and whatever we say about architectural form can be applied mutatis mutandis to the formal properties of works in other arts—for the concept of form, like those of expression and imitation itself, is infinitely elastic, though if one stretches such concepts too far they may not snap back into shape. Music, notoriously, is Pythagorean from the beginning, if only because musical scales are constructed on (or found to embody) mathematically specifiable proportions. A painted likeness must be arranged on its support in a specific fashion and must have a form independent of what it depicts; a statue must have determinate proportions. Some theorists contend that the principles of right proportion can be (or indeed have been) discovered and stated; others hold only that they must be postulated to account for the way in which judgments of formal excellence coincide. The latter possibility gives rise to some equivocation, as in the view attributed to Mannerist theory by Anthony Blunt: "Beauty was something which was directly infused into the mind of man from the mind of God, and existed there independent of any sense-impressions. The idea in the artist's mind was the source of all the beauty in the works which he created" (1940, 140–141). For the idea in the mind of God must be unknowable, or knowable only by analogy, and the idea in the artist's mind can function only as subjective ideal. We seem here to be within a hair's breadth of Bell's theory, but really we are not; for whereas Bell insisted on an ecstasy felt on apprehending the overall look (or sound) of a work, the sort of formal theory we are exploring limits itself to that aspect of the look which is due to formal proportions, and it assigns the excellence of those proportions to principles that are real and effective even if not actually discoverable.

Like expression, then, the concept of form begins as a dodge for bringing a new class of works under the umbrella of "imitation," but is immediately recognizable as a dimension of the value of some works in all the imitative arts and probably of all works in any of them. *Embarcation for Cythera* by Watteau *depicts* a scene, *expresses* a subtle nostalgia, and satisfies the mind by its formal organization; Elgar's "Dorabella" variation *represents* a girl's stammer, *expresses* a playful affection, and gratifies the mind's demand for formal organization by its concise elegance and its oblique relation to its theme. Even buildings are expressive and may be representational: Coventry Cathedral is a powerful and elaborate symbol of agony overcome, and Angkor Wat diagrams the cosmos.

Imitation theory has now provided us with three modes of whatever it is, having different roles in the different fine arts. A recent tendency has been to make the formal demand paramount in all of them except possibly literature,[81] but to allow that painting *may* legitimately add representation and *can* express feeling, while music *ought* to express feeling but *ought not* to represent. But such judgments are irremediably controversial. Perhaps, in any of the fine arts, works and styles may appear in which one or other of the three modes dominates. In painting, one could argue that abstract expressionism exalted expression, cubism and de Stijl isolated the formal demand, and some Victorian genre painting subjected everything to representation. Rhapsodic music of the Romantic era is predominantly expressive; some contrapuntal music is almost purely formal. And a dance, even within the formal tradition of ballet, may be abstract or principally expressive or predominantly mimetic.

Despite the variability in emphasis to which I have just referred, one need not think of the three modes of imitation as being in competition, though on a given occasion they may be found so. It used to be supposed, for instance, that because Greek sculpture became more naturalistic from the sixth century to the fourth, it *must have* become less interesting formally; but it is surely *possible* that formal control should have increased as representation became more subtle, and I for one think it did. In any case, the three modes of imitation (or three things that "imitation" is taken to mean in defiance of linguistic propriety) present a striking though imperfect analogy with the three "dimensions" that a number of influential aestheticians from different backgrounds have independently ascribed to every work of art—I will say something about them in chapter 6.

The fact that each of the three major kinds of imitation is exemplified by each of the arts of "imitative play" means that the latter form a more closely knit group than one would have expected. But though I insisted that the theory of mind-gratifying form does belong in this context, the position of architecture in this group of arts rests on a quite different footing from the others. All the other imitative arts are developments of activities that are inherently charged with meaning and proper objects of attention. Each of them is the elaborated, disengaged, and endotelic use of something we commonly do to express a meaning to ourselves or others: telling becomes literature, showing by models becomes sculpture, showing by marks becomes drawing and painting, showing by acting out becomes drama, showing by gesture becomes dance, showing how one feels by body movement becomes dance, showing how one feels by use of the voice becomes music; and the abstract (nonrepresentational, nonexpressive) versions of these arts still rely on the symbolic repertories and resources of these means of communication. But none of this is true of architecture, which, if it is a fine art at all, is the elaborated and disengaged use, not of a means of communication, but of useful organization of space and firm structure. The appeal to "form that expresses the mind's demand" applies to the process of elaboration by which building becomes architecture, not (as in all the other arts) to what is elaborated on. Architecture, therefore, remains very much the odd man out.

Imitation theory is certainly versatile. But its contortions, though they give an impression of vitality, are the convulsions of despair. It is because the arts it brings together are obviously not united by being representational in any plausible sense that theorists have been driven to ingeniously rich analysis of their more recondite effects and potentialities. No doubt the best theories in every field derive their energy from the determination to save an outrageous thesis. Philosophers raise a dust, not to blind themselves, but to have something to make pearls on.

It is unfashionable nowadays to say that the fine arts are arts of imitation. The versions that made them all a matter of likeness making were originally formulated to debunk the arts rather than to explain them. But the versions that rely on the concept of expression are still current and pass for the normal form of a theory of fine art among persons of old-fashioned tastes. The generality of the theory, however, can be saved only if we replace the expression of an independently describable feeling or viewpoint by an abstract expressiveness; and this cannot be differentiated otherwise than rhetorically from the effective articulation of forms, which in turn is only another way of saying "beauty." Why, then, should we not simply say that the fine arts are the "fine" arts, the arts of beauty? It seems safer, and it is certainly simpler.

When the interpretation of the fine arts as arts of imitation is reduced to the highest common factor of its variants, it passes over into the interpretation of them as arts of beauty. But this alternative interpretation would not have satisfied the anatomists of interpretation. Far from it. It was the complications that interested them. Plato, in particular, was interested in the fine arts largely because of the specific ways he thought they were imitative.[82] Admiration of an artifact that expressed a virtuous personality, he thought, might lead one to reconstruct the form of the artifact in one's mind and thus introject the value structure, and hence the values, of the personality. Expression through copying thus made it possible to effect moral education by means of activities that the agents valued for other than moral reasons and in which they saw no moral significance. And yet, the reasoning behind this curious doctrine demonstrates another way in which arts of imitation may be reinterpreted as arts of beauty. The alleged process works by enticing people into morality and could only be effective if what immediately attracted people to works of art was their beauty, as opposed to their expressiveness or whatever moral or other worth they might have. Plato has characterized the fine arts in the way that answers to his own special interests; but they will meet his need only because they are also, and more immediately, arts of beauty, arts whose works exercise an immediate and unanalyzed attraction.

The Uses of Imitation

Granted that Plato and others may have had special reasons for their interest in arts of imitation as such, is there any reason why those of us who lack such reasons should not trade in that notion on the more straightforward idea of "arts of beauty" or "fine arts"? There is. The lasting strength of the concept of imitation is that it takes a work of art to be something, not isolated in mental space from everything else in the world, but essentially related to the rest of the world.[83] The arts are taken seriously by being referred to a human or more than human context. Historically, it is when they were interpreted as arts of imitation that the fine arts came to be thought important and not merely agreeable. Perhaps the arts choke in a vacuum.[84]

Opponents of the interpretation of the fine arts as imitative have tried to hide its advantages by supposing that all imitation is likeness making, that the understanding can be engaged no further than in identifying the original of the likeness, and that appreciation of the likeness is vicarious enjoyment of the original. They then ask why there should be arts of imitative play, since such arts must demand laborious triviality from the artist and indulge frivolous superficiality in the public. The question is no more than a tiresome conundrum, for connectedness is more than replication, and we have amply seen that the underlying supposition is a mere pretense.[85]

The question why there should be arts of imitative play may, however, be posed in a more serious way—not indeed with reference to expression, the point of which is obvious enough, or to form, which is related to imitation only by an intellectual artifice, but with reference to likeness making. The Stoic definition of an art postulates an entrenched human value as the end by which an art is identified and governed. And what, in this case, could that end be?

The question why there should be arts of imitative play in general, and of likeness making in particular, is a complex one, and attempts to answer it have formed much of the substance of theorizing about the arts. The first complexity arises from the number of different questions that can be asked with the word "why." In the present case, the question why there should be such arts could be answered by specifying drives (what impels people to go in for them), functions (what useful ends they achieve), or purposes (what people mean to encompass by them). The drive or drives involved could be any general urge to acquire knowledge, to give form to thought and feeling, or to mimic; or they could be as specific as you please. The theorist has considerable freedom. Drives are postulated rather than observed, and they have a rather vague place in psychological speculation. Whatever drive one postulates, however, will hardly serve to explain so highly organized a form of activity as the fine arts unless we suppose that artists and their publics become conscious of it and act on it, and then it will function not as drive but as purpose. If one prefers an explanation in terms of function, a similar difficulty arises. The function in question could be specified in terms of any interest of any individual or collective whose relevance could be established; but, again, no function can explain why any activity is systematically undertaken by free agents unless it either also functions as a drive, a blind impulse that must somehow acquire eyes before it can do what is required of it, or becomes recognized as a need and hence once more functions as purpose. One therefore seems reduced to explaining why there are arts of imitative play by ascribing purposes to artists and their publics. But that is not very satisfactory. Questions about purpose are not inherently problematic, but can be simply settled by asking people why they do things. But one can't ask everybody, and one hardly knows what to put on a questionnaire for random sampling; and the answers one got would explain only why this or that individual engaged in the practice once it existed, not why the practice itself was established and maintained.

I have made things look worse than they are. Drive and function are usually reduced to purpose in a quite straightforward way: an artist, it is said, is a person who discovers that he has to undertake certain complex enterprises if he is to relieve his inner tensions, and his public consists of those who feel his work to be important, though they cannot explain how. Explaining why the arts exist is identifying and explaining these hidden needs. The question why there should be arts of imitative play thus takes on some such form as the following: What is the deeply felt need whose obscure gratification accounts for the fact that artists are obsessed with their arts and that their products are esteemed by others? The stated purposes of those involved are too diverse to explain the uniformity of the practice of art and too slight to explain the high value set on it. There must be a hidden payoff. What could it possibly be?

Before we glance at some answers to that question, two further complications must be got out of the way. In the first place, we saw that the Stoics' attempt to individuate arts by function does not answer to the way things actually happen. The transferability of skills and the inertia of sustaining institutions provide alternative ways in which arts may coalesce. So there need be no one function that an imitative art performs; in fact, we can be certain that any skill will be put to all the uses it can be made to serve and be made to satisfy all the appetites it is capable of gratifying. At most, then, if we concede that an art must at least begin by fulfilling a need, whatever extraneous forces may sustain it thereafter, we can hope to find one function sufficient to originate it and at any later time one function sufficient to sustain it; but we cannot hope to rule out a plurality of functions, and we have little hope of deciding which of any set of alternative functions should be assigned priority either in time or in importance.

In the second place, even if we were to decide that some one function or purpose furnished the unique answer to the question why there should be arts of imitation, it would not be clear how that purpose should be related to artistic practice. Would it be that each and every work of the arts in question fulfilled the assigned function? Or that most of them did? Or that the works that fulfilled it were somehow identifiable as typical, however few? Or that the works that fulfilled the function were the only important ones, all the others being a necessary wastage? Or that perhaps no work by itself fulfilled the function, but all did together? Or even that no works fulfilled the function, either individually or collectively, but that the practice of playing imitatively was what was important? These are all real possibilities, and the differences between them are important. We must not forget them, but nothing I want to say in this book depends on them. Their immediate relevance is that they enable us to forestall an objection that could be raised against any proposed function for the imitative arts: that not all art does what any of them says. The objection, we now see, is easily countered. One has only to say that the supposed function is the normal one for art, what accounts for the rise and maintenance of the practice. Once the practice exists, of course, it and other practices like it will be carried on in the interests of any purpose that it is possible for them to serve or to be thought to serve. It is a general truth about human affairs that everything is used for everything it can be used for. That does not stop us distinguishing between what a thing is for and what this or that person may happen to use it for.

Suppose we did, in spite of everything, want to answer the question why there should be arts of imitation by specifying some single benefit they confer, what would that benefit be? Our answer must specify some nonutilitarian and perhaps not obvious but somehow valuable deployment of the cognitive faculties. Without taking into account the fact that expression and depiction might feed very different and unrelated hungers, one can distinguish at least nine kinds of answer satisfying this general form.[86] I do little more than list them here.

The first possibility is that the mere free play of the cognitive faculties might keep them in trim and develop their potential resources. By depicting and describing without serious occasion and by observing the results of such activity in others, we might renew our capacity for the recognition of form and for expressive utterance.[87] Second, it may be that the human form of adaptation is to impose order on an alien world, taming the enigmatic cosmos and the inner chaos of inchoate feeling.[88] Farmers must see the landscape as potentially agricultural land, soldiers as the field of strategies. When such ordering is done authentically and afresh and not in terms of existing schemes, and when it is done for its own sake and not in the interest of a practical purpose, what we have is one or another of the forms of imitative play we call the fine arts. This popular notion assumes that conceptual and other ordering schemes fulfill a general need of the mind as well as practical purposes of all degrees of generality. The third possibility is that imitations that lack obvious utility serve the concealed purpose of bringing to light one or another sort of concealed reality or hidden tendency, enabling us to envision clearly what otherwise we only half suspect.[89] A fourth possibility is that art reveals the divine: art makes the invisible visible, makes the transcendent immanent. When this hidden function becomes conscious purpose, art ceases to be play and becomes a form of theurgy or liturgy, a suggestion that opens up a quite different train of thought from any embraced in the notion of a fine art and, viewed as the mystic line, will be the topic of a later chapter. Fifth, it may be held that when imitation and expression are exercised in abstraction from any practical context, their subject is revealed as a pure essence, something existing in and for itself and not as an integral part of a situation. This enables us to get a good look at it.[90] Sixth, the playful use of the cognitive faculties may free our imagination for ideals and extrapolations, presentations of what we would become or avoid. Seventh, in the unconstrained play of imaginative imitation we might find embodiments of archetypal structures, constant patterns in mental structure or in cultural need, collective memories or dreams, the main themes in the experience of all men or of a civilization. By the celebration of these concealed constancies we might be thought to achieve a measure of desirable stability. The eighth possibility would be the converse of this: that the imitation in art might serve to present new forms of order, to acclimate the imagination to new technologies, or to educate perception in a world where patterns and rates of change are ever changing.[91] But there is always a ninth possibility: that, after all, the imitative play of the arts is only play, an amusement analogous to solving jigsaw puzzles, yielding such plain cognitive pleasures as that of seeing new patterns and interpretations emerge, affording vicarious experiences, or pleasing by the novelty or strangeness or even the unexpected accuracy of the relation between what imitates and what is imitated.[92] And what then of the supposed seriousness of the arts that was supposed to rule this sort of possibility out? The artist's devotion to his art could be that of any hobbyist to his hobby; the seriousness of critics and dealers could be merely a racket, so long established that hypocrisy has hardened into true devotion; the solemnity of the public could be comparable to that of the dupes of a false Messiah. Or we could say, as Aristotle said, it is natural for people to delight in the disengaged use of their cognitive faculties. For a free, rational being, there is no higher activity than this and, therefore, none by which it can suitably be justified; and there is nothing better for a person to be than a free, rational being. This is, of course, the exact converse of the Freudian claim that art exists to ease our repressions and would not be needed in a healthy society, and of the Marxist claim that art exists to alleviate our alienation and would vanish with the end of alienation. Anyone who wants to can easily put the three together: when humans are free but not rational, Freud will justify their art; when they are rational but not free, Marx will do so; when they are free and rational, Aristotle will come into his own again.[93]

IV

THE CLASSICAL LINE
3: ARTS OF BEAUTY

Beauty

We have seen that any theory that considers the fine arts to be forms of imitative play is obliged to recognize that they are in the first instance arts of beauty: that is, that they are directed toward the production of objects whose primary value is exhausted by the quality of the experience to be obtained in cognitive relation to them, in perceiving, understanding, investigating, contemplating, and so at last or first enjoying them.[1] The function of imitation theory in relation to this initial thesis is to explain why there should be such arts and what special kind of contemplables they produce. Imitation theorists know that there are arts of decoration and amusement that produce contemplables that are in no sense imitative, but maintain that such arts lack the dignity and significance that unite the imitative arts and make them worth serious discussion—nowadays, they express this by denying that such arts are "really" art "in the strict sense." But we have also seen that the required concept of imitation is complex to the point of incoherence, so it makes sense to try to develop an adequate notion of "arts of beauty" that does not bring that concept in.

The expression "fine arts" itself originally meant, and should probably be construed as still meaning, "arts of beauty." "Fine" in this context is a misleading word. It invites a contrast with "applied" that makes it equivalent to "refined" or "purified." The *fine* arts would then be thought of as rarefied or uncontaminated arts, not spotted by the world; and indeed they are sometimes thought of in that way, and the word "fine" then captures some of the meaning that the word "play" has in imitation theory. But a "fine" woman is not necessarily a refined or pure woman; she is beautiful, and a fine day is a beautiful day. Perhaps, then, the fine arts are beautiful arts—arts of beauty, arts devoted to producing beautiful objects. In German and French the equivalent phrases to "fine arts" are *schöne Kunst* and *beaux arts*, respectively, and it is in these languages rather than English that the tradition of thinking about the fine arts has flourished.[2] "Fine arts," in fact, is simply (according to the *Oxford English Dictionary*) a translation of *beaux arts*.

What is the beauty to which the fine arts are devoted? The sense required by our argument is just that classically formulated by Aquinas: *id cuius ipsa apprehensio placet,* "that of which the very apprehension gives pleasure." But we must be careful to take these terms in the senses our argument calls for, not in any narrower senses they may have borne in our preconceptions or in their scholastic home. *Placet,* "gives pleasure," is not to be thought of as the conveyance of a peculiar sort of agreeable feeling.[3] We might better have rendered the term by "can be appreciated" or "is found worthwhile" or "is esteemed"—*placet* is how one registers a favorable vote in Latin. All that is meant is that whatever the relevant positive value is, it is in the *apprehensio* that it is found. *Apprehensio,* for its part, must not be thought of as immediate perception, a first glance. It is not meant to rule out close inspection, investigation, examination, contemplation, or any process through which enlightenment may be achieved, but only to exclude utilization, consumption, and discussion from the area wherein the relevant value is to be found. The products of the fine arts, then, are objects that can be fully appreciated, will give all that as such they have to give, without being put to any use or consumed for any purpose but simply by being perceived in whatever is the appropriate way. And to speak of "the appropriate way" is not to invoke any supposed "aesthetic attitude" uniquely appropriate to beautiful things or to works of art as such. All it asks is that the particular work be looked at, listened to, pored over, or scrutinized in whatever way may be necessary to appreciate the performance. The attentive bestowal of the appropriate sort of regard is sometimes called contemplation, to signify that the awareness of an object of art may demand absorption and attention, and I will use the word myself, but one has to admit that the word has unfortunate associations. It suggests both that a passive sitting back and looking is all that is required and that the appreciation of art goes with tranquillity.[4] But to isolate a performance calls for active interpretation, and such interpretation may well require effort.[5] And the appreciation of certain works may be inseparable from a mood of wild excitement or even from exhausting physical exertion. A slightly less misleading word is "appreciation" itself, to appreciate something being, not to perform any cognitive act in relation to it, but to have succeeded in getting out of it whatever can be got from realizing what it is.

The fine arts, then, could be defined as arts directed to the production of proper objects for appreciation; and the value of such objects as such must accordingly lie wholly in their appearance as thus appreciable, whatever other values they may have in other capacities.[6]

The appreciated as opposed to the used, and the apparent as opposed to the substantial, together with the contemplative as simply opposed to the discursive, jointly mark out a domain that we can call *the aesthetic*. We can thus say without further theoretical commitment that the fine arts are the arts of the aesthetic. But we shall see later that this apparently innocent move is a dangerous one.

Some theorists impose a further restriction on the domain of the aesthetic or that of the fine arts. They require that the contemplation be sensory, in the sense that it essentially involve the use of one or more of the five senses and not be a purely intellectual meditation or survey, and that the appreciation of the performance be at least partly an appreciation of its sensible qualities.[7] The restriction is attractive, catching something that seems essential to music and painting. But it appears to exclude literature: neither sight nor hearing can be essential to the appreciation of a literary work, which is the same work whether read or recited. Some would say that literature is primarily for the ear, that the written word is merely a sign for the word that one must speak inwardly. When one thinks of lyric verse, the thesis seems to have some force. To the objection that the common audible component can only be a phonemic structure that different speakers will realize in widely different patterns of actual sound, one could reply that readings of musical scores by different performers, and realizations on different instruments, give rise to similar variations without anyone being led to deny that music is largely an art of sound. The patterns of literary sound retain sufficient identity through all variations of dialect and idiolect, which affect the quality of the elements in the pattern rather than the pattern itself.[8] But whatever may be true of lyric verse, it is hard to believe that much of a novel's effect can be traced to the sound of its words, whether real or imagined.

That intelligible but imperceptible things may be beautiful and reward contemplation is an entrenched doctrine of our civilization.[9] That works of the fine arts as recognized by that same civilization are available to the senses, and derive much of their nature and value from that availability, is a mere truism. If we think of the fine arts as arts of disengaged communication, it seems to be a conceptual truth; if we think of them as arts of beauty, it is less clearly so. But, in any case, by adopting the Aristotelian slogan that there is nothing in the intellect that was not first available to perception, we can reduce it to triviality, asserting no more than that if airy nothings are to be made the matter for an art, the artist must at some point and in some fashion give them a local habitation.

Whether they accept the restriction to sensory contemplation or not, many theorists insist that the only senses that can be principally engaged by works of the fine arts are those of sight and hearing. There are three related reasons for this. First, these are the senses whereby we perceive at a distance the other senses, because they operate through actual contact with, or ingestion of, their object, are too bound up with gratification through consumption for it to be possible to achieve appreciation through awareness alone. This is a weak reason: it finds the sense of smell guilty by association alone and imputes to all humanity what may be a weakness only in some. The second reason is stronger. Sight and hearing are the only senses that convey enough fine structure for the ordinary perceiver to find a complex gratification in a scrutiny of their products rather than merely savoring their commingled quality. We do not know how to construct or decipher patterns in flavors, scents, or tactile textures. The third reason is linked to the other two: these are the senses on which humans rely for communication and are thus already engaged with habits of attention and scrutiny. The restriction to sight and hearing is perhaps more persuasive than the one that excluded intelligible orders; if we accept it, we equate the fine arts with those directed to the production of things to look at or listen to, visual and auditory performances. Incidentally, this restriction agrees well with the definition of *kalon* proposed for discussion in a fine-arts context by the Socrates of Plato's *Greater Hippias* (298 A): *to di' akoês te kai opseôs hêdu,* "that which pleases through hearing and sight" (my translation)—a definition from which the scholastic formula adopted in this chapter no doubt traces its lineage.

Adoption of the restrictions just mentioned does not entail any formalistic view of the fine arts. It might be thought that it would follow that the most appropriate analysis of fine-art performances would be in terms of the proper objects of sight and hearing as such and that these visibilia and audibilia would be patches of color or stretches of sound in relation. It does not follow. Experientially, one sees things and people and their aspects and groupings: mother, a woman, a complexion, a scene. It is a mistake to think that what is immediately available to experience is shapes and sounds as such. The mistake is that of confusing the end product of one kind of analysis with the data from which a construction is elaborated. Investigation may show what changes the auditory and optic nerves can undergo, and hence what must be the properties of what can stimulate them, and it is easy to infer that whatever one sees and hears must in some way be analyzable in terms of these properties and changes.[10] But that does not mean that it is easy or natural to see things as colored shapes or hear things as mere sound.[11] It is not: it is all but impossible—it is not a recovery of a primitive innocence but a sophisticated achievement. Practically, the thesis that the proper concern of the fine arts is to produce such pure objects of perception restricts (and is meant to restrict) the visual arts at least to a small part of their range.[12] But it is one thing to say that most painters paint badly or in the wrong way and quite another thing to say that most of what they do is not really painting at all. Such polemical moves are for pamphleteers, not for theorists. And, of course, there is the problem of literature. A formalist reduction of literary works to arrangements of visibilia or audibilia is absurd. Literature is made of words, and to be a word is to be a possible element of linguistic structures, which are inherently meaningful. Formalism in literature goes in quite the opposite direction and makes literary works into structures of pure meanings—entities even more dubious than visibilia, but certainly not reducible to them.

A current way of dismissing the myth that the visible world is constructed out of elements of pure colored form (visibilia) is to say that whatever is seen is seen *as* something. This phrase covers a wide range of phenomena, not all on the same logical level. The basic point is that if, for example, I see someone coming in the door, I immediately, without needing to go through any conscious inferential process or to find words for what I see, recognize the entrant—as a person, as a particular kind of person, often as an individual. I do not have to look for clues, and often cannot specify what made recognition possible. In special circumstances I can see the entrant as a silhouette, as a patch of color against a ground, as a three-dimensional bulk in space. I may even learn the trick of seeing a thing *only* in these ways, blotting out for the nonce my normal recognitions. But though it seems that such "seeings as" may be rivals of the former sorts, the phrase "seeing as" is being used in rather different senses. Part of my seeing the entrant as mother is that I do not doubt that she is mother; but it makes no sense to say that I do not doubt she is a patch of color against a ground.[13] Visual experience is a part of life experience: "seeings as" may involve all sorts of identity assumptions, existential assumptions, and abstractive efforts.

The ways in which we see things in settings constitute one set of phenomena of "seeing as," the basic set. Here is another. Looking at a line drawing on paper, I may see it as a lot of lines; or (not isolating the lines) as a marked surface; or as a single unified two-dimensional form (a *Gestalt*); or as an arrangement of lines; or as a drawing of a person coming in a door (seeing it as a drawing of a scene); or as a person coming in a door (seeing it as a drawn scene). Neither in this sort of case nor in the other is there any possible experience that can be described as *simply seeing what I see* not in any particular way. It cannot *say* what I have seen without saying *what* I have seen, thus describing or identifying it in one way rather than another; and this simple logical fact is a reflection of the phenomenological situation just outlined.

The language of "seeing as" can be misleading in two ways. First, since a thing may be seen as many different things, there is a suggestion that what is seen as all of them must be some neutral factor like Aristotle's "prime matter" that is the substratum to which all interpretations relate. But that would be a mistake. As in the Aristotelian analogy, in the phrase "seeing x as y," both x and y can only be determinate ways of referring to some definite object. If what I see as y you see as z, we see the same thing in different ways; but the "same thing" cannot be specified in some miraculous way that suffices to identify what we both see, yet fails to identify it in any specific way whatever. It is largely because it has seemed natural to suppose that there must be some such common visual substratum that is variously interpreted that the analysis of perception in terms of sense data or visibilia has claimed epistemological priority. But the claim cannot be allowed in any other sense than the one I have admitted, that one or more such reductions must be presumed possible because there is a clear sense in which we cannot see more than our optic nerves transmit.

The second way in which the language of "seeing as" may be misleading is related to this first one. It is the implication that there must be some one *normal* or unmetaphorical way of seeing in which "seeing x as y" takes the special form of "seeing x as x," seeing a thing for just what it is. The objection to this is to the supposition that there must be some one description under which something must be seen if it is to be seen normally. But this seems to be a mistake. Although "seeing a tree as a fountain" refers to a strained or imaginative sort of vision, an injection of metaphorical content into my visual experience, whereas "seeing a tree as a tree" does not, that latter phrase seems to have no privilege over "seeing a birch as a tree," "seeing a tree as a birch," or (in the same situation) "seeing a birch as a birch." "Seeing a tree as a tree" (and in general "seeing things as they are") is simply a matter of not being deceived, not allowing one's identifications and interpretations to be colored by inappropriate, imaginative, or metaphorical descriptions; it need not be implied that there is only one such way of identifying or interpreting anything.[14] Nor can one specify any one "normal" way of seeing, for how one specifies what is normal depends on what sort of abnormality one is ruling out. One can indeed say that the norm for our visual experience of nature is provided by our common experience of solid objects in motion, as built up from an innate basis through our learning to move in the world, and that the norm for our experience of the visual arts is provided by further learning through exposure to prevailing traditions of artistic practice, and that a general condition of normality is freedom from such mechanical deviations as presbyopia, color blindness, and whatever else the eye doctors cure or deplore. But all of this means no more than that normal vision is that with which one can see what most other people can see.[15] It does not entail any definite way of specifying what on any occasion one can truthfully be said to see anything as.

Few subjects are more complex than the psychology of perception, and making perceptibility a condition of beauty risks introducing many of the complexities into the theory of the arts of beauty. Many theorists hedge; even Aquinas, whose definition of beauty I started from, gives alternative definitions: *id cuius ipsa apprehensio placet,* "that of which the very apprehension gives pleasure," and *quod visum placet,* "that which gives pleasure on being seen." Whether we hedge or not, the strategy of my argument demands that the beauty with which the fine arts deal be defined in Aquinas's sort of way and no other. If we define beauty as "the proper excellence of objects of the fine arts," which it can mean, we make our definition circular and useless for specifying the scope of these arts. If we follow Edmund Burke and equate beauty with the source of a special sort of sensuous gratification, we falsify the nature of the fine arts by restricting them to a small part of their actual scope. Moreover, more significantly from the point of view of our argument and in the context of the scholastic definition, we must not follow Vasari (himself following Augustine) in distinguishing beauty as "a rational quality dependent on rules" from grace as an "undefinable quality dependent on judgement and therefore on the eye" (Blunt 1940, 93). On the contrary, it is the latter that answers directly to *quod visum placet*; the former is that formal beauty which I said belonged to imitation theory as answering to the requirements of the mind.[16] What I am now saying about beauty and the fine arts is meant to be purely formal, imposing no concrete requirement whatever on practitioners or publics of such arts. Among all possible theories about what things are beautiful, what makes things beautiful, whether beauty is subjective or objective, relative or absolute, what aims artists should pursue and how they should pursue them, my accounts are neutral. For such arts as I have described to exist, it is not necessary that any particular sort of taste or tradition should prevail or even occur. All that is required is that there be a public given to the appreciation of such organizations—perceptual, or conceptual, or both—as may be artificially produced and that this public should be stable enough for there to be a skill of accommodating it. And we saw that this condition is so readily fulfilled that in the limiting case an artist may be his own public.

The notion of beauty has been thought to have implications that go against the sense of the last paragraph. Kant observed that people who call something beautiful usually imply that the thing must please everyone, or that whoever it fails to please is somehow defective. It is only because this claim is implicit in them that "judgments of taste" are worth discussing. True. But the prevalence of such claims does not entail their validity, and the project of making things to give universal and necessary pleasure could be operationally regulative without being even theoretically capable of succeeding.[17] All we are entitled to infer is that the public believes itself to be right, and thinks it makes sense to think so. Such objectivist or universalist notions of beauty might seem to be supported by my use of the Thomist formula *cuius ipsa apprehensio placet*, "of which the very apprehension gives pleasure," without a grammatical object. It looks as if *placet* here is short for *omnibus placet*, "gives pleasure" meaning "gives everyone pleasure" or (more insidiously) "*normally* pleases" or even "pleases absolutely." But in fact I have insisted that no more is required than that *some public or other* should be pleased. It would be better to follow "gives pleasure" by "to someone," *placet* equaling *alicui placet*. But the expression is best left incomplete. Different specifications of who is to be pleased answer to different theories about what the fine arts are and are for. The fine arts clearly do produce objects for appreciation. It is less clear whether those objects are to be appreciated by anyone, by everyone, by connoisseurs, by critics, by other artists, by the artist himself, by members of the artist's culture or subculture, by the pure in heart, or by whom. By saying "everyone" or "someone," we commit ourselves to some of these alternatives and cut out others. Better leave it open.

My account does embody one restriction. It gives the view, not of the artist, but of his public, even if the public is only the artist himself in another capacity. The artist at work must think of the actual material he works in and what he is making of it, and the production of something to be appreciated may not be in his mind at all.[18] Perhaps beauty is even, as some have thought happiness to be, an "end beyond the end" that can be attained only by ignoring it and concentrating on the task in hand, so that the pursuit of beauty is self-defeating. That could be either a psychological thesis or a logical one. The psychological thesis would be that worrying about beauty (as about happiness) makes one self-conscious and spoils one's performance; it is a sounder policy not to ask how well one is doing. The logical thesis would be that beauty (like happiness) is an overall outcome, arising out of the summed qualities of an entire work (as happiness is the quality of a whole lifetime): logically, such a totality cannot serve as an objective, and the question how well one is doing, all-important as it may be, can have no operational significance. In either case, the argument amounts to little. Neither version denies that the fine arts have the rewarding of attention as their proper end, by the attainment of which their products are properly judged. In fact, what I call the point of view of the artist is his only when he is actively immersed in detail, not when he is thinking reflectively about what he is doing. The very notion of a fine art is a public-oriented notion, and an artist who thinks of himself as practicing a fine art must in the long run be a public-oriented artist. Notions about art to which this viewpoint is repugnant are those that find the very concept of an art inadequate or inappropriate to artistic activity or to the artist's calling. I reserve consideration of such notions for part 2.

Beauty and Significance

The notion of fine arts as arts of beauty serves as well as that of arts of imitative play to distinguish from all others a set of real or possible arts. Like the other, the notion can be gerrymandered to include or exclude what one wants in or out. The two notions can be used to delimit the same set, or different sets: in particular, the arts of beauty are hospitable to decorative arts, but keep magical practices out, and arts of imitative play have precisely the opposite tendency. In relation to the way we nowadays practice art and think about it, the notion of an art of beauty has a directness and generality that the other lacks, and we have seen that the other can be so stated as to presuppose it.

The two ways of differentiating fine arts from other arts are problematic in similar ways. Given that there could be arts of imitative play, one had to ask why play should take that form. Given that there can be arts of beauty, one has now to ask why such arts are needed. The world is full of things to look at and listen to: we have only to attend to whatever our eyes and ears present to find inexhaustible interest and delight.[19] If the senses become jaded, what is needed is a spiritual technique of reinvigoration rather than a fresh lot of stuff to become bored with. Nor is the plenitude of beauty outside the fine arts a mere theoretical possibility. The things whose beauty it is our way to celebrate belong to at least five kinds, of which works of the fine arts are only one. First, we find beauty in Aristotelian natural objects—that is, in organisms and in such lifeless things as are formed by a systematic process of unified development. To this class belong the bodies of people and animals, seashells and snowflakes. Second, we find it in non-Aristotelian natural objects, in things that have a measure of cohesion but are produced or modified by a fortuitous interaction of forces. Cascades and pieces of driftwood are of this kind. Third, we find beauty in collocations that form a unity only as observed from a particular viewpoint, such as sunsets and picturesque landscapes.[20] Fourth, beauty is found in products of the useful arts, especially in those, such as machines and bridges, whose form is imposed by stringent functional requirements. And fifth are the products of fine arts. These five kinds of perceptibles, classified here by how they get their forms, cover (with their borderline cases) pretty well the whole range of visibly formed things.[21] Preferred sounds seem equally various: bird song belongs to a class like the first of our kinds of preferred sights, the sound of waves on a shore to one like the second, soundscapes to one like the third, the noises of steam trains to one like the fourth—and then there is music.[22] So it seems not only that anything can be chosen as an object for aesthetic contemplation, but that objects publicly agreed to be preferable objects for such contemplation may belong to almost any kind of perceptible thing. Beautiful objects abound: providing them cannot be what the fine arts exist for. Just as one could object to "imitation" theories of art that it is not necessary to duplicate the world, since it already exists and one is enough, so one can object to the present theory that there is already so much beauty that we need no more.

The objection outlined in the last paragraph is specious. Books are for reading, but no book exists merely to provide "something to read"; similarly, to say that the fine arts exist to provide things to look at and listen to does not entail that they exist to gratify a single sort of desire that can be specified no more precisely than as "wanting something to look at or listen to." There are at least six conditions under which abundance of natural beauty would still leave a place for arts of beauty. They are not mutually exclusive. Any one of them would justify the existence of some such art, but different practices may need different justifications, and one practice may be justified in more than one way.[23]

First, and most simply, arts of beauty could provide beauty where there was none before or not enough. Abundance does not guarantee proper distribution. Such a defect might be remedied by importing extant (natural) beauties rather than by creating new ones, but it is sometimes easier to make something than to fetch something. It is true that, in theory, no situation can be wholly deficient in beauty, since anything may be found beautiful; but not everything is obviously or notoriously beautiful, and some such findings call for special education (or lack of miseducation) or special efforts of attention, which it is not reasonable to expect everyone to undergo or make. The task of the fine arts on this understanding would be to maintain supply and distribution of *appreciable* beauty. Second, different situations might call for different kinds of beauty. The task of the fine arts would then be, not to regulate the supply of culturally acceptable beauty, or to create any characteristic kind of beauty, but to provide *suitable* beauty. This would make of the artist a sort of environmentalist or environmentalist's aide. Third, the fine arts could provide novel kinds of beauty. Nature, however bounteous, holds nothing like the domes of Isfahan or the quartets of Shostakovich.[24] Fourth, it could be that their beauties are more intense. Surely something expressly made to be looked at could be better worth looking at than anything produced in another way. Its not being so would be either miraculous or evidence for some unintelligible teleology of vision. Fifth, it might be that the fine arts could achieve a beauty not more intense but purer than any in nature. Perhaps natural beauties (or some kinds of them) are always infected by irrelevances or blemishes that the observer has to think away. If so, the fine arts might produce similar objects with this editing process already performed, landscapes without pylons.

The sixth way in which arts of beauty could be vindicated is more complex than the others and requires discussion. It might be that the fine arts existed to provide beauty of some special kind, distinguished not merely by availability or suitability or purity or intensity or difference but by characteristic qualities whose production was what called for an artist's vested skill. And one can guess what sort of qualities these would be. The very fact that works of fine art are produced by people for other people suggests that their function is to communicate something that matters to people. And the fact that governments spend vast sums on music and painting, and justify this expenditure, not (as firework displays are justified) by the pleasure they give, but by their cultural significance (that is, they are recognized to be important whether you like them or not), suggests that what they communicate not only matters but matters greatly. Apparently the fine arts are thought to be ways of furthering some important human concern. That phrase "furthering some important concern" could lead us badly astray; we must be careful not to let it. It could mean that the arts of beauty are valued as means to some extraneous end, as midwives of revolution or stiflers of revolt; and so they often are, but those are not the values internal to the art by which its transactions are judged. Or it could mean that their practice serves as a means, not to some end that could be equally served by some other means (as other distractions may stifle revolt, other incitements move to revolution), but to some obvious good that only an art of beauty could achieve. So it may be, but it need not be so; for to assume that it must be so is to presume that there are interests in life higher and more vital than those realized in the arts themselves, and we are not entitled to presume that. All our argument entitles us to say is that the beauty achieved by the fine arts matters (or is thought to matter) in a way that bespeaks an important role in human affairs, which could not be the case if it were a mere double of natural beauty. But the role might be that of being beautiful in a human way.

If the fine arts produce beauty by way of furthering some important human concern, what human concern would it be? Our earlier argument requires us to say: any that could be furthered by their means. The identification of art with imitative play explored one set of possibilities, and there may be none that that protean concept could not embrace. It could be an endless intellectual pastime to think up new ones. One or many, the concerns would have to be among the following kinds, which are (though roughly formulated) logically exhaustive.[25] First would be a concern for order and pattern as such, not satisfied by natural beauties because the interest lies at least partly in the signs of ordering and patterning activity. The human mind does its work by imposing on the world elaborate organizing structures, such as Chomsky shows grammars to be and J. J. Gibson shows spatial perception to be. When this activity is carried on for its own sake, it issues in the uselessly complex structures that are characteristic of the fine arts: we recognize such structuring as our proper business as human beings. The second kind of concern would be some other covert but explicable need of the mind, perhaps (as suggested before in another context) a need to humanize one's psychic resources and environment and tame them by showing patterns they can fall into.[26] Third would be some inexplicable concern, a quirk of the cortex not otherwise describable, perhaps some byproduct of the genetic mechanism, a kink we are stuck with because it happens to be carried by the same gene as something needed for survival. Fourth, it might be some overt interest consciously shared: a demand for icons to fix one's thoughts on supernatural beings, a need for loud rhythmic noises to coordinate muscular activity, an interest (such as great novels gratify) in the possible depth and variety of human experience.

The complexity and variability inherent in the organization of any art is such that (as we saw when we were considering arts of imitative play), even if the importance attached to the fine arts demands that they be thought to further some important human concern, it does not follow that every work of art should further the same. The importance attached to their practice is sufficiently explained if a high proportion of their output can be found important; their common character could still only be that they produce objects for appreciation. Further, it might be true that one concern was characteristically satisfied by some one of the arts, and another by another; or it might be that no such relation between specific concerns and specific arts obtained. Above all, we should bear in mind that the importance attached to the arts need show no more than that some or all of the activities associated with them are among the things to which a cultural consensus may attach importance.

Substantive theories of the fine arts are commonly designed to support some of the possibilities canvassed above. Their usual project is to reconcile the requirement of endotelicity with that of human significance, to vindicate the independence of the arts from subservience to immediate utilitarian purposes without reducing them to triviality.[27] My own project does not require me to espouse any such theory or to favor any type of such theory. If the products of the fine arts are to be construed as performances, however, it does seem to follow that they differ from natural objects in being necessarily construed as meaningful. It is characteristic of human making that a man could pursue other ends and could essay other means in their pursuit: a work of art inevitably represents a system of choices.[28] Even if an artist makes it his objective to produce objects whose beauty is indistinguishable from that of natural objects, he has eschewed human significance and not merely bypassed it: he has chosen to hide the signs of his choices. If we do not know that he has done this, we may enjoy what he has made, but we cannot appreciate what he has done.[29] One could then maintain that the fine arts are those whose products are proper objects of connoisseurship and perhaps also of criticism, not merely of agreeable contemplation. It might seem that this conclusion could be easily avoided by saying "art lies in concealing art": appreciation of such works is unnecessary, enjoyment suffices. But it can hardly be denied that most works of art require to be construed as systems of choices: their structure must be investigated in search of meanings. Hence, if one knows that something is a work of fine art, one must at least test it for meaning and ascertain if no such investigation is required. A work of fine art that is to be enjoyed exactly as natural beauty is enjoyed would thus have to be one of which no one knew or suspected that it was not natural. A civilization in which the fine arts were like that would be one very different from ours; I cannot imagine what it would be like. But I think it would have a different concept of nature from ours, for our concept of the natural is one that excludes human intervention. Part of our enjoyment of natural beauty comes not merely from gratification of mind and senses but from the sense that the gratification is gratuitous.

Kinds of Beauty

I have given reason to expect that the beauty to which fine arts are directed will normally be of certain kinds, roughly designated as those that lend themselves to an elaboration of shared experience. But I also gave overriding reasons for denying that the fine arts can be confined to such beauties. My definition, as I interpreted it, forbids us to place any further restriction on their products than that their primary value is found in cognition before use. But it may be asked whether it is not possible to say what are the kinds of beauty that the fine arts may achieve. Of course it is. The kinds of beauty will be as many as there are kinds of cognition and kinds of value that may be found in cognition. But we have no ready-made way of classifying such kinds, and we can have none without a comprehensive phenomenology of man's engagement with his world, which must either rest on or supply the foundation for an equally comprehensive theory of human nature or the human condition. And we have no ground for preferring any such theory over any other.[30] We must, therefore, content ourselves with the general thesis that any intelligible distinction between modes of awareness (such as perceiving and recalling), cognitive operations (such as investigating and watching), and attitudes to the cognizable (such as reveling in and being astounded at) will differentiate kinds of beauty that we have no reason to exclude from those possible to the fine arts, and so too will any distinction between kinds of value that may be found in cognizables.

The scope of the last clause is unclear. What counts as finding a value? We have warned already against equating the *placet* of beauty with any sort of pleasant feeling or charm or with enjoyment. One may like to do things one does not like doing. Art may be shocking, scandalizing, intimidating, titillating, absurd, repulsive, and so on, so long as people are prepared to submit themselves to shock, scandal, and the rest without ulterior end. Some artists have claimed that even boredom is an appropriate response to art, for a person who is bored is not merely negligent or indifferent; distaste and dislike are yet more positive responses. But here a distinction must be made. If a person submits himself to experiences that he professes to dislike, to find distasteful or boring, we must choose among disbelieving him, quarreling with his terminology, and concluding that the kind of distastefulness, boringness, or whatever that he has in mind is such that he judges his life would in some respect be poorer without it. But our definition of an art of beauty does exclude the imposition on a public of experiences such as they would not choose to undergo but rather would avoid if they could. Anyone who claims that it is the function of art to give offense in *this* sense is saying that art cannot be explained as "the fine arts" as we understand that expression. He has a choice. Either he can modify the definition to say that a fine art is any whose products take their primary significance from, and are primarily to be judged by, the kind of experience they yield to appropriate cognition, or he can say that art has only an incidental relation to the fine arts and is essentially to be explained in quite other terms—perhaps in such terms as we shall introduce under the label of the purist line.

Although our argument requires us to admit that the kinds of beauty can be neither enumerated nor restricted nor classified on a single principle, there is one distinction that has played such a significant part in the history of the theory of art and beauty that we should single it out for special attention: it is that which contrasts beauty with sublimity. The "beauty" that figures in this contrast is never that which figures in our preferred definition, as we have understood it, but one that takes *placet* in some more restricted sense. In its simplest form, the distinction contrasts two fundamentally different ways of rewarding inspection: whatever is beautiful satisfies the observer, whatever is sublime staggers him. Expectation may be fulfilled by perfection or overwhelmed by excess. But the distinction corresponds to a contrast that goes far beyond aesthetics: Plato's distinction between the values of appetite and the values of "justice." According to this venerable thesis, it is characteristic of the intellect to look for exact fulfillment of a precisely and objectively determined demand, and characteristic of desire to hunger for unlimited gratification of an indeterminate appetite. Plato presents this contrast as one between two radically different and complementary systems of evaluation and behavior (cf. Sparshott 1966b). If we assimilate the beautiful to one of these systems and the sublime to the other, the beautiful is for the intellectual who knows just what is required, and the sublime is for the emotional person who knows only that he wants *more.*

The above use of the word "systems" may mislead: each of the alleged systems is little more than a loosely associated set of properties and tendencies whose differences are as important as their affinities. Instead of a single contrast between complexes designated as "beauty" and "sublimity," we should rather speak of a number of contrasts often made in conjunction, the terms "beauty" and "sublimity" being loosely used to imply one or more of them.

The contrast between intellect and desire, between the cerebral and the visceral, can be split off from that between the fitting and the overwhelming: surely the intellect can be dumbfounded and desires can be satisfied. Certainly the satisfaction in something's being got exactly right demands a care in scrutiny and a coolness in judgment that is not only unnecessary to being taken aback by sudden splendor but apparently incompatible with it; but to interpret such astonishment as an extrapolation of the daydreams of greed is gratuitous, to say the least. Nor is either of these contrasts the same as that between the charming and the shocking, which figures in a confused way in the most famous of the polarizations of the beautiful and the sublime, that of Edmund Burke. What Burke contrasted with the sublime under the title "the beautiful" was precisely the winning, the seductive, the beguiling; and the opposite of such a "beauty" is not so much the overwhelmingly tremendous as the agreeably thrilling.

It is a commonplace that the sublime has disappeared from our art. If this is true, it may be because the three contrasts have separated. Insofar as the sublime was to appeal to feeling and not thought, its role is taken by pop music and *Kitsch* generally. Insofar as its function was to overwhelm by magnitude or force, electronic amplification can do this for the ear and steel-frame construction for the eye, without any profound spiritual commitment. Insofar as its function was to shock, to jar perception from its ruts, its part is now played by the absurd, which subjects our sensibilities (as it were) to horizontal rather than vertical jolts. The theater and literature of the absurd present us with what defies comprehension, not because it is beyond the normal scale, but because it defies our understanding of causal and personal relations. If these three have indeed temporarily replaced the sublime, it may be because the sublime makes pretensions and is thus vulnerable to irony. The absurd makes no pretensions: it is itself a fruit of irony and exploits the "psychoanalytical" ways of thought that lend modern irony its most facile support. The other two evade irony because they make no pretensions but are abject. Any fool with enough money can equip himself to make as big a noise or as big a building as he pleases, and no one pretends otherwise; and if the *Kitsch* artist can be made out to have done more than give himself and others an agreeable time, he is shown to have failed. But to evade irony is to earn contempt.

Yet another set of contrasts that has affinities with that between the beautiful and the sublime is that between the beautiful and the ugly, the fair and the foul, the lovely and the obscene, the gratifying and the fascinating. Every culture must define a set of experiences that are taboo, forbidden, not to be entertained. But what is thus pushed out of sight is not merely ignored: the unthinkability of eating human flesh is not like that of eating elm leaves, something that simply does not occur to us. One function of art may be to stabilize what is thus forbidden within the culture by celebrating it in a sublimated form and a segregated context, not merely to enhance the positive, but to redeem the negative. It is by no means unthinkable that one function of the arts should be thus to complete culture by integrating what must not be admitted but cannot be excluded. But that function, even if it were the more important, would not displace beauty's function of embellishing the everyday.

Fundamental to the Platonic foundation that I have detected beneath the antithesis between the sublime and the beautiful is a contrast between emotion and thought, between feeling and intellect. The contrast is facile, if not quite misconceived. What is essential to the sublime is not that thought is bypassed but that it is surpassed: it is a *recognition* of superiority and transcendence, not a mere feeling of awe, that defines the sublime and makes it vulnerable to irony. The appreciation of beauty (in its broad sense) of any kind requires cognition as well as reaction. We have no ground for feeling any way about what we do not recognize; and if we do not feel any way about what we recognize, it is hard to say what we mean by finding value in the recognition. Even Plato could only save his dichotomy by reinstating feeling within the intellect and tacitly endowing feeling with a capacity for cognition. Nonetheless, it does seem possible to distinguish two groups of reactions. On the one hand, one may be soothed by the bland, stimulated by the piquant, held by the gripping, and so forth; on the other hand, one may be enthralled by the engrossing, intrigued by the paradoxical, captivated by the ingenious, or just interested by the interesting. The first set are reactions to the overall qualities of stimuli; the second are ways of engaging a problematic reality. Perhaps, though, this distinction might better have been called that between the passive and the exploratory; and one might then reflect that the word "contemplation" in its ordinary use suggests passivity, but belongs on the intellectual side of any likely distinction between thought and feeling. Perhaps we can neither eliminate nor improve on the old metaphorical contrasts of head and heart, brains and guts.

Conditions of Beauty

The kinds of beauty cannot be enumerated, for want of any single perspicuous principle to compile a list on. Can we say anything about the conditions of beauty? Apparently not: anything can be found beautiful, in an unrestricted number of ways. Our formula defining beauty by the satisfaction taken in it discourages us from distinguishing between what is found beautiful and what really is so otherwise than by drawing distinctions between different groups of beauty finders; and though it does not preclude such distinctions, it lends no support to any one of them.

Because anything can be beautiful, nothing has to be. There can be no criteria that will effectively differentiate beautiful things from other things. One can specify no conditions that an object must satisfy in order to be a thing of beauty, and no conditions such that if it satisfies them, it will certainly be one, other than the conditions it must satisfy to be apprehended in the first place.

That beauty can be found in anything is a principle which, though hedged around with restrictions and qualifications no less important than itself, has a crucial part to play in my ensuing argument, in which I will have occasion to repeat it again and again. Its truth, insofar as it is true, rests on interpreting the phrase "that of which the very apprehension pleases," not as picking out a class of objects, but as designating the proper object of a certain kind of interest. And insofar as interest is *taken* rather than *found*, anything whatever might satisfy the definition and thus be properly termed beautiful.

That everything is beautiful in some relations and in some respects is a basic tenet of the scholastic theory from which our definition was borrowed: whatever is real is beautiful just so far as it is real.[31] The scholastic originators of the theory did indeed stipulate three "conditions of beauty," unity, integrity, and brightness, and these seem to make beauty more than what pleases the eye. But the appearance is deceptive. When applied to what people do, the first two can be taken simply as defining performance: what is performed is singled out as one thing (*unitas*) from its context, and to be a performance is to be complete (*integritas*). That leaves *claritas*, which need be taken as saying no more than that the performance must attract. More generally, whatever can be said to exist must be ascribed unity and integrity: it is said to be in some sense one thing, even if only one collection or one assortment or congeries, and has integrity because even to be a congeries or heap it must have all the components it has, or it would be a different and smaller heap.

Formally, and with more specific relevance to the beauty of art, the three requirements may be taken as negating the three ways in which *apprehensio* may be thwarted—by being unable to pull everything together into a single context, by finding something missing or out of place, or simply by not finding anything worth looking at. And this thwarting cannot successfully overcome the tenacious seeker of beauty, because everything must have some order, integrity, and clarity in order to exist, and whatever has these has beauty (cf. Kovach 1974, 264).

Not too much should be made of the ubiquity of beauty. For whatever reason of nature or nurture, most people find it easier to take interest in some things than in others, and someone who claims to find as full satisfaction in staring at a blank wall as he does in listening to the *Hammerklavier Sonata* played by Kuerti impresses us as either a saint or a poseur or tone-deaf. "It is not quite the case," J. N. Findlay remarks, "that anything whatever is a suitable object of aesthetic concern: for an object to come before us aesthetically it must do so perspicuously and poignantly" (1968, 137). But we note that he speaks of suitable objects, not of possible or actual objects, and that in speaking of the way in which things come before us he leaves open the possibility that anything whatever might come before someone in that way. As for the argument I cited from Kovach, it can mislead us if we fail to notice that it is symmetrical. Certainly, everything really does have some unity, order, and clarity, and may please thereby; but also everything except God really lacks some unity, order, and clarity, and this absence of beauty is every bit as genuine and noticeable as the beauty itself.[32]

It would appear, then, that if beauty and its converse have necessary and sufficient conditions, those conditions are not of any practically interesting sort: in everything a beauty can be found that it really has.[33] Not all things are obviously, or notoriously, beautiful, and in some the beauty may require heroic effort or derangement to discern; but the fact may not be relevant to the fine arts, which clearly cannot be devoted to such easy and obvious beauties as may be found everywhere. It is true that the fine arts of any time and place restrict themselves to a narrow range of products, but this is not because the range of beauty is narrow. It is because for an art to exist, for a skill to be effectively developed, the range of effects and means must be brought down to what an institutional complex can encompass through its constituent schools and their members. It is not arbitrary that there should be some such restrictions, but the particular restrictions themselves are arbitrary.[34] But even if no firm criteria can be found for distinguishing things that are beautiful from things that are not, it does not quite follow that nothing can be said about conditions that must be fulfilled if beauty is to be discerned and ascribed. Everything can be found beautiful, but not everything always is, and it may be that some things never are. Perhaps all and only that is found beautiful which fulfills certain conditions—conditions, of course, such that in suitable circumstances anything could fulfill them. Some such conditions, in fact, there must be, although they might amount to no more than "being subjected to whatever cognitive operation is necessary for their beauty to appear." We indicated that the "unity," "order," and "clarity" of the scholastic definition are conditions of this kind and that the "poignancy" and "perspicuousness" required by Findlay might be too.

The question "What are the conditions of beauty?" when translated into terms of the definition I have adopted is the same as "What makes anything worth attending to?" and admits of a purely formal and general answer: significant departure from the anticipated. Whatever is totally expected must be completely meaningless, redundant, and hence unnoticeable; whatever is totally unexpected cannot be related to anything and must again be quite meaningless.[35] Beauty occupies the ground between cliché and chaos. One may steer closer to one than to the other. It does not follow that the maximally beautiful is whatever presents the most identifiable differentiation from a discernible order. That would be the requirement for a perfect communication, a bearer of maximal information, not for a perfectly beautiful object. We are entitled to assert only that what lies quite outside this middle ground cannot serve as an object for looking, listening, or meditation, for there would be nothing to look at, listen to, or reflect on.[36]

To say that beauty holds the middle ground between cliché and chaos seems to belie the claim that no criteria of the beautiful can be specified. But it can and should be understood in such a way that it does not. What is anticipated and what surprises depends on the context of presentation. The structures and the psychological preparations that determine anticipation and surprise can be and are varied by many kinds of devices of radically heterogeneous sorts. What is a middle ground can always be changed by shifting frontiers. Seen in this light, the requirement that beauty depart significantly from the anticipated suggests a more positive function for artistic traditions than the merely simplifying one already noted.

They provide familiar norms from which departures may be observed. Without such norms one's attention must be unfixed, one cannot tell what the artist has done. Thus, in music, rules of harmonic sequence and consonance serve, not as laws that must be obeyed, but as norms for expectation, from which various kinds of departures provide significance. When departure becomes so frequent as to be nonsignificant, the norm ceases to function and must be replaced by another.[37] Similarly, the principles of word order and word choice normal in a language may provide a standard by violating which a poet gets his characteristically poetic effects. And, in this light, we can see various modes of likeness making not as defining the fine arts but as furnishing them with potent resources: they yield a singularly complex but easily recognizable norm of expectation, many sorts of deviation from which can be observed. Thus, figurative artists have at their immediate disposal an immense range of effects that the artist who eschews representation denies himself—just as a painter who nowadays insists on making his work representational denies himself a whole world of possibilities, which happens to be the new world that his contemporaries are exploring and colonizing.

Departures from any norm may be for the better, for the worse, or merely for the different. So we should expect to find idealizing and pejorative (satirical or ironic) modes in art.[38] But in arts that do not use language or employ representation of some sort, this distinction may not be easy to apply: if the norm defines, as in the arts it usually does, not the level of attainment or satisfaction one expects, but simply the normal way in which something is done, what counts as "better" or "worse" becomes indeterminate. A more generally useful distinction may be that between variation in form and variation in content. As I have observed already, the terms "form" and "content" notoriously lack a fixed application, even in arts of imitation where they seem most at home; but in practice it is not usually hard to distinguish in any performance between what is done and how it is done. Whenever such a distinction can be made, artistic beauty may be found to exploit variations in the one rather than the other. Thus, we may distinguish medium-emphasizing from message-emphasizing works.[39] The difference between exploitation of form and of content is also realized in the distinction between the romantic and the classical, in one of the less common interpretations of that polymorphous polarity.[40] The romantic, in this version, relies on a fantastication of surface qualities, harmonies and timbres, "some strangeness in the proportion," unexpectedness in vocabulary and syntax, or at a deeper level oddity of incident and character. The stock example among writers used to be Seneca. The classical relies on perfection in deployment of matter, art concealing art in the use of the medium, musical structures rather than effective sounds, plain words and regular syntax, coherence rather than oddity in character and story. The stock example among writers was Cicero.[41] Lovers of the romantic often use a trick of definition to exclude the classical from the proper domain of the fine arts. They point out that, since beauty must please through being cognized, its worth must lie in "appearance," and they then equate appearance with what is immediately striking. Thus they exclude from consideration the level on which classical effects are achieved. But we have already seen that this is a mistake. There is more to appearance than meets the eye. We may say that the classical is differentiated from the romantic by its concern with structures rather than fragments and with perceptible realities rather than surfaces, but its concern remains with the evidence of the evident.

Recognition that anything can be found beautiful precludes us from accepting that variation on a norm is a necessary condition òf beauty unless we add to the romantic and classical a third and quite different possibility: the rediscovery of the ordinary through a framing device that isolates it for renewed attention, so that it seems fresh if not odd. What hides the familiar from notice is only the fact of its familiarity; a breach of habit can restore its significance. When a radio station has been off the air, its carrier wave becomes an important message. However, the obvious way of bringing this third possibility into play is by developing a general technique of shifting frames, a way of looking at anything, rather than by using fine-arts techniques to provide specific objects to be looked at. Either the shock effect of novelty wears off quickly, or the object is presented together with a framing device to ensure that the effect is renewed. In the latter case, the proper object of artistic skill is the whole *including* the frame—the artist is a creator of setups.[42] And it then becomes a moot question whether the appreciation of his work requires taking account of the frame, failing to notice it, pretending to ignore it, holding one's awareness of it in suspense, or any or all of these. The whole status of the enterprise becomes equivocal.[43]

Among cases where the beauty of an object is that of a familiar thing restored to freshness, we must distinguish between those in which what is presented in the frame is an arbitrary fragment of the perceptible world (as in some of Cage's work) and those in which specific qualities of the recaptured objects are relied on (as in some of Duchamp's ready-mades).[44] In the latter case, the specific qualities must amount to some determinate form of complexity or subtlety that will enhance experience on repetition; and this complexity or subtlety must be assignable to the what or to the how, to the classical or the romantic mode.[45]

The famous slogan "unity in variety," an old defining formula for beauty, looks like an equivalent for what I have called the conditions of beauty. Variety ensures departure from the banal, unity ensures freedom from the other extreme of chaos. Like *quod visum placet*, the demand for unity in variety can (and, on the way of thinking developed in this chapter, should) be taken in a purely formal way: it simply reminds us that what interests us in any work of art or any beautiful object can be assigned to the specific interest of the details and parts or to the way in which those details and parts combine and the general character of the whole in which they do so.[46] But there is a standing temptation to take it more concretely. After all, if the fine arts engage the interest through perception, it is natural to suppose that the higher achievements of those arts will reach a high degree of intensity in the demands they make on, and the rewards they offer to, perception. And to do that they must surely combine in an irreducible creative tension the most powerful tendency to order (in novel and rigid structures) and the strongest tendency to disorder (in novel and strongly individualized details).[47]

The demand for a coherent complexity, pushed to the utmost in both aspects, is indeed a very plausible one. But the notions of variety and complexity are obscure. They seem to call for complication and fussiness, although simple forms are often more rewarding than busy ones. One therefore tends to say that by complexity one means some relation of relations rather than a mere multitude of surface changes. But (to invoke Hume's principle once more) anything is related to anything in indefinitely many ways—that is part of the reason why anything can be found beautiful; the demand for complexity seems to mean either nothing or the wrong thing.

As merely complicated things can be denied to be complex "in the required sense" (though no sense has been specified), so one can deny that seemingly plain things are simple by saying that they are subtle. But what does that mean? It could mean that, although a thing has (as everything has) abundant internal and external relations, these are of such a kind that they cannot be explicitly analyzed out into discrete sets of relations and relata—it being supposed that the term "complexity" is reserved for a plethora of separately identifiable and describable relationships satisfying some criteria for observability or relevance or both. But it would be extravagant to suppose that everyone who calls something subtle, whether justifiably or not, should be construed as claiming to have discerned a rich indeterminate interrelatedness. Perhaps his calling it subtle means only that, although it is obviously very simple, he is determined to call it complex, because he sees that it is beautiful and knows that whatever is not complex cannot be beautiful. Not that it is necessarily wrong to save the appearance of a theory in this way: anyone who finds a thing richly rewarding and cannot say wherein the richness lies is right to say that its richness is concealed.

Whatever use may be made of such face-saving terms as "subtlety," any talk of unity in variety or coherent complexity, and any postulate calling for departures from anticipated norms, must somehow come to terms with the fact that tag phrases and snatches of melody that one would not ordinarily hesitate to call simple may come to have a powerful and obsessive attraction, and that the pull of this attraction is felt by enough people for dictionaries of quotations and themes to be compiled and used. And it certainly seems that at least part of the compelling force of such simplicities lies in the simplicity itself, a weight of inevitability that has little to do with the "inevitability" that critics have traditionally ascribed to fully integrated intricacies.[48] The great conundrum for all discussions of taste and beauty is not the status of the classical, which can be easily enough handled in terms of an underlying complexity rich enough to afford indefinitely renewable consummatory experiences in a variety of cultural contexts,[49] but that of the "old favorite," the touchstone line.[50]

Even if a way can be found of accommodating the familiarity that rightly breeds love rather than contempt, the idea of departure from a norm confuses more than it clarifies. There seems to be no way of giving the notion of a norm any precise and appropriate sense. I have spoken of departures from the anticipated: but since artistic effects are supposed to rely on such departures, anyone who knows that he is confronted with a work of art must expect them. Again, to call something a departure from a norm is to imply that it is in some way a defect; but the departures in question here are in no way defects, for all aesthetic value depends on them. For a fine art to be recognized and practiced, there must be some set

126

of variables as a medium and some repertoire of normal devices for their use; but these, like the pieces and rules of chess, only determine what counts as a game and not what games are interesting. What a given person will find a dull chess game or a dull work of art depends on what his knowledge of the rules enables him to be surprised by.[51] The rules are not what are violated by surprises, but what makes dullness and excitement alike possible. And since surprise is not the sole aesthetic value, and no one has decreed that it is the task of art to maximize information, there may be at least three ways of delighting: surprise by controlled variation of the rules or unexpected use of them; elegance in normal compliance; and familiarity, the recognition of a well-tried and well-loved pattern.[52] But it is still hard to see how the last candidate can be brought under our rubric. Shall we say that banality is significant when we are not sure beforehand that banality is forthcoming? To say that is to reduce the whole thesis to triviality. But if anything whatever can be beautiful, it had to be trivial anyway: as I said at the beginning, the question could not be whether beauty lay in significant departure from the anticipated but only what sorts of departure and anticipation there might be.

The Concept of the Aesthetic

I said that the defining characteristics of the fine arts—their direction toward appreciation rather than consumption and use, their concern with the apparent rather than the actual or substantial and with the presentational rather than the discursive—also served jointly to mark out the domain of the aesthetic, so that the fine arts could be termed, without change of meaning, the arts of the aesthetic. But I also warned that the substitution was risky. The fact that the fine arts comprise all and only those arts whose concern is the aesthetic does not mean that they necessarily take the whole of the aesthetic as their range or that the aesthetic is limited to what they range over. Their concern could be with special kinds of appearance and modes of presentation, leading to special forms of appreciation. Indeed, the word "aesthetic" is often understood as designating a quality or a set of qualities rather than as marking out a domain. There are, in particular, three assumptions one must be careful not to make: that because the typical products of the fine arts reward contemplation (or sensory contemplation, if one prefers that restriction), what makes all such works rewarding is some further set of qualities that they all share; that because the typical works of the fine arts *and other things* (such as certain natural objects) reward sensory contemplation, what makes all such objects rewarding is a further set of shared qualities; and that all the qualities that can render *any* object thus rewarding must be shared by all such objects. Any of these propositions, of which each is stronger than the one before, could prove to be true, but none can be assumed to be true. To assume their truth is to obliterate all possible distinctions between performances and natural objects, between kinds of performances, and between kinds of fine arts, with no other reason than that one had adopted a vocabulary with certain tendencies.

The root of the trouble with the word "aesthetic" is that it is a semitechnical term. Everyday terms arise in the marketplace, and their use is kept in line by their users' sense of familiarity. Technical terms are introduced by definition, and their use is controlled by their restriction to a technical context in which the meaning of the definition is fixed. But a semitechnical term like "aesthetic" is controlled in neither way. It is a jargon word used by theorists, but not controlled by any effective stipulation. Rather, it is subject to pulls in two directions. In effect, it is derived from "aesthetics" and subject to the vagaries of the latter term, which we have already noted. Briefly, "aesthetics" was introduced as a word for the study of whatever in nondiscursive speech might correspond to validity in argument, and was immediately extended to cover the "imitative" arts whose effects were supposed akin to those of poetry. But from there the idea branched in two directions. Those who saw no difference between the beauties of art and those of nature converted aesthetics into the study of beauty; those who saw the fine arts as significant because of what differentiated their beauty from that of nature made aesthetics into the theory of art. Accordingly, the term "aesthetic" in theoretical discussions has two distinct meanings. First, it means something like "pertaining to sensory contemplation and its objects."[53] Second, it means something like "pertaining to the fine arts as such." Most writers confuse the two, combining in a single discussion statements that require each meaning to the exclusion of the other.

Serious as the confusions outlined in the preceding paragraph may be, others are worse. The word "aesthetic" is most often used in the context of certain set phrases, and in these it takes on special meanings. Being a semitechnical term, the word can be submitted to all kinds of manipulation of this sort without effective interference either from the learned world or from the public at large. "Aesthetic" in such phrases tends to stand for some specific characteristic that the theorizer conceives to be essential either to sensory contemplation or to the fine arts as such. Some such phrases have a fairly constant meaning of this sort, assigned by some influential theorist who has made the phrase his own. Others have rival meanings. In either case, the special sense of "aesthetic" involved is likely to become confused with one or both of the two general senses I have mentioned. The confusion comes about as follows. There are two ways of introducing such phrases. Either one can make it a matter of *definition* that the aesthetic point of view (or whatever) is one having certain describably psychological (or whatever) characteristics, and then *assert* that this point of view is commonly taken, or is uniquely appropriate, to works of art or to beautiful things (as the case may be), or one can *define* the aesthetic point of view as that usual or appropriate to the said objects and then *assert* that this point of view is found in fact to have certain describable characteristics. It is then all too easy to forget which path one has followed, and to suppose that both the describable characteristics *and* the unique suitability are guaranteed by definition. Even without this false step, the very use of such a phrase as "the aesthetic point of view" assumes what is too seldom proved, that there is some one point of view (and so on) that is either commonly taken or properly taken to all beautiful things or works of art.[54]

There is never any doubt as to the general area picked out by the term "aesthetic," namely, that covered jointly by beauty and the fine arts. But because most writers use the term, not in this fully vague sense, but with such various more precise meanings as I have suggested, it is advisable to ask some questions whenever one meets the word in serious discussions. Our discussion suggests at least the following three. Is the word being used in a more restricted sense than to allude vaguely to this joint domain—and, if so, in what sense? If it is used in a restricted sense, has the writer seriously tried to establish the existence and unity of the phenomena the term purports to refer to? And is the writer in effect using the word simultaneously in the vague sense and in a restricted sense?

It seems that the word "aesthetic" is a danger signal, especially when someone is trying to prove something. For this reason, many philosophers think the term should never be used. To those who object that this would deprive aesthetics of its prima facie subject matter they reply that, if the unity of aesthetics depends on the use of a question-begging term, it is better disrupted; instead of throwing ambiguous words around, one should spell out whatever it is one means and describe whatever phenomena one has in mind. These scrupulous thinkers have a good point, but the word does have a certain use in marking out a domain for which we have no other term and which can be at least roughly mapped out by discovering affinities and marking distinctions. As for the dangerous ambiguities, they can be neutralized by being recognized and are no worse than those that infect such expressions as "art," "work of art," "beauty," "form," and "convention," some of which those who refuse to speak of the "aesthetic" are bound to employ unless they are to abandon this sort of subject matter altogether. Philosophy cannot be made foolproof.

Recapitulation: Arts of Beauty

It is possible to mark off from all other arts those that manipulate real or ideal materials with a view to producing beauty, that is, in such a way that the value of the performance as such is exhausted in the cognition of its apprehensible qualities: "beauty is that of which the very apprehension pleases." The necessary condition of beauty is that it must be noticeable: the products of such arts as we are discussing must be distinguishable from other things that are near or with which they might be compared in imagination. They might be so distinguishable at first glance, or only on close inspection; by their qualities, by their relationship to their setting, or only by the kind of attitude that the manner of their presentation was understood to demand.

The definition of beauty allows for at least three principal kinds of variation: in who is pleased, in how he is pleased, and through what mode of apprehension. It also allows for other modes of variation in the nature of what is apprehended and so pleases. The term "fine arts," originally a translation of *beaux arts* in which the word "fine" functions as a transferred epithet synonymous with "beautiful," is applied to any such arts as there may be; but it may be restricted as an *appellation contrôlée* to only some such arts, distinguished from the rest by some superiority along one of the dimensions of variation considered. Only what calls for scrutiny,[55] or repays repeated viewing in many contexts, or pleases the cognoscenti or the pure in heart, will be allowed by some to qualify as "fine art."

The foregoing restrictions on the types of beauty available to the fine arts are optional, answering to different theoretical requirements and historical accidents. But there is at least one necessary restriction: that the beauty they aim at must be one demanding skill in its production and meeting a demand from a public for just that beauty. The restriction is necessary because anything can be found beautiful: therefore, the production of beautiful things, though it serves to define a set of arts, does not suffice to characterize them. The restriction imposed could take any of many forms. It could be something as nugatory as the demand for artificial beauty,[56] or beauty produced by certified purveyors; or it could be a specific demand for beauty of some definable type whose production demanded a correspondingly specialized skill. The required skill might be no further definable than the ability to give pleasure in a certain defined context ("Get out there and do something"), or it might be equated with the ability to handle certain media expertly or with dexterity in certain set types of performance. All that is clearly necessary is the restriction to skill-demanding performances. In practice, however, it seems likely that skills of the fine arts almost have to be confined in any given cultural context to certain set kinds of performances; otherwise it is hard to see how skill could be developed and its outcome appreciated.

Despite the prevalence of local restrictions (such as the differential cultivation of genres), it is arguable that in time every art that can be developed will be. Or rather, since arts are so indeterminate in identity that the phrase "every art" is improper, whatever comes to be recognized as a mode of cognition or a means of satisfying cognition will at some time be brought within the range of the fine arts, and ever new modes and means will be sought and explored. To recognize a limitation is to envisage its transgression, and there is always some satisfaction to be found in transgressing limitations. If this is so, then the fine arts as a whole will serve endlessly to explore and expand the range of conceivable and available cognitive experience. And this could be used to justify the inference that it is the task of art (in relation to the history of mankind) to push back the frontiers of the imaginable.

The requirement that the beauty of fine arts must be in some fashion such as only they can supply (since otherwise the arts would not exist) has a corollary. Art is made for people by people, and in the fine arts publics are served by organized producers. Art thus appears among the social transactions of mankind, and it is reasonable to suppose that it meets some such need as men may meet in men. This could be any need, but it is more likely to be a need for something in the way of a communication than for bare visual or auditory stimulation. Even ornaments and cosmetics are *cosmos*, components in the cultural structures we build together.

There is a further corollary. The beauty of the fine arts is *additional* beauty, a beauty superadded to that of the natural world. Is it not then reasonable to suppose that much of its significance will lie in its additionality, in its relation to what is natural? A call for an artificial beauty may include a call for artificiality in beauty, hence a beauty that lies partly at least in the exact ways in which it relates to what is natural. The typical beauty of art might then be a second-order beauty: most pictures once were, as most literary works still are, *about* the world if not *of* it, and an inventory of their interesting features would include as a major part a list of the ways in which they differed from the real. And some theorists argue that this holds even of abstract or nonfigurative works, which are construed as rearrangements of materials derived from nature or as realistic projections of nonreal objects or as demonstrations of methods of seeing reality.[57]

If we construe the corollaries outlined in the last two paragraphs, not as descriptions of probable tendencies, but as tasks and defining characteristics, we find ourselves equating the fine arts with arts of imitation: that is, precisely, arts whose beauties are second-order beauties and lie in all the kinds of variations on and from nature that could be developed.[58] But the equation cannot be made without exploiting the ambiguities of "imitation" in a highly tendentious way. In any case, it follows from the initial definition of the fine arts that, whatever the educational or other value of their performances might be, the value relevant to their consideration as fine arts lies simply in the appreciation of their cognizable qualities. As such they properly belong to the realm of culture and not to that of the workaday; they are a part of what makes life worth living, not means to other ways of making it so. They may not be useless, but it is not their business to be useful. Artists work at them, but they are arts of play.

Enjoyment and Understanding

We have two alternative definitions of the kind of art that produces contemplables: as fine arts, arts of beauty to delight eye and ear; and as arts of imitative play, whose products are valued for something that is mediated by one or another kind of recognition. But these alternative definitions seem to determine different ends for art and its contemplation: enjoyment and understanding. Are these ends really different, and, if they are, what kind of difference is it?

People certainly do produce and study works of art as sources of knowledge or understanding or illumination or something of that general cognitive sort, and in that context the question "Did you enjoy it?" or even "Did you like it?" strikes one as inappropriate if not inapplicable. It certainly seems strange to say that one goes to an exhibition of a serious artist in search of pleasure—we go to learn, to seek enlightenment. That is part of the reason why it seems so very much the wrong thing to say that questions of artistic worth are matters of *taste*: when confronted with a work of any pretensions and complexity, especially a major masterpiece, personal reactions, likings or dislikings, are simply irrelevant: the object has the structure that it has, and it is up to one to come to terms with this formidable entity. It is ludicrous to say that one likes or dislikes, enjoys or is put off by, Raphael's *School of Athens*.

The split between enjoyment and understanding is certainly not absolute. The end of critical interpretation is usually said to be appreciation (cf. *CC* 129–145), and enjoyment that is not based on understanding and thus does not amount to appreciation is irrelevant because it must be enjoyment of something other than the actual performance that the work is. And one is inclined to go further and say (as indeed our discussion of the meaning of "pleasure" encouraged us to do) that the split is illusory: if the understanding of the work is thought of as acquiring information or other useful mental equipment, the work is not being treated as one of fine art. The experience of illumination must be valued for its own quality of illuminatingness, and any directly valued quality of experience counts as pleasure and hence as "enjoyment." That is true, and the point should not be forgotten; but it has something in common with the notoriously deceptive argument in ethics that whatever a person does he must *want* to do (he has, after all, chosen to do it), and, therefore, unless he does it as a mere means to an ulterior end, he must like doing it, must enjoy doing it, must derive pleasure from it. That too is true in a way, but only in a way. It is true that what a person really does for its own sake he must find worth doing, it must be what he wants to do and in that sense (and in that sense alone) *likes* to do. But to go further and say that therefore the person must like doing whatever it is and therefore must enjoy it is to extend those notions illegitimately: it is to blur the distinction between things we do because we find them fun and the things we do because we judge them worthwhile and find satisfaction and fulfillment in doing *because* we judge them so. Similarly, in the arts, we must not allow anything to cover up the fact that *The Importance of Being Earnest* is enjoyable in a way that *King Lear* is not—or, less tendentiously, that most people attend the former in the reasonable expectation of being beguiled, but the latter because something important is taking place. The fact that "all men by nature desire to know" does not make learning a form of entertainment. From *A la recherche du temps perdu* one may or may not learn much about the anatomy of love, the structures of social ambition, and the organization of French society in the early twentieth century, but one certainly learns the important truth that it was possible for a human being to write that novel, and it is to widen and deepen that knowledge that we go on reading it.

Can we say that the fine arts are what we go to solely for such knowledge, moved by the thirst for enlightenment, and that what is enjoyed is only entertainment? No. Mozart and Haydn were, and knew that they were, professional entertainers; Shakespeare, even in *The Tempest*, maintains the posture of someone putting on a show. And no one holds that those artists and works are trivial, or descended to triviality insofar as they entertained. Nor do the suffering and intransigence of Van Gogh, and the visionary novelty of the visual world he stubbornly created, render absurd the actions of the plain people who hang reproductions of his works in their living rooms.

There is certainly a split of some sort between understanding and enjoyment as alternative ends of the fine arts. The question is what kind of split it is, and what, in consequence, is the appropriate thing to do about it. One obvious solution is the Aristotelian one, in which the fine arts exist to produce specifically cognitive pleasures—in other words, experiences in which the cognitive aspect itself is what is enjoyed, and enjoyed for its own sake. The split then comes down to a matter of emphasis: some theorists will explain the arts as producing cognizables (in the cognition of which, of course, enjoyment or satisfaction of some sort or other will be taken); others will say that they are arts for generating satisfactory experiences (the experience being in each case a cognitive one). The handling of the split then becomes a challenge to rhetoric rather than to theory: one may, for instance, be prepared to say such things as (following Aristotle himself) that humans prize knowledge so highly that they would not willingly return to a state of childish ignorance, even though such a state is blissful in contrast with the anxious pains of responsible adulthood; but one will at the same time have to find a way of saying that some pleasures must be more equal than others, since such a person must find more value in his present pains than in his former joys. There is no problem of substance here: it is merely a matter of choosing a suitable vocabulary and stipulating appropriate senses for it.

An alternative solution to the apparent problem of the split would be to agree that in every case the proper object of the fine arts is to produce objects that shall be the occasion of cognitive satisfactions, but that in particular works the emphasis may be laid on either side, or that even within a single complex work the emphasis may shift as between parts and aspects of the work. This is, in fact, a refined version of a classical solution: *omne tulit punctum qui miscuit utile dulci*, "the best work is that which both teaches and pleases," says Horace, with the clear implication that it is possible to do one without the other, or to emphasize one at the expense of the other, while still remaining within the boundaries of poetry. All we have to do to make this position our own is to reinterpret "teaching" as the offering of a purely cognitive entertainment in which what one enjoys is one's engagement with what one understands, and to reinterpret "pleasing" as the offering of a more sensuous delight in which what one enjoys is the felt quality of sights, sounds and surfaces. But this solution could well be challenged on the ground that the original distinction between the useful and the pleasant is perfectly intelligible, but our substitute for it is not. On the contrary, it insinuates falsely that the satisfactions taken in works of art fall neatly into two classes, the intellectual and the sensuous, whereas what we have in fact is an immense and indefinite variety of cognitive attitudes and of modes of satisfaction on which it would be arbitrary to superimpose a priori any dualism derived from a different field of discourse.

A third way of handling the split would be to say that it is no more than a confused and misleading way of alluding to the fact that, if the fine arts produce objects for cognitive satisfaction, they may be regarded with equal legitimacy in either of two ways: as producing works or as producing the experiences for which those works are the occasion. In fact, any account of those works will have to attend now to the properties of the works themselves, now to the experiences for the sake of which (or, in slightly less tendentious terms, with a built-in capacity for engendering which) those works exist. If these two aspects are kept apart, the work as such, and attention to the work as such, will be described in terms of what is to be perceived and understood; and, since perception and understanding as controlled by the work are thus already dealt with, what remains to be spoken of as the experience of the spectator is only the affect derived from the work, the attitude taken toward it, the kind of satisfaction found in the perception and understanding that have already been characterized in artificially neutral terms. In other words, the alleged split proves to be an artifact of our method of inquiry.

Whatever our solution to the apparent problem of the split, two things are certain. First, the contrast between interpretation and evaluation is not the same as that between understanding and enjoyment. Despite some tendentious theorizing to the contrary, evaluation and enjoyment have no immediate connection.[59] Objects of understanding can be evaluated on many scales of value without reference to any pleasure that may be taken in them. And second, there is no close connection between either of those contrasts and the availability of two rival ways of defining the fine arts. There is no reason why the products of arts of imitation cannot be evaluated and also enjoyed as such, or why the products of arts of beauty cannot be at least partially understood and explained.

V

THE CLASSICAL LINE
4: ARTS OF IMAGINATION

The two rival definitions of the fine arts could be unified in the concept of *arts of imagination*, were it not that the term "imagination" itself may be equivocal at the crucial point. I say "may be": the equivocation would be between imagination as the quality of being imaginative, quick to see possibilities to which others are blind and to invent freely, and imagination as the mere human capacity to form mental images and do other things related to but not identical with perception. But whether that is an equivocation or simply the verbal counterpart of a breadth of scope in the use of capacities within which no clear division of function can be identified is a matter of debate—pointless debate, perhaps, but that too is debatable. For the word "imagination" is most readily understood as standing for a faculty, a general human capacity to perform any of a large class of kinds of activity among which theorists detect or postulate a functional affinity; and there is no agreement as to the appropriate strategy for thinking and speaking about such faculties. The most cautious and therefore the most respectable position is to maintain that "abilities" and "faculties" are mere inventions, the corresponding reality being the individual acts that people perform and the other acts that *we say* they would perform in certain unfulfilled circumstances, plus whatever anatomical facts justify our saying so: if I say that I can (have the ability to) recite the alphabet backwards, I am not saying anything that could be true or untrue of myself at the present moment, but merely making an indefinite (and rather mysterious) prediction, unless I am covertly alluding to certain brain traces, or pathways, laid down in my cerebral cortex by the animal spirits with their little asphalt spreaders. On that supposition, the trouble with "imagination" as with other "faculties" is that the vagueness of the predictions suggested, and the corresponding nebulosity and implausibility of the anatomical machinery implied, go far beyond anything that science or sanity can tolerate.

The doubts raised in the preceding paragraph obviously rest on the presumption that "imagination" is used as a term in psychological theory. But "fine arts" is not a term in psychology, and "imagination" in "arts of imagination" need not be either: all that is required to make the latter notion workable is that "imagination" have a *conceptual* unity, that we can assign to the term either a single functional meaning in articulating overt practice or a range of meaning in which we can find (and, ideally, demonstrate) coherence. Rather than waste time on a priori justifications to meet methodological demands that themselves can be neither precisely stated nor justified, let us just sketch out what the required notion of imagination and arts of imagination would be.

The term "imagination" derives from a latinization of Aristotle's term *phantasia*, which meant, approximately, the ability to conjure up "mental images," quasi appearances qualitatively like the perceptible appearances of actual things. But there is also implied a secondary meaning, whereby imagination is the ability itself to have sense data, to see-or-seem-to-see and hear-or-seem-to-hear whether anything to see or to hear is actually present or not. If one hears the telephone ring, one is not imagining it, but one is exercising imagination in this last (artificial) sense. If one thinks one hears the telephone ringing, but in fact not only is it not ringing but nothing within earshot is making a telephonelike noise, one is not hearing the telephone but only imagining it.[1] But also, without being the victim of any such illusion or error, one can deliberately conjure up the sound of a telephone, make oneself hear it in "the mind's ear" or in imagination—an entirely different situation from the last, in which one neither hears nor seems to hear, and certainly does not think one hears, but as-it-were-hears in the sense that one is directly aware of the sound one would be hearing if one heard a telephone. Different as they are, and confusing as it is to call them all imagination unless one is consciously using that as a blanket term, all of these senses are such as to make it appropriate to call the fine arts, conceived as arts of beauty, arts of imagination. That is certainly true of the first and third senses. The fine arts are arts that have to do with sensory orders as such, prescinding from questions of actuality or representation; they are also arts in which the free invention of such orders is embodied. A hardy theorist can make out a case, though not a very good one, for the relevance of the second sense as well: the fine arts, one says, are arts in which the order of sound in motion or the ordered pigment on canvas or whatever creates for the spectator, auditor, or reader the illusion that he is present in worlds or present to realities that the presented order itself constitutes as real.

As perception is to the real, so imagination is to the unreal and possible. As Aristotle and Sartre have insisted in their various ways, action as such depends on the possibility of envisaging alternative situations to the one in which one is placed.[2] Without such envisaging, what the organism "does" is merely a reaction to a stimulus: it cannot properly be said to have done anything at all. The fine arts, on any interpretation, are arts that exploit that possibility, not in the interests of free action, but merely for its own sake, so that the imagining is itself the action. The arts of representation (or as representational), we saw, deal not in replications but in projections; they envisage possibilities rather than record appearances. Insofar as they do in fact record appearances, as of course they very often do, the fact that they do so is irrelevant to their status as fine art: if that were all they did, and insofar as that is their function, what they produce would be, and are, mere records, data, or keepsakes, not works of fine art at all. By the same token, arts of expression are those that make disengaged use of the means of functional expression, hence create what they (purport to) express and are thus exercises of imagination; and the same must hold good of formal arts in which the mind's requirement of order is met by inventions wherein appropriate orders are manifested and celebrated. Arts of creation, which imitate nature by exercising creativity on novel objects for cognition, are preeminently exercises of imagination; and, as we have seen, arts of beauty exemplify imagination in the sense closest to the wider of the senses Aristotle originally endowed the term with. A quick survey thus suggests that, after all, "arts of the imagination" is the most illuminating as well as the handiest designation for the fine arts as the classical line identifies them. There is one apparent exclusion, which as we saw before is in any case a matter of controversy: it looks as if the arts of imagination might exclude arts, if there are any such, of nonsensory contemplation—not in the fashion in which literature is such an art, for literature furnishes us with imaginary worlds, but in some other fashion that perhaps we are not in a position to specify but only to envisage as an abstract possibility.[3] However, it is no use worrying about that: when we are confronted with a claimant to the title of fine art that we might want to bring under such a head, it will be time to consider what to do about it—whether to reject its claim, to stretch the notion of imagination as the notion of imitation was so freely stretched, or what.

I have sketched briefly some ways in which various aspects of the fine arts as here defined could be thought of as arts of imagination. I will now start from the other end and sketch (equally briefly) some ways in which alternative views about what imagination is, or alternative meanings of the term "imagination" as used by theorists, yield alternative views as to what the fine arts as "arts of imagination" would be.[4]

First, imagination may be identified as the general faculty of imaging—the general capacity to have sensory presentations, of which the capacity actually to perceive real things would be but one manifestation (though by far the most important one). Answering to such a notion would be arts of sensation, of pure appearance, producing objects for sensation that are (of course) perceptible, but in which the fact that there is *a real object to be perceived* is of no account: the work of art is "mere appearance," "pure semblance," or even "illusion."[5]

Second, imagination may be identified as the faculty of forming *unified* appearances, visual fields and auditory worlds: not isolated objects of sense, but integrated and total fillings for the sensory spaces with which we are equipped—the ability, in short, to have the kind of unified sensory experience that is most importantly exemplified by the world as perceived. Answering to this notion would be arts of unified sensibles—sensibles that would be integrated in the way suggested by the scholastic conditions of beauty, namely, wholeness and order.

Third, imagination may be identified as the faculty not merely of imaging but of imagining, forming images in the absence of any stimulus—and doing so, let us add, at will, not as the passive victim of hypnagogic imagery and such other shows as one may well believe to be the mere excreta of one's organs of sense. Answering to this notion would be arts of pure semblance once more, but this time with emphasis on their creative status: they do not merely provide but invent sensibilia.

Here is a fourth way of identifying imagination, related to the second view of what imagination might be in the same way as the third was related to the first: as the faculty of forming coherent concatenations or complexes of imagery without identifiable stimulus. Here we come close to what plain people think of as imagination, and the associated view of the arts would treat them as arts of *creating unified possibles*. The artist of the fine arts, on this showing, does not simply provide occasions for pure experience, he creates unified and patterned complexes of sound or color that constitute

alternative virtual realities. And it should not be difficult for someone with the appropriate commitment to formulate a view of that
sort in such a way as to yield a perfectly acceptable account of what
painters and musicians (if not practitioners of other fine arts) evidently do.

Fifth and last, the faculty of freely conjuring up simulacra can
be freed from its confusing association with "imagery" or quasi
pictures, the epistemological status of which has been a bugbear of
philosophy for a long time. The ability to perceive (and the habit
of image forming or as-it-were-perceiving) is one sort of thing;
imaginativeness, the possibility of conceiving or conjuring up alternative realities, is quite another—the possibilities thus envisaged
may be present to the mind without illustrations. When I read a
novel, I enter the world of the novel, which I recreate from the
author's cues, and the world I recreate is identical with the world
the author created. Whether he and I imagine the same world has
nothing to do with whether or not we have any mental images at
all, and nothing to do with (what we can never know, and never
think of asking) whether or not such images as he and I may have
are like each other.[6] Imagining in this sense is simply envisaging
alternative realities; and the view of the fine arts that corresponds
to it is one that sees the artist as creator of possible worlds—this,
as we saw, is one of the transformations of the view that the artist
imitates nature in its process.

But what is it, we may ask, to "envisage" or "conjure up" an
alternative reality? Old men who dream dreams and young men
who see visions may have no doubts about the matter, but philosophers are uneasy. Is it a single phenomenon or a whole range of
phenomena that we have in mind when we use such phrases? The
uneasiness is not diminished by the realization that we do not know
exactly what the problem is. A thoughtful answer, drawing on much
classical and contemporary philosophizing, forms the conclusion
of Mary Warnock's book on the subject. What a good portrait does,
she writes, is not so much resemble its subject as "convey the sense
or significance of the individual. . . . It is for us affectively as if the
absent object were present" (Warnock 1976, 171). What the artist
of the imagination does, then, is not merely to create a simulacrum
but to make something real for us, whether that something be a
world suggested by his work or the work itself as a living presence.
And the mental power that Kant identified as the ability to envisage
a unified world (in fact, as the inability not to do so) should rather
be thought of as "a power . . . which enables us to see the world,

whether present or absent as significant, and also to present this vision to others, for them to share or reject. And this power . . . is not only intellectual. Its impetus comes from the emotions as much as from the reason, from the heart as much as from the head" (ibid., 196). Like all good answers in philosophy, Warnock's revision of the idea of imagination raises at least as many questions as it allays. One question that arises is: in what sense can the power that enables us to see the world as significant really be the *very same power* that enables us to present its significance to others, and is the imaginative power of those to whom we present that significance exercised in sharing that vision or only in finding a significance that no one has yet seen and presented? But I do not know at all how she would, or how I should, go about answering such questions, so I set them aside.

Closely related to the interpretation of imagination as conjuring up alternative realities is the notion of imaginativeness, in which the faculty of imagination as the ability to envisage alternative possibilities is transformed into creativity, fertility in new ideas and unprecedented solutions to problems. Whatever we finally choose as the most apt characterization of the fine arts, it is obvious that the originality they require will make imaginativeness a main asset in their practitioners; but imaginativeness is a general mental excellence that is not peculiar to any particular field of activity, so that there can be no specific "arts of imaginativeness."

In the concept of "pleasures of imagination," in which Addison in 1712 first mooted the notion of arts of imagination, the foregoing notions of what imagination is are not separated. Writers in his tradition may assume that invented images are all derived, at some remove, from the data of perception, thus glossing over such distinctions as might most readily be made. But Kant notoriously identifies the pleasures, and hence potentially the arts, of imagination with the operations of a faculty that unifies perception in lawful and quasi-lawful ways. The trouble with this notion, as Podro (1972) points out, is that, according to Kant, whatever is sensed is sensed as part of a sensory manifold that is necessarily fully unified in a field and should therefore be apt occasion for whatever pleasures of imagination there may be: everything is beautiful. But that should disturb us no more than the scholastic thesis that everything that exists has beauty disturbed us when we defined the fine arts as arts of beauty; all we have to say is that those things are judged beautiful that lend themselves to such unification in a special way, presenting and celebrating relatedness, not in a perceptual field, but in a particular object or within a frame. (For more on this aspect of Kant, see chapter 13 and Appendix A.)

The fine arts could be arts of imagination in an Addisonian sense simply by addressing themselves to sense in one way or another; they can be arts of imagination in the Kantian sense (though we must emphasize that the idea is not one that Kant himself formulated or would have tolerated) only by producing emphatically unified objects. But one may wonder whether or not there can be such arts, if arts are to be organizations of knowledge and skill. And these misgivings are sharpened when we recall Coleridge's post-Kantian separation of imagination from fancy. "Fancy" (significantly, the word comes straight from the Greek, whereas "imagination" is derived from the Greek by way of a Latin intermediary) is the power of conjuring up and concatenating images in ways that may charm and beguile; the word "imagination" is reserved for the faculty of creating coherent unities in which no part exists separably from the rest but each has a significance mediated by the whole. If this distinction can be made intelligible, it is obvious that the consequence of making it will be that there can be arts of fancy and that that is exactly what the fine arts will be; but one does not see how there can be arts of imagination, since the unity of every product of imagination will be such that it cannot be constructed but can only be generated or secreted as an organic whole.

It can be argued that, if the fine arts are to have the importance claimed for them, they must be arts of imagination in something like the Coleridgian sense and that there can be no such arts. It is in fact the necessity of partly acquiescing in this conclusion that will eventually take us out of the classical line of argument altogether: to accommodate it, we will have to introduce the modern notion of art and embark on what I shall call the poetic line and its derivatives. But one might protest that the idea of an art of imagination is after all only mildly paradoxical at worst, and should perhaps rather be thought of as scandalous in the way most successful operations of the mind (and, in consequence, faithful accounts of such operations) are scandalous. An art of imagination in its broadest sense would be the converse of an "art of beauty": what the public sees as an art of beauty, because the art issues in what the public esteems for beauty (if for anything), must be envisaged by the artist in a different light: to engage in an art of beauty would be to give the public what it wanted or ought to want, not to concentrate on the work itself. But what is it in the work that the artist concentrates on? Not so much its beauty as its unity, the inner integrity of its fidelity to what on completion proves to have been its central or pervasive idea. To work thus is to exercise, precisely, one's imagination; and since the artist is an artist, skilled in his profession, there must be arts of the imagination, whether we like it or not. The artist must start somewhere, must have interesting ideas; but artists notoriously cultivate and develop skills of interest, scan the world for données, which they take before they are offered, and develop ways of producing unified wholes: an artist's mastery of his own style is nothing other than his control of his personal method of unifying and unfolding. Such skills fall well within the range of arts as the classical line understands them.

It may still be urged that, although there can indeed be arts of the imagination in every sense but the Coleridgian, that sense at least necessarily escapes the boundaries of the fine arts altogether. But if it does so, it may be by stipulation only. I have sketched the way in which developed skill may be used in developing a complex work from a single idea or in producing a unified work from disparate material: what is the extra something that takes the Coleridgian imagination into what is said to be a different realm? Only, apparently, that the seams don't show—that, in fact, the work is very well done. And, of course, it is not within the compass of any art to ensure that what a practitioner does on any occasion shall be exceptionally well done. What more than that is implied by "imagination" in Coleridge's sense is partly a matter of mere psychological description, stipulating that the artist shall or shall not proceed in a certain order or that he shall or shall not be aware of the appropriate descriptions of the steps into which his procedures may be divided, and partly a matter of vindicating this or that degree of mental dignity or indignity for this or that alleged process.

What gives us pause in the assertion that arts of imagination in the Coleridgian sense must altogether escape the boundaries of the fine arts is only the word "altogether." We cannot ignore those aspects of art that do lie outside those bounds; there are thoughts that we insist on thinking about art that the classical line does not capture at all. We must, therefore, trace alternative lines. But before we do so, we must see what the classical line makes of works of art and of artists.

VI

THE CLASSICAL LINE
5: WHAT WORKS OF ART ARE

The Primacy of the Work

Once we have adopted a definition of a fine art of the sort given in chapter 4, we can define a work of art as the performance of a practitioner of a fine art in the practice of his art. But although we can do that, we would be ill advised to do so for a number of reasons. In the first place, the status of the definition of a fine art is in some doubt. The fine arts are arts of beauty in the sense indicated, perhaps only because the concept of arts of imitative play proved unmanageable, and that concept, though unmanageable, may remain to haunt our thinking. If it does, the alternative ways of thinking about the fine arts generate, respectively, a thin sense of "work of art" as beautiful performance and a thick sense of "work of art" as performance making disengaged use of the means of representation, expression, and formal construction. One can, however, accommodate both thin and thick senses by first adopting a minimalist definition of a work of art and then providing for a richer interpretation of (or enriching gloss on) the definition, which one can apply to preferred or normal cases. The present chapter will make provision for such a strategy.

A more serious objection to defining the work of art in the way first suggested is that it lays an unwanted stress on the institutions of the arts and on their secondary as opposed to their primary standards. Any art exists presumably for the sake of the improvements it organizes knowledge and skill to bring about, not for the sake of the knowledge and skill themselves, and still less for the sake of the machinery by which that organization is effected. So the work is what matters.[1]

Most theoretical treatments of the fine arts do start by considering the work of art, as though it were an independently existing entity. In fact, most recent philosophers of art treat "work of art" and "art" as interchangeable terms—apparently, since they do not explain their practice, without realizing that there could be any relevant difference; and in doing so they are not dissolving the work of art in the art that generated it, but are eliding art in its works. The work thus attains primacy by default. Part of the reason for this elevation of the work to a position of isolated primacy is the disappearance from the contemporary consciousness of the classical concept of technical thought; another part is the recently fashionable equation of thinking with verbalization, so that a work of art can be an object of philosophical concern only insofar as it becomes a target for critical or appreciative discourse. But there is a better reason. The legitimate interest of the public in works of art lies in the works themselves, not in what goes into them.[2] What goes into them is either conceived as the performing of the performance, which must issue entirely and effectively in the performance so that it would be otiose to consider it, or else figures as mere biographical anecdote, irrelevant to the work itself and of interest only to those who are more interested in gossip than in the fine arts.

However we choose to explain it, the practice of starting one's consideration of the fine arts with the work of art itself, considered as an independent object, is well established and easily defensible. But the independent consideration of the fine arts as organized practices was no less defensible. The two lines of thought obviously cannot be guaranteed to meet each other head-on. In turning from the fine arts to works of art, we must therefore be ready to make a fresh start that may take us to a new destination.

To call something a work of art is not usually to say anything about the artist's credentials. Nor is there any reason why it should be. If a work of art were defined as the product of a fine art, one could not call anything a work of art until one knew not only what skill went into its making but also how that skill was organized. That would exclude from consideration both objects about whose exact provenance nothing was known and objects in whose making aesthetic factors were not paramount: cave paintings would not be works of art because we do not know anything about their painters, and carved canoe paddles would not be works of art if they were made to paddle with. One could accept such restrictions, but they are pointless if our concern is with such objects as do in fact issue from the fine arts, but not with the fact that they so issue. The sense we want to give the expression "work of art," if we are to lay our previous discussion under the greatest reasonable obligation, is approximately "the sort of thing the fine arts produce." But that needs to be made more precise, because, as it stands, it looks too much like what we rejected: the sort of thing the fine arts produce is their product. And if we do make it more precise, there are various options open to us. We could use the term evaluatively: something good enough to have issued from the fine arts. Or we could use it judgmentally: something that meets the standards laid down by and for the fine arts.[3] Or we could use it descriptively: something that has some (enough, presumably) of the properties that workers in the fine arts characteristically impart to their works. Or we could use it sortally: something that belongs to one of the kinds of things that the fine arts produce.[4]

What sort of account should we give of what works of art are? It cannot, in any event, be an account of what most people mean by the phrase, for the phrase is paronymous: that is, things are called works of art for a variety of different reasons and in a variety of senses, all related in some way or other to the group of practices we lump together as art, but not at all in the same way. I have already remarked that the phrase is used evaluatively, judgmentally, descriptively, and sortally. A related point can be made more directly by saying that there are at least three quite different sorts of reasons for saying that something is *not* a work of art: that it is not related to the institutions of art in some stipulated way (is not the work of a competent practitioner; does not belong to a recognized art form); that it is not related to whatever the *function* of the fine arts is taken to be;[5] and that, though related to that function, it does not fulfill it in an adequate way.[6] More importantly, a unitary definition of "work of art" could be of little interest. There are a number of questions into which the topic "the nature of a work of art" naturally enters, and they call for quite separate treatments: there are questions of teaching methods, which require emphasis on intention and accomplishment; questions of aesthetic value, which call for emphasis on perceptible qualities; questions about the function of the fine arts; questions about the relation of technique to inspiration; and so on. The account of "what a work of art is" that will illuminate one of these questions will be useless or even harmful for others, and discussions of the merits of proposed definitions of works of art are likely to be disguised debate about what sort of question shall take priority over all others. Such debates, if their nature were recognized, would at once be seen to be absurd. It follows that debates about the merits of rival definitions of the work of art tend to be absurd, too.

What sort of account, then, are we looking for, and what do we want it for? The impetus of our account, which should carry over as much as possible from previous chapters, calls for something like a characterization of "the sort of thing art historians talk about." But not all art historians talk about the same sort of thing: even in this rather restricted context, the expression "work of art" is not only paronymous but vague.[7] For instance, corresponding to the idea of arts of imitative play is a conceptualization of works of art as (to use Nelson Goodman's phrase) characters in symbol systems, intrinsically intelligible and in principle presumably wholly explicable; corresponding to the notion of arts of beauty, on the other hand, is a conceptualization of works of art as objects for contemplation and appreciation, in principle not wholly explicable. Each of these ways of thinking about works of art has evident advantages that the other clearly lacks: choosing between them would be silly, unless one made the choice for the purpose of some particular thesis one wished to expound or of some discussion in which one wished to engage.

An account of what a work of art is cannot, therefore, describe the way the expression is used, because its use is irreducibly various; nor can it be stipulative without absurdity, since any stipulation would impoverish or hamper discussions in which we ourselves might wish to engage. We seem to be left with four likely courses of action. One is to content ourselves, as Morris Weitz did in his famous essay (1956), with insisting that the concept of a work of art is an open concept, necessarily undefinable. The trouble with that is that it is completely unilluminating, a condition that is not alleviated by insisting that there is no light to be had. The second course would accordingly be to chart all of the different things works of art are said to be, all the reasons for calling them so, and all the different things the phrase "work of art" is used to mean, with a full treatment of how these uses and appellations relate to different contexts—ending, no doubt, with a "to be continued" clause to leave the ways open for future history. That would be an interesting thing to do, but since we already have a context here and now, this is not the time and place. A third course would be to define "work of art" in some completely trivial way (e.g. "a work of art is anything anyone calls a work of art"), so that the real issues lying beneath discussions of what works of art really are will have to be discussed in more illuminating (and, presumably, more appropriate) terms. And a fourth course of action would be to hazard an ad hoc definition for present purposes. The fourth course is the one I mean to take, with wistful glances back at the third.

The present purpose my ad hoc definition is to serve is to clarify certain relationships between ideas. The relationships themselves are not arbitrary, though the decision to use a particular phraseology in the course of clarification is admittedly arbitrary. Definitions are useful, if not indispensable, for fixing one's ideas. And fixing one's ideas is a good thing to do, so long as one is prepared to unfix them again and use the resources of unfettered and informal speech, floating with its context, to give the agile intelligence play.

Ten Definitions

In order to make precise the idea of a work of art required by the classical line in art theory, I propose to offer ten definitions, the eighth of which defines a work of art. The others either contribute to this definition or define other terms that need to be distinguished from "work of art." All the definitions are artificial and have no other purpose than to clarify an obscure notion. My starting point is that a work of art is not necessarily a product of the fine arts, but is the same sort of thing as such products are. The question my definition should answer is: In what ways must things be like the typical products of the fine arts for the same kind of discourse to be appropriate to them? On what conditions can a thing enter a fine art context without being a fine art product? Four kinds of answer seem possible: one, in terms of the qualities of the object; the second, in terms of the social function the object fulfills; the third, in terms of the way the object enters that context; and the fourth, in terms of the immediate end the object serves. The first kind of answer is generally rejected, and I reject it too, if only because my definition of "beauty" forbids me to foreclose on what kinds of perceptibles will yield what kinds of satisfaction. The second has been brilliantly expounded by Paul Ziff, but in terms our classical line cannot accommodate.[8] The third has been tried out by George Dickie, but with doubtful success.[9] That leaves us with the fourth kind of answer, which in any case fits the argument of chapter 4 best.

My first definition assigns a special sense to the word "contemplate," as suggested in chapter 4. To contemplate something in this sense is to attend to what it is like as opposed to what it is or what can be done with it: to seek out and dwell on appearances and on structures conceived as appearances or as structures of appearances. Ways of contemplating include looking at things and watching them; listening to them; savoring flavors, aromas, and textures; reading texts and imaginatively realizing what they present; and mentally dwelling on systems of intelligible relationships. Insofar as anyone is contemplating, his attention is disinterested in the sense that it has no ulterior motive, has no further end than the attending itself.[10] Whereas in common use the word "contemplate" suggests an attitude of peaceful, detached, passive receptivity, what the term designates here may be excited rather than calm, exploratory rather than passive, involved and engaged rather than detached.[11] "Contemplation," wrote Dewey, "designates that aspect of perception in which elements of seeking and thinking are subordinated (although not absent) to the perfecting of the process of perception itself" (1934, 253–254), and it might be thought that I would be disagreeing with him (or, rather, using the word "contemplation" in a sense other than his). But Dewey speaks of *aspects* of perception, not of occasions, and a contemplative perception may be what it is only because of the intense search of which it is a part: it will accord with my usage to call it contemplation insofar as the perception is assigned a value of its own. Beyond that, I do not mean to suggest that the various attitudes and activities that are collected under the heading "contemplation" have any features in common.[12]

My second definition is of an "aesthetic object," which I define as "anything whatever *insofar as* conceived as a fit object of contemplation." There are three things to note here. First, no restriction is placed on the kind of contemplation. In discussing the fine arts, I entertained restriction of the aesthetic or of the fine arts to seeing and hearing or to sensory activity. Such restriction is now repudiated. Part of the reason is that literary works, despite the arguments cited before, are not in general essentially sensuous. Though a literary experience may be auditory and must be temporally extended, with duration and sequence, it is not susceptible of temporal measure. Essentially, it is a construction of meanings and meaning bearers. More important, even if I had adopted such a restriction for the fine arts, nothing in the definition I have adopted confines aesthetic objects to the fine (or any other) arts. God could be an aesthetic object; in fact, if He can be an object at all, He obviously is. The second thing to note is that the phrase picks out a viewpoint, not a class of objects. The only things excluded from being aesthetic objects are those that can never be fit objects of contemplation. But since, as I have said and will have to say again, one cannot set limits in advance on the kinds and sources of value discoverable in contemplation, one cannot exclude anything from being a fit object for contemplation otherwise than by stipulating special standards of "fitness," which my account, having said nothing at all about what fitness amounts to, leaves as a possibility, but not as a very promising one. Meanwhile, to call something an aesthetic object is to affirm that one conceives it fit to contemplate, and that is implicitly to claim that one knows of something in it that does in some definite fashion reward some particular mode of contemplation. And the third point is that I do indeed speak of a fit object, not a possible object. If English afforded a precise equivalent for the Latin gerundive, I should use it—I speak of *contemplanda*, not *contemplabilia* or *contemplata*. But fitness is not pleasantness, and the contemplation called for might be a horrified stare. To judge something a proper object of attention is not to say what there is about it to be attended to, or how such attention is repaid.

My definition of an aesthetic object does not specify *who* conceives it a fit object of contemplation. One might wish to make some such move as George Dickie makes in his definition of a strictly classificatory sense of work of art, according to which the status of contemplability is freely conferred, a conferring that of course cannot be either true or false, though it may be wise or foolish. One may know of an object that others conceive it a fit object for contemplation, though unwilling so to conceive it oneself. An object may draw attention to itself as an object for contemplation by conventional features (frame, pedestal, spot lighting, fancy printing), or have attention drawn to it by the context of presentation, though in fact one may judge that the promise to reward contemplation can never be fulfilled. I have urged that everything whatever must in principle be a fit object of contemplation from some sort of view in some circumstances: whatever exists must be capable of being perceived or conceived, and whatever is perceived or conceived must be such that some interest can be taken in it. But the plain sense of my definition is to discount the effect of this principle and distinguish the fit from the unfit. We may then apply the phrase "putative aesthetic object" to those objects that obtrude themselves as intended for contemplation, even though we wish to deny the possibility or legitimacy of any interest taken in them; only those putative aesthetic objects to which we are prepared to concede actual fitness will be allowed to be aesthetic objects *sans phrase*.

My next definitions contribute to our study only indirectly. The third definition is of appreciation. To appreciate anything is to recognize in it what value it has in a certain respect understood to be the relevant one, and to value it as the object of that recognition; to appreciate it fully is to recognize in it all the value it has in that respect, and to value it for that. Accordingly, it makes no sense to speak of appreciating anything unless the relevant values are clearly delimited by the context of discussion. To appreciate an aesthetic object is to recognize that in it whereby it is a fit object of contemplation, and to value it on the basis of that recognition. Art appreciation classes purport to teach their students to identify the values to be recognized and esteemed in works of art of specific kinds.

The definition of "appreciation" adopted here does not stipulate that only performances can be appreciated, though the stipulation is one I have no quarrel with and have myself made in other contexts. But the present definition does call for something analogous in requiring a firm prior decision as to what values are understood to be the relevant ones, for this prior decision can only be embodied in an established context of practice or of connoisseurship, a context that, like the concept of performance itself, carries the implication of a determinate relationship to actual and possible intentions. That being so, the notion of appreciating an aesthetic object raises a curious difficulty. Appreciation requires an object that is in principle determinate, so that it makes sense to speak of recognizing all the value it has. But the way I defined an aesthetic object suggested considerable indeterminacy: a thing might be a fit object for contemplation of many different sorts, or might be fit for contemplation because of any of many different sets of properties. But this difficulty is easily resolved, if it is a difficulty at all. An aesthetic object is anything conceived as "a fit object," hence as one object: it follows that anything (any space-time region or whatever) may be conceived as, and thus be, a number of aesthetic objects, in much the sort of way indicated by Virgil Aldrich (1963).

It is conceivable that contemplation in the sense we require could be defined in terms of appreciation, as whatever cognitive operations might be necessary for the appreciation of any aesthetic object: what those operations would be would of course depend on what was to be appreciated. But we would then need a way of differentiating aesthetic objects from other appreciable objects.[13] It is probably better to start with contemplation and define aesthetic objects in terms of that, so that aesthetic appreciation is nothing other than the appreciation of aesthetic objects.[14]

My fourth definition is that of an artifact, by which I shall mean any material object whose characteristic form was given it by an agent whose action was directed to giving it a form of that kind. Such terms as "material object" are notoriously hard to make quite precise, but I intend the expression to be taken in a common-sense way: I would number among material objects statues and paintings, but not such doubtful entities as the performance of a musical work, even though such a performance might be said to consist materially of a set of sound waves. In the traditional and archaeological sense of the term, an artifact is something a person can pick up and handle. I mean to depart from this usage only by omitting the size restriction—in my present sense, Cheops' pyramid is an artifact. By "characteristic form" I mean something Aristotelian—the "best answer" to the question "What is it like?" Whether or not a material thing is an artifact thus depends on whether changes deliberately made in its apprehensible qualities by some agent amount to giving it a new form, or merely modify the form it already had. I do not convert Mount Rushmore into an artifact by carving a head on it, but I do so convert that hunk of the mountain which I carve. By "agent" I mean a living being capable of forming and following plans, deliberating and contriving. Unless an ape has such capacities, and devotes them to its painting, an ape's painting is not an artifact in the present sense; if there is no clear answer to the question whether an ape has such capacities or uses them thus, it follows that there is no clear answer to the question whether its paintings are artifacts.[15] The provision that the agent's action *was directed* is to be taken literally as referring to a matter of fact. Whether or not something is an artifact is determined by its history, not by what critics may say of it after the event, though it may be up to the critics to decide how the artifact is best described. Finally, the provision that his action was directed to giving it a *form of that kind*, rather than *that form*, is meant to allow for errors and lucky successes but not for serendipity. A man may produce a better or worse work than he planned, may incorporate accidental smudges in his work, without our questioning its status. But I want to rule out any cases where a man acts rather as a force of nature than as an intelligent agent. A man might accidentally drop a bucket of paint and have it turn into a fine painting, or casually split a rock and find himself confronted thereby with an uncovenanted statue of Hercules. But by the proposed definition the product of such a freak event would not be an artifact.

The fifth definition must be that of a performance in the special sense discussed at length in chapter 2. I there offered a number of allegedly equivalent definitions. For present purposes, I offer a new variant: "any self-contained thing that is done or made, conceived strictly as the outcome of the doing or making in question"—that is, insofar as its characteristic form was given it by an agent in and by his agency. Here the phrase "self-contained thing" excludes nothing a priori and is really otiose: anything whatever can be self-contained, that is, perceived or conceived as an isolated whole in abstraction from everything else (even though in practice it may be hard to think of some things as such wholes). I put the phrase in because it is important that whatever is thought of as a performance is thereby thought of as self-contained.[16] In any case, my earlier discussion showed that things made and done, whatever may be true of other things, can be isolated only by acts of attention, critical or purposive. Anyone who construes something as a performance is taking it to be a certain isolated whole and, in so taking it, constitutes it as just that whole; and it is that person who must be doing the "strict conceiving" specified in the proposed definition. It is unnecessary though harmless to add "and whatever qualifies it as such a single outcome," for such a whole can be qualified only by what constitutes it. The same strictness excludes from consideration any features of any resulting artifact, of the motions gone through while performing, and of the individual doing the performing, that form no part of the relevantly criticizable outcome; it forbids us to equate performance with artifact, but requires us to equate a performance with the sum of the relevant changes made in the artifact if there is one.

In the present context, I reject my alternative definition of a performance as "an object of criticism as such," because it implies that a critical intervention can make a performance where there was none. For present purposes, it is more important that a critic who criticizes a piece of driftwood as a sculpture is making a mistake than that the mistake he is making is not a critical one. There is a contested area here, which I shall leave contested: is one necessarily *mistaken* if one criticizes a man's dancing when what he is really doing is trying to save himself from falling? There is no simple answer. What I do stipulate is that there really is an agent or agents and there really are motions of the minds and bodies of those agents from which performer and performance can be abstracted. A performance is at least something done or made, not something thought to be done or made.[17]

The sixth definition is that of a design, taken here to mean "all those aspects of any performance that constitute it a single aesthetic object." In ordinary use, the word "design" approximates either to "intention" or to "pattern," but neither approximation is to the point here. There can be as many types of design as there can be types of aesthetic objects that are also performances (or abstracted from performances) and, hence, as many as there are reasons for attending to what things made or done are like. In the case of a typical work of fine art, if we suppose that a work of fine art is an aesthetic object, we shall say that its design consists of all its aspects as performance: not the painting itself, perhaps, but everything about the painting.[18] But a performance may be conceived in a more complex way and (like our carved canoe paddle or a ritual mask) be at once an aesthetic object and something else. We may abstract from this abstraction in one way and say that the maker has done two things at once, combining an aesthetic performance with a performance of a task related to boat propulsion; or we may perform the abstraction in another way and say that what he has done is to carve a paddle that is both ornamental and useful, but that we wish to attend to the system of the aesthetic properties he has given it. The latter way has advantages: we may want to insist that he has made and done one thing, not two.

All kinds of beauty that are not excluded by the inapplicability of the concept of agency are kinds of design. What kinds of design (and hence what designs) a given individual or society will accept as such will depend on what he or they can conceive as a way of directing or organizing attention. A design may be invisible because the artist's way of looking has been lost, or even because no one has yet learned to look in the appropriate way. Who knows what ready-mades of the future await their Duchamp?

Among designs—among those aesthetic objects that we think of *as* performances—we may differentiate three kinds: messages, expressions, and patterns. To construe a design as a message is to take it as comprising properties given it by someone for someone else to take note of. To construe it as an expression is to take it as comprising properties that reflect agency in some integral way but are not directed to conveying anything to anyone else. To construe it as a pattern is to prescind from any considerations about agent or public and attend to the intrinsic properties it has, as though it were a natural object—or better, as though it would be a matter of indifference whether it was a natural or an artificial object if it were not taken as a manifestation of skill. So long as what is attended to is the apprehensible qualities that constitute the design and not the content or pragmatic import of the message as a social transaction, or the life interest of what is expressed, messages and expressions are not less designs than patterns are. The distinction is not sharp, and one may slip from one viewpoint to the other. But it is as well to keep in mind that a design as such may have the quality of an expression or the quality of a message.[19] Otherwise, we may slip unawares into the supposition that only patterns can be designs.

My seventh definition is that of a "design act." A "design act" is any action or set of actions of any agent or set of agents, not necessarily contemporaneous with or knowing about each other, that issues in a single design—that is, of course, in the design of a single aesthetic object. The idea is supposed to work like this. Suppose we have an aesthetic object, such as the King James Version of the Bible taken as a literary work of which Genesis is the beginning and Revelation the end. Taken as a performance in our sense, the work projects a single performer and a single act of performing (corresponding, incidentally, to the Holy Spirit and His inspiration). But, of course, the performer projected by the work is a fictitious one, or at best one perceptible only to the eye of faith: the unitary act of creation never took place, and there was no one person or *group* of people to perform it. But the literary work, still taken as a performance, has a design, a set of aesthetic properties (literary excellences and potential excellences) that were in fact imparted to it by the real historical actions of a large number of people doing very different things at very different times and places. It is those real actions that issued in what we view as a performance (and hence as the outcome of idealized actions) and gave it the design that it has, which I call a design act. To take a different sort or case: consider someone making a ritual mask. In discussing my definition of "design," I said that we might wish to say that he was performing two performances, making a ritual object and making an aesthetic object, which projected two different performers and two different performings, theurgic and aesthetic in character, respectively. But we might prefer to say that he undertook a single performance, in which we discern aesthetic aspects (the design) and other aspects. Now, even if we take the latter approach, I shall want to say that the design we find in the mask actually issued from the historically real actions of giving the mask its aesthetic character; and those real actions I shall once more call the design act.

The idea of a design act is one I will be making use of later. I have misgivings in introducing it, not because of any unclarity in the idea, but because of its mixed character: the "design" of the performance is isolated by one sort of abstraction, the identification in the object of its aesthetic characteristics, and the design act is then picked out by another sort of abstraction, the selection of those episodes in history that we deem relevant to the production of those characteristics. Moreover, it is untidy to have the concept of performance side by side with the closely related idea of a design act. But so be it. Overelaboration is better than confusion and falsification.[20]

My eighth definition is that of a work of art. Borrowing a phrase and part of an argument from Joseph Margolis, I define a work of art as a performance "considered with respect to its design."[21]

The stipulation that a work of art is a performance, something done or made, is not meant to be an arbitrary or external restriction. To think of something as a work of art is to relate it to human agency and, hence, to the enterprise of social living in which we are ourselves engaged. We enter into implicit conversation with its putative maker.[22] Typically, our interest is neither in the outcome of the making alone, as it might be in the physical properties of the resulting artifact, nor in the person of the agent, but in the *thing done*, including the manner of doing and the agent qualities shown—assuming all these to be inseparable. Artistry, artist, and artifact are not in practice to be considered separately. If indeed a piece of driftwood is sincerely said to be a splendid piece of sculpture, as Morris Weitz supposes (1956), it is not merely because it is beautiful but because it seems splendidly *sculpted*—it bespeaks a carver who appears in it.[23] This is no less true if we are mistaken in supposing it to have been carved, or do not believe that it really was. Nor is our relation to the performance any the less essentially fixed within the human world if the artist (like Warhol in his ostentatiously dehumanized silk-screens, unmistakable in their abnegation of personality) stresses his impersonality and anonymity.

The performance that is a work of art is defined as one considered with respect to its design. Considered by whom? The openness of the definition admits of appeal to any real or imaginary elite or consensus, or even to the ideal sensibility and comprehension of God. In dealing with an analogous definition of "beauty" as that which pleases on being perceived, we said that the question "Pleases whom?" was a real question that remained open, and was better left so. Different answers corresponded to different views that were all tenable and all actually held. So here too it may be that different answers to such questions as "Considered by whom?" and "Occasionally considered or regularly considered?" and "Regularly in what community?" will answer to different views as to what works of art are, or to different applications of the expression "work of art" in different contexts of discussion. And we may recall in this connection that, although we said in chapter 2 that every art has a public, that public could in the limiting case be the artist himself on a single occasion.

The failure to specify who is to do the considering opens our definition to at least three different readings. On the first reading, which we may call the normal reading both because it seems the natural way to take it and because it invokes normality, "considered" means "habitually or regularly considered"—presumably within a readily identifiable community. That is how a dictionary definition would be taken: when the lexicographer defines a cassock as "a long, close-fitting garment worn by priests," he does not mean one occasionally worn by this or that priest, but one that forms part of a typical priest's regular wardrobe. So the natural way to read "a performance considered with respect to its design" is as referring to any performance that is regularly so viewed. It would not be unreasonable to stand by this natural implication of the wording we have chosen and thus preserve a distinction between a work of art and something that is for the time being being treated or considered as one.[24] To do so would fit well with the blunt statement that began our opening chapter, that there are some things that everyone knows are works of art—a statement that makes sense only if there are other things that everyone knows are not.

Even if there are some things that everyone knows are works of art, it is not easy to say how everyone knows it. It is even less easy to say how everyone knows of some things that they are not works of art. Nor is it easy to say just who is included in the "everyone" who has this knowledge, or what proportion of the world's putative art is covered by this facile consensus. As Danto shows in a trenchant refutation of a claim of this kind (1981, chap. 3), radical and widespread error is possible here. One might then opt for a second, more subtle way of reading our proposed definition that may be called the interpretive reading. This reading exploits the normal reading's presumption that there is an identifiable community within which the considering regularly takes place and takes "work of art" to mean a performance that is regularly considered with respect to its design by whatever appropriate reference group one has in mind, so that what is claimed by calling it a work of art remains indeterminate unless and until that group is identified. (This definitional strategy was elaborated in its application to words like "good" in Sparshott [1958].)

The third reading our definition admits is an open one, according to which "considered" simply means "considered by someone." This is a reading our definition really does admit, and it does have the consequence that it is within the scope of the classical line to classify as works of art all performances that anyone ever considers with respect to their design, though, of course, there is nothing in that line to oblige or even encourage anyone to take this view. The openness, as we shall discover, is not so disconcerting and scandalous as it sounds. But one might reasonably prefer to reserve the classificatory use of the phrase "work of art" for the normal or the interpretive sense, and to say that in the open sense the phrase is used not to classify performances but to refer to an aspect of them. One would then be construing our rather ambiguously worded definition not as "any performance that is considered with respect to its design is a work of art" but as "any performance, considered with respect to its design, is a work of art." This sense, and this use, would be as well or better captured by saying that "to consider a performance as a work of art is to consider it with respect to its design," provided only that one does not then construe "as a work of art" to mean "as if it were, as a matter of classification, a work of art."

My present task is to expound the classical line as such, so it is not incumbent on me to opt for one specific way of reading a definition of which the ambiguity is deliberate. Its ambiguity derives from a sort of openness already built into the concept of design. What any person or society accepts as a design, and hence what he or it can accept as a work of art, will depend on what he or it is able or prepared to expect from designers, that is, on what could *conceivably* be performed or apprehended in a performance. But no kind of performance is such that it cannot be considered with respect to its design, as I have insisted before: a waiter's manipulation of his tray among tables may be considered with respect to whatever aspects of it constitute an aesthetic object (a sort of dance), though what he is "really" performing is not a dance but a clearing of tables.[25] Though any performance may be considered with respect to its design, however, not all are equally easily and suitably considered so. A pipe layer's trench could be considered a work of art, and, *if* so considered, it would, on the appropriate reading of our definition, be a work of art, though we may guess that it would not be a very interesting one. If we exclude the trench, we will be unable to include the carved canoe paddle without appealing either to the carver's intentions (which we need not know), to the presence of ornamentation (which seems to make ornateness a defining property of works of art), to the excellence of its proportions (in which case we must commit ourselves to a decision about what proportions are admirable before we can decide what is or is not a work of art), or to the consensus of some elite—and who shall say which is for all time the right elite?[26] We know very well that most people will not in fact consider the trench so. They will assume it is not worth looking at (or smelling). It will not occur to them that any of its properties as a performance, the aspects of its digging and dugness, will have been the sort of features that could conceivably have formed part of any design, or could enter into any designer's mind. We need not fear that our catholicity will pave the way for a mob of anarchic iconoclasts cramming the artworld with tedious trenches. All the same, we cannot rule out a priori the possibility that a cult of trench connoisseurs should arise, or even the possibility that, if it did, we might be missing something if we failed to join the cult. Meanwhile, if a lot of people whose judgment you know and respect urge you to come out and look at a trench with them, I would almost be inclined to advise you to go along with them, if you can spare the time and it is not raining, because it just might turn out to be the damnedest trench you ever saw.

Anything, we have insisted, can be an aesthetic object: every performance is such that a design could be found in it, and it could be considered with respect to that. But it does not follow that every performance, including any random pipe layer's trench, is a work of art, even a bad or uninteresting one. It does not follow, because of what at first seems a puzzling feature in the proposed definition of a work of art. That definition speaks of *the* design of a performance. Its design, if we follow our definitions through, is nothing but the aggregate of those features that render it, as a performance, a fit object of some mode of cognitive action. That certainly sounds as if it implies that there is a determinate set of such features, which combine to make it an object with a single determinate character. But how can that be? If anything whatever can be an aesthetic object (or even if it is only in principle possible that anything whatever *might* be), it is reasonable to suppose that for every performance there will be an indeterminate number of sets of such features—otherwise, we should be postulating the miraculous coincidence that for every performance and indeed for every thing there will be one and only one way of cognizing it as an aesthetic object.

The puzzle can be readily resolved. In the first place, I was careful not to begin with aesthetic aspects or features and build the aesthetic object up from them: rather, the aesthetic object is conceived first, and its "features" or "aspects" are identified only by their contributing to its design. There is indeed no such "aggregate" of features as I just invoked. In the second place, to call something a work of art is indeed to imply that it is a single aesthetic object and has a single design. One must accordingly at least know how to begin specifying its relevant features, though no doubt one never knows how to end and cannot be certain one will not be successfully contradicted by sharper or more sensitive souls. Anyone who calls that pipe layer's trench a work of art is claiming to have identified in it a design that characterizes it as a performance, and has thus implicitly limited the kinds of beauty that may relevantly be found there.[27] It follows that, although I have for purposes of this chapter set aside my alternative definition of "performance" as "any object of criticism as such," a performance answering to a specific critique may be a work of art strictly by virtue of the design the critique established for it.[28] Calling something a work of art thus implies that one is in possession of a definite way of interpreting it and, in the context of utterance, this definite way is the one right way. And this is not trivial. It implies that to call something a work of art without having actually identified in it a considerable design is fraudulent.[29] Trickery in art does sometimes take this form of falsely claiming to have identified a design, as when one seeks to have accepted as a work of art some byproduct of a manufacturing process in the hope that the experts will be conned into pretending to appreciate what is not there to be appreciated. But this fraudulent intent does not guarantee that the hoped-for victims, when thus inveigled into trying to identify and appreciate a design, will not really succeed in doing so. That is why the successes of artistic hoaxes are so often doubtful or ambiguous.

The practical point of any definition of a work of art lies in the inclusions and exclusions it requires. The definition proposed here excludes natural objects even if they have significant aesthetic properties, whether or not this exclusion violates the ordinary usage of the expression "work of art."[30] It includes suitable artifacts made with no aesthetic intent. It includes fakes and frauds, for their fraudulence lies not in their failing to be performances, but in their failing to be performances of the particular provenance they claim.[31] It includes aesthetically unsuccessful performances, though the positive connotations built into the concept of design threaten to exclude them: an object may be considered with respect to its design and in that respect condemned, and what is contextually determined to be a fit object of contemplation may frustrate the contemplation it invites. For the same reason, the definition includes *Kitsch*, if that concept is countenanced.[32] But it excludes performances to which no one has ascribed a determinate design.

It may be argued that the practical point of a definition of a work of art lies not only where we have placed it, in the inclusions and exclusions it prescribes, but, more subtly, in those it does not require but invites or insinuates and, consequently, in the redirections of practice it solicits or declines to solicit. That is the point, it will be said, of even those definitions whose authors repudiate any such interest and claim merely to provide tools for the clarification of thought. And my own definition, taken without stipulation as to who is to do the considering, identifies a work of art, not as a member of a limited set of performances or things, but as any performance considered from a point of view that may be taken to any performance at all. In admitting an open reading it encourages such a reading.

Although the open reading of our definition is not the normal one, I am far from repudiating it. I would even urge that, as the most inclusive reading, it takes theoretic precedence and there are good reasons, while admitting the normality of a different reading, for allowing the open reading the central place in ordering one's thoughts and attitudes. The history of the changes of taste, and the successive introduction into the art world of new objects for appreciation, show that to adopt a definition that definitively excludes anything is to risk committing oneself to the exclusion not only of things that a changed critical fashion may embrace (which might not matter) but of things that one may oneself want to keep within the ambit of his discussion and the context of his philosophy of art.[33] What we needed was therefore an all-inclusive term that merely showed what it is for a thing to enter into this context. And the term "work of art" seemed not only to be the term most available for this catholic definition but to be already used in theoretical discussions in a sense at least approximating this. For our exclusions, we will propose other expressions differently defined.

Justified or not, our catholicity may cause uneasiness. If this malaise is merely a shadow of that caused by the shifting boundaries of acceptability in the art world, it is not my responsibility to do more about it than to advise you to hold onto your hat—and, of course, your wallet. I would certainly advise you not to take any wooden nickels, but to expect a definition to help you to tell wooden nickels from buffalo nickels shows the wrong attitude. It is unwise to look to a verbal formula as a shield. A formula is no substitute for wisdom in the ordering of one's judgment, which calls for experience, cunning, and generosity of spirit. And a desire that one's judgments should ever become *safe* is likely to prevent one from ever finding much value in anything. People who do want to be safe need no help from theories; they can easily be so by reflecting that despite their ignorance of art they know what they like.[34] And if they don't even know what they like, they can't expect the rest of the world to bother with them.

A more legitimate ground for uneasiness with my catholicity than its failure to stem the tides of change is that in countenancing the exceptional and marginal case it fails to capture the normality of the normal case. Most of us, when discussing works of art, rightly hold in the front of our minds the typical case, an accepted product of one of the fine arts. That typical case does indeed provide a norm, not because it is the commonest case, but because it is the case in which nothing is accidental, nothing is diverted from its original use, nothing is more plausibly seen in any other light than that of the concept of a work of art. The reasonableness of the charge that a catholic definition errs by its neglect of this norm appears perhaps best in George Dickie's remark that the nature of the work of art as he conceives it appears best from Dadaism (1974, 32); for Dadaism, the insertion of unassimilable objects into the fine-art context, which is supposed thereby to be afflicted with acute indigestion, worked only by exploiting the superficial reactions of a snobbish and ignorant bourgeoisie. The jest of *L.H.O.O.Q.* falls flat for anyone who appreciates Leonardo's painting.[35] The point is made in a variety of words by different writers. Wittgenstein (1966) insisted that to give prominence to judgments framed in terms of "beauty" was to misunderstand aesthetics, because serious critical judgments have to do with whether or not specific points of detail have been got quite right yet. John Berger points out that an artist's art differs from "child art" in being born of a serious effort, which the public recognizes.[36] Paul Valéry observes that the old Italian masters did not fear that mastery of their craft would inhibit them, or suppose that it was up to them to create their own "aesthetic," because "the aim of their work was not to catch the eye, but something quite different: to be looked at for a long time" (1960, 224); and Michael Fried insists that not everything that can be seen as a painting in such a way as my definition countenances can compel conviction as a painting.[37] All these critics in their various ways are pointing to the chief implication of the idea of the fine arts in the classical line: that an art such as painting, sculpture, or music is a serious business, not to be mastered without study and not to be appreciated without assiduity, and this serious business is not to be confused with casual amusement, entertainment, and *coups de théâtre* of all kinds. And no more it is. But the question immediately at issue is whether or not the definition of a work of art is the right place for pointing the contrast. My argument must be that it need not be: that a definition of the work of art as such must point to the dimensions of artistic quality, but need not stipulate degrees of quality. The contrasts between the serious and the frivolous, between the casual and the committed, between the deep and the shallow, gain no extra point or depth by being encapsulated in the supposed meaning of the phrase "work of art." Just because the normal case is central, however, a definition that fits all cases including the marginal, trivial, and eccentric ones should also fit the normal case in an eminent degree. One could, of course, adopt some less catholic definition for work of art and define or describe what an open definition includes near its borders as quasi art of this or that kind. But I have given reasons against some kinds of restricted definitions, and other kinds may be ruled out by the consideration that there are, after all, two different kinds of borderline cases, those that are marginal, frivolous, or freakish and those that are problematic, exploratory, uncovenanted, and extreme. I know no way of devising a formula that will exclude the one lot without excluding the others.

In what remains of part 1, I will follow out the implications of the foregoing discussion by taking my defining formula in the open sense that the generalizing character of my project requires. A work of art is a performance, considered with respect to its design. But while my own theoretical exposition of the classical line calls for this reading of the formula, it would be wrong to suggest that theorists working within that line are likely to think anything that the open reading captures. On the contrary, the interpretive reading or even the normal reading will better serve to articulate their likely positions. The uncertainty and the divergence arise because, whereas the considerations brought forward at the start of this chapter call for a conceptual gap between the fine arts and works of art—a gap we all observe in practice even if our theories make no provision for it—those reasons do nothing to determine how wide the gap shall be.

Works of art as we have defined them are to be distinguished from two other sorts of things that critics and theorists discuss, which I shall term "art objects" and "works of fine art." My use of these words is in some measure arbitrary, though I think not unnatural. The distinctions themselves are real and important.

My ninth definition, then, is that of an "art object."[38] By this I mean anything that anyone intends to be taken as a work of art, or that within any community is habitually regarded as such.[39] By anyone I mean anyone: the most likely person to form such an intention in the first instance is the producer of the object (the "artist" if there is one). But the intention may be that of an impresario or dealer, who selects and builds up as a "work of art" some object, natural or artificial, chosen on any or no grounds. The intention may be that of a private individual, although we shall not concede reality to his intentions unless, like the impresario, he does something about them.[40] The definition specified "anything," not "any performance": unlike works of art, art objects need not be performances. There may be no performance relevantly involved other than that of the impresario who presents the object in his salon or gallery, in a context where works of art are usual. It may be that we should think of the impresario as the artist and of his act of presentation as the performance that is the only work of art involved; but that is not what we mean by calling the things he presents art objects. It follows from my definition that all art objects that are performances are works of art, being considered with respect to their designs; but not every work of art is an art object, for no one may bother to put it into circulation.

Although an art object need not be an artifact or a performance, it follows from my definition that it is taken, or is to be taken, as if it were one: the act of presentation or the fact of acceptance implies that it is taken, or is to be taken, as having a design. It is the kind of aesthetic object that works of art are, not the kind that seashells or scenery or crystals are. To borrow Nelson Goodman's ideas (1977, 16–17), a natural object that is made an art object is made so by being taken to *exemplify* (to display, flaunt, show off, manifest) certain of its properties. But which ones? A child who brings a pretty pebble home from the beach does not make it an art object, and a gallery director who displays natural objects is not repeating the child's act. The context must somehow make evident a *right way* of taking the object, and the right way can only be one that recognizes something tantamount to a design.

An objection may suggest itself here. R. G. Collingwood (1938) contrasted art "properly so called" with rhetoric, the former being confined to pure spontaneous expression. Whatever was intended to be taken in any particular way he relegated to the inferior realm of rhetoric. On that showing, the concept of an art object as I have defined it lies in the domain of rhetoric and not in the realm of art at all. This objection does not move me. Even those who accept Collingwood's arguments (which in fact have no place in the present context, but belong to an expressive line of their own) can hardly deny that the making of something into, not a work of art, but an art object must always be a deliberate act or a historical process. It is not an act of creation but one of interpretation and publication. The world of art is a public world; the mystique of expression can play no direct part in its operations and should not be allowed into a description of those operations. Nor can we admit that the public status of art objects has *nothing* to do with art, unless we wish to deny that it is the destiny of works of art (even conceived as Collingwood conceived them) to become art objects. If we wish to save the spiritual virginity of the artist,[41] we can do so by conceding that, as artist, his intention may be no more than that his expression as already achieved, or whatever expression he might come to achieve, should be available to afford intuitions for others.

Perhaps nothing is more important in reflecting on art today than to make a sharp distinction between the two concepts I have defined under the names "work of art" and "art object." The fact that it is in many cases a distinction without a difference is precisely what makes it important.

My tenth and last definition is that of "work of fine art": it is defined as a product of skill and knowledge of the kind that the fine arts organize. It is not necessary that the producer of such a work should have been trained in the accredited institutions of such organizations, but it is necessary that his work should manifest the same kind of skill as such institutions (if any) impart.[42] The distinction is important. We want to include the self-taught and the naturally gifted, but to exclude the lucky novice. The test is repeatability, not necessarily of success by the primary standards of the relevant art, but at least by its secondary standards.

Is a work of fine art necessarily a work of art? Not according to my definitions. To be a work of art is to be considered in a certain way. To be a work of fine art is to be in fact the product of a certain kind of skilled operation and has little to do with how anyone considers anything. I say "little," not nothing, for to *call* something a work of fine art is indeed to consider it in respect of the skilled work that has gone into it. A Rembrandt used to replace a window blind, a Praxiteles built into a church wall, though they are still indeed the products of skill, are not functioning as such but are reduced to mere canvas and marble.[43]

None of the terms I have defined means "a performance intended *by its performer* to be a work of art," although that phrase picks out what we surely think of as the typical case: a painter, who thinks of himself as a painter, paints what he means for a painting and takes it along to his dealer. The dealer may say "That's not what *I* call a painting," but that is not for him to decide.[44] The public pays (or starves) the piper, but the artist calls his own tune.[45] I decided not to use this natural notion in defining a work of art not only because as formulated it is circular but because it would entail that we never know whether objects of unknown provenance are works of art. Besides, with works of known provenance, it may be charged with committing the "intentional fallacy" of substituting what a person meant to do for what he did.[46] My theoretical caution installs dealers and publics in a place of authority and reduces the artist to a mere source of raw material.[47] That looks bad. But the classical line requires this reduction: the fine arts, like other arts, exist for the service of mankind. Nor does the reduction undermine the artist's priority, for that rests not on definition but on fact: painters can paint, and dealers cannot. Nor can self-styled painters, come to that, and many art school graduates can't paint worth a damn.[48]

What gives the true artist the edge, once his identity is known, is that dealers and publics both learn that he knows better than they do what they will turn out to have wanted—a privilege that belongs, as Plato already observed, to the expert practitioner of every genuine art, the heart of which is the knowledge of what is really good and bad (and hence what will in the long run satisfy) within the compass of his experthood.[49]

If we wished, we could pick out some hitherto unused piece of terminology (say, "artwork") and make that the *definiendum* of an eleventh definition: "any performance meant by its performer to be a work of art."[50] But it hardly seems worthwhile, and it is perhaps better to remember that this is the *normal case* of an object that is also a work of art.[51]

Most of my definitions, then, fit together like this. An "art object" is anything the status of which is intended to be that of "a work of art," which is a performance considered with respect to its "design," which is that the value of which is recognized and valued in the relevant mode of "appreciation," and, being the product of a "design act," is the totality of the properties that render a "performance" (a thing done or made qua done or made) a putative "aesthetic object," which is anything considered as a fit object of "contemplation," which is exclusive attention to what a thing is like. The only definitions not included in this chain (aside from that of "an artwork," which would have been any performance intended by its performer to be a work of art) are that of "a work of fine art," which is a performance performed with the kind (or one of the kinds) of knowledge and skill that the fine arts organize for the production of works of art, and that of "an artifact," which in the relevant case is the embodiment of a performance.

All the terms now interrelated have been turned into semitechnical terms. That is, they are not controlled by any context, either by the dense usage of a natural language or by the formalized context of a science. They cannot, therefore, really be *used* in just the senses they have been given, though one may give oneself the illusion of so using them by taking enough care. What, then, is the point of them? The point is to show how concepts fit together. What you do at one point in the system affects what you do at other points: to modify one's views on what I have called contemplation involves modification of one's views on all the related concepts.

The Identity of a Work of Art

Many people have thought there was a problem about what kind of thing a work of art is. Michelangelo's *Moses* is a hunk of marble: we know where to go to find it. But Milton's *Paradise Lost* is nothing and nowhere in particular. It exists in countless copies; but if all the copies were destroyed, the work would remain if someone remembered it by heart. And it is debatable whether, if the copies remained but mankind (and all other language-using species) were destroyed, the marks on the paper would still be words. Our account seems to have got round this sort of question by making it merely a contingent fact that a work of art should be embodied in an artifact or artifacts.[52] To be a work of art is to be a performance, an upshot of performing action, conceived in a certain way; and in such a performance there need be nothing obscure. If one tries to identify Beethoven's C-minor Symphony with an object or a set of objects, one hesitates between the manuscript score, the sum of the occasions on which the piece is played, or whatever. But there is nothing relevant in the performance that seems to escape us as we think of Beethoven writing in his notebook, humming, playing, transcribing, editing, sending manuscripts to publishers, their being engraved and printed and circulated, then rehearsals, editions, performances of the work, recordings, themes whistled. . . . All that, conceived as the establishment and preservation of a design, is what the C-minor Symphony is, and just that is what it is. Nothing is added to our understanding if we try to apply to the result some classification or principle of individuation that, having been worked out to fit some other sort of subject matter, is most unlikely to be fully appropriate. Once a system of qualities has been established by the completion of a design act, it can in principle be repeated. The only question is what counts as a repetition rather than as a fresh design act.[53]

When do we speak of one work of art rather than several? We might have (1) two photographic prints made from the same negative with the same exposure; (2) ditto, with different exposures;[54] (3) two copies of the same state of the same engraving; (4) copies of different states of the same engraving; (5) performances of the same production of an opera on different nights; (6) two productions of the same opera; (7) two attempts by the same artist at the same painting; (8) unrevised and revised versions of a symphony; (9) a poem and its translation; (10) the poems of Propertius and Pound's *Homage to Sextus Propertius*. In the first case, I would be surprised if anyone said there were two works rather than one. In the last case, I would be shocked if anyone said there was one work rather than two. In the other cases we might be uncertain, or different people might confidently say different things. Can such hesitations and certainties be justified otherwise than by appealing to "what we would usually say"? Our system of definitions helps us to give a general account of how such questions are settled, although (fortunately, in my view) it does not purport to resolve doubtful cases so much as to indicate what it is that is in doubt.

Since the design in respect of which a work of art is considered is the design of a performance, we speak of a single work of art only in virtue of a double unity: that of the design as a system of qualities constituting a single aesthetic object and that of the design act from which it issues. But the unity of this act, as of all acts, rests primarily on (if indeed it is not constituted by) the possibility of recognizing a single *thing that has been done*, which involves a unity of the agency no less than of the outcome. What one point of view shows as a single action may be several from the other: many men may cooperate on many occasions in what is determined by its unified outcome as a single action, and a man in one swift and complex movement may bring about several results and so have done many things.[55]

Problems about the individuation of works of art are of two kinds: those where many acts issue in a single performance or a single artifact and those where a single act terminates in many artifacts or many performances. A situation may belong to both kinds at once: a playwright writes a libretto, a composer sets it to music, other men design scenery and costumes, a director arranges the ensemble, and the outcome as realized by a group of performers is a single performance; but their performance may then be repeated night after night.[56] Criticism may fasten on individual contributions taken as isolated achievements or on the whole as a single work, on the production or on the production as performed on one particular night. Even in the last case, two ways are open. A critic may take as his object the production-as-performed, a single design to which all from the librettist to the chorus have contributed in one communal action; or he may take the production as given, and fasten on what the performers have made of it (their performance *of it*) on this particular evening. Whenever in a corporate performance we can distinguish contributions to which a design can be assigned, we can and in fact habitually do consider and criticize those contributions as independent works of art, whether or not we choose to call them so.

Multiplicity of agents or of occasions for action seems to be irrelevant. The responsible agency may be one man on a single occasion, as with Kuerti's rendering of the *Hammerklavier Sonata* on a particular evening; one man on many occasions, as Goethe's exudation of *Faust* throughout a lifetime; many men collaborating on one or many occasions, as in the National Ballet's *Kraanerg*; many men of whom some are unaware of the others' contribution, as when Wren sought to complete Yevele's Westminster Abbey by adding new yet deliberately harmonious towers; or many men without thought for each other, as when generations of traditional builders produce a harmonious townscape. Apparently all that matters is that the common result of designing activities on however many occasions should be such that it can in fact be seen as though it were intended. Whether one views Canterbury Cathedral as a single work of art or not is hardly affected by one's knowing whether one of the west towers is a nineteenth-century addition, or whether the builders of the nave really meant to leave the old choir standing.

It depends rather on whether the parts blend into a sufficiently coherent whole.[57]

Unity of occasion seems then to be irrelevant. But unity of design is not enough without unity of action, constituted either by contribution to a single performance (so that we speak of a *single* work) or by unity of origin (so that we speak of the *same* work). Individuations depend on provenances as well as similarities. Where provenance is doubtful, identity is doubtful: plagiarism suits hinge, or used to hinge, on accessibility as well as on coincidence of design.

We are now in a position to elaborate our previous distinction between types of case. In the first type, those where what is problematic is the aesthetic unity of a single complex individual, there are some cases where the distinction between one or many turns on whether later or independently contributed parts, themselves such that they could be considered independently as substantive designs, are in fact thought of as mutually integrated with the original or with each other; there are other cases where the question is whether later modifications in a design, themselves not such that they can be conceived as independent designs, are so extensive as to make of the whole a new design or merely complete the old. In the former kind of case, but scarcely in the latter, the parts may be either heterogeneous, as when one puts music to words, or homogeneous, as when one adds an annex to a building. If they are homogeneous, the resulting work of art (if any) is a new and more complex individual of the same kind as the old; if they are heterogeneous, any resulting work of art is an individual of a new kind.

The second of our main types of case was that which turned on whether or not a number of similar or partly similar individuals represent the same work. The question here depends on whether one traces all the putative exemplars to a single design act or to many. If their designs are judged to be the same and to stem from a common origin, we speak without hesitation of "the same" work; if the identity of design were judged to be coincidental, we would not call the works the same, but such a coincidence would be so odd that we might wonder what we should say. (I return to this later.) The cases in which we might speak alternatively of one work or more than one are those in which the design is supplemented. Such supplements are of two kinds. In some, as in making an engraving from a drawing, the additional features belong to the very process of reproducing the original design.[58] In others, the late comer deliberately or negligently adds something of his own.

In cases of both kinds it may be a matter of opinion whether the new version has enough independent character of its own to be thought of as a new work.

In all types of cases the principle to be observed is the same. Whenever we refer what is done to a single design act, we speak of a single work of art; when we decline to speak of a single work, we impute disunity to the responsible agency. And whenever we recognize a single work of art, we use the proper name of the work to designate what we recognize. When we think of a postcard of the *Mona Lisa* as reproducing the panel in the Louvre with only accidental modifications, we speak of it as "The *Mona Lisa*" with no less aplomb than when we speak of a copy of *Paradise Lost* as "*Paradise Lost*" or of a performance of the *Nelson Mass* as "The *Nelson Mass.*"

The question of whether a design is preserved through vicissitudes of one artifact seems no different in principle from the question whether it is preserved through the production of multiple artifacts. Yet some people have thought that the latter case raises logical problems as the former does not. In the former case, there is a single spatiotemporal continuant to which alone the name of the work of art properly applies; and the individuation of such continuants is a problem too familar to philosophers to hold any terrors for them. But there seems to be a different kind of problem when the name of a work of art, which seems to be a proper name rather than a common noun, is alleged to be properly applied to a lot of objects and situations unconnected in space and time. In such cases, what are we talking about when we discuss the work of art? Not necessarily about any one of them. Presumably what we say will be equally true of each of them insofar as it does enshrine its identifying design.[59] Indeed, what we say will be universally true: it will hold of anything whatever provided that it has the defining properties of the work in question.[60]

The foregoing argument invites us to identify a work of art with the class of all those performances (or artifacts) to which the name of the work is properly applied, propriety of application being determined by the possibility—whether logical, practical, aesthetic, or social—of tracing in all a single design act to which (though, as we shall see, not necessarily only to which) all may be referred.

A work of art cannot conveniently be equated with its instances. The consequence would be that, if the class with which the work was identified were an open one, an artist could never know that his work was completed; and, if it were (implausibly) a closed class, his work would not be done until (implausibly) the last copy of his novel was printed, or his music performed for the last time. But that does not mean that a work can exist otherwise than as instantiated. The design act is not some mysterious spiritual entity, an "intuition" whose external manifestation is a matter of indifference. Actions, whatever they are, are not substances (whatever *they* are), and actions do not exist otherwise than as enacted.

If there are difficulties in equating a work of art with the membership of a class, there are also difficulties in equating it with the class itself. What is true of a class is not for that reason true of its members, but what is true of my postcard *to the extent that it is a work of art* is true of the *Mona Lisa* (and vice versa), and true because it is that work (and that is the only work it is), not because it is a member of it. For this reason, it has been fashionable to use the terminology of "types" and "tokens" introduced by C. S. Peirce (1933, 4, §§537ff.), applied to literary works by C. L. Stevenson (1957), and applied to works of art of all kinds by Margolis (1965) and many others—most recently by Sharpe (1979).[61] The terminology works as follows. If I speak of "the first word in the preceding sentence," it is quite unclear whether I mean "the word 'the' " in general, a word that can be used on many occasions, or the particular markings on paper that make up this occurrence of that word. We then speak of the word conceived as repeatable as the "type" and of the particular instance of it as the "token." The point of the terminology is that whatever is true of the type will be true of the token insofar as it is a token of that type, and vice versa. It seems likely that this relationship holds only for such entities as are constituted by their own formally significant properties. We call these entities signs. Words, sentences, and all repeatable verbal structures are signs in this sense. For this reason, applying the type/token terminology to poems and other literary works seems to raise no problems. But it can further be held that all works of art are signs in this sense. On the definition of a work of art that I have adopted this certainly seems to be so: a work of art is a performance considered with respect to its design, and a design is so defined as to be a system of formally significant properties. If I point at an etching and discuss its merits, it makes no difference whether I am taken to be referring to the particular print on my wall or to any prints of the etching there may be. But beyond this point we find ourselves in trouble. What I have just said really only applies to cases like those of the poem and the etching, where all relevant features are fully present in each exemplar. It cannot be extended to reproductions or even to such items as an etching that exists in several states or a piece of music that is performed by different conductors. The *Mona Lisa* is a type of which there is one token, the panel in the Louvre. The cut of the *Mona Lisa* in my copy of volume 17 of the 1958 edition of the *Encyclopedia Britannica* is not a token of this type, but of the type whose tokens are all such cuts in all the copies of that volume of that edition, cuts that will differ only because of accidents that befall particular copies during and after printing. I therefore follow Stevenson in introducing a new term, "megatype," for what stands to the class of all artifacts or performances to which the name of a given work of art is properly applied in the same relation that the type stands to the class of tokens. A work of art can now be identified with a megatype together with all its tokens, its tokens being all the members of that class with which, a few pages back, I provisionally identified the work.

Sometimes a group of types belonging to the same megatype is set off from all other types by a set of relevant differentiating properties. Such a group of types I shall term a "mesotype." Since we do not want to allow artistic relevance to accidental vicissitudes of exemplars, the relevance required of the differentiating properties must be relevance to design and, beyond that, to design acts. A mesotype answers to the modification of a design by an act, whether that act be more nearly one of reproducing or one of varying. Because designs can be successively reproduced and varied, mesotypes may form a hierarchy; and each may be considered not only as a mesotype of a megatype but as a megatype setting up a work of art known by its own name. Thus, my copy of the Golden Cockerel Press edition of Pope's *Iliad* is a token of that type, which is a type of the mesotype "Pope's *Iliad*," which is a mesotype of the megatype *Iliad*. But the Golden Cockerel edition is a work of art in its own right and may be considered as such, and so is Pope's version. Each may then claim the status of megatype defining a work of art that consists of itself and its tokens.[62] It seems desirable to stipulate that a group of types constitutes a mesotype only where it *can also* be taken as constituting a megatype. In developing my argument, then, I can and will ignore the complexities introduced by the possibility of one or more hierarchies of mesotypes. But the possibility is real and important.

If we ignore the necessary genetic relationship introduced by insisting that it is design acts rather than designs that individuate works of art, the relation of megatype to mesotype and type is that of genus to species, with the type as *infima species*. Are we then to say that the tokens of a megatype are not strictly tokens of it, but instances? No. A megatype is a type, and the logical equivalence that holds of type and token holds of megatype and token. The difference is that tokens belonging to different types of a megatype have less in common than they would normally do if there were but a single type. A megatype such as "the Bible" is a shadowy entity. But demonstratives, proper names, and definite descriptions are still applied indifferently to megatype and token. If we cannot perfectly explicate the conditions of identity of a work of art in terms of the type/token relation as its inventor originally conceived it, this is not because a better terminology lies to hand, but because the relationships to be articulated are characteristic of works of art, so that it is not to be expected that any set of terms developed to account for other relationships will quite do.[63]

One thing about what I have been saying seems quite wrong. Although I have insisted on the primacy of a designing act, I have usually written as if all types and tokens had equal status—as if all that distinguished the panel in the Louvre from my cut in the encyclopedia was that the former happened to be the sole token of its type. But, of course, there is only one *Mona Lisa*, which is (one hopes) the one hanging in the Louvre, and not my cut. Besides, it is on *this very panel*, and not on any class or its defining megatype, that Leonardo worked.[64] Different sorts of design acts have different sorts of outcomes, and these differences account for different relations among types and tokens. In particular, there is a fundamental difference between tokens that are derived at one or more removes from other tokens that are their originals and tokens that are not so derived.

A token stands as *original to* another when it is the sole source of the other's design insofar as that other is conceived of as the same work of art. *Originality to* and its converse, *derivation from*, are transitive relations. It can be true of at most one token of a megatype, and need not be true of any, that it stands as original to all other tokens of its megatype and as derivate to none. Any such unique token I propose to call an original token or prototype. If any megatype has more than one token, and if one of its tokens is a prototype, then each of its tokens must stand to some other token either as original to derivate or as derivate to original. These conditions outline the essential relationships among tokens of those works of art that have an original token. Not all works do. But since works of art are individuated by their design acts, it must be possible to recognize the design act that determines a work. It follows that where there is no original token there must be some other definable point or process of origination.[65] It is up to me to say what these other kinds of origination are.

Among design acts that do not issue in prototypes some issue in artifacts that are not themselves works of art but are templates or other objects from which, by mechanical or quasi-mechanical means or by precisely specified procedures, a number of artifacts can be produced all of which are tokens of the work and from which all other tokens are normally derived, but of which none is more original than any other.[66] Such templates and so forth I shall call archetypes. An example would be the copper plate from which an engraving is printed. The tokens directly produced from an archetype in the appropriate way I shall call ectypes, and an example would be the prints pulled from the plate in a suitable press. Prototypes and ectypes are *primary tokens*. Of primary tokens, and of these alone, it is *never* legitimate to deny that they *are* the work of art whose name they bear. When primary tokens of a work are not the only ones, it is equally legitimate to say of any of the others that they *are* the work in question, or that they are not it but only replicas or reproductions of it. It is more common (though not more legitimate) to say of prototypes than of ectypes that they alone constitute the work of art, for uniqueness is more readily attributable to a single individual than to all the members of a class taken jointly, however few they may be (for example, the six copies to which editions of bronzes are conventionally restricted).

What seems to be the most serious objection to what I have been saying runs as follows. It is true that if you point to my cut of the *Mona Lisa* and ask "What's that?" it is correct for me to reply "It's the *Mona Lisa*." But it is quite wrong to infer from this that my cut *is* the *Mona Lisa*. It is, of course, a reproduction of the *Mona Lisa* and nothing more. To be a *copy* of a thing is necessarily not to be that thing. Part of the meaning of calling one thing a representation of another is that they are two different things. Is it not similarly true that part of what one means by calling something a reproduction of a work of art is that it *is not* that work of art? Granted, my account included the claim that a reproduction may be said with equal justice to be and not to be the work it reproduces; granted, too, that my account distinguishes reproductions from primary tokens, and thus squares with the fact that what is ordinarily contrasted with a reproduction is not a work but "the original"; should we not have recognized that to be a reproduction of a work is never to be that work *in any sense?* The fact that one answers with the name of the work when asked what it is, is neither here nor there. If you were to point to a photograph of Niagara Falls and ask "What is that?" the appropriate answer is "Niagara Falls," not "A picture of Niagara Falls." That does not mean that the picture is in any sense a waterfall. It is just the accepted way of talking about pictures. I don't say "It's a picture," because you can *see* it's a picture. The waterfall "in" the picture really is Niagara, and the object "in" the picture really is a waterfall; if you had asked "What is *that picture?*" a different answer would have been appropriate. Just so, the picture "in" my reproduction really is the *Mona Lisa;*[67] but the reproduction itself is really a picture of the *Mona Lisa*, a picture of a picture of a woman. This objection certainly has some force, but not enough. I defined the work of art as the performance, not the artifact, and the performance considered with respect to its design. And the design, the ensemble of aesthetic properties, *is present* wholly or partly in the reproduction. The reproduction *re-produces* the work as the picture of the Falls does not re-produce the Falls; for to be a waterfall is to be a lot of rock with water going over it, and nothing of that sort is in the picture.

I have urged that we do right to speak, as we habitually do, of reproductions sometimes as being the work they reproduce, and sometimes not. It is important to preserve this ambiguity. There are gradations of acceptability in likenesses (in scale, form, and color) and variations in contexts in which different standards of perfection in reproduction become relevant, just as some contexts call for stronger light and a closer look than others do. And it is a mistake to suppose that it is always the original that affords the best view: there are many cases in which the original is inaccessible, or cannot be seen from a good angle or in a good light, or has faded or deteriorated.[68]

The cases we have been considering are those in which the design act issues in a single prototypical or archetypical artifact that either constitutes or generates a primary token or set of tokens to which or to one of which all other tokens can be traced. Not all cases are of either of these two kinds. Sometimes the immediate outcome of the act is not an artifact but a prototypical performance that has the status of a primary token. For example, in an oral culture a composer may introduce a song by singing it once in public. His performance may then be copied by others who sing his song. But sometimes what is produced is only a score or notation, not a template, but a set of instructions for producing tokens of a work.[69]

The status of such a score is much more equivocal than anything we have had to consider before. It is both logically and psychologically possible for a composer to work at the score itself, which thus becomes the original of his work. But he may equally work the music out in his head or by singing or playing it aloud, and then perhaps make several attempts at transcribing it.[70] He may, as many choreographers do, slowly evolve his composition with members of his company in the course of rehearsals and performances. In such cases there is certainly a performance in my quasi-technical sense, but no single original artifact or performance and no formal set of instructions to play the part of prototype or archetype. What there is instead is an identifiable process of production that at a certain point is found to have reached a measure of stability, issuing in a design that, after a certain point, varies only in a limited way. Margolis observes, justly, that in such cases those accustomed to the use of scores and the like tend to postulate a sort of ideal or shadowy score or notation as the "original" from which all actual tokens can be imagined to be derived. But this is a fiction. What we actually have is a set of tokens marked out as privileged by the details of their production by the artist and his colleagues. We may define "privileged tokens" as those produced directly from a notation in the appropriate fashion—that is, in whatever fashion follows most closely the directions embodied in the notation in accordance with the best authenticated rules for compliance, adding no further design features beyond those without which a token could not be produced at all; or, where no such notation exists, are such as we should consider to have stood in that relation to the imputed or reconstructed notation that we posit. We note that, whereas the task of identifying the *primary* tokens of a work is one of establishing a historical fact, deciding what is a *privileged* token demands judgment: even where there is a notation, no precise and uncontroversial account can be given of what constitutes the "appropriate" fashion of producing tokens from it. I will say more about this element of indeterminacy later. Before doing so, I will consider another problem of individuation that may arise when there is no single artifact or token in which the design act unequivocally issues.

Suppose a composer were on two occasions to play what, so far as any hearer could tell, was the same (unwritten) work, but asserted that on the second occasion he was improvising. Should we then say that it was not the same work after all, since he has assured us that his second performance issued from a design act separate from, though exactly like, the first? Surely not. But why not? Would our reason be merely that he must after all be, at least unconsciously, remembering what he had done before? But then, suppose someone else composed a piece using the same notes in the same order? It has become customary to cite in this connection Borges' story of a man who performs the almost impossible task of reinventing part of *Don Quixote*, word for word (Borges 1962). Or suppose one were unknowingly to recreate some masterpiece of art—after years of inspiration and toil to learn that one's creation already existed under the title of *La Bohème*. Would one then have created a new work of art? The design act would certainly be entirely different, but would not the design be exactly the same? Borges insinuates that it would not be, because the rejected alternatives represented in Pierre Menard's version, and hence the meaning of what was finally written, would be entirely different from those of Cervantes' work. To borrow the language of the French structuralists, the codes according to which the two "identical" texts were to be construed would have to be entirely different. But then the structuralists' argument leaves the text itself indeterminate and, in fact, eliminates the concept of design (and with it the concept of a work of art) altogether. And in Borges' exposition of the different meanings of two identically worded passages from Menard and Cervantes the element of arbitrary fantasy becomes obtrusive. It is distressing to observe how many writers discuss Borges' story as though he were solemnly narrating something that really happened, or at least that really could happen.[71] Of course, he is not: his wisely playful demonstration of what it would be to acquire a twentieth-century frame of mind of which the text of *Don Quixote* would be an appropriate expression sufficiently shows, if it needed showing, just why it could not happen. Unconscious plagiarism is quite common and accounts for all credible cases. It is a fundamental error to discuss these issues on the basis of what is "logically possible": what is at issue is what is culturally possible.[72] We do not need to fall back on the philosopher's standard defense and say that the distinctions we make do not envisage, and hence do not provide for, this or that kind of fanciful eventuality, so that we cannot say in advance what (other than "Gorblimey") we should think or say about them.[73] We can say more directly that no conceivable case has yet been presented, and that no case that is conceivable promises to offer any further difficulty than one is accustomed to encountering in reality.[74]

Works of art whose privileged tokens are public performances by persons other than the artist himself are typically produced from a score, that is, a set of instructions for producing tokens. Such instructions can seldom be exhaustive. There are few cases of any kind in which anyone can tell anyone else exactly what to do in the sense that one makes no use of his judgment but only of his mechanical compliance. Such works then not only expect but rely on a supplementary design act from each interpreter. A playwright can do no more than provide his actors with the clues from which to construct readings of their parts, and this is as true when his stage directions are prolix as when they are minimal. And, though the language I have just used suggests that this is a weakness of the playwright's art, it may with equal justice be thought to be the glory of the performing arts that they allow such free cooperation. Works whose design act issues in an archetype may also, but do not always, rely on skilled interpretation in the production of tokens. This sort of interpretation, on which the artist relies to fill out his design act, must be distinguished from two activities also called interpretation that take place after the performance is completed. The first of these is exemplified by what a photographer does when he "interprets" a sculpture by artful lighting, choice of camera angle, illusions of scale, and so on. Of such cases one is inclined to say that the photographer has taken one performance and used it as the occasion for another. The second "interpretation" is that whereby each spectator or auditor of a work of art makes sense out of the finished performance that confronts him. Some writers insist that the true work of art is what thus appears in the minds of the public.[75] It seems simpler to say that designs may be variously read. Insofar as a design is unreadable, it might as well not be there. But it *is* there. There is an obvious and crude sense in which *Othello* is what Shakespeare wrote and is as he wrote it, no matter what anyone else may make of it. The fact that each of us can only know of it what he can make of it should not stampede us into neglecting or denying the fundamental truth that Shakespeare was there first.[76] But even if one equates the work of art with an "aesthetic experience" resulting from a process within each member of the public that one chooses to call interpretation, such interpretation cannot be placed in parallel with the interpretation whereby a musician interprets a score; for whenever this latter form of interpretation occurs, the resulting performance will require "interpretation" within the public's minds no less than any other token of a work of art. The arrangement must be in series. The composer's score says "play something that complies with this."[77]

The interpreter's performance, on this rather eccentric way of thinking, says "hear something that complies with this" or "construct an auditory work of art using these materials."

The distinction I made between processes and artifacts as two kinds of outcome of design acts answers to one between two ways of working, two kinds of objects of an artist's attention, of media to be worked in and of materials to be ordered. Sometimes artistic composition literally consists of giving shape to a definite material, whether prototype or archetype. Sometimes it lies in inventing sequences of sounds or words or events that are intrinsically repeatable, in that the relations directly worked on hold among types rather than tokens. To compose a poem is to arrange a system, not of marks or sounds (even if one does write or speak in doing so), but of words considered strictly as repeatable. The same sort of thing is true of musical and dramatic composition. But an engraver is engaged in actually engraving one particular plate, even though the plate he works on is not a token of his work but an archetype for it. This distinction is fundamental.[78] But it is also true that an engraver may use several plates in the process of perfecting his design.[79] And a painter may use several canvases in pursuit of a single design to which he makes several approximations or on which he constructs several tentative variants. As processes of approximation, these productions of successive rejected artifacts seem not to differ in any significant way from those whereby a poet produces successive drafts or a musician successive versions of the same piece. If the differences between versions are considerable, they may be thought of either as different but closely resembling works or as attempts at the same work; and this seems to be as true of designs carried by artifacts as it is of those that are systems of types. Nor do we restrict ourselves to speaking of "different versions of the same" only when the earlier versions are intermediate stages in a creative process of which the last version is the consummation, for we may use the same terminology in cases where the later workings are judged inferior, perversions rather than perfections.[80]

The division between works of art originating in a process and those originating in an artifact nearly coincides with that between works of the "time" arts, whose design depends on being taken in a certain temporal order and with a certain temporal patterning, and works of the "space" arts, whose design depends on spatial relations that are presented simultaneously and can be grasped all at once or in any order.[81] It seems reasonable that a work whose design is structured sequentially should be generated by a process determining a typical sequence, and that the sequences themselves should be the object of artistic endeavor. And such a sequence cannot exist as a durable physical object, since its way of existing is to be a succession of evanescent parts. Bluntly, if a work of the "time" arts cannot be an artifact, there is no a priori reason for an artifact to be used to generate it, but since primary tokens of the "space" arts usually are artifacts, and the easiest way to fix any spatial pattern is to embody it in an artifact, it is most likely that the object of the artist's immediate concern will be an artifact.

The division between "space" and "time" arts also corresponds roughly to that between arts of which the typical outcomes are, respectively, determinate and indeterminate. Since what is generated in the "time" arts is a specification for a type of sequence, it is not necessary that the primary or privileged tokens of this type should be indistinguishable from each other, and perhaps they seldom can be. If all "time" arts used scores and notations, and all scores and notations required interpretive choice, such indistinguishability would indeed be a rare coincidence.

There seem to be important exceptions to what I have just said. A poem as a poet writes it may be taken as a score for a reading. But if it is not to be read aloud, there is nothing in it that is schematic and requires interpretation in any other sense than that in which a spectator must "interpret" a painting, that is, notice certain potential design features and miss others. The poem is a "time" work in the sense that its structure is linear and must be taken sequentially; but, as a purely linguistic structure of sentences rather than of utterances, belonging to "language" rather than to "speech," its structure is fully determinate. For an "eye" reading this is all; but if the poem is to be read aloud or voiced inwardly, the written text is an incomplete notation that fails to prescribe any actual set of velocities, accelerations, and intonation. The reader has to supply these as a cooperative interpreter. This difference is so striking that one is tempted to say that the term "literature" is used for two fundamentally different sorts of work: poetry for reading or reciting aloud and poetry for reading with the eye (cf. Sparshott 1979).

One way of giving a process an invariant outcome is by reducing relevant differences to those between types, as in the case of the written poetry we have just considered. Another way is to use a mechanical device to generate the tokens. Electronic music can be performed only by running the manufactured tape, or a replica of it, through an appropriate playback machine. Electronic music is inherently uninterpretable because nothing can "read" the tape except a machine. If the machine is wrongly adjusted, the music is not interpreted but spoiled.[82] Yet what the composer produces is in many ways more like a score than it is like an archetypal template.[83] The composer does not primarily work on the tape itself: certainly, the qualities of the tape (its distribution of electrical charges) are not what he has in mind as he works. What he does to the tape itself is limited to cutting and splicing. The major work lies in producing the sequences of sounds that the tape captures, or in generating the electrical charges that will magnetize the tape. Analogously, in much contemporary popular music what is created is not a song or composition in the old sense but a recording, in the production of which the engineers are as important as the writers and (in the old-fashioned sense) musicians. Here again what is done is to produce sequences of sounds that are combined and preserved on a tape that is part artifact and part score.[84]

Privileged tokens of works of art admit a sort of indeterminacy by their possible differences. In a quite different way, even the primary tokens are indeterminate. As performances, in relation to their performers, we may say that they are determinate in that the *opus operatum* is nothing other than what the operator has done; but as actually embodied in artifacts they do not always make this postulated determinate entity available. In fact, primary tokens are subject to at least three kinds of indeterminacy, some of which are remediable and others are not.

First, there are changes in the medium: stone crumbles, bronze patinates, pigments fade and crack. Most of these changes are irreversible chemical and thermodynamic alterations; but some may be reversed, as when oxidization of metals is reversed by electrolysis. Somewhat similarly, in arts of process that lack primary tokens, pronunciations and meanings of words change, techniques of constructing and playing musical instruments change, practices of intonation and voice production change. Some of these changes are reversible: one can reconstruct antique instruments and sometimes learn how they were played. But some are irreversible; realizing and ornamenting an instrumental part in the "authentic" way may be possible only for someone whose imagination is limited to the possibilities of the day, and this limitation can hardly be recovered. Another kind of change affects the primary token, not by making it physically inaccessible, but by making its design unreadable. Traditions of emphasis and preference change. Later generations will mostly be exposed to material of a different sort than once prevailed, and this must so form their expectations that they pick out for emphasis aspects of design that were originally subordinate and discount what was the original focus of attention. The most striking changes of this sort, which result in the submerging and reappearance of reputations, are reversible. But cultural situations can never recur, if only because the earlier situation must form part of the history of the later; and, consequently, the fine structure of the expectations and emphases that people bring to the reading of designs changes as steadily and irreversibly as the physical condition of an artifact.

There may be a third form of indeterminacy in recoverable designs, related to the second but differing from both the other two in that it is not related to the passage of time. What the performer has done may be such as to impel his public to engage in a sort of editorial complicity in order to find a design with which it can be satisfied. The implanted forms may need supplementation, being suggestive rather than explicit and in themselves too meager to satisfy, or they may call for pruning, being too rich to form a single comprehensible structure.

All three forms of indeterminacy make critical interpretation necessary. It requires a special knowledge of history or science, or a special effort of insight, either to recover in imagination what in the past was available without effort or to make available to less attentive minds something that they can fasten on.[85]

The foregoing considerations make it possible for us to distinguish more effectively among various kinds of doubtful, marginal, or odd cases in which we are not certain whether a given token or type is properly spoken of as the work of art to whose megatype we would refer it. They are distinguished by the different kinds of vicissitude that have befallen the original design. In one kind of case the original design is partly lost, to the point where it is disputable whether it can be identified at all: bad copies, faint impressions, damaged survivals, garbled recollections, shards. In a second kind of case the design has not been worn away but has been filled out, supplemented, edited. These cases are interpretations and are themselves of two sorts, one sort consisting of tokens, performances that represent barely possible readings of a score, and the other sort consisting of types, ways of interpreting artifacts or reading scores, whose validity is similarly questionable. For we have remarked that the conventions governing the reading of scores can never be quite comprehensive, and no score can include binding rules as to what latitude may be used in its reading; there must always be a margin between the permissible and the intolerable, and where there is a margin there must be marginal cases. Finally, there is a third kind of case in which the original design has been made the basis for what may amount to a fresh design, so that it is debatable whether what we have is a new work or a very special type of the old.[86]

Before this section ends, some of the distinctions it makes need to be blurred. Consider a pianist improvising at the piano. What he does is something that could be copied, whether or not it *can* be copied; and in fact it seems clear that anyone with a good enough memory or tape recorder and a good knowledge of music could copy it. But, in copying it, what he would do, in effect, would be to analyze it into a reconstructed score and an interpretation. Moreover, the "score" could almost certainly take several different forms: it must often be a matter for discretion whether one represents what one hears as a series of short notes or a single arpeggio and so on. And now it occurs to us that the case is really no different if we are working in a tradition that knows nothing of scores: a musician who listens to another playing or singing, with a view to making that song or tune his own, will in fact identify in what he hears that component which he takes to be significant, which in his own rendering will have to be "the same." And, again, the case is the same when someone copies or makes an engraving or any sort of a reproduction from a painting: he must identify in it what is to be the same, and this component has precisely the same function that the score has when one plays a piece of music composed in the Western tradition. Any prototype or privileged performance of a work can be read, and read in a diversity of ways, as a system of instructions for producing other tokens of the work: it is as though there were built into the work a score together with a set of instructions for execution. The copier or reproducer must interpret the work as saying "do this like this." Something in the "instructions" that he reads into the work he will take to be mandatory, as essentially constitutive of the design; something he will take as recommendation, to be preserved or approximated as may be, subject to his own good judgment; and something he will dismiss, if he notices it at all, as nugatory or irrelevant.

If we accept the formulation just given, we see that someone who acts *Hamlet* or plays the *Appassionata* can be taken as doing two things. He is producing a single realization of a set of instructions that another (or he) has composed; but he is also producing an interpretation of the part or of the piece that another could take as instructions for his own realization. If Garrick portrays Hamlet in a way that sheds new light on Hamlet's character, then others may give their own readings of Garrick's Hamlet. This possibility, which we often see realized, is seldom talked of otherwise than with a sneer, because Shakespeare and Beethoven have left us score and text that we think should have no rivals for the position of *what* is to be done, and to elevate any *how* into the position of an original is felt to be either a confession of one's own incapacity or an insult to the original artist—like adding trombones to Mozart as though in rebuke of his weak orchestration. But this attitude speaks more of the antiquarianism and pedantry of this age of the knowledge explosion than it does of its artistic conscience.

Like several other passages in this section, but even more than they, the blurrings introduced in the preceding paragraphs run counter to the thrust of Nelson Goodman's analysis, with its division between autographic and allographic arts and its contrast between notational schemes and the kind of dense scheme exemplified by picturing. I mean no disrespect: no one in our time can legitimately be ignorant or neglectful of his classifications, or can ignore the differences he demonstrates between arts like literature that are in some aspects notational, arts like music that are in part notational, arts like dance that are potentially notational, and arts like drawing that are in no way notational, and the concomitant differences in the ways arts as they become notational are thought of and their works identified. But my blurring is necessary too. Goodman's system is designed without taking explicit account of any peculiarities that differentiate the use of symbol systems in the fine arts from their use elsewhere, and in the context of the arts, as I have remarked before, his universal requirement of strict criteria of identity is a handicap. It implies the adage that in a (perfected) work of art "nothing can be changed," which, however often and however high-mindedly it is repeated, is wrong. A small change may ruin a physical object, reduce it to rubbish: a small hole in a contraceptive or in a reactor's cooling rod spoils all. But works of art are tough and resilient. They resist fading, fragmentation, restoration, and misrepresentation in a remarkable way, as a person's character survives the vicissitudes of a tough life. The force of the design act carries through all. That is why an account of works of art as characters in symbol systems will never do. There is no place in such an account for that vitality of design of which Focillon (1942) has spoken. Against Goodman's indisputable truth we must set this equal and opposite truth. Philosophers of art must speak with forked tongue.

Such a hierarchical schematism of types as I have set out in this section might serve to validate the disputed concept of art. The schema is complex enough that we may assign a common character to anything it applies to: it is conceivable, then, that whatever is suitably individuated by its means is a work of art, whatever medium it may be conceived and executed in. The hierarchical structure itself is probably applicable to any field in which artifacts are designed, made, copied, and improved and (as Harrison suggests) to all cultural objects. It is where the relations among types and tokens are relations of design and essentially depend on design acts that what we have is a work of art. Of course, as I have been at pains to insist, any performance whatever can be regarded as and hence could be a work of art: it can be considered with respect to a design that can serve as a megatype generating mesotypes, types, and their tokens. But I also insisted that not all performances are equally suitable for such consideration, and it is obvious that only some performances (art objects) are habitually so regarded. Multiplicity of tokens is prima facie evidence of the suitability of so regarding a performance, though uniqueness of the token is by no means proof of its unsuitability.

The Dimensions of the Work of Art

Art may be a simple matter. But works of art are complicated. Like people, they are many-sided, and to speak of them without falsifying the familiar subtleties of our transactions with them calls for mental openness and agility. An aspect of this complexity is what has been called their multidimensionality. Many modern aestheticians, belonging to diverse schools, have arrived from their different directions at the conclusion that a work of art, simply in and for itself and without taking account of the multiple ways it enters into our lives, has three "dimensions" or "layers."[87] These may be introduced and justified very simply in terms of our system of definitions. First, then, simply as an object of contemplation, a work of art must have a presence: it is primarily an object of experience, something really and simply there in its wholeness. Second, as a performance, a thing done, it must have an analyzable, describable, unravelable structure: that by virtue of which things can be said about it that are informative and true. And third, since its character as a performance must be that of outcome of a single doing, it must represent what is or could have been a single mental act.[88] That is, the work must have an expressive dimension: it must speak to us of a shaping, affective agency. The felt present unity of the contemplated work is also thus perceived as the work of a unifying imagination, and what this unifies has the character of expression.

I will not now embark on yet another elaboration of this theme: a majestically proportioned version can be found in the work of Mikel Dufrenne (1953), for one. Rather than repeat what has already been well and often done, I will mention a couple of variations. For the consensus that exists is only a rough one: different theorists seek to integrate into the threefold scheme this or that added complexity, or to produce partial versions of their own.[89]

One of the main sources of variation on the three-dimensional structure is the anomalous status of any representational element in art. For the structure as I have outlined it could take no account of representation, being meant to apply to all works of art whether they are representational or not. The concept of representation is in any case, as we have seen, a confusing one because of the extremely elusive and equivocal nature of any element of actual reference to what exists in the world outside the work. It is therefore not surprising that different theorists have integrated the representational aspect of art into this threefold scheme in different ways. Dufrenne handles the matter as follows. We see the affective, representational work simply as one presence: the person in the painting is present to us directly as part of what the painting is, and so is the mood in the work, the unifying presence. But *what* is represented, the *fact that* this or that is shown, belongs to the second level: not that that which is represented exists outside the work, but that the fact that the person present to us in the painting is this or that person doing this or that belongs to the second, analytic level. Dufrenne actually calls this second level as a whole the level of representation: it is simply the whole analyzable and describable content of the work, whether the analysis be in terms of structure of any sort or of representational content.[90] Similarly, though the work as present is expressive, what is expressed, its expressiveness as such, as relating to a projected personal quality, constitutes a third dimension.

At this point Dufrenne makes an important move. At each of the second and third levels, he says, the work generates a world: it comes to us as representative of both a represented and an expressive world. By this he means that on each of the levels apart from that of sheer presence, where it is a thing done and complete in itself and for us, the work represents a way of doing in which other things could be done—it generates the idea of a personal style; and it represents a kind of thing done such that other things of the same kind, or more of the same thing, could be done. The former of these, the style, represents the expressive world to which the work belongs: it is not merely that another work could have the same feeling tone, or that in point of historical fact an artist can do more than one work that is characteristic of him, but that the performing personality that the work projects is *projected as* one from which further works might issue and of which they would be recognizably characteristic, even though their feeling tone were to be quite different. Having heard a person laugh, we think we know how he might weep. To recognize a personal quality in anything anyone does is necessarily to have the implicit idea of the person doing something else—a person is, precisely, someone who might do something different. The represented world, in Dufrenne's treatment, is (as we should expect) two-sided. If one looks at a painted landscape, what is conveyed along with what one sees is an implicit idea of how the landscape might continue beyond the painting's edge—and, one step further, by the same token how another scene from the same painted world might look. Thus, the landscape painted belongs in a very straightforward fashion to a represented *world*, though of course this world is a mere indefinite possibility subtended by the painting, and we know nothing of any scene it might contain.[91] But Dufrenne develops this simple notion into another, equally simple: if the painting were not a representational one, it would still be true that the handling of the paint and the spatial relations must be such as to suggest, supposing the painting to be continued beyond the actual edges of the present canvas, one sort of continuation rather than another, and to suggest, if it were merely one part of a large work or a member of a set of works, what the rest of the work or the other members of the set might be like.[92] Dufrenne argues that the recognition of a common style among works or artists is best thought of as the discovery that this always present possibility of a subtended world is, to all appearance, realized.[93]

Dufrenne's insertion of representation in the second dimension, which is that of potentially describable and analyzable content but is perhaps better characterized by the notion of a continuable world, may be sufficiently explained and defended by just that notion of

189

the representational world, which must be one of formal and representational properties alike. Another way had been chosen by Santayana (1896). His first dimension or lowest stratum is that of sheer presence, as before; his second dimension is that of analyzable form; his third dimension is that of expression. But this last level, "expression," includes representation. Santayana's reasons for this grouping are the same as those that led the theorists who thought of the fine arts as arts of imitative play to take representation and expression as different modes of "imitation." He is considering his dimensions in terms of the kinds of relations involved. At the level of presence, no relationships are recognized; the second level is that of internal relationships; the third level is that of external relationships. That is, both expression and representation are conceived as referring to something outside the work, whether this is something actual or something projected (an intentional object).

Of the alternative placings of representation, Dufrenne's answers more nearly to the account of the work of art suggested in this chapter, and avoids the notorious difficulty of marking a precise division between purely formal relations and representational aspects. Yet Santayana's way has a rough justice to it, and one should beware of denying the obviously true merely because it is untenable.

That works of art do have three dimensions can hardly be denied.[94] At least, the first dimension must be conceded: without an actual presence, there is nothing to be contemplated, and the "aesthetic experience" becomes an attenuated and abstract feeling that may be attributed to anything or nothing. As Souriau remarks (1947, 30), though a work of art may be called a quasi object because of its status as performance rather than artifact, it really exemplifies as nothing else can the status of a substance, a self-contained entity that confronts us as an object and not at all as an instrument. There has been some controversy over the implications of this primacy of presence, as we have seen: to some, it has implied sensuousness and seemed to exclude literature; to others, it has meant that works of art exist only in their particular instances, so that the tokens are everything and the type nothing. But these doubts and qualms arise when we stop considering the status of the work as object and start thinking about its ontic quality in terms of material conditions or what not. It is enough for us to say that a work of art as such is considered in respect of its design, that is, of those qualities taken together that render it a contempland, and, therefore, to be a work of art is to be an object present for contemplation: whatever the modes of possible presence are, they are the possible modes for a work of art.

The second dimension seems almost as necessary as the first. There could no doubt be such a thing as an undifferentiated object of contemplation, the correlate perhaps of a mystical intuition.[95] But it is hard to see how any performance could be such. There must be something definite done, something for criticism to engage with. And without the third dimension what we have cannot be a performance at all, for either it must lack unity or its unity cannot be that attributable to a design act: it will be a mere thing, at best an art object and not a work of art.

VII

THE CLASSICAL LINE
6: WHAT WORKS OF ART ARE LIKE

The Classification of Works of Art

What different sorts of works of art are there? All sorts. The question is absurd. Classifying works of art seems to be a problem only if one feels that one has to criticize those systems of the arts that philosophers from Plato to Souriau have attempted. But perhaps it is worth saying that the best way to classify works of art is not necessarily by enumerating and classifying arts. Since we define a work of art as a performance considered with respect to its design, the appropriate classification of such works would follow the proper ways of classifying performances and designs, and neither the accepted systems of the fine arts nor anything that might plausibly take their place would be likely to do that. The phrase "works of art" is often used to designate the genus to which paintings, sculptures, poems, and such belong, and we know they are paintings and so forth before we know they are works of art—they are works of art *because* they are paintings or whatever. But in my terminology what is thus classified is "works of fine art" rather than works of art. If it is the classification most commonly used, that is because the practices of the fine arts are so institutionalized as to impose it.

The traditional professional practices of the arts provide names for arts and their divisions (painting, portrait painting), accepted media (oil on canvas, piano solo), recognized genres (comedy, opera), and set forms (fugue, sonnet). Institutionalized practice thus supplies the culture of any particular place and time with a limited repertoire of standard methods, media, tools, and forms, which the professional employs with facility; but it may also admit of free variation. A painting may be acrylic on canvas—or it could be anything; a poet may write a sonnet—or a poem of any structure that occurs to him. Set forms, and the like, do not constrict their expert users, but offer a set of precisely controllable variables whose use makes certain precise effects possible. The design requires that the public (and, above all, other practitioners) know what the form is within which the variations are made. Different epochs vary in the extent to which their output of works of fine art falls within the scope of such accepted forms and means. It seems unlikely that any theory could explain why any particular set of restrictions should be accepted, or why any set of preferred forms or media should be chosen. Someone tries something new; a few others see possibilities in it; it catches on; and soon the thing to do is to write rondels or to compose by field.[1] The concept of a fine art logically requires that there should be a substantial set of preferred methods (whether material or formal) of some sort, but it is not logically necessary either that actual output should be confined to rigidly determined forms or that it should not be so confined.[2]

It is conceivable that a classification of works of fine art might proceed more or less a priori by charting the inherent interrelations of skills: one would enumerate possible modes of cognition, possible elements and relations discernible and manipulatable within the sphere of each of these modes, the effects thus achievable, and the resulting characteristic emphases. (I say "more or less" a priori because, when speaking of practice, one must rely on experience to suggest possibilities as well as to provide realities.) That would be an enormous and indeterminate task. More realistically, one might base a classification on the characteristic effects and problems of the fine arts as they are actually practiced. The distinction between monodic, contrapuntal, and chordal-harmonic music, for instance, is not a mere cultural whim, but reflects inherent possibilities and choices in the means of music to which nothing of comparable significance in any other art corresponds. Or again, the place of representation in any form of music is quite different from what it is in painting, and the ways in which it can be carried out and its significance when carried out are different as well, so that a distinction between representational and nonrepresentational painting will not have the same sort of classificatory function as a distinction between representational and nonrepresentational music—or so one would suppose, and it would be worthwhile to check out the suspicion and explain the result. Again, an analysis of the possibilities open to cinematic technique might shed light on the selection of the set of those possibilities that is most frequently explored and constitutes the film as we know it—or it might shed no such light, and the inexplicability would be equally significant (as demonstrating, perhaps, the autonomy of the semiotics of cinema).

The prospects of such grandiose anatomies of the arts, and the classifications of works consequent on them, are questionable. The fine arts, if they are to be arts (and they are), must have describable areas of expertise (and they do); and the boundaries of these areas determine the accepted classifications of their works.[3] But that fact itself is entirely consistent with the classifications themselves being accidental. Certainly our definition of a work of art had nothing directly to do with the fine arts and did not invoke fixed forms or procedures. It called only for the possibility of identifying a performance to which an aesthetic point could be assigned. It may be that the notion of a kind of performance that engenders an object fit for contemplation always carries with it the belief that only certain types of performances are likely to reward such contemplation and, hence, the expectation that designs will be recognizably like other designs—the old romantic dream of a work of art that can be taken on its own terms, in that its design is transparent to the innocent eye or ear, is only a dream. But in the development of mankind, languages must have been generated, by however easy stages, from nonlanguage behavior patterns, and art forms come from different forms and ultimately from no forms at all; and every child starts his own development from scratch, both in learning languages and in learning to appreciate beauties, however sophisticated. The most that can be thought innate and universal is the ability to discern grammatical structures and aesthetic forms of the most general actual sort; no unchanging cross-cultural repertory of actual forms or kinds of forms can be supposed necessary. The strongest case we could make would be the following. Given some clues as to its possible context and reference, any message of sufficient length can be decoded, and so any artist who is persistent enough can create the taste by which he is enjoyed. But that takes time, and the public may not have that much time to give, especially if many other artists are demanding the same effort of decipherment, each of them concerned to establish a separate set of factors that he is varying. Unless one starts with a knowledge of what is to be looked for, one can interpret a complex, variegated surface as a putative design in indefinitely many ways. One must know how to direct the attention before one can register any of them, especially since the most satisfactory designs may be such as do not register at once. The *Gestalt* mechanisms of vision will do something, but not enough; and what they do may be the wrong thing, for the line of least resistance is not always the best line. We cannot fix limits a priori to the possibility of detecting designs.[4] But we can be reasonably sure that if too many artists operate beyond the range of a repertoire of accepted formal possibilities, the accessibility of designs will be limited. It is for just such situations, as Lewis (1969) shows, that conventions are devised (cf. chap. 3, n. 38, above).

The demands of definable expertise that provide the works of fine art with a fixed classification are thus matched by a looser requirement of intelligibility that may impose a similar sort of classification on art objects and, hence, in effect on works of art; and one would expect the classifications to be the same, for why should they differ? But a classification, not of generally accepted works of art, but of *all* works of art should be in terms of *possible* types of performances and *possible* types of designs. The classification by the arts to which the works are affiliated and their subdivisions is sure to figure somewhere, but one would expect it to appear rather late in the discussion. Its lateness would not make it trivial. As in biological taxonomy, divisions having great systematic significance may be sparsely represented in real life, and the most striking and familiar differences may appear only in the topmost twigs of the branching tree. To a botanist, cabbage is virtually indistinguishable from Brussels sprouts, but not to a cook. Nonetheless, to get the whole picture straight and in focus we should start with what is systematically fundamental, even though the greatest practical interest attaches to what differentiates closely allied species.

If works of art are properly classified by kinds of performance and kinds of design, some familiar modes of classification are excluded. The kind of material the artist uses is irrelevant except insofar as it affects the type of design. His motives can be relevant only marginally and indirectly, if they somehow affect the way his performance is to be construed. Psychological characteristics of artists, and times and places of origin, can only have an indirect relevance through correlation with design types. Such exclusions are easy enough. It is much harder to say how performances and designs are most appropriately to be classified, what the main dimensions of variation are, which are the most important of them, and how far they can be reduced to a single system. Once more we feel inclined to say that there are all sorts of performances and designs, and let it go at that. A system of classification serves only as a challenge to produce a rival system. But our earlier discussions have laid the ground for some classifications, and it seems appropriate here to list a few without making any strong claims for their status. I will start by considering variations in the ways in which performances may be (or may be thought of as) design acts, proceed to aspects of the performance emphasized in the design, and end with types of design produced, which may be classified by types of element ordered and by types of order introduced.

The most basic classification reflects our distinction between works of art, works of fine art, and art objects. Some works of art are performances systematically produced by means and in circumstances that suffice to claim for them the status of aesthetic objects. Others, though lacking full institutional warrant, are put forward as aesthetic objects by their performers; others are of a kind that, regardless of the performers' intentions, are generally recognized as aesthetic objects, institutionally adopted by a public or its representatives. Others are merely taken for the nonce as aesthetic objects by some person or persons. The last category is residual, including all performances that are taken to be works of art although they belong to none of the other kinds.[5]

A second classification goes by the relative emphasis placed on producer, recipient, and medium. A work of art by our definition is taken to be done or made as an aesthetic object, that is, to be cognized and appreciated. It therefore has the nature of a communication, and any communication can be taken in any or all of these three ways. Medium-emphasizing designs are those taken as patterns, abstract and impersonal, even though the content is of the kind called representational. Producer-emphasizing designs are those taken as relating to a real or possible experience or feeling or thought of the performer or of someone for whom he is spokesman. And a recipient-emphasizing design is one construed as conveying something to a real or possible public. These distinctions must relate to a context of presentation from which the performance is inseparable and, more properly, to the qualities of the design itself; the actual circumstances in which a work happens to have been produced make no difference to our placing it in one class of works of art rather than another. Thus, as I observed in the previous chapter, to consider a poster as a work of art need not be to consider it as an abstract design, and must not be to respond to its message or to consider its effectiveness as message, but is to consider it as a public design of a special sort. To consider a lyric poem as a work of art is not to consider it as a verbal pattern, not to respond to it as to a cry from the heart, not to consider its efficacy in relieving the poet's heart from a feeling of oppression, but to consider it as expressive design: a verbal design that works by articulating a possible attitude. The three emphases are cumulative. First, there must be a discernible pattern. This may then be complicated by an implied reference back to a pattern maker, and this complex may be further complicated by an implied link forward to a supposed public. But this order of complications does not mean that message designs end by being more complex or subtle than others: on the contrary, the added reference to the public is often associated with crudity on the levels of pattern and expression.

The distinction between patterns, expressions, and messages can be broken down further by distinguishing the most significant types of each, though these might serve rather to characterize than to classify works, unless they were adopted by the typology of traditional practice. A typology of patterns would go by the kinds of element ordered (specified, presumably, in terms of medium rather than of material) and by the kind of order imposed. No such typology will be attempted here, though the topic will be resumed in the next section. Expression types might be differentiated by the degree of involvement they imply, from the confessional to the impersonal, and perhaps by what is expressed. For the expressiveness of a work may be related to an emotion or mood; to a whole persona; to a community or class, however defined; to mankind as a whole; or even to the universe as a sentient whole, for art may be the proper domain of such mystical fancies. Message types would be differentiated by what audience, if any, the work implied and by whether the work was cast in an informative, a hortatory, an emotive, or an interrogative mold.[6]

It is probably under this heading of message types that one should include the most basic differentiations of subject matter and manner of representation: whether a work is in any sense about something and, if so, in what sense. It is true that some people hold all works of art to be representational on the ground that there can be nothing produced by imagination or intellect that was not *given* in some form in sensation, and others maintain that representational aspects are never aesthetically relevant. But such all-or-none inclusions and exclusions, once one has seen their point, fail to sustain one's interest—just as a declaration that all men are sinners arouses less sustained interest than information about who has been committing what sins lately. They neither undermine nor assist our differentiations. In any case, visual works do differ significantly in the ways in which they exploit the forms of objects. If those forms are assumed to be familiar to the public, they may be made the subject of various different sorts of comments and variations, which the public may be expected to recognize for what they are. A work may produce a likeness of such a form or distort it or take it as theme or take it as suggestion or allude to it. In much the same way, a literary work may have a theme (such as sentimentality) or a subject (such as the fall of Rome) of whose general nature the public is supposed to be sufficiently aware to appreciate what the author has *done with* his subject or his theme. Here the relevance of the known reference point is that it affects the nature of the design. But in other cases the work assumes that its reference point is unknown and is so presented as to make that point its subject matter, what the work is about. A painting may be of, and a book may be about, a real or imaginary person or place or event, and be so presented as to suggest the function of telling the public about this thing or happening or person in which the interest is supposed to lie.

The difficulty of working out a single, systematic, preemptive classification of works of art becomes startlingly visible when we reflect that a third classification, no less plausible than the second, could be based on the three dimensions of works of art differentiated at the end of the last chapter. Thus, a work may be primarily one of presence, a single object making its main impact through the *claritas* of a commanding whole; one of structure (Dufrenne's "representation"), the design being principally a web of relationships, whether internal to the work or relating the work to a suppositional entity beyond itself; or one of expression, chiefly a revelation of personality or of a quasi-personal emotive reality.[7] Since the three dimensions were not unambiguously identified, they do not determine a unique classification; but it certainly looks as if no classification worked out on these lines could stand alongside the one we derived from the possibility of emphasizing origin, pattern, and message in communicative performances. Expression and origin orientation come to much the same, or would overlap in a confusing way; structure and pattern are the same. But presence is not commensurable with the relations of our second classification at all, nor does message orientation sit comfortably with the third. One could certainly take a firm stand and insist that these two classifications have nothing in common, arguing that the second classification characterizes works as private, public, or self-contained in their mode of presentation, whereas the third distinguishes style, structure, and presence as alternative emphases, so that the apparent overlap shows only that the words "expression" and "representation" are radically ambiguous, as we already knew. But the argument rings hollow.

A fourth classification goes by the mode of contemplation that the work imposes. Some aesthetic objects exist to be thought about rather than to be perceived. Chess problems, like mathematical proofs, have an order that in no way depends on any sensory medium or on any spatiotemporal order in which they may be set out.[8] A chess problem is the same problem whether set out on the board, diagramed, or recorded in any notation; although its primary mode of existence is to be realized on the board, it gains nothing aesthetically by that realization. Chess problems, though works of art within the terms of our definition, are perhaps seldom art objects.[9] But recent years have seen the rise (and, after a few months, the fall) of a "conceptual art," many of whose works were nothing other than "things to think about" and owed nothing to any mode of perception. Other aesthetic objects do depend on sensory order. Dances and drawings are to be seen or heard. Even if the significance of their ordering lies in some nonsensory intellectual or spiritual realm, the order itself is a sensuous order of sensuous material. A musical score is like the notation for a chess problem in being a set of instructions, but unlike it in that the instructions are to produce something that one can hear or can imagine hearing.[10] Other works again require a mixed mode of contemplation. Literary works, as we noted before, have an order that is in some measure sensuous, for words do have sounds (or, in *poésie concrète*, looks), but form components in literary works by virtue of their meanings. It is as intelligible structures that literary works exist; but, as seemed not to be the case with the chess problem, the exact order of the intelligible components *as perceived* is of the essence of the form.[11]

Continuous with the distinction between sensory and nonsensory modes of contemplation is the distinction between the senses and their characteristic objects—in practice, that is, between audible and visible works. In part this answers to the distinction between "space" and "time" works, to which I return in a moment; but, as Marshall McLuhan used tirelessly to insist, the senses have characters of their own, which offer considerable scope to investigation and speculation.[12]

A fifth classification, linked to the fourth, follows the basic modes of origination sketched in the last chapter—process works, artifact works, and so on. And one of the kinds there identified, the executant's interpretation that is a work of art applied to the work of art it interprets, suggests a sixth classification: the distinction that Kant formulated as that between free and tied beauties. Some works are to be taken as free creations, independent designs; others as solutions to problems. A building may be an impressive organization of space, but the same building may also be an elegant and thrilling solution to a tricky problem posed by an awkward site or by a complex pattern of use. If it does both things, it may do them independently or in such a way that the free and tied aspects of its design reinforce one another; and one would suppose that the last would be the highest achievement of architecture. There seems also to be a mixed sort of beauty intermediate between the free and the tied, in which the tricky problem that is finely solved is a purely technical one within the scope of the design itself, rather than one imposed on the designer by the conditions of his work. Thus, we were told in school that Gainsborough's *Blue Boy* triumphantly overcomes the recessive tendencies of cool colors, and that those with technical knowledge of painting derive added delight from the way in which the artist has succeeded in something that is very hard to pull off. Certainly critics and expositors often do say that an artist "has set himself a very difficult problem here," and one must suppose that they find this relevant to their appreciation.

Our seventh distinction, as intimated above, classifies works by the fundamental dimensions of their order. Some works are spatial—not merely spatially extended, but having designs in which the relevant relations between the parts are all spatial and no determinate sequences of events or experiences are presented or specified.[13] Of spatial works, some are two-dimensional (flat, rough, textured, or worked in low relief) and others are three-dimensional, presenting a plurality or continuity of significant aspect. The difference in design is far-reaching. The former works have a design that postulates a single viewpoint.[14] The latter have a design whose appreciation depends not merely on its being seen from all sides but on the changes in relation that appear as the viewpoint is changed. And of three-dimensional works some are permeable and environmental, others are impermeable and encompassable.[15] There are complexities here: an environmental sculpture has a permeable order of a different sort from a building, and that from a garden, and that from a city; and walking through an arch may not differ fundamentally from walking around a monolith. But it remains true that a building establishes a quite different sort of significant use of space from that which is set up by even a colossal statue.[16]

Other works again have a temporal order, their design consisting of one or more *successions* of elements and complexes whose spatial relationships have no significance for the design.[17] Other works, again, combine in their designs temporal and spatial orders. These tend to belong to the arts of visible motion and the arts that combine sight with sound: drama, dance, film, and the like.[18] Among these, the motions of some are mechanically sustained (as with films) or self-sustaining (the flight and burst of fireworks), and the motions of others are sustained by continuous control. Most of these latter are works of gesture, constituted by bodies in movement; but in some (as in puppetry) the artist maneuvers his work more or less indirectly. This seventh classification of works answers to the familiar distinction between "space" and "time" arts. This is because differences in dimensions of order answer to equally wide distinctions in kinds of skill required and, hence, in the organization of those skills, as well as in the circumstances required for suitable exhibition and, hence, in the institutions that mediate the works to their publics.

The bases for classification now mentioned do not cohere into any satisfactory system, though it might not take too much violence to make them do so.[19] At least they were all justified by general theoretical considerations. But, as I said at the beginning, the classifications that prevail in practice often relate to design traditions and are to be explained by history rather than by theory. Theory shows only that there must be some such traditions. It is a fundamental truth about the arts that, although anything can be found beautiful, so that the possibilities open to the fine arts are unlimited, skill cannot be cultivated and appreciation cannot be refined unless these possibilities are limited in range. What forms and means are preferred at any place and time, and how restricted the effective range is, may or may not be explicable by historians and social scientists. The most obvious explanation makes it a matter of opportunism. An artist limits his task by borrowing and developing the most promising or congenial lines opened up by his fellows or by reacting against their excesses or by using their resources to meet some challenge presented by his own condition. The range of actual challenges, opportunities, and repertories need not determine all that is done, but clearly covers most of it, however the total resultant may be explained. It is by such opportunism (though my word travesties his argument) that T. W. Adorno contends the arts can maintain integrity and autonomy in a world manipulated and flattered by advertisers, propaganda ministries, and public relations persons of all sorts: the artist works at a specific task determined by the solutions most lately reached by other artists to their own tasks, the sum of these tasks and solutions constituting the state of the art (Adorno 1956). But it will be seen that his view of the matter generates a classification only insofar as the tasks and solutions fall apart into identifiable lines of development.

There is no need for us to recapitulate here the seekings and findings of historians. An exception might be made in the case of what in *SA* I called syndromes, the classifications like "romantic" or "mannerist" that historians and critics use sometimes to group works by place and time of origin, sometimes by characteristics thought typical of those places and times, and sometimes by what are deemed the same characteristics regardless of when and where they are manifested, which are then related to timeless classifications of personality patterns or social situations. But even these it will be convenient to treat in the next section under the rubric "characterization."

One might suppose that the relevant classifications of works of art would have to fall into the classes now considered: design types are either systematically describable or historically observable and either do or do not involve reference to the performing dimension. But design was defined in such a way as to relate it to contemplation, and there are fundamental differences both in the context and in the manner of contemplation. As the distinctions we made before rested on an implicit analysis of the possible variables in designs and of the conditions that made the contemplation of identified designs possible, the distinctions we now make must rest on an implicit analysis of conditions for contemplation. No such analysis has been carried out, and I do not know what the primary differentiae for such conditions should be; I proceed on the unjustified assumption that they are the contrasts between the special and the ordinary, between the regular and the casual, between the recurrent and the unrepeated, and between the involved and the detached.

Our first distinction might be that between the sacred and the secular. Some works are to be taken as special, remote from everyday concerns, proper objects of awe and dread and circumspection; there are others whose enjoyment is properly continuous with the concerns of everyday life. At least some of the objects we think of as works of art seem once to have been placed in the former category, and perhaps some still are; in a later chapter we shall have to consider the proposition that all art properly belongs to the sacred, and that our relocation of it in the secular world amounts to sacrilege. A weakened version of the same contrast would be that between the ritual and the occasional. Some works exist to be encountered whenever the mood or the occasion arises, or make their appearance when the artist or his agent feels disposed to exhibit or produce. But others are tied to a feast or a season, and can be enjoyed or properly produced only in the context of a ceremony. Christmas carols are not (as yet) sung in August; tragedies were once performed only at Dionysia. Being a fit object for contemplation may be a seasonal property. With the seasonal as with the sacred, a socially structured attitude of expectation may dispose a public to react in a particular way to designs of a particular type.[20]

More generally, works may differ in the manner and degree of personal involvement they require of their public. The most familiar distinction here is one related to that between the secular and the sacred, namely, that between Apollonian and Dionysian art; but that is a complex and subtle distinction, and it will be more appropriate for us here to deal with its aspects and its approximations one by one.[21]

One of the distinctions akin to that between the Apollonian and the Dionysian is that drawn by Michael Fried (1967) between "theater" and "art," which in less question-begging terms is that between works that confront the spectator with an object for contemplation and those that involve him in an experience for which they provide the occasion. Our thesis that "anything whatever can be found beautiful" relates to the latter kind of work, in which the performance is simply that of moving or engaging the spectator; works in which the performance relates to a specific problematic context or formal achievement pertain rather to the former kind.[22] Fried, as his language shows, considers the kind of work that serves merely as occasion for an experience, usually within a manipulated context, as the antithesis and enemy of art as it is understood by those who take art seriously; the fact that the approach we are taking here precludes this polemical maneuver does not prevent anyone from making the value judgment it implies.[23]

Close to Fried's distinction is Eco's (1962) classification of works as relatively "closed" or "open," to which I have alluded before: that is, between works that require the spectator to participate in their completion or realization by constructive action of his own and those that require him merely to appreciate what the artist has definitively achieved. Eco picks up, as it were, the formal side of

Fried's global distinction, and a paper by R. W. Hepburn (1966) picks up its affective side. Some works, Hepburn points out, have qualities to which the vocabulary of human feelings seems appropriate: we find them sick or dizzy. But others are such as actually to arouse feelings: they are sickening, not sick, and dizzying rather than dizzy. And in between there is a third set that does not so much arouse as solicit feeling, invite one to be sickened but in such a way that the invitation can be accepted or declined. There is clearly a difference between provoking a response, facilitating a response, and providing the pattern for a response: as we observed before, a recipe is neither an invitation nor a permission, much less a command.[24]

Closer to the original contrast between the Apollonian and the Dionysian is the contrast between the detached and the involved. Contemplating something as an object in a calm and steady way differs from being involved in it as a process. In listening to a piece of music one may be moved indeed, but still react at each moment to the whole of the music as concentrated in that moment, making it an object for one's awareness as though it were always statically there to be listened to. But, alternatively, one may be caught up by and swept along with music in such a way that the essence of the experience lies in the dynamic process of one's changing states. Associated with this contrast between experience as cognitive relation and experience as psychic process is that between participation and observation. One may observe a work that others are performing, or be aware of it through one's own performance. And the latter mode of awareness may take several forms: it may involve the muscular feeling of effort or the feeling of being part of a whirling pattern.

A performance is necessarily accessible in some aspect to its performer, but necessarily in a different aspect from that accessible to anyone who is not performing. There is a continuous gradation from square-dancing, through dancing before onlookers, to ballet; or from playing house, through acting while people are watching, to acting as a form of work; and in general from knowing-through-doing, through doing-and-showing, to exhibiting. This relation between contemplation in performance and contemplation of performance from the outside admits of elaboration in terms of the numbers of people involved in the two capacities of agent and experient. In some works, the performer is alone while performing and has no audience. He works for himself, and his awareness of the work, fused with the feeling of doing and creating, must be different from that of any other possible public.[25] The joy of doing, of being aware of what one is doing, is a primary kind of aesthetic delight whose importance no theorist of art must forget. On other occasions a single performer plays or writes (or whatever) for one other person, as Achilles in the *Iliad* played for Patroclus. Here we may suppose, unless the victim of the serenade is unwilling, that the contemplative delight may be shared equally, that the work serves as a vehicle of communion. And then there are cases where one person works for many persons, to whom he is related as performer to public. The audience may then be critical or enraptured, may admire or enjoy, but in any case can enjoy no more than an illusion of intercourse with the man who is set apart, literally or figuratively on a stage. To these three cases involving the single artist correspond three where the artists are many. Sometimes there is no audience, as when people play quartets or sing madrigals or enjoy a jam session or dance together: joy lies in how one joins harmoniously with others within a design that enfolds one. Or the audience may be many as the artists are many, and there is a public show. And symmetry demands that we single out the third kind of case, which in itself seems of little consequence: the command performance that many put on for a single person, as in the royal masque or pageant—where the true audience for the work may be the proud performers rather than their illustrious victim.[26]

Musicians often complain of theorists that they wrongly suppose music to be written for hearers and not for players.[27] And some critics have argued that action painters, if no others, paint for themselves alone. I have made fun of the latter view as incompatible with the behavior of such artists in the matter of sales and publicity, but it is true that defining a work of art as a thing to be contemplated does not entail that it is to be contemplated from the outside, by a public that is other than the artist, let alone by one that confronts him rather than enjoying solidarity or empathy with him. Patently, that is often the case; but there is no reason to suppose that the case has any privilege.

If the discussion of the classification of works of art, which I now terminate rather than conclude, is amorphous to the point of indeterminacy, that is because the notion of a work of art with which we have been working is itself indeterminate on the relevant points. It has to be so. Unless we are to exclude candidates arbitrarily from the status of art, we must accept that no one can say what a work of art is not, for that would only be a useful challenge to artists and their friends to produce and acclaim (and, more important, to force us to acclaim) a work of just that kind; but, for all that, the phrase "work of art" is by no means empty. That is, the concept of a work of art is open, but its openness admits of analysis. We have seen that it is open along many dimensions. Given that to take anything as a work of art is to take it as a performance, classification may go by how the decision to take it as a performance is reached and by how the performance is related to its performer or to his actions or to the upshot of his performance. Given that it is a fit object for contemplation, one may classify it at least six ways: by how one decides it is worth contemplating; by the basic reasons for contemplating things in general; by the reasons for contemplating performances in particular; by the different modes of contemplation; by the ways in which contemplation is rewarded; and by occasions for contemplating. And all classifications rest on knowledge of what is possible as a design act and, hence, as a design. But none of this tells us how to classify. It only tells us what to classify.

In addition to the classifications inherent in the institutional practice, historiography, and criticism of the fine arts, two important kinds of classification have been omitted here because they do not follow directly from my definition of a work of art. One of these, which differentiates works by the part the artistic practice to which they belong plays in the general context of cultural activity, is assigned to an appendix (B, on "Kinds of Art"); the other, which classifies works by the ways in which they perform a function assigned by the theorist, is relegated to a long note, thus.[28]

The Characterization of Works of Art

From problems of classifying works of art we proceed to those of characterizing them, from what kinds there are to what they and their parts are like. Sorting is not the same as describing, but either can form the basis for the other: saying what a thing is like is enough to put it in the class of things like that, and assigning a thing to a class usually tells something about what it is like—but not always, for one may classify by origins or circumstances.[29] Thus, one might expect a discussion of characterization to follow the lines of one of classification, leaving out the bits that classified extraneously. A satisfactory and comprehensive classificatory system should provide us with a classification of the epithets appropriate to works of art, which would need only to be supplemented by an account of predicates (such as "artistic" and "OK," perhaps) appropriate to works of all sorts. Lacking any such system, we might let the matter rest. But in reality matters are not so simple. The kinds of words used to characterize works of art do not answer to our classifications even when they seem to. For instance, one kind of word whose habitual application to works of art has (as we shall see) led to a lot of talk is the mood word, such as "cheerful." One might think at first that this answered to our classification of expression designs, as opposed to message designs and pattern designs. But we shall see that this has been contested: not only can cheerfulness be variously construed as a message quality (a cheerful work is one whose character is that of a message of good cheer, for instance) but it can be taken as a pattern quality: one can argue that cheerfulness is a quality of patterns, describable in pattern terms, that has merely appropriated the name of a mood, much as Brussels sprouts have borrowed the name of a city, for no reason that anyone needs to know about. We must therefore make a fresh start.

If a work of art is defined as any performance considered with respect to its design, to characterize a work of art appropriately must be to say what there is about it that makes it a design or that makes it one sort of design rather than another: that is, to say why it is worth contemplating or what there is about it that makes it worth contemplating. The qualities that are those of works of art as such will be those that play a constitutive role in such characterization. But if any performance may be a work of art, and whatever can be construed as a performance can be taken as a work of art, it seems to follow that any quality that can be contemplated in a performance or that makes it capable of being contemplated may also make it worthy of being contemplated. Just as the only adequate answer to "What sorts of works of art are there?" was "All sorts," the only answer to "What are they like?" is "Like anything." It seems to follow from this that the qualities of works of art as such must be arranged in sets such that it is logically necessary that a work of art should have one of the members of every set of which it is logically possible that it should have any.[30] That is, if symmetry is an aesthetic quality, so must asymmetry be; if coherent complexity is an aesthetic quality, so must incoherent simplicity be—even if, as may well be, we feel that one of these pairs is likely to be exemplified more often than the other.[31] If every visible thing must be either symmetrical or asymmetrical, a visible work of art may be either; and, when one is attending to its design, one must attend to whichever of these qualities it has. Speaking of an artifact merely as an observed object, one may note that as a matter of fact "It is symmetrical"; as an aesthetic object, "How symmetrical it is"; as a work of art, "How symmetrical he has made it!" Thus, one may qualify the design of any performance by using terms that are in themselves neutral members of such exhaustive sets but by their use in such a context become first jointly and then severally charged with evaluative import.

It seems, then, that the characterization of works of art depends less on the use of special words than on a special use to which words are put: what it is relevant to say about a work cannot be determined independently of the decision or discovery that it is one. However, as we have seen, though any performance could be a work of art, not every performance is. Most works of art are *art objects*, and the history of art can be written. So we shall expect to find that there is, after all, a terminology characteristically applied to works of art, over and above the more general vocabulary I have mentioned. And, in fact, the considerable discussion of "aesthetic qualities" in recent decades has centered on judgments of a specific sort and on the vocabulary typical of such judgments. The received wisdom about such judgments, adjusted to our own terms, would look something like the following. Since a design is what makes a performance worthy of contemplation, qualities of a work of art as such must be such as to ground an overall appraisal of worth (or an avowal of overall appreciation or enjoyment). Such appraisals and appreciations must obviously be based on the contemplable properties of the work. But since anything can be a work of art (or, at least, one cannot stipulate a priori what contemplable performances cannot be works of art), the aesthetic qualities that are cited in support of evaluations of works of art are such that possession of them affords neither necessary nor sufficient ground for the evaluation: it is always logically possible, at least, that a work to which the same predicates were applicable would be differently evaluated, and that a work similarly evaluated should have different qualities. And, of course, the overall appraisal itself will always be contestable in principle and usually in practice, and overall avowals of enjoyment cannot always command concurrence. At the same time, these qualities that ground evaluations are such that possession of them cannot be deduced from any physical properties, or other properties possession of which can be empirically verified. And yet one can learn to make such judgments and use them to conduct meaningful and illuminating discussions of particular works of art. It seems to follow that the meaning and import of such concepts depend in a particularly strong way on the context in which they are uttered.[32]

It is not that a particular color scheme confers gaiety and gaiety confers excellence, but that the excellence *of this particular work* at least partly depends on the gaiety it gets from its color scheme. And it seems to follow that the ability to use such a vocabulary in an acceptable way must be acquired through some rather special sort of education or indoctrination or both, the nature of which calls for elucidation. The words for such "aesthetic qualities" ascribe observable merits or observable demerits. They resemble other evaluative terms in being Janus-words, combining a descriptive with an evaluative function.[33] With one face they look back to the demonstrable attributes of what they characterize; with the other face they look forward to its adjudged excellence. As calling a man brave tells one something about the sort of thing he does as well as praising him for behaving meritoriously, so calling a picture harmonious conveys something about what sort of picture it is, as well as suggesting that it has at least some merit. What differentiates aesthetic judgments from other evaluations is, not this, but that both the descriptive and evaluative aspects are challengeable in ways that are somewhat distinctive. And now one must philosophize at some length to establish wherein this distinctiveness lies and to produce a coherent statement covering what one wishes to preserve of this conventional wisdom in an accurate and defensible form.[34]

It would be wasted labor to add yet another story to the monument of philosophical prose in which this favorite issue has been enshrined. Let it suffice to say that in terms of our analysis the matter falls out somewhat as follows. Aesthetic judgments and their characteristic terminology no longer serve as intermediary between incontestable statements of observable fact and contestable evaluations. On the one side, performance as such cannot be neutrally described. What has been performed on any occasion is always a matter for interpretive judgment. On the other side, the qualities of a work of art as such already have evaluative import. So the supposed tripartite structure collapses. Certainly there must be, on the one hand, some neutral observation statements that could be made and, on the other hand, some general evaluation that could be passed or reaction that could be avowed; but these are really artifacts of this or that mode of quasi-logical or epistemological analysis, pure ideology, and have no practical bearing on the matter in hand. A work of art as such is a contempland, an appreciable thing, and to characterize it as a work of art is to say what there is about it to appreciate.[35] To perceive its design is already to *understand its value*, though not necessarily to prize it. Now, we have seen that not all designs are perceptible to all men. Not only must one be able to entertain the thought that a certain sort of design falls within the range of human possibility—and the history of taste and criticism is largely a history of incapacities and incredulities in this regard—but one must be able to discern the actual design; and such perception may depend on learned skills of discrimination. In addition to this, critical debates on the interpretation of complex works show that what the design of a work actually is may be a controversial question even among those presumably best able to apprehend it. What a performance is is always a matter for judgment, and not all such judgments are accessible alike to all men. It follows that the aesthetic qualities that constitute a design, and hence the performance whose design it is, are not necessarily perceptible to everyone.[36]

Even if we repudiate the model whereby aesthetic qualities have the function of mediating between publicly verifiable descriptions and controversial evaluations, it remains true that two questions can be asked of any putative work of art. First, does it have the qualities that are alleged to make it appreciable? And second, if it is agreed to have those qualities, do they afford sufficient grounds for contemplating it? It seems reasonable, in the light of what we have said, to suggest that answers to the first question are a matter of education rather than indoctrination, since they depend on the training of perception and imagination; but the answers to the latter might be rather a matter of indoctrination, not of education. The proper outcome of a course in art appreciation might then be, not that one would come to love works of the sort one was exposed to, but that one would know what one would have loved them for if one did. More precisely, appreciation of a design is compatible with a number of different sorts of rejection: one may decide that such a success is not worth achieving; that one sees the point but has no time and energy for such points; that for moral or political reasons one must close one's heart against such achievements; that one personally simply fails to respond to things of this sort or to this particular thing; that one's ability to respond has become jaded for the time being or forever; and so on. And such responses differ in the measure of their critical irrelevance. Yet we feel that there is something amiss, even grotesque, in such discrepancies between appreciation and liking, between comprehension and love.[37] We can scarcely endure the thought that anyone should thoroughly understand what we love and fail to love it, since our own love seems but the function of our comprehension. We can scarcely evade the thought that the other's indifference reflects a shallower or a deeper comprehension than our own: surely he must either have missed or have seen through what we know we have seen.

What I have said about the training of perception in the appreciation of design might repay elaboration. To attribute a design character to a performance one must draw attention to those aspects of it that taken together make it worth contemplating. This can be done only on the basis of a prior understanding of what can be a design, and only for persons who at least partly share this understanding: one is inviting them to "Look at it *this* way," and the invitation will be in vain unless they are already initiated in the tricks of attention and discrimination that constitute the way of looking and have some training in the appreciation of designs of the sort that such attention and discrimination will bring to light. The acquisition of any form of discrimination or refinement of perception calls for training in material of the kind in question: one cannot read aerial photographs or decipher the scratches on bullets without intensive training in doing precisely that. Analogously, we would expect that aesthetic discrimination would *ordinarily* be the product of prolonged exposure to works of art, even if some people have an "uncanny knack" or "instinctive ability" that seems to bypass the ordinary procedures of learning; and we would further expect that the ability to appreciate designs of a given type would be acquired only through exposure to designs of just that type.[38] (In fact, one might envisage a typology of designs based on discovering exposure to what designs facilitated appreciation of what other designs.) One sees and responds to what is really there—one does not need to postulate a mental construct that is the "real" work of art—but one is seeing and responding with emphases and suppressions, picking out some relations and not others, in a way comparable to that in which one exercises any perceptual skill. For learning to act effectively in any sort of situation, whether it be learning to read, learning to drive a car, learning to chop down trees, or learning to follow philosophical arguments, requires that one come to respond to all and only those cues that call for a possible response in the situation in question. A child's life is notoriously vivid because a child responds to everything alike; but it is because of this that he cannot act effectively in any situation. Adults become incapable of responding to anything in a situation that they cannot use. This notorious fact is often used to contrast childlike aesthetic awareness with everyday awareness, but in fact aesthetic awareness is as sharply focused and differentiated as any other—children, one might rather say, respond aesthetically to everything *except* works of art. The alternative to the adult mode of selective discrimination is not total discrimination, for there is no such thing, but absence of any discrimination: the "blooming and buzzing confusion" of James's famous phrase. All that makes the discrimination of the qualities of works of art a special case, if anything does, is that the "use" that governs response is not a practical purpose but the qualified discrimination itself.

Different people may differ in their responsiveness to designs that they read in just the same way, though the possibility makes some people uneasy.[39] But it is more likely that their different experiences with designs will affect their reading of the designs themselves. One interprets forms by analogy with other forms, and exposure to different sets of forms must afford a different set of analogies. An age like ours, in which the repertoire of available art goes beyond anyone's possible comprehension, is bound to be one in which a cohesive public is replaced by a multitude of mini-publics, each with different competences, the membership of which shifts from work to work. The persons with whom I share the expectations that govern my hearing of Boulez are not those with whom I share those that govern my hearing of the Mothers of Invention, far less those that govern my seeing of Les Levine.[40] It is because vision thus depends on experience that critics and historians adduce plentiful comparisons to show how any work they are discussing fits into the traditions of the arts.

There are at least four ways in which a person's experience of designs may be expected to affect his reading of further designs. First, it will facilitate his attending to and looking for and, hence, seeing some relations rather than others, and it will affect the importance he is disposed to attach to those he does see. Second, it will govern whether the symbolic meanings of certain features are matters about which he has (at best) information, or are ways in which he has come to see without making an effort or even without being aware of doing anything special. Third, familiarity with the appropriate tradition will enable him to gauge the range within which variation is achieved. And fourth, familiarity with such traditions will enable him to place a work in relation to the area of human creative endeavor of which it forms a living part.

It is quite generally true, if it is true at all, that, since every man's experience differs from every other's, the way he sees the world must be unique to him, and in particular areas of experience the way he sees things will be most like the vision of those whose experience has been most like his own. The only respect in which aesthetic contexts are peculiar in this regard is that the relevant discriminations, being themselves the main object of concern, are cultivated intensively and in isolation from any factors making for community of experience. It is thus easy to believe, even if it is not actually established, that aesthetic judgments vary more widely than other judgments. Differences in perceptual skills, in experience references, and in preferences might combine to make the attribution of such qualities as harmony and delicacy limitlessly contestable to the point where the question whether a given work *really* had them would not be worth asking. But even if that were so, such attributions would still be related in definite ways to describable experiences, so that they could hardly be called arbitrary. Though the question whether a given work *really is* delicate had no fixed answer, the question whether it can *justifiably be called* delicate might well have: it asks whether there is an acquirable skill and a viable design tradition in relation to which delicacy can be found in the work, even if it may be complicated by asking whether the skill is one worth acquiring, or whether the relevant tradition is anywhere prevalent or current.

The position reached in the last paragraph has an element of exaggeration in it. One must distinguish between the obscurity of a design for those unversed in the relevant habits of perception and the ambiguity of a design for the initiated. Whatever may be true of works of art in general, and even of art objects, it is ridiculous to suppose that artworks can support indefinitely many radically diverse readings. Within a community reasonably identifiable as that of the artist, the important distinction will be between those who only see a mess or hear a racket, those who roughly grasp what is going on and react to its gross features and associations, and those who perceive the design with more or less fine tuning and whose responses are shaded toward different aspects of it. Among the last two groups, and to a limited extent even in the first group, we would expect to find that different individuals would choose different words for their spontaneous characterizations of a work, but would dispute the applicability of the characterizations of others equally well informed only insofar as they were grossly evaluative (that is, if the forward-looking face of Janus were much larger than the backward-looking face). And even then, though I would disagree with your calling a work boring, I should be able to see what bores you in its heavenly length. In fact, though it is true that it is less precise to say that a certain work *is* delicate than to acknowledge that it may *fitly be called* so, it would often be mere pedantry to insist on the point.

Insofar as the question whether a work is delicate is simply one of saying what sort of design it has, then, the recognition of delicacy calls for education rather than indoctrination. But insofar as a work's delicacy is assumed to be something good about it, indoctrination may be called for. Even if you recognize in a work what I call its delicacy, understanding all I say about the work and perceiving everything I indicate in it, seeing what I like in it and even realizing why I like it, you may still refuse to dub it with what you consider a laudatory term, preferring to think of the work as effeminate or finicky or timid. An attribution of delicacy may be fitly supported not only by indicating, for instance, the relations of elements but also by a rhetorical discourse setting forth more exactly how I feel about the work as a whole, and thus at least conveying what *sort* of delicacy I would like you to look for. But to find this sort of delicacy may require not merely fine discrimination (or lack of discrimination) but a system of preferences (or "taste") without which the required emphases will not in practice be accessible to you; and you may well resist what really comes down to an attempt to remake you in my own image. This situation is in some measure typical of evaluations: attributions of such moral qualities as courage are supportable in just the ways described, and the support is more likely to fail of conviction in the latter way than in the former. You are not likely to be unable to identify the actions that make me call the man brave, but you may well not appreciate the kind of man I extol so warmly.[41]

Like other terms whose use tends to carry evaluative implications, the terms used of works of art vary among themselves in the manner as well as in the proportions in which they mingle description with evaluation. Some both indicate what rewards attention and suggest that attention is indeed rewarded, as "harmonious" and "delicate" do. Other terms, like "interesting," "trivial," "frivolous," "sublime," "ugly," and (above all) "beautiful" tell little about what the work they are applied to is like, but serve primarily to praise or dispraise it for rewarding or frustrating attention in some very general respect. Others again, like "ironic," carry very little suggestion of praise or dispraise, but indicate only the manner in which attention is rewarded insofar as it is rewarded at all. But the serious use of even such minimally descriptive terms as "frivolous" is usually thought to do more than express a merely personal response. It should at least do that: if I am in earnest in calling it frivolous, and not merely quoting common cant, I should be expressing the frustration of my own (serious) attempt to find a way of taking it seriously. But in saying not that I was thus frustrated but that the work is frivolous, I imply in addition that the work is such that no one could succeed in taking it seriously, that my response, in fact, is normal. I use such terms, not when I am out of my depth or in doubt as to the appropriateness or normality of my reaction, but when (whether from knowledge, from bravado, or from sheer insensitivity) I am confident in my experience. Lacking such confidence, I either confine myself to reporting my own reaction as such, or I hedge. This presumption of normality is by no means peculiar to aesthetic or even to evaluative contexts, however. One has something of the same hesitation before committing oneself to a factual assertion in any field or on any matter on which one stands open to correction from those one concedes to be better informed than oneself. The difference in this regard among aesthetic judgments, and between aesthetic judgments and others, lies only in the degree of vulnerability, or of evidence of vulnerability, in claims.

It is notoriously true of Janus-words that either aspect of their meaning may be taken as primary in a given context. If one fastens on the pejorative sense of a term like "obscene," for instance, one will refuse to apply the term to anything one does not deplore; if one fastens on its descriptive aspect, and makes a supposition such as that whatever literally describes or depicts the sex act is obscene, one will refuse to admit that whatever is obscene is *pro tanto* to be condemned unless one happens to believe that the sex act should never be described or depicted. In either case, one may simply prefer to avoid terminology whose use seems to commit one in advance (like the word "nigger") to an involuntary automatic association of a description with an evaluation.

I said a few pages back that one could ask two questions of a putative work of art: whether it really had its alleged appreciable qualities and whether the appreciable qualities it did have rendered it worthy of contemplation. Somewhat analogously, the discussion in which we have just immersed ourselves suggests that there are two ways in which the characterization of a work could be problematic. It might be that the property in question was indubitably present—the painting is executed on a seasoned maple board three inches thick—but dubiously relevant to the characterization of the work as such; or it might be that the characterization would be indisputably relevant ("It is a masterpiece of tragic insight expressed with the utmost delicacy of feeling") if only one could be certain that it applied. Many characterizations seem questionable in neither way. That a piece of music is a fugue in four parts is a plain fact about what sort of work it is and what sort of design it has, and, though the listener may not need to notice the fact that it is a fugue, the fugue quality of its structure is an aspect of what is there to listen to. What may be problematic is only whether the fact of its being a fugue is part of what makes it a satisfactory design, or serves only to classify its design. There is, however, a third way in which some characterizations have seemed problematic. It may be that a character is admittedly present and admittedly relevant, but that there is something puzzling or disquieting about its attribution. The first two of these ways in which a characterization could be problematic have been sufficiently enmeshed in the meanders of the discussion we have now concluded. The third remains to be dealt with, in a manner that must be no less intricately indecisive.

Among the terms whose attribution to works of art seems both evidently proper and yet logically inexplicable none are more notorious than the terms whose primary application is to human or other sentient beings, such as "cheerful" or "sad," which are among the terms most frequently used to characterize musical compositions and performances in particular. One may have no qualms in calling a piece of music cheerful, and have no doubt that its cheerfulness is an important aspect of its specifically musical quality, and yet have doubts about the sense in which a piece of music can be called cheerful at all. Prima facie, these terms are expressive in character in that what they ascribe to the work bears the name of something that the fine arts as imitative would be held to express. Accordingly, as one handy way of dividing the terms to be discussed, I will refer these terms to designs conceived as expressive, and follow my treatment of them by saying something about the characterization of designs as messages and designs as patterns. After that, I will say something about those global characterizations that in *SA* I called syndromes because they combine heterogeneous characteristics mutually linked by a bond whose nature and status are the very questions at issue.

I was saying that one might be certain that a piece of music was relevantly and truly to be called cheerful and yet be doubtful about how such an appellation could be justified. Such doubts may be of three kinds. It may be that one feels some impropriety in using such terms at all, on the ground that really only people can be cheerful—to be cheerful is essentially to *feel* cheerful. Or it may be that one thinks the application perfectly proper, yet evidently secondary to the primary application to conscious beings, and is then puzzled by the transition from one use to the other, for which some psychological explanation or quasi explanation seems required. Or it may be again that one thinks the application to art to be neither improper nor derivative but somehow autonomous, and is then puzzled by what connection, if any, there may be between the aesthetic and the personal applications. The topic has a long history, in the course of which every possible position has often been taken. One can hardly hope to add anything new, but it may be worthwhile to run through an argument linking some of the positions together.

How can it be proper and evidently fitting to ascribe such a feeling tone as cheerfulness or sadness to a work of art? Perhaps the first and best thing to say is that works of art are more like people than they are like things. Our knowledge of them is like our knowledge of people, requiring intimacy and delicacy rather than technique; we relate to them by living with them rather than by using them; the practically important differentiae are the finest discriminations rather than the gross contrasts; our contemplation of them is more like a communing with them than like an observation of them.[42] So why should we not apply to them a range of epithets otherwise only applicable to persons? Why not, indeed. But our use of such terminology is metaphorical, it will be said, because only a person can *feel* cheerful and thus *be* cheerful, literally. The work only *looks* cheerful. But what do we mean when we say that it looks cheerful? There seems to be no problem, because works of art, especially musical works, have in an extreme degree what many other objects of experience have—a brooding landscape, for instance, or the innumerable laughter of the waves. They come to us "suffused with affect," which may strike us immediately, before we have registered those structural properties whose presence may be easier to vindicate in the face of skepticism. But (especially in such cases as that of the landscape) we do not believe, and often do not feel, that the ground of this affect is a state of consciousness in or behind the object. Should we not then say that the feeling ascribed to the object is actually and literally in ourselves—that cheerful music is music that cheers us, a brooding landscape one that induces broodiness in the beholder, who then simply projects his feeling upon its stimulus?[43]

The short answer to that question is no. Sad music does not sadden me, nor does cheerful music cheer me. Perhaps I am exceptional in this regard; but surely it cannot be generally true that sad music saddens people, or no one would willingly hear sad music. One might try to save the position by saying that sad music produces a "distanced" sadness, a sort of sadness that is disengaged from one's practical concerns. But what does that mean? Either it only means that the sadness is causeless, in which case we repeat that no one would then willingly submit to sad music, or it means that the sadness is not suffered but relished. But then we should rejoin that a sadness that is not suffered is not a feeling of sadness at all. To speak of a sadness that is not suffered is a way of saying "sad" without meaning it, a mere verbal subterfuge. It would be more honest to say at once that sad music is so called because it causes, not sadness, but a special sort of surrogate emotion, an "aesthetic emotion" that is called sadness because it is somehow like sadness. Some people have said this; but one is inclined to reply that the only feeling that could be like a sad feeling in a way that would give me good reason to call it sadness would be another sad feeling. This retort is indeed sophistical, because it fails to hold if it is really true that people are susceptible to a sort of shadow range of aesthetic feelings somehow analogous and isomorphic with the range of real-life emotions. Yet the retort is effective enough, because the postulation of such an elaborate set of psychological machinery is the sort of move one would rather avoid. So perhaps the initial supposition, that cheerful music is so called because of any sort of way it makes anyone feel, was mistaken.[44] The connection between the cheerfulness of tunes and that of chaps must be of some other sort.

If we are not to invoke the alleged feelings of the listener, the obvious alternative is to invoke those of the musician. Shall we then say that in sad music we recognize the composer's expression of his own sad feeling? That would be absurd, as almost everyone recognizes. If one were composing an opera with scenes of lament and triumph, would one have to wait until one was grieving or triumphant before setting to work? And suppose one were composing an ensemble in which various characters were simultaneously giving voice to their rage, glee, chagrin. . . . Besides, it is sufficiently evident that the music that would express the composer's sadness, were he sad, would have had just the same character if he had composed the same music without being sad; were it not so, the connection between the feeling and the music would be magical rather than musical.[45] The least correction that requires to be made is that which S. K. Langer makes (1953): music expresses, not the composer's feeling, but his knowledge of feeling, to which we through our own knowledge respond. But this way of talking seems needlessly roundabout. One could equally well, and equally needlessly, say that, if a composer writes for clarinets, his music expresses his knowledge of "clarineticity." In that case, it would be simpler to say that he knows how to write for clarinets and does so; and we know that he does so because we hear the clarinets play. Just so, we should say that what the composer knows is how to write sad music, and we recognize its sadness. And it would be no less sad if he had written the same notes fortuitously or randomly, without "knowledge of feeling." The music simply is sad, and we recognize the sadness because it is there to be heard (cf. Prall 1936, chap. 5). After all, when we recognize that some person is sad, we do so because the sadness is actually manifested in what they do and say.

We have come full circle. We have failed to identify any person to be the bearer of the feeling of sadness by virtue of which we find the work sad. But we have still to meet the objection that started us on that wild-goose chase, that a work of art cannot have feelings and cannot be literally sad. It seems easily met, though. It is met if we can maintain that sad music is in some way iconic with those utterances or gestures by virtue of which we call a sad person literally sad. Its rhythms might be those of slow and despondent body movements.[46] This is an attractive position, but I am not sure that it can be maintained, at least in any simple form. The sadness of the music is more evident than the analogy supposed to explain it: one first notes the feeling tone and then looks around for something to explain it. Perhaps we might construct a fanciful genealogy. In the beginning there are sobs and cries of grief. These become formalized and ritualized into laments and keenings. Then the musical materials characteristic of laments and keenings become recognized as hallmarks of sadness in music. So that now we simply recognize sad music by its likeness to other sad music—that is, to other music that our musical culture assures us is properly called sad.[47] But now we see that the genealogy is irrelevant to our present experience: what is relevant is that it is now established that some music is properly called sad, that its character is recognizable, and to call a new piece sad is simply to draw attention to its affinities with these current paradigms. In fact the genealogy is so irrelevant that we can deny it altogether, as Hanslick (1854) did: all such attributions are merely conventional and rest on associations of which one can say for certain no more than that they exist. That is to say, as Stravinsky says (1936, 91-92), that music is by its nature incapable of expressing anything, but (though Stravinsky obscured this point) that would not prevent music expressing things *by convention*. It would not even rule out such a language of music, with its own vocabulary and syntax of precisely identified feeling tones, as Deryck Cooke (1959) outlined.[48] If someone wishes to deny that music can *really be* cheerful or sad, at least he cannot deny that such language is widely used; he must then hold that it is used, though widely, wrongly. But one may counter that a way of talking that is widespread establishes its own correctness; the only plausible error would be that of maintaining that the use of vocabulary had certain implications that, as we have now ascertained, it could not have.[49]

Our résumé of some possible positions about the etiology of the feeling-tone vocabulary has thus far declined to avail itself of an obvious resource. Every work of art, in our view, is a performance and thus projects a performer. Is it not to this necessarily projected agency, rather than to the artist as a person, that the feeling expressed in the work is referred? It is surely in this dimension that the work's sadness lies. But we should beware of saying what this suggests: that the work *is as if* an outpouring of grief, but that the griever is a fictive being projected by the work. Sad music does not closely resemble a moan. It has indeed the distinctive quality that we call sadness, and that is not to be found elsewhere than in sad music. What makes the feeling-tone vocabulary apposite, however, is not merely that our relation to works of art is (as I said some pages back) in some ways analogous to our relation with people. It is rather that, because a work of art is essentially a thing done, questions about design must always admit and often invite formulation in terms of how this or that was done, so that the full vocabulary of qualities of persons and their actions fits into a large prepared place in all our discourse on art.

All that can legitimately be meant, it seems, by calling a piece of music sad is that it has a design whose characteristics include a prominent set that is either naturally or conventionally associated with sadness. But a complexity remains to be introduced. What we have just said encourages us to say that, of course, sad music may be written by someone to express his sorrow, and sad music may sadden someone. But sad music may equally well be written by cheerful or placid or businesslike people; only we will not then say that it expresses their mood. And it is no more likely to sadden than to amuse or invigorate or soothe or cheer the auditor. Why, then, do we single out those cases in which the mood assigned to the music bears the same name as that ascribed to the composer or induced in the listener and say that in such cases the mood is "expressed" or "communicated"? Perhaps it is no more than a simple mistake, a gratuitous and slovenly assumption. But it might be more: such language might signal a recognition that the mood of the music has a sort of conceptual fittingness to that of the person. And it might be more yet. It might signify a belief that a composer's or a listener's sadness may be linked to that which it causes or follows from in music in either of two distinct ways. Sometimes the relation is merely causal: a man's grief might be among the causes of his writing sad music (or, in precisely the same way, of his writing cheerful music). But among the sad music people write in their sadness, there is some that is not merely caused by the sadness but in some fashion articulates, gives a voice to, the very sadness they feel. In such cases we shall say that the music expresses the composer's grief. Similarly, among the sad feelings that sad music arouses, some are merely caused or aroused by the music, for whatever reason there may be (and, in exactly the same way, cheerful music could sadden and sad music cheer or irritate); but some sad feelings are not merely aroused but somehow shaped (and, again, given a voice) by the mood that the music articulates.

If expressive relationships of the sort mooted in the last paragraph are possible, it seems that two things follow. First, such terms as "sad" are used of music in a radically ambiguous way: sometimes they refer to a quality of the musical design as such, sometimes to a complex function of musical form and compositional or auditorial psychology. A man humming a tune dolefully is indeed humming a doleful tune, but not at all in the same sense that Tchaikovsky in the slow movement of his sixth symphony is writing one. Second, the term "express" is susceptible of a like ambiguity. Sometimes one means no more by saying that a tune expresses gloom than that it is a gloomy tune; but sometimes one means that it expresses, gives form and voice to, the gloom of the tunesmith.[50]

It may be in place here to interject a double caveat. First, the fact that I have dwelt at such length on this theme is not to be taken as implying that music is inevitably expressive, or essentially related to feeling, in the sense that all or most music must be related to some emotional mood in one or other of the ways sketched. Many have held, on various grounds, that that is the case; but my present argument is concerned only with what the sense of such terms must be if and when they are applied to music, however often or however seldom this is done. Second, and perhaps more important, my procedures should not be taken as implying that, if all music is expressive, it must be so in the sense that there is no piece of music to which no mood word is appropriate, or that no music is expressive unless some such word is applicable. Just as practically everything anyone says is expressive in that its tone and rhythm convey a continuously vital meaning (and nothing is more expressive than to speak "without expression"), but very little of what one says is appropriately dubbed with any mood word, so it could be that all music is expressive in its variations of tone and emphasis and rhythm, but relatively little of it calls for the application of a mood word.[51] That is presumably what Mendelssohn meant by his celebrated observation that the emotional meaning of music is *too precise* to be put into words (cf. Cooke 1959, 12). It has a human meaning; but that meaning cannot be expressed otherwise than by performing the music itself.

The terminology of feeling, which I have been discussing, is more regularly and readily applied to music than to the visual arts, for reasons which I have touched on, and which have been often explored. Our moods are less spatially differentiated than worked out in the tempo of our actions and experiences. They naturally find expression in shrieks, laughs, shouts, moans, mutterings, which have their rough affinity to the raw stuff of music; but not in colors. Yet a painting may be called cheerful. Almost all I have said about the application of such language to music will apply mutatis mutandis to painting; only the ground of supposed original metaphor must be different, and we have seen that this is essential, not to the use of such terminology itself, but to its use in a certain ambiguous fashion. In the case of painting, however, and in general whenever a work has referential content, a complexity may be introduced that calls into question the usefulness of referring such terminology to the expressive dimension of the design without further qualification. Guy Sircello (1972) has pointed out that there are three distinct ways in which a painting may be, for instance, lighthearted. Mondrian's *Broadway Boogie-Woogie* might be called lighthearted simply because of its formal properties, beginning with its tonality of predominantly bright yellow with numerous small areas of other primary colors and proceeding through the handling of the paint. Here the lightheartedness is a property of the painting itself, but on reflection we might wish to explain this by saying that the performance projects a lighthearted performer: it looks like the sort of thing we should find it natural for a person to conceive and execute in a lighthearted mood, even though in painterly and historical fact we are not in the least inclined to make any suppositions about anyone's frame of mind. On the other hand, we might find a painting lighthearted in a quite different way, in that it presented a glimpse of a way of life conceived as lighthearted: for instance, Fragonard's *The Swing*, in which we do not need to invoke a performer as locus for the feeling tone because the persons portrayed in the work itself are shown as sharing in the attitude that the depicted event evokes, and with which nothing in the manner or form of the painting quarrels. But there is also a third way in which such vocabulary becomes appropriate: one might construe a painting as lighthearted because, no matter what episode was portrayed or what abstract formal properties it had, something about it conveyed the character of *not being taken seriously*. Sircello's own example is Brueghel's *Peasant Wedding*, which he finds an ironic painting because the caricatured quality of the faces and gestures is at odds both with the festive nature of the occasion and with the gladness evident in the expressions of the agents, while the formal properties of the picture do nothing to support the gladness against its apparent undermining. Here the attribution of the feeling tone to the performer is much blunter and more direct than in the first case—so much so that Sircello acquiesces in the common habit of going outside the painting itself and attributing the ironic vision to Brueghel personally rather than to him in his capacity of performer, although nothing in his argument requires him to do this. In the case of the Mondrian, the lightheartedness was immediately located in the painting: that simply is the sort of painting it is. But in the Brueghel, though the irony is indeed in the painting and nowhere else, the quality of the painting is that of a thing *ironically conceived*. It might be sensible, indeed, to register this difference by a distinction in usage: to say that the Brueghel *expresses* irony, but the Mondrian *is* lighthearted, and so in its different way is the Fragonard.

What I have just been saying suggests, if it does not require, the modification in our original position of which I gave advance warning. It was too simple to call such properties as sadness and lightheartedness "expressive" properties. Prima facie expressive they certainly are, in the sense that they attribute to a work of art a predicate literally applicable only to persons, and the sense of metaphor involved in that use is so attenuated that, rather than "literally," one is tempted to say that they are "more strictly" or "primarily" applied to persons. But on reflection it appears that such a term as "cheerful" sometimes imputes an expressive character and sometimes does not. A cheerful work may be one that is most fitly described by imputing good cheer to the putative performer. But cheerfulness may equally be a property of certain patterns, those whose elements are of such a sort and disposed in such a fashion that cheerfulness is the proper term for the result, whether or not one could specify precisely what features and what arrangement were in this instance necessary and sufficient for the cheerfulness. And one does not see why cheerfulness should not also be a property of the work in its aspect as message, a cheerful work in that understanding being one in which a cheering quality was evident—not that it cheered one, which would not be a property of the design itself, but that aptness to induce cheer should be a part of its eviden⸱ character. There is no reason to suppose that such words as "cheerful," which are very far from being technical terms, should have any one use in critical discourse, and as little reason to suppose that the point of the use of such a term on any one occasion should necessarily be clear. No doubt "cheerful" is always used by virtue of something somehow relatable to the kind of human feeling, behavior, and intercourse to which the word "cheerful" may be presumed to have its primary application; but it is likely that the implied relation will be sometimes of one sort and sometimes of another sort and most often of no definite sort at all. Or, if we prefer the material to the formal mode of speech, we may say that the property of cheerfulness in art is a complex one, that of pertaining to, and somehow manifesting something relatable to, good cheer.

I have dwelt for a long time on the ambiguities and complexities in the use of prima facie expressive characterizations of works of art, because these seem to be the most far ranging as well as by far the most discussed. But questions of justification and significance may arise with other sorts of characterizations. For instance, such properties as that of being "rousing," "baffling," or "obscure" are surely prima facie "message" properties in that on the fact of it they have to do with designs conceived as oriented toward contemplators rather than in themselves or as stemming from designers. But it is not clear at once what such terms mean, or whether (or in what circumstances) they ascribe properties to a design rather than referring to a contingent relation between a work and its public. In one way, and up to a point, it is perfectly clear what is meant by calling Albee's *Tiny Alice* an obscure play: "obscure" is plainly a more appropriate epithet than "simple" or "straightforward." But in another way, and beyond a certain point, it is not clear at all what is meant. Is it simply that the task of unraveling the meaning in fact baffles all but a few playgoers? Possibly. But it may rather be that the play is felt to have a quality of obscurity even by those who believe (as I do) that there is no hidden meaning to be brought forth and no complexity to be unraveled. A pervasive air of meaning withheld is recognizable even by those who do not think that Albee is withholding any meaning from them. The ambiguity of "obscure" in such cases is far-reaching and irreducible: if a work is relished by many of its public as presenting real difficulties of understanding, it is unreasonable to deny that it is a property of its design that it does so; equally, it may be a property of its design that it comes across as withholding meaning. The term "obscure" seems equally fitting to both, and it is certainly not the case that any firm usage or convention assigns the term one meaning rather than the other. Similarly, and perhaps even more simply, I may call a Sousa march rousing because it stirs my blood in such a way that I surmise that the blood of others will be also stirred; but I may call it rousing because of the snap of the rhythm and the prevalence of cymbals, even though it fails to rouse my sluggish blood and I neither know nor care what it may do to the circulation of anyone else.

The sorts of ambiguity that are common to message properties and expression properties are those that arise from the apparent outward look of such characterizations: a property of the design in itself seems to be linked with a property of the design as looking back to a performer or forward to a public, and these in turn seem to be linked with relationships between works and their actual producers and publics, respectively. But there are also pattern properties, qualities of designs that do not in any obvious way look forward or back, which cannot reasonably be taken as referring in any way to artist or public, even if on epistemological reflection we consider that artist and public must be presupposed in their recognition. The way our discussion has gone so far might make us expect that pattern properties would be unproblematic—if we except those subtle ones that cannot be perceived without trained discrimination and those Janus-faced ones that cannot be ascribed without taste because to ascribe them is to register not merely recognition but appreciation. But we shall find this expectation falsified.

Meanwhile, the exception just referred to is an enormous one. Because a work of art as such is something fit to be contemplated, it is regarded as existing for the sake of discrimination and appreciation; and for this reason its most relevant and interesting properties will be those that are problematic because they are on the borderline of trained perception or are irretrievably bound up with habits of relishing. Still, that would seem to leave us with a large and comfortably unproblematic realm of pattern properties that are verifiably present and indubitably relevant. That a pattern has certain elements, and that they are put together in certain ways, is surely ascertainable by direct inspection and as relevant to design as anything could possibly be. There is indeed an enormous area of this sort in which our conversation is easy. But when we come to the ensemble properties of patterns overall, we find ourselves once more in a problematic area. At least three factors enter here. First, since the design significance of a pattern as a whole must lie in its being just the one unique pattern it is, there must be some looseness of fit between the assigned pattern and the denumerable features on the basis of which it is assigned. But this is true of anything that is said of any complex situation and requires no special consideration.[52] Second, patterns may be read in different ways: even a checkerboard is indifferently an arrangement of black and white squares, a black square with white squares on, a white square with black squares on, or a linear grid with particolored interstices, to name only the grossest alternatives, and its nature as an aesthetic object is a function of the way in which these and other more complex possibilities interact. And third, it is seldom clear whether an overall pattern character has or lacks an evaluative component. Symmetry, it might seem, has none, provided that term is interpreted as identity of design on either side of one or more axes; grace, on the other hand, seems highly value laden, though grace too could be defined descriptively in terms of appropriateness to organic movement.[53] But it is really seldom clear how the matter stands, because one presumably would not bother to mention the symmetry or the grace unless one thought the property aesthetically significant—and, reverting to our second case, one may now add that one would probably not think it worth saying (assuming, as we are entitled to do, that the context is one of works of art) that, for instance, the side of a checkerboard square measured 1.75 centimeters unless one meant to imply that the design was one in which exact measurements were relevant to a proper appreciation of the pattern.

We might now wonder whether it is true, as it seemed at first to be, that at least some pattern characters are indubitably present and indubitably relevant. That confidence rested on the certainty and neutrality of discourse about elements and combinations. But

I pointed out in the last chapter that what is to count as an element in a pattern must depend on the pattern it is an element in—or, we should perhaps rather say, an element *of*. If what we have to do with is a visible pattern rather than an audible or legible one, whatever is an element in the pattern must be something inherently visible, hence belong to the surface as surface rather than the pigment of which the surface is made. But what parts of the surface are elements in the pattern? *Minima visibilia*—but how determined, and from what distance, and with or without what lenses? Or the elements that mechanically form the surface, if these can be determined—brush strokes, color dots in screen processes, continuous lines in drawings of the appropriate sort? Visibly homogeneous patches—but on what criterion of homogeneity? Or gross units, whether homogeneous or not, that are the lowest one can get on some preferred description or dissection of the pattern—the end of the little finger in a figure painting, a blade of grass in a landscape? One descends to facetiousness, because it soon becomes ludicrously obvious not only that what sort of thing is an element depends on how one reads the pattern overall but that the notion of an element has no clear and uniform application outside of notational and quasi-notational systems in which pattern making is methodically reduced to an assembling of units.[54] Typically, our recognition of the design starts with a sense of the whole, as a unity or as an assemblage of complexes, and our analysis then reaches downward along no fixed channels and with no determinate end. Given that one was in perfect agreement with someone else about the pattern and composition of a picture, it does not follow that one would be committed to a single analysis of its composition, determinate and exclusive down to the last detail. Typically, one switches from one mode of analysis to another freely: the test of agreement is not that two people say exactly the same but that neither dissents from what the other says.

One set of characterizations of works of art remains to be dealt with: the terminology of styles. Such terms as "mannerism" and "cubism" allude to bodies of practice united historically and synergetically: in *SA* I called them syndromes. Such terminology may be regarded with equal justice as classificatory and characterizing, for it serves indifferently to pick out a body of coherent practice and to indicate where its coherence lies. But it may also be used purely to classify, with sole reference to social or spatiotemporal connections, or purely to characterize, since what is deemed to impart coherence to one body of practice could always in principle impart a like coherence to like bodies elsewhere. It is therefore not surprising that the problems about the use of such terms are among the most tangled, refractory, and notorious in criticism. What makes such terms especially problematic is that so much theorizing is invested in them. They are weapons of critical and historical debate. On the one hand, critics and historians put such terms to such strict service in their own systems and schemes that one is tempted to say that the terms must be redefined to fit their function in each new theory. On the other hand, since it is in debate that they are used, those who use them so diversely can and do meet each others' minds; to say that the debaters are talking about different things is to miss the whole point of what they are doing.

The terminology of styles is far from homogeneous. Terms vary greatly in the extent to which they are bound to particular historical manifestations, or are associated with alleged phases in historical cycles, or impute psychological or social tendencies, or straightforwardly connote design characteristics, even though any such term is such that it could be put to any of these uses. Thus, the term "fauve" is used primarily to mean "produced by the group known as Fauves during their fauve period," and only secondarily to mean "characteristic or reminiscent of the Fauves," while the term "classical" cannot be pinned down at all to any one period or group of artists, but denotes indifferently a way of doing things and a historical status and only secondarily designates this or that actual group of persons or period. Most style terms are in fact ambiguous, and on different interpretations have affinities with different sets of other style terms.[55] An anatomy of style terminology would thus be an endlessly intricate and tiresome affair; actual discussions of such terms as "romanticism" achieve interest by ignoring some of the complexities of the conceptual framework in which such terms operate.[56] This said, I proceed to sketch some of the things that may be implied by such a term, bearing in mind that on any one occasion it may be quite unclear which of these implications such a term is supposed to have. Just as a term like "placid" makes a vague gesture in the direction of expressiveness, but is commonly used without any clear implication of what relation to literal placidity would prove on reflection to be the most relevant one, so a term like "romantic" makes a vague gesture in the direction of a vast range of familiar historical, cultural, stylistic, sociological, and psychological phenomena without its usually being at all clear which of the innumerable possibly relevant associations are the most relevant ones. Saying "romantic" is like saying "over there" with a casual wave of the hand.

The clearest use of a stylistic term is that of a word like "fauve" or "vorticist" to designate the work of a small group of artists working together for a while and elaborating a shared way of doing things. This will ordinarily include expressive, message, and pattern qualities as well as social connections. Provided that the group is clearly identified by its own members and by others, it may even be relatively easy to decide roughly which works are most characteristic of the common style—are, let us say, quintessentially fauve. Stylistic terms become progressively unclear as a group's practice becomes less homogeneous and as more and more extravagant suppositions are made about the implications and grounds of such homogeneity as there is.[57]

The first such complication arises when it is assumed that a style prevails in, or dominates, the art of its time: one speaks of the "romantic era," as if romantic artists had things all their own way, and then uses "romanticism" as meaning little more than "belonging to the art of the epoch when romantic art prevailed." A second complication comes in when it is supposed that the style not merely prevails in an age but also expresses the character of that age. One then supposes that the age has a character to express; the style is not a contingent collection of traits that might indeed be quite fortuitous, but is assumed to have an internal coherence corresponding to the cultural coherence of the *Zeitgeist*, whether or not one has independent reason for supposing such a *Zeitgeist* to exist.[58] A third complication is now possible: it is supposed that the defining characteristics of the age, being mutually coherent, are not historically bound, but could recur as a perennially possible cultural configuation: one then speaks not merely of "the baroque age" but of "baroque ages." A fourth complication, less important, arises if and when the coherence of the style is imputed to a complex personality type, which is encouraged in some cultures and phases of art history and relatively suppressed in others.[59] And, of course, it makes little difference to our argument whether on any given occasion it is really supposed that the artist as human being was possessed of this character, or whether the performance that is the work has its coherent quality by projecting a performer of this character. A fifth complication arises when it is supposed, as it often is of some style terms, that a style plays a specific role as reaction in an evolutionary or dialectical history of styles: that, for instance, mannerism inherently represents an inevitable reaction to the impossibility of either repeating or surpassing or ignoring the achievements of classicism, for now to call a work mannerist is to place it within a dynamic of art history. And from this comes a sixth complication: it is now easy to suppose, as many have supposed, that there is a natural history of styles in which processes of stylistic change repeat themselves analogically; in any sequential art history, we shall look to find archaic periods followed by classical ones, these by manneristic ones, and so on, and to call a work manneristic will be to assign to it properties deemed characteristic of ages overshadowed by classicism. As an alternative to these progressive complexities or confusions, one may use a stylistic term simply in relation to the initial uncomplicated common practice of a functioning group, but extending the term to whatever individual works and artists at any place and time *are as if* they had been produced by members of that group, in some preferred fashion or to some required degree. We are then free to say that the appearance of such a group of artists sharing a common practice draws attention to what that practice proves to have been a permanent possibility of style, by focusing attention on a possible congruity, the congruity that makes it possible for the group to develop their cohesion and their common practice in the first place. What were Rabelaisian humor and Kafkaesque situations called before Rabelais and Kafka? We don't know, but Rabelais and Kafka showed that such things had always been possible.

We recall that the reason why an element of dubitability entered into the ascription of pattern properties no less than into that of the more evidently problematic expression and message properties was that their aesthetic relevance depends on them being design properties in our sense, that is, on their being the ground of the appreciation of a performance. They therefore rest like the others on a sense of what could conceivably be intended, on what it makes sense to do; and this basic judgment, however self-evident it must often seem, rests ultimately on a psychological and historical comprehension. It is in stylistic properties, where the interpretation grounding appreciation is one relating to a specific constellation of intentions, however "natural" it may be, that this aspect of the ascription of properties becomes most evident. Such understanding, we have amply seen, cannot be determinate: we cannot ever justifiably place limits on the possibilities of human autonomy and freedom, and the limits of our understanding are only our limitations. It is for this reason that it was fashionable in the early decades of this century to decry all use of style terminology or ascription to genres: it was felt that this ascription was invariably restrictive, never illuminating.[60] But surely we can say now that such ascription, however provisional, is necessary and necessarily involved in all appreciation—so much so that Hirsch found it useful to coin the notion of the "intrinsic genre" of each individual work (1967, 80), the unit class to which it alone belongs, which in our terms coincides with the recognition of just what performance it is.

One use of style terms seems unproblematic: the use of a term like "fauve" to designate the shared quality of the characteristic works of a small group of mutually interacting and collaborating artists at a given place and time. And if, on a larger scale, we could bring ourselves to apply such a term as "mannerist" to a perceptibly shared quality of the work done by the members of a historically identified movement, without implying that that quality has any particular etiology but admitting that it may be a mere fortuitous congeries, the term would have the innocuous meaning of "done by a member of this group in their characteristic manner" or "done in the manner characteristic of this group." Theoretically this might be so. But in practice the artistic movements that give their names to such styles are neither homogeneous nor historically sharply delineated: different people do different things, members come and go, the group itself gains and loses coherent identity in ways that call for historical judgment to chronicle.[61] To take one notorious instance, different critics purport to correct each other by defining "mannerism" in different ways. They choose different starting points, different diagnostic features, and different paradigms of what is typical or quintessential mannerist work, as well as invoking different historical and psychological etiologies. A person might perhaps wonder why the critics involved in such controversies insist, as we noted above, on debating with each other by calling what they are doing a redefinition of mannerism, rather than the definition of a somewhat different configuration (paramannerism or something). Are they not needlessly quarreling over a word? But the answer seems to be that the function of such terms as "mannerism," when historically bound in the way we are considering, is to make the history of art intelligible by reducing it to a finite number of "movements" whose progress and interrelations are comprehensible in the sense that we can see the point of what was done and what happened, to explain the influence of what was influential, and to leave as little work as possible inexplicable, or explicable only in terms of fortuitous concatenations of chance events. And such historical explanation has a double purpose: it must make plain what happened in terms that are not anachronistic, that answer to what a deepening historical knowledge will continue to find nourishing, and must make that history comprehensible to us today, explain changes by reference to features that contemporary criticism can recognize and accept. It is then possible to view controversies about the nature of mannerism, not as logomachies, but as rival attempts to arrive at the one true and finally best account of the history of art. But it is not at all necessary. It may be that the revisionary seeks merely to produce an account that will fit into a history that his contemporaries will find a greater aid to comprehension. And it may equally well be that one person will find several views of mannerism, covering many of the same works but adopting different perspectives, equally attractive and complementarily necessary to his fuller understanding. We do not ordinarily find it the best way to study the history of a period to confine oneself to a single narrative, nor do we treat alternative accounts of the same events as contributing simply as parts to a whole ideally comprehensive narrative. To commit oneself permanently to a single meaning for the term "mannerism," or to refuse to accept for the time being a critic's redefinition of mannerism as definitive for one viewpoint, would be a comparable impoverishment of the understanding.[62]

We began this discussion of the characterization of works of art with some idea that the peculiarity of the concept of a work of art might generate a characteristic terminology—an assumption that seems to have guided the discussion of many aestheticians and theorists of criticism in the present century. And we have passed under review a number of different sorts of terms that are used in discussing art, whose peculiarities have been involved in this debate. But it has surely become clear, especially from our discussion of prima facie expressive characterizations, that an effective discussion of the characterization of works of art cannot work back from considering the peculiarities—the logical grammar, as it used to be called—of individual terms, but must proceed from a consideration of critical needs. Rather than consider what the term "mannerism" has been taken to mean, and how it has proved ambiguous, we should consider (as glancingly we did) why the history of art is written and hence how it must be written; we should then be able to see how a term like "mannerism" might fit into such discourse in this way or that. Rather than discuss the implications of calling a piece of music cheerful as we followed the example of many philosophers in doing, we should consider, for instance, that works of art as we have defined them must have an expressive dimension and the variety of ways in which this dimension enters into discourse; we can then see without further ado how "cheerful" might be used in such contexts and for such purposes, without wasting time on what other things someone might mean by "cheerful" in other contexts. It is clear, then, that the next task that confronts us is a brief consideration of the whole activity of criticism in relation to art.

VIII

THE CLASSICAL LINE
7: THE CRITICAL FUNCTION

Our discussion of characterization showed two things. First, certain doubts about how works of art are fitly to be described, and about how descriptions agreed to be fit are properly to be understood, reflect a contestability, a floating quality in designs themselves. Second, discussion of the terminology used in ascribing qualities of works of art must be inconclusive unless it forms part of a more general discussion of the kind of discourse in which it figures. On both accounts, our next move should be to say something about such discourse. The topic certainly seems to be a standard one in the philosophy of art: the nature and function of critical discourse. But can that be right? My introductory chapter urged that the philosophy of criticism is not part of the philosophy of art but a study all of its own, so that one could not expect a treatment based on the classical line in art theory to coincide with it. But perhaps that need not concern us here: if we say what the occasion demands of us, we need not worry whether a general theory of criticism might not look entirely different. In practice, it will be easy to find a line to follow, because the classical line is that strand in art theory to which the concept of criticism in all its transformations is congeneric. But it may be as well to mention three complicating factors.

First, if we consider the concept of criticism in its most general acceptance, we find that it is not only art that is criticized: one can criticize anything done or made, for to criticize anything is simply to consider how well it is done or made. This is the concept of criticism examined in *CC*; I will not repeat that examination here.[1] "Criticism" in this most general sense may be defined as "discourse apt to ground evaluation of performances," and not all performances are works of art. Since discussions of the logic and function of critical discourse do not usually take this into account, they do not consider how much of what they isolate as peculiar to art criticism is common to all criticism, and how much arises from the special character of artistic performances and our relation to them.

A second complication is this. For reasons that will soon be clear, if they are not already obvious, most writers assume that critical discourse is expert discourse: the critic is an authority.[2] But by no means all discourse apt to ground the evaluation of performances, and by no means all relevant discourse about works of art as such, is authoritative. Writers who ignore this fact fail to consider how much of what they say is relevant to all critical discourse and how much is peculiar to expert and authoritative discourse, and, conversely, how much is generally true of all expert discourse and how much is peculiar to criticism proper.[3]

The third complication, like the second, comes from thinking of criticism not merely as a type of discourse about a special sort of subject matter but as the type of discourse characteristic of the professional utterances of a special sort of person, the professed or professional critic. One identifies the critic as a writer on art or literature. But such a writer will be likely to consider art and literature in all relations—biographical, historical, or whatever. Writers on art, as a group, will write whatever interests them about art and also whatever they think will interest anyone else.[4] Thus, if we attempt, as some do (e.g. Weitz 1964), to arrive at a characterization of criticism by induction from what recognized critics do in business hours, the concept of criticism as a function or as a type of discourse must evaporate completely.[5] Yet it is hard to have as much faith in one's abstractions as one does in the observable character of a corpus.

The fact that an alternative and legitimate notion of how criticism is to be conceived, as any kind of expert writing on books or art, may lead people to identify as criticism whatever anyone who is an expert on books or art may say in the course of a work that is largely but not exclusively devoted to books or art, and even to call criticism whatever a professional critic writes for money, may remind us of something we left unsaid at the outset. Granted that we turn to critical discourse as to the wider context in which the vocabulary of criticism is deployed, what is the unit of discourse to which we should attend? Is it, as Frank Sibley (1959) supposed, the single proposition? If so, the unit of critical utterance must be something like a Kantian aesthetic judgment, a pronouncement whose warrant is the taste it expresses; but the real reason it must have that logical character is not anything epistemologically fundamental, but simply that the isolated pronouncement of a verdict was the unit chosen. Or is the unit of criticism the whole opus, the book or article? If so, much of what counts as critical discourse will be so only contextually, and any further pronouncement on the logical or rhetorical character of critical discourse is automatically precluded. Should we then, following the line of much philosophical writing of the last half century, identify criticism proper with arguments in which the vocabulary of criticism provides the terms? But, then, how is it established that critical discourse properly consists entirely of argumentation? Arnold Isenberg wrote a classic paper (1949) that could be construed as urging that in criticism proper there are no true arguments, only quasi arguments, considerations apt to determine the mind only in a context that the critical discourse indicated but could not specify. So perhaps we should say that the proper functional unit of critical discourse is the critique: all that part of the critical opus which bears on grounding the evaluation of performances, either in some determinable fashion or presumptively in that its irrelevance is not evident.[6] If there is a certain awkwardness in choosing among these alternatives, that may show something about the irremediable (because functionally necessary) vagueness of the concept of a context, the concept of discourse, and by inference the concept of criticism itself: we are speaking of strategies of the understanding.

Such labyrinths we may leave to their native minotaurs. Our thread is tied firmly to our definition of the work of art as a performance considered with respect to its design. That is, the work of art is an object for appreciation; and discourse relevant to works of art as such will be discourse expressing appreciation, elucidating the grounds and precise quality of an appreciatory experience or judgment, and guiding toward appreciation. This tells us at once what we must take critical discourse to be. To reward contemplation there must be something to contemplate, something to look at it, and that means that the work must have at least such complexity and richness as might in some circumstances resist comprehension.[7] There must then be a place for informed or wise discourse to assist in identifying the performance: saying what has been done; in elucidating the performance: enabling the hearer or reader to perceive what has been put there to perceive; and in evaluating the performance: providing some guidance and assurance as to whether the labor of coming to see what has been done, of training a sense and forming a taste, will be repaid, and how it will be repaid. And that really is the gist of what I have to say; it remains only to reiterate and elaborate.

What I have just said of specifically artistic criticism is quite generally true of any criticism of any performance. The concepts of criticism and performance, let us recall, may be defined in relative independence, or they may be interdefined. A performance is what is performed by a performer in his performing of it, anything done or made conceived simply as the outcome of its doing and making. Criticism is discourse apt to ground evaluation of anything done or made. But a performance may also be defined as the proper object of criticism as such, and criticism as discourse appropriate to performances as such. To speak of a performance is to fasten on an area of space/time and to pick out within it those goings-on that, taken together, constitute getting something done. And to say what the performance was is to say what got done, that is, to identify the task in which success was achieved or missed; and that should require two things—that one establish a generic kind of end that was to be encompassed and that one say what constituted the actual achievement. We need to know what the performer was up to as well as what he brought off. Finally, I insisted that the notion of getting something done includes that of succeeding where one might have failed, the idea of an achievement, so that, to that extent, the concept of performance is inescapably evaluative. So if criticism is to be all and only that discourse that is peculiarly appropriate to performances as such, it will have a generic aspect (identifying the type of task performed), a descriptive and interpretive aspect (explaining just what the performer's performance was, what he did, and what he was doing when he did it), and an evaluative aspect— not in the sense that the intent of such discourse is always or usually to reach a summary verdict or appraisal, but in the sense that everything said implies that the performer was doing something in which he might succeed or fail, the point of the activity being to succeed.

At this point we come across what seems at first a paradox in the notion of criticism. In everyday speech, to criticize someone is to draw attention specifically to the failures in his performance in the light of a presumed superior knowledge of what he should have done instead, or how he should rather have done it. But the account given in the preceding paragraph made it seem that criticism should rather be positive in tone, in that whatever in a performance fails of success is rather a misperformance: to speak adversely of a performance can only be either to show that the wrong thing was performed, or that what took place failed to be a performance.[8] But really there is no paradox. Criticism in its most general sense is an exercise of the judicial function, playing the *krites*, the (Greek) judge. But the obvious occasion for doing this, when it needs doing and needs no special gift to do, is when clear standards for performance are applicable and have not been met, that is, when there is an easily recognized and clearly authenticated right way of doing something, and this has not been taken. If everything has been done right, there is no need to call in the judge, no need to talk about it.

Such facile criticism, predominantly negative in tone and depending on prior notions of a task to be done and a standard to be met, is not typical of criticism in art.[9] It is easy to see why. The only task by which the artist's performance is fitly judged is that of producing an object for appreciation; the only criteria of success is in the quality of appreciation achieved and allowed. The critic of such a performance cannot proceed by enunciating standards or rules or go on to denounce deviations.[10] His criticism must be an exercise of connoisseurship, of self-aware appreciatory skill. Rules, standards, general principles, will be cited only to explain why the attempt to appreciate has foundered. For in the last resort (as every charlatan knows), the critic of such a performance can be more secure in his positive judgment than in his negative judgment. He knows that what he appreciates can be appreciated, but he can only know that a performance that resists appreciation does so under certain aspects, the aspects he has tried and been able to think of; he may suspect, but can never be certain, that there is no aspect under which the work might delight or reward.

The primary skill of the moral or legal critic is his knowing what to condemn and how to condemn it: his laws, standards, rules, conventions, shibboleths, are means to that end. But the primary skill of the critic in the arts is his knowing how to appreciate, his ability to make fine discriminations surely—not indeed infallibly, but without being taken in by the meretricious, the fashionable, and, above all, the spurious. If he knows how to condemn, it is because he more importantly knows how to appreciate where others fail to do so. And his social function tends to be positive: to recommend for purchase or favor or patronage or reward, rather than to censure for failure to fulfill a social demand.

I argued in chapter 26 in *CC* that works of art are preeminently proper objects for criticism. This is partly because they have eminently the character of performances, combining the isolation and the reference back to agency in a most marked way. But it is also because they are the kind of performances they are, in which so much is so clearly relevant to comprehension and enjoyment. Since the justification of the existence of a work of art is that its contemplation should be valuable, the evaluative function cannot be amiss; and since its justification further requires that its way of rewarding contemplation shall be distinctive, the interpretive function is likely to be in place. This is the more likely in that, as we have seen, the design of a work of art is inherently contestable, is attributed rather than possessed; and we should expect it to be often hard to find just that reading of an object's surface which will enable us to see in it a coherent performance. And at least in ages like ours, where the public for an art extends wider than its practice, the traditions of design that make comprehension a practical possibility as opposed to a merely theoretical one are certain to change faster than the reaction of any public that cannot devote to its appreciation a measure of time and energy comparable to that which the artist has expended on production. An informed body of go-betweens will be needed to keep the uninitiated informed on how to look and what to look for and, in more general terms, on what current patterns of expectation (that is, genres) prevail to which works may be profitably related.

The critical function becomes important whenever a public becomes estranged. The estrangement may be that of students confronted with the deposit of a culture that has become alien, of grandees investing their wealth in objects whose immunity to future depreciation—or whose conduciveness to present prestige—they must take on trust, or simply of people with no leisure to keep up with all the studio trends.[11] But what of the situation in which traditions are limited and fixed—where the acceptable value of a new work is only that it does very well the sort of thing that has long or, as such a community is likely to say, always been done?[12] In such a situation the critical function would be, if not quite abrogated, greatly modified. The task of interpretation would be to detect just those refinements that constituted the excellence of the latest variation, that is, in what precise way the deviations from expectation must be taken, or what they must be divined to be, if one is to appreciate the potentialities of the design. The very certainty of the expectations aroused and relied on by a sure tradition would surely afford ground for a subtle play upon them, and this should afford scope for the critic's interpretive art.

In such a time of unquestioned tradition, however, the generic function of criticism should vanish. Those people who oppose generic criticism often suppose that the practice of referring works of art to kinds antecedently known presupposes that an exhaustive repertoire of such kinds is current. This seems improbable. Rather, the availability of such a repertoire makes generic criticism otiose: what kind a work belongs to ceases to be a critical question. As for the evaluative function, that would tend to split into two. There is the question of whether the work succeeds in meeting the requirements of its assigned category; and, if it does, the critic will still have the task of evaluating the success and the scope of its operation within these terms of reference. There is, in a sense, a set task to be performed, such as that of writing an epic or whatever; but the question of artistic excellence is not thereby reduced to that of whether the task has been properly carried through.

I have been writing as if there were two possibilities for art: that a set of generic possibilities should prevail without question, or that genres should have a merely provisional and heuristic value for artists and critics alike. But this is not so. Works of art as we know them could not be produced if generic traditions were so rigid that the only evaluative question for criticism was that of conformity, for design acts would then be impossible; and if no generic similarities at all could be identified, designs themselves might well be unidentifiable, as Bond (1975) argued. The only domain hospitable to art would be that in which generic possibilities are recognized but not imposed, questioned but not precluded. I proceed to some explorations of this domain.

The Generic Function: Originality and Tradition

I have urged that the recognition and appraisal of performances, and the appreciation of designs in particular, rest on presumptions of what could conceivably be attempted and hence on notions of what is in principle acceptable as a design—what could be used as an element, what could be significant as a relation.[13] But these presuppositions may function in two ways. They function inarticulately and without being thought about: we simply construe the design intuitively, and it is only on reflection that it occurs to us that our intuition rests on such presuppositions. But they also function explicitly as critical weapons. If our intuitions about the design are to be conveyed, explained, and defended to others whom we do not know beforehand to be like-minded with ourselves, our presuppositions must be made accessible—first to our private comprehension of ourselves and then to others. This will require that they be articulated with some measure of formality into notions of what different sorts of designs are possible in principle and likely in practice.

It used to be argued that generic reference in criticism was necessarily mistaken, as showing that the critic had his mind on something other than the work under discussion—the "something other" usually being the standard works that established the type by which his expectations were organized (see Prall 1936, 185ff., and cf. *SA* 171–172). But such reference may be apposite, since at least the more public anticipations about form often enter into designs as vital elements or principles of organization: it is sometimes inept to read a design otherwise than as a variation on a type of design that has become established. A critic may indeed make the mistake of condemning *Paradise Lost* because it purports to be (or he takes it to purport to be) an epic, but is unlike the *Aeneid*, just as someone might commit the absurdity of condemning a Picasso portrait as nonnaturalistic. But it is not that the *Aeneid* and the practices of naturalistic portraiture are irrelevant. Rather, part of the point of *Paradise Lost* is that it is unlike the *Aeneid* in specific ways, and one could hardly appreciate *Paradise Lost* without being aware of those differences; and part of the point of Picasso's designs is that they depart from ("distort") in certain precise ways the schemes of representation that we identify as naturalistic.[14] One could hardly come to terms with Picasso unless one already knew what naturalistic painting was like and took it as some kind of norm.

The opponents of generic criticism might concede what I have said and still dismiss it as relating only to special cases, however numerous such cases might be in this or that historical situation. It remains the besetting sin of critics, they might insist, that they have unduly narrow notions of what could have been attempted or intended in a work. And it is certainly true that this is one of the ways in which critics most frequently and seriously annoy creative artists. But an abuse does not discredit a proper use, and a tendency among critics to be too narrow in their preconceptions does not mean that they can do without preconceptions altogether. I urged a little while ago that the "what" in "what has been succeeded in" could be wholly internal, to the point where one could rest content with saying of a work that "It is what it is and it does what it does," the further specification of its success being in terms of encomium. But that does not mean that a design can be confidently read off from a work in the absence of any understanding of the relevant tradition and of the general attitudes of the culture to which it pertains; and, in consequence, it cannot be explained to another unless either such understanding is already shared or else the critic says something to indicate what those traditions and attitudes are (or were) like.[15]

Every work, no doubt, must justify itself through its uniqueness. It is sometimes thought that this requirement implies that what makes any work valuable must be what differentiates it from all other works, that a work is unoriginal and hence unsuccessful insofar as it belongs to or refers to any artistic tradition.[16] But this doctrine belongs, not to the tradition of theorizing about art we are now exploring, but to the quite different tradition that equates art with expression; and even there its legitimacy is not beyond dispute. The oddness of the view outside of any special theoretical context can easily be seen by considering an analogous case. To the lover, the loved one is unique, irreplaceable. But that does not mean that she or he is loved only for what differentiates him or her from all other persons. She is loved for the special way she does what all do: the way she talks, walks, hugs; her nose and her knees are more precious than any other knees or nose, but it is a nose, and they are knees. Her uniqueness includes her special ways of being a woman, being Irish, being a professor of French. Her way of sharing cannot be valued separately from what she shares. So with our argument. The classical line requires that the work of art be worth contemplating, and I have argued that it must thereby be such as can be ascribed to a design act. But we saw that such an act must often, if not always, take the form of variation within a tradition, and in such cases the value of varying cannot be sundered from the value of what is varied. Nothing in our argument assigns any exceptional value to cases, if such there be, in which the design act takes other forms.[17]

That the required uniqueness of the work of art is not unrelatedness or independence of tradition is at once evident when we consider that open-mindedness is not the only demand we make of a critic. We demand also that he be well informed.[18] Artists are as likely to accuse their critics of being ignorant as of being hidebound. And the ignorance in question can only be that of relevant practices and traditions.[19] To say that every work has its own unique character and quality is not at all to deny that it can be understood only in relation to other works; it is only to say that its qualities could not be reduced without remainder to those of other works.

Suppose one were to take the extreme position, here repudiated, that every work of art must be considered entirely on its own terms, hence without reference to any previous work. Still, to demand this treatment for a specific performance would be to demand that it be considered as a work of art, that is, in respect to its design. But what could warrant such a demand? Surely among the conditions would have to be *some* relevant likeness to *some* extant work of art.[20] It will do us no good here to argue that if works of art are each sui generis in the strongest possible sense, there could be no art critics, because there is no reason a priori why there should be art critics; and those who hold such an extreme thesis about art are likely to deny that criticism is a legitimate activity. But we may be allowed to repeat our old question how a performance could be isolated and identified at all, if not in the light of some idea of what might be being performed. How, indeed, could we consider a work of art on its own terms unless we could establish what those terms were?

Notoriously, an analogous argument can be developed from the artist's point of view. A poet cannot know what a poem is, so that he can set about producing his own unique poems, otherwise than from his experience of extant poems. The poet must write in terms of what poetry has been, whether to continue or to counter it; the critic must explain what is new, but such an explanation can only proceed by relating it to what is old. Tradition and originality are not opposed, then, in the sense that one can proceed without reference to the other. Yet there is clearly some tension between the claims of the past and those of the future. It would be agreeable to settle for some simple formula, such as that tradition provides the matter for which the artist's originality devises a form. But that could be misleading, if it suggests that the relation between the new and the old is always the same. An artist may exploit a tradition in such a way that the relation of his work to some predecessor is part of his subject; he may work within a tradition in an unself-conscious way; he may equally unself-consciously ignore tradition in such a way that only the hindsight of later critics detects in him the historical dimension; he may make the relation to the historical process itself the center of gravity of his art.[21] We can only be sure that to have artistic and vital significance a work must stand in a definite relation to an artistic situation,[22] just as a person cannot act effectively and freely in the real historical world except by taking effective account of a definite situation in that world.[23]

The tradition that stands in perpetual vital tension with originality is not to be understood simply as whatever has been done in the past, as some of the phrases used above might suggest. It is rather what is at a given time available from the past as a resource in the way in which it is available. And its availability lies in its appearing as what is ready for change and, hence, as in itself not static but the transmitter of preceding change. But here a difference appears. For the artist or critic who defines a situation as revolutionary, it is a practical necessity to define "the tradition" as static, immovable, monolithic, whose dynamism is only one of energetic self-perpetuation; for artists and critics who define themselves either as reformist or conservative (or who do not define themselves at all, for it is always the way of naive conservatives to think of themselves as unpolitical), tradition appears as endlessly changing. It is the reflective in both camps who perceive that every revolt finds a new monolith to measure itself against.

The tension between tradition and originality works itself out in familiar critical debates, which are as polymorphous and perpetual as that tension itself. They are irresoluble, like many theoretical controversies, because each side has hold of a half-truth that is in constant danger of being denied or forgotten; and the cool irenic mood that would give each side its due seems to do no justice to the passion and concern of either. It will do no harm to glance briefly at some of the pairs of opposed terms in which these debates are couched.

The work-in-itself, to begin with, stands over against the work-in-relation. On the one hand, each work is meant to stand by itself, to be received and appreciated by a public that has nothing before its mind but the work it perceives and understands. On the other hand, each work belongs to an oeuvre that it extends and in which it is rooted and nourished, to a style that it enriches and from which it takes resonance, and to a personal and social context of which it is a vital part.

A second antithesis is that between the aesthetic, the purely contemplable, conceived simply as characteristic object of a special sort of perception or attitude, and the artistic, the knowingly contrived for contemplation. For it may be argued that, insofar as a work is truly original, nothing can be said about the conditions of its making that can be relevant to its understanding or appreciation: it is indeed as if it had not been made at all, for the processes of its production, however factually necessary, are in principle inaccessible to the public, a sort of *Ding an sich*. Slightly different is the contrast between genius, the gift for the unprecedented, and craftsmanship, which is a versatile handling of what is in some sense already mastered. In this contrast, it is not necessarily supposed that nothing can relevantly be said about how the work is produced:

rather, it was once fashionable to liken the work of genius to spontaneous and organic growth (which follows no precepts, but is nonetheless orderly) and to equate craftsmanship with mechanical processes of addition, replication, and manipulation *ab extra*. Again, the autonomy of the work, the requirement that its own inherent tendencies establish the canons by which it is understood—that it, or the group of works of which it is a member, create the taste by which it is to be enjoyed—runs up against the equally inescapable demand that the work be understood in its proper context or frame of reference; yet both these demands call for the same thing, respect for the integrity of the work, which may be held to be violated equally by wrenching it from its vital setting (as when a totem pole is taken from its village setting and placed in a museum) and by taking it simply as a function of its environment. Similarly, when the symbolic reference of a work to its setting is conceded, the tension between originality and tradition reappears as that between the way every work symbolizes itself and expresses its artist's personality in just that phase of it which the work does give expression to, and the not less evident and necessary way in which the work must typify an aspect of its age that it also expresses, since his and its way of manifesting their individual selves will be, inevitably, ways of expressing a manner of work and a mode of life that took their meaning from that age. So too, finally, the innovation demanded of the artist (for which the critic must bare his innocent eye) is balanced by the requirement that he be serious, responsible, not arbitrary.

So far, then, are tradition and originality from being incompatible that the most original work is likely to be the most thoroughly traditional, for it takes account of tradition *up till now*; the "traditional" work that serves up a pastiche of past styles uses the past, not as tradition, a transmission of vital meanings, but as a junk heap of materials to be exploited.[24] If, then, the antithesis of tradition and originality is understood as one of relative emphasis on continuity or discontinuity between a new work and its predecessors, which are in either case wholly relevant to it, it seems related both to the polarity of chaos and cliché that we saw marked the limits of intelligibility in communication and to the polarity of freedom and reason that R. M. Hare (1963) has emphasized and explored. Free and responsible action, Hare argues, must be principled, must be based on a decision for which there are reasons; but it must also be free in the sense that one takes full personal responsibility for it. A fortiori, an action cannot be moral if it is undertaken without regard for the standards, demands, and expectations of the community one belongs to; but this affiliation and allegiance do not entail compliance, or reduce morality to conformity, or absolve the individual of responsibility to his conscience.[25]

Interpretation and the Hermeneutic Problem

The generic function of identifying a performance is not sharply distinguished from the interpretive function of elucidating it. In both cases, it seems, one says what has been done, and fully to identify the task performed is one and the same thing as fully to describe the performing of it. But though the operations may thus be identical, the functions differ. The generic function has to do with our relevant anticipations, what we are to look for; the interpretive function has to do with what we find. The generic function seeks to identify the performance, interpretation assumes that it has been identified. And, as we have just seen, the generic approach assumes, as the other does not, that what the performance is has been fully determined by a performer in the context of a practical tradition. The problems of interpretation thus admit of independent treatment.

Performance and criticism are interdefinable terms. The reciprocity might make the practical relationship between them equivocal. A successful critique, one supposes, is one apt to what has been performed. But might not a performance be constituted by the success of the critique itself? This is not a merely empty or facetious suggestion. Art objects are constituted such retrospectively, by adoption; and, though this could not be true of works of fine art as here defined, there is nothing to prevent it holding for at least some works of art. We have indeed ruled out as mere mistakes (though not as *critical* mistakes, only as historical ones) those cases in which a performance is divined where there really was no performer. But where there was intelligent agency, the matter becomes cloudier: people often do things without thinking about them, do things without knowing that they do them (in a fit of absence of mind). In fact, a person can do something he *could not know* that he was doing (we often say just this when what was done is the initiation of a train of events); and the creation of a work of art is just such an originative act as leaves us unsure of the limits on what may properly be said of it.

There is a distinction to be made here. The "camp" sensibility that converts bits of old tat into objects for appreciation does so by developing a perspective, a critical stance, from which they can be relished. The objects of such a sensibility end up as being art objects rather than works of art, in that the campy person congratulates himself on his fancy taste rather than the artisan on his creative power or technical prowess. A quite different situation is exemplified by the *politique des auteurs* that discovered works of art and artists among the Hollywood studio output of the thirties, once more by discovering and developing a way of perceiving and a critical position and method, but this time one that isolated and recognized artistry. The studio technicians and directors seldom thought of themselves as artists, nor were they thought of in that way by their employers and initial audiences: here surely, we feel like saying, the critic has created the work of art in retrospect, rather than the artist producing a performance that the critic had only to appreciate and explicate. Yet it seems utterly outrageous to generalize from this case to the point where one says that Bach's *Art of Fugue* was a mere inchoate mass of notes until some critic or critics came along, blew the dust off, and made it into a work of art by their creative insight.[26]

One might try to deal with the irritating paradox or conundrum we have just generated by distinguishing a successful critique from a valid one. A successful critique determines performance by isolating an entity that it shows to be meaningful, picking out from the phenomena that prima facie constitute such an entity some significant set; but what constitutes a relevant and valid critique is determined by the actual structure that a real live performer imparts to his performance.[27] But a more straightforward and common-sense answer serves us better. The case of Bach and that of the director of Hollywood B movies are really different in an obvious way that we should respect. Why should we not say that the performer determines what his performance is, not by decreeing what it shall be taken to be, but by performing it, and does so precisely to the extent that his performance is fully determinate and fully successful (which, as we saw, may come to the same thing);[28] but insofar as it is incompletely determinate or partially unsuccessful, the critic (some critic, any critic, a consensus or rabblement of critics . . .) has the task of determining what the performance *is*—and hence, retrospectively and generously, of constituting it what it *has always been*? It is, no doubt, a matter of degree: the critic can always find leeway in the determinate and must have something to go on in the indeterminate; but cases may tend indefinitely toward either end of the continuum.[29] One cannot decide, however, which of these situations prevails (or may be more properly judged to prevail) otherwise than by oneself exercising a critical judgment on the performance itself and on whatever critical performances purport to determine it—for a critique, being itself a performance, must be subject to the same potential ambiguities as any other performance (cf. *CC* chap. 9).

Should we say that a successful critique gives a viable, or convincing, interpretation of a performance, and that a valid critique interprets it correctly? Perhaps; but the concept of interpretation, on the face of it, sorts ill with the notion of performance. An interpretation is the work of an *interpres* (etymology does not, I think, deceive us here), a go-between; as such, its function is that of a translator-interpreter, namely, to complete a communication that without it would be incomplete, abortive. And the concept of a performance is essentially of something complete. In one way this does not matter, for it costs us nothing to say that what is perfect in itself may be imperfect as a communication, that the artist's work may be complete and determinate, and yet the interpreter be faced with the open task of fashioning something new that will serve as analogue of the old work in a different context, and to repeat that a work of art is an ambiguous object that is both perfected thing and utterance in the conversation of mankind. But in another way, it does matter; that was too easy. The work of art is inherently interpretable; its typical perfection is a perfection of richness that lends itself to commentary.[30]

The contrast between perfected performance and incomplete message is precisely the wrong one to shed light on critical interpretation in the arts. It is the perfection of the work that lends itself to interpretation, that makes it worth interpreting; and the imperfection of the message that the translator must handle is typically, not that of formal defect that requires supplement or exegesis, but that of an object (presumed perfect in itself) that needs to be complemented by a precise counterpart. The criterion for a perfect translation-interpretation is, first, that it get the message right—that is, understand the text completely and correctly in the light of its intended and actual structure; and, second, that it provide a counterpart that conveys precisely this message to its intended recipient, without omission, addition, or distortion. This criterion has no application to art. If one could ascertain with certainty that a work was correctly understood (which presupposes that there can be a correct understanding, which may be the point chiefly at issue), interpretation would be needed only where the public's lack of special historical knowledge required expert supplement. The point emerges clearly from a consideration of the central thesis of Hirsch's *Validity in Interpretation* (1967). His argument that, if there is to be a single standard that establishes one uniquely valid interpretation, the standard must be what the artist intended his work to mean, seems incontrovertible. His contention that this standard is in principle applicable, because the meanings of works are intentional objects, not psychological events, and so can be objects for many minds, seems reasonable (to a phenomenologist, it is obvious). But he quite fails to meet the well-established objection that such meanings cannot in practice be recovered. Except in some very special cases where an ambiguity can be removed, a fully realized intention cannot be distinguished from the work itself, since the relevant intention must be the articulation of a design; and an unrealized intention is of doubtful relevance and questionable authority. A certain melancholy interest may attach to what a botcher or a novice thought he had done, or hoped he was going to do, but the interest is a marginal one to the business of criticism. So "what the artist meant by his work" turns out to be what the work must be taken to mean in the light of the most relevant available evidence.

It may be that the only place for the notion of validity or correctness in criticism of the arts is in connection with the sort of historical exegesis that explains obsolete iconography or provides glossaries for archaic or dialect terms, where, in fact, the critical interpreter acts as translator. A view of critical interpretation on these lines was once proposed by Monroe Beardsley (1966b). An interpretation, in this view, is a purportedly correct reading and, as such, is possible only when rules of correctness can be applied— when, for instance, there are systems of representation that can be learned or symbolisms of which one might compile an iconology. But though this view has a straightforwardness and a demystifying air that recommends it, it seems inadequate. It suggests that no critical interpretation could ever be illuminating, and that there can be no more than one acceptable interpretation of a work. But that is a curious view to hold, unless one merely wishes to place a restriction on the word "interpretation" and use something else ("reading"?) for what "interpretation" used to mean.

If we reject Beardsley's view as claiming too much for correctness, we might go to the other extreme with C. L. Stevenson (1962).

249

Stevenson thinks of an interpretation as an evaluation of approaches. The interpreter invites his public to view a work in a certain light; and his interpretation admits only of pragmatic support, by the actual persuasiveness of what he says and the real or promised advantages of what he proposes. To say that his view of the work is a *good* one would only be to express approval of it and recommend it; to claim that his view was *correct* could only be to say that it coincided with that of the best judges—and to say that they were the *best* judges would be merely to recommend that their judgment be accepted. But Stevenson's view, though like Beardsley's it has an attractive directness, is also like his in not being quite believable or often believed; for, though we may concede that calling an interpretation correct can seldom be made out to mean more than Stevenson says, Stevenson's view also forbids us to mean more by calling an interpretation *incorrect* than that we agree with those who disagree with it—and surely some purported interpretations are just blunders, mistakes, absurdities.[31] One's failure to understand a work may be such that one does not reach that level of comprehension from which all critical disagreements start.[32]

Evidently, what Stevenson calls interpretation starts where what Beardsley calls interpretation leaves off. But I would say that anyone who undertakes the task of interpretation is going to have to do both sorts of things, and the word "interpretation" is usually taken to cover both of them. And we may take it, I think, that at least the elements of an interpretation may be correct or incorrect. Even at Stevenson's level, an interpretation may be found incorrect, though a claim of positive correctness would be harder to make out. We need not dissent from Stevenson's dissolution of incorrectness: we may, if we wish, concede that what we call a simple blunder is simply an interpretation that would convince no one, in the sense that nothing that could be said in its favor could be traced to anything in the work itself or in the relation of the work to a context. An interpretation that could be so traced would then be *not incorrect* even if not *correct*.[33]

Whatever we may think of the applicability of the concept of correctness, and whatever we may concede to Stevenson's logical claim, a pragmatic criterion for evaluating interpretations is at once given if we accept that the interpreter's task is to make sense of something not at once intelligible.[34] To make sense *of the work* and not of something else, he must start from a choice of performance-constituting phenomena that are initially plausible as a coherent entity. To *make sense* of the work, his interpretation must fulfill two conditions: it must leave as little as possible unexplained (or inexplicable), and it must make the performance out to be as successful as possible. To make sense of a performance as a performance is to show its structure, how as many as possible of its elements cohere in as many ways as possible. A critique is shown up as inferior by how much of what prima facie should be included it has to leave out as irrelevant or accidental, and by the poverty and paucity of the justificatory relations revealed among what it does include.[35]

It is an apparent objection to what I have just said that it makes it impossible that a good interpretation should function as an exposé, whereas it would be a proper exercise of the interpretive function to reveal the meretriciousness and poverty of a work that had taken in all the fashionable critics, or to rescue the essential simplicity of a work from the overelaborations of its sophisticated exploiters. But I do not think this objection holds. The exposé makes the work out to be as successful as possible, but shows that that is less than we had previously thought possible. Attempts to debunk tend to fail just insofar as their derogations fail to meet the detail of the case that had been made out on the other side. And to rescue the simplicity of a work must again be to show that the complex relationships imputed by other writers do not obtain; otherwise, it is the claim to simplicity that fails. The criterion must always be whether the alleged elements, relations, qualities, and so on, were really discoverable, or were gratuitously imputed by critics or fraudulently suggested by the artist. This, since *ex hypothesi* alternative claims have been advanced, must always be a matter for judgment; but although our criterion for a satisfactory interpretation is not one that can be applied impersonally or automatically, it may serve to articulate what it is that we ask of an interpretation: that it enable us to see relations we were blind to before, that it deliver us from the spell of persuasive illusions, and that it account for the presence in the work of all that we find there, including what was otherwise inexplicable.

Having criteria for a good interpretation, or knowing what form such criteria should take, is not enough to give substance to the notion of the *best* or the *most satisfactory* interpretation. For it may be that divergent interpretations are compossible, and their divergence rationally explicable. That possibility would rule out the notion of a single interpretation that would be *the correct* one; it leaves ambiguous the notion of *the best* one, because the situation with interpretations might (as in Stevenson's analogy) be like that with views: we might agree that the best view of a building was obtained from a certain spot, without in any way suggesting that other views might not be good in their way, have something of their own to show, be nice for a change, and so on.

We are certainly accustomed to think that with plays, at least, a familiar play may profit from a novel production that, even though eccentric, sheds an intriguing new light; and opinions differ widely as to the endurable limits of such variation, their justification as performances *of the play* (and hence as interpretations thereof), and their proper relationship to standard or traditional performances within a cultural milieu.[36] Without entering the domain of the recognizably offbeat, it is clear that *Hamlet* can be read and played as the tragedy of a man who could not ascertain what his situation was; or of a man who, for reasons of state, was unable to do what he should and was unnecessarily bothered in his conscience about the resulting delays; or simply as a play whose author either was prevented by his neuroses from reducing it to a coherent order, or cynically spun out the action to fill up five acts with a series of loosely connected and insufficiently motivated pretexts. All of these things have been believed and acted on by people as intelligent, learned, and sensitive as ourselves—and much more famous.

How, in general, are divergent interpretations of the same work possible? The first thing to note is that there are at least three different ways in which they may diverge. First, the divergent interpretations may not be rivals, but partial treatments that might conceivably be combined into one grand whole. Theoretically, it looks as if this should not be so, for we required of an interpretation that it be comprehensive; but in practice, as our sample readings of *Hamlet* suggest, a critical interpretation singles out for emphasis one set of relations, and takes much for granted, leaving it to the reader's acumen to perceive how much fits in with the preferred reading and how little tells against it. It is then thinkable that an interpretation emphasizing certain relations should be supplemented by one emphasizing others, the likely relation being that in each case what one interpretation singles out for emphasis serves as coherent background for the other. But to say that such interpretations can be *summed* is a bit strong. What is foreground cannot at the same moment be background, and a combination of emphases cannot yield a version that emphasizes everything equally. Part of the meaning of such a partial interpretation is that it claims overriding significance for what it picks out.

Second, it is possible that two interpretations, though not summing, should not contradict in the sense that either asserts what another denies. They might correspond to the realization of different possibilities, much as two painters, using the same motif, might provide alternative representations, differing in style and treatment, but not ascribing to their common object any incompatible properties. Actual critical interpretations are analogous to such paintings in that normally they do not consist of such isolated assertions as we gave in connection with *Hamlet*, but are rhetorically complex prose structures. It may well happen that what one critic says is very unlike what another critic would say, and cannot be combined with it to make any consistent or coherent whole, without their definitely conflicting with or contradicting each other.

How should two such interpretations be compared? We face a choice of metaphors: they impose different structures, see in different lights, filter through different grids, view from different angles, distort with different prisms. No doubt different metaphors will impose themselves for different actual comparisons. It is at least clear that in reading a critique by an informed and sensitive person with a powerful personality and an effective style of his own, like F. R. Leavis, we learn something of how such a work appears to him. We get some idea of what it is like to be a different person reading the work. This is always interesting and enjoyable. It can tell us much both about the work and about the critic, and be very valuable on both counts; its value is comparable to that of a novelist's view of life. But, although we might be convinced by the interpreter that there is much in what he says, it is absurd to think that anyone of integrity would adopt as their own the critic's view in all its nuanced entirety, for that would be to become like the critic and unlike onself. As Leavis himself is fond of saying, the most positive response to the critic is "Yes, but. . . ."[37] With works of art as with other matters, one does not discuss matters with one's peers in order to acquire or impart opinions. Rather, one shares perspectives to supplement and correct one's own without losing its distinctive character. After talking to a powerful or striking personality, an impressionable chap like me may come away spouting his views, but these involuntary impersonations are eroded by time and erased or overlaid by counterimpressions.

We have been discussing a second form of divergence between interpretations, in which there is neither summation nor conflict. The third possibility is that there should be conflict. Hamlet cannot be both pathologically indecisive and fully justified in his abstention from murder; and this incompatibility remains, however nuanced, individuated, and elaborated the interpretations may be in which

the conflicting judgments are enshrined.[38] There are now two possibilities. Either at most one interpretation can be right, and all
others must be wrong, or else more than one of the mutually incompatible interpretations can be, not of course the *right* one, but
tenable, justifiable, reasonable.

Of the possibilities we have canvassed, the last is the most interesting. The ideal totality mooted in the first proves, as we saw,
impossible, and the case has no other interest; the interpretations
covered in the second case seem rather to add new structures to
that attributable to the work (as the landscape painter adds or
imposes an order that is not, and is not meant to be, that of the
scene) and, to that extent, escape the terms of our problem; and
the first version of the third possibility suggests a condition that
cannot be proved to obtain. Even if it did obtain, it would do us
no good: either we could not say which interpretation was correct,
so that it would be idle to postulate that any was correct, or, if by
chance we should be able to show that one interpretation was indeed
correct, its rivals would thereby be revealed as mere *mis*interpretations, demonstrated errors removed from our terms of reference.

There seem to be at least four different cases in which different
and incompatible interpretations of one and the same work of art
would be equally tenable. (I touched on these already in discussing
the identity of works of art.) The first case would be that in which
the relations presented in the work were unmanageably complex
or imperfectly consistent, so that different selections of relevant
sets were equally supportable but required ignoring or discounting
alternative sets. This might seem to cause some awkwardness for
our conceptual maneuvers in defining the work of art, for the
targets of such rival interpretations would by our definition be
different performances and hence different works of art. But this
awkwardness is one we need no definition to land us in; there is
that obvious and familiar sense in which warring critics are not
"talking about the same film" (though we usually treat this way of
speaking as a hyperbolic metaphor). The awkwardness is anyway
easily removed. Performances are contextually defined in two ways,
both relevant here. First, prima facie, a literary work consists of a
set of words bound up together; a painting of marks on canvas; a
musical work of the notes prescribed by the score, which we can
read, or by the playing or singing of a musician, which we hear. It
is true that our interpreting these as constituting a performance
involves some "editing" of a familiar sort, but we should not allow
that to conceal the blunt fact that by and large the ballet is what's

going on up there on the stage between the raising and lowering of the curtain. But there is a second way in which the performance is contextually defined, by the unity of the performing act itself. And this depends, not simply (as in our earlier argument) on what we conceive to be possible as a way of making coherent sense, but on our sad (or joyous) familiarity with the perversity, weakness, instability, fickleness, and confusion of the heart and the mind. When the musician improvises, we make allowance for fluffs, interruptions, squawks, and all sorts of distracting concomitants that we assume to be no part of the performance.[39] But we also allow for his forgetting what he was doing, trying to do two things at once, changing his mind about where he is going, starting more hares than he can chase at once, picking up where he thought he had left off but resuming what was not quite there in the first place, discovering and pursuing tendencies in what he has done that would have taken a rather different form if he had thought of them at the time, and so on.[40] These are all part of his performance, tied together in a single web of intention, a single aesthetic object, though an inconsistent one. This seems to be the normal condition of art. According to some theorists, it is a failure of art, for perfection of design requires total integration and consistency, a coherent whole mediating all its parts. But others will say that that expresses a preference for meagerness over generosity, that the greatest works are those that impress us as being as ample as life itself, as possessing an order that eludes our grasp because we never come to its limits.[41] And there seems to be no reason why alternative structures should not be equally discoverable in any large and complex work and serve equally well to articulate our sense of the complex meaningfulness of the whole.

The converse of the ambiguity that comes from ungraspable and irreducible richness is that which comes from meagerness of evidence. Relations on which a design depends may be adumbrated rather than stated; a sketch may project more than one set of relations in such a way that different supplementations may complete equally plausible *Gestalten*.[42] Such ambiguities may well be as ubiquitous as those that come from *embarras de richesses*. Whatever I say or show makes sense only by implying much that is not explicitly said or overtly shown (a woman whose face I see in a portrait must be taken to have a back to her head and a brain inside it), and no rule can separate what may be inferred from what must be inferred. In practice, it cannot be often that a work lacks any feature on the basis of which a critic could infer an apparently unstated significance that other critics deny or ignore; and surely (since anything can be related to anything) there is a sense in which every work potentially contains an infinite number of relations, so that a critic must in any case start by making a selection even if he is not conscious of doing so, and even if the initial selection is imposed on all critics equally by convention or by the authority of the work.

A third occasion for interpretive divergence may rest on critics' preferences among emphases that have sound but incompatible justifications. One may find satisfaction in a work because it speaks to our condition; hence, one may emphasize certain aspects of it that give it contemporary relevance, although these can have had no especial significance for the artist and his initial public, whose own preoccupations will have led them to emphasize aspects to which all but the most deeply historically minded are nowadays blind or at best indifferent.[43] Historical reconstitution may properly be judged necessary for the recovery of the original and actual work; but it seems equally justified to reject such insistence on reconstitution as pedantry and to insist that the work *for us* must be that which has reached us across the years, as we cannot but see it in the light of our current preoccupations.[44] Similarly, what is tired convention in a work's own tradition may become exciting novelty when it is injected into an exotic culture. To the casual museum goer it may be that all West African carvings look much alike, their significance lying in their shocking or exciting African look, whereas to the artist's communities the similarities might be unnoticeable, the aesthetic significance of the carvings lying in the differentiations of forms that the individual carver has introduced. Again, when one reads the translation of a Japanese novel, one's primary impression may be of a certain strange feeling tone in a narrative that itself may strike us as being somewhat inconsequential. But to the Japanese author and his compatriot readers the events must have social implications quite lost on us; it is a different story they are telling—one less inconsequential, or one whose inconsequences do not fall where we find them. To them, too, with their different knowledge and expectations, the characteristic feeling tone of the story, whatever it is, can hardly be the one we find there. And when it comes to the detailed interpretation of the formal design in a work, every degree of immersion in or estrangement from the originating culture must make its difference.

Fourth, different interpretations may reflect preferred differences of emphasis at a more self-conscious level, such as a differential selection of explanatory myths and similar systems of explanation. Notoriously, and obviously, one can read *Alice in Wonderland* in terms of sexual symbolism from Freud's dream book.[45] I trust it is equally obvious that one does not have to. But, if one does not, one may try a reading in terms of solar myth, Jungian archetypes, Marxist class relations, and so on endlessly. And these readings seem to be alternatives, rather than supplementary.[46] Their attraction for their public is that they are the *one true* explanation, so that *we alone* are the truly scientific readers. Supposing, now, that one admits that some such reading is applicable—that a Freudian reading of *Alice*, say, *works*. Does one immediately conclude that it is relevant? That will depend on several things: on what one thinks of Freud's doctrines and methods (if they are rubbish, who cares if they can be applied?); on one's commitment to Freud's view of art (one may agree that a Freudian reading is informative about the artist's psychology, but find it an irrelevant distraction from the work of art as a system of aesthetic attributes); and on the extent to which one finds explicit consciousness of general implications relevant in appreciating the qualities of designs.

It is tempting to discuss alternative interpretations in terms of idioms of the verb "see." We have a rich store of expressive phrases. Different people see the same thing in different ways, see it as different things, see different things in it. If I cannot sympathize with another's appreciation of a work, I may say that I don't know what he sees in it—the implication being that the object has qualities or relations that I have failed to discern, perhaps because he only imagines them. But expressions like "see in" tend to be ambiguous: idioms are idiomatic and seldom lend themselves to purposes of clarification. When a gypsy sees death in a man's hand, what she sees is something she takes to be really there, and in using this language of her we have acquiesced in her vision. But when a man sees pictures in the fire, he sees what he thinks is not there, and in saying this of him we concur in dismissing his vision. And when I say that I don't know what you see in a work, it may be excessively literal to suppose that different forms are accessible to your eyes and to mine. More likely, all I mean is that I don't know what value it has for you. Similarly, different evaluations of a work may lead us to say that we do not see the work in the same way; this may mean that our perceptions are somehow differently organized, but it need not, for the phrase "the way I see things" most often refers to my practical estimation of the factors in a situation that call for action. As for "seeing as," the manifold complexities of that phrase in the matter of *merely seeing* were touched on above (chap. 4 and

n. 14). In the light of our present concern with ambiguity, we must beware of taking as paradigm the sense in which an ambiguous figure may be seen as white cross on black ground or black cross on white ground. That is a very special case, in which two determinate ways of seeing are built into the pattern. Either one manages to see, or one cannot help seeing, these alternatives. This is very unlike anything that happens with works of art, in which the possibilities are not by any law predetermined or of any definite number.[47] If, in a work of art, I say that I see X as Y, Y may be a thing with which in some frame of reference X may be identified ("I see Meursault as a Christ figure"), or Y may be something that I know X is not and do not propose to identify with X in any frame of reference, but which I use as a superimposed analogue to determine a reading of the form ("I see the draperies as a wave breaking around the rock of the right knee").[48] Neither of these has much in common with the "aspecting" of ambiguous figures.

The flexibility of the "seeing" idiom of English has a certain mild interest.[49] It is in some way illuminating that although the question "Have you seen *Alice's Restaurant?*" can ordinarily only be answered by yes, no, or "I don't remember," people who find they are inclined to describe that film in different ways may express their difference by saying "We didn't see the same film"—the point of which is, of course, that both know they *did* see the same film. But the effect of this flexibility is that the terminology of "seeing" cannot be used to make or explicate distinctions, but only to comment on distinctions already made and understood.

The most striking and troublesome cases of mutually incompatible but defensible interpretations are those arising from the passage of time and the consequent shift in the understanding and expectations that the passing generations bring to a work. Such cases are troublesome and pervasive because in any civilization the monuments of art and letters are a heritage: they are what we receive from the past, and they define the continuity of our culture. Yet our forefathers were different from us, thought otherwise, lived otherwise: surely a horse sketched or spoken of in the days before trains cannot have looked or meant the same as a horse in our day of the airplane. We cannot take the works away from our forefathers, for they are theirs; it would be unjust to do so.[50] Yet we need them for ourselves. And again, what can it be that we need of them, if not what they had to give? The problem of what to think and do about this situation is the "hermeneutic problem" that gives rise to the alleged philosophical discipline of hermeneutics.

We reminded ourselves in our introduction that the problem and discipline of hermeneutics are in origin theological, arising from the peculiar quandaries of a "religion of the book." Every sacred text must be responsibly and faithfully interpreted. That means that its original meaning (and of course its original text) must be preserved or, if necessary, recovered. But to be the holy book for a living religion, on which contemporary belief and cult can rest, its meaning must be made alive for each successive generation of believers. These demands are blatantly contradictory and rest on contradictory assumptions: the first supposes that the text transcends cultural conditions, the second that it does not. From the time of Schleiermacher, it has been recognized that this problem must be confronted by the exegete. And with the simultaneous rise of the historical consciousness and of a reverential attitude toward the fine arts that mark the early nineteenth century, the student of works of art has been in the same theological fix. But it is not agonizing for him as it is for the man of faith. If the latter cannot maintain that the meaning of his text for its successive contemporaries is the same as well as different, the same message perennially renewed, either his religion risks irrelevance or it loses any but an institutional and historical ground for its identity. But if the student of art finds the present and the past falling apart, he can without blasphemy proclaim a new era and divide the labor of understanding between antiquarian pedants and with-it appreciators. His inescapable problem is only the intellectual one: how is communication across the generations possible?

Every work of art reflects the environment of its production, for even a man born out of his own time stems from the time out of which he was born. The work was appreciated by its primary public in terms of the preoccupations of its time and in terms of the expectations generated by the aesthetic experiences available then. Even if a historian can find out what these were, we cannot make our experience the same as theirs, or be preoccupied by what preoccupied them: we have our own lives to lead, and the pretense to lead the life of another must always be a hollow one. One might then expect that works would have short lives, and some do; but others live on, and yet others go under for a while and then surface from time to time. This faces us with two problems: first, how can we, and, second, how should we, come to terms with the cultural deposit of the past?

The actual historical problems of understanding particular works are fascinating, but on the general problem of how understanding is possible at all there is little of interest to say. One begins by distinguishing, as hermeneutists distinguish the kerygma from its literary integument, the meaning discoverable in the work itself from the personal or social resonances it may have from time to time, its significances for the lives of this or that person. Then, we can say, it is not surprising that a topical or modish work is popular for a while, then loses favor, and will not recapture interest unless the mode comes round again. And some modes recur oftener than others.

It is doubtful whether the pure distinction between meaning and significance can be explicated or maintained in practice, except in cases where the significance is plainly idiosyncratic: a meaning that is of no significance to anyone is of no interest. Though a symbol system may suffice to determine a meaning, the meaning it determines is effective only through the actual use of the system. In principle, one supposes, every text belongs to infinitely many symbol systems (or, as Barthes would have it, sets of codes), but is actually referred only to one such system or set, and this one enshrines the range of concerns of its users. And the fact that meaning thus shades into significance raises a further consideration for the differential availability of works of art. Significances will be widely shareable, because the maintenance of a human body in a terrestrial ecosystem, and the conditions of coexistence with other humans, must impose a large common element on human societies; but significances will diverge, because it is just as obviously characteristic of man and earth that there is no limit to the variability of actual ecosystems or of actual specific responses to similar systems. But this consideration clearly lays down a pattern of differential availability of cultural phenomena, one to which works of art conform. The durabilities and revivabilities of designs will vary with the degree of their dependence on the perpetual, on the recurrent, and on the idiosyncratic factors in cultures; but the variation will not be a simple dependence, since, as we have seen, it is always the interestingly different that attracts.[51] The situation will be further complicated by factors of a different order, themselves apparently impossible to assess. It may be that some design elements or principles have an unfailing interest because of biological or other factors unrelated to culture. It may be that works of very subtle and intricate construction are endlessly interesting because they lend themselves to endlessly various interpretation—this might simply be so, without our being able to explain it further.[52] And it might be that any reputation, once established, is self-sustaining for two reasons: a famous work becomes "the thing to see," a tourist attraction, and a sufficiently close and confident scrutiny can find its reward anywhere.[53] If anything can be an aesthetic object, it may be that something is perennially interesting because people perennially take an interest in it.

The problem of how understanding is possible across the ages and between cultures is largely factitious. Every artist, after all, is an individual whose personal history and training are different from those of any of his colleagues and any member of his public. His work cannot have the same meaning for them that it does for him any more than it can have the same significance. And even if his background and training were (as they cannot be) exactly like theirs, except that he had produced this one work and they had not, it still cannot mean to them what it means to him. To him, it is the design he has excogitated, which grew on him as it grew in him; to them, it is the design they are confronted with. Yet, not only is it true that people with their own different histories contrive to appreciate his work, but it is their understanding and appreciation at their best, not the artist's own, that are our standards for understanding and appreciation.[54] So the problem of mutual comprehension arises already between individuals in the same community; extending the problem to remote places and times does not change the issue, but merely dramatizes it.[55] Our first problem thus reduces to this: how can anyone understand what anyone else says? And to that the answer is that (insofar as what they are doing is speaking a language, which is the extent to which "understanding what someone says" makes sense), if it is the same language they are speaking, why should they *not* understand it? That is what languages are for. And if it is not the same language, we are launched on the enormous literature on translatability. The fact that I know you are speaking your language guarantees one level of comprehension; that I can unravel your syntax guarantees another; and on that basis we can erect all our misunderstandings.

Our second question in the hermeneutic zone was that of propriety: how ought we to come to terms with the cultural deposit from the past? On the one hand, it seems a failure in our responsibility to our forefathers, and to the human enterprise in general, if we simply take over their works and exploit them for whatever we with our different interests get out of them. On the other hand, the dead to whom we have this alleged duty are dead and no one can have any duty to them, whereas we are alive and we owe ourselves something, even if it were not impossible to make ourselves over into living anachronisms. Different positions have been vehemently adopted, but it almost seems a nonissue: insofar as it is difficult and irksome for us to enter into the minds of our ancestors, the line of descent is effectively broken. To think otherwise is to confuse physical lineage and family with cultural heritage. And if the line is not broken, we do not need to decide where our duty lies. Does one keep up the family tombs to placate the ancestors, or to keep up the family feeling, or simply because the rice grows well among the headstones (cf. Han 1965)? Such questions are made not to be answered.

What the hermeneutist dreams of is to excogitate the principles of an interpretation that will avoid pedantry and iconoclasm alike, combining vitality and fidelity; but I do not know of anything substantial that has been worked out or is likely to be, and the world goes its own way.[56]

The Evaluative Function

Every human being uses and exploits, takes means to ends, formulates plans and works to fulfill them both by himself and together with others. It is obvious that, accordingly, people will need to know whether things, artifacts, actions, and persons do what they are meant to do and carry out what is expected of them, in what ways they do so and in what ways they fail. They will need to know this whether the task or need in question is one that an object was made specifically to perform, or one that a person has explicitly assumed, or one that is imposed on a thing or person already sufficiently provided with purposes. It is accordingly to be expected that a good deal of what people say to each other will be devoted, directly or indirectly, to the collection, correction, and dissemination of such information. Aristotle indeed thought that .such intercourse was among the salient features of humanity, at the foundation of human language and society.[57] Man is a value sharer, and his communities are defined by the values they share and agree to share. Whether things and persons fill their various bills clearly depends partly on their characteristics and partly on the bills they have to fill. So much seems beyond reasonable dispute. For discourse of just this kind we shall use the term "evaluation." We can now say that no human community or individual can get by without constantly evaluating things of all sorts.[58] What is not so clear is the logic of such discourse, namely, how to describe the character of the arguments by which one comes from a recognition of the qualities of a thing to a final verdict on its adequacy. There is a vast literature on this general topic, to which I have added (Sparshott 1958 and 1970a); I will only remark here that some of the very worst problems need not trouble us, since they arise specifically in cases where it is not clear whether the evaluator has any specific bill to be filled in mind, or, if he has one, what its specifications are.[59] If our concern here is the critic's function as evaluator of works of art, and if works of art are defined (as they are here) in terms of the sort of bill they must fill, we have to do with what the authors of such theoretical analyses are able to treat as a special case that is relatively free from the problems that plague them.

There is one problem about evaluation in general that may concern us here. Is there not perhaps some one final Bill by their filling of which all things, persons, deeds, and thoughts must be weighed? Or do we not sometimes speak and think as though there were? By common consent of philosophers, discussions of art are relatively exempt from such problems, since the realm of art is in large measure an autonomous enclave within which each work is a walled garden of its own. But does a critic have the additional task of deciding whether a given work is not only a good work but also a Good Thing in that it contributes to whatever positive end for all mankind he or we may envisage? Here we may be brusque: some critics make that their business, some do not, and the abstention of the latter is as intelligible as the commitment of the former. If one can give any sense for oneself or others to the notion of a good thing in the light of a universal end, of whatever sort that end may be, it must be a reasonable project to consider how any thing contributes to that end—and reasonable in the double sense that it is an undertaking whose justification is plain and that the very notion of such an end guarantees that anything whatever can be related to it. On the other hand, if a work of art is a performance, it must be equally reasonable to discuss its success in the narrower and more specific context that presumably determines its character as performance. The latter mode of criticism is possible and intelligible without the former; and, though the former can hardly proceed without presuming the latter, a fair division of labor may take the latter as read, as Plato attacked Homeric poetry on moral grounds while assuming without argument that a favorable aesthetic verdict had been returned and would stand. It is humanly understandable, though not intellectually defensible, that exclusive practitioners of either sort of criticism should condemn the practitioners of the other as misguided and perverted. Persons with no ax to grind should recognize that both are desirable, and that there is no compelling reason why a person should not do one without the other, though it would be agreeable if there were some persons who would at least attempt to combine the two.

The same problem of the scope and context of evaluation recurs within the realm of that aesthetic judgment which considers the work of art as such, as performance. We saw that criticism has a generic function, placing a performance by type and context and hence by the sort of bill it is to be taken as filling, as well as an interpretive function that seeks to determine just exactly what it does by way of filling what precise bill. But the assigned contexts and types may be differently chosen for different purposes, and the question then arises of how the evaluations related to these assignments are to be related to one another. One usually explicitly and always implicitly evaluates something *as* something, that something being ultimately definable in terms of some real or supposed set of purposes. One speaks of "a good portrait," "a good painting," "a good Carlo Dolci,"[60] "a good work of art."[61] The last of these expressions, though not in very general use,[62] might seem to have a privileged place as the most general and the least qualified: in this overall judgment, perhaps, our most fundamental evaluative principles for aesthetic affairs are called into play. But that is not necessarily so: the vagueness and generality may merely reflect some doubt or hesitation as to what sort of thing one is confronted by.

The relations between pairs of such judgments seem not to follow any very simple rule. A painted portrait is a painting, let us say; but is every good portrait a good painting? Probably; for if it were not, we have at hand a ready phrase, "a good likeness." But every painted likeness is a painting, too. Again, just as every burglar is a person, but no good burglar is a wholly good person, so it may be that not every good Carlo Dolci is a good painting, because (let us suppose we agree) Carlo Dolci is not a good painter and those who like his paintings do not like them in the same way that they like those paintings that they call good paintings.[63] Well, now: is every good painting a good work of art? And if it is, is its being so a contingent or a necessary truth? One might argue that, in the present conceptual condition of our discourse, it is necessarily true: to be a work of fine art is ipso facto to be a work of art, and to be a work of fine art is nothing other than to be a work of one of the fine arts; the total range of values of works of fine art can only be the sum of the values appropriate to the specific arts. Yet one could as well argue the opposite: that painting could, whereas works of art as such could not, come to be judged entirely by secondary standards and craftsmanlike compliance. It seems to me to make perfectly good sense to say of a painting that it is a bad painting but a good work of art, meaning thereby quite specifically that it violated certain secondary standards for painting that one wished to uphold although by primary standards it excelled, or that it excelled as a work of art but did so in a mode inappropriate to painting. Such things are in fact often said.

The lesson of all this might be that to assign to criticism an evaluative function is not to lay on the critic the task of issuing a single summational judgment, as though there were only one thing the artist could appropriately be considered to have performed.[64] For any object said roundly to be good, the question "a good *what*?" admits of many answers, to no one of which can any preemptive position be assigned. It may be that the task of critical evaluation is to find complex defensible answers to precisely this question, provided only that the answers or partial answers describe or adumbrate possible ways of being a work of art. To do that would be to give the fullest possible account of the work as appreciable, even though in doing so one would either compromise the integrity of the work as a performance and hence as a work of art, or else describe it as a performance of indeterminate ambiguity. Since an interrelation of appreciabilities is itself in principle appreciable, nothing stands in the way of those many critical thinkers who would make ambiguity a possible excellence of art.[65]

I have argued repeatedly and at length that the very concept of a performance in general and the concept of an artistic performance in particular have at their heart the idea of an object that can be evaluated; so that, insofar as discourse succeeds in being relevant to a performance, it cannot but have implications for evaluation: it discusses successes and failures in achieving purposes, whether these be projected (as in interpretation) from the performance, or implied (as in generic discourse) by a putative structure enveloping the performance, or actually intended by the performer or his public. And the function of evaluation is as multiply implicated in the practice of criticism as in its object. It is implicit in the logic of the practice itself, it is equally implicit in the meaning of the very term "criticism," and it is commonly required of the critic by his public.[66] And it is the commonest spur to critical activity of all sorts that there is revaluation to be done. It must, therefore, come as a surprise to find that "evaluative" criticism is sometimes despised as an inferior sort, proper to journalists but not to scholars, barely deserving the high name of "criticism" rather than the low one of "reviewing." But the explanation lies to hand. The objection is in fact directed, not against the processes of evaluation, but against blanket judgments of merit or demerit, especially those issued without qualification or without support.[67] It is observed that people most often call works of art good or bad, or use equivalent phrases of them, when they are unfamiliar or not understood; acquaintance and understanding issue in more nuanced judgments, commonly to the effect that this or that specified detail was right or wrong or might be improved in such and such ways.[68] The objection to "evaluation" is then directed partly against false evaluation, the mere expression of a reaction masquerading as an assessment, and partly against what might indeed be part or outcome of an evaluative procedure, but confines itself to summations instead of specifics, or substitutes a verdict for an argued case.

No simple verdict that a critic might reach can have any other value than that of a guide to what to look at first when there may not be time to look at everything, or of an estimate as to whether time spent in coming to understand something initially not understood or appreciated would be time probably well spent (cf. Harrison 1960); nor can it have any interest beyond that of the light it sheds on the critic's preferences—an esoteric interest, indeed. Roger Fry (1939, 9–10) pointed out, finally and devastatingly, that an authoritative pronouncement on the merit of a work of art would be worse than useless. As matters stand now, if someone whose judgment we respect commends a work to us, we examine it earnestly to see if we can find in it what he finds there; but, if we cannot, we can put it down to difference in taste, or suspect that he has been taken in for once, or simply leave the matter open. But suppose we knew for certain that a work was excellent, and we could see nothing in it? And, given the actual diversity of preferences, this must often happen. How would the knowledge of our incapacity benefit us? We still could enjoy by no taste other than our own. What we need from the evaluative critic is not information to shame us, but guidance to aid us, to show us where to look and to help us to see what is there to be looked at (cf. Crittenden 1968).

Although works of art are preeminently criticizable, and criticism is ultimately always evaluative at least in the sense that its organization must be intrinsically ordered toward evaluation, we now see that there is a sense in which the evaluation of works of art is pointless. No one needs to *know* what is good art, as people need to know what is good food: the closest analogues of such indispensable information are assurances about what we will like in the future and how prices will stand up. This may seem to verge on paradox, but does not. Criticism in other fields is less needed because the needed knowledge, just because it is needed, is widely diffused. It is because art fills no specific set of needs that its forms ramify in the way that calls for the systematic practice of criticism. Criticism flourishes where it is called for, in societies where claimants for aesthetic attention are too numerous and clamorous, and aesthetic traditions too widely and rapidly ramified, for the informal processes of communication to keep up. We need someone who has been there before, to show us where he has hit pay dirt. Every critic may often mislead, as any guide may lose us; but that does not enable us to travel without critics or guides.

There remains always something perilous in the critic's performance of his evaluative function that reflects a problematic aspect of the function itself. Judgments made within clearly delineated and unchallenged traditions may be soundly based, but judgments of the merits of works of art as such that seem to reach beyond the boundaries of traditions and genres are more problematic. The bare notion of good design and of a good work makes perfectly good sense. But any application of the notion seems indefensible. Tastes vary from person to person, and social habits of taste change, too: anything, we keep saying, may be an aesthetic object; and it seems in principle impossible ever to prove of any object that it may not in the right light and with the right preparation be the object of the most profound and delighted interest. Nor can the critic appeal to anything beyond the actual experiences that may be had from, the actual activities of the mind in relation to, the work itself without taking his discussion outside the whole sphere of art as circumscribed by our classical line: if there is discrimination among works, it must be in terms of the number, the certainty, the profundity, the intensity, the probability, the durability of the interests and joys that can be taken in works—in fact, the classical line confines the critic's possible theoretical support to something like the felicific calculus of Bentham as modified by Mill, though it is unfashionable to allow this underpinning to show through.[69] The critic and the theorist of criticism are thus faced with that favorite problem of the eighteenth-century aesthetician, "the fluctuating standard of taste": how is criticism possible when the object of passionate attention from connoisseurs in one generation is despised by the next? Ruskin had the most detailed reasons for his praise of Millais' portrait of himself, which to us is little more than technically expert; Eskimo ivories for which we scramble to pay high prices were almost unsalable eighty years ago (after a previous mild boom) and may be so again; Rosa Bonheur's prices were the highest ever paid to a living artist before Picasso; and so on.[70] The interpreter's task of recovery of meaning, though impossible in principle, is not too hard in practice, and a recovered meaning is intelligible. But the evaluative critic, though not prevented by any difficulty of principle from achieving and imparting a relish for anything, or at least from recovering the use of the standards by which it has once been judged good or bad and may so be judged again, seems by this very facility debarred from achieving any firmness in upholding any one standard against any other.

No argument can prove the excellence of any work; the proof remains the appreciation of the individual with the taste he himself has formed, whether many others or no other have formed like tastes with him. Are the pretensions of art and criticism not then vain? But if they are vain, how are we to explain the appearance of rationality in criticism and the relative orderliness of the art world? The impossibility of escaping such subjectivist and historicist traps tends to obsess beginning students of aesthetics, though their elders, no longer self-conscious about their values, find it a great bore.[71] Why should not a man's taste and a critic's judgment be forever at risk? Safety and continuity, emancipation from death and the processes of history, are what human beings cannot have and should not want. Or, if we wish to say with Schopenhauer that art stops the turning of Ixion's wheel, the eternal truth and beauty revealed to us in experience need not be ascribed to the specific designs that occasion the emancipating vision.

The fluctuating standard of taste, the fact that one cannot find in one's own experience, or in the words of any critic, anything that one can be sure of always being able to hold on to, hardly poses a problem for philosophers—it is to be expected that people, having different experiences and learning from those experiences, will learn different things. What would call for explanation would be not change but the absence of change; and what in fact concerns philosophers of culture is not the fact of variation but what the manner of variation might show about the nature of human rationality. The mere fact of fluctuation does, however, pose a problem for two sorts of people: the intellectually ambitious young and the prudent collectors. It was the latter group whose interests directed the eighteenth-century discussions. It was important to defend civilization and the fragile enlightenment against barbarism and superstition; it was also urgent to protect the investments of the gentry who were beginning to put their money into the works of acknowledged masters whose value might be expected to hold up, rather than having a picture done that would do for now. The interests of the collector, however, are largely satisfied by a changing taste, so long as it changes relatively slowly: a gentleman plants and purchases for posterity, but cannot be expected to think beyond his grandchildren's grandchildren. And indeed a perfectly established and ascertainable scale of values would have its disadvantages. One who buys on the word of an infallible Berenson may have a permanent price tag on his purchase, but Berenson is in the public domain, and such safety debars one from the thrill of backing an outsider. As for the other group of anxious value conservers, the young, they deserve our sympathy. They divine that their future tastes will have been formed by decisions they are now consciously making, decisions to attend to some sorts of things and to neglect others. Naturally they are anxious not to corrupt their future selves either by bypassing the excellent or by being bamboozled by the meretricious. History shows them that at no time are current reputations reliable indexes of subsequent consensus. Young people urgently need to know at least whether it makes sense to say that one sort of work is better than another. But we must harden our hearts. Of course they cannot know any such thing; if there were such a thing to be known, the situation that troubles them would not have existed. There is no way in art any more than in manners or morals of bypassing the agonizing uncertainties of growing up in a complex society.

If it is conceded that all men have similar bodies and live on the same earth and have similar brains, and live besides in complex communities whose complexities are defined precisely by the way they structure and share their values, nothing further needs to be said to explain how tastes can be individually unique, historically articulated, and practically reliable. The logic of how intelligible structures of values can be generated from atomic experiences has been explored by philosophers in ways beyond which we have no present need to go (Lewis 1946; Von Wright 1963; Hartman 1967). The terms within which we operate were laid down once for all by Francis Hutcheson (1725): it cannot be that all taste is a matter of cultural conditioning, or the very notion of beauty could not have arisen—taste can be modified culturally, but the capacity of taste itself could not be generated culturally; but one cannot deny that taste is deeply affected by such conditioning, since the known history of its variations shows that it is. Since the metaphor of taste derives from feeding, one may compare the phenomena of food preferences.[72] People must eat to live, and their food must meet nutritional requirements if they are to live in health; but the food preferences of different cultures, including what they define as food, do not at all correspond to the presence or absence of the required nutrients. Some available foods are selected, some rejected, some not recognized as possible food at all. In the case of art, nothing quite corresponds to the nutritional constraints; whatever we may think of the survival value of this or that form of aesthetic competence, no one actually dies of aesthetic starvation.[73] Attempts to determine a priori what could become a culturally acknowledged aesthetic object have not got very far. Perhaps all we are entitled to say is that we cannot tell what traditions may arise, but that within traditions judgments may be firm, and traditions there must be: the differential development of perceptual and appreciative skills makes some choices readily available, but not all, and the development of skills in relation to traditions guarantees that only certain kinds of objects will at any time be readily available in suitable contexts.

Up to now I have been dealing mostly with the problems generated by a criticism that is not initially committed to any particular frame of reference, but assumes that the world is its oyster, or that it inhabits a museum without walls. We have assumed that criticism as from within a tradition can be ignored because it raises no problems. But Wittgenstein (1966) notoriously began his lectures on aesthetics by saying that aesthetics was an entirely misunderstood subject just because it devoted itself to the criticism I have been discussing, whereas serious discussion of art has nothing to do with the beautiful and the ugly or with good or bad, but has to do with expressing recognitions of what precisely is right or wrong with specific aspects of specific objects. The assumption is that aesthetic discussion proper takes place within enclaves in which artist and public share a common level of understanding and, above all, in which the members of the public are in a position to tell the artist what to do.[74] As always, his remarks are penetrating; but, as often, they are betrayed into superficiality by an inadequate grasp of what there is to say, what has been said, and the reasons why it needed saying. The ideal Vienna in which the cultivated Wittgensteins with their seven grand pianos were integrated into a milieu of impeccable cultivation was a city in which advanced musicians found it hard to get a hearing;[75] and it is usually only in very small circles indeed that the sort of mutually corrective criticism that Wittgenstein takes as paradigm is the norm. In wider circles, even among the most aesthetically sophisticated, merely directive and eulogistic or appreciative-descriptive talk has its place. Poets seldom talk technicalities with other poets, for what they say is likely to be either obvious or irrelevant, and most likely both; what we need to know is who has written a good book lately. Still, talk of what is right or wrong has its inalienable place. Rather than guiding to appreciation, it starts from the other end and supposes that the object of criticism is already appreciated, that satisfaction or disquiet is already felt or may be readily aroused; its objective is to locate the source of the satisfaction or disquiet, to make intelligible an experience whose quality is already determined.

The point made in the last paragraph suggests that much of the anxiety attendant on critical evaluation can be removed by interpreting critical discourse as hypothetical. The critic may be taken as answering the question: Why does this work affect me in the way that it does? (There is some presumption that the critic is strongly moved, one way or the other, but the presumption is not necessary; all that is necessary is that the work should be felt as having a notable character, without which it would not have called for comment.) And this question splits into two: What is it about the work that moves me, and what exactly is the way in which I am moved? The former question is to be answered by describing and explaining the work—the interpretation, we now see, having rather the character of an *explanation of the description* of the work; the latter question, perhaps, by similes and analogies ("Like stout Cortez . . ."). Then, since the criticized work has presumably been published or exhibited, and is thus at least to some extent shown to be publicly viable, it is reasonable to suppose that others are also moved by the work; and, if it is reasonable to suppose that, it must be because it is reasonable to suppose them to have been moved in the same way; and, if that is the case, they should find that the critic's elucidations and analogies illuminate their own experience. If anyone is not so affected, the explication will simply pass him by; if he is (by some coincidence) quite *otherwise* affected by the same work, then another critique will no doubt be illuminating for him and for those who share his reaction.

IX

THE CLASSICAL LINE
8: THE ARTIST

This can be a short chapter, because it is a mark of the classical line that the artist is no big deal. That line encourages us to define the artist as an artificer, one who produces a certain sort of product. In no other way than in this, the exercise of his functional role, is it implied that he is in any way special. He is defined solely by his having the ability to produce works of art, or works in one of the fine arts, and by his actually using this ability. Thus, a painter is simply one who has mastered the art of painting pictures and does paint pictures. In antiquity, in the Middle Ages, in the Renaissance, perhaps until the end of the eighteenth century, this is how the artist is usually thought of. Nor is the view obsolete; it has a sturdy, obvious, and inexpugnable rightness that keeps it current alongside whatever more recherché and ambitious definitions of the artist may come into fashion from time to time. When the chips are down, the painter recalls that he, after all, is the person who knows how to paint, has the will to paint, and does paint; and he expects to be recognized, and is recognized, in such terms as these. It being agreed that that is what an artist is, disputes may rage about how important he is, whether he can be a gentleman or must be a menial, and about the extent and kind of the knowledge he must wield. Renaissance painters sought to maintain their dignity by claiming that a painter must have knowledge of all the kinds of object and quality that could appear in his work, and thus he must be a scholar if not a seer.[1] More subtly, the same age saw a shift from the notion that the artist was a purveyor of a certain type of product to customers to the notion that he freely produced such products *for a public*. The difference is profound: in the former view the artist is literally an artisan whose hand is ultimately at the service of another's directing mind and whose activity is thus in essence servile; in the latter view his hand and mind work freely for the good of the commonwealth in which he is an equal partner. At the start of the nineteenth century, with the rise of the common man, or the demand of the petit bourgeois that attention must finally be paid to such as he, the idea of the artist begins to take leave of the classical line. For those who now masquerade as the artist's public are neither his betters nor (as in the Wittgensteinian paradigm with which we ended the last chapter) his equals: they are swine before whom he must cast his pearls in hungry contempt.[2] If he is to be enjoyed, he must create the necessary taste, and so cease to be merely a producer of works of skill and become a changer of minds: an educator or a revolutionary.

Within the classical line as such, the artist has no special theoretical importance, whatever his social dignity. His importance is that of the works he produces and the skill he embodies or of the profession he represents. But as soon as we say that, we realize that the classical line leaves the concept of the artist ambiguous or indeterminate, for we saw that the concept of a fine art and the concept of a work of art are somewhat loosely related. An artist might be defined in terms of either or both. An artist might be the possessor and user of the knowledge and skill that identify one of the fine arts, or he might be a producer of fit objects for appreciation. And one could obviously be either of these without being the other.

The difference between defining the artist in terms of his art and in terms of his works appears already in the implications of the scholastic definition of art (in its primary manifestation as a quasi virtue of the artist) as *recta ratio factibilium*, the rightness of reason in the sphere of making things: for the definition of art itself is herein torn between the rightness of rational principles of making and the rightness of the end product.

Wherever there are rules, the scholastic definition implies, the artist must know and apply them; but there is nothing to say that there have to be rules in the sense of principles consciously enunciated. All the definition requires is that the making show right reason whatever the relevant rightness might be. The appropriate model might be that of the Aristotelian intellectual virtue of prudence or practical wisdom rather than of an Aristotelian art: the man of practical wisdom has an intuitive (educated and habituated but immediate) grasp of the nature of human well-being and a similarly immediate grasp of the moral implications of any situations he finds himself in; if there are maxims, rules, slogans, or laws that help him figure out how to achieve what, their function is subsidiary. Just so, it might be, the fine artist has an acquired taste (a sense of beauty or of his own "thing") and a sure feel for what to do in any situation. How and where systematic thought has entered into his becoming a person capable of such intuitions, and whether and how they can yet be teased out of his practice, are interesting questions indeed but secondary: the excellence of art depends strictly on that of the work, and his actually reliable practice is all we can in strictness demand. It then becomes a contingent fact that art, the rightness of reason in production, should ever become such that it could be codified in arts, bodies of knowledge and skill. Since it is a fact, it is a very important fact, probably deserving the epistemological attention Plato and his successors gave it. Where they erred was not in that, but in supposing it to be necessary that the rightness of productive reason should take that form.

The artist as practitioner of a fine art is one who has the knowledge and wields the skill appropriate to one or more of those arts whose defining knowledge, skill, and institutional exoskeleton are explicable only on the supposition that their characteristic objects are contemplables. The skills by which the artist is defined may still be variously chosen. One could, and sometimes does, bestow the title simply for the possession of secondary skills, the technical know-how involved in the successful production of the appropriate sort of performance—these are quite notable enough to define a profession and, indeed, to strike the layman with awe. It is under this rubric that commercial artists are so called. But one may urge that commercial artists are no more artists than Salisbury steak is steak, and insist on the primary standards of the art. The requirements can then become quite exalted. If the fine arts are arts of imitation, it is at this point that we insist that an artist have knowledge of that which he imitates, whether that be the secrets of the human heart, the truths of geography and medical science,[3] or the determining laws of natural structures. If the fine arts are arts of the aesthetic and nothing else, the appropriate skill may include a facility in "design" in our special sense. At these high levels we once more approach views of the artist's status more readily associated with other lines than the classical. The artist becomes creator, hence godlike in a way that other men are not.[4] As imitator, he creates a mimic heaven and earth; as artist of beauty, he produces genuinely novel entities, ontological originals.[5] Yet so long as we keep to the classical line these remarkable dignities are still circumscribed: the artist's preeminence is his ability to produce things that have remarkable qualities. It is when the excellence of his product is taken as testimony to the presence of a spiritual excellence more important than any of his works that he turns into a phenomenon for which the classical line has no place. This remarkable transformation is less likely to happen when he is regarded as a maker of likenesses or of beautiful things than when the arts of imitation are construed (as we saw they may well be and have been) as arts of expression and when the arts of beauty are thought of as arts of imagination. When the fine arts are understood in those ways, what they demand of the artist is primarily the cultivation of a faculty or personal gift rather than the development of a skill, however rarefied, and it is then a short and easy step to the position that the faculties and powers of an exceptional person are more to be prized than anything that could issue from them.

I began this chapter by saying that the classical line encourages us to conceptualize the artist, the person whose activities most centrally embody that mode of productivity or activity which is formalized in the fine arts, in either of two ways: as practitioner of an art or as producer of works. Neither of these is an unambiguous notion. The most natural and common way to think of a practitioner of a fine art is as a wielder of systematized skill. But that is not the only way. Since a fine art, like most other arts, usually has an exoskeleton, a sustaining institutional shell of schools, unions, and such, an artist may be such primarily because he is an accredited member of his profession (as in the case of Von Dutch Holland, cited in chapter 2). And insofar as the arts are institutionalized, the artist can acquire the status, not of an accredited member of a profession, whose standing among his peers is thus assured, but of an attested occupier of a social role. He is the person you go to for art, as the doctor is the man you go to for pills—of course, the basic idea is that the doctor knows what pills to give you, but in fact he may not, and respectable people get their paintings done by proper painters by way of genuflection to the principle of division of labor: it is the function of wealth "to give employment to the artisan."[6] And incidentally, but not unimportantly, one should not forget that the division of social roles, of which the institutionalization of arts is one manifestation, generates trade stereotypes: everyone knows what millers, tailors, and airline pilots are like, and what they look like too, even (perhaps especially) if we have never met one. Painters, poets, and movie directors similarly have their icons in everyone's mental gallery. And so, once we are tempted to move out of the classical line by assigning the artist an importance other than that of the actual practice of his art, we find that an impetus inherent in the classical line itself has already made that separation easy for us.

Suppose, on the other hand, we derive our notion of what an artist is from his relation to the work of art. We do in fact always refer to the producer of a work of art as "the artist," without necessarily implying that he is *an* artist—that is, that he is the kind of person of whom such production is characteristic; although, if his artistry is extremely atypical of his usual mode of behavior, our referring to him as "the artist" even in relation to this specific work may be touched with sarcasm. But the kind of person we call *an* artist because of his productivity is one who either regularly produces works of art or occasionally produces works of art of notable merit. Either quality or quantity suffices with very little of the other, although of course the best artist is one who combines productivity with excellence. It follows from this, almost of necessity, that the best artist must go through a number of different styles (unless he dies young), as did Beethoven and Picasso: if his later works are simply more of the same, it is hard to see how they could still fulfill the requirement of eminent contemplability for one familiar with his earlier work or even (more significantly) for himself. But "almost of necessity" is not quite "of necessity," and there is nothing in this version of the classical line's view of the artist to rule out someone producing a new and brilliant cantata every Sunday through a long lifetime without any stylistic development at all: one presumes that such an artist would have to wield a formidable repertory of resources from the beginning, but there is nothing in the classical line to suggest anything about the sequence in which such resources should be deployed in time. In any case, the artist on this variant of the classical line is one who, by will or habituation, actually turns out many works or good works of art or both, or at any rate more or better works of art than most people: that is, he is one whose designs are many or worth contemplating or both. But the requirement that his many design acts issue in things eminently contemplable has its own ambiguity. Anything *can* be contemplable, as I keep saying; and although a man may be recognized as artist because his designs tend to be found worth attending to by some suitable reference group (everyone, the newspapers, the best people . . .), their contemplability might be largely a matter of intention: he thinks they are worthy of note and thrusts them on the attention of an indifferent or even a reluctant public. This is very important in the world of art. A painter is not necessarily a man who has a special gift: he may be a man of determination, a man who will not give up painting and bringing his paintings before the public. Horace may have been right when he said "It's not good enough to say 'I write wonderful poetry—Devil take the hindmost' " (*De Arte Poetica* 416, my translation), but Aristotle was also right when he pointed out that races are not always won by the best runner among those present: they can be won only by someone who enters for them and keeps on running until he breasts the tape, no matter how many brilliant sprinters are sitting in the bleachers. But determination is never *quite* enough. It is more generally true that the contemplability of the artist's work by virtue of which he is held to be an artist is a matter of social recognition. In the version of the classical line we are now considering, what is socially recognized is not a professional affiliation. It may be just a matter of common experience that in fact his work is generally found worth attending to, or is found by some appropriate authority or reference group to be so. But social recognition may also be simple acknowledgment of status—his works are to be attended to because they are his. And, although such status is no doubt usually attained at least in part by appropriate achievement, it can be acquired by politics and propaganda, and it could even be arbitrary or accidental.

However numerous they may be, cases in which the artist is deemed such because he is a source of plentiful or excellent works not de facto but de jure or ex officio may justly be dismissed as pathological. The primary sense of the term "artist" must be that of the de facto producer: the actual wielder of imagination and creative ability and energy—and, we must add in this context, wielder of them no matter how obtained, for we are distinguishing this usage from that which relates the artist to the disciplines of the fine arts. The reason for insisting on the distinction must be that the skills of the fine arts and their training are in fact either unnecessary or insufficient for the production of appropriate works.

The ideas of what an artist is that stem from considering, respectively, the fine arts and works of art do not coexist peacefully. They are in conflict. It has long been recognized that the fine arts are not enough. The artist must produce works of individual character, and this cannot be taught: even if we say, as we did at the start, that an art may incorporate as one of its requirements that each artist develop an individual style, that style cannot as a personal skill contain anything to guarantee the individual effectiveness of works.[7] By concentrating on the individual aspect of the work of art, a whole set of concepts has been worked out to differentiate the artist as producer of wholly uncovenanted works from the artist

277

as wielder of an inherently repeatable skill. The artist, one says, is a genius, a creative force unaccountable even to himself, as opposed to the mere man of talent who knows how to do things well and can account to himself and others for his knowledge. The artist works by imagination, a power of forging perceptible unities, not by fancy, a skill in working and fitting details. His procedures are organic, flowing out of each other as continuously as a flower unfolds, rather than mechanical, step following step. The mere product of a fine-arts training, as such, is not an artist at all: he is no more than a craftsman.

The conflict between the two ways of thinking about artists has something factitious about it. Surely the two ways are easily reconciled and naturally combined. The *complete* artist, we should rather say, is one who habitually and successfully wields the skills of one or more of the fine arts to their appropriate ends and, in doing so, shows a distinctive flair, amounting in the extreme case to genius, but in any case contributing its element of *je ne sais quoi*.[8] The combination seems natural: it might seem odd that anyone should apply himself to the fine arts without having some temperamental gift or predisposition, since as sources of livelihood they have seldom been reliable and never (especially considering what they demand in talent and energy) outstanding. It would be strange for anyone gifted and dedicated not to take pains to equip himself with whatever resources of knowledge and organization may be available. And I think it is true that we do consider the artist in this double light: we expect him to have a gift, and we expect him to have been trained and to belong to the appropriate organizations. Surely, then, it is no more reasonable to speak of a conflict between the implications of inspired production and those of acquired expertise than it was, in discussing criticism, to find opposition between originality and tradition, or indeed to find a conflict between the primary and secondary standards of any art. We said before, in discussing how works of art should be defined, that the normal case is that in which potentially divergent criteria are all fulfilled. So here, the normal case of the artist is that of the productive expert who unites skill and inspiration. So what comes of the alleged conflict? Well, it still goes on. However much skill and inspiration may need each other, they pull in opposite directions. And it is a literary commonplace that the fiercest hatreds spring from the closest relationships.[9]

In any case, the combination of creative gifts and productive know-how is not necessary: we have no hesitation in calling a sufficiently gifted and productive person an artist without inquiring into how he has made himself such, and there is a sense in which we do call the practitioner of a fine art an artist merely as such, though with a certain reservation that some philosophers have formalized by saying that we use the term "artist" of such persons in a purely descriptive and not at all in an evaluative sense. But I think it is also true that the further away we get from both parts of this meaning, the more conscious we become that we are using the term "artist" in a way that is partly hyperbolic or metaphorical or tendentious.

I mentioned earlier the possibility of a trade stereotype of the typical member of an artistic profession. Another stereotype long prevailed of the artist as creator: that of the melancholic "born under Saturn,"[10] whose fits and crotchets were thought not only a likely concomitant of the gifts of creativity (which would be a psychological hypothesis of little theoretical interest) but appropriately symbolic of the lonely responsibility of someone who sees for a living what no one else has yet seen. One might expect such insistence on the personality of the artist to be an offshoot of romanticism, with Beethoven as its archetype, since (as I began this chapter by saying) the artist must for the classical line be no big deal. But in fact it is earlier: the prime example is Michelangelo, with his *terribiltà*; and long before him there is Euripides. Such paradigms of artistic melancholia are coupled in the tradition with models of serenity: Euripides is contrasted with Sophocles, Michelangelo with Raphael. In terms of what I have just been saying, it seems that the members of these contrasting pairs represent, respectively, those in whom originality quarrels with craft and those whose originality is the flower of craft, in whom craft itself is integrated (as the Stoics insisted every art as such must be) into the prevailing values of a flourishing social order.

Finally, two marginal or subsidiary versions of the idea of the artist remain to be noted. First, there is that of the artist as "man of art," the denizen (so to speak) of the *Lebensform* that answers to all the artistic side of life. In the context of the classical line, this notion is very marginal indeed, for we saw that the fine arts as such cannot generate a *Lebensform*: and we may add that, though art as *recta ratio factibilium* might do so, that form would be indicated by some such term as "productivity" and would be irrelevant to our concerns. If the fine arts as arts of beauty are associated with a form of life, that form would be designated rather by "the aesthetic," and its typical denizen would be not the artist but the aesthete. The artist simply as identified by a way of life or general type of interest or area of concern belongs rather to some of our alternative lines of thought, to the poetic line to some extent, and above all to the purist line.

The other marginal version of what it is to be an artist is more relevant. This is the notion of artist as *auctor*, as whoever stands in the same relation to anything that an author does to his book or any artisan to his artifact—and, of course, as the artist conceived in some more usual fashion stands to his work. Among the artistic manifestations of the 1970s, which have very various significances, some have had to do with authorship in this sense. The artist's work has essentially taken the form of *establishing himself as author* of a segment of his life not otherwise interesting or even recognizably individuated, and thus establishing it as a work (or, as it has become fashionable to say, a piece). Such maneuvers fall within the institutions of the fine arts and belong firmly to our classical line: they have nothing to do with the purist line, in which ploys that are superficially similar are given exemplary significance and so have the very different role of establishing some rarefied excellence in the artist and his life.[11]

To conclude, the double demand made of the artist by the claims of repeatable skill and the claims of unique work is what holds the classical line together. But the unity, as we have repeatedly seen in this chapter, is precarious, and its fragility continually pushes us, in one way or another, toward a concern with the artist in whom it must be embodied. There is then a tendency, which we have also found elsewhere in our discussion, to abandon the classical line altogether in favor of alternative lines in which the center of interest lies, not in performances as we conceive them, not in the making and doing of what is done or made, but in the human interest of a more diffused mode of activity. For this activity the name is art, and it is to lines of thought that make art, rather than arts or works of art, their center that we now turn.

X

THE IDEA OF ART

The way of thinking about artists and their arts and works that has hitherto occupied us, and the explication of which we have now ended, has some claim to be considered normal. What it is based on and articulates are the irreducible and ineluctable facts of practice and institution, and even of history, with which any theory of art must deal. It is because institutions, objects, and practices exist to which what we have said is immediately and evidently appropriate that there is a theory of art. What leads us to say that art exists is, ultimately, the fact that this conceptual nexus has been brought together. When the nexus comes unknotted, art will be living on borrowed time: either it will be replaced by something different, as the novel replaced the epic or the miniskirt the bustle, or else the whole idea and institutional complex will fall apart, and we will be left with painters, musicians, and such—but no *artists*; and perhaps none the worse for that.

We traced the growth of the idea of the fine arts through a series of stages. First, the occasional exploitation of specific analogies leads to the general recognition that certain organized practices can be grouped together as arts of imitative play or as arts of the aesthetic. Then, it comes to seem that what joins these arts to each other is more significant than any common factors linking any one of the practices in question to any art not so definable, so that the fine arts come to be thought of as a single area of human concern. Then, this community becomes embodied in institutional linkages, educational, political, and other. And at last it seems a fact of nature that the fine arts are species of one genus.

The classical line in the theory of the fine arts stops at that point. But the impetus to thinking of the fine arts as a unity has not yet exhausted itself. The supposed unity partly depends on the unifying institutions, but those institutions were themselves called into being in the name of a unity of a different order. And that original unity, as we saw, is inevitably construed as a common significance, which necessarily extends beyond institutionalized practice. The arts of imitative play have the general meaning of cognitive exploration and of "expression," and the arts of the aesthetic prove to be arts of the imagination; the concepts of expression and imagination strain against the confines of the classical line's underlying notion of skilled and organized practice. The deep significance that lies beneath the unity of the fine arts is that of a domain of human experience or spiritual achievement. It is this domain, and this achievement, that are to be captured in the contemporary concept of art *as opposed to* the fine arts; and they are the central concern of the philosophy of art as that has been generally understood.

In the double development just sketched, whether that be a historical fact or a logical fiction, the idea of the fine arts and of art are gradually clarified, slowly separated from the accidental encumbrances of their history and prehistory, much as the idea of philosophy had been clarified centuries before and the idea of science was being clarified at about the same time. To possess these ideas of philosophy, science and art in a fairly clear form can be made out to be the hallmark of our civilization or even of civilization as such, so that to identify a civilization as alien (in the first case) or a culture as uncivilized and primitive (in the second case) it is enough to show that the civilization or culture lacks one of the three ideas.[1]

That the concept of art in general, like the concept of the fine arts, developed late in the history of our civilization tells nothing against it. The development in fact exemplifies the evolution that Hegel traced in the life of the mind, from the subjective through the objective to the universal. At the most primitive level we have the aesthetic impulse (or whatever) as felt by this or that person and expressed in this or that private act. This widely distributed impulse becomes objectified, achieves a determinate reality, in the institutions and practices of the fine arts. And the impulse as thus given institutional being achieves self-consciousness in art as such and as a whole. The universal, then, is the aesthetic impulse (or whatever); the particular is the fine arts; and the individual is the artist as genius, the artist in relation not only to his specific art but to what now stands revealed as the unified and living tradition of art as a whole. In this light, the concept of the fine arts is revealed as superficial and provisional, even if it is also indispensable.[2]

What we presented as the classical line is defective in two ways. *Fehlt, leider! nur das geistige Band*, someone will say.[3] The principle of intelligible and vital unity is lacking. The unity ascribed to the fine arts is extrinsic, a matter of shared characteristics; and, although the practices we mentioned have been allowed enough motivation to make them intelligible, what could be thus motivated would be both less unified and less important than the arts are taken to be and doubtless really are. Though each art is an art, and painters are not more likely to be poets than practitioners of any other practice calling for brains and taste, there is an important sense in which the arts are special cases of something else, which we may as well call what everyone else calls it, namely, art.

The other defect is that the classical line either omits or devalues everything of general interest—an objection against which my Preface seeks to defend this book as a whole. The sort of thing it does, at once intricate and banal, is not what people interested in aesthetics and the philosophy of art want to hear. And why should they? What they want is something simple and uplifting, namely, a philosophy of *art*, not to increase analytical understanding, but to symbolize their feeling that what is at stake in the fine arts is supremely important.[4]

But what is this art, that which is at stake in the arts, that of which they are special cases or manifestations? It can hardly be an object or a class of objects or an organized practice or set of practices.[5] That use of the substantive without an article suggests an entity or construct of a different order—more ethereal or more nebulous, depending on the intellectual climate. What is the theorist of the classical line to say about art? He may dismiss or deride the notion, but to win the right to do either he must first come to grips with it. And this he can hardly do, for the way of thought he has chosen to travel has its own ends and limits. Art as the general human capacity to generate and practice particular arts is within his scope, and so is "art" as a word used to gesture vaguely toward the aesthetic. Even art as a *Lebensform* associated with the fine arts and works of art he can come to terms with, though not easily. But more than that is required.

The term "art," in the familiar sense that now concerns us, functions as a generalization bearer. It is by no means clear how such terms are to be understood. Not that the unclarity bothers many people, even theorists. Just as people who use the term "man" in a phrase like "man makes himself" seldom show any sign that there might be a need to justify the apparent attribution of an indeterminate degree of solidarity or of metaphysical unity to members of the human species as such, so those who use the word "art" in such phrases as "art and its objects" seldom see the need to explain how there can be an "it" suitably called "art" and capable of having objects. A book that claims to be systematic and yet starts at this point, as so many do, without explaining how such expressions are to be understood and what metaphysical claims underlie their use, can hardly be taken seriously as philosophy. And yet we all do use the word "art" in this carefree way; and, since we appear to understand one another, it is to be presumed that we are making sense. That presumption would not be defeated even if we proved unable to explain the workings of such language in terms of some mode of discourse that formal philosophy was better able and more willing to take systematic account of, for the task of accounting for such discourse and finding ways of translating it might lie in philosophy's future rather than in its somewhat limited and arthritic past. But that inability should itself not be too lightly assumed. It might be, not that we lack the resources to explain such locutions, but that we lack ingenuity in the use of such resources as we have, or that the resources themselves have gone rusty from disuse. In any case, there is no reason to suppose that the use of the term "art" is inexplicable merely because it is often not adequately explained.

Actually, the meaning of "art" is not all that obscure and needs little explanation. People who talk about "art" in ways that take them beyond the limits of the classical line generally mean something like a spiritual capacity of human beings and the collectivity of the manifestations of that capacity. "Art" is whatever shows that human beings are (or that some are and hence all may be) beings of a certain kind, having a certain ability. And the alleged ability or capacity is of a sort that can set men apart from all animals: those who talk of "art" in this way usually think of art as a defining property of man, or as a special manifestation of a defining property. The difficulty in comprehension lies not so much in grasping the way the word is used as in ascertaining what on any occasion is presupposed by its use. It is claimed that human beings have and exercise some capacity, that this capacity is distinctively manifested in the fine arts, and that the capacity has some importance in itself and in relation to what makes human beings human. But one might reasonably deny that any such capacity exists.[6] To accept the term "art," it seems, is to accept a claim of indeterminate extent. What more is meant by invoking a capacity than the acknowledgement that the fine arts exist and are cultural phenomena? Typically, the word "art" is used to demarcate a spiritual terrain, a province in the country of mind or soul. Insofar as that is the case, its use is inherently tendentious, for marking out spiritual areas is not something one can do without serious intellectual commitments, like sectioning an orange or surveying a tract of prairie. Use of such a word in such a way is a form of spiritual lifemanship, insinuating a theory that is neither clearly stated nor (apparently) clearly articulated in the minds of its users, but which one suspects of vague extravagance.

If art is a capacity and its manifestations, it is presumably a good thing, because capacity is better than incapacity. But the actual capacities invoked turn out to be rather various. There are in fact at least five grounds on which special dignity may be, and has been, claimed for art.

First, one may claim superiority for the artist, who is somehow above the ordinary run of mankind. The alleged superiority may be of several sorts. It may be thought to lie in the purity of his motives: he is uncommitted, uncorrupted, indifferent to success, not concerned to please. "Vissi d'arte," he says. "Art" thus comes to stand for the possibility of disinterestedness in a commercial world. Alternatively, the artist's superiority may be ascribed to the exceptional refinement and delicacy of his perceptions: he sees what others miss, feels what leaves others cold. The value of art is then the value of refinement. Again, the artist may be thought better than other men because of his creative power, whereby he brings new things into the world—but if we put it that way, his glory is only reflected from his works, so let us say rather that the artist is set apart by his *imagination*. We came across this polymorphous concept before and will meet it at least twice again: in the present context it stands for imaginativeness, creativity, the ability and will to extend the scope and range of one's thought beyond practice and experience. Finally, the artist may be thought of as a marked man, a scapegoat, a pole squatter, who suffers needlessly because art is after all superfluous, but who compensates by his gratuitous pains (of gestation or something like that) for the easy lives that people who have the leisure to think about art but are not themselves artists may be supposed to be leading. Art then becomes an exemplary anguish, a means of atonement. Thus, the artist may be distinguished by disinterestedness, by refinement, by imagination, or by sacrifice from other men; and in this distinction he yet celebrates or symbolizes the uniqueness of humanity, for we certainly do not suppose that the brute beasts consciously engage in gratuitous action, or strive to impart delicacy to their perceptual transactions, or take broad views of their world or beyond it, or seek purification for themselves or others.

These values ascribed to the artist might be anatomized in terms of the ways of life differentiated by Arendt (1958): she argues that, whereas most of us nowadays are possessed by the values of labor and consumption, according to which merely staying alive is the sole objective—and, thus, what sets us apart from the brutes is only the manner of operation, plus the fact that for us this way of life is the preferred one, not the only one possible—other values have in other ages been recognized as prior and have determined other ways of life. There is the contemplative life, in which schooled awareness is supreme and takes a timeless value from the eternity of the objects it contemplates; the active life, in which the resonance of fame among fellows is all; and the life of making, the way of the artificer who is to be justified by the lasting changes he makes in the world's fabric. On the classical line, the artist is evidently to be distinguished by the last of these, but the kinds of preeminence we have now touched on are appropriate rather to secularized versions of the contemplative life or to negative counterparts of the active life.[7] (One might conjecture that if and when these other ways of life are restored to positions of honor in the everyday life of our society at large, art will revert to the sphere of fabrication, its original home, instead of standing in as a surrogate for the missing satisfactions of mystical adoration and political involvement.)

A second possibility is that the honor of art should be sought, not from the exaltation of the artist, but from the very unpopularity of art, which thus becomes contrasted with "life" or with "entertainment." This contrast may lie in its having a special and rarefied appeal, which only the cognoscenti or some other designated elite can understand, thus affording an enclave of difficulty and difference from the commercial enticements of a degradingly manipulative society; or the contrast may lie in its being actually offensive, subjecting the bourgeoisie to a deserved and salutary shock. In either version, this second possibility locates the honor of art in its provision of an alternative set of values, lest one mediocre custom should corrupt the world.[8] And here especially we notice how apposite it is to use the sweeping word "art" rather than the more precise phrase "works of art" or "the fine arts," for what serves this purpose is no set of objects or persons but a way of life with everything that belongs to it, all our engagements with it and commitments to it by virtue of the character we attribute to it—and, above all, what it stands for.

A third possibility is that art should be accorded dignity through the ontological singularity of its objects: created forms, species with temporal origins, a whole order of objects that but for man could never have existed. What is thus exalted is not the artist or his work, which in themselves might have no special merit, but precisely art itself, the very fact that such a pure origination should be found in the world.

A fourth possibility is that art should be thought of as a sort of magic or visionary power, through which man is related to some sort of cosmic force. Of course this possibility can only be realized where the reality of such a power is either recognized or feigned; but we shall see later that this condition is often fulfilled.

Finally, and most commonly, art may be assigned a cognitive priority in the articulation of spiritual energies. By "art" we now mean, or think we mean, or (as R. G. Collingwood put it) try to mean, that faculty whereby man achieves a truthful expression.[9] We find our way around the world and communicate with each other by using languages, systems of gestures, and other symbolic systems. No nation lacks these. But before they can be used they must be developed. It must therefore be characteristic of humanity that people can develop and acquire symbolic systems, which they previously lacked.[10] The symbolic inventions of art are the focus of activities that manifest, celebrate, and keep alive the most originative and therefore most fundamental aspect of this necessary ability to generate meanings and systems of meanings.

The following chapters will expound briefly three ways of thinking about what art really is that answer to three of the above grounds for the exaltation of art, together with the concomitant notions of a work of art and of an artist. We will find less to say about the concomitant views of what an art is, for the very notion of an art is proper to the classical line. Other lines of thought cannot deny the existence of the fine arts (indeed, we have urged that they are parasitic on them), but tend to find them an embarrassment or a scandal.

The views we are now to look at can be thought of as united in the following way. They all agree that the phenomena that define the classical line exist and are much as we say they are; but they take these phenomena to be, not the original datum, but the original problem for a theory of art. What really is all this stuff for? Why do people trouble themselves so? Granted, the classical line provides answers to these questions, but most of those answers are in terms remote from those by which the classical line defines art and its works; they have the air of excuses or afterthoughts. The views we are to examine take such reasons for art very seriously, and define art as what they are reasons for; consequently, they think of the established institutions as almost always adversaries or perverters of art as it should be—as indeed it must be if it is to do what it is for. These, then, in what they and we take to be the situation of artistic practice, are reformist views. Only some of what is generally called art will serve the proposed purpose and thus be worthy of the name of art: the rest will be "art falsely so called," spurious art, vestigial or degenerate art. But because those who hold these views define art in terms of a capacity and its manifestations, they will not only be reluctant to give the name "art" to those purported works that do not directly manifest any such capacity but may bestow that name (or wish that it might be bestowed) on much that in their eyes manifests the capacity, though it is not generally thought of as art.[11] We encounter, in fact, a problem of epistemological continuity, for which the classical line afforded no real counterpart. The theory of the fine arts takes it for granted that what the fine arts do is formalize, organize, and develop what already exists in an informal, unorganized, and less developed form. But if art is a manifestation of a special capacity, or something of that sort, we begin to wonder whether we should think of art as occupying some distinct sphere or as representing in extreme form tendencies that are manifested elsewhere than in art; and whichever answer we favor, either the evident continuities or the evident discontinuities are likely to cause us some theoretical trouble.

It is the contention of this book that, having expounded the classical line, we can readily present the other lines as departures from it in this direction or that, whether as true alternatives or as supplements, and no other starting point would afford such ready access to its alternatives. If that is made out, the claim to have presented a normal approach to art theory is so far made good. If not, the claim can only be that the approach taken here is no worse than others.[12]

What I have already said of the alternative or supplementary ways of thinking about art that I am about to expound indicates a curious ambivalence in the notion. On the one hand, we find traces of what is in fact a widespread notion that it is through art that a society finds expression of its common life, that the function of art is to unite men in feeling. On the other hand, art is conceived negatively as a protest against worldly or comfortable standards, as having as its main function, not to reconcile, but to shock or surprise, to oppose and destroy the ordinary conceptions of society.

This apparent contradiction could be reconciled in two ways. First, one could say that if art is a capacity with all its manifestations and effects, it is in the nature of capacities to be ambivalent, to be usable for good or ill. What unites can also separate, for every *us* is opposed to a *them*. The other thing one could say would be that it is indeed ideally the function of art, and the nature of art, to unite all men in feeling, but today's societies are such that this cannot be done. They are alienated and alienating, not true societies at all: all "everyday" communication is merely a failure to communicate, so that only art remains as a testimony to the possibility of *real* society and *true* communications. It is in the act of bearing this testimony that it opposes the false bonds and spurious communications that prevail. The pattern of thought that this attempt at reconciliation exemplifies is one familiar from theological and other ideological propaganda: one proves that every alleged white is off-white, and takes this as showing that black is the only true white. The pattern can be persuasive if the examples of off-white are carefully chosen and presented, and if one attends only to the presented case and fails to remind oneself of the general run of one's experience; but to recognize it is to rob it of its persuasive power. In the present case, one might reflect that people do live together in complicatedly interacting ways, and understand each other well enough to do so: even to generate a misunderstanding or a communications breakdown takes a great deal of preliminary communication.

Rather than try such desperate measures of argument, it might be better to let the contradiction stand. There are then several lines left open. One can say that some art unites and some confronts, some communicates and some affronts. One can say that true art affronts, and only entertainment or flattery pleases and joins;[13] or that true art unites in feeling, and whatever affronts is not true art but antiart;[14] or, with Tolstoy (1898), that true art unites in feeling and neither pleases nor offends as such, but false art is designed to please some and thereby offends others. Or one might say that by art we mean whatever expresses something (in the appropriate sense) successfully, and in the nature of things what is expressed will get through to some (can be intuited by them) and not to others. Or one may say that art does something else entirely, and whether it separates or unites people has nothing to do with its status or success as art. But one line that has lately been popular among theorists seems closed to us. We cannot now properly say that "art" is merely a collective term for works of art, and works of art form a class whose membership is determined simply by de facto acceptance of its individual members, so that any statements about the unifying or sundering functions of art are merely speculative ornament. For the very concept of art in the aspect under which we are now considering it is that of some sort of spiritual capacity and its manifestations; the reason for talking about "art" as opposed to works of art was precisely to accommodate that meaning. And we might add that those who embrace such alternative views of art as we are now undertaking to consider do not in fact coincide in their views of what is properly to be recognized as a manifestation of art. The layman is at liberty to extend the label "art" to all manner of *Kitsch* and hokum; and, though the high-minded theorist of art deplores such lax usage, he does not dispute its propriety, for it is exactly suited to the layman's ignorance and Philistinism. But he will no more acquiesce in it for himself and for those who are as thoughtful and serious as himself than an ornithologist will take the layman's word for what is a sparrow,[15] or a connoisseur of wine accept the Ontario vintner's word for what is champagne. Like the theorist of the fine arts, the layman uses the word "art" in a way that reflects his own legitimate interests and concerns and the level of his understanding. The theorist of art holds that those interests, concerns, and understanding are trivial or superficial.

How, in general, is the free-floating concept of art related to our classical line? That the views invoking art as a spiritual capacity can be construed as intelligible deviations from that line is a claim I hope to make good. But there are several possible relationships we have to bear in mind.

First, we must remind ourselves that generalizations about what art is and does can be taken in at least three ways. First, it can be held that each and every operation and object that is properly called a manifestation of art manifests the nature or fulfills the function in question. Second, one might hold that, whether any individual object or operation is or does what the theory requires or not, art *as a whole* is or does it. One is speaking about a total practice or cultural manifestation, to which particular objects and actions might contribute in a variety of ways that perhaps might not be individually demonstrable, just as what my brain does (or what I do with my brain) might not be reducible in practice to the sum of what individual neurons can be properly said to do. Third, one might hold that it is the nature and task of art to be or do whatever it is, and this nature or function is borne by particular operations and works, but it is not a defining property of works of art: the practices of art provide a matrix within which particular works fulfill the function in question and exist for the sake of those works, but other works that do not fulfill that function may nonetheless be proper cases of the practice. This third possibility exemplifies a pattern of thought that is very common and seems to me quite legitimate: it is the pattern appealed to in the cant phrase (ubiquitous in sermons and television commercials), "Isn't X (love, flavor, giving) what Y (marriage, beer, Christmas) is all about?" And if generalizations about art are taken in either of the last two ways, they cannot be rebutted by counterexamples of indubitable works of art that do not do the job art is supposed to do.

Second, we must not lose sight of the uses of the general word "art" that we found established within the classical line itself. The word is used, we recall, to mean the general human capacity and tendency to develop arts—its logic in this use is somewhat akin to that of the word "reason," or that of "language" when we take language to be a distinctive property of man, meaning that human beings all use some language or other and must be supposed to have whatever it takes to develop, learn, use, and understand languages. And we acknowledged another use of the term somewhat akin to this one: we pointed out that the term "art" is very commonly used without theoretical commitment, simply by way of gesturing vaguely toward that whole department of life that is concerned with the arts and their objects, artists and galleries and all that; and in this usage the logic of the term is akin to that of "sport" or even of "life." I have insisted that a large part of our conversation depends on such vague gestures being accepted and understood with appropriate flexibility. And the vagueness may take either of two forms. The word may be used to pick out something unspecified in the general direction indicated, the precise referent or significate to be determined, if at all, by the whole context of the conversation in which the term is used.[16] Or it may be used to designate the *Lebensform*, the whole domain as a type of context imparting a certain character to all that falls within it.

The foregoing general uses of the term "art" may be dismissed as innocuous, theoretically indifferent to any purposes of ours. But it is important to recognize both that they do prevail, and account for much general talk about art, and that thinking of art as a spiritual capacity has the way prepared for it by these humbler uses.

Another way in which talk about "art" can be related to the classical line relates to E. W. Hall's (1959) distinction of three ways in which behavior is subject to social control: technical, formal, and informal. The part of human behavior that is related to the fine arts and their products is very extensive and pervasive, and reaches in many ways into the avocations and pastimes both of children and adults. A lot of people spend a lot of time in a lot of different contexts doing things that are evidently related to what artists do expertly and professionally. Dancing, drawing, painting, designing, singing, and playing are not things we leave to specialists; and, though much of what we do is unpretentious and uninteresting to anyone except us who do it and our intimate associates, and may even be thought of as antithetic and inimical to "high art," it so obviously belongs to the same area of life that to leave it quite out of account would deprive one's work of any theoretical interest.[17] The classical line as I developed it treats the arts and their works from the point of what Hall calls the technical: as a mode of behavior in which ends and the means thereto are established, which is openly taught by recognized teachers, and the procedures of which are open to analysis and, if necessary, correction. It seems likely, however, that the segment of our behavior loosely designated as "art" should rather belong to what Hall calls the formal, or should have formal aspects. Hall's "formal" comes close to what philosophers have thought of as appropriate to morality: behavior that is deeply entrenched in society, its standards not open to rational criticism, thought of and judged in terms of (absolute) right and wrong, and imparted not through technical instruction but through deliberate encouragement and inhibition by people at large. The tone and manner of a Plato, a Ruskin, a Tolstoy, even a Croce, and the deep and ready response they have found, not to mention the moralization of aesthetics by the dictatorships of the first half of this century, suggest that art at least does not escape entirely the ways of formal thought and cannot be confined within the technical. To this extent, art, like morality, functions in our thought as an unqualified and unlocatable entity, the source of an absolute demand. And if art is not a mode of behavior confined to either the technical or the formal, we might expect to find it partaking also of what Hall calls the informal: the sort of behavior we simply pick up, apparently spontaneously, that is taught by example, compliance with which is not required or formally expected, but deviance from which merely becomes observable to the deviant and his compeers. And so of course it does. The things that "everyone" in this or that community simply does as a matter of course often if not always include activities within the broad domain of art. No doubt every such domain, every concrete complex of behavior, every *Le-*

bensform, partakes of the technical, the formal, and the informal alike. Art is too important to be left to the artists, or to the critics. The word "art" or some other linguistic device is thus indispensable, not as a way of indicating loosely the modes of behavior that the conceptual structure of the classical line more precisely articulates, but as a way of designating the entire complex of behavior patterns, no doubt far from self-contained, within which the classical line provides adequate articulation only for the technical component.[18]

The most significant way in which talk about "art" arises from the classical line is none of the above, but comes from the internal development and the internal disintegration of that line itself. On the one hand, each way of looking at the fine arts begins to turn them into something that goes beyond the concept of an art. Arts of imitation become exercises of creative power analogous to the fecundity of nature; arts of expression become disclosures of the depths of personality; arts of beauty become uses of imagination, and imagination is a faculty rather than a set of skills. On the other hand, the concepts associated with the concept of a fine art tend to break loose from it. When we turned from the concept of a fine art to the concept of a work of art, we found it expedient to define the latter, not as the actual product of the former, but rather as the sort of thing that such an art might produce. Then we defined an artist, not primarily as one who wields an art, but rather as one who has a propensity to produce works of art. And we identified a strong and familiar strain of thought according to which no skill or technique, and thus no art, could suffice to produce works that would serve as paradigms of our definition, though it might produce works that would exemplify it well enough. Consequently, proficiency in a fine art would not suffice to make someone an artist, in the sense of someone whose tendency was to produce paradigm works. Because of this insufficiency of the fine arts, we might (and often do) introduce "art," not as a generalized capacity whose specific manifestations are or include the fine arts, but as a supplement to them: the specific capacity, answering to the "originality" demanded of the artist, that runs beyond describable and transmittable skills and answers to whatever is inexplicable, unforeseen, uncovenanted in the man-made aesthetic object, that in it which cannot be explained but only recognized after the fact, because to accept an explanation of it would be to claim to know in advance what was significant in its outcome, and hence make examination of the work itself superfluous.[19] Art as thus thought of would indeed be a spiritual capacity. It would keep in touch with the classical line insofar as it was construed strictly as an ability to produce adequate aesthetic objects, however much dignity was devoted to the phrasing of that construction and however the ability excelled the skills it supplemented. But in speaking of indefinite capacities of persons we open the door to all sorts of extravagances, and it is through this door that modern departures from the classical line have mostly been made.

It is unjust to insinuate, as I just did, that to depart from the classical line involves extravagance. It may be argued that the inner disintegration of that line amounts to a blatant contradiction: that a performance merits contemplation precisely insofar as it is original and presents something altogether new to eye or mind, and hence escapes the scope of any art, whose operations can serve only to provide as it were a neutral vehicle for the work of art as such. And it is a mere pretense to say that in the fine arts a creative or imaginative capacity supplements skilled operation: art lies only in the former, the fine art only in the latter.

Many theorists who assign the word "art" a strategic place in their thinking do so because they think the notion of a fine art to be a contradiction in terms, and as a way of repudiating the classical line. For the pretense that creation supplements skills in a single operation they substitute the fiction that art depends on a creative power that could function in the absence of skill, rather than on a skilled use of such power or a creative use of skill. If challenged, they might concede that this was indeed a fiction, but a fiction that should be maintained because it isolates everything in art that is of interest to theory and of value to contemplation. One might retort that this isolation is as artificial as that which allegedly (in chapter 8) separated the original from the traditional, but such retorts do not always carry conviction.

The generalized reaction to the internal inadequacies and contradictions of the classical line, a reaction of which the programmatic use of the word "art" is the symbol, is familiar in history as the rise of Romanticism.[20] The actual development of that complex movement has been copiously and variously chronicled and analyzed in histories of literature and art, and it would be out of place to repeat the story here. Our interest in it is not as a historical reaction but as a permanent possibility, indeed a permanent necessity. As a standing position, equating art with creative imagination as it issues in objects for contemplation, I call it the poetic line, and I will give a perfunctory sketch of it before I go on to the three lines of thought that will concern us most: the expressive line, in which art is a sort of epistemic organization; the mystic line, in which art unites us with the divine; and the purist line, in which art is a manifestation of unworldly or antiworldly values.

The Poetic Line

There cannot be arts of beauty, because the beauty proper to art depends on difference; works of art cannot be manufactured, but must be created by means of a "creative process" in which the deployment of means toward an end does not figure. Art is altogether creative, a purely innovative action that springs from a purely innovative thought.[21] From what is created rules may be generated; but whatever is made by those rules will not have the status of art. The capacity for such originality will be of a very special sort, not a heightening of skill, but of a different order.[22] Since the eighteenth century the term "genius" has been reserved for it and contrasted with the "talent" that is a heightened aptitude for skill. The thought of the person of genius does not proceed by planning and contriving, but *ex hypothesi* must unfold in him spontaneously, like a natural growth: it is customary to speak of his thought processes as "organic" rather than "mechanical."[23] Ideas occur to him, and the result of putting those ideas into effect gives him further ideas: his critical and contriving faculties are confined to monitoring the flow and seeing where inspiration has run dry, or discarding the less promising of two alternatives, or taking care that casual inspiration does not destroy the main thrust of a work or lead it into irrelevance, just as a topiarist can do no more than clip off those shoots of his yew that weaken the shape it has taken.[24]

The dominant notion in this line of thought is that of "imagination," in one or more of three of its dominant senses: the bare ability to frame images, to have appearances present to one; the ability (Coleridge's "esemplastic power") to mold the objects of one's thought or vision into a coherent unity;[25] and the ability to conjure up, for contemplation by oneself or others, entities that owe their being to mental energies and not to any condign stimulus from the world outside. In our chapter on "arts of imagination," we sought to pursue these ideas in relation to arts of the aesthetic, within the bounds of the classical line, but we found it hard not to trespass beyond those bounds. We may note now the significant hint of sorcery in the phrase "conjure up," as if the artist were evoking a living object whose life did not depend on himself; and we saw in our earlier chapter how Mary Warnock found in this uncovenanted sense of induced vivacity the core of the notion of imagination itself. In the theory of art, the origin of this notion is Longinus' concept of the sublime, the inexplicable stroke that goes beyond the reach of rhetorical skill to suggest inexhaustible life and power; and his prime example was the injunction "Let there be light" in Genesis. To equate this intense but diffuse power of the creative utterance with imagination, and then to make imagination the whole of art, seems to take two large strides. But the move is not unjustifiable. To imagine is, in any case, to conjure up or frame a coherent appearance. Such an appearance, insofar as it is imagined, depends on the creating and sustaining work of the imaginer and is as such, as Sartre insists, an *unreal* object—one which, as imagined, we assign to a place in the world only secondarily in view of its "place" in the mind. It is then easy to argue that whatever is imagined, however sketchy, is always imagined *as* a whole, not constructed out of parts. God and Dr. Frankenstein, being respectively almighty and imaginary, can first construct bodies and then breathe life into them, but human creators have no such two-stage process available. One does not first imagine Mr. Pickwick's gaiters, then his glasses, then his bodily bits and pieces: one imagines, first vaguely and then less vaguely, a living presence who does not acquire gaiters and glasses but becomes gaitered and bespectacled; and the processes of refining and reworking cannot really be systematic or methodical, however much they may seem so to the casual or careless observer, for the intent of such revision can only be to render the original vision brighter or more coherent—that is, the existing whole suggests the whole into which it may be transformed.

All imaginative activity, we may say, conjures up lively wholes; but they may be idle, mere phantasms whose vitality is, as it were, exhausted in sustaining their own momentary being. To give them a definite and stable form, so that they can be contemplated by oneself and others, is what takes the creative power of genius. Anyone can say "Let there be light"; the test of the creative force is that there *is* light. The kind of imaginative activity that issues in contemplables, and is as such susceptible in principle of refinement through a creative process and not merely replacement as of one reverie by another, we may call (as Coleridge did) *poiesis* or poesy, or simply art.

If we think of art in this way, how shall we think of the fine arts? They are at best trivial, and at worst an embarrassment. They are trivial because what is essential to art is the creation of an imaginative (because in the first instance imaginary) object, and what differentiates one fine art from another is merely the type of matter that is given form or the type of form that is imparted to matter. They are at worst an embarrassment because if art is simply imaginative power, we should expect (as Socrates in Plato's *Symposium* expected, at the end of a hard night) not merely that every writer of tragedy could write comedy as well but that the typical artist would turn his hand equally to painting, music, poetry, and sculpture. The sculptor who is only a sculptor should be an exception to be explained away; the prevalence of sculptors who are only sculptors is something of a scandal.[26]

What in effect happens when art is thought of as primarily an affair of the imagination is that the place of the arts is taken by art history. Instead of reflective and systematic thought about artistic production being practical, productive, and prospective, it becomes reconstructive and retrospective; and, as we observe elsewhere, the artist's thought about his work comes to be dominated by an attempt to forecast how his work will fit into the eventual story of the art of his time, if it will be part of the main narrative or a mere excursus or footnote.

What, then, of the artist? His status is that of creator, envisager of new possibilities and maker of new being. But this status is an ambiguous one—an ambiguity that may be extracted from a dictum in a book review by C. R. Brighton. There are, he says, two ways of responding to the apparent chaos in the contemporary art scene. One response deplores the loss of traditional values. "The second, the radical response, argues the opposite case. It holds that the traditional values of art do not lie in the values presented by individual objects, but in the originality and creativity of artists and maintains that it is this which characterizes the greatest art of all ages" (Brighton 1971, 105). As it stands, the wording of this statement is odd. It suggests that to create and originate is not to create and originate anything in particular. Would not such production be exemplified in a mere striving after novelty or in a blindly productive force like a cancer? But that cannot be meant, because such mere productivity would not "characterize the greatest art of all ages." So what is meant is probably one of two things, though one cannot tell which. First, it might be meant that the value of a great work lies in the quality of originality discernible in it (and, of course, in others like it), not in its compliance with set standards. The quality of the performance (to use my own jargon) testifies to the excellence of the performing and hence to the merit of the performer—and perhaps to the corresponding personal merit of the artist, the person who the performer is.[27] But, second, it might be meant (and the language used, contrasting the values presented by the work with those possessed by the artist, strongly suggests that it is meant) that the value of the work lies in nothing discernible in it; the work is valued merely as the byproduct of the personal qualities of the artist. Whether intended by Brighton in this context or not, the latter move is fateful. It leads to the notion (which we shall return to in the purist line) that, if one is the right kind of person, it is not necessary to create art in order to be an artist. If the work is no more than evidence of the artist's merit, it is that merit itself which alone has value—just as, on Aristotle's view, fame and applause have no other value than that of testifying to the presence of the applauded qualities, which would be the same whether they were applauded or not. Indeed, if art (as opposed to the fine arts) is some kind of spiritual level, the conclusion that nothing matters except the inner attainment of that level becomes one that theorists require ingenuity and determination to avoid.

The same destination is reached by a slightly different route. The artist's status of creator and envisager of new possibilities and realities is shared with original scientists, mathematicians, philosophers, and so on: creativity is not the prerogative of art. And we can hardly define him by his product, since the refusal of status to the arts goes with an equally programmatic refusal to accept that one knows what sort of thing will be found worth contemplating. So the artist comes to be defined contextually by the idea of art: he is a creative member of the historic community, the communion of secular saints, that art history and allegiance to that history define. He is a plaything of the cunning Hegelian reason. But since we cannot wait for history (because history will not wait for us), the context by which the artist is defined is actually an institutional one: the artist is one who devotes himself to art, goes to art school, exhibits at art galleries, and generally occupies the role of trainee and producer in the world of art. And since, as we saw, his occupation of that role is contrasted with the actual production of recognizable sorts of things, it will be enough if he is identified with that role by himself and others.

What, finally, of the work of art? The situation here is ambiguous. If we take the poetic line as contrasting organically creative art of the imagination with mechanical production of bijouterie or mere craftsmanship, there seems to be no problem: it was from the idea of the work of art extrapolated from the classical line that the poetic line took its start. The work of art is simply a product of the imagination directed to contemplation. If we wish to complicate our account by saying that contemplation is itself an exercise of imagination and by trying to relate this reconstitutive act of imagination to the original creative act, we may do so; many people have done so, and Croce found it necessary to do so in the context of his version of the expressive line, but for the poetic line in general it is not necessary.

Although it is open to the poetic line to deal with the work of art very simply and directly, in the way just sketched, we have seen already that complications may be introduced. Emphasis on the artist and on his qualities tends to relegate the work to an inferior position. There are other considerations that may have the same effect. Because the arts are replaced by history in this way of thinking, the work of art becomes a part of the historical process and in itself a mere abstraction (in Hegel's sense), something whose meaning lies not in itself but in its relation to the mental realm of which it forms a part. There is thus a very real tendency for the idea of a work of art to vanish: it is the artist's creativity, the art act, that matters; the work is at best a sign that art has been here. So, like the classical line, the poetic line generates a disintegration that amounts to a contradiction: as, on the classical line, the arts must be but cannot be regular means of attaining the irregular, so here the work of art as created is (to draw on Souriau once more) the most thinglike of things, but as essentially dependent on the creative act a mere abstraction. As with the classical line, the contradiction is easily avoided by those who wish to avoid it—one has only to repudiate the role assigned to history. But some people think it smarter to embrace contradictions than to eschew them—one has to be very *deep* to contradict oneself *and mean it*—and others like to think of history rolling ever onward and carrying us all with it, like fleas on a dog.

The notion of art in general that is presented by what I have here called the poetic line is widely current, though seldom explicitly developed. Theorists rather neglect it, though it has respectable ancestry. Its roots are Neoplatonic, and it could be teased out of the hints on the nature of beauty in the plastic arts dropped by Plotinus (*Enneads* V. 8.i). Plotinus derives the beauty of the work from two timeless sources: the beauty of the original idea to which the content of the work relates and the beauty inherent in the art as it exists in the artist's mind. In other words, he writes as if the Aristotelian "final cause" of the work were not a sort of blueprint for it in the artist's mind but rather his sharing in the intellectual capacity to generate forms of that sort. Aristotle himself had said that it was the art of building that was the form of the house (*Metaphysics* Z,9, 1034a24), but he had not made the art a principle of beauty. The idea of a double source of beauty of this sort is developed by Jacques Maritain (1953); for our purposes, what it involves is that the artist not only must be able to divine the beauties latent in things but must himself be the channel for an independent source of beauty not reducible to anything in the world that stimulates him. And this is an aspect of the generic notion of art as developed in the poetic line. It is mildly paradoxical to father this notion of creativity on Plotinus, for whom the artist cannot be truly creative, but can only be a channel for the manifestation of beauties whose principle is eternal. But the paradox is a very mild one: in the first place, since the sole reason for invoking an eternal reality is that the evidenced power runs beyond any material exemplification, the distinction between antecedent reality and created novelty can be made only on a priori grounds; and, in the second place, proponents of the poetic line are ever ready (as we have seen Klee was, see note 23) to ascribe the creation of novelty itself to a higher source, for which the artist is a mere channel. A creative artist is a mystery to himself, obviously, and must therefore be equally a mystery to whoever takes his creativity seriously.[28]

There are three reasons why the poetic line as expounded here is not favored by theorists. The first is that its leading exponents (like Coleridge) are specifically theorists of literature in the very dense historical context of the Romantic movement, and are felt to repay study most fully when related to that context in all its occasionally arbitrary richness. The second is that, if the implications of the Neoplatonic background are accepted, new theoretical considerations are introduced, which take us into what I shall discuss later as the mystic line. The third is that its characteristic ideas, or their counterparts, take on more precision in the expressive line, to which we now turn. In fact, the expressive line is what happens to the poetic line if one tries to make a theory out of it. For these reasons, I have not treated the poetic line as a full-fledged type of theory alongside the other four.

XI

THE EXPRESSIVE LINE
1: ART AS EXPRESSION

Of all those alternatives to the classical line that find their natural expression in speaking of "art" as a single significant entity rather than of "arts" or "the fine arts," by far the most influential and widespread has been what I here call the expressive line. Not only was this approach the one generally taken by theorists of art in the early decades of this century, but more recently, as the entrenched doctrine, it was what theorists conscious of their originality felt they had to present themselves as combating.

What I mean by "the expressive line" is the various developments of the idea that art is that in which one makes one's truest feelings clear to oneself and others: in a phrase, that art is "the expression of emotion." But that phrase can be very misleading.

The concept of expression has already occupied our attention in several contexts within the domain of the classical line. What we are about to discuss is something different.

First, the theory that the fine arts were in whole or in part arts of the expression of feeling, of the subjective aspect of experience, appeared as one variety of the theory that those arts are arts of imitation, representing the disengaged development of the cognitive faculties. But such an art is a presentation of a kind of material, which can be worked up and exploited: the artist's true feelings, and his potentiality for feeling, are a resource for his art. And the work that is the outcome of such exploitation is a work for a public: if the artist is the first member of his own public, that is merely incidental; and if he is the sole member of his own public, that is exceptional and (usually) unfortunate. The underlying thesis of the expressive line is very different. What is essential is that the feeling in question be made clear. That is, it was not clear before. The process of clarification is therefore one of pure discovery.[1] There can be no art or skill of it and especially no question of *working up*: immediacy, in one sense or another, is essential. And we said that the artist makes his feeling clear to himself and others.

But it is obvious that he himself is the sole judge, if not of the clarity, then of the fact that what is clarified is what was to be made clear. And the others are not so much *the public* as witnesses of an achievement of clarity that can only take place within the artist's mind.[2]

Second, we previously identified an expressive aspect of every work of art as corresponding to a dimension of performance: as a thing made or done, a work of art may require for its appreciation more or less attention to its implicit performer and manner of performing. But that expressive aspect was a factor in the design, part of the aesthetic quality to be appreciated in the work, and as such shared the status of pure fiction (that is, we recall, questions of truth and untruth were as such irrelevant, even factual veracity being aestheticized). What the expressive line holds is that the actual accomplishment of a real clarification is important: so far from veracity being fictionalized, fictions are valued for such real insight as they represent.

Third, we noted in the classical line that many aestheticians attributed three dimensions to every work of art, of which an expressive dimension was one: closely akin to the "expressive aspect" just mentioned, but belonging to a rather different context, the expressive dimension was the stylistic one, the "way of doing" a work projected. But this dimension is one dimension among others, an aspect of something whose other aspects are no less important: the work of art is not simply an exemplification of style, and does not exist for the sake of style. And, if it did, the style as something projected by the work and shareable by other works (so that, as we said, the work potentially participates in an expressive world) is not that unique feeling which (according to the expressive line) the work of art exists to clarify, and of which ideally it is nothing but the clarification.

Fourth, our exposition of the classical line used the concept of expression when we considered the characterization of works of art, and gave special attention to those epithets of art whose home ground was in the domain of human feeling. The use of such language has no direct bearing on the expressive line. Not only (as we saw) is the use of such language equivocal, so that a sad piece of music might be sadness showing or sadness producing or simply sad-in-the-sense-in-which-sad-music-is-sad, or more likely something more complex than any of those; in any case, such attributes are merely some of the aesthetically relevant attributes that works of fine art may have. However important, as attributes they do not constitute the essence of that to which they are attributed. The only bearing of such language on the expressive line is indirect: if indeed art is that in which feeling is brought to clarity, the feeling thus clarified might well be one to which some such general label as "sad" would be (though not very illuminatingly) applicable, so that the prevalence of such a vocabulary would come as no surprise.

It is obvious from the foregoing that not every use of the word "expression," and not even every theoretically responsible use of it, pertains to the expressive line. The interests of clarity would certainly be served if that line gave up the word "expression" altogether, and used some word (such as "clarification" itself) not already heavily committed elsewhere. But it is too late for that. "Expression" is what the leading exponents of the line (and all their followers) use. And they might object to our allegation that the word is *already* committed elsewhere. They might urge that the word "expression" is introduced into the philosophy of art to mean very precisely what they mean by it, by Herder and his contemporaries, and it would be cowardice to acquiesce in the slow corruption and contamination by which its pristine meaning has been beclouded.

Whatever the priorities and proprieties, the English word "expression" has associations that are inimical to the expressive line. As Tormey points out (1971), what we speak of as "expressed" is usually something that has an intentional object, which can be stated in propositional form: I express the fear, the belief, *that* something is or may be the case.[3] In other words, the expressible is (as it were) parasitic on discursive language; and that is the very opposite of the situation envisaged by the expressive line, in which what is expressed is supposedly an emotionally charged intuition the clarification of which is the discovery of a meaningfulness incapable of any reduction. Nor is the expression, on the other hand, a mere revelation or disclosure of something antecedently felt: the feeling and the expression are one. Thus, expression in the required sense has to be distinguished from betraying, evincing, or otherwise giving signs or indications of mental states.

If what the expressive line means by "expression" is something that can be understood only by following an exposition of the line itself and attending to the specific phenomena it picks out, and not by looking up "expression" in a dictionary, even a dictionary of musical terms (cf. Tormey 1971, 110ff.), the terms "emotion" and "feeling" are no less misleading. Those words make it sound as if what were in question was the venting of some sort of mood, like sadness, by discovering a qualitative analogue of it that could be imparted to a perceptible object.[4] But a mood is not the kind of thing that can be clarified. What is intended is rather that one attain a clear and distinct idea, in which the object of experience and the quality of the experience are one; Croce prefers the word "intuition," and I will later follow him in this. It is characteristic of the expressive line to make the programmatic claim that in any clear, attentive, and honest experience the precise object of awareness, and one's precise feeling about that object, are mutually determining, so that neither can be specified without specifying the other—and that it is in art that experiences of this character are achieved.[5]

It is clear from what I have been saying that the expressive line is in sharp contrast with what is said of "expression" in this or that context of the classical line: it holds that what is essential to art is something that escapes in principle from the net of the fine arts. The classical line is wrong from the start. What is now meant by "expression" is something to be defined as the distinctive character of art by the theory itself, whether or not what is thus defined overlaps with what is elsewhere called expression. Most critiques of "the expression theory of art" are quite unaware of this contrast. Thus, although they are effective ad hominem against careless statements of the expressive line, they sink into futility because what they attack is the thesis (seldom if ever held) that art is essentially expression in one or more of the senses that belong to the classical line. That is, their authors are ignorant of the doctrines they purport to challenge.[6] That is not to say, of course, that the expressive line in any of its versions is tenable or even intelligible. It is only to say that it is the expressive line that has absorbed the energies of the philosophy of art for the last two centuries.[7]

To castigate the critics of the expressive line as careless and ignorant, as I just did, is not fair. It would be truer to say that they have neglected to meet (as a philosophical critic should) the purest and most forcible version of the doctrine under attack. For it is not only the critics who are confused. Many, perhaps all, of the exponents of the expressive line itself occasionally use language and even avow opinions that pertain to the classical line.[8] In particular, theorists of the expressive line are indeed given to speaking as if (and therefore, presumably, actually *supposing* that) the kind of clarification they painfully expound has something to do with "self-expression" in an everyday sense. What one finds in nature, all too often, is a hybrid mishmash of mutually incompatible notions: my expressive line is thus to some extent an abstraction. But the abstraction is true to the plainly avowed intent of the leading theorists of the line.

I began this chapter by saying that the expressive line has been the most widely held theory of art as such. One can go further. Until recently, and to some extent even today, the thesis that art is the expression of emotion, understood in a rather confused way, has remained "obviously true" in that it has been the accepted line for persons of general culture to take when talking about those works or occasions of production that are taken as paradigms of art—and are taken to be paradigms just because the language of expression can be applied to them without the appearance of paradox.

I have said some of the things that the expressive line is not (but with which it is often confused). It remains to say what it is. But that is not easy. The central notion that art is the expression of emotion sees in it a joint (and mutual) refinement of perception and feeling, or (in Hegel's terms) the finding of an adequate form for an idea—a form that can be adequate, we must add, only because the idea was initially framed as its own adequate form. But this central notion represents the confluence of three quite different impulses, any one of which may dominate (or which may be variously combined) in a given version, and which are not easy to reconcile with each other.

The first impulse toward the expressive line sees in art a matter of feeling as opposed to artifice. In most utterance what is said and meant embodies hearsay, habit, convention, which not only conceal the nature of what they refer to but evade and falsify and hence degrade and corrupt the experience itself that should find expression in them. Art represents, by contrast, a directness of utterance (in whatever medium) that has the quality of a simple gesture, the outward form of a clear eye or ear and a simple heart.[9] The utterance is not an artifact to clothe, reveal, disguise, or modify an experience separable from it: the achievement of the utterance and the having of the experience are one. If a language is used, it is as if the language were minted for the occasion and the utterance itself were a single original word or gesture.

The second impulse toward the expressive line stems from what was said in the last sentence of the preceding paragraph and expounded in chapter 10. All language, and all artistic convictions, rely on the manipulation of symbols of which the meaning is in a sense already established.[10] But before languages can be used they must be invented: suitable symbols must be coined. Human beings

307

must therefore have had, and presumably still have, the capacity to produce mental contents that are not parts of extant symbol systems but are that on the basis of which such systems can be constructed. There must, that is to say, be a level of basic intuition that is the epistemic origin of all discursive thought, a grasping of unitary complexes of thought and feeling.[11] That level is art.

The third impulse that drives toward the expressive line stems from considering the significance of the epistemic origination I just mentioned. Man is the symbol-using animal: humanity and language use are coextensive.[12] The achieving of basic intuitions is then the essential step in the humanization of mankind. In expressing emotions we come to have expressible emotions, that is, civilized emotions. Art as the expression of emotion is then at once the invention and the discovery of mankind.

The three impulses just mentioned, though intimately linked, diverge. Spontaneity and directness as such have little or nothing to do with clarification or authenticity—an unconsidered word or gesture is as likely to be a cliché as not. And clarification is something one can work at, eliminating what was due to slackness and inattention. Clarity can be *achieved*; a gesture cannot. As for the humanization of mankind, that should surely be a slow and cumulative business, not confined to a series of intuitions achieved and then remembered and combined. Rather, the humanization of man should be a matter of achieving a certain level of lucidity in one's life as a whole, and this has little to do with the attaining of particular insights and intuitions. The expressive line, then, seems to point us toward three linked notions of what art is: direct gestural expression; the achievement of clear and purified intuitions; and the attainment of clarified consciousness. Theories belonging to the expressive line tend to take one of these three directions without any clear consideration of the alternatives.

Let us consolidate our position by recapitulating half a dozen basic contentions or insights that constitute the expressive line, as first formulated in the eighteenth century and since refined and distorted.[13]

First, what characterizes humanity is articulate culture, which can be equated with language in a broad sense: ways and forms of life organized through the syntactical deployment of an integrated set of concepts or analogous mental objects referring to reality as experienced.

Second, the use of language presupposes the invention of languages, which depends on the recognition of significant occasions:

the archetypal language-generating act is the devising or discovery of a sound or movement or mark (a "gesture" in any event) that stands at once for something worth noting, what is worth noting about it, and why it is worth noting—the reference, sense, and significance of the gesture.

Third, in the life of every individual his learning of his language is his becoming human. It is also his becoming the individual he is, because to learn the common language of one's people is at the same time to invent one's own language. Language is a device he takes over and makes his own. Its possibilities are resources for making his own language (his own system of references, senses, and significances) and thereby his world (as he lives it and lives in it) and himself.[14]

Fourth, both in the life of an individual and in the development of a society or culture, routine and habitual experiences and attitudes (the "everyday") are referred to and characterized by repeating and combining established linguistic means, but new experiences and new approaches can only be realized in new symbolizations—new linguistic forms, new art forms. More accurately, insofar as anything is experienced as new, that is, insofar as it is experienced at all, it must be enshrined in an original linguistic gesture, and every such original gesture enshrines a new experience that it alone makes possible.[15]

Fifth, it is the function of art to provide these new intuition-releasing gestures. Strictly, though not in common speech, art is nothing other than the provision of these original expressions. Every such expression, however unself-conscious, humble, transient, and unnoticed, is art no less than is the masterpiece that is recognized as molding the consciousness of its people and its age. In the next chapter, we shall see if there are not reasons for softening this position, and ways of doing so, but the basic position is this intransigent one. In any case, nothing is properly called art that is not such an expression: common use, based on the institutionalization of the fine arts, conceals the true significance of those arts themselves, as everyone would realize if they stopped to think—and having stopped, thought honestly.

Sixth, art as thus identified necessarily has the status of absolute origin in the economy of mind. Its having that status has two consequences. First, a work of art as such cannot be analyzed. It may, of course, consist of words, pieces of stone, discrete sounds, and definable harmonies, but cannot be properly described as a system of such parts, which must be fused in it into an integral whole.[16]

Second, though the work may stand in a felt relation to some antecedent observation or feeling or experience that it may be said to record or express, that relation cannot be formally described or categorized but is necessarily indeterminate, because to precede expression is to be indeterminate. The experience expressed in the work cannot be formulated otherwise than in the work itself.[17]

The first of the foregoing points has its antecedents long before Vico and Herder, in the view of human life put forward in Aristotle's *Ethics* and *Psychology*. What is characteristic in human life is that part of it which is amenable to conscious control: man is a rational animal. That is, a human being is a living thing whose life has a complex order. Human seeing does not merely register the differential impact of light rays, as a photographic film does: it selects and arranges in the light of memories and projects. A human action is not a mere response to a stimulus, but involves generalizing, arranging, and conceptualizing: actions reflect attitudes and enter into plans. When a human being eats, he does not merely browse or graze, but takes a meal, the selection, preparation, and ambiance of which all form part of a way of life consciously developed and pursued and saturated with meanings. The course of one's life among other people is something of which one is aware, although (since it is all-embracing) it cannot be captured by any formula: it must, therefore, have an ineffable order by virtue of which it is graspable, and this order or style is imparted to it by the actions of which it consists. The actions that make up our lives are, therefore, saturated in an activity, ceaseless and pervasive, whereby our lives become meaningful in their parts and as wholes— an order not imparted to lives that would still be something without it, but an order in living. Some parts and some aspects of this activity are routine or ritual, repetition or rearrangement, but these parts and aspects conceived as separable do not constitute the intimate fabric of our experience. It is to the unified underlying order in the life of an individual and, in a lesser degree, of a society, rational because full of meaning but not reducible to concepts, fully interrelated but not separable into relations and *relata*, that the expressive line looks. To say that art is expression is to say that art is the whole or part of this shaping activity; to equate art with expression is to affirm that whatever truly has this quality of being through-and-through meaningful has the status of art.[18]

The equation of art with expression, as thus conceived in the context of an Aristotelian anthropology, has the happy consequence that a life lived in full consciousness would be a life of art, the only possible perfect work of art. This idea has in fact attracted many, but it is not normally espoused by proponents of the expressive line. The seamless unity of such a life could hardly go to build up a linguistic or cultural deposit of achieved forms, and bears no simple relation to those limited objects we know as works of art. It is one thing to say (as the expressive line delights to say) that common notions of what a work of art is err alike in their inclusions and their exclusions—that they do not quite hit the target they aim at; it is another thing to say that they aim at the wrong target altogether. That would be just nonsense. Exponents of the expressive line accordingly confine the status of art to particular coherent complexes of experience, saturated with meaning in the way I spoke of, but delimited and self-contained and thus able to serve as objects of cognition—in fact, a class of what in expounding the classical line I called performances. A work of art as thus conceived is really nothing other than a clear and distinct idea, as that notion was formulated within Cartesian philosophy. What is necessary to clarity and distinctness is that the flux of experience shall not only be a rich and orderly flow but shall admit of being ordered in its parts, so that, through memory or perception or rumination or however, a moment of experience can be given form: it will be clear to the extent that nothing in it is unformed, irrelevant, or unexamined, distinct to the extent that it is complete in itself, self-explanatory, not essentially related in its meaning to any other idea. It is true that, according to Cartesian rationalism, poetical ideas or intuitions can only be clear, not distinct, but that is because distinctness depends on differentiation, which requires logical definition.[19] Perception does not involve negation. But the inference "not logically differentiated, therefore confused" begs the question: it must be the contention of the expressive line that the self-contained nature of the clarified intuitions it postulates involves a *haecceitas*, an element of being-nothing-other-than-this. The substitution of nothing-other-than-this for this-rather-than-that captures what was meant by distinctness.[20]

An "expression theory of art" would either be one in which notions of the foregoing sort were made precise (for instance, by specifying what distinctness was, by defining rationality or substituting for rationality some comparable concept, and by establishing criteria of clarity) and their relations specified, or a specific version of the classical line's reduction of imitation to the expression of subjectivity, or a psychological hypothesis about the conditions in which art originates and flourishes and by which works of art come about.[21] These are different sorts of theory, as I have insisted, but a particular theorist may confuse them or deliberately try to combine them; it is by no means certain that this cannot be done without confusion, however much confusion may have been thus engendered in the past. Within the expressive line, a theorist must in effect choose whether to emphasize the lyrical and gestural quality of art or its freedom from unclarity; its spontaneity or its character of achievement; its epistemic originality or its humanizing synthesis. And he must also in effect decide (for there is no reason why such a question should be explicitly posed rather than revealed as solved in the lucidity and consistency of exposition) whether to treat such pairs of alternatives as occasions for choice or as poles between which tension must be preserved without sacrificing either. For one may well argue that in dealing with the life of the mind, which is strenuous and full of conflict, a theory that is free from internal tensions cannot contribute much to the search for truth and can be of only mild interest.

Up to this point, I have tried to characterize the expressive line generally. In what follows I shall restrict myself more closely to one version of that line: a purified version, derived from the opening pages of Croce's early *Aesthetic* (1901).[22] For our purposes, though not historically, the version in question appears as an attempt to reform that version of the classical line which treats the fine arts as arts of the aesthetic, the skilled production of objects for contemplation, by first eliminating the extrinsic aspects of that notion and then removing the trivializing features of what is left. The most obvious result, we find, is the elimination of the fine arts. First, all secondary standards are ruled out: no criteria of skill can be relevant, since the test of a contempland is contemplability. Next, we rule out any supposed benefits of contemplation, which would undermine its nature as contemplation. At the same time, rules are eliminated, since what has to comply with a rule need not be contemplated, but only checked out. By the same token, we deny that such knowledge of artistic practice as is involved in critical reference to genres and set forms is relevant to artistic appreciation: such reference makes us stop contemplating and start comparing. Again, we exclude from our theory of art any reference to purposes that contemplation may serve: not only such political benefits as conservation, revolution, and reform, and moral betterments such as encouragement or improvement of life, but even such immediate payoffs as instruction and delight. We contemplate, not to learn or to amuse ourselves, but for the sake of the contemplation itself.

So we will follow Collingwood (1938) in contrasting "art proper" with rhetoric (which seeks to persuade), with magic (which seeks to enchant), and in general with craftsmanship (which seeks to encompass preconceived ends). It is even misleading to say that the end of art is only to be art, for no work has so general an end, and the concept of art has no more place in the generation of art than any other concept: the end of any operation of art is only to bring its own proper object into being. The work of art is not even (as our language has thus far suggested) *to be contemplated*: it is contemplable only because it is already contemplated in being achieved. Art is nothing but the generation-in-contemplation of the contemplable, and has no more future destiny than past history.

The basic concept in the expressive line as I will now develop it is that of an intuition: a logically primitive entity that is yet both cognitively and affectively full of meaning. An intuition is an idea, image, or thought that is clear in the sense that it is pellucid, has nothing in it that is obscure or confused or unformed, and distinct in the sense that it is different and sharply separate from every other. Though previously attained expressions may genetically contribute to such an intuition, they can form no part of it: a new intuition, formulating in its clarity and distinctness a genuinely integral view of some moment of lived experience, makes a new beginning. And there can be no method or art of arriving at such intuitions, since an art requires at least a logical and practical distinction between matter and operation.

To grasp what is meant by "intuition" in the relevant sense, it is best to consider some actual work of art that one takes to be entirely successful and to consider how a scrupulous critic would see it and what he would say of it (a hostile commentator would say: to consider a carefully chosen aspect of that). Consider, then, El Greco's *Burial of Count Orgaz*, supposing this to be in our eyes a perfect work of art. Obviously, we can describe its form and its color scheme, enumerate its parts, say who is portrayed in it. But in doing that we are not saying what it is that makes it an excellent work of art or even a work of art at all; such a description has exactly the same form as that of any colored snapshot. We can, perhaps, say how El Greco came to paint it and how he did so: who commissioned it, what inducements were offered, then what sketches he made, how he worked them up, who helped him with backgrounds and ground his colors. But nothing in that story has any bearing on the painting as a work of art: every detail in the story could be quite different, and if the resulting painting looked just the same (as why might it not?) it would be just the same painting. We can relate the style of the painting to post-Byzantine formal conventions and to post-Titian colorism. But the use El Greco made of those was not as items in a repertoire, as one selects this or that tie to wear at a wake; rather, what in a bungler might have been conventions here become the very stuff of vision. If we need to learn about them, it is only to forestall an impression that we have to do with intrusive strangenesses.[23]

The foregoing remarks are the merest clichés of criticism, even if it is the influence of the expressive line that has made them so. In other words, the notion of an intuition is a familiar one, and is reached by considering what is already recognized as the way of thinking about art most appropriate to the tenderest critical conscience. What is new is the insistence that even so elaborate an object, set in the midst of a cultural life to which it is integral, has an epistemological simplicity that belies its evident historical and compositional complexity, coupled with the assertion that this is not just one way in which tender-minded critics think about an aspect of masterpieces but the only proper way to think about any work, works to which it is inappropriate being dismissed as spurious or contaminated. Either intuition has been achieved or it has not, and whatever is not achieved intuition is not art. As intuition, moreover, a large and complex painting is on exactly the same footing as any gesture or exclamation in which a perfect expressiveness is achieved. In fact, the advantage is on the side of the humble gesture, which is more likely to be free from construction and contrivance. Any work on a large scale is likely to have slack parts, unassimilated aspects and bridge passages, and so is less likely to be a true work of art than its humbler counterpart.

Reflection on what has just been said about complex paintings and the like brings to light a problem that may prove insuperable. The initial paradigm of an intuition is an ideally integrated masterpiece of art. But, as the El Greco example suffices to show, such a masterpiece can only be a product of a mind already civilized. Similarly, a poem, however indissolubly unified in its meaning, is erected on the basis of a conceptual structure in which each concept must rest, at some depth, on an original intuition, a gesture of mind past. The work of art, then, cannot really be on the same epistemic level as the basic intuitions that our most naive expressions still embody. It must belong to some higher cycle of integration, one that cannot form the basis of language, but either remains in its own right as a flower of experience or is reintegrated into the unified life of the cultured mind that itself becomes a sort of second-order "language" or symbolically ordered totality. Perhaps, then, we should say that only such higher level integrations should be called art, but proponents of the expressive line have mostly opposed this move as subverting its deepest intent. We shall return to the question in another context.

Meanwhile, we cannot but recognize in this theme of second-order unification a complication (if not a problem) that arose already within the concept of imagination (see chapter 5), but to which we paid little heed at the time. We have seen that Coleridge distinguished between fancy, the ability to join separate images in striking new combinations, and imagination, the ability to generate unified images—the esemplastic power that is characteristic of art. But within the general framework of a Kantian epistemology the existence of a single world of space-time must itself be the product of a unifying power of the mind: the mind does not combine data that come to it from elsewhere, but generates a perceptible world by generating not only percepts but perceptible relations in such a way that, for instance, we are aware of a continuous and continuing "visual field." How does the primary unifying (esemplastic) power of imagination whereby we generate a perceptible world differ from the power of imagination that generates specific intuitions and, therewith, art? The same problem is posed by Kant's theory of the aesthetic judgment. The significance of such a judgment is that it responds to a pure orderliness, a directedness without specific direction, and thus deploys the faculty of imagination that, by linking actuality to teleology, secures the unity of the human mind. But has this not been done already in the unity of apperception that presents the world as a unified whole within which the sense of actuality can be deployed? The world is itself the work of imagination, so there is no need for any additional field or mode of judgment to provide the imagination with a sphere of operations all its own (cf. Podro 1972). The world is already beautiful (and purely so: there is no *concept* of a world in accordance with which we judge our world perfect); so what, really, is the status of those things (including works of art) that we call beautiful? In Kant and Coleridge, as in our general consideration of the expressive line, we seem to be confronted with a superimposition of originations: absolute novelty is claimed for a form generated on the basis of what is already formed.

The solution to the little puzzle we just posed is not far to seek. In Coleridge's case, we start by saying (as he said) that there are two levels of imagination, a primary and a secondary. Primary imagination, the world-generating function that every idealist must postulate as the primary work of mind, is epistemologically the more significant, but the order it generates is weak in that its orderliness is not evident. Since the world is everything, it cannot manifest a single order, because it must embrace whatever is most disorderly, casual, or adventitious (unstructured interplays of regularly operative forces, unplanned intersections of subplans in a master plan, unlegislated effects of freedom within the law). And, insofar as it is experienced as order, it is an order that the subject encounters as object, one in which the felt and inchoate demands of the heart are not so much rebuffed as excluded. What the secondary imagination of art creates is an order in which subjective and objective are fused, in which feelings take symbolic shape and objects are expressive of feeling: a finite order in which the cosmogonic power is evidently at work in every part. Similarly, in the Kantian context, a perceptual unity that the mind imposes just so that it can have something to perceive will not have the character of an evident unity. Transcendental reflection reveals that it is ordered and thus orderly in a way in which it might not have been— or rather, we would like to say "it might not have been" but cannot, because no world not thus ordered could be a world for us, and that fact is a measure of the weakness of the order it has. What we find beautiful is what affords to imagination a special opportunity, in which orderliness is not revealed by reflection but is at once evident and the open-ended and accommodating orderliness of the world as a whole is supplemented by a closed and intensive order. The ordering faculty is the same, but in this special use its exercise is facilitated and encouraged and is thus raised to the level of delighted consciousness.[24] The aesthetic judgment that deploys this emphatic use of imagination is symbolically (and for the philosopher systematically) significant, but not epistemologically, except that a mind incapable of aesthetic judgment could not perceive or envisage a world at all.

The application to the expressive line is immediate. The perceptible world is in its own way a repertory of clear and (in a way) distinct ideas, in that the intelligent eye and ear encounter no limit in apprehending and distinguishing. What is seen fuzzily is seen as just as fuzzy as it is; and if the eye cannot distinguish between two resembling shades or two mutually approximate magnitudes, then the imperceptible distinctions are not perceptual indistinctions: they function as unclarities and indistinctnesses, not in the moment of perception, but in some intellectual maneuver carried out on the basis of perception, so that (as we saw) attributing indistinctness to ideas of sense begs the question by intruding an intellectualist bias.[25] Our perception of the world then has, in some sense, the status of intuition.[26] But within the world's order limits are too easily imposed, and their imposing is a matter of indifference: it is not that the world "given to sensation" is a blooming, buzzing confusion, but that the world taken in perception is overabundantly ordered. That is the world of nature. Art begins with separate intuitions, strongly ordered as in Kant, fused with feeling as in Coleridge, the isolation of which (whether in apparent discovery or in evident invention) is not a matter of indifference, because the feeling fixes and defines its object and the object focuses and defines the feeling. The line we draw between nature and art may be better described, not as one between intuition and what is preintuitive or subintuitive and hence of a lower epistemic order, but as a line within intuition, between the ad hoc and evanescent unities within the unity of perception and the significant, isolable, and hence repeatable unities of gesture, which, being repeatable, can serve as foundation for the different kind of stable order that we call culture.

Let it be supposed that a defensible account of intuition can be given by fastening on the relevant aspects of perfected works of art and critical discourse on them, making precise the sense in which whatever requires such discourse must figure in any epistemic structure as an origin, not as a construct, and specifying conditions that every intuition must fulfill by way of recognizability, unity, and significance, not to mention clarity and distinctness. The pure and simple version of the expressive line I have selected for exposition then runs as follows. Art is the expression of intuitions, and a work is nothing but the expression of an intuition; an intuition is derived from an impression, a crude datum from the artist's life; an intuition is the same as its expression, so that a work of art is never a perceptible particular but always the object intended by a mental act; the perceptible particulars we usually call works of art are merely the externalizations of expressions, and it makes no difference to an expression as such whether it is externalized or not; and an expression can (mediated by its externalization and an associated impression) as such be the object of a further intuition, so that what the artist saw in his work as such should be exactly what a properly attentive and not misinformed member of the public sees in it. Our task is to test the links in this chain, to make clear which in a series of apparent relationships are identities and which are not, to say what the relationships that are not identities are, and to explain why the identities should appear to relate differentiable terms. The pairs of terms to be related are: impression and intuition; intuition and expression; expression and externalization; externalization and reimpression; and reimpression and reintuition. The last two of these pairs seldom figure in expositions of the expressive line, but they are always discussed under some rubric or other and cannot be ignored.

Impression and Intuition

The relation between the artist's intuition and the impression, the raw experience, on which it is based, is crucial for the expressive line, because on its adroit handling depends the distinction of the expressive line from that version of the classical line which assigns to the fine arts the function of expressing feeling. And the distinction is vital, because to neglect it lays one open to Hospers' question (1955, 324): Why should one say that the artist expresses feeling rather than any of the other things (such as messing around with paint) he may also be said with perfect truth and relevance to be doing? The expressive line is a complete answer to that question, but only at the price of most carefully eschewing anything like the classical line, which makes of the fine arts organized practices to be interpreted. But the relation between impression and intuition is often fudged. This is partly because the authors in question are confused, or trust too much in their powers of synthesis; but it is also partly because the relation is a hard one to handle and indeed (as we will see at the end of this section) is one that in the end the expressive line must be careful not to commit itself on.

The artist's intuition must obviously be based somehow on his experience. But how can it be? If we say that his creation and intuition consist in clarifying what was before obscurely and confusedly felt,[27] we are open to the objection that what is clear cannot be what was confused: the essential character of the intuition is its clarity and distinctness. Those who speak in this fashion are bemused by images of light, in which one and the same visible object is first dimly and then brightly lit, seen first in fog and then in full day, or peered at first with the naked eye and then through the necessary correcting lens. But that image is inapposite, for to separate the work of art from an object to which it relates is the distinguishing mark of the related version of the classical line. But if we then say that what the artist does is substitute a clear idea for a confused impression, what kind of substitution can we have in mind?[28] The clear idea cannot play the same part in his mental economy as the confused one did, for several reasons: because it is an original discovery, not an episode in a life; because it is intuited, not undergone; because it is in the present and in a sense timeless, whereas the feeling unclarified was in the past and is time bound. If we say only that, whereas previously the artist was disturbed in his feeling and is now (ex officio) serene in his intuition,[29] the same effect would be produced by any spiritual activity that took his mind off his troubles. If we say that the intuition is the same as the impression because it has the same occasion, we invite the retort that the original feeling must have been occasioned by some stimulus in the course of the artist's life, and, if it is proper (which is at best doubtful) to speak of the occasion of an intuition, its occasion must be the feeling itself and not the occasion of the feeling. If we say that impression and intuition have the same object or content, we are refuted by the fact that *ex hypothesi* the object or content of an intuition is specified and specifiable only by the intuition itself; if the object or content of the impression could be specified, it would itself be an intuition—either the same intuition, in which case it cannot be related to it as origin to outcome, or a different intuition, in which case it is a separate outcome in as much need of an origin as the other.

In relating impression to intuition, the expressive line seems to confront a Scylla and a Charybdis between which it cannot steer. Either the impression can be identified or it cannot. If it can, it is either formed or unformed. Thus, if the impression is identified, we commit the absurdity of either equating what is unformed with what is identified solely by its form or equating one form with a different form. But if the impression is not identifiable, the having of an intuition, unrelated to any past or current life experience, becomes simply the generation of ideas for art, the creation of pure forms. That works of art are based on having and developing ideas for works of art is not exactly news—it says, at most, that works of art are created and are seldom if ever created instantaneously. And if the intuitions of art are created out of nothing, we seem to rob the expressive line of that promise of giving art a strategic place in the development of human consciousness which is its chief reason for being.

Having reached this impasse, one is tempted to give the expressive line up as a bad job. But, before one does so, one should consider that the difficulty is not one peculiar to the theory of art. Socrates confronted the same hard choice, though he never showed himself aware of it.[30] A man, he said, should transfigure his life and specifically his virtues by making its and their basis fully conscious. But since their unrestructured form was not fully conscious, whatever intellectualized basis was uncovered would be the basis, not of that life and those virtues, but of a different life, whose virtues, if any, would be quite different. But the original virtues were praised for what they were, and it was that praiseworthiness that made it worthwhile seeking intellectual underpinnings for them. There is therefore no warrant for supposing that the new intellectually based life would be similarly praiseworthy or indeed praiseworthy at all. We might only succeed in converting a saint (if he would let us) into a prig.[31] If Socrates was not put off by this objection, perhaps we should not be too hasty in succumbing to its analogue.

Pleading Socrates in extenuation prompts the question of what philosophy has been doing for the last two millennia. We must try again. One expedient that offers a model for the kind of mitigated identity that should unite impression with intuition exploits the notion of articulation. The unexpressed experience, the impression, is inarticulate, hence inchoate; the expressed experience, the intuition, is the same experience articulated, given coherent voice (cf. *SA* 413-417). But this image, whatever its worth, is precisely the opposite of the one that we yearn for here. To articulate something is to impose a more simplified or emphasized, and hence graspable and describable, form on what was already fully formed. That is, rather than generating the seamless unity that intuition and expression have to be, articulation emphasizes divisions that were already there, if it does not introduce new demarcations of its own. The model of articulation is grammatical speech distinctly uttered; and it is with speech characterized in just that way that intuition was, in the fundamental intent of the expressive line, to be contrasted.

If the idea of articulation is rejected as inappropriate, one might try Langer's thesis (discussed in chapter 3) that art expresses, not feeling, but knowledge of feeling. What a work expresses is in no sense what the artist as a human being felt or experienced, but the complex of feeling that the artist intuited. He experiences the possibility of feeling and seeing in a certain way, and this possibility is immediately an actuality, because to envisage its possibility is to envisage itself; but it is experienced, not in relation to the course of his life, but in relation to his work as an artist. It is, then, the idea for a work of art; but in terms of the expressive line it is an idea that is already a work of art, and it is an idea for a work of art only because it is an intuition, a fused complex of formed vision and feeling. The gift of a great artist is one of imaginative sympathy with a multitude of lives not his own. What, then, is the impression that corresponds to the intuition? At this point things get tricky. If we say that it is nothing but the intuition itself, we answer the question only by refusing to countenance it; if we say that it is the artist's acquired knowledge of feeling, his repertoire of vicarious experience, it appears that the status of the intuition as epistemic origin is lost, since what the artist is doing is practicing this or that art of expression as a variety of representation. In either case, if what is expressed is knowledge of feeling, then the relevant feelings already exist to be known and, as knowable, must be already intuited and hence formed in the only sense relevant to our purposes.

Langer herself does not differentiate between the expressive line and the related version of the classical line, but her own treatment of the relationship that concerns us does offer a way out of the impasse we have just formulated. According to her theory, it is just because the artist's (and other people's) repertory of "knowledge" of the possibilities of feeling is not available as knowledge but exists as a sort of empathetic capacity that art is necessary to symbolize the modes of sentience. The conundrum that her critics pose for her, that we cannot know that art does this unless we can already recognize the symbolized modes of sentience, so that the symbolization is unnecessary, is readily solved: all that we know is that the work of art before us gives form to *some* form of sentience; *what* form that is we can say only by describing the work. In other words, we can extract from Langer a reply to our initial question, namely, that the "impression" is a diffused life-experience the sole function of which is to enable us to find works of art significant and to use our own sense of significance to create works of art of our own.[32]

In the last resort, it might be that the solution we have extracted from Langer will be the only one that will save (if anything can) the expressive line. But a last resort it is. It violates one of the ideas in which the expressive line is rooted, that of feeling about an object. If the feeling is to be one about the object itself, it can only be a feeling about the object as perceived or cognized, so that perception determines feeling.[33] But it is integral to the expressive line to urge that perception is determined by feeling: our interests determine what we pick out from the supposed flux of experience to constitute an object, and further determine what in the object picked out constitutes its essence, what makes it just the object it is. Sense fixes reference, interest fixes sense. There is, then, a reciprocal relation between feeling and perception, and the original locus of this reciprocity is art. Lack of this sense of discovery and insistence on perception returns Langer's theory firmly to the classical line as soon as we insist on the alternatives.

From the recognition that feeling and perception are related reciprocally we may go either of two ways. I will go some distance in each direction in turn, beginning with the one I take to be the more promising. Since the relation between feeling and perception is reciprocal, it obviously cannot be a causal relation: the relation must be a noncausal one of mutual determination. But the notion of mutual determination is obscure. It cannot mean a sort of reciprocal causality, for that is the nonsense we invoked it to rule out. It must therefore be a relation of meaning: feeling defines perception, and perception defines feeling. But it is not an abstract relation of meaning that we are speaking of: we are speaking of what is actually involved in feeling about a specific object. And we must, I think, conclude that the ideal case is that of a single experience of feelingful perception or perceptive feeling; any feeling that is left over when the perception is defined is subjective, unfocused, extraneous feeling; and any perception that is not saturated with feeling is extraneous, nonvital, aberrant, and irrelevant—it is fragmentary perception unworthy of the name. In fact, we are driven to the notion of an intuition as the expressive line conceives it; and if the sequence of thought leads us to the reflection that such intuitions are rare, certainly not the normal stuff of life, the theorist will gladly accept that most of what we call feeling and perception is secondhand, inauthentic, spurious.

Now, what of the impression? The only things that could qualify for that role were the object as perceived, or the object for perception, and the feeling that impelled us to select and define the object. But we have seen that both of these are swallowed up in the intuition. So there is nothing of any interest for the impression to be. The impression must be something extraneous and fundamentally irrelevant, some unfocused and unrealized element in experience that plays no part in the intuition and has no meaningful relation to it.

Shall we then say that the impression is related to the intuition only causally? We cannot say that if we mean that there is a causal law relating the two—it is in fact the ambition to conceptualize such a law without the means of doing so that gives rise to those theories of "the creative process" that give the expressive line a bad name. Feeling and perception are mutually determinant in a way that leaves no room for any overdetermination because together they comprise all that can be experienced in the intuition. The relation of impression to intuition is therefore either unspecifiable or such that it can be specified only historically. On some occasions we shall say only that the artist created this or that, had this or that intuition: we must suppose that he would not have had it had he not been the man he was with the experiences he had, but no particular experience can be specified as especially relevant. On other occasions, when life and work form a pattern or when work alludes to life, as when we recognize in a novel a scene we remember, we shall say that the artist felt or saw such and such, and on the basis of that he created what he did; but although we use such a phrase as "on the basis of," we must concede that the experience was not a sufficient condition of the work, for obviously one might have had the experience and made nothing of it, nor a necessary condition, for obviously another novelist might have created the scene out of whole cloth—we do not suppose that novelists depend on their life experience for every incident that occurs in their work, or that anything in our experience of the work will reveal what in it was and what in it was not related to a specific experience.[34] Experience and creation are only contingently related, by a sort of narrative connection. If we speak of a causal connection in such a case, we postulate or discover in the artist's life suitable antecedents for his work on the basis of our own notions of congruence, and then devise a covering law ad hoc to supply the required causal link. Some theorists regard the devising of such nonce-laws as a fraud, others think of it as a benign expedient.[35] In any case, it comes to no more than saying: since causality reigns everywhere, and since these events were followed by that event, we are obliged to suppose that these events plus certain unknown conditions are such as to give rise to that event. But that thesis is trivial, for a similar claim may be made with equal right for the connection between *any* two events that we know to have actually taken place, if we are prepared to let the unknown conditions be rich enough. All we can say is that those who feel the need of a causal connection or other genetic story will insist that there is such a story to be told, such a connection to be established. Since it is impossible to verify that there is such a story or such a connection, the insistence on it has no significance for criticism or for epistemology.

It is important not to lose sight of the basic incoherence of the position we are trying to develop here. The notion of an impression that it uses is that of something necessary but inexplicable: it insists on the one hand that intuitions are absolute origins, cannot be related to impressions as to causes or necessary conditions, and impressions are entities of a different order from intuitions; and on the other hand that it is human beings who have intuitions, which must arise within the order of experience; and the order of experience must be an order, in that impressions can occur and be recognized and intelligibly related to each other. However we twist and turn, we cannot rid ourselves of the fact that impressions, to play their part, must already have the character uniquely assigned to intuitions. The only way of rescuing the whole enterprise is to introduce such a two-level theory of imagination as we have spoken of: whatever is experienced must be unified and coherent in some fashion; art and intuition stand for a more intense and meaningful unity. In the eighteenth-century versions that speculated on the origins of language, it is to be presumed that, before men invented linguistic expression and became human, they were successfully living the lives of apes, with sensation and memory functioning well enough to equip such a life as a baboon may enjoy. The man who in Herder first finds a name for his sheep must already have had the fleecy bleater well enough individuated and integrated into his life to tell what was a good name for it (Herder 1772). But as soon as we admit this lower level of coherence, the plausibility and attractiveness of the expressive line are destroyed, because the distinction between two levels comes to seem arbitrary. Why two levels, rather than three or indeed a multitude? Why make a sharp distinction between levels at all? It is easy to use Hegelian language and say that what was unified at the lower level is sublated (*aufgehoben*), at once canceled (in its individuality) and preserved (in its deeper meaning) by being taken up into a more comprehensive context—or that it undergoes a sort of reverse *Aufhebung* in which depth and individuation go together. It is much harder to make of this language anything more than a name for the problem and a declaration of the will to solve it.

I said that there was a second, less significant, route that could be taken from the point where one conceives of feeling and perception as mutually determinant. According to this alternative, the mutual determination takes place by mutual adjustment. What starts us on this road is the reflection that, after all, the relation described was not symmetrical. The interest that led to the definition of an object was not obviously the same as the interest taken in it once defined; and then one reflects that this latter interest should, by parity of reasoning, lead to the redefinition of its object—to which, again, a new refinement of attitude would become appropriate. Thus, a dialectic would be generated, not wholly unconnected perhaps with that dialectic of contemplation and desire which in Plato's *Symposium* leads the lover from philandering to philosophy. But it is hard to see where this road leads, if not right outside the expressive line; for now, instead of a sharp contrast between unformed impression and perfectly formed intuition, we have a smooth progression from the dimmest inkling to the most exquisite discrimination. And just as in this progression there is no call for any distinct first term—indeed, how could there be? for the impression as such cannot be distinct, which is what sank us on the other route also—there is no obvious place for a last term. Plato starts with sex, which is where we do start, and ends with beauty itself, because there is nothing higher; but in what shall our dialectic end? Well, in an intuition, certainly, than which nothing is more perfectly unified and therefore, in the required sense, nothing higher. But how can a finite intuition that has been reached by such a dialectic have any finality? To make sense of this picture, we have to postulate each perfected intuition as standing at the end of a blind alley. But what we have thus outlined is something very different from the stark theory I picked out (in the name of the early Croce) as the truest embodiment of the expressive line. The pattern of thought is much more like Collingwood's, which I rejected as too subtle for our purposes. Subtle or not, it seems we have to look at it now.

The schema proposed in Collingwood's *Principles of Art* (1938) is elusive. One version appears to be conceived psychologically. According to this, the artist, or other expressor, begins with a vague disturbance or inkling; then, slowly or in a moment of triumph, he comes to an expression, an adequate counterpart of what was vague, in which he recognizes the meaning adumbrated in the initial disturbance. The initial stage is characterized by its coming first and requiring clarification, the end stage by its coming last and providing clarification. The trouble with this as a version of the expressive line is that the clarification is essentially relative to the initial disturbance or obscurity, of which it is no more independent than a solution is of the problem it solves; the expression is thus epistemically an end rather than a beginning. Accordingly, Collingwood provides another version, which we may take to be the official one, in which the criterion of successful expression is simply the coherence and self-contained nature of what is expressed, a coherence that is so far from being related to the artist's felt need that he may fail to recognize it and go on to spoil what he has done. In this version there is no place for an initial impression at all: there is nothing for the expression to be true to—for, if there were, expression would be a matter of craftsmanship, like achieving a faithful likeness in a portrait. It seems to most readers that Collingwood either runs these two versions together without noticing the discrepancy between them, or tries to combine the dynamism of the one with the epistemic self-containedness of the other without fully realizing the difficulty of doing so.[36]

Collingwood would rejoin that our charge of confusion or overconfidence reflects our own commitment to the obsolete categories he seeks to supplant. His own schematism is as follows. Human awareness and life function on three levels: the psychic, the conscious, and the intellectual. Each episode at each of these levels carries an affective charge inseparable from it. What we are calling impression belongs to the psychic level, the preconscious and subaware continuum of vitality that is the whole of what is available to our awareness though we are not clearly aware of it, the unexamined background of our lives. The affective charge on experience at this level is sheer reaction, mere elicited response. The conscious level consists of that part of this mess to which we attend and, by our attention, on which we confer a specific character that our attentiveness discovers—and, if our attention is unremitting, fully discovers. The feeling charge on such revealed and clarified experiences is emotion, which, since it reflects attention, has the precise character of the cognition on which it is the charge. (The third level, the intellectual, is that at which we reflect on our conscious experience, conceptualize it and think about it; the experience of such intellection has its own feeling tone, which expresses the experience that is the specific thinking of the thought in question in just the same way that emotion answers to conscious experience.)[37] Language and art are just the fully conscious experience that comes from unclouded and (if necessary) unflinching attention. What is there in this to be accused of confusion or overoptimism? It is true that in the transition from an enraged yell to a curse we make the transition from what is merely undergone to what is actively done, but the relation of this transition to the artist's personal history has no systematic interest. The transition is nothing other than the passage from the unclear to the clear, from the inchoate to the consummate, and, by the same token, from mere psychic event to something that is meaningful and hence can be incorporated in a system of meanings (and can form the basis, accordingly, of intellectual constructs). The key move is to make the transition from the *pair* of psychic half-awareness and its associated vague response to the *pair* of intuition and emotion, and therewith to eliminate the contrast between psychological and epistemic transitions.

Our only reply to Collingwood's rejoinder would have to be that the problem we began with still remains. What is it that is attended to? It cannot be the impression, which is as unformed as ever. It cannot be the intuition, because it is the act of attending that grounds the intuition. "Attention" turns out to be a metaphor, returning us to that deceptive model of the observer scrutinizing an external object that is *there to be seen* if conditions are right. What is called attending can only be, for the artist, responsibility in original creation. Once more, the "impression" is left without definable status or intelligible role.[38]

Principles of Art has an air of haste, which, together with its philosophical power and its author's open contempt for other thinkers guilty of the sort of fudging he seems to descend to here, tempts one to seek clarification in those of Collingwood's other systematic works that seem most relevant, the *Idea of History* (1946) and the *Essay on Philosophical Method* (1933). Initial results are encouraging. From the former of these works we gather that historical understanding, the recapture of the works of mind, consists in rethinking the problematic of other agents, which suggests that the only way to understand a work of art is to reconstruct the clarification that constitutes its meaning, whether that clarification was an actual psychological progress from dark to light or a blinding flash in which the problematic was merely implicit. And from the latter work, fundamental for all of Collingwood's mature philosophy, we gather not only that the end state of an intelligible process determines the meaning of earlier states (an idea so widely shared and so often systematically developed that we may leave its complexities unstated here) but also that concepts exist only as historical entities. And it seems evident that an expression should operate under the same rules as a concept, since each operates as an indivisible unit of thought.[39] But this promise of aid from Collingwood's other works ultimately proves delusive. The model of historical understanding does not fit. The historian must understand what *was* done, the beholder of art must appreciate what *is* expressed. It is nothing to us whether a work of art solves its artist's private problem: we come to it from the depths of our own predicaments, not from his. Or rather, a historical understanding of the work is indeed possible, and a work may be understood as part of its author's life story or part of the story of art, but such understanding is contrasted with the intuition capturing the expression that the work is, which is the only proper response to the work of art as such. Any phase of a historical process is what Sartre (1943) calls a detotalized totality. Like an individual's state of mind at any given time, it is an integrated whole, organized into foreground and background identified in relation to a coherent set of envisaged changes—what something is to be done about, what is to be borne in mind, what can wait till later, what can be ignored. But this ordered whole is what it is only as a phase of a process or a life, and it is shaped by a dynamism that will itself destroy the total order and substitute for it a new distribution of emphases and changes, no less integral and no less unstable, in terms of which past events no less than future projects will be assigned new meanings and new values. To be a work of art is precisely not to be this sort of unstable entity: it is to be a monument, the dynamism of which lies in the ceaseless dialogue it maintains, in its integrity, with a succession of interlocutors in successive historical contexts (for the expressive line, it rather maintains a monologue). Collingwood historicizes concepts in the way I mentioned just because he exempts works of art and other expressions from history. A concept is a historical entity and dialecticized in that its status as unit of thought is denied: it is integrated into language, and language changes as speech is continued. We may protest that works of art also change. Handel's *Messiah* changes as styles of performance change, as audiences change in social composition and musicianly competence, as musicology provides ever new backgrounds of knowledge and illusion, as the advance of music puts Handel's procedures in ever new perspectives. But it is the central thesis of the expressive line that through all these changes the work of art itself remains unchanged. As a fully expressed meaning it remains, it *must* remain, perfectly recoverable. If Collingwood thought his other works provided underpinning for his theory of art—and there is no evidence that he did think so—he was wrong.

If we are determined to retain an intrinsic relation between intuition and some antecedent that will serve as impression, we may return in desperation to the thesis that intuition discloses what is already potentially or obscurely present, or at least significantly nonpresent. Heidegger's rhetoric is richly expended on the notion that intuition is the occasion of truth, and truth (*aletheia* "the unhidden") is the standing forth into the light of what was visually nonexistent because dark. But intuition, as we have observed before, now loses its status of origin: the Being of which it is a disclosure is an antecedent reality.[40] In vain we insist that human being, *Dasein*, is the only determinate being, the only place where Being can be revealed, so that the antecedent reality is dispensable or chimerical: unless its antecedent status is recognized, the whole rhetoric becomes pointless, and Being becomes a mystery that we cannot see in the dust we have so industriously raised. The model for this way of thinking remains that of the figure seen through a mist that is dispelled, or seen in a shadow that our light banishes; that of the expressive line is the picture in the fire from which the artist evokes a landscape.

It is time to give up. We cannot steer between the Scylla of irrelevance and the Charybdis of identity. One chooses Scylla, of course, but the real difficulty is that of preserving two insights, equally valuable and appropriate to the same general attitude toward art, but tending in opposite directions: that art is a continuously humanizing force, and that art serves epistemically as absolute origin. The former requires continuity, the latter discontinuity, between intuition and any antecedent impression. And there is no sufficient reason for favoring one insight and tendency over the other, nor is there any reason to associate art with one rather than the other. The expressive line is called into question by its critics not only because it tends to confuse both these insights with each other (as well as with the theory that the fine arts are arts of expression) but also because if the insights are examined separately both of them have unwelcome consequences. The notion of a continuously humanizing capacity of expression seems, in the first place, to have nothing specially to do with art; if such a process or capacity exists, it seems rather to be roughly equivalent to the whole of culture, within which art has a specialized and perhaps quite a minor place. In the second place, there seems no good reason for assigning humanizing and socializing and educative forces to any one process or set of processes; certainly the word "expression" does not suffice to single out anything recognizable and unified that would serve the turn. More fundamentally, the basic idea that within human behavior there is some subhuman stratum that requires to be made over into humanity seems doubtfully true, even if it is intelligible: we hardly know what sort of existence to assign to it. I have already cited the old Aristotelian contention that, except in the newborn, all human activities other than those amenable in no way to any conscious control are "rational" in the sense that their form is characteristic of the sort of animal that has a nervous system such as ours: our lives are the lives of beings such as we are, and that means beings with the mental capacities we have. Why should we suppose those lives to be somehow mysteriously superimposed on the life characteristic of a type of animal that we are not? But, if we do not suppose that, there is no fundamental function for art as expression to perform.[41] We might as well go back to the classical line and simply talk about the fine arts and what they in fact are and do. The other insight, that something must serve the mind as absolute origin, and that this origin must be such as to admit of the development from it of articulate structures and therefore must have an irreducible distinctness and clarity, fares no better. The idea that epistemic systems must have determinate starting points seems nowadays no more than a reflection of the naivety of Euclidean geometry. A starting point is useless unless one knows where one is to go from it: it derives its status from the system, and cannot generate the system itself. An expression in itself remains an exclamation or an achievement: the very success that guarantees its status prevents it from even functioning within a system, let alone giving rise to the idea of a system. If we wish to say that the expression serves as thesis in a dialectic on the Hegelian model, we reflect that an expression as such is free from contradiction and hence can give rise to no dialectical movement of diremption and reconciliation. The work of art as achieved expression can figure in such a dialectic only as the final synthesis. In short, if the expressive line falls or stands by its ability to formulate correctly the relation, or any relation or lack of relation, between an intuition and any antecedent impression, it falls. And that may partly explain Croce's tropism for a crude, romantic version of the expressive line according to which the true work of art is a spontaneous gesture, the lyric cry. Such a view of art may be ridiculously false and theoretically trivial, but at least it avoids combining theoretical ambition with incoherence and a complete lack of applicability.

If any attempt to formulate the relation (or unrelatedness) between an intuition and any specific impression is fatal to the expressive line, it follows that the best bet for that line is to assert that the relation may be "anything or nothing." In general, intuitions must be formed on the basis of something like Collingwood's "psychic" level of life, or of the "feeling" that Croce said was formed in its own terms but not in terms relevant to intuition and hence cognition; but that is only a general truth that becomes obvious when one reflects on the situation. On any particular occasion, no antecedent impression is to be invoked. The essential thing to bear in mind is that it is a main contention of the expressive line that there is no determinate relation between intuitions and impressions. The mistake that leads to the dilemma that has troubled our argument, and to all the twists and turns that have ensued, is to accept the challenge to clarify this relationship, as though its not being specified were a weakness of the theory and not a necessary part of it. As for the apparent paradox (not really in point here, but involved in our discussion) that an intuition that is clear and distinct, and thus essentially isolated from all else, is in some fashion available for, assimilable into, cultural structures and humanized life, this should not be treated as an objection, but made a matter for discussion, a problem. It is, after all, just the same problem as that of accounting for how a definable word, whose use one can indeed learn pretty well from a dictionary, can be used as an integral part of a specific context. One would need to be an idiot to take that hermeneutic circle as proving either the impossibility of speech or the uselessness of lexicons.

Above all, it is prudent for the exponent of the expressive line to avoid moralizing. Collingwood, notoriously, denounces as "corruption of consciousness" the failure or diversion of attention that fails to bring emotions to their full clarity and falls back on stock responses. But not everything that is begun can be completed, and one cannot attend to everything; and to speak in this way almost inevitably leads one, as it did lead Collingwood, to use language that implies that one's moral duty is not to flinch from the painful task of confronting one's own feelings. Humanly, practically, it may be excellent advice that an artist should be true to his innermost self, his deepest impulses, his basic insight, or what not; but as soon as one indulges in such moralizing, one speaks as if the artist had a choice between two ways of working, each of which was present to him as an option. And if one speaks thus, it is almost impossible to preserve the original integrity of intuitions.[42]

Intuition and Expression

In contrast with the relation between impression and intuition, that between intuition and expression is straightforward. Intuition and expression are identical. The assertion of this identity is almost the defining characteristic of the expressive line, and its clarity and decisiveness are purchased at the price of making the relation between impression and intuition problematic, and that between expression and externalization rather surprising. In other words, all the problems are pushed back or forward so as to preserve identity here.

Intuition is not passive receptiveness of a mental content performed elsewhere. It is a mental act, a single act that creates in grasping and grasps in creating. Expression is not giving form to something that without it would be incomplete: once the act of intuition is performed, there is nothing more to add. There is no musical insight in a work separate from the musical structure itself, no thought behind the words of an utterance that the words may not adequately express: if the thought can in principle be verbalized, then until the words are found the thought does not exist.

Two questions about this identity seem worth asking. First, if there is only one entity, why are two terms needed? To this the answer is that they are not needed. I have used "intuition" almost exclusively, and Collingwood confines himself to the term "expression." One might say that the two terms refer to two aspects: we talk about intuition when we are thinking of the facet that is a grasping of something, a cognitive achievement; we speak of expression when we are thinking of the facet of the same act that is a making manifest, to oneself and hence potentially to others. Neither of these precedes the other. To create a piece of music is to hear it in the mind. The hearing, of course, cannot precede the creation, but there is nothing that could count as creation that might precede the hearing.[43] The talk of two "aspects" or "facets" is troubling. If the intuition-expression is a single, simple act, how can it have two facets or aspects? But this trouble is needless. To speak of two aspects is not to divide the act into parts, but to relate it to two contexts, to consider it from two points of view.

The second question about the alleged identity has to do with its status. Is it a *thesis* that the two are the same? If so, just what is the thesis, and what countertheses is it meant to exclude? Obviously it is not an assertion about English or Italian to the effect that two words are synonymous; it is evident that they are not synonymous. Is it then the announcement of a discovery, like that of the identity of the evening star and the morning star? That also is impossible; the analogue would be a discovery in psychology that two familiar entities were manifestations of the same underlying reality, as though one were to discover that schizophrenia and hysterical aphasia were symptoms of the same viral infection, and that is not what is meant at all. The assertion is rather that, if you think carefully enough about what an intuition really has to be if it is to be entirely clear and distinct, you are bound to realize that nothing need be added to it to make it an expression; and, conversely, if you consider what we mean by the term "expression" in a sense adequate to the romantic theories of the original force of language, you will see that it can neither add anything to the intuition it expresses (or would be said to express, if the two were different), nor fall short of it, because in either case it would not be the expression of just that intuition. So the only clearheaded and sensible way to use the two terms is in such a way that whatever can be called by the one name can also be called by the other. And the theses combated are primarily two. First, it might be held that an initial impression plus the feeling for how to go on from there is what an intuition is, and it suffices for expression of that intuition that one be faithful to that combination of notion and hunch, which seem, as Dufrenne (1953) observes, to draw the artist irresistibly on to their inevitable fruition. The argument of the expressive line is that there is no such inevitable fruition, that the feeling of inevitability is an illusion, that the incept of a work of art is not a recipe for it. The other thesis combated is a variety of the first, and lies in the common feeling that what differentiates me from Mozart is not that Mozart had musical intuitions and I do not, but that Mozart knows how to put his musical intuitions into musical language and I lack that skill. To this the reply is that if you do not have the notes, you do not have the music. Again, we have no unexpressed thoughts that are really complete and waiting only for the words. If you don't have the words, you don't have the thought; when you find the words, you will have found the thought, and not till then.

Expression and Externalization

If we say that intuition and expression are the same and also equate the work of art with expression, it seems to follow that what the public sees, hears, and reads cannot be the work of art itself, but must be something else; for it is the artist alone who intuits his intuition, and what I intuit is my intuition, and what links the two is a mere vehicle, which we may call the externalization of the work. And expression and externalization cannot be the same if the expression is simply a clear and distinct idea, for one may certainly have such an idea without giving it any outward and visible or audible sign. Moreover, the externalization is likely to be an imperfect embodiment of the expression: *ex hypothesi,* it cannot add anything to the expression, and it is only too easy to see how it may fall short, in arts requiring manual manipulation, through sheer accident. Is there any difference in principle between the accidents that befall a painting in the centuries after a painter's death and those that befall it before the paint is even dry?

It seems to many critics so scandalous that the expressive line should entail that no one has ever seen a work of art that they reject it out of hand on that ground alone. But it is not easy to see what they are objecting to, other than a mildly paradoxical turn of phrase. If by "work of art" we mean the *opus operatum,* what the artist did in his work qua work of art, not the artifact subject to all the vicissitudes of fate, the distinction between work as expression and externalization seems no more than a recognition of the most familiar facts about art and our dealings with it. It is not in the least paradoxical to say that someone may compose a poem in his head, and that he then adds nothing to his creative work by reciting it or writing it down. Similarly, a musician with a good memory can compose in his head without a piano to play on or a pencil to write with, and without humming to himself either; and if he then performs that music or writes it down, performance and writing add nothing to the act of composition as such. In principle, the same would be true of an architect: it is merely a contingent fact that it is unlikely that anyone could complete the design of a building in his head without jotting down or drawing the details. It is no doubt true, as I once wrote (*SA* 356), that the real Saint Peter's is not Michelangelo's design or Bramante's but the one that got itself built, but that is a fact about Rome, not about the art of Michelangelo or Bramante; and the oeuvre of Le Corbusier, for instance, includes the many projects that never got off the ground as well as those that got onto it. It is only with what Goodman has called autographic arts, those in which the direct exercise of manual skill is essential to making the work just the work it is, that we feel uneasy. But even here it is not clear how much of our unease is warranted. Such works are often to some extent planned before work begins—a sculptor will think twice before he starts hacking away at an expensive hunk of marble, and a fresco painter's medium makes improvisation risky—and such planning could obviously be very extensive. The challenge of the expressive line is to ask whether it is *in principle* impossible for a painter or a sculptor to work his painting or his carving out in every detail before he sets brush to canvas or chisel to stone. A sufficiently experienced artist, it is argued, may know *how it would be* to paint precisely this or that: he could, as it were, feel it in his hand. It need not be suggested that any artist has ever proceeded thus, or that he would be a better artist for proceeding thus, nor would the case be strengthened if it were discovered that someone did so. The question is in fact better put hypothetically: if a painter did know just how it would be to paint a painting and just how that painting would look, so that all that remained for him to do was to paint, stroke by stroke, exactly what he had decided to paint, would his creative enterprise be in any respect incomplete? If so, *what* creative act would remain to be performed? Would not the act of actually painting be even less creative than the act of someone making a laborious copy of an existing painting, since in the latter case one would at least have to make decisions of one's own about how to achieve the required likeness? Unless common sense has seriously asked itself just this series of questions, the objections of common sense to this feature of the expressive line do not deserve a hearing.

Those who equate intuition with expression and divorce expression from externalization are not denying that people see and hear what they are ordinarily thought to see and hear, nor do they urge that people should stop saying they have seen the *Mona Lisa*. All they are doing is making the readily comprehensible point that the creation of the type of order that is a work of art is logically independent of this or that particular material exemplification of that order. If the work in question is a painting or a musical composition, then the look and the sound are the very substance of the intuition: it is a musical and audible order or a painterly and visible order that is created, not an abstract system of relations, a mathematical formula, that the visible or audible order would merely illustrate. The argument is not that music and painting are such that they are necessarily imperfectly accessible to ear and eye, but that in *every* case what is heard or seen *may or may not* be the precise audible or visible form that the artist intuited and thereby expressed.

Before going further, one should get a firm grip on the position laid down in the preceding paragraph. What follows amounts, in the end, only to a muddying of the waters, an attempt to trick the expressive line into this or that falsification of its position. That position is that it is possible *in principle* for a work to be completed in imagination without being given a material embodiment. The difficulties we shall raise rest on attempts to undermine this position by arguing that "possible in principle" is an empty phrase, or that the phrase "completed in imagination" is deceptive.

We may begin by confronting the expressive line with a stark alternative. Either paintings and musical works are essentially visible and audible orders or they are not. If they are not, then the real work of art is after all some sort of abstract equation; and this suggestion surely is as objectionable as common sense could fear. But, if they are, then must we not say that actual hearing and actual seeing are the relevant manifestations of mind? But if that is the case, externalization becomes essential: until the painter has painted something he (and others) can actually see, his expression, if it is to be a visual expression, is necessarily incomplete. By the same token, if the order in question is necessarily perceptible, his intuition will be incomplete too.[44] And if we then balk at saying that a musician has not completed his musical work until he plays it or hears it played, on the reasonable ground that it makes perfectly good sense to say that years elapse between the completion of a work and its first performance, and that we do not want to say that the composer of a work first performed posthumously completed his intuition after his death, the reply may be that if a work of music is essentially audible, then a composer as such, as distinct from the composer-performer of the good old days, does not create works of art but only recipes for works of art. Croce himself was a literary critic and, according to anecdotes, little interested in the material manifestations of the concrete world (cf. *SA* 419); and this professional and temperamental bias, which should have been irrelevant, may have led him to underestimate the difference between the inward vision and the precise shock of the realm of light.

Croce's literary bias, which tempted him to allow more pragmatic reality to the split between expression and externalization than it deserved, was not shared by Collingwood. Collingwood's artistic connections were with painters (his father had been Ruskin's secretary), and the motivation of *Principles of Art* was a concern for the contemporary state of painting in England. Collingwood rejects the whole notion of externalization, as resting on a false dichotomy between mind and body.[45] What there are is people: it is the person who acts, and an expressive act involves the whole person. Just as a speech act involves tone and gesture and not merely a verbal structure, a painterly expression involves the whole action of painting, in which the generation of a visible form is inseparable from the action of painting a canvas. But, having insisted on this point, he does not explain it. The painting, after all, is what the public sees and all there is for the critic to appreciate. Does Collingwood want to say that the visible painting, the achieved expression, is equivalent to the track of the dancing brush, and this in turn equivalent to the dance of painting? He offers no clue. If we take his few words at their face value, the expressive act is the action of painting, and this is (one supposes) accessible only to the historical understanding that retraces the action. But I said before that I could see no way of reconciling this form of understanding with the thesis that a work of art is an achieved intuition.[46] We may give Collingwood credit for good intentions, but we must say that, instead of cutting the Gordian knot, he has merely tagged it with a label reading "any fool could untie this."

Let us return to the issues. The stark alternative that was supposed to confront the expressive line is easily seen to be factitious. A painting does not require externalization to save it from being some sort of abstract equation. It is indeed a visual order, even if not yet visible: it is imagined, imagined visually and imagined for vision. But now we can return to the attack and once more confront the devotee of the expressive line with what looks like a hard choice. On the one hand, one may admit that the expressions of art are inseparable from their visual or auditory manifestations. To Ryle (1949), actually seeing and actually hearing real sights and sounds are mental activities in good standing, of which seeing and hearing in the mind's eye or ear are imaginary or at best ghostly simulacra; and to Descartes seeing and hearing are (provided that we do not treat them as "achievement" verbs by including an implied reference to an external object) perfectly good examples of "thinking" in the sense required for his *cogito*. And a consensus of Descartes and Ryle, we might think, is a formidable consensus. But, then, if these are perfectly good examples of thinking or mental activity, we cannot suppose them to be, as mental activities, identical with their counterparts in imagination, even if one act of seeing may be quite isomorphic with another act of seeing (seeing the same thing, presumably, in the same circumstances). But then we cannot say that expression is complete without externalization, though it may (for the reasons suggested in our previous argument) be a matter of indifference whether the externalization is in this specific material embodiment or that.[47] And now we have to choose between

337

saying that intuition is not achieved without externalization and abandoning the equation between intuition and expression. But to abandon that equation is in effect to abandon the expressive line altogether; certainly it is to abandon the only point in it worth fighting for. Yet to say that expression is impossible without externalization is to abandon the whole line of argumentation we ran through to the contrary, without which again the expressive line loses at least much of its attraction.[48]

Once again, the embarrassment with which we have threatened the expressive line proves to be factitious. If actual vision is indeed relevantly different from imagined vision—different, that is, in ways that affect its nature as clear and distinct idea[49]—it is quite true that the artist cannot know his painting until he has actually painted it and looked at it: it may always surprise him. The imagined painting and the actual painting might both be works of art, but they would be different (though similar) works. If that is not the case, then the alleged differences between imagination and actual vision do not have the consequences that the opponent of the expressive line requires of them. But in cases where such differences between the imagined and the sensed do obtain, the concept of externalization has no application. The systematic position of externalization remains just what it was in all cases where it does have application and hypothetically wherever it may or might have had application. Nothing whatever of any consequence for the expressive line hinges on there being an actual difference between expression and externalization, though the differences in general epistemology may be quite radical.

The same considerations hold for a better-known argument most tellingly stated by Bernard Bosanquet (1915). In the manual arts, the argument goes, the physical experience of handling the paint, the resistance of the stone, the feel of the modeled clay, are not extraneous to the act of creation: an artist works *in* his medium, not merely *through* it. A painting simply is manipulated paint. Thus the expressive line, according to which the manipulation of paint is relegated to externalization, is false to artistic experience.

Bosanquet's argument makes a good point against Croce and other followers of the expressive line who do sometimes phrase their doctrines as though it were necessary for the process of creation and the act of externalizing the creation once achieved to be, psychologically and historically, two separate processes. But this is not essential to their theory; in fact, there is no point in maintaining it. They are not concerned to describe a process in two phases or stages, but at most one with two aspects. Historically and externally, there is a series of stages through which some material passes, from raw material to finished work. Internally and meaningfully, there is a passage from obscurity to clarity. But this passage, as we have seen, is not a process with a history: it is an achievement, and a passage only in the sense that an achievement presupposes a time at which whatever it is was not achieved. What then comes of the objection that painting is necessarily expression *in* paint? It seems to fall into two parts. The first part claims that the experience of painting (or its counterpart) is psychologically necessary to creation in autographic arts.[50] The second claims that it is logically necessary that creation in paint be creation in paint. But it is now at once evident that the first part of the objection is merely a contingent claim about how some, most, or all painters need to set about their business—if they felt no such need, that could not possibly affect the quality of their painting. And the second part is trivial: obviously, the expressionist will say, until the painting is actually painted, it is not yet a creation *in paint*; but what of that? What the objectors require is that it should be *logically* necessary that a man could not create a painting without the feel of brush on canvas—not the imagined feel, but the real feel—together with the resistance of the paste and, above all, the formal inspirations that he receives while he paints from his awareness of the emerging forms themselves in their very physical presence. But it does not seem likely that any such necessity could be made out.[51] Even the psychological necessity, which in any case would be irrelevant, seems hard to maintain: how do we distinguish between someone's merely habitual procedures (always wearing a felt hat while painting), the normal conditions of his success (having a good north light), and the conditions *sine quibus non*? He may discover that he can paint quite well in semidarkness, wearing a cloth cap, with the brushes strapped to the wrists of his paralyzed hands, if he has to.

The expressionist is surely on firm ground if he says that the artist's perceptible achievement is his achievement no matter how he set about painting his canvas. It then becomes very hard to block his next move, which is to say that the artist's achievement would be the same even if he had never set brush to canvas at all. It may not be enough to say that he must make his painting visible: the expressionist can agree that that is true and still say that "it is all over bar the shouting"; the final act of externalizing is, however necessary, merely the completion of a formal requirement (like mailing a manuscript to a publisher, or getting planning permission to erect a cathedral). Perhaps after all the best point is one made by Sartre (1946) in a somewhat different connection. The only conceivable evidence that anyone, even the painter himself, can have that he can paint a picture is that he paints it. That he has successfully painted before is no evidence. Perhaps this time, for the first time in his life, he only *thinks* he knows exactly how his painting will go, but when he comes to do it he will discover some appalling lacuna. Only when he sees it set down will he know that there was no mistake.[52]

In conclusion, the distinction between expression and externalization is that between creating a perceptible order and producing something that people can see. If the former cannot be done without the latter, the impossibility is not a logical one, but either epistemological, in which case the distinction retains a hypothetical interest, or psychological, in which case the distinction retains its full force. Or does it? One may well protest that it is absurd to dismiss as *merely* contingent, *merely* psychological, an aspect of our lives that is inseparable from our whole way of being in the world. But we cannot here argue for or against the basic strategies of phenomenology.

Expression and Recovery

Perhaps the most difficult equation that the expressive line must establish is that between the expressed intuition that is the work of art and the intuition that any member of the public who appreciates the work must derive from it. The equation must surely be strict, for the whole point of the expressive line is the determinacy and autonomy of the expression: as absolute origin, it can owe nothing to any parts into which it might be analyzed, or to any relations to anything else, or to any generic features that might be assigned to it. It follows that, unless there is a failure at the level of externalization, what the public can see is just what the artist expressed, and the function of the critic is not to interpret the work but merely to remove interpretations, which are all necessarily misinterpretations. The public's intuition and the artist's expression must be identical. Of course, the public does not have access to the artist's experience of working in his material, of painfully excogitating his design. It is presumably necessary to the experience of painting that one face the terror or thrill of making a start, the perpetual risk of going wrong, as well as the manipulation of paint; and none of these is accessible to the public, who are necessarily cut off from the act of painting that particular canvas and are confronted only with the finished painting.[53] Any difficulties the public may have in intuiting will be very unlike the difficulties the artist faced. The public starts with the knowledge that the artist's difficulties were not insuperable, since he overcame them, and it is just his ignorance of this that is the artist's worst difficulty. Again, if the work is assigned the status of a clarification of an initial confusion or distress, the public cannot recover the clarification because it can only be by improbable chance that they share (or are in a position to divine) the initial confusion.[54] But these considerations are beside the point; what we infer from them is not that the artist's expression and the public's intuition cannot be the same, but that the artist's expression as such must be divorced both from the actual process of achieving it and from any status as clarification that we might assign it. As expressed intuition it is what it is regardless of context. One is tempted to say that if it is a clarification, it is because it has the evident character of a clarification and thereby makes known what it clarifies; if it is the solution of difficulties, it is because it presents itself as a solution and hence reveals the difficulties it resolves. But one who keeps strictly to the expressive line may deny that this can truly be the case: to assign to a work this or that character, even if it be that of a clarification or a solution, and even if "clarification" and "solution" are reinterpreted so that they refer only to the internal structure of the work, is to analyze what cannot be analyzed and to say what can only be true of some parody or paraphrase of the expression that lacks its totally fused quality.

The position just outlined is more strict than judicious. How, one wants to ask, if total fusion overcomes all analysis and description, can we know that we have to do with a parody and a paraphrase of just *that* expression? How can one recognize that a work is copied or derived from another? How can we even make sure that two people are talking about the same work if it happens that they can remember everything about it except the name and location? It is obvious that the expressive line is in constant danger of leading us into a quicksand of absurdity. It cannot deny that many statements about a work of art as such may be true. Even if we say that all simple statements about works of art are misleading, because abstractions (but by the same argument any simple statement about anything whatever is misleading if we suppose, absurdly, that it purports to be the only truth about its subject, or to capture the whole nature of what it is about), we can hardly say the same about qualified statements. It is in no way misleading to say that the *Aeneid* is a poem *rather than* a gambling casino, in Latin *rather than* in Urdu, *more of* an epic than a lyric, about Aeneas *as opposed to* Tallulah Bankhead—and so on and on and on. Of course works of art can be described, because we describe them. What could be meant by saying that we do not describe them *as works of art*, or that their describability detracts from their status as expressions?

Does the expressive line really commit its holders to saying such extravagant things? Some would say yes: it is precisely such commitment, such lack of intellectual mawkishness, that differentiates it from suitably sophisticated versions of the classical line. But I doubt if that position is justified. Why is it not open to the expressionist to say that *of course* a work may present the character of clarification, and may work by making its public experience *as it were* a clarification, just as it may be written in Latin, carved in marble, and so on? The point is that Latin, marble, clarification, become in it something they never were before. And now, the expressionist may continue, how can we deny that insofar as something is expressed it can also be intuited? To say that something is fully expressed is to say that it is altogether clear, that nothing in it depends on adventitious aids for its understanding, that where it is vague or ambiguous its vagueness and ambiguity are precise parts of the design. Think of the *Aeneid*: two millennia have gone by since Virgil, and it does not even make sense to say that his poem is enigmatic. Its structure imposes itself. Individual readers, or whole generations, may find their own significances in it, but what they find them in is a commanding unity. If few works of art are like that, well, art is not easy. One must, of course, learn the language, and a little history and geography; but this is genuinely public in the sense that it is the kind of thing that anyone can get up to the relevant level, and the inner meanings of persons, places, events, and words are made accessible by the powerful expressive field of the poem itself. What cannot thus be intuited with the help only of factual information cannot have been expressed and is a failure of art.

The position developed in the last paragraph does not suffice to carry the point now at issue. Is it not possible for the spectator of a work of art to derive from it an impression that will ground an intuition that is perfectly clear and unified in the way required but still not be identical with the equally clear and unified intuition of the artist? After all, in the theory of the work of art that we developed in the classical line, whatever is judged to be a work of art is judged as a performance, that is, as a clearly articulated and achieved outcome of action, while it is expressly conceded that the supposed performance may not be what the artist intended to do or thought he had done. There is no way in which the alleged identity can be shown. On the contrary, it is common knowledge that not only is it rare (if not unknown) for there to be no disparity between the ways in which competent critics read a work but artists are generally resigned to accepting that no one will ever see in their work all they have put there to be seen. Suppose we have achieved complete agreement in interpretation through a lengthy discussion, we still cannot be sure that some point will not arise on which disagreement will be found, a disagreement that may alter the whole light in which the work is seen; and the expressive line itself requires that the relevant differences may evade explication. One might indeed say, if one had a taste for paradox, that complete agreement in description would be conclusive evidence that the two intuitions were not the same, since the life experiences of any two persons must so differ that the same words have subtly different meanings for each of them.

How can the expressionist meet this objection? His best response might be to dismiss it as a typical empty ploy of skepticism. Of course, he will say, the identity cannot be proved, just as I cannot prove that whatever looks to me like a dog does not look to you like a rabbit (that is, as a rabbit looks to me), but we never discover this because of some obscure difference in our use of language. In this latter case, the impossibility of proof is so unimportant that no one is going to bother to ask if the required adjustments of language would really be possible or not—no one is going to waste time on a hypothesis so strained, so silly, so arbitrary. Just so, the expressionist will say, it is ludicrous to suppose that what to me evidently forms one perfectly unified and perfectly clear intuition will to someone else form an intuition equally clear, equally unified, but quite different. That supposition, he will say, surreptitiously invokes the illegitimate analogy of rival interpretations of designs that are themselves ambiguous or indeterminate, in ways indigenous to the classical line. For the rest, he may appeal to one version of that polymorphous principle, the identity of indiscernibles. We cannot directly compare two intuitions, one mine and one yours, to see if they are the same: it is sufficient if from your expressed intuition I myself receive an intuition of equal perfection. If for every intuition expressed I intuit an expression, it is useless to ask if the two intuitions are the same or not.

The thesis that any expressed intuition can, if adequately externalized, be reintuited by another has one unfortunate consequence. The artist, we said, expresses his intuition merely by having it, and his externalization of it adds nothing to the expression. But now, if we say that the member of the public has the very same intuition, and thereby expresses it, and if his externalization of the work also adds nothing to the expression (for the full expression of the work must extend to every nuance), it follows that everyone who truly appreciates a work can reproduce it exactly. Something like this has indeed been argued by Gisèle Brelet (1951), according to whom only a virtuoso performer can appreciate any piece of music; but it seems a bit steep. According to the expressionists, incomplete expression is not expression at all, and every failure in art is absolute. From this it seems to follow that whoever cannot *perfectly* reproduce a painting is *totally* unable to understand it. If that is so, so far from its being the case that every work of art is a new acquisition for the cultural life of mankind, every work is a dead end, and art turns out after all to be, not an important dimension of the life of the mind, but a mere curiosity.

I have laid myself open to the objection that my version of the expressive line, like so many, has relapsed into ridiculous parody while purporting to reveal extravagances. But does the expressive line really have at its disposal an alternative way of relating the artist's expression and the public's intuition that will escape the devastating consequences of equating them? The obvious alternative is simply to admit that they are different. The artist's expression may be complete, but because no two human minds are the same, being formed by different experiences, his expression can only be the occasion of a different intuition in others. (Yet, because all human minds are both human and minds, any expression will be partly accessible to anyone else; and, as Collingwood emphasized [see note 54], to the extent that we share a world and a way of life we do share the impressions that serve in the last analysis as material for our intuitions.) This means that the artist's expression serves, not directly as intuition, but as the ground of an *impression* that stimulates, and forms the elaborated basis for, the intuitions of others. But now we meet the difficulty that the most promising version of the expressive line made the impression quite extraneous to any intuition to which it might lead. Moreover, what serves as impression need hardly be the intuition expressed by the artist; in fact, insofar as it enters into the common cultural stock, it can do so only as generalized and approximated.

It is easy to see what has happened to the expressive line here. It has pitched its claims for art too high, made the distinction between what is art and what is not art too absolute. It results that what the spectator gets from the work must be either the same intuition or a quite different intuition or a mere impression; and none of these will serve to ground the kind of dialectical transformation that we originally had in mind when we devised the expressive line to give art its place in the life of the mind.

But now, having said that, we can see what we have been doing wrong. We have been trying to develop the second round of the dialectic, so to speak, without developing our ideas concomitantly. So what is it we want to say? Never mind about the dichotomy between impression and intuition, which makes sense only on the ground floor, in the immediate operations of the mind. What happens when the spectator, or the artist himself, looks at what he has done? It cannot be a mere impression, because *ex hypothesi* its unity commands the eye and mind; but it cannot be intuition, because the intuition is complete. Or rather, it is intuition, but repeated intuition. It is, in fact, impression derived from intuition by way of externalization. That is, it is predigested experience. It has a special status that is perfectly evident simply from the description of the situation in which it occurs, and which is not to be reduced to anything simpler than that description prescribes. And, since the unity of the expression has been definitively achieved, whoever recaptures it can safely reinsert multiplicity into its unity (which is, after all, the next stage in a Hegelian dialectical movement),[55] note in it what can be generalized, how it differs from other things, how it is constructed. It is as a unity that is apprehended at one and the same time as the unity it is, and also in the fullness of its relations to other real and possible things, that the intuition enters into the developing life of the mind and the work of art enters history. It was a peculiarity in the classical exponents of the expressive line that they refused this step. To take the step is in a way to betray the expressive line, to abandon its glittering hardness; but to refuse the step seems to leave one with a choice of intolerable absurdities.

That is not quite all that needs to be said about the recovery of expressions from their externalizations. But the remainder will appear more suitably when we come to the theme of artist as everyman in the next chapter.

XII

THE EXPRESSIVE LINE
2: ARTS, WORKS, ARTISTS

The standard form of the expressive line holds not only that all art is expression but that all expression is art. If, having established that expression is a fundamentally significant form of mental activity, we then concede that art is a special case of expression, we need a separate argument to establish that its specialness does not lie in its being marginal or trivial. But if what makes it special is not its triviality but the kind of importance it has, then the philosophy of art is the theory of that kind of importance and not the expressive line as such, and there is nothing to show that the required theory will not lie outside the confines of that line. Again, if expression is a necessary component in the life of the mind or a necessary aspect of all cognition, art as a *special case* of expression cannot itself have that necessity. If art is necessary to anything, it remains to establish what, and how. Thus, all the attraction of the expressive line as a way of thinking about art is lost.

If, on the other hand, we treat "art" and "expression" as synonyms, or make the relation between art and expression biconditional, we run into a fresh set of difficulties. It is easy enough to explain away (as we have seen) the admitted fact that not everything defined as expression is commonly called art, by attributing the fact to vulgar or snobbish error. More serious is the fact that (as, again, we have seen) every exponent of the expressive line must take as his paradigms of art and expression the admitted masterpieces of art—otherwise, neither he nor his readers will accept that his theory of expression is a theory of art. It is all very well for the theorist to insist that there is no sharp line, no difference in kind, between the simplest expression and the most formal and elaborate art; such insistence concedes that there is a line or a difference of some kind, perhaps one of context or one of degree.

The expressive theorist may, and would perhaps be wise to say, that his citing acknowledged masterpieces has only pedagogic or heuristic value: the point is not that they are egregiously expressive but that they are so by common consent. He can then go on to say that the very notion of art as a distinct form of expression, even one distinguished only by context or degree, should be abolished. One could argue, for instance, that it is a sign of our civilized sickness that, instead of recognizing that our lives are or could be expressive and intuition heavy throughout, and making them so if they are not already so, we confine our expressiveness (or our recognition of expressiveness) to restricted areas where it becomes, in consequence, overemphasized and perhaps falsified.

The strategy just outlined has attracted many exponents of the expressive line, with good reason. But it has problems that may be insuperable. It claims that all expression is art, while conceding that not all expression is called art. But claim and concession alike admit that the distinction between art and (other) expression is one that is in fact regularly and successfully made. That is, the distinction itself cannot be illegitimate; wherever a distinction can be made, there must have been a distinction to be made, and all that can be illegitimate is the interpretation of the distinction and the theoretical or practical weight assigned to it. What, then, we must ask, would be the point of depriving (even if only in theory-spinning contexts) the term "art" of this distinctive application and reducing it to a synonym for "expression"? We already have, after all, a perfectly good word for "expression," namely, "expression" (not to mention "intuition"). If the point of this conceptual juggling is to capture the prestige of the word "art" for other forms of expression, in the way Stevenson (1938) described, the move defeats itself: it concedes what it would deny, that is, that the importance now attributed to the fine arts rests on their being something other than the locus of expression.

Perhaps the intended strategy behind the equation of art and expression is rather that described by David Hume (1757). The theorist begins with a consensus in favor of the importance of art, as a matter of experienced value. He then argues that this value, on examination, can be irrefutably traced to art's being the expression of intuitions. He then points out that other things than recognized works of art are demonstrably expressions of intuitions. He then urges that the same value should be discoverable in them as was recognizable in accepted works of art, and invites his readers to consider their own experience frankly and see if this is not so. In other words, the only way in which art is a special case is that its value has been generally recognized: nothing but negligence, inattention, and bad custom stands in the way of equal recognition for all expression. The analogy with Hume is, however, imperfect. What Hume had in mind was the pedagogic use of a dialectic to advance from particular observed cases to unobserved but observable cases. But, as we remarked before, the transition demanded by the expressive line is from a differentiated set of phenomena to a wider set, and we are stuck with the fact that what differentiated the initial set cannot be the same as what will justify its inclusion in the larger set.[1]

It seems that if art is expressive activity, we will have to concede either that art is a special case of it or else that the concept of art as ordinarily conceived is that of a special case or cases. The question is, which, and, in either event, what sort of special case. The problem for the expressive line is then not to find a way of refusing the concession but a way of rendering it harmless. The line of argument that brought us to this point suffices to suggest a plausible line of attack. Art is expression that is in some way conspicuous. It remains to consider in what way the expressions of art are conspicuous. This must obviously be the whole or part of what *could* make an expression conspicuous. There are at least five possibilities. The expressive line is on firm ground if any or all of these both fit whatever facts need fitting and are compatible with the theoretical commitments of the line.

First, the expressions of art might be conspicuous through their perfection. But to accept that would take us out of the expressive line, for which the simplest expression may be perfectly expressive and all expressions as such are perfect expressions of intuitions, which in turn must be perfectly clear and distinct or they are not intuitions at all.

A second possibility is that the expressions of art are conspicuous through their context: expression produced in a context where it is looked for and dwelt on is art. Just as for the classical line any performance isolated for contemplation is a work of art, and any aesthetic object in a fine art context is an art object, so here any expression produced within whatever context defines for the nonce the practice of art is art.

A third possibility, akin to the second, is that the expressions of art are distinguished by their self-consciousness: an expression produced in the name of art (or in the name of expression) is art. But this possibility makes one uneasy. How can the having of any intuition be subordinated to any conceptual requirement, even if the concept be that of intuition itself? The outcome would be accepted or rejected, one supposes, by *criteria* for intuition, by meeting or not meeting *standards* of clarity and distinctness. And if "in the name of art" means anything more than that, the attempt at art sets up a shadowy end to which what should have been one's intuiting becomes a means. Alternatively, the artist becomes one who sets out deliberately to rid his mind of impurities, and this nudges the expressive line toward that very different theory according to which the artist is someone whose mind is exceptionally beset by impurities in the first place.

A fourth possibility is that the distinction is one of elaboration: where expression is systematically developed, or where we have very complex expressions, we have art. But this position seems hardly acceptable: in the first place, complexity seems excluded by the stipulation that an intuition and its expression be utterly simple; and, in the second place, even were that not so, we have seen in another context that the concept of complexity has no critical value, because elements and relations cannot be enumerated without presuppositions of exactly the sort that the context here precludes. To flesh out the notion of complexity for present purposes, one is tempted to have recourse to something like the following: it is generally conceded that even the most direct and natural gestures have something conventional about them and rely on something languagelike, some expectation that certain forms will have a certain significance; so every expression uses conventions, and an expression that uses a very elaborate set of conventions we assign to art. But this temptation must of course be resisted. It is essential to the expressive line that it either redefine "gesture" in such a way as to ensure that gestures are in no way conventional or deny that gestures have anything to do with expression; and the same must hold of art a fortiori. To make complexity a matter of elaboration, and hence almost of necessity a matter of convention, is to admit, if not to invoke, the institutions of elaboration and the systematic development of expressive means. In short, it opens the way to the fine arts, which can no longer be considered extraneous to art conceived purely as expression; and that is simply to abandon the expressive line.

A fifth possibility rests on the observation that the expressions called art are in practice those in which what is expressed is not private but public or communal feeling or experience. The expressions of art, then, are not private gesture but public symbol. A version of this thesis, as we saw in the preceding chapter, was in effect Collingwood's position: art is a vocation within a community.[2] That would fit in with our practice of referring to "the arts" of a civilization or a tribe, rather than of an individual. The position, certainly, has difficulties. All feelings are feelings of individuals, it will be replied; and, even had that not been so, an expressed intuition cannot be evaluated by, or meaningfully referred back to, any supposed feeling that served as its impression. Moreover, the equation of art with what is public suggests one of two things, both absurd: either that art as such has to do with public themes, so that a government poster may be art but a love lyric cannot be, or that art deals with what is general (and can thus be common to many) rather than specific—whereas generalized expression is, for the expressive line, a contradiction in terms: generalization is exactly what is opposed to expression and art alike. Still, one might say, to call something art brings it into the public domain: it is to say not merely that it repays attention as an expressed intuition but that it plays a part (or is fit to play one) in the public life of conversation and culture. That is quite consistent with saying that what so fits it is a matter of mere fashion or cannot be further specified, in which case the appellation of art may be retrospectively bestowed or abrogated, as needs or fashions change. It is also consistent with Collingwood's position that real communities really share and exchange thoughts (cf. Collingwood 1942), so that it makes good sense to distinguish (whether as "art" or otherwise) expressions that positively relate to this sharing and exchanging from expressions that do so only of necessity through the inevitable participation of everyone in the life of his place and time.

Which of the foregoing possibilities is most promising for the expressive line? One might argue that there is no reason to decide, since for that line as such it is "expression," not "art," that remains the key term. It is quite reasonable to hold that "art" is a term loosely applied to expressions conspicuous for any or all of the above reasons. In fact, once the expressivist has conceded that the distinction among expressions between those that are or are called art and those that are not must be acknowledged, it is consistent with the impulse of that line to defuse the distinction as much as possible by making "art" out to be an ordinary language, family resemblance concept of open texture, rather than one capable of defining some theoretical concern that might divide attention with the theory-laden concept of expression itself. But this returns us to a familiar difficulty, namely, that on this showing the expressive line is not a theory of art and cannot incorporate such a theory, but is a theory to *replace* a theory of art. Perhaps, then, the best option for the expressive line is the fifth of the possibilities listed above, or perhaps some other possibility yet to be mooted. One such possibility we will meet in the next section: that the fine arts and the distinctions between them are interesting only on the level of psychological or historical description and are of no philosophical consequence. The failure of the expressive line to be a theory of art as such can then be equated with its fidelity to a canon of philosophical relevance.

Expression and the Fine Arts

The classical line begins with the concept of an art conceived as an organization of knowledge and skills. The expressive line has no place for that concept. The Platonic notion of general or universal knowledge organized for the production of specifiable kinds of change is precisely what the expressive line was designed to exclude. The Stoic version, in which acquired knowledge and skill is exercised together for a valued end, is not quite so bad, because the "exercising together" takes off the curse of generalization; but the idea of an end for which the art organizes the means remains, and that too is anathema to the expressive line.

On the other hand, the expressive line cannot deny that the fine arts, as organized practices in connection with which the most striking expressions have been formed, do exist and are historically linked to art as expression. To deny the connection, or to say that the distinctions between the different arts are unreal, is to put oneself in the same unhappy position as the Trobriand Islander, with whom it is a matter of faith that the father plays no part in begetting children—he is all right so long as he only has other Trobrianders to talk to, but he comes in for some awful teasing as soon as he leaves home. And the devotee of the expressive line finds himself among people (like Hospers) to whom it is obvious that the organized practices of the fine arts have at least as much to do with art as expression has.

The expressive line cannot, then, deny that the fine arts exist and have some relation to art. What the devotee of that line cannot admit is that their relation to it is central. And it is hard to deny that centrality without seeming to deny the prestige and power of most that is valued as art in every civilization, which would really amount to denouncing the whole of civilization as a confidence trick.[3] The position is, therefore, one of some delicacy.

The expressive line does not have the option of denying that the fine arts are historically important. But is it necessary for the line actually to include a theory of those arts? Perhaps it is, if only to defeat the challenge they appear to represent. At the very least, it needs a metatheory: a sufficient explanation of why it is all right for the expressive line to ignore them.

One way of handling the problem is suggested by Collingwood's observation that "if [the fine arts] are merely embodiments of the aesthetic spirit in different kinds of matter, a philosophy of art, *as distinct from an empirical description of art*, would prefer to ignore them; if they embody that spirit in different degrees, as some have thought, they are generally recognized as belonging to its subject-matter" (1933, 56-57 [my italics]). Setting aside the question of what it means to "embody the aesthetic spirit," a notion perhaps incompatible with the expressive line as Collingwood later developed it, the observation is ambiguous, being susceptible of a stronger and a weaker interpretation.[4] On the weaker interpretation, which the phrasing rather suggests, what can be ignored by philosophy is the particular facts about the arts and their differences, the general fact that there are indeed arts in which the "spirit" is embodied retaining its philosophical importance; on the stronger interpretation, the philosopher as such need take no account of the fact that there are arts at all.

There is much to be said for the proposition that it is important, from the point of view of the expressive line, that there should be arts, but of little or no consequence what they are. One then has the opportunity of reinterpreting the arts in a nonclassical way, so that they cease to be an embarrassment. One might, for instance, argue as follows.

It is not surprising that the fine arts should be the home of the most developed expressions. The civilizing or humanizing process must be cumulative: a certain level of expression affords the starting point for a new level. The refinement of means makes new effects possible. Only against an established body of practice can one do one thing *rather than another*. Each new expression is, of course, completely unified and unanalyzable; but it is so only against the background of a structured situation, which is the current state of one's art. Just as (in Croce's original view of the matter) the basic intuitions that humanize mankind and generate mentality become re-fused into syntheses at a higher level, so that eventually there is a sort of diffused intuition that constitutes culture or civilization as a single unique totality, so in the fine arts the original intuitive creations of naive artists form the experience from which sophisticated artists create both their original individual works and the arts themselves, the bodies of experience that constitute the world of art. These bodies are articulated in the sense that they have describable historical structures, but they can be and are experienced as dynamic unities. One's sense of the history of painting is not of this painter influenced by that but of the vital development of painting through all painters, a development in which one as painter takes a living part. The techniques of the fine arts function, not as knowledge to be learned and applied in the external way described in Collingwood's account of craft, but in the way described by Sartre—one's technique becomes as natural a way of expressing oneself as one's native language, becoming something to be thought of only in the learning stage, or when one moves temporarily out of the domain of intuition into that of problem solving and has to think what to do instead of merely doing it.[5] Technique as such, in fact, has precisely the status of impression: it is removed from the substance of what is intuited and relegated to a merely biological level. And not only techniques but one's knowledge of the repertoire and history of one's art has this same status: it belongs to the life out of which one freely acts. Schiller's distinction between the sentimental and the naive artist becomes one between the artist into whose vital experience the historic material of the arts has entered and the artist whose formation does not include any such component. The expressivist can thus easily incorporate into his position the practices of the fine arts: since in any case something must play the part of impression, and this must in any case have at least enough structure to count as experience, there can be no reason for excluding the experience of the arts as such from this domain, or for denying that anyone engaged in conspicuous intuitions (whatever they may prove to be) will be drawn to precisely what has been intuited in the past by his peers and esteemed for its expressive value ever since.[6]

The foregoing train of thought seems reasonable in itself and consonant with the expressive line, but the proponents of the line have been reluctant to adopt it, to the point where some have blurred or denied the fundamental consideration that the level of impression must be largely formed of experiences that are in their own context formed, individuated, and recognized.[7] The reason for this coyness is that it is hard to go only thus far and not go on to make concessions that make the expressive line, if not untenable, unattractive or trivial.

In the first place, if refined expression depends on a refinement of means so that fine discriminations can be made and perceived, this refinement can hardly stop short of the exploitation of set forms. A symphonist knows what symphonies are and have been, and in his writing a symphony may depend on his and his audience's sense of how what he is doing differs from what has been done before (Meyer 1956; Rosen 1971). But this is to admit what the expressive line exerted itself to deny, that artistic genres are relevant to criticism. It is not, of course, as expressivists like to pretend, that we suppose that every work must bear the name of some set form, and is to be judged by its conformity to canons for that form; but we must concede that a work is to be perceived in relation to some works rather than others, and is to be understood in part by its specific relations to them. But now what is left of the expressive line, with its insistence on the autonomy and isolation of intuitions? In the second place, to admit the refinement of artistic means in this way seems likely to sacrifice the expressive line's promise to provide an epistemic origin. The work of art, based on works of art and forming itself a basis for others, becomes an integral part of an artistic order, expressing artistic experience and no other. What is autonomous is not the work but the world of art, or the world of music. None the worse for that, no doubt; but we have thrown over everything the expressive line had to offer. We are back with the classical line, with the fine arts as arts for elaborating aesthetic objects.

There is nothing in the preceding paragraph that need reduce the adherent of the expressive line to despair. He can insist that to intuit the expression that a symphony is, one not only need not but must not compare it with other symphonies; one must sense it as the expression it is, in its integral uniqueness, and with this uniqueness its difference from other symphonies will be immediately given.[8] But perhaps this concedes too much to the traditional interpretations of the fine arts. It is open to the expressivist to take a tougher line. Whatever requires reference to set forms, however indirect, he may say, has nothing to do with art as such, but belongs to the languagelike use of art. Only what is really irreducible, genuinely independent of antecedent intuitions in any other form than as source of impression, counts as art. And even within this narrower version of the expressive line one can still account for the existence of the fine arts, as follows.

The expression of intuition requires some means of formalizing fine discriminations. The sensory manifolds of sight and hearing, through which our knowledge of the world around us is mediated, afford such means. The plastic arts and music are just the expressive use of these manifolds. Since physical survival requires us to move in the world with precision and grace, and social survival requires us to be especially sensitive to the movements of our fellow humans, arts of dance and gesture are as naturally available as musical and plastic arts. And then, of course, there is language, in which we must acquire the ability to say just what we mean. The fine arts thus correspond pretty well to the discriminatory skills we must in any case acquire. If the actual range of the fine arts at any time is more specific than these general considerations call for, we invoke once more the consideration that if discriminations in the form of *this and not that* are to be exploited, one must confine onself to a limited repertoire, and this limitation may be entirely arbitrary.[9] The situation we would expect to find would be that the general realm of art, expression through the discriminatory skills that all possess, will be *supplemented* by the development of limited repertoires that few will wield. Those that wield them will no doubt be professionals—that will be precisely what their professionalism will consist in. But the fine arts as such have no special preeminence, nor are the finest works of art *necessarily* produced in their domain; it is just that someone who concentrates his intuitive powers will tend as a matter of course to do so by exploiting what affords the most opportunity.

Although the position just sketched seems consistent with the expressive line and offers a way of accommodating what in the fine arts has to be accommodated, it is not the kind of thing any exponent of that line would say. The rhetoric is wrong; and expressivists don't like to talk about that sort of thing. If they were to accept it, they would probably want to add immediately that the opportunities afforded by our special discriminatory capacities afford not only opportunities but temptations and a constant grave risk of perversion. The temptation is to facility and slickness, threatening a relapse into technique. The risk is certainly real, but it may be a mistake to dwell on it too much. For it may be no worse than the opposite risk: false naivety, demonstrative ineptitude, the substitution of sincerity for expression. Sincerity is here to be understood as closeness to experience (hence, remoteness from artifice); and such closeness is all too readily identified with Collingwood's "psychic," preconscious level. Another perversion that threatens is exoticism, the overspecialization of impressions leading to a predominance of useless expressions: in short, the elitism with which "high art" finds itself everywhere charged. But that issue, a complex one, has nothing specifically to do with the formulations of the expressive line; it reflects a social fact that every line of thought must wrestle with as it can.

It is possible to argue that the tempting enticements of the fine arts, with their promise of an expression that has ever more to express as discriminatory skills ramify and artistic resources grow, are deceptive. The purest and deepest expressions are those of primitive art or of genuine naivety. To maintain this, it is necessary to explain away the evident fact that the greatest expressions do seem to be found among works of the fine arts. Partly, one says, that is illusion; but, as we have pointed out, it is implausible (and inconsistent with the pedagogic strategies of the expressive line) to make that the whole explanation. One must somehow explain how it is that the greatest artists of the past took up one or other of the fine arts. And the explanation lies ready to hand. It is that they had no practical option. Children of their age and sharers of its illusions, they naturally supposed that expression was possible only in the arts, just as the English unquestioningly suppose that chop suey cannot be eaten without chips. Art, refined and elaborated expression, grew up unnoticed in the midst of craftsmanship, rhetoric, and magic, from which it must now shake itself free, in just the same way as painting grew up contaminated with the requirement of representation from which it did not free itself until our century. The great painters of the past were figurative painters, but we do not therefore suppose that the great painters of the future will be so; and the fact that the great artists of the past practiced an art does not show that the great artists of the future will do so. Indeed, it is already noticeable that the same sort of thing is being done in the name of art by artists swearing formal allegiance to music, the dance, the theater, and the gallery arts. The attraction of this line of thought is that, as I indicated in chapter 10 and as is generally agreed, the idea of art did grow up in this way, unawares, as it were, as an inner significance that had to be discovered retrospectively by isolating the relevant features of certain arts hitherto thought to be only loosely and externally connected. The difficulty with this line of thought is to find plausible support for the contention that expressions of comparable force to those of the best art can flourish outside the arts, since the examples that come to mind are either (like the avant-garde practices referred to above) marginal and specialized and even less fitted to fulfill the vital expressive function of art than the fine arts were, or else spontaneously gestural and "expressive" in the ordinary-language sense of that word rather than in the sense developed and required by the theory. And that is not at all surprising, since the technical notion of expression was developed precisely to accommodate the distinctive character of the most successful works of the fine arts.

We saw that Collingwood's position about the fine arts was ambiguous between saying that the distinctions between the arts are philosophically insignificant (except on a certain hypothesis) and saying that the development of any arts is insignificant. In one of his later papers (1919), Croce outlines a position that is more carefully nuanced but equally puzzling and more disconcerting. The divisions between the arts, he says, are superficial, resting on such facts as that painting is an "imitative" art and music is not, whereas in truth there are no imitative arts (1919, 357-359). Lines, colors, tones, and such "are metaphors, metonyms, synecdoches to designate the motions of the soul," but not "signs or symbols of feelings which they are employed to convey. . . . We mean to say, in a literal sense, that the sentiments themselves are really lined, coloured, shaded, illuminated, and are all one with those forms," and all are given together, "for it is only by an abstraction that we can think of one portion or one aspect of life being given without the others." The critic's task is then "to penetrate rationally . . . the state of mind expressed in the work of art, which is called its inspiration or lyricity. This should need no arguing, for if the painter is an artist and not merely a mechanical combiner of lines and colours as a game or pastime, if his artisthood as a painter grows from the roots of his manhood, then he must have been inspired and guided to take up his brush and to paint his canvas by a feeling; and it is to this inspiring feeling that the critic, retracing not the technical process, far less the personal and practical biography of the artist, but the creative process, must make his way, resolving the intellectual problems to which this creative process has at each stage given rise." And he meets the anticipated objection that such criticism replaces the determinacy of visual form by abstract spiritual categories with the comment that, in any case, critics must use concepts and not merely retrace the works on which they comment (ibid., 362-364).

What are we to say about this remarkable statement? Is it a tissue of contradictions and absurdities (with its *literally* striped feelings), or a nuanced *via media* with the minimum of metaphor? If the latter, what it says is that the feeling expressed in a painting is not something that could exist separately from the painterly means

357

employed, but it is not equivalent to them either. It is dynamically related to a feeling that the painter had before he began painting (logically rather than temporally before: his having the feeling was a condition of his painting a work of art). That feeling was neither something personal to the artist as individual, nor something purely internal to the business of putting paints on canvas, but rather something related to the "roots of the author's manhood." But since we are told that those roots can be his neither as individual nor as painter, they must be his as generically human: the original feeling was then his *as man and artist*, that is, as expresser of intuitions, not as person or painter. So far, so good. But have we not after all run into a contradiction? We cannot both say that the painterly expression is not a sign of the feeling but an inseparable attribute of the feeling itself, and also identify it with an "inspiring feeling" unconnected with painting and yet so determinate in form that the critic can reconstruct it.[10] We have a choice: either we reject the inseparability or we reject the lack of connection with painting.

In terms of the impetus of the expressive line, the former of these options is far the worse. But does Croce's presentation allow us the second? In fact it does. What was inseparable from the painter's expression was not paint or painting in general but this particular formation of paint; what is inseparable from a musical work of art is not notes in general but the actual notes in which it is written or performed. So there can be more affinity, in terms of what is expressed, between a particular piece of music and a particular painting than between that piece of music and another piece of music—as indeed it is easy to believe there can be: it is not obvious nonsense to say that a Fra Angelico panel has more in common with a Palestrina motet than it has with an oil by John Martin. And if that is so, the fact that the inspiring feeling proves when expressed to be necessarily a feeling-in-a-painting does not link the feeling *generically* with painting, but only with the way paint is used in the specific painting in which it is expressed.

If, on the other hand, we are seduced by Croce's talk of "spiritual categories" into making the other choice, and abandoning the inseparability of the inspiring feeling from its painted expression, we run the risk of making the fine arts merely alternative means of externalization, equivalent not merely in the sense that none of them has a describable range of feeling in which it alone can be used for expression but in the sense that, given an inspiring feeling, the artist has a choice as to which art to use for its embodiment.

And if an artist has that choice, there must for each poem be some possible musical work that expresses just the same feeling—and presumably also some painting, some sculpture, and some work in each of an indefinite array of actual or possible arts.[11] But that notion, even if not preposterous in itself, is alien to the expressive line: it is a version of the classical line, in which the arts are mutually intertranslatable languages for representing feelings that, having their own distinctive character, stand in no need of expression.

Croce's formulation (1919, 362) plainly rules out the idea that the arts represent mere sensory gamuts that are neutral embodiments of feelings to which they are extraneous. I have commented on the way in which his thesis avoids assigning specific characteristics to specific arts. But can this avoidance really be carried through? The brush stroke, says Croce, is integral to the feeling. But does that not mean that the feeling is in one aspect a brush-stroke feeling? And is not that something Croce is anxious to rule out? And if we do not rule it out, how can we deny that painters are exceptionally prone to brush-stroke feelings, and thus (since these feelings go back to the roots of their humanity) find in the practice of painting their characteristic way of being human? In fact, this would be far more characteristic of their humanity than being "an artist" is, since to be an artist is only to express intuitions, which is after all the common form that everyone's humanity takes.

Croce's strategy, in short, seems most unlikely to succeed. It might be better to go back to our earlier suggestion that the fine arts simply afford means of discrimination—or, perhaps better, that it is inevitable that in expressing intuitions people should use the sensory and motor capacities they have, and the fine arts are what that use develops into. But if he wishes to pay pious respect to the original hunch that what is intuited and expressed should be dynamically related to levels of life below the epistemically clarified, the exponent of expression can without inconsistency espouse the thesis that the specific developments of arts and genres answer to broad areas of deepest concern: our sense of our selves, of society, of earth and heaven, of body and mind, of place and past—in the manner of such theorists as Langer, Frye, and Heidegger. There need be no inconsistency so long as he maintains the position that the articulation of the arts corresponds, not to specific contents, but to diffused and pervasive preoccupations. He might argue that the association between arts and concerns rests on some inherent suitability, or he might make it out to be a matter of historical accident, or he might be content to leave the question open. It is true that there seems to be no likely way of developing such a thesis that would be specifically appropriate to the expressive line rather than the classical line or some other, but that is all to the good. Even if the fine arts are not a scandal and an embarrassment to the expressive line, it has no special love for them, and it would be out of place to pay them more than the necessary minimum of attention.

The kind of thesis just mooted, then, though not integral to the expressive line, is consistent with it, and something of the sort may be thought a necessary concession. But it does have the consequence that the apparently arbitrary or accidental specialization of professional practice in the arts entails a specialization in what is expressed. The professional artistic practice of a place and time reflects or generates a style of experience that at that place and time is dominant at least in the sense that it commands public attention. It follows that at any place and time only persons of the right temperament or inclination or interest will become professional artists; an artist out of key with his time must produce an art oblique to the practice of his fellow professionals. But to the expressive line, he is no worse an artist for that: he will suffer social and financial inconvenience, and he will have (like Blake and Schoenberg) to forge for himself the terms in which he imagines and to create the taste by which he is enjoyed.[12] But that is what the proponent of the expressive line would like to say (and if he has a weak enough sense of reality actually does say) every artist does in every work, in any case.

In the end, to accommodate the fine arts, all the devotee of the expressive line really has to do is to concede the frailty of human character. To achieve expression requires in the adult, oppressed by the quotidian and harassed by cares, both strength of spirit to purify his vision and freedom from distracting business. To buy such freedom, unless he is independently wealthy, he must achieve such expressions as will move the wealthy to endow him with leisure (through sales, sinecures, or pension); and strength too will come from the positive reinforcement of praise and reward more dependably than from lonely pride. There is, therefore, nothing in the facts of prevalence of fashions and styles, not only in the artistic professions but in art itself as the expressionist sees it, to gainsay the absolute egalitarianism of expressions on which the expressive line takes its stand.

The Work of Art as Intuition Expressed

Unlike the classical line, the expressive line directly determines an account of what a work of art is. It is the expression of an intuition (or an emotion, if that term is preferred). Whereas in developing the classical line we had to be almost arbitrary in making the important decision as to what sorts of things should be called works of art rather than art objects or something else, because many different sorts of things stood in more or less appropriate relations to the fine arts from which that line began, the expressive line with its programmatic concept of art proceeds directly to the work of art. In fact, the centrality of the concept of the work of art as expressed intuition is what differentiates the expressive line from more generalized versions of the poetic line. If the theorist concedes that not all expressed intuitions are usually (or suitably) called works of art, a name reserved for those produced or published in certain contexts or achieving a certain public character, he will, as we have seen, refuse to allow this habit of nomenclature any deep significance.

The protracted and tiresome distinctions that the classical line brought together under the heading "The Identity of a Work of Art" fall by the wayside: as it was there the design act that in the end determined identity, so here the original insight of the expressive line traces identity without more ado to the unified expression of intuition—the end result is similar though simpler, difficult cases are brushed aside,[13] and there is no fuss. Whereas in working out the classical line we had to grapple with the identity of physical objects, the expressive line finds that topic irrelevant, since the work of art as a single meaning cannot be identified, or in any way essentially linked with, any specific physical object in which it might be externalized. The appropriate characterization of works of art, on the other hand, becomes more problematic, since there is a certain awkwardness in admitting that the supposed primitive unity of an intuition can be characterized at all. Since all intuitions are equally successful and perfect, characterizations can in any case have no room for good-making characteristics and Janus-words; and formal descriptions will be irrelevant and misleading at best. In fact, the only appropriate descriptions will be those that indicate the kind of experience that finds expression in the work.[14]

The classification of works of art is something the expressive line must reject totally on pain of violating the uniqueness and originality of the intuition. It is true that the rejection cannot be carried through in practice, since it is hard to deny that Beethoven wrote five extant piano concertos and one violin concerto. To write without ever mentioning such facts is an absurd affectation (comparable to the party game in which one has to carry on a conversation without using the sound *s*), but the expressionist will insist that such "facts" can only distract attention from the work in hand. In saying this he is on stronger ground than one might suppose, since every theorist in every field will dismiss many indubitable facts as irrelevant to the theoretical task he has undertaken, and unwillingness to do this is a sure sign of theoretical incapacity—stupidity or inexperience or invincible ignorance or frivolity, as the case may be.

In approaching the task of criticism, the expressive line will discard the generic function completely, assigning the study of genres to the history of ideas. Evaluative criticism is not eschewed completely, but takes the form of diagnosing different kinds of failure and different modes of falsely pretending to the status of art. In addition to this, it is not out of place for those adepts of the expressive line who admit a public dimension in those intuitions assigned to the category of art to say something about the values of utility or necessity in that dimension, about "greatness" or even "sublimity," which are not characteristics of art as art but have to do with the way art fits into life. But, in saying that, pure-minded expressivists will say we have only revealed the insidious dangers that lurk in the discrimination between expressions we will call art and other expressions. What remains for criticism is the interpretive function, the task of which is to aid the public in their recreation of the original intuition by clearing obstacles from their path. And, since the expressivist critic, like all other critics, chooses what to criticize, in his interpretive capacity he will automatically assume the task of the cicerone, the role of truffle hound for the expression hunter.[15]

In saying that the expressive line makes the work of art its starting point, one is running afoul of a widespread conviction that it is precisely to the work of art that that line fails to do justice. The main reason for that conviction is that what the expression theory dismisses as externalization is integral to the work, so that whatever it is the expressivist does justice to cannot be the work itself in its physical actuality. If that is all that is meant, we have said enough on the matter already. But some critics carry their strictures a step further. Thus, Peter Jones, citing G. H. Lewes' complaint that J. S. Mill "has looked at the creative *mind* of the artist, not at the *work of art*," adds that "this criticism, which he applied also to Hegel, is one of the earliest formulations known to me of a salient objection to the whole expression theory of art" (Jones 1975, 60). And this is quite wrong on almost any likely interpretation—conjecture is necessary, for Jones does not elaborate usefully. If, first, it implies that expression theories are concerned with the biography of artists rather than the criticism of works, that is simply not true of the major theorists by whose positions "the expression theory" is usually defined.[16] On the contrary, the insistence on the autonomy of intuitions means that the "mind of the artist" has no status whatever. The objection as thus interpreted confuses impression with expression. If, second, the objection is that expression theories treat the work of art as performance rather than as artifact, that is no doubt the case; but I have argued that only thus can one do justice to the way we think about art and must think if we are to make sense. If, third, the objection is that expression theories concern themselves with an expressed content existing antecedently to its expression, and thus with intended rather than with actual works of art, the point is highly debatable. The whole force of the expressive line goes to deny that what is expressed can be something that previously existed unexpressed. One might argue that in theory it is possible for someone to achieve an intuition that (because he was paralyzed or deprived of access to his paints or whatever) he could not externalize, and that the expressive line would then say that such an intuition would be a perfected work of art. But in such a case it is not the artist's intention but his achievement that is taken into account, and it is very strange to read this as a contrast between the artist's mind and his work. If Jones is relying on such passages as Croce's reference (quoted above) to an "inspiring feeling," we find on examination that that feeling is detachable (so to speak) from the artist's biography but not from its specific embodiment in the work. If, finally, what is meant is that expression theories are concerned with an artist's art in general as opposed to his specific works, that is incompatible with the distinctness of intuitions. What Lewes said was very likely true of Mill, who was passionately interested in human virtue and uninterested in the arts as such, and is certainly true of Hegel. But it is not true in general of theories that take the expressive line; and it is not even true of theories on the classical line that are concerned with the arts as expressive of antecedent states of mind, for it is not really a common characteristic of representational theories that they transfer interest from the work of art to that outside the work which the work may be deemed to represent.

363

We may return to a point made in the last chapter: although in principle externalization is separable from expression, in practice it is only through the processes (externalization or other) that issue in what the vulgar world calls a work of art that the achieved intuition is accessible either to the artist or to his public. Only the laying of the cards on the table reveals the four-flusher.

The Artist as Everyman

The classical line offered us three possible accounts of what an artist might be taken to be. He might be the wielder of one or more of the skills that are institutionalized in the fine arts; or he might be a skilled or gifted practitioner of one of those arts; or he might be someone who regularly produces works of art (or who has notably produced one or a few conspicuous works). And we saw that in fact our use of the term "artist" wanders among all these as our discourse fastens on one or another of the ways in which producers are related to the arts. But the expressive line offers no such choice. Technique is excluded from art altogether, and the arts are admitted if at all (and our insistence that they must be does not correspond to any overt admission by the exponents of the line) only on sufferance and by indirection. We might then expect to find that the expressive line means by an artist always and only one who regularly produces works of art. But we have seen that every expressed intuition is a work of art, or at least (on the compromise version) that the difference between works of art and other expressed intuitions has no importance in principle. And since every human being, simply in the process of becoming human, provides himself with the intuitions that form the groundwork of the world of meanings he inhabits, and in fact expresses an intuition every time he comes to clear knowledge of any occasion, the expressive line is often taken to entail the thesis that every man is an artist, even though not every man is called so. This thesis, however, is too strong for everyday use. It is usually watered down into the statement that every human being is *really* an artist,[17] but for practical purposes we confine the use of the term to those whose expressed intuitions are publicly conspicuous in some appropriate fashion (the specification of which, as we saw, is no integral part of the expressive line).[18]

To say that every human being is an artist allows everyman more authenticity of intuition than many will allow him: since it is characteristic of the expressive line to hold that even the arts are riddled with *Kitsch* and routine, we can hardly believe that the man in the street will have a purer mind than the artist in the academy. We will therefore likely say that the minds of adults are for the most part sunk in everyday routine repetitions of mental clichés; it is only children in whom it is usual, because unavoidable in their ignorance of clichés, to express intuitions. Every child, after all, has to express intuitions, because it has not yet learned a language and is still creating its own language; an adult, having created its language (and learned the language of others), can go ahead and exploit it. What would be the use of learning a language if one were going to make no use of it? It is every child, then, not every human being, who is an artist, until his fresh eye and tongue are spoiled by training. And this has indeed long been common cant. It is common to see exhibitions of child "art" or read collections of children's "poems," all carefully artless, assigned artistic value by their impresarios on the ground that they express the untaught and therefore unspoilt vision of the child. The hankering after a lost innocence of childhood, for which the corn is orient and immortal wheat,[19] long antedates the expressive line and even the romantic theories of language that are its antecedents.[20] But it has provided excellent grist for the expressivist mill.

If not every person but every child is an artist, what shall we say of adult artists? Presumably that they are childlike, have preserved the innocent eye of childhood.[21] The artist differs from other people not, as on most versions of the classical line, by what he knows, his acquired skills, but by what he does not know, by his failure to socialize his imagination and acquire the common speech and vision.

The child's expression of his intuitions is the natural mark of his condition, as one who has not yet acquired a language. But that is not true of the adult artist, despite what was advanced in the last paragraph. It is not that he has no language, but that he retains and exercises on suitable occasions the gift for intuition.[22] His intuitions, his works of art, are achievements, not residues. In fact, the equation of the artist with everyman or everychild assimilates expressed intuitions to the model of gestures rather than to that of cognitive achievements; and this model, as we have had occasion to remark, provides only inferior versions of the expressive line.

Everyone except a mother or a kindergarten teacher, I suppose, has noticed that child art on the whole *lacks something*. Those whom the world calls artists can, by and large, do something that other people, even very small children, can't. Not only does an artist know how to practice his art (a knowledge that the expressive line denies or discounts); he can produce something that is worth attending to because it is new and vital, and not just another tedious manifestation of a fresh and unspoiled sensibility.[23] The artist is, in fact, a specialist. A poet may be born and not made, in the sense that without an uncovenanted grace of intuition he can do nothing in art; but the choice to convert this grace into works involves determination or at least acquiescence in an overpowering impulse. Poets are not persons to whom poems happen to happen, but at least persons who have decided to make welcome such poems as may happen. If we are to remain within the expressive line, we must say that technical training and practice are in principle irrelevant; but we are not obliged to say that they may not be in fact aids to intuition and that a refined sensibility and purity of heart cannot be cultivated—much as the would-be mystic goes through the discipline that is known to induce, though it cannot guarantee, the vision. Technical training is largely replaced by spiritual preparation: the artist, we may say, is not everyman but rather the person who achieves intuitions such as an appropriate preparation might be thought to induce.

A central contention of the expressive line is that man as a symbol-using animal must first be (or have been) an expressive animal—the faculty of expressing intuitions is at least among those things that set mankind off from less mentally elaborate creatures. But then, if artists are specialists in expression, are we to say that artists are specialists in being human? Something like this rather startling thesis was indeed propounded by Schiller.[24] If the common man has fallen into everyday routine from a level of constant intuition, the artist represents a paradigm of unfallen humanity, a saint or hero of authenticity—a thought that will be developed in our last "line." But if we say, more modestly, that the artist's specialization lies, not in the fact that he expresses intuitions at an age when most people have lost that gift, but in his doing so in a publicly accessible and notable way, his art becomes not a sign of redemption but a celebration of humanity. And a position such as this seems to fall within the ordinary scope of the expressive line as its proponents would have it (rather than, as with some of our ventures, violating it in order to reconcile it with a "common sense" they would despise).

The notion that artists are best thought of as specialists in expression might be thought to invite paradox. It suggests that the normal artistic progress would be from specializing in general expression through specializing in one of the arts until finally perhaps one discovers one's métier in one particular manner or genre, for surely this is the normal pattern of specialization. Or, at least, musicians would be artists who have chosen to specialize in music. But that is not the way things are. Musicians, painters, and poets are usually different people from the very beginning and seldom if ever cross boundaries, although the process of coming to specialize *within* the art one practices is so common as perhaps to be the norm.[25] In other words, the expressive line leads us to think of musicians and poets as essentially artists who have chosen different specialisms, rather than as persons practicing different things that for certain purposes it is handy to consider as species of the same genus. But in fact there is nothing here to give the expressive line pause, unless it be the repeated reminder that the arts do have characteristic media and the expressive line has seldom taken these into systematic account. All that was meant by speaking of the artist as a specialist in expression is that he has in some area and on some occasions retained the initial purity and energy of the child's creative mind and employed this with an adult's strength and scope. It is because there is an area and there are occasions on which he notably does this that we confer on him the distinctive name of artist.

Conclusion: Status and Prospects of the Expressive Line

The expressive line is not exactly trendy. Old ways are often best, and the author of a book designed to reinstate classical concepts is in no position to deride old-fashioned things, but the old claim of the expressivist to be making precise what the best minds were already less articulately thinking no longer holds good. The fire has gone out. It would, I think, be very difficult to restate the line nowadays with the kind of conviction that sustained Croce. But that does not mean that we can safely forget about it.

In one way, the expressive line is a purification and culmination of the development that converts arts of the aesthetic into arts of imagination, and arts of imitation into arts of expression. In this aspect, the expressive line is related to the classical line as a sort of vitamin or dietary supplement, without which the classical line is inert.

In another way, the expressive line is not a supplement but, as

Collingwood saw it, the converse of fine-arts academicism. In this light it represents a necessary corrective, a falsehood that complements the opposite falsehood of the classical line. Since there is no getting away from the classical line, the correction is permanently necessary.

In a third way, the expressive line makes plain, as the classical line does not, that (and how) the fine arts are not merely recreation, a superficial ornament of life, but a central function in human culture. Since the official culture of the English-speaking world finds it difficult either to deny that centrality or to come to terms with it, in this aspect too the expressive line has permanent worth as a necessary scandal.

In somewhat oblique relation to the epistemic centrality of what art exemplifies, one may point out that to many thinkers, not necessarily in accord with his basic positions, Collingwood's *Principles of Art* has seemed the one essential book in aesthetics. Part of the reason has been its passionate concern with the centrality and seriousness of art, but another part is his recognition of the risk in art. It is not only the artist, as I said before, who is at risk, though he risks more. The critic too is always unsafe. It is not that the knowledge and skill of artist and critic are of no use to them; it is that they can never be relied on to do what is asked of them—they cannot preserve the artist from total insipidity and the critic from total incomprehension just when each seems most secure in his prowess and his judgment. One does see the point when Kendall Walton says that art is a game of make-believe for which the artist provides the props; but if it is, it is a gambling game in which the stakes are high and the playing and the wagering are one and the same act. Of all writers on art who are not artists, Collingwood seems most alive to this danger, and it is for this reason that he is almost the only writer on the subject whom artists will always take seriously.

For all that we have been saying, the status of the expressive line remains ambiguous. It is necessary to that line that it be, not a correction or an additive to the classical line, not a reflection on the significance of an already known and identified something that we know as art, but an independent alternative to the classical line establishing what art essentially is. The classical line, that is, is not merely inadequate but false from the beginning, and one would be better off if one had never known it. But if that claim is taken literally, it certainly becomes difficult, and I would say it becomes impossible, to make good its claim to pick out a level of mental attainment, be it epistemic origin or humanization, in a way that combines necessary precision with credibility and with relevance to what even its own exponents will be able to bring themselves to think of as art. That is, it surreptitiously invokes the classical line, the prior knowledge of what art is that only that rival line articulates. I think the only way the proponents of the expressive line can escape that charge is by saying that they speak with the vulgar because they themselves must, for the time being, think with the vulgar. A world from which fine-arts thinking and all its objects had vanished would be a better world, a world in which art would appear in its true purity. But no advocate of the expressive line has yet said quite that. Those who come closest to it are advocates of the mystic and purist lines, which we have yet to examine.

If we do take the expressive line on its own terms, as an attempt to explain from the beginning what art as an essential function of the mind truly is, I think it has been superseded, probably for ever, by structuralism. The reason for this is that the expressive line, at bottom a theory of language of an exceptionally high level of abstraction, rests on a view of language (as old as Plato and doubtless older) that starts with *naming* and thinks of language as the combining of names. The lexicon comes first, grammar comes next. But in the last thirty years our thinking about languages has reflected our development and increasing use of computers, the theoretical basis of which is the logical analysis begun by Boole in the middle of the nineteenth century and given its decisive form by Russell and Whitehead two generations later. Linguistic creation now becomes code construction and encoding. In structuralism, the union of nature and culture is effected, not by the immediate fusion of an intuition, but by a process of mediation; not by a succession of syntheses of insight and feeling, but by a process of superimposing natural and cultural codes. Conformably, the center of interest in art is no longer the work of art, but *arting*, the activity and not the act; it is significant that for Lévi-Strauss the paradigm artist is Wagner precisely because of the inexhaustibility of his modification and interweaving of motives (1964, 14).

Strictly, expressivism and structuralism are complementary. A formal language is one thing, its interpretation as relating to some content or aspect of experience is another; the activity of using codes is one thing, the creation of works (or of myths) is another. It is, as I have observed, a glaring weakness in Barthesian structuralism that it purports to deny what its exponents cannot but show that they know very well, the integrity of works; it is a defect of the expressive line that it programmatically refuses to admit what its exponents are mostly expert in, the analysis of works. Neither has found a way out of, or a way of remaining comfortably within, the hermeneutic circle.

XIII

THE MYSTIC LINE

At the beginning of chapter 10, I recapitulated the story of how the observed or imputed likenesses of certain practices generate the idea that those practices are variations of a single practice, that of the fine arts, and how that notion in turn generates the concept of art as what animates that practice. Once isolated for inspection, the concept of art gives rise to a new spirit of practice: "art for art's sake," a devotion to the production of objects that cannot be mistaken for anything other than objects for contemplation because they are conspicuously divorced from the service of any other possible interest, or (as the expressive line has it) to the expression of uncontaminated intuitions.[1]

What is thus represented as a transition from contaminated to uncontaminated art, and in a larger perspective as the rise of art in the midst of and on the basis of what is not art, could equally well be thought of as a transition or degeneration from a full art to an impoverished or empty art. What from one point of view is essentially aesthetic, because purely contemplable, is from another viewpoint thin, because there is little in it to sustain repeated or interested contemplation: the idea of a pure art may be connected, as it is by Jakob Rosenberg, with the impoverishment of life inherent in the division of labor.[2] The missing fullness of art may be variously identified. Marxism locates it in a vital relationship to the economic interests of the rising class (ultimately, of the proletariat as the irreducible producing class), in which alone a concentration of the gaze does not distract attention from the only reality there is; others, more in the tradition of Dilthey, find it in a relation to the fullness of the cultural life of a historically situated epoch; the expressivists working in the classical line look for it in the relation between art and the real life interests of individuals, and more especially those common to all or many folk, or between art and whatever among the deepest human concerns needs symbolic expression. Or the fullness of art might be thought to lie in some relationship to an ultimate reality specified without reference to human needs and conceived to be independent of them.

To deplore the (alleged) impoverishment of art by the vogue of "art for art's sake" does not necessarily take a theorist outside the scope of the classical line, which was indeed originally developed by theorists innocent of such purism.[3] What attracts and rewards contemplation is what interests in any mode. It was only through a quibble that formalists could present the "aesthetic" as necessarily devoid of any life interest and then opt for the former as opposed to the latter—as though interest in what was presented in a work must be interest in some other thing "outside" the work and represented by it.[4] In fact, the quibble was so implausible that one is inclined to think of it as a mere debater's trick.[5] But if we take the last version mentioned, in which the fullness of art lies in its relation to reality, we have stepped outside the classical line, and our theory undergoes an unheralded transformation in kind. Since ultimate reality cannot be presumed to be identical with any set of appearances, and in fact no one talks of ultimate reality unless they have something in mind that goes beyond appearances, the relation that is now to constitute the fullness of art is one that need not be, and strictly cannot be, mediated by contemplation. We have thus opened up the possibility that the inherent power of art should have some noncognitive link with natural or supernatural forces, to which link the perceptible power of art is merely a testimony. For this reason, this interpretation of the required fullness of art generates a line of its own, distinct from either the classical or the expressive line. The point of this line is that art is essentially not a production of objects for contemplation or an expression of intuitions, even though art may involve these incidentally by some derived necessity; its operations and products have a primary significance that is radically other than the aesthetic. We have accordingly to add to the classical and expressive lines of thought about the arts a third, independent line. It would be agreeable to call it the power line, but the phrase has misleading associations; so let us call it the mystic line.

The family of theories and opinions comprised in the mystic line may be defined by the following three theses.

First, there are, or are thought by some relevant group of persons to be, powers operative in the universe other than those defined for the purposes of theories of positive science (whether physical, behavioral, or social). Such powers are exemplified by God, gods, the world soul, élan vital, *numina*, *mana*, demons, and so forth, but their character need not be specified, nor need they be associated with any particular religion or cult beyond what is implicit in the practices of the relevant arts themselves. Because positive science knows nothing of them, let us call these occult powers.

Second, the proper domain of art lies in relating some or all human activities or passivities to the said powers: the human concerns in question may be those of some or all of the artist, his public, his society (or religious group, etc.), and mankind at large.

Third, within that domain of the relation of mankind to occult powers, the special province of art is those processes or products that represent, symbolize, or control those forces in a way that to a suitably sensitive observer is evidenced by the character of the processes and products themselves. That is, art is a bearer of evident power, and that in it which is the ancestor of the aesthetic (and thus could generate the arts in the secular guise in which we know them today) is the expressive evidence of power.

The three theses above, which determine the mystic line, must be contrasted with three other theses, popular in themselves, which persons unsympathetic to the mystic line often suppose its proponents to be maintaining. These other theses do not take the theorist out of the classical line and have no particular interest for the theory of art as such. If they are true, they belong to the politics or to the empirical sociology or psychology of artistic production as conceived by the classical line.

First, then, it is no part of the mystic line to argue that art has as one of its functions, or even as its sole function, some religious purpose. The mystic line has to do with the nature of art, the kind of affair it is, not with the use to which art (having a nature and belonging to a setting otherwise defined) may be put. A theory about the function of art is a theory about the uses to which contemplable things may be put; the mystic line has to do with what art is when it is not perverted into the production of contemplables.

Second, it is no part of the mystic line to contend that art, artists, or works of art ought to be placed at the service of religious institutions—for some such reason as that, for instance, God is the master of all and all should be at His service, or that the power of art should be at the disposal of those most truly dedicated to the service of goodness. That is not a theory about the real nature of art, but about the organization of practice.

Third, it is not within the scope of the mystic line to maintain that religious themes, because of their inevitable social and psychological punch, are so eminently proper a subject for art that only a spontaneously religious age can possibly generate a great art. This might indeed be the case: it might be that great secular art exists only as a fallout from great religious art, and the very idea of greatness requires a religious setting; but it is a thesis about the conditions in which one can expect art to fulfill criteria that are defined in terms consonant with the classical line, and has only a peripheral interest for the general theory of art.

Just as many writers combine the characteristic theses of the expressive line with assertions of a very different character that can only be construed in terms of the classical line, upholders of the mystic line will often maintain one or more of the extraneous propositions I have just referred to, usually without being aware that their position has any internal complexities. Many of them are high-minded persons more interested in religion than in theory and more fearful of impiety than of unclarity or even of inconsistency. The fact that diverse propositions are associated or loosely combined in their minds does not suffice to show that there is any logical relation between them.

Confronted with the mystic line as exemplified by some version of our three theses, one's first impulse might be to ask in what sense what confronts one is a theory of art. It can hardly serve as a stipulative definition of art, since it normally presupposes that we already know what art is and that what best conforms to the theory is practices and products other than those that serve as the agreed paradigms of art. Nor can it be taken as a generalization about art defined in some other terms appropriate to the classical or expressive lines, for when thus taken it is manifestly false. It singles out a different set of practices and products from those singled out by the other lines; in fact, it is usually meant to do so, customarily appearing in the context of a denunciation or depreciation of secular art, whose right to be called art is, however, not denied (as the expressive line typically does deny the title of art to what it excludes). Why is it not a theory of theurgy or the sociology of religion, involving practices and products that only contingently are also to be deemed art? This is a question that will occupy us at some length. Briefly, the answer seems to be that what the mystic line offers is a reformative definition. The underlying contention is not that all art complies with the theory, or that the confines of art should be redrawn to exclude all that does not so comply, but that the human activities of art make sense only in the defined context, so that until that context is restored, neither the practice nor the theory of art makes any sense.[6]

How is the mystic line related to the classical line? It implies that the latter, taken at its face value, is a perversion of the truth in that it makes something peripheral in art, the aesthetic effect, into the center, much in the spirit of someone who buys a book for its binding. It implies that the classical line is at best the wrong sort of theory to take as one's starting point in considering art: that line, if not a complete misstatement of the nature of art, is formalistic and wrongheaded, describing the superficial character of art rather than its inner dynamic; and art, like any other form of human practice, must be understood primarily in terms of its fundamental location in the network of human purposes.

The mystic line is in some ways closer to the classical line than the expressive line is. It admits the idea of expert fabrication, which is at the basis of the classical line, and which it is the main concern of the expressive line to eliminate from the consideration of art. It accommodates specific arts and regards the fine arts as perverted only in that they are the wrong sorts of arts, not (as we have seen the expressive line does or would dearly love to do if it could) because art has no place for any arts at all. But in another way the mystic line is further from the classical line than the expressive line is. The expressive line, though in theory extending the range of art far beyond the fine arts and excluding much of the latter from that range, in effect takes as its paradigms of fully achieved expressions some or all of the acknowledged masterpieces of the fine arts, being in fact derived (as we saw) from the most sophisticated practice of the criticism of such masterpieces. But to the mystic line art criticism and connoisseurship are wholly alien: the works it singles out as most significant would coincide with the acclaimed masterpieces of art, even of religious art, only by accident or through the operation of some psychological or sociological causality the efficacy of which it is no part of the mystic line to affirm. A magical image is not as such meant to be contemplated or appreciated. It may be, as I shall argue, that efficacious magical images tend to be beautiful or (more likely) striking or vital or awe inspiring, but those qualities are not independently identified and asserted to be as such the ground of the efficacy. An aesthetically insignificant image would do equally well if it happened to do the job, for the same reason that there is no need to employ a graceful gesture in crossing oneself.

How is the mystic line related to the expressive line? It must regard the latter (especially in its impure and romantic versions) as a secularized version of itself. What, after all, could the object of an intuition be? We should not call it an intuition unless there were something really intuited; but what is intuited is *ex hypothesi* something unified, and a nonevident unity at that, or there would be nothing for the artist to do. The intuitions of art must therefore really penetrate appearances to find some underlying unifying power; it is sheer hypocrisy for the expressive line to deny this evident and glaring truth. As for the dialectical versions of the expressive line, in which the cumulative reintegration of expressions on the basis of expressions generates culture, what are they but bowdlerized versions of the Hegelian self-unfolding of Mind (cf. Croce 1906)? And the Hegelian Mind, as a sophisticated version of a Neoplatonic One, is explicitly presented as the successor of the Gods of organized religion, *agnôstos theos*, the unknown God whom they all ignorantly worship. But the mystic line must be flatly opposed to the expressive line for essentially the same reason that it is opposed to the classical line. To the mystic line, the work of art is not endotelic, does not have its reason-for-being in merely existing: its production is nothing more than a means to an external end to which other means could equally well have been taken if they had proved equally effective. No doubt magical works do express the sense of the numinous felt by the artist or his society, but that expression is not their function: there is supposed to be a real force to be controlled or manifested, not simply a belief in such a force to be expressed, so that what matters is what will actually control or embody the force in the relevant way. One used to dance the rain dance, now one seeds the clouds; that the latter procedure is less deeply satisfying than the former is neither here nor there, so long as it rains just the same.

The popularity of the mystic line is disproportionate to the historical evidence by which, as we shall see, it is most often supported, and is independent of any religious or metaphysical convictions that might render it credible or intelligible to this or that sector of the intellectual world. It simply seems to be how a large number of writers on art like to think. One example may serve for all as typical of the level at which much of such writing is carried on. In a review of a book on surrealistic and marvelous theater, Donna Wilshire writes of its practitioners:

> All share the attempt to discover and celebrate the natural powers of the universe. All the practitioners of the marvellous are striving to create a magical aura, a force, an atmospheric tension through which we can learn of the vast "surreality" and achieve a higher spiritual state (1977, 498).

Wilshire is not a trained philosopher or other professional theorist, and such persons might ridicule her words as sentimental rubbish. So they may be; but they are also the expression of a superior intelligence seriously engaged in the rationale of a public professional practice to which she is responsibly committed. What she writes is, therefore, if not a theoretical position to be seriously debated, a phenomenon that deserves attention.[7] We notice, then, that these sentences presuppose, first, that there are "natural powers" at large in the universe; second, that these powers may be discovered by artistic practice and not only (if at all) by scientific work or theological investigation; third, that knowledge of these powers either constitutes or normally accompanies the achievement of a spiritual state that is (for some unspecified reason) to be ranked as higher than that in which most people otherwise pass their time; and, fourth, that the arts in question succeed in achieving this knowledge and elevation through the creation of an "aura" and a "tension," a perceptible force and excitement that must be presumed in some way analogous to, respectively, the reality of which knowledge is required and the state of enlightenment that is to be achieved. It is not clear whether a "magical aura" is an aura suggesting magic or an aura having magically efficacious properties, and it is possible that the author is writing without full awareness of the distinction, or is aware of it but would deny its legitimacy. In any case, there is nothing in the content or context of what Wilshire writes to indicate in what sense she believes what she is saying to be literally true, what arguments or evidence she would adduce in its support, or to what religious or metaphysical systems she would relate it, if to any.[8] But it is clearly presented as the frame of mind in which practitioners of the arts in question appropriately approach their tasks.

One may well ask why anyone in tune with our scientifically informed age, or why any educated person in any age, should indulge in such loose talk about powers and auras. One might, in disparagement, point to the current popularity of bizarre cults and magical playthings among adolescents as an analogous phenomenon. That testifies, it may be said, not only to the thinness of the educational veneer imparted in an egalitarian society but to a twofold revolt in the name of a meaningful life against the emptiness of a society ruled by a mercenary positivism and in the name of childish wish fulfillment against the realities of adulthood and responsibility.[9] But such disparagement, even if the downgrading of the alleged analogue be accepted, is unnecessary. One might equally well admit that some art is not merely charming or bizarre but evidently wields some power, and that whatever in art lacks such power, and especially whatever excludes or denies it, is trivial, so that the first requisite to speaking the truth about art is that its power should be acknowledged. The vagueness and looseness complained of are simply the effect of refusing to go beyond what is evident into irrelevant domains of abstract speculation or arid dogma.

That art wields evident power could be doubted, or held to be meaningless.[10] One's argument might therefore be strengthened by pointing out (once more) that art is customarily accorded a public importance and respect that are incompatible with its having the status of mere decoration, mere pleasure, or mere imitation, and by urging that the attempts to explain this fact away by claiming a recondite importance for all forms of "play," of which art is one, are implausible in themselves and fail to meet the case, because the public importance accorded to art is different in kind from that accorded to any kind of sport or game. Now, whenever we find respect paid to anything for which no present ground can be discovered, one looks to the past to see if that respect is not a carry-over from some situation in which the bearer of that respect did in fact merit it by whatever canons are or were appropriate: one may find respect paid to a former prime minister even when it is evident that he is now nothing but a garrulous old fool.[11] The present unmerited prestige of art has similarly to be justified by looking away from the arts as practiced in classical and modern times and examining the prehistory and dark ages of art.

Such a turning away from the institutional presence of art seems at first scarcely legitimate. But to begin one's reflections with the concept of art rather than with that of the fine arts automatically emancipates one from the current history of art. If art is presumed to be a spiritual accomplishment or an epistemological function, one no longer is obliged to account for, and cannot reasonably confine oneself to, what has been done in the name of art lately. Rather, one seeks or postulates a function that is necessary to the workings of the human mind or to society, something without which no individual or no group can function effectively, which art may be plausibly alleged to serve, and the lack or mishandling of which in our own civilization can be credibly linked with an alleged failure of that civilization to flourish.[12]

A proponent of the mystic line might well complain at this point that he is being traduced. He will urge that, so far from postulating a function and then casting around for evidence to demonstrate its relevance, his position is the only one that can be reached by any honest inquirer. Once one has decided that what is currently practiced under the name of art is functionally inexplicable and incommensurate with the reverence paid to it, all one has to do, and all one can reasonably do, is to seek for the explanation of art in some comprehensible function that practices historically related to our own or clearly analogous with our own do serve. One has three places to look. First, one may investigate what is common to the analogous practices of other civilizations, such as the Indian and the Chinese, on the ground that what is found common to these will testify either to a common origin or to a universal need, and more likely both. Next, one may examine the practices of nonliterate ("primitive") cultures. The traditional justification for doing so was that, as the word "primitive" suggested, their practices approximated to those in our own prehistory; but that historical assumption has come to seem doubtful, since nonliterate societies must be supposed to have pedigrees as long as ours and to have been no less susceptible to change.[13] An alternative though equally romantic excuse might be that they are unself-conscious, their motives neither falsified by sophisticated rationalizations nor sicklied over by the pale cast of literacy. If something is shared by all peoples not given to critical reflection on what they traditionally do, this common factor may be supposed connatural to humanity.[14] And, finally, one may delve into prehistory itself, examine the earliest relics of what we can recognize as art and figure out their likely significance.

Proponents of the mystic line can urge that all three routes lead to the same destination. It is widely agreed that if one looks at the worldwide use of such objects and practices as we would assign to the fine arts, one finds that their function is neither to instruct nor to please beholders but to capture and regulate, and sometimes to impart, powers that would not be otherwise amenable to human control: occult forces, divine powers, the vital forces of beasts hunted or hunting. Support might be found in Coomaraswamy's (1977) interpretations of Sanskrit authorities; Chinese and Japanese insistence on an artist's cooperation with, or induced subjection to, the way the world goes (e.g. Sze 1963); and the tendency of ethnographers to assign religious or magical functions to most ornamentation and image making in nonliterate societies. But it is likely that the greatest impetus of all to this way of thinking has come from the discovery of the paleolithic paintings of France and Spain, the earliest known art, to which it has seemed obvious to ascribe the magical function of securing power over game animals.[15] Art, it seems, is originally and, except for ourselves, universally religious, not in the sense that it is taken over and put to priestly service or that its subject matter is the divine, but in the sense that it is itself a fundamentally theurgic or liturgic practice.

I remarked on an earlier page that the mystic line might be hard put to it to explain why it is a theory about art, rather than about something for which a different word—say "iconopoiesy"—would be more appropriate. One might, after all, present one's doctrine in the form of an anatomy of and encomium on iconopoiesy, the manufacture and use of theurgic or liturgic imagery, accompanied by a denunciation of the practice of art.[16] But one reason is supplied in our general chapter on the concept of art. The introduction of that concept prepares the way for the contention that the fine arts, the institutions in which the spirit of art is for the time being factually embodied, represent a distortion of art or have temporarily taken a wrong turning; and if we allow "art" to stand quite generally for *whatever* important function the fine arts enshrine, however imperfectly, there is no reason for not retaining the word "art" for the mystic line, with the understanding that rival notions of what art is represent misunderstandings of the fundamental and original purport of what has turned into the fine arts. In fact, though, virtually all proponents of the mystic line maintain that at least some modern and even contemporary works retain their proper ambiance and aura, and may thus save the fine arts for art as the ten righteous men would have saved Sodom.

It is perhaps harder for the mystic line to meet the objection that it confuses the nature of art with the origins of art. I have already cited Nietzsche's observation that the origin of an institution does not by any means determine its principal function in any later age, and I remarked in *SA* (212) on how misleading it is to say that one thing "is originally" another, thus insinuating without evidence or argument that what it first was it still must fundamentally be. One does not suppose that the autonomy and authenticity of the concept and practice of the fine arts are undermined if it is shown that those practices had originally been utilitarian representations in which an aesthetic element was first accidentally discovered, then indulged in as incidental enhancement, and at last made the sole concern; in fact, one must suppose that every special practice arose in the midst of unspecialized activity from which it was not at first distinguished. Why should we not then invoke the names of Collingwood (1938) and Lukács (1963), and say that aesthetic power, to which many are susceptible without religious involvement, grew up in the context of magical power, with which it was at one time confused, but has now become distinct?[17] The practitioners of marvelous art, to which Wilshire refers, would then be artists who specialize in aesthetic effects of the powerful rather than the charming sort; they are, after all, dramatists and not Magi; and if they go in for magical practices, they notoriously do so in a way that impresses the religiously committed as aesthetic and frivolous for all its ostentatious solemnity.[18]

It is by no means absurd to suppose that art, though magical in its origins, should be nonmagical in its nature. Its discovery would be more than a lucky chance, like the discovery of penicillin; it would arise inevitably from the nature that religious symbolism almost inevitably has.[19] The form of an artifact that is to ensnare or represent an occult force cannot be known to be determined, and, therefore, for practical purposes is not determined, by that force itself; otherwise, the force would not be occult. The pragmatic end leaves the artist (or the artistic tradition as a whole) free in effect to determine the shape of his image, however unfree he may feel. How then can the form of the image be determined? If it is not to be entirely fortuitous and arbitrary, a mere mystification by a cynical exploiter secure in social power, the form can only be judged by some perceived congruence with what is supposed by the artist, or by his clientele, to be the purport of the force entrapped or the powerful being to be controlled or made present. Whether such a standard is explicitly invoked or subconsciously operative, the work will be found satisfactory only if it conveys a sense of a particular kind of vital power, or of a kind of ideal, or expresses the sense of the powerful movement invoked or subjugated. But that is to say that the images produced must be in fact proper objects of contemplation and have the properties that the classical line ascribes to works of art; and, since they satisfy a deep personal or social need, they will probably be works of expressive power. No doubt the very holiest images will not be of this kind, but will be amorphous or commonplace objects or locations whose presumptive efficacy is entirely a matter of association, and the magical nature of whose power is indeed attested by their apparent ordinariness. But these are objects around which sanctity has grown. An image cannot be *made* to be of this kind; what is made to have sanctity must be given a head start, must derive sanctity without delay, either from the rituals of its manufacture or from the qualities perceptibly imparted to it, and most probably from both. On this showing, the mystic line is reduced to a thesis about the origin of art: the need to make images of power leads to making images whose nature is such that they seem appropriate to their function, and at last it becomes apparent that the power inheres in the work itself and is not an external force controlled or invoked by it. And that is the discovery of aesthetic power and either the discovery of art or an element in that complex discovery.

The proponent of the mystic line must in any case admit that the magic power of art, however genuine, is a power manifested in appropriate formal and expressive properties; what makes him speak of art is not the presence of power nor even the feeling of power, for surely he does not think that to feel awe or dread is as such an artistic experience. It is the perception of power in an artifact or performance. It is then hard for him to reply effectively to the contention that magical art is but one sort of art, exploiting one range of the possibilities of formal and expressive organization, even if it is a specially important sort; and that it is the only important sort is also hard to maintain. It is tempting to assert that art devoted to pure expression or pure aesthetic effect invariably does become impoverished as soon as the impetus of a religious or other similar tradition wears off, that great art always has been art put to another service, and indeed conceived within the framework of some other and greater interest than the aesthetic, and that this service is typically religious. It is customary here to cite the vapidity of African masks made for the tourist trade ("airport art") and of European visual arts since the Renaissance. If one conceded that such degenerations were the rule (and one need not concede it[20]), one could dismiss it by insisting that the relation between motive and effect is merely external and causal. But the satisfaction to be derived from saying this is rather thin. If God is dead, and only the living God can innervate art, then, for there to be a vital art God must be somehow resuscitated. The practical proponent of the mystic line might well concede that a devotional or theurgic motive or ambiance is logically neither necessary nor sufficient for aesthetic worth or interest and is causally insufficient, provided that it were granted him that it was causally necessary. But even to assert this invites the lie direct. There certainly seems to be great secular art. What of *King Lear, Eroica, The Night Watch?* To relate these to a religious ambiance is preposterous.[21] To deny their greatness is perverse. One may find no power in them, but to deny the power that others find there is of a piece with an atheist's denial of the depth of the religious experience he lacks, or with a ten-year-old boy's scorn of sex. No one bothers to argue with such a boy. A safer line for the proponent of the mystic line to pursue here is to claim that the power that is found in such works is not secular (what indeed could such a secular power be?), but is derived from some cosmic force working through it, as the cunning of the Hegelian reason works through the selfishness of individuals. The artist would probably not deny this, if he were asked; and, if he denied it, we would not have to believe him, for we were not speaking of his intentions but of the source of the power of what he does, over which in any case the artist can have no control.

It now appears that the mystic line can be reduced to a very simple position. Art is so generally conceded to be important that it must really be important, and, if it is, its proper place in human affairs can be no trivial or peripheral one. It is natural to associate this importance with the evident power that some works wield. But a merely psychological effectiveness would not be a power of the requisite importance, and any power that goes beyond this must be assigned to the occult forces in the world. Why? Because to speak of a felt power that is not mere psychological impressiveness is already to speak of an occult power.

The triumphant Q.E.D. with which I ended the last paragraph was premature. The mystic line must still meet the objection that it is entirely gratuitous. There is absolutely no intelligible connection between the harnessing of power or any other form of magical efficacy and the actual procedures of artists, which as procedures remain mimetic and ornamental. Why on earth should such procedures be supposed to have such efficacy, and how could they? One might retort that it simply happens to be the case. This just is how powers are harnessed—the inscrutable cannot be scrutinized and the ineffable cannot be uttered. After all, some things do just have to be accepted as raw data, as one just has to accept that whenever the priest says *Hoc est corpus meum*, something comes over the bread. Why should the world not be odd? But such a contention is likely to be ineffective, for there are an infinite number of odd things one could believe, and one must be given a reason for accepting another person's favorite oddities. In fact, however, people who think in this way find no difficulty in specifying the ways in which magical powers are exercised, and contrive to make such exercise comprehensible to themselves and others. The principle depended on is one of congruence. Making a visual or oral likeness (replica) of a being "captures" it and thus harnesses its forces if they are beneficent, or neutralizes and controls them if they are maleficent. Appropriately chanting the right name (like dialing the right number) of a deity forces him to attend,[22] as does drawing the appropriate hieroglyph or symbolic design that serves as his personal "seal." Adam had power over the beasts because he had named them, and "whensoever he shall be able to call the creatures by their true names he shall again command them" (Bacon 1734, 222). A dance that catches the rhythm of an animal's movements captures its rhythm and controls its motions, and the same may be done for the movements of the heavens. Building a temple that is correctly aligned with the heavens and reproduces the main divisions of the universe not only symbolizes and humanizes the world order but encourages that order to be more orderly. Musical speech encourages the muses to impart their secret knowledge. An ecstatic dance unites the dancer with a deity. If we ask how the right name, the right dance, the true likeness, are found, the answer must be that they are found by the artist's skill and recognized by their felt congruence with what is believed of the power in question. But for the mystic line to take this approach is suicidal. It amounts to a concession that the criterion of art is a mode of aesthetic effectiveness.

In the end, the mystic line must fall back on the simple claim that there are many uses of symbolism, many ways of organizing patterns in space and time, and many ways of relating to whatever powers the world may hold. The coincidence of these three defines a domain, and this domain plainly belongs to the practices we call art and has the significance we claim for art. Whatever its difficulties, this claim has for many people a strong attraction, and the attraction perennially outweighs the difficulties in finding a version of it that is immune to familiar objections.

Variants

It is appropriate to speak of "finding a version" of the mystic line, because that line does not confront us, as the expressive line did, with a single preferred theory or group of theories. Although I defined the line at the outset by three specific theses, it is not usual to find these developed and defended in any systematic argument. The line represents a style of feeling rather than a class of solutions to a kind of problem. The doctrinal forms in which those feelings find expression are radically heterogeneous; and to specify a doctrine is to specify social, psychological, and cosmic relationships that as such cannot be controlled by any self-contained theory of art, but of which the relevance to art, and still more the degree of importance for art, cannot be specified by sociology, psychology, or cosmology because the concept of art is not initially one that is defined in terms of those disciplines. Most versions of the mystic line are either specific doctrines about the specific nature of particular procedures and classes of works, or general assertions that provide little beyond the affirmation of some or any religious or magical context that art belongs somewhere or other within that context. Because many such relationships are possible and about equally plausible, there is a great variety of versions of the mystic line, varying along a number of different dimensions—or, if one prefers it so, the appellation "mystic line" is a vague one, designed to capture a miscellany of views among which it may be only the metatheoretical compiler (me) who discerns a family likeness. In any case, I proceed to outline a number of ways in which such views may vary, without the support of any system that would show my catalog to be exhaustive or impose a hierarchy upon it.

The first kind of variation is one expounded in chapter 3 and applicable to theories of art generally, but peculiarly relevant to the mystic line. Whatever relation to a religious context or function is postulated may be ascribed to each and every work of art, so that whatever fails to manifest it is for that very reason a spurious work or a work only by courtesy and in some secondary sense; or it may be ascribed to only some works, it being understood that the rest, though works of art indeed, really exist only as part of a practice whose sole meaning is that it sustains the privileged works that carry the religious meaning; or it may be ascribed not to individual works but to the totality of the art produced in a given community (whose relation to the Whole or to the Wholly Other it unites to specify or whatever), or indeed, in a Hegelian manner, to the totality of art produced by humanity at large. In the latter two cases, the relation or function is effectively imputed to the practice of art rather than to the works in which the practice issues. And in the mystic line, as contrasted now with the expressive line, we must distinguish between views that ground the relevant connection in the processes of production, so that the work itself is properly to be regarded as a byproduct, and views that find the power in the work itself. Among the latter, some will ascribe the efficacy of the work to the properties evident in the work, and others only on condition that the work is produced under the appropriate conditions.[23] The status in this regard of music and the dance, which are among the arts that play the largest parts in the mystic line, is ambiguous. When David dances before the Lord, is it the dance that he dances, the figure his motions mark out, or is it the dancing of it, the motions that he makes in dancing, that are important? Or is it his acceptable will in dancing, so that it would not really matter what the dance was if his heart was appropriately pure? Of course it might be any of these, but it is quite likely that in a given context there would be no way of telling.[24]

Another way in which versions of the mystic line may differ is in the nature of the postulated relation to whatever powers may be invoked. The intention may be to exercise power over them, whether to harness a beneficent power or to neutralize or avert a power for ill; or it may be to transmit that power, to afford a channel for grace; or finally it may be simply to symbolize and celebrate a power, to afford it a location and thus make available a convenient way of relating oneself to it. And the supernatural power itself may be variously conceived. It may be thought of as transcendent, a controlling power (or part of a hierarchy of controlling powers) behind the world order; or it may be conceived as an immanent aspect of the world order itself, some pervasive force like Nature or the *Tao*; or it may be some quite specific force, either independently operative in the world or animating some place (a genius loci) or vitalizing some living thing or things. In the last of these three cases at least, the force related to will be deemed supernatural only from the standpoint of a nonanimistic physical theory.[25]

Whatever the alleged power, and whatever the supposed connection with it, a theorist's interest in postulating the connection may take any of several forms. In considering the other lines, it is irrelevant to take such questions of animus or motivation into account; but with the mystic line there is good reason to do so, for in this line we are relating art to a kind of interest that is normally focused elsewhere and can in any case be separately identified. It is possible for the theorist to adopt a posture of indifference, alleging simply that the matter stands thus, though I do not recall any instances of such detachment. It is more usual for the theorist's claim to take the form of a demand that art be thus, and this demand may be made in the interests of mental health or of social well-being or of the stability and order of the cosmos; or the connection may simply be deemed good in itself, something that ought to exist for its own sake, in the manner explained by G. E. Moore (1903). It is even possible that the demand should be made for purely aesthetic reasons, and, in fact, it often is; but to do so seems rather frivolous, and one suspects that it is seldom thought through. Such, for instance, seems to be the thinking behind the practice of deploring the decline of West African carving and ascribing it to the substitution for a religious motivation of a commercial (or even aesthetic) one, on the ground that the secular work is vapid and formally weak. Either those who do the deploring believe in the powers to which the allegedly powerful works related, or they do not. If they do not, it is frivolous to promote what one believes to be superstition on aesthetic grounds; if they do, it is frivolous to make one's grounds for deploring apostasy merely aesthetic.[26]

A theorist's interest in pushing the mystic line is most likely to reflect, and can hardly avoid being affected by, his religious beliefs and disbeliefs, because these will determine his views about the existence and nature of the powers to which art is to be related and, in consequence, the kinds of relations that he thinks possible and desirable, as well as his estimate of the intelligibility, plausibility, and truth of the beliefs of others. In general, it seems obvious that the most important factors differentiating variants of the mystic line will be questions of belief, and the basic issue is whether there are any real powers in the world that are accessible to the artist in his work—over and above, that is, the power that his own mind and work must generate, reveal, and exercise if his activity as an artist is to amount to anything. The question arises in different forms for different people: for the artist and his clientele, for the theorist of the mystic line, and finally for the metatheorist who (as in this chapter) approaches the mystic line from the outside. As metatheorist I have tried to renounce any such stance, except that ironic evasion is itself a stance; and this has no doubt led to difficulties in interpretation. One might complain, for instance, that it is impossible without commitment to define what would count as a "power" in the required sense. But we may reply that this difficulty of definition matters little: even the irreligious have been exposed to enough religious discourse to be able to identify a force of the required kind by the rhetoric associated with it, or simply by the absence of the reductive rhetoric of naturalism or positivism.

A theorist of the mystic line may or may not believe that the powers to which he holds that art must be related really exist. If he thinks they do, he is likely to hold that the only true or proper art is one related to these real powers. He may, however, take the view that art is properly related to whatever powers the artist and his community believe in, since a man can worship no gods but his own, but that to stand in this relation, however appropriate, is vain, futile, blasphemous, idolatrous, and so on unless the power is correctly identified and characterized—unless, in short, it is the One True God.[27] If, on the other hand, the theorist does not believe in any such powers at all, or does not believe that art can stand in any such relation to them,[28] he may think that the artist's task is mythopoeic, to generate images to which power can be ascribed and which make religious attitudes posssible (and thus do in effect generate a real power); or that the artist's task is to generate powerful images, which, however he thinks of them, will in effect unconsciously symbolize obscure social, physical, or other forces that are real enough but not supernatural; or he may simply think that a belief in such forces, however valueless or even socially and intellectually harmful it may be, is good for art. In the last case, he may hold that the artist must believe in the forces he invokes, so that the agnostic would-be artist has no hope but conversion, or that the artist is free to invent (as Yeats and Blake did) such mythology as his art requires or implies.[29] Both of these last alternatives, of course, are straightforwardly psychological hypotheses about the conditions in which it is possible or easy to produce works of art that are acceptable on other grounds.

Supernatural forces to which art can be essentially related may or may not exist, and may or may not be believed in by the artist or by his public. There are thus eight possible structures of belief and disbelief. It will be instructive to go through them one by one, with brief remarks.

The first possibility is that the supernatural is real and both artist and public must believe in it—for the good of art or the health of society or the orderliness of the world or whatever. This may be termed the Catholic Utopian, or millennial, view, and may be taken as the normal form of the mystic line in the sense that if any one of the three is required—the reality of the supernatural, or belief by the artist, or belief by the public—we need some special explanation of why the other two should not be.[30]

The second possibility is that the supernatural is real and the artist must believe in it—his mind, that is, must be attuned to it—but the public need not. This amounts to the causal hypothesis that a real harnessing of a real power is necessary for an aesthetic effect, or for an aesthetic effect of the appropriate sort, with the proviso that the working of the power is effected through the normal conscious operations of the artist, whether or not special religious exercises are required to give those normal operations the requisite form. Unlike the first possibility, this one is not in the ordinary sense religious, because the powers involved, although real, are *ex hypothesi* either not the objects of any cult or, if they are, that cult is divorced from artistic praxis. It is a view of this sort that is attributed to Sanskrit authorities by Coomaraswamy (1977).[31]

The third possibility is that the supernatural is real and the public must believe, but the artist need not. The artist, on this showing, is the unconscious channel through which the deity communicates with the faithful. The relationship is exemplified in a nonartistic context by the Delphic oracle, in which the priestess does not know what Apollo utters through her mouth. I am not aware that anyone has ever supposed that this could be the normal condition of art, although one might be led to it through espousing the mystic line while trying to avoid the intentional fallacy.

The fourth possibility is that the supernatural is real and a relation to it is essential to art, but neither artist nor public need be aware of this. On such a view, secularists would be simply mistaken about the nature and ground of aesthetic effects. The view seems not to be inherently implausible, in that every theist must hold quite generally that, whatever the secondary causes of particular phenomena in the world may be, God is their primary cause. Since that is true of everything, it must be true of human expressions and communications, including art. But that is not good enough: as elsewhere, to say that God is prime cause of everything means that He cannot be invoked as specific cause of anything except by way of a miracle—that is, explicitly as an exception to the general run of things, not (as here) as the general run itself. To make this view significant, then, one would have to add some explanatory rider, such as that Beauty is one of the Divine Names, or that aesthetic objects make available some special revelation or dispose of some special power, whether anyone is aware of it or not. A view of this sort affords the substance of the well-known literary trope whereby the Heavens declare the Glory of God, or this or that pretty thing reveals the divine handiwork to the initiate; how many of those who use and enjoy this trope would subscribe to it as a matter of doctrine is another matter.[32]

The four possibilities thus far enumerated assume that some supernatural power is real and is such that art can be essentially related to it. Without that assumption, one would obviously be less likely to espouse the mystic line, but it is worthwhile looking at the four possibilities left open. Our fifth possibility, then, is that the supernatural should be unreal or not relevantly accessible, but both artist and public must believe in it. This might be termed the anthropological view, treating art as a social custom with a component of intellectual commitment from which the observer prescinds. Something of the sort is to be found in Nietzsche's (1872) invocation of myth or in Francis Fergusson's (1949) contention that a vital theatrical movement depends on a view of reality that artist and audience must share; but it requires that we superimpose on that view, as a general requirement, something like Wilshire's special characterization of magic or surrealist theater as simulating or generating an aura of the supernatural, an atmosphere charged with awe.

The sixth possibility is that there should be no available supernatural force and the audience need not believe in one, but the artist must. One might interpret in this sense the view of poetry put forward by Plato in his *Ion* and *Phaedrus*, according to which the mythological figures of the Muses (in whom Plato cannot be supposed to have believed) symbolize the "madness" requisite for poetry, the inability to rely on predictable techniques of fabrication. But the Platonic texts suggest that the poet may be puzzled by his creativity (as Ion is) rather than attribute it to divine afflatus, and the irrationality of the appeal of his art for others is identical in kind with that of his poetic process; so the exemplification of this possibility is incomplete. Another approximation to it is the psychoanalytic view of art according to which the essence of successful art is the artist's neurosis or infantilism, which the audience does not share—for was not Freud himself a connoisseur of the arts? But even if we accept that artists must be mentally deranged, and that a common form of such derangement would be to associate one's work with some improbable cosmic force, neither Freud nor anyone else has ever tried to establish for artists as such either an extraneous causal link or an intrinsic connection of meaning between artistic success and the content of any such belief.[33] Thus our sixth possibility remains effectively unrealized.

The seventh possibility is that no available force exists, and the artist need not believe in any, but his audience must. The theory would be that whatever attitude artists may take to their work—cynical, commercial, common-sensical, workmanlike, or whatever—the health of art requires that it be taken seriously, not as an object of delight or instruction, nor in any utilitarian or socially helpful way, but as an object of or adjunct to reverence. It is conceivable that someone should argue thus: such an attitude may be thought implicit in the ordinary procedures of art in those fantasized Middle Ages when all art was religious but every artist was a humble workman, and has its analogue in the contention of Paul Valéry that the inexplicable in poetry lies, not in the artist's creation, but in the public's understanding of that creation (1964, 143). But in fact no one has taken quite this line, probably because few people who disbelieve in supernatural forces regard a belief in them as beneficial in any other way than by enforcing such a solidarity in feeling as our fifth possibility envisaged. The Wizard of Oz is nobody's hero.

Finally, the eighth possibility is that there should be no such forces and no reason why anyone should think there are. This, one might suppose, excludes the mystic line altogether. But in fact it generates one of its more interesting variants: a phenomenology of art according to which "everything happens as if" artist and public were linked in a religious communion, a religion with priest and congregation and the service of the altar, but no god. The essence of art, one would argue, is the quasi-sacred character of this bond itself, and it is a true insight into the character of the bond, together with a natural but mistaken inference to a set of beliefs such as accompany such bonds in the religious contexts to which we have been persuaded to think them confined, that affords the real ground for all other variants of the mystic line. So far as I am aware, however, this eighth possibility has never been developed in contradistinction to the others.

Critique

The introduction of a phenomenological version of the mystic line as one of its most interesting variants suggests a fundamental criticism of the line as a whole. A power that is made fully evident by art is a power that is evident *in* art, and should be recognized simply as the power *of* art; insofar as it.is not made fully evident by art, that in it which is inevident has no bearing on art, but is an intrusion into the aesthetic of irrelevant dogma. The manifest power of art is one of the evidential or emotional bases on which dogmatists illegitimately erect their theological constructions. Why should we not say that the mystic line is simply a mistake, an illegitimate inference from a perceived quality to an unperceived reality? No one of even moderate education can seriously believe that there are at large in the universe any such powers as could be controlled by the techniques of art, much less believe in any particular set of such powers and techniques with enough firmness and definition to warrant taking the alleged belief seriously.[34] People may mouth such phrases and even experience powerful feelings of conviction in relation to them; what they cannot do is integrate such beliefs with the theoretical and practical approaches they necessarily adopt to the world as they experience it and live in it. The beliefs remain on the level of playacting or pious hope or nostalgic wish. As for the saving expedient whereby one appeals to a phenomenological version of the mystic line, one must retort that such phenomenological démarches in areas of concrete experience such as art are inevitably and notoriously arbitrary in their selection of the range of phenomena to be correlated with the essence of the object under discussion, and, specifically, that in this instance the appeal to phenomenology is merely a self-indulgent expedient to remove one's whimsies from effective criticism.

Initially, we noted that the mystic line claims support from the world history of art and its ancestors. Such support, we must now say, would at best be extraneous, justifying, not the truth of any version of the mystic line, but the expediency of holding it in the interests of better or more prestigious art. But in fact the evidence is not adequate. Certainly the evidence cited for societies other than our own is copious, but the generalization to all art even in those societies is hazardous. Of the general nature of prehistoric art we really know nothing (cf. n. 15). Assigning all the art of great civilizations other than ours to a religious connection really amounts to defining all of their cultural phenomena as religious simply because they do not fall within the scope of a concept of secularity that is defined in relation to the particular tenets of Christianity and cannot be legitimately applied outside Christendom; and the assigning of all preliterate art to a specifically religious ambiance owes less to observation and analysis than to the early missionaries' dismissal of their victims' entire system of values as benighted idolatry.[35]

Even if we were to concede that outside our own civilization all art was religiously based—or rather, since such phenomena as work songs, political praise poems, and ornamentation for its own sake cannot be denied existence, that all *significant* art is and was so based—we need not accept any inference to the conditions of art among us. Our civilization covers a vast range of human experience; in fact, there are good reasons for saying that, like it or not, Western civilization, with its associated habits of technological method and critical thought, is the only form of human organization that can nowadays be taken seriously. Those living under other systems define themselves as deprived or underprivileged precisely insofar as they cannot conform to its norms, which without exception they are adopting with all convenient speed. If that claim be rejected, on the ground that one of the Gadarene swine might claim that every pig he knew was rushing down the cliff with him, we might resort to the less openly value-laden version of it I introduced in an earlier chapter. It would be ridiculous, I said, to accept an account of science that preferred the practices of other civilizations to our own: "science" simply refers to a complex of practices developed within our civilization, which other civilizations neither match nor modify. So too, I for one would argue, with "philosophy." That term stands for a complex of practices with its own justification and its own history, and its own stringent criteria: to apply the term to systems of thought serving other purposes and conforming to other principles (usually principles against which philosophy was with great labor developed as a protest) is merely a sign of confusion. And we might then go on to say that it would be equally muddle-headed to allow the name of art to anything that stands outside the institutions developed within our own civilization, except insofar as those extraneous phenomena can be subsumed under the same values that the term "art" in its modern use has developed to enshrine. Art is art as we know it, and art as we know it is defined by values that simply are not such as the mystic line envisages. In fact, Lukács (1963, 377-411) uses an argument like the one I used above for the prescriptive right of Western philosophy: the secular values of art as we know it were developed in reaction to, and as part of the defense against, the superstitious and magical miasma within which they grew up. To revert to a religious significance for art in the name of piety toward origins is simply to give up on civilization and humanity.

On the present showing, the prospects of the mystic line are not good. Art certainly cannot be defined or redefined in its terms; it is not true that all art does function in a religious ambiance, that every work is in fact a bearer of religious value, import, or power; and if it be said that (on grounds provided by the theorist's cosmology) every work of art as a whole cannot but fulfill the required role, we might reply that a power so diversely manifested can exclude nothing and simply becomes the world: all that is being said is that vital art relates vitally to reality.

What, then, if the mystic line takes refuge in the full generality of its original contention and insists that the proper domain of art demonstrably lies within the religious concerns of mankind, in the context of the relations between men and the unseen powers of the world, because in the absence of such a context it obviously and admittedly becomes pointless, vestigial, trivial, a mere distraction from the important concerns of life, as every red-blooded American accountant knows it to be? Then three strategies are open to us. First, we may give the lie direct, as we did above, and insist that there is great secular art and the valuing of art as art is a central fact of our society, chambers of commerce notwithstanding.[36] Second, we can point out that the allegation requires that nothing in human life is serious and can impart seriousness other than the relation to occult powers: the devaluation of secular art requires the total devaluation of human life.[37] And third, we can reply that, even if the facts were as stated, the proper conclusion would be, not that the context of belief should be restored somehow, but that, since the context is now known to be delusive, art is now obsolete. Man has become Man and must put away childish things.[38]

Matters cannot be left there. Religion, notoriously, however often debunked, is never disposed of. It merely assumes another form. All that happens if you crush the infamy is that you get left with a lot of crushed infamy. Where the rosary was, there shall the *I Ching* be. Ours is not a secular age after all, and seems to be so only to the extent that the rise of commercialized mass media as enshrining the visible image of the times has restricted public prominence to the marketable, and has paid to the mindlessness of the unreflective a respect that it never had before. People in the ordering of their lives still orient themselves by supposed unseen powers, however successful we may have been in freeing our technology and all the manipulative specialisms of our lives from their influence. So long as such values are accepted, at whatever level of sophistication or with whatever reservations or irony, they will occupy a crucial place in people's lives, and it is not to be expected that the values of art can be purified from them or would benefit from such decontamination. In fact, if the mystic line cannot serve as a theory of the nature of art, it remains uneliminable as a recognition of an irreducible aspect of artistic practice. As Rader and Jessup (1976) argue, the attitudes it enshrines seem essential to expressing the depth of people's feeling for reality, and hence for overcoming alienation by uniting oneself in love or in dread with all that would otherwise be alien.[39]

There is no question, it seems, of defeating the mystic line altogether. The question remains, if one is not to surrender to it (and we have seen that that is hardly possible), what the terms of coexistence between it and the other lines of thought should be. Specifically, on what terms might it be acceptable to someone inclined to scorn all magical and religious practices as backward and ignorant? Roughly, there seem to be three likely expedients. One is to say that since art is plainly important and is properly located in the domain of the occult, the proper domain of the sense of occult powers is the world of art. One cannot prosaically maintain that the world is haunted or impelled by proper objects of awe and worship, but it is poetically proper to imagine it so. There is no obvious reason why one's imaginative attitude to the world should coincide with one's practical and analytic understanding of it, provided that one does not confuse the two ways of thinking and allow either to usurp the other's place—a division of labor that most people throughout history have found it easy enough to observe.[40] Such a nonfactual sense of wonder may be not only good (or even necessary) for mental health but also epistemically valuable: scientific confirmation is governed by measurement, but discovery, including scientific discovery, is the work of imagination, and (obviously) of an imagination open to the unsuspected; there is nothing absurd in the contention, first, that such an imagination finds its most natural expression in the dramatization of the world as the haunt of powers and, second, that the proper means of sustaining such imaginative structures is in the symbolism of art—and even, third, that the essential use of art is to sustain it.

The second expedient is to euhemerize the occult forces in the symbolization of which art finds its unique force: the forces harnessed and neutralized by art are not such as less sophisticated ages postulated but social bonds whose power is dimly sensed rather than perceived (as in Durkheim), archetypal forces in the mind (as in Jung), or whatever else may come to mind. Even a primitive animism, it may be urged, is a less absurd system of belief than one that denies that there are *any* occult forces in the world with which we must come to terms.[41]

The third expedient is to turn back upon the objectors one of the objections against the mystic line to which I gave summary expression, and, without specifying the powers harnessed by art, say simply that art in its evident power relates us to the world as a place of powers whose reality is evident but whose nature is beyond any simplifying grasp—a single devolving power or a field of fields of forces. Of course, art in this context cannot be an instrument of theurgy in the old sense; but, as I suggested in outlining the first of the three expedients, it may play the only theurgical part that such a view of the world's dynamism allows, by affording insight and acclimatization—for knowledge is power, and familiarity breeds contempt.

The best bet for the mystic line may still be that suggested by a phenomenological approach. Art is a matter of experience; and, within experience, what seems to be, is. Art has evident power, and an evident power is real; a seeming relevation must be a real revelation, if one makes evidence one's criterion of truth.[42] And if art is the only way we have of making ourselves aware of the world, not as the merely cognized world of objects or the world organized as instrumental to our concerns, but as present power, then we can say that there is a sense in which it is only in art that Being is unveiled and hence (so far as we can be concerned) real—for to be, as Plato observed (*Sophist* 247-249), is to make a difference, to be powerful. Primitive notions of theurgic or apotropaic uses of art now become readily understandable errors. The undisguised presence of reality is taken for the presence of an occult power lurking behind reality; allowing something to reveal itself is mistaken for exerting power over it, compelling it to come clean. It is easy enough to accustom oneself to this paradoxical rhetoric, which at first makes it look as though Being and Reality were special sorts of entity; or, if the rhetoric is found offensive, it can be avoided easily enough by periphrasis. That done, it is necessary only to persuade oneself of two things: first, that one has not merely substituted for specific myths a myth that seems to be more than a quaint superstition only because it is vague and abstract; and, second, that one has gone significantly beyond acknowledging that art as a whole stands as a record of what artists have done by way of producing original contemplables from their experience.

One further step may be taken in demythologizing the mystic line. Instead of saying that in the evident power of art the mysterious dynamism of reality also becomes evident, one can say that art holds the sacredness of its power within itself. The power evident in art is itself occult in the required sense, because it cannot be brought without remainder within the scope of any science. An artist's power is mysterious even to himself.[43] It is, if not supernatural, paranatural. On the basis of this recognition, one may make a move analogous to that made by Thomas Aquinas when he said, after proving to his own satisfaction the existence of an unmoved mover, "And everyone understands that this is God." So, in the face of whatever shrivels the soul, one may exclaim, "Everyone understands that this power is God." But that would be ambiguous. On the one hand, one could be thinking Hebraically and equating the object of one's frisson with the God of Abraham, of Isaac, and of Jacob, or with a Heideggerian Being; but that would be hazardous. On the other hand, one could be using the word "God" in the Hellenic sense as a predicative concept, and mean no more than that whatever manifests such power has the quality by virtue of which whatever is holy is agreed to be so.[44]

A perceived power in art such as to inspire awe is not the only ground on which art might be deemed inherently sacred. One might, as suggested before, point to the relations of artist, public, and art object within the sanctifying museum world as exemplifying patterns of behavior characteristically religious and sufficient to constitute a religion of art with the work at its sacred center. Or one might identify the religious life with the *vita contemplativa*, which is essentially what Plato and Aristotle both did, so that inherent contemplability becomes the necessary and sufficient condition of divinity, and then point out that the *vita contemplativa* has manifestly found its contemporary refuge in art even as the classical line conceived it. Alternatively, one might look at the Protestant view of the prophetic voice, disturbing mundane order and suspending the ethical, and then say that this voice is in fact the voice of art, which nowadays many people feel should be neither pleasing nor instructive but alarming, disruptive, disquieting, uncanny.[45] But perhaps this feeling is better accommodated by what will be our fourth line, according to which art is a form of exemplary activity as such, without any added reference to cosmic forces of any sort, whether intrinsic to art or alien to it. The same observation holds equally of an even more diluted version of the imputation of sacredness to art, according to which everything is sacred that is not secular, that is, that is set apart from practical concerns and made the object of special attitudes. Such specialness may be a recognition of the power felt in works of art, but belongs with equal right to the creative activity, to putting oneself in the way of inspiration. What is thus effectively recognized is nothing but the seriousness and specialness of artistic activity.[46] Such recognition really belongs to a line of thought separate from the original impetus of the mystic line.[47] But before we turn to this line, our plan requires us to say something about what the mystic line may make of the arts, of works of art, and of artists.

Arts of Power

The mystic line does not require the concept of an art, since the power invoked may be a spirit that bloweth where it listeth. But, unlike the expressive line, which positively resists the notion of the arts and is likely to be damaged by whatever acknowledgment it makes of their existence, the mystic line lends itself readily to the notion. Most versions of the line stipulate an end to be achieved over and above the completion of a contemplable object. Usually, there is a specific power to be harnessed or revealed, and it is likely that there will be accepted criteria of success in doing so and, consequently, accepted ways of meeting the criteria. The extent to which procedures can be codified will depend on the nature of the power invoked and on its relation to other powers and, hence, to one's general cosmology: demons will be as subject to the general laws of the universe as anything else, but a Supreme Being must be approached with circumspection. In general, however, magic and theurgy are nothing if not professional. Powers are always dangerous, and require special techniques for their handling.

Typically, what is conceived as efficacious in the mystic line is not the production of a certain kind of artifact by whatever means may serve to bring it about but the performance of a set of ritual observances that issue in a work of a given kind. As in any sort of divination or theurgy, the substance of the art is a set of procedures that one learns from other initiates. Even if the tradition is that the initiate chooses a lonely place and there awaits the inspiration of an indwelling spirit, he must undergo the right preparation and choose the right lonely place, and he must do so within the ambit of the traditional understanding.

The idea of a fine art, or what is equivalent thereto, is affected by the mystic line in two ways. The art may be conceived either theurgically, as controlling a power through symbolic action, or cognitively, as revealing a power through the special enlightenment of the artist. It looks as though the former modification would be more external, in that the controlling effect of an image is something quite distinct from the perceptible qualities of the image itself, whereas the special discernment of the illuminate shows itself in the quality of the revealing image. But it need not be so. It is more likely, in fact, that the artist will need his special enlightenment to be aware of requirements made on his iconography (and of qualities in the resulting icon) that are revealed to him and his peers alone and that the profane must take their word for, whereas the image that constrains a spirit is likely to do so by virtue of its own evident impressiveness. Mastery is no secret.

In general, arts conceived in the light of the mystic line would most naturally be individuated, not by the medium or the radical of presentation, but by the type of power related to, the kind of relation to it that the art establishes, and the type of means employed to establish that relation. On the face of it, such a classification could correspond to one indigenous to the fine arts only occasionally or by coincidence—statues, for instance, are permanent in a way in which musical performances are not, so that the latter seem more suitable for establishing evanescent relationships and the former permanent ones. If then we find, as very often we do, a proponent of the mystic line putting his views forward as a general view of the nature of art, which he takes to be roughly coextensive with the fine arts, and accepting the traditional divisions of the arts without question as affording at least a partial articulation of his discourse, we are entitled to suspicion: his practical commitment is to the fine arts, and his espousal of the mystic line is merely exploitative, a takeover bid. The more reputable proponents will either rework all relationships, or confine themselves (as Wilshire did) to a single practice that they are not concerned to integrate with other fine-art practices as such.

It will obviously be difficult for the mystic line to sustain a theory of the arts on its own terms, for much the same sort of reason as it is difficult for the expressive line either to accommodate or to reject them. Let us suppose, for example, that we wish to interpret a specific musical tradition or practice as invoking cosmic forces to undergird the social order. The musician's training will involve mastering his instrument, learning the scales and phrases that make up the vocabulary and grammar of the tradition, learning what sounds pertain to the relevant forms of control over the relevant forces (and, equally important, what sounds are dangerous), and undergoing whatever ritual purifications and preparations are necessary for his music to be efficacious. Then those present when he makes his music will be able to tell from the sounds he makes that he has mastered what an outsider might call the musicianly side of his art;[48] but to tell that he has performed the ritual requirements they must follow him backstage, or infer his conscientiousness from the success of his machinations.[49] And to know that precisely the right occult force is embedded in his music in just the right way, they must share his theology. We saw that, on the classical line, one way of individuating arts is by the transferability of techniques and the functional interrelation of skills; but on the mystic line the connections between aspects of skill are extraneous—at most, a matter of accepted propriety. It may be that no one reared in such a tradition can bring himself to perform unless he has washed three times and bowed to the north; but so far as any perceptible effect on the work goes, it is hard to see that this differs from the personal compulsion a secular artist might feel to put on his old felt slippers. One is tempted to think of a fine-art tradition with a ritual component as only an impure sort of genre: as any genre is defined by an arbitrary restriction of possibilities that provides a structured situation for artists to work in, so a magically defined art provides a psychological and social setting to which composition and performance can be related. If the proponent of the mystic line insists that the aesthetic value of the work lies in the power that is visible or audible in it, and that ritual and technical preparations naturally converge to this end, he is open to the familiar objection brought against those who say that an artist must be personally sincere: it is what is visible and audible that can be seen and heard, not the means whereby they can be achieved. And the ritual remains extraneous to the effect in a way in which the technical is not.

No proponent of the mystic line will accept the argument just put forward. He will insist that we might as well have said that painters need not learn to paint because the skilled application of pigment to surfaces is irrelevant, a mere external means, and what matters is only that the painting have aesthetic significance, however achieved. That would be absurd, because (to repeat one of the standard objections to the expressive line) paintings do not exist without being painted; in exactly the same way, power does not shine through a work to which it has not been imparted. There may of course be exceptions, but so there are on any view—a man hacking in fury at a block of wood might indeed make there the image of a cow. But I wouldn't count on it if I were you.[50] It takes a holy man to sing a holy song. If we repeat that it is obvious how learning to paint is relevant to painting, but it can never be obvious how any magical practice is relevant, because *ex hypothesi* the powers invoked are occult and the means of invocation not to be excogitated by reason, the reply will be that the suitability of his means is as obvious to any magician as the use of gesso is to a painter. Our objections have merely begged the question by assuming that aesthetic means are extraneous to religious or magical effects, and magical means extraneous to aesthetic effects. What we pretended was an internal difficulty in the mystic line was merely a refusal to entertain it.

Our argument has evidently suffered the common fate of discussions of religious topics, caught in the dreary round of mutual incomprehension between believers and unbelievers. The critic might try to force the issue, as follows. Either the occult power invoked or captured is perceptibly present as a mode of aesthetic power, or it is not. If it is not, a theory to which it is relevant is only indirectly a theory of art, and the mystic line is simply a bundle of mistakes. But if it is so present, it is relevant only as aesthetic power; its reality as power has nothing to do with art. The mystic line is then swallowed up in the classical line, to which it merely adds riders about the institutions of art and about the hierarchy of aesthetic qualities. Counterexamples to the alleged connection between real power and apparent power may be expected to abound, and leave us a choice between three things to say: that the connection is not after all strict; that the causal conditions have after all been met unbeknownst; or that the aesthetic effect is illusory. In any case, on any such view the alleged magical or religious connection, however interesting to magicians, will be to the theory of the arts neither more nor less interesting than such other popular but peripheral contentions as that successful artists must have unhappy childhoods, be drinkers or abstainers, have or lack a special chromosome, be sociable or solitary, be married or unmarried, or have or lack any other characteristic or follow or abstain from any other pattern of life.

The objection to such attempts to force the issue is that it is precisely the implied divorce between values, or between spheres of interest, that the mystic line is most concerned to reject as degraded if not blasphemous. "We are blessed by everything"[51]—the locus of value is the whole praxis, in which magical efficacy and aesthetic success are integral. To isolate one of these as an aspect for attention would be to violate the whole tenor of life, as disastrously as Herrigel's premature attempt to hit the target by aiming at it.[52] It is to exclude oneself from a way of seeing and feeling the world.

The Work of Art as Sacred Symbol

If the mystic line is to be taken seriously as an account of art, it must take the work of art as experienced to be, or to be taken to be, in some appropriate sense identical with an occult power. It is, for once, legitimate here to say "in some sense," because the notion of identity is notoriously elusive: one is never sure, in the absence of a familiar context, what exactly is meant by saying that two things are the same. "The same *what?*" we ask, and the intellectual resources of the mystic line will be expended in spelling out a suitable answer. One can think of several analogues for such an identity or partial identity. Plato's theory of "forms" affords one: the tallness in a tall person is not something other than tallness itself, though the latter is eternal, real, and perfect, and the former is none of those. We may say equally that it is that tallness, partakes in it, or is a likeness of it—the advantages and disadvantages of Plato's theory, and the problems in understanding it, seem likely to hold for the mystic line. Again, an artist may say of his work that it is what he is, a living presence that lives with his life and is not merely a record of his efficacy. A third analogue might be the sense in which (I said before) the post card bought at the Louvre is the *Mona Lisa* and not just a likeness of it; a fourth would be the rather different sense in which a performance of a musical work is that work. A prudent proponent of the mystic line will urge that the relation of which he speaks is one that can only hold between occult powers and what manifests them, and that if it is not grasped directly in experience, it can be but dimly grasped through such analogies.[53] Let there be a power (call it Dionysus): its way of being, just because it is a power, is to be efficacious, and wherever it is effective it is present; objects to which any of its efficacy is imparted, or in which its efficacy is revealed, simply are that power—the leader of the dance is Dionysus.[54]

Works of art achieve (or testify to the achievement of) this identity through some likeness or affinity of form. They cannot be likenesses or replicas of the power, since obviously an occult power cannot be portrayed, not only because it is occult but just because it is a power rather than a strong thing or person. Rather, they have perceptible properties whereby they have an affinity, whether explicable or inexplicable, with whatever it is that makes the power in question to be the very power it is, and not another power, and presumably also with what makes it a power and not something inert.[55] I remarked in *SA* (389-390) on how the conventional representation of the bear in Haida art looks more like a bear as one might expect to meet it in the bush than any photograph of an actual bear; and we can now add that it not only looks bearish but is bearish, because the claws it emphasizes are the bear's strength and, above all, because its powerful stylization has bear power. It is not enough that the identity in fact obtain, and that it be achieved through formal affinity, for both of those might be true without anyone's knowing it; it is also necessary that the supposed identity be testified to by a felt expressiveness in the image.

As thus interpreted, the mystic line determines a specific view of the work of art, whether the line be interpreted as historical comment, as normative hope, or as essential penetration: it is an image that is also an expression of what it images and a part of what it expresses.[56] Because of the latter relationship, and other similar relationships mentioned earlier, the concept of a performance as we introduced it in the classical line, which seemed thoroughly at home (some would say, suspiciously at ease) in the expressive line, is alien to the mystic line. Not that it cannot be fitted in, for as a formal concept one needs only patience and ingenuity to show how anything complies with it; but the difficulties that we encountered toward the end of our discussion of the arts are here pointed up. The artist's performance in the mystic line falls apart into his success in fulfilling the prior task of bringing about a real presence, and the endotelic task of artistic expression. If the mystic line insists, as we have urged that it must, on the fusion of these two aspects, we confront again the problem that the requirements of presence cannot be divorced from the rituals of sorcery, but the latter cannot in any way be contained in the work of art itself as *opus operatum*.[57] One might respond that the concept of a performance has no prior claim on our respect; but one might also say that the difficulty merely shows that the concept of a work *of art* is alien to the mystic line, because it insinuates an isolation of values that it is the main concern of the mystic line as a theory *of art* to deny.

Some versions of the mystic line are likely to restrict the scope of works of art severely. If one accepts only a small class of occult forces, it is to be expected that only a small range of products and practices will be found to embody them. Even if, whether as a believer or from a metatheoretical position, one accepts an unlimited variety of forces, but thinks of them as specific powers, it is likely that works of art will be limited to works whose subject is essentially single: icons whose background is merely ancillary to the central figure, buildings with a unified schematic plan, poems (like the *Homeric Hymns*) limited to celebrating a single deity. It is only if one takes or admits a universalizing or pantheistic view of the indwelling power of the universe that the scope of art can conveniently be expanded to include the discursive subjects that have occupied much of the most compelling work in the fine arts; and, whatever one might think of the downgrading of the whole fine-arts tradition that animates many versions of the mystic line, it seems strange to single out for especial depreciation that in it which is expansive or discursive in topic. Not impossible, indeed; but strange.

If one thinks in terms of demons, of scattered or localized or specialized powers, one is committed to a world of mantic and theurgic operations of which we need say no more, leaving each adept to his own dark road. But if one thinks of a single divine power in the world, one is emancipated from such crippling dogmas; and our characterization of the work of art as an image that is a part of what it expresses is in fact akin to the idea of a symbol popularized by Coleridge in relation to a single unrestricted power conceived in Neoplatonic terms. Such a view certainly looks more promising as a theory of art that will be adequate to all the phenomena we (like Coleridge) wish to include. But its advantages bring drawbacks with them.[58] The symbol becomes a living and expressive part of a single undifferentiated divine reality. The work is indeed meaningful, but its meaning cannot be specified by referring to the underlying reality, because that is undifferentiated and therefore cannot specify anything. Thus, the meaning of the symbol cannot be captured or defined otherwise than by exhibiting the symbolic work. No harm in that; but are we not now simply restating the familiar expressivist position, that the work's meaningfulness lies in its having achieved meaning? The only possible reply is that the work harks back to a real undifferentiated realm of spiritual possibility, which according to the expressive line is exactly what there cannot be: there can be no mental or spiritual reality apart from perfected expression. The mystic line postulates a higher reality, which is a (presumably transcendent) God. According to Aquinas (*Summa Contra Gentiles* III.56), God knows all things by knowing his own perfections as in certain respects imitable; so human beings, it may be said, can know the perfections of their works only as imitations of the divine. But that is exactly what cannot be known. What humans know as imitable and thus imitated cannot go beyond the imitation itself. To allude to a God whose perfections they are adds nothing to what can be known in the work.

The foregoing remarks are based on an essentialist theology to which God is a perfected reality. A more sophisticated theology would be existentialist, identifying the divine with an initially undifferentiated activity. The Neoplatonic version of such a theology thinks of the world as emanating from such a divine reality: to be is to be creative; the highest reality is a unity beyond definition, but generates an intelligible and a perceptible world, and in discrete perceptible particulars is still present as a power. Because it is present, there may be modes of consciousness in which the diversity of particulars is bypassed and the original unity is somehow accessible in all its lack of particularity. Traditionally, the means to such knowledge is a withdrawal from particulars; but since the One is in fact present in them too, it is not impossible that access to the One should also be gained through particulars, in special circumstances. If that is the case, it may be that works of art are the appropriate particulars, and aesthetic experience is the appropriate means of transcendence. But even if one were disposed to accept the view of reality enshrined in this view, and then to violate its deepest tendency by converting selected particulars into Mother Carey's backstairs (cf. Kingsley 1864, chap. 8), it would be hard to reconcile the privilege of art with the perfect generality of the metaphysics. In all things that are on the same ontological level, the deployed force of the One must be present in the same manner and to the same degree: all particulars are equally particular, all minds are equally mind. The work of art can have no special privilege. It cannot symbolize the One because none of its distinguishing features can be relevant, since the force it was to symbolize has no differentiating character. Even if we are less ambitious and say that what the work of art symbolizes is not the One but the next highest grade of reality, the intelligible archetypes that account for the formal regularities in the world, we meet the familiar and insuperable objection that they were postulated precisely in order to lack perceptible characteristics: the perceptible excellences of works of art do not bring them any closer to this higher level of reality than other things. And to seek to approach the intelligible ideal by somehow bypassing the perceptible and renouncing perceptible excellence would not be to produce an exalted art but to destroy everything that could be of artistic relevance.[59] Plotinus, the clearest head among the Neoplatonists of whom knowledge survives, was quite clear about this. If an artist's work is inspired and inspiring, it is not because he has access to an intelligible archetype as a sort of supermodel in addition to whatever visible model he works from, but because he brings to that model his art and his vision of beauty: his technical knowledge and skill and his understanding of which possible forms to choose for his artifacts and which to reject.[60]

Although the work of art cannot symbolize the One or any ideal archetype, Plotinus does give us two positive alternatives. First, in its beauty it may symbolize the radiance of the divine beauty; and second, in its exemplification of the artist's art it may symbolize creative power. The former of these alternatives is open to the objection already stated, that all created reality is beautiful and symbolizes beauty in the same way. The objection can be met by saying that not everything symbolizes beauty to the same degree or with equal evidence; but this is a contention that it is hard for a Plotinian metaphysic to reconcile with the nonreality of matter, and in any case it plunges us into the uncertainties about the relation between beauty and reality that baffled us in chapter 4. The other alternative seems more promising: all the perceptible world, we now say, is in fact an emanated reality, a divine creation in which the creator should be evident; but it is not manifestly so, except to the eye of faith. The work of art is manifestly so. The esemplastic power of the creative imagination (to use once more the words and thought of Coleridge), that faculty whereby disparate entities are forged into an indivisible unity through the symbolizing power of the mind, is what is essential to true works of art; and the creative pressure toward unity-in-diversity thus expressed reenacts, and doubtless expresses, the diffusive force of the eternal creative love. The power of the work lies, not in its somehow capturing a useful derivative of divine power, but in the effect of its consciously or unconsciously reminding people of the operations of the universe that are at the same time the deepest workings of their own minds.

By creation, then, Creation is celebrated. The notion is attractive, lends itself to endless elaboration, and has a certain evident truth in it—if the world is a created world, it is best symbolized by creating. But for our present concerns it is hardly relevant; it is a straightforward theory of art as imitation of *natura naturans*, and as such we found it at home within the classical line. In any case, it does not hang together, for it rests on two different analogies that work in opposite directions. The analogue for the single power working itself out in creative diversity is not the single work of art but the artist who, in his love of the highest reality (cf. Plato's *Symposium* 206 B), produces many entities that are independent realities but also partake in the being of their progenitors, the reality as beloved and the artist as lover. But, as in the universe at large, the unity of these artifacts is not the formal unity implied by the notion of imaginative power but the mere fact that they are one person's works, just as the diverse creatures in the world are limitless in their diversity and united only by their compresence in the same world.[61]

The esemplastic power that issues in a work of art whose parts are fused into a single whole, which was to have supplied our analogue for the world's unity-in-diversity, works in the opposite direction, which from the present point of view is the wrong one. Instead of a whole devolving into multiplicity, there is an initial diversity welded into one, differing from the work of fancy only in that an organic or chemical unity is achieved rather than a mechanical unity of composition. If that is what imaginative creation is—and it is certainly what the word "esemplastic" implies—it bears no analogy to divine creation.[62] Is it then possible to find within the process that issues in a single work, and is perceptibly enshrined in the completed work, some analogue for emanation and devolution of power? There seem to be four possibilities. The first possibility is that the animating idea of the whole work should be initially present or dominant throughout, and should determine its parts and aspects successively by progressive specification, in a way roughly analogous to that in which the genetic material of an embryo realizes itself in ever more specific forms. No doubt something of the sort can happen—an artist may know the general tone and theme his work is to have before he knows or plans any of its details; but there is no reason to think that this is always the case, or that the works of which it is true differ from other works in the kind or measure of their manifest unity or in any other way. It is indeed commonly related that, whatever the original conception of a work may have been, as soon as something specific is actually done it tends to exercise an overriding control over what is done elsewhere: the tensions and vectors set up by the work actually done call for certain continuations and not others, and those continuations themselves will impose new directions that the unity of the work shall take.[63]

A second analogue for emanation and devolution would be the evolution of a work from the implications of a single theme or motto, as in the system of continuous variation envisaged as the mainstay of musical composition by Schoenberg. In an earlier age, one may think of Beethoven's Fifth Symphony as simply flowering out of the first four notes. But, even if this were the typical case and not just one sort of example, the analogy is remote. In no sense is the work contained in or implied by its motto, although one to whom it is familiar may read later developments back into it; rather, the work is written in such a way that its motto is contained every-where and is felt to pervade it.

Third, the "original idea" from which the work is devolved could be not a motto but a module or a system of imagery, a formal device that by its pervasive presence imparts a common tone or an over-riding rhythm to the whole. But this will hardly serve: such a per-vasive feature is a unifying rather than a generative device (the same module can be used in many buildings).

The fourth and last possible analogue for emanation and dev-olution is simply the personality of the artist as artist, envisaged not now as a personal style unifying an oeuvre but as a power of mental force making each work a unity through its felt presence, however that presence may be related to that felt in other works by the same or other artists. As the universe would speak of creative being in general, but cannot do so in an expressive manner because creative being as such can have no distinguishing character, so the work of art is eloquent of a specific creative being. The work par-takes of and is a specific expression of and thus symbolizes the artist's mind, which in turn bears the same threefold relation to the divine or universal mind, so that the work also bears that three-fold relation to the created reality that is the perceptible world. This fourth analogue of emanation and devolution is probably close to what Coleridge had in mind, although "esemplastic" hardly seems the most suitable coinage to cover it.[64]

The Artist as Seer

Any theory according to which art normally disposes of some sort of control over occult powers must have a distinctive notion of what it is to be an artist. The essence of his art is mastery through knowledge. Such mastery is not, like that of the classical line, some-thing in which one may show any degree of ineptitude or profi-ciency; nor is it, as in the expressive line, one in which one must succeed completely or fail utterly. The power may elude one's grasp altogether, and (as in the case of the sorcerer's apprentice) there may be conditions in which approximations to knowledge are but aggravated ignorance; but adepts of such arts differ in the extent and variety of their powers. On each occasion, however, the req-uisite manifestation occurs or fails to occur. Each work is a separate successful deployment of knowledge achieved. There is, one would think, no analogue function that relates acquired knowledge to expert practice. Not erudition but intuition is the appropriate form. But since the classical line also thinks of an artist's knowledge as tested individually by his works, it may be that in any context and on any understanding the knowledge appropriate to art is primarily a matter of isolated insights rather than of the concatenated understandings and evidences that "knowledge" connotes in the arts and sciences generally (cf. Sparshott 1967a).

Corresponding to the difference between theurgic and mystic versions of the mystic line is a difference between two relevant views of the artist. According to the former, the artist is an impresario of the demonic, like the traditional conjurer or practitioner of the black arts: a craftsman who wields secret skills. And insofar as this model is adopted, the mystic line is simply unworkable as a theory of art, because it completely severs the power captured in the work from the work in which the power is captured, like a genie in a jug. Though some writers in fact use this model, they do so without taking its implications seriously. According to the alternative model, his special knowledge is a form of privileged insight, and it is this model that most influences the way we think about art.

On the mystic line, then, the artist is one who has effective access to, knowledge of, and hence control over, that occult power whose effective presence is the hallmark of art. This knowledge, which constitutes his specialized expertise, is not likely to be thought of as an alternative to the skill that on the classical line makes the artist an expert producer of a special kind of performance, or to that whereby, on those variants of the expressive line that concede specialism to the artist, he excels others in the intensity, interest, or elaboration with which he does what everyone does anyway, but rather as superadded to either or both of these, and affecting the way in which they are exercised. But what makes him an artist, as opposed to an entertainer or a daydreamer, is his knowledge of hidden reality. And one who has knowledge of hidden reality is a species of sage: the artist is wielder of an uncanny wisdom, a seer.

> Hear the voice of the Bard!
> Who Present, Past, & Future sees
> Whose ears have heard
> The Holy Word
> That walk'd among the ancient trees. . . .[65]

For such an artist the shaman may serve as paradigm: the singer whose function is to put himself into a trance and, while in this condition, to journey below, over, and above the earth, and then, returning, sing or tell of what he has seen (cf. Eliade 1964).

Whereas on the classical line the preferred notion of the artist was derived from that of the work of art rather than from that of an art of the relevant kind, in the mystic line the opposite is the case: in fact, the artist as shaman does not quite fit the idea of the work of art as sacred symbol. It is easy enough to see why this divergence should have occurred. In the classical line, the fine arts have significance only as sources of contemplables, so that when we think of the artist it is most appropriate to think of him as himself such a source; in the mystic line, what is ultimately important in the work is its relation to reality, so that when we think of the artist, it is natural to think of that in him whereby the necessary relation is guaranteed.

The belief that artists have mysterious access to knowledge is quite widely held by persons who are not otherwise committed to the mystic line, and many of whom do not see the connection and would repudiate it if they did. Among university students of literature, especially, one meets many who seem seriously committed to the view that the writers they study somehow know things they have not learned, have a privileged insight into the way things really are. And, if that view is taken seriously, it can only mean that there is a reality apart from the way things appear to be, and knowledge of this reality is achieved, not by any investigation, but by some immediate access; and that is simply a vague version of the mystic line. It is only because the students in question are innocent of epistemology and ontology, and indeed unacquainted with any kind of sustained and critical thinking, that they can espouse such views with insouciance.[66]

The most startling appearance of the artist as seer is in the social realism of Karl Marx and Friedrich Engels. Engels, in particular, once committed himself to the proposition that it was to the artists rather than to the theorists of an age that one should go to learn of the real pressures operating in the contemporary phase of the class struggle and the emerging shape of the future.[67] But the professional training of the artist is in the handling of his medium, whatever it may be, rather than in sociology or economics. An artist's professional interest might make him observant of significant trends that others failed to notice, or of events to which others were blinded by conventional thinking, and more sensitive to symptomatic nuances of behavior. But none of these could suffice to reveal the shape of the future, or indicate which of the observed events would prove decisive and which trends prevail. The knowledge postulated is not natural knowledge, not an ideology subsequent to material reality; it is a prophetic faculty, analogous to divination—a mysterious "sense of history" more readily explicable in relation to Marxism's Hegelian background than in terms of its professed materialism.[68]

Since an artist's knowledge of the true nature of reality is not acquired through critically tested procedures of inquiry, the authenticity of his revelations cannot be confirmed by the correctness of his methods (although in the theurgic version this would be the right way to check), but only through their conformity with what one otherwise knows to be the case. With prognostications, this is possible; in other cases, it can hardly be. If the artist sees things the way one is oneself inclined to see them, to accept his revelation is only to flatter onself; to acquiesce in his vision because of its power is merely to be gullible. Of course, one may come to see the world with the artist's eyes, but perhaps that has no more epistemic significance than the well-known fact that one who has suffered prolonged exposure to the work of a landscape painter may see on the face of nature the look of one of his paintings. No doubt the appropriate model for the confidence with which the artist's insight is to be met is that of some such other divinely authenticated knowledge as the oracle at Delphi. The veracity of such an oracle is not in question, so there can be no question of verifying or discrediting its utterances. The suppliant knows a priori that somewhere in the world he will find the facts that will prove the truth of the oracular dictum; it is up to him to use his acumen to discern those facts.

What the artist reveals, the gods will bring about. Thus, for practical purposes, the artist becomes an agent of divine power by the very act of disclosure. So, for Engels, the artist's revolutionary insight becomes a means of revolutionary action; and so, for Shelley, the poet is the unacknowledged legislator for the world. So, too, Arthur William Edgar O'Shaughnessy (1874), having said of the poets "Wandering by lone sea-breakers, / And sitting by desolate streams" (the familiar vigil preparatory to vision) that they are "World-losers and world-forsakers,"[69] affirms that nonetheless they are "the movers and shakers / Of the world for ever"—but then the requirements of rhyme intervene to make an honest man of him, and he adds "it seems."

It does not seem likely that any version of the mystic line will pass current as the only way, or even the most important way, to think about art. But so long as art remains something of central importance to many people, and so long as what is of central importance is linked in one way or another to the operation of forces not reducible to the parameters of the exact sciences, the kind of thinking that the mystic line enshrines will be with us, however swathed in metaphors and hedged with apologies. And the most popular and durable part of the mystic line is that which treats the artist as a visionary legislator, wielder of uncanny insights and incantatory powers. If, then, the main part of our thought about art and the arts is couched in other terms, we have to decide how such views of the artist can be reconciled with and integrated into our theory of art as a whole.

The mystic line's view of the artist might define an alternative stereotype for "the artist" as we think about him, or it might define an alternative role that some artists could actually adopt. But it can only define a functional role if some real power is accessible; otherwise, the role itself degenerates into a posture and reduces once more to a stereotype. As an alternative stereotype, it will function as such things do, serving to save mental labor in matters and contexts where fine discrimination is not needed. It is by no means unusual for one person or group to use several different stereotypes for the same social role or other visible group. In such cases, one slips from one stereotype to another according to what the context suggests, and adopts different representative persons or role models accordingly. Sometimes, when one speaks of artists, one is thinking of (say) Winterhalter and people like him, technicians of imagery. Sometimes one is thinking of people like Mallarmé, ascetics of the ivory tower. And sometimes one thinks of such as Blake, prophetic eye rolling in a fine frenzy. A given context of thought and conversation will suggest to one's mind only those aspects of artistic practice, and only those practitioners, who conform to the relevant stereotype. But no doubt this slovenly habit of thinking would not be so easy for an intelligent person to fall into if the suggested roles were not mutually compatible, even if no one could be found to exemplify all of them to the full. When we think of the artist as a visionary, we are not thinking of him as a professional; but if we are brought to think of it, we may agree that *of course* he also has a studio and had teachers and is connected with a gallery, and *of course* his works formulate self-contained intuitions that are somehow exemplary for his fellow citizens, if not for all his fellow men.

Being a visionary legislator, then, is one of the things we expect of an artist, but do not demand of him. It is an option that an artist may take or leave aside, which he may aspire to or despise as hokum. But if an artist does take that road (or is found on it), it is essential to his being an artist in the way he is an artist. Blake was not a poet and a prophet, but a poetic prophet and prophetic poet; and what being a poet means to poets who are not prophets is fundamentally affected by the fact that being like Blake is one of the things their poetry might have meant to them.

So in general: if we think that the mystic line is altogether false in all its possible versions, it remains true that art can be what it is only because it is as if the mystic line enshrined a system of possible truth.

XIV

THE PURIST LINE

Let us review our progress once more and see what remains to be done. The classical line derives the notion of the fine arts, and the more general idea of art based on that notion, from the emphasized affinities of certain bodies of skilled practice. These arts specialize in the production in this or that medium of suitable objects for absorbed contemplation, and may be alternatively thought of as arts of representation, presenting and interpreting the world or an alternative world in image; as arts of expression, presenting and communicating the artist's vision and hence his feeling; or simply as arts of the aesthetic, devising especially beautiful or interesting objects to reward the attention they attract. And, since all these characterizations are possible, or can be made with a little ingenuity to seem acceptable, we can easily arrive at the idea that art ideally does all of these, and does each by doing the others.

The classical line is comprehensive, including within its scope most theories of art. But it is not so all-inclusive that its articulation can serve to articulate the entire domain of art theory. It is essential to all forms of the classical line that the idea of art and of the arts is focused on the work of art as contemplable product. And the propriety of this focus can be denied. It is possible, and therefore necessary, to supplement the classical line with the expressive line, a type of theory for which the facts that the work is a product of skill and that it can be appreciated are strictly irrelevant. Art is now conceived as the imaginative formulation of intuitions, mental contents that are epistemically original so that there can be no art or skilled practice of producing them. This line offers an alternative perspective to the classical line. It cannot drive it out or replace it, since the continuing efficacy and power of the institutions of art are evident facts; at most it can discredit that line as concentrating on the inessential and countenancing the spurious. It is perhaps best regarded as offering a better answer to the question why art as the classical line conceives it should be deemed more than informative, pleasing, or self-indulgent.

The classical and expressive lines together do seem to take every-thing in. But they do so only on one condition: that the world as experienced and man as acting and experiencing are all that anyone need take account of. If that view of the matter is radically wrong, and men, individually and socially, live out their lives in the midst of a world of definite but obscure spiritual powers to which they are dynamically related, and if men can use the symbolic and form-ative means of the arts to control their relations to these powers, then this is an aspect of art that can neither be subsumed under the classical and expressive lines nor ignored as extraneous. If such control is a function of art at all it must be a prime function, and it is one that completely bypasses both the appreciability and the intuitive function of art. Thus we must add what I have called the mystic line to our repertoire. But this line, unlike the other two, cannot make out a reasonable claim to be true of the whole province of art as we know it, and resists coherent theoretical development. It introduces into art theory a complexity of a rather annoying sort: after an initial promise to vindicate for art an essential place in the economy of human life, it ends by providing nothing but an array of unprofitable but (to a conscientious observer) unavoidable baf-flements, half-truths, qualifications, and special pleadings.

Can we at least stop there? We cannot. In the last few decades, fashionable writing on art has been taken over by a new rhetoric, a development from familiar themes of romanticism that has turned into something new. In the other three lines, the arts and the artist have their importance, if any, from the work of art, whether that be conceived as contemplable performance, as intuition achieved, or as magical liaison. This new line, which I shall call the purist line, allows the work of art no independent value at all. Such value as it has is symbolic; what it symbolizes, and what has independent worth, is the activity of art as the way of life of an exemplary person.

The purist line, even more than the mystic line, exists as a climate of opinion and a style of obiter dicta rather than as a family of theories. It may be defined by the thesis that the main if not the only point of art, or of what is to replace art, is to exemplify and celebrate a way of life and a scale of values that are better and purer than those of ordinary people because they are not subor-dinated to and do not acquiesce in economic determinants. It is necessarily a recent phenomenon, then, for it is only since the eighteenth century that it has occurred to anyone that the "profit motive" might reign supreme, so that what art must rise above could be recognized as existing, or believed to exist. This line involves the exaltation of the artist and the downgrading, if not the elimination, of the work of art; it also calls for a redefinition of art, and either demands the elimination of the arts as such or accords them a merely incidental status.

The purist line is closely related to some aspects and versions of the mystic line. As we saw, a minimal or residual version of the latter would think of art as a sacred activity, not because it was tied to a specific theurgy or theology, but because it inherently occupied a spiritual territory segregated from the workaday. If we make the occupation of that territory itself the essential factor in art, what we have becomes the purist line as soon as we replace the concept of the sacred or holy with a merely secular and moral equivalent. Again, we said that the institutions of art seem in some important respects to be modeled on religious forms, with priest, church, rite, and congregation, but with no god, and that from this point of view art seemed to generate its own quasi-divine power. As soon as this phenomenon is divorced from the reference to an implied power, it becomes a merely special and holier-than-others activity in which the pretension to superiority neither supports nor is supported by any metaphysical claim. And finally, the version of the mystic line in which art is rendered intrinsically holy by the power of the work itself becomes the purist line when we take the power of art as testimony to the spiritual power of the artist as exemplary figure.

The relation of the purist line to the expressive line is less immediate than its relation to the mystic line, but is close enough, since the expressive line already thinks of art as representing an essential spiritual function of mankind that is in perpetual danger of being obscured by the banality of routine. The purist line simply transfers this function from the artist's vision to his way of life. The expressive line also prepares the way for the purist line by its denial of skill. It is true that artistic skill was at first merely discounted as irrelevant to originality of expression, but a few short steps take us from constating the essential irrelevance of skill to announcing its needlessness, thence to declaring it harmful and making a virtue of ineptitude, and at last to the hypocrisy that simulates clumsiness. In the expressive line, the last step at least is a perversion. But in the purist line, in which, as we shall see, skill is associated with all that aspect of life from which purification is sought, a willed abjuration of skill is a legitimate device. Third, in addition to downgrading skill and denouncing routine, the expressive line makes absolute the divorce of art from economic ends and indeed from all ends, whether ends beyond the work or aspects of the work isolated as conferring value on the whole. This absence of ends is what the purist line picks out and converts into a positive value: art is valued as conspicuously useless and pointless activity—pointless, but not thereby valueless.

With the poetic line, that generic line of thought to which all theorizing about art as creativity belongs, the purist line shares a tendency to protest against the fragmentation of man. In creative activity, as opposed to all the specialized activities undertaken in a society that divides labor, a human being is thought of as wholly engaged and expressing his whole self in creating something that will engage another human being in the wholeness of his receptivity. And in the purist line the repudiation of specific goals and of subordination to the economic has as its positive side a celebration of wholeness. The artist preeminently does his own thing, the thing that he is.

One must not think, then, of the purist line as an unexplained takeover of the concept of art. Like the mystic line, it can claim to recapture a significance that was already evidently present in the practice of art and in the attitudes that stabilize the institutions of art in their meanings. Even in the classical line, art as imitative play is located firmly in the domain of enjoyment and the prized rather than that of utility and the priced: the fine arts are placed among the arts that contribute directly to the substance of a good life, and do not merely provide means to it. But in the classical line this does not suffice to define art or its significance, because other arts, practices, and pursuits also go to make up the substance of a good life: pure thought, the conversation of friends and lovers, and whatever fully engages one's interest and mastery. It is necessary to the purist line that these alternatives should be blocked, that all ways of life should be contaminated with the alienating shadow of economic utility except those that are devised with no other aim than to get clear of the shadow; and if these are called art, it may be because art alone still offers that bright refuge, or it may be because the corruption that has overtaken even the institutions of art has not yet contaminated the concept of a pure art.[1] Even the purest intuitions of the expressive line turn out, in the end, to be externalized in salable commodities; but if one could engage in an art that no one wants, the original significance that art once shared and is now that of art alone can still be maintained. Seen in this light, the purist line is profoundly pessimistic, a total despair of institutions that are totally depraved; but it preserves its faith in humanity, in a salvation that is always available though always under threat.[2]

The purist line can thus be made out to be a distillation of the values of the other lines under stress. Another way of looking at it is as the combination of the view that takes art to be inherently sacred, or to have a special status analogous to that of the sacred, with the negative aspects of the alternative lines. The expressive line, as we saw, proceeds largely by negating aspects of the classical line: it accepts the status of the work of art as eminently contemplable object, but rules out all considerations of skill and all determinate values (grounds for appreciation) that may be found in the work; the only demand is that the work represent an authentic and unadulterated insight, a demand that in the less cautious and more popular versions becomes a call for sincerity in the expression of emotion. To the classical line, on the other hand, sincerity is irrelevant and the concept of expression even in its most sophisticated form is gratuitous, since what makes a work contemplable is that it has the form it has. If we combine these negations they yield the notion of art as having to do with objects that need be neither beautiful nor expressive, that conform to no preconceived requirements at all, and that are singled out only by their combining uselessness with the status of claimants for attention and a certain sacredness. And then we may add the further negation from the mystic line, that the significance of the work lies not in its contemplability or in any specific properties that challenge attention, and conclude that art celebrates uselessness, demanding that attention be paid to that which has no other distinctive characteristic than that of belonging to the realm of art.

The thesis that anything whatever can be an aesthetic object, which hitherto has functioned as a concession or loophole, now wins central importance—not because all things are equally beautiful, but because all are alike indifferent. Whether or not the mind is passive in sensation, attention is paid and actively directed, and art can simply be the practice of providing objects for attention unmotivated otherwise than by the readiness to attend. Art can thus provide the resting place for Ixion's wheel that Schopenhauer wrote of (1818, III, §38). Schiller had already assigned to art the function of providing respite and recuperation from practical values, and one obvious function of the sacred has always been to provide an inner sanctuary, to relieve the mind from secular pressures. But classical art theory and classical religious theory supposed that the relief could properly be afforded only through objects that had some specific property, such as beauty, or stood in some specific relation to a divine being. But this proves to have been a mistake or a gratuitous stipulation. Such specifics are, when freed from their institutional constraints, mere concessions to human weakness, as John Cage (1966) has argued that composed music merely panders to a degenerate unwillingness to exercise one's ears on whatever may float into them. All that is necessary to stop Ixion's wheel is a break in continuity;[3] and work with computers has made it even more obvious than the behaviorists' work with rats had done that the best way to make a fresh start is to introduce an element of randomization—the shuffle before the new deal. If art as conceived by the classical line functions between cliché and chaos, we now find that cliché is the prison from which we must break free and that chaos is not to be feared. Anything can be art, but the paradigms of art will now be objects and activities that conform to no expectation and answer to no demand, and therefore make no sense.

Paul Ziff's idea (1953) that art is a practice with a floating function, whose nature can be determined only historically and in relation to a specific culture, is most at home with this aspect of the purist line. If the value of art is that of inutility, of a clean break with all determined values, then what art is at any time will be an inversion of the values prevailing at that time, its affirmations determined by what it has to deny.

If art is to celebrate uselessness, mere uselessness of act and product will not suffice. The superfluous act or object must be made conspicuous, attention must be directed to it. No one seriously maintains that everything useless actually is art, even if it could be: the furthest one could go would be to maintain that anything can become art when it is isolated for attention, even if nothing is needed to effect the isolation other than a purified and purifying eye.

How is the combination of inutility and conspicuousness to be contrived? Despite the de-emphasis of the work of art, most methods rely on the conspicuous inutility of some form of object or performance, and are thus more suitably postponed to a later section of this chapter. But we can say now that, if the requirement of valuelessness be added to that of uselessness, conspicuousness may be hard to come by. The trick is to make or do something useless, valueless, and pointless and have it recognized and attended to as art. This could hardly be possible otherwise than by exploiting institutions of art that have been established by other means. The habit of solemn attention to the useless could hardly originate with such objects, since the whole point of them is that there is nothing in them to make them inherently worthy of being singled out for notice. The resulting situation is confusing, because ever since the Impressionists it has been common for persons behind the artistic times to say of recent works that "a five-year-old child could have done that." Some of the works and operations we are considering now are intentionally such that a child could indeed have done them—but no one would have paid any attention. An artist, it appears, is someone who can do trivial and pointless things and get articles written about him in the glossies. And to do that he must establish his credentials, which is not easy and is impossible unless there is a credential-bestowing set of institutions in operation; and there must be glossies already in existence (and, accordingly, with paid-up subscriptions and advertisements), whose attention can be attracted.

The point may be illustrated by one of the exploits of Marcel Duchamp, who had a geometry textbook hung out in the weather to expose it to experience.[4] Moderately witty people, one would think, do such things often, to the momentary amusement of their friends, and no one thinks anything of it; Duchamp gets into the histories of modern art. What makes his action different? At least four factors are involved. First, one has to allow for the *je ne sais quoi*, the master's touch, which here as in so much of art and life confers inexplicable inimitability; but that is not the only factor at work.[5] Second, there is the fact that Duchamp had a whole oeuvre of such ploys, variously presented and chronicled, so that the geometry book figures as one ready-made among others in the Duchamp story.[6] But that is not all, because what such a series of anecdotes established Duchamp as might have been a practical joker or a typical "bright young thing" such as figures endlessly in the pages of memoirs of the twenties. A third factor is decisive: that Duchamp had already established himself as a serious painter and hence an artist, maintained his position in the arts establishment, and carefully prepared a fine-arts context for his activities—we note that, before the geometry book disintegrates, an oil painting is made of it. Duchamp is a prime illustration of Arthur Danto's thesis that whatever an artist does is art—cannot, in fact, but be art (one could go further: Duchamp and his direct imitators are the only illustrations of the thesis, and are so because they take great pains to win that acceptance for what they do). But a fourth factor is necessary as well and is what most concerns us here: as an insider in the art

world, Duchamp has and exploits access to the realms of art reporting.[7] As he told Pierre Cabanne,

> The artist exists only if he is known. Consequently, one can
> envisage the existence of a hundred thousand geniuses who are
> suicides, who kill themselves, who disappear, because they didn't
> know what to do to make themselves known, to push themselves,
> and to become famous (Cabanne 1976, 70).

It is a familiar truth. But if the genius's work is a monument or a
document, its dependence on publicity is indirect. In the case of a
gesture like Duchamp's, and other such exemplary actions that (for
reasons I will expound later) the purist line tends to favor, conspicuousness depends wholly and immediately on publicity. As Les
Levine says, "All process oriented works rely on the viewer and the
art critic for their final definition as works of art. If it is neither
photographed nor written about, it disappears back into the environment and ceases to exist" (1969, 37).[8]

At this point we encounter a disconcerting ambiguity in art, a
confusion between the artworld and the public relations industry.
Before the art of exemplary acts became fashionable, the public
had become resigned to publicity stunts and their political analogues, nonhappenings turned into events for political or commercial purposes by the media,[9] or even invented by them; and
the heyday of that art coincided with the heyday of the demonstration in which a dozen youths holding up placards for the TV
news camera did duty for a crowd expressing its rage. The effective
political action there was the action of the TV station manager in
sending his cameraman; and the effective art action in the other
case is that of the critic or editor in mounting a feature or writing
a story—or, more likely, reprinting the publicity handout.

What makes that ambiguity so disconcerting is that the public
relations industry epitomizes just those values of commercial degradation of experience that the purist line affects to repudiate. But
there is a deeper ambiguity just behind it. If the work depends on
the means of publicity for its very existence, perhaps the truer view
of the matter is that the work of art is the whole package, publicity
and all—a possibility that Jack Burnham has spelled out.[10] The
"artist," however personally paradigmatic of the values of purism,
is just one member of the team that produces the work, which as
I remarked in part 1 is a straightforward performance in the understanding of the classical line, a work of the fine art of stuntsmanship.[11]

Purism, it seems, treads a narrow line. The more plainly its exponents try to dissociate themselves from the consumer-oriented traditions of the fine arts, the harder it is to differentiate what they do from the yet more directly consumer-oriented arts of public relations—and also, incidentally, from displays of auctoriality, in which pure affirmations of originative status are divorced from the qualities of any particular originated entity and purism is lost in an egoism that has much in common with the inverted possessiveness of the potlatch. Many people, of course, who are construed by themselves and others in the latter modes are not interested in purism, and some have purist rhetoric thrust on them by well-meaning critics; but if anyone were to commit himself as an artist to purism, he would have a hard time disambiguating his position.

The solution to the problem just raised seems clear enough. The problem arises from the requirement of conspicuousness. We may believe Duchamp and Levine that conspicuousness is practically necessary. But is it conceptually necessary? I have argued that in the classical line and even in the expressive line it probably is, but not in the mystic line. What about the purist line? Can purism accommodate the praxis of an unknown artist? To do so, one must find an alternative strategy to differentiate art from other things. And this, as we will see when we turn to the question in another context, presents difficulties of its own.

Variants

The theses and attitudes I am assembling under the rubric of the purist line are only loosely connected to the identifiable practices and institutions of art—necessarily so, because by definition purism is concerned with values symbolized rather than embodied. Consequently, they are a heterogeneous lot, by no means mutually compatible. What I propose to do now is to enumerate some of the alternatives facing the purist—or rather, since it is not to be supposed that people first flutter into my pigeonholes and then wonder which corner to nest in, some of the alternative ways of conceptualizing art as a source or buttress of a way of life governed by values higher than the economic. The alternatives are in practice dynamically linked by a variety of dialectics, some of which will be briefly explored in text or notes; I will try to strike some kind of balance between tidiness and relevance, but the artworld is full of tangled things and texts and aching eyes, and I have no reason to claim that my arrangements and proposals are the best possible.

The main alternative versions of the purist line are those that see in art a saving alternative to prevailing social values and those that see art as actually condemning those values. And if art condemns, it may do so in three ways: by the fact that what it typically represents and does is such as to be a standing reproach to respectability and economic viability; by embodying a direct onslaught on them; or simply by the fact of its existence, shining like a good deed in a naughty world.[12] Obviously it is hard to keep the two main versions apart, especially if the second takes the third of its forms: one can only mount an effective attack on social values if one at least represents a set of arguably higher values, and alternative values inevitably stand as an inherent threat to established but vulnerable values. Still, there is a fundamental difference between an adversary stance and an exemplary one.

A second difference lies (as the wording of the previous paragraph indirectly suggests) in the kind of values from which art is to purify its beneficiaries. They may be simply the values of the marketplace, as in the discussions of notes 10 and 11, or they may be all values economically determined.[13] Or they may be all socially accepted values, on the understanding that society is wholly corrupt (the vulnerability of this understanding will be discussed in a later context); or they may be, and very often are, identified as "bourgeois values," the values that dominate a specific way of life, which itself dominates society—an identification that we shall see is also vulnerable, but in a different way.

A third difference among versions of the purist line lies not in what is opposed but in the supposed instrument of opposition. One possibility is that it is art as we know it, art as a whole and as typified in the fine arts, that is pitted against the corrupt world. Alternatively, one may follow Adorno (1956) in pitting serious art against a seductive society, including frivolous art among the agencies of seduction. Such serious art is to preserve freedom by being unpleasant and difficult and, above all, by being independent of the wishes of artist or public: it must rely on its own dialectic, each work responding to the artistic situation created by its predecessor—just as for Kant the bondage of causality is avoided by making the sense of duty one's only motive, and just as Plato called on measurement as corrective to emotion. Now the battle lines are clearly drawn: art becomes a domain of strict freedom,[14] and art institutions are opposed, not because they are institutions, but insofar as they serve a clearly recognizable purpose of seduction in a given historical context.

Adorno's version requires that a main stream of art be identified and made the sole means of artistic purity. Another alternative in our third kind of differentiation makes mainstream art itself the chief enemy, as identified with the Establishment and hence corrupted by power, if by nothing else. Purity is sought by means of an alternative art, whose marginality is its saving grace. Mainstream art, whatever form it may take, assumes the status of *the aesthetic* and becomes identified with its qualities. But these qualities are eminently enjoyable, and thus cannot constitute the purifying nature of artistic activity, the way of life that is to be higher than the ordinary; and once such qualities have been found irrelevant, they can only be a distraction and an irritation, and thus once more relevant but in the opposite sense.[15] The marginal art opposed to mainstream art may be identified with vanguard art: it is tempting to do so, because the avant-gardist is readily thought of as lonely, misunderstood, heroically sacrificing all to the new truth, and so on. But the identification is treacherous, because the concept of a vanguard is opposed to that of marginality—where the vanguard is now is where the main force will be soon, if the advance continues; and if the main force goes in another direction, the supposed vanguard proves to have been at best a patrol or a diversion, and at worst some unfortunates who took the wrong turning. So it may make better sense to think of the alternative art as marginal in some other way. The situation is obscured by the very looseness of fit between the pathos of purism and the actual practices to which it relates, which forms the starting point of our argument in this section. The obscurity is deepened by the fact that there are polemical advantages to be gained by making the purist pathos one's own, so that the claim to superior purity is often used on behalf of art practices and movements for which very different values are also claimed, without much regard for consistency.

That last alternative within the third kind of difference among purisms, the pitting of outsider art against establishment art, leads directly to a fourth difference; but before turning to that I will offer some discursive comments on the one we have just examined.

The thesis that art takes its significance from its embodiment of activities having values other and higher than those of society at large runs into a grave difficulty. At least some art of the past, and perhaps the greatest art of the greatest periods, has shown its strength in celebrating the values of the society in which it originated, or some of its values, or the values of some sector in it.[16] The practice of art thus harbors contradictory tendencies: in its content, it typically celebrates the values of society as a whole, but in its essence it manifests a set of values wholly other than, if not opposed to, those it celebrates.[17] To avoid this contradiction, it is usual for purists to argue that the practice of art represents an attack on established society or at least on its ruling class and institutions. But art itself is embodied in social institutions. The purist thus has a choice: either he can say that those who argued that art symbolizes in ritual and myth the emotional bonds of society were simply mistaken, and art's real function is to shock, to disrupt easy habits and acceptances, to confront the bourgeois with an astringent alternative; or he can say that art as it ought to be, or as it must nowadays be, is anarchic, disruptive, and antisocial, and is pitted against traditional art and its institutions no less than against the rest of the bourgeois establishment to which it belongs—the argument then being that official art is not art at all.[18]

The need for the purist line to decide between speaking for all actual art or only for adversary art, whether to claim the institutions of art as its allies or attack them as compradors,[19] reminds us of the ambivalence in the expressive line about the fine arts, which are at once the eminent manifestations of art and its deepest corruption, and the ambivalence of the mystic line toward the arts of the aesthetic, which may be either blasphemies or revelations of an unknown god. Revolutions in all fields face such choices (and in the end are destroyed by them, whichever way they choose). But it is not always evident which choice a theorist has made, or even whether he knew there was a choice to make. For instance, Sartre writes:

> Art, of its essence, is opposed to that which exists; its task is neither to glorify nor to explain; its value is one of terrorism; it is a weapon against traditional values and morality; it is aggressive, challenging, destructive; it leads established society to deny itself through the medium of the culture which it demands. This is the great lesson of de Sade and the true Surrealists (1973, 75).

Whether or not one agrees that de Sade teaches this lesson and that Surrealism leads established society to do whatever it is through whatever it is, it is quite unclear from this quotation and from its context whether Sartre thinks de Sade and the Surrealists have revealed what is true of all art since the paleolithic, or whether he thinks that only art like theirs is (for some unexplained reason) properly called art. Why would we go to de Sade and the Surrealists, even the true ones, to learn what art is in its essence, whether that essence be real or nominal? We do not know because we are not told. We are left, in any case, with a problem. Proponents of the purist line tend to make things seem easy for themselves by the anachronistic pretense that the institutions of art are the bailiwick of official art, which in turn is equated with the academic art of the mid-nineteenth century—much as communist cartoonists used to simplify their rhetoric until quite recently by pretending that the American economy was run from Wall Street and that Wall Street was populated by fat men wearing top hats. By this facile equation the proponents of the purist line could imagine themselves attacking all their enemies at once. But there is nothing to prevent the prestigious institutions of art being taken over by confrontationists. And who is to be fired on then? Does one speak in the name of all art or only of some? Does one oppose institutions as institutions or only those that are at the service of an enemy one has already identified? Is art pitted against society as such or only against some aspects of society? That blessed phrase "the Establishment" no doubt covers all, but blanket terms make strange bedfellows.

Let us return to our listing of variants. We had just considered one in which a marginal art is set as pure over against impurities shared by normal, official, or mainstream art. A fourth difference among versions of purism is that between those who associate purity at least with some form of art and those who count art itself among the enemy and ascribe purity to an alternative institution and practice contradistinguished from art, an antiart. And there are two ways of thinking about antiart: either as destroying art from within, a sort of fifth column, or as replacing it from the outside. Both alternatives are beset with difficulties, which will occupy us in the next section.

The variants of the purist line hitherto distinguished have all had one thing in common: art itself has been given a prominent place in them. Our fifth distinction must contrast all these with a view more often manifested in practice than espoused in theory. This equates art with dropping out, abandoning oneself to the *Tao*: straight society and its institutions are not confronted but evaded or casually exploited ("ripped off"). Since one's life acquires a spontaneous rhythm, one's actions are likely to include the production of recognizable art of a not too strenuous sort, but no division is recognized between this and the rest of one's life. All art that does not fit into this style of life is ignored.

Sixth and last, there is a distinction that cuts across the others. Whether salvation is sought in all art or only some, the values the purist line promotes may be taken either as reinterpreting the traditional values of art or as replacing them. Contemplation, as Roger Fry pointed out, is a biological luxury or blasphemy,[20] and to delight in beauty is already to delight in something that holds no promise of being in itself profitable. If aesthetic pleasure is delight in appearances and hence in the useless, it may be thought to include a delight or absorbed interest in the fact of uselessness itself. Alternatively, one may regard the newly discovered value of inutility as replacing the values that art formerly had. On this showing, the purist line would join the mystic line in treating aesthetic pleasure as irrelevant to the true value that art has always really had: we discover that art was never anything other than *serious play*, that beauty and representation are unimportant, and the discovery frees us from the aestheticism and hedonism under which the true value of art was long buried. But the former alternative is hard to maintain: there is a perversity, obvious though familiar, in saying that we mistake the nature of our values, although we may well mistake their significance.

The difficulty of maintaining that what traditional art is traditionally prized for (aesthetic value) is something other than what it overtly is, is comparable to the awkwardness (which I have mentioned already) of upholding a version of the purist line that endorses all traditional art. Such art has a definite, positive character of its own, which seems to determine already the kind of place it has in human life; and the purist line has to discount that character. The expressive line can be reconciled with the classical line because intuitions and contemplands may well coincide. But the comparable move in the purist line, as we have just seen, makes the inutility of contemplating the sole reason for contemplation. And in traditional moral theology this is a notorious perversion of the value of contemplation, comparable to going to a movie to get out of the rain. Awkward as it is, however, the move is not impossible: the movie may afford the only shelter there is.

The Work as Weapon: Problems of the Adversary Stance

We have seen that the purist line does not necessitate commitment to avant-garde forms or values, but may take forms that involve reinterpretation of established works and movements. Historically, however, purism is associated with Dadaism and its successors during and after the 1914-1918 war. Italian Futurism had proclaimed a new art of violence, involving a protest against the idolization of immobility and permanence by conservative culture as they saw it; the Dadaists, horrified and disgusted by the contrast between the degradation and mass murder they saw and the pretensions of bourgeois complacency, developed that rhetoric into an antiart of gestures directed against the values of Western civilization and its arts and culture as a whole. This is no place to recapitulate that history, but it is the place to look at the type of phenomenon it represents.

I said at the beginning of this chapter that the purist line allows no independent value to the work of art, which is reduced to being a symbol of a way of life or of an attitude wherein the value lies. Nonetheless, most of this section and the next have to do with works and quasiworks. This is because it is essential to the form of purism under discussion, and to most others, that the attitudes in question be symbolized, and whatever carries the symbolic function is in effect either a work of art or something that functions by being like one in some relevant respect. So I could have made these sections subdivisions of my treatment of the work of art as seen by purism; but it seemed better not to do so, because the problems of symbolization here discussed are continuous with problems in what is symbolized.

The variant of the purist line we are now to consider condemns art and its institutions as part of the corrupt bourgeois culture that creates total wars and slumps: it confronts them with antiart, actions of accredited artists operating within the official culture whose point is to lack and hence mock the values of beauty and culture. But it is this movement and its derivatives that have come to represent the main body of the avant-garde in art—a development that represents a complex ideological catastrophe, whose ramifications are hard to unravel. It has two aspects: first, antiart inevitably becomes art—the attack on art had to be made from within the institutions of art, and those institutions corrupt everything into art that comes into their clutches;[21] and second, the vanguard of art (that was once antiart) becomes, if not the main body of art, at least something that is related (as a paradoxical phrase in the preceding sentence was meant to suggest) as main body to a patrol or skirmishing force yet further out. These transformations are a double catastrophe, because the movement from which they sprang defined itself polemically, and its rhetoric was part and parcel of it; consequently, the practitioners and spokesmen of the successor movements cannot rationally decide whether they are with art or against it, and, if the former, whether they speak from its center or from its edge.

There are in fact at least three reasons why antiart should turn into art, acquiring conventional art values and entering the bourgeois artworld. The first is that, since anything can be an aesthetic object,[22] nothing can long resist the pressure of the transmuting context of the institutions of art. The second is that, to make the attack on art effective, the presented image had to be sufficiently offensive or grotesque in the art context to arouse rage and dismay. But hostility is a reaction that proves the positive value of what evokes it: it takes as much power in an image to provoke cries of rage as to elicit tears or sighs of admiration. And, third, and far the most important, the designation of antiart evidently relates, not to the nature and quality of the work produced and the act performed, but to the intentions of the producer and performer. To be a protest is not a formal property of a work or a part of its content but a property ascribed to it in the context of its presentation.[23] The notion of antiart belongs to the domain of criticism and commentary rather than to that of the works and operations of art. And the Dadaists were, had to be, persons of character and ability, so that whatever the properties of what they presented as antiart, their presentations themselves had style.

Any work that can be construed as failing to conform to whatever academic standards one erects as norm or butt can be thought of as antiart, for nonconformity can always be interpreted as rejection. Thus, Whistler's tasteful arrangements could be taken as flinging a pot of paint in the face of the public, and Cézanne's painfully elaborated constructions dismissed as mere insults to the picture-viewing gentry.

The habit of fastening the label of protest on anything that is not utterly conventional has become depressingly common. Consider an exhibition by the Bulgarian artist Christo (Javacheff) some years ago. Christo's works have tended to take the shape of wrapped and tied forms, which some critics have found evocatively sinister, and he has conceived imaginative projects for wrapping enormous shapes, covering whole landscapes with tarpaulin and rope. When invited by the Museum of Contemporary Art in Chicago to mount an exhibition, he very sensibly took the opportunity, instead of showing a lot of small bundles, of having the whole museum, inside and out, wrapped and tied. One would say that the artist was carrying through the implications of his *idée maître* or obsession in an appropriate and consistent manner; yet the director of the museum wrote an article claiming that his wrapping of the museum somehow expressed a condemnation of the art world, the museum establishment, and the like.[24] Certainly his action could be so taken, although it would have been more plausible to do so if wrapping the unwrappable had not already been what the artist was known for, and if transforming environments rather than providing objects had not been a fashionable mode of exhibition at the time, and if he had not been invited by a member of the museum establishment to exhibit, and if he had not accepted the invitation, and if the museum's director had been displeased at what he did instead of writing an article about it. But there is no reason for taking it as condemning anything, either in addition to or—still less—as an alternative to other ways of taking it: as a mere spectacle, as one in a series of wrappings, as a joke, or however.

The difficulty just raised is a pervasive one for the purist line, not only in its antiart phase but in any version that makes the activities of art constitute a rejection of some or all conventional values. Rejection is a very concept-bound activity, for it is only by explanation that one can make it plain what one is complaining about or protesting against. And art remains, however expressive, dumb. It often used to be said of works of the pop art that some years ago subjected commercial images and technological commonplaces to scrutiny that they offered oblique comments on contemporary civilization. But those who said so faced a dilemma. If they left it at that, saying neither what the comment was nor how they knew a comment was being made, few readers would be so naive as to fall for so facile a maneuver; but if they specified the comment, it became evident that the claim was entirely arbitrary. Harold Rosenberg wrote about a large model of a slice of pie made out of cloth by Claes Oldenburg:

> But its looks are beside the point. It exists as a demonstration model in an unspoken lecture on the history of illusionism as it occurs in both painting and the streets of big cities. Since the purpose of the pie is to dispel illusion, it might more properly be called a criticism object than an art object (1964, 63).

If the lecture is unspoken, how does Rosenberg know what it says? But in fact it is spoken: by Rosenberg, then and there. Oldenburg, so far from speaking or leaving a lecture unspoken, has made an object and shown it. The object will serve to illustrate, more or less appositely, any lecture the viewer may care to address to himself or to the public. One does not see why Oldenburg should receive either credit or blame for the lectures, or have the content of any or all of them attributed to him.[25]

Even when the context makes it obvious that a work has to be construed as a comment or critique on conventional values—when that is, in Austin's terms, its illocutionary, rather than its perlocutionary, force—it may not be clear what the comment is.[26] For instance, in 1919 Marcel Duchamp exhibited an oleograph reproduction of the *Mona Lisa* with a mustache painted on it, bearing the legend *L.H.O.O.Q*. Obviously some sort of point is being made, and a shock reaction is intended; but what exactly is the point? Many possibilities suggest themselves, some mutually exclusive, and none better than the others.[27]

Another example of a work in which a comment or message seems plainly implied (although not in this instance necessarily a protest), but there is no way of telling what the comment is, is John Cage's *4'33"*, in which the performer comes on stage and sits silent before the piano for that length of time.[28] If one knows that Cage has said on occasion that the composer of traditional music is a tyrant over performers and audience, dictating what they shall play and hear, though they are quite capable of playing and hearing for themselves ("our ears are in excellent condition"),[29] one may infer that the audience is meant to be freed by the pianist's silence to hear whatever sounds may happen along: the rustling and coughing in the hall, the cars outside, the sigh of the air conditioner, and whatever else, all as intrinsically interesting as any composition could be.[30] But this is not a reasonable or probable interpretation of the event as such, since the expected effect of the context of a musical performance would be that one would try to tune out any sounds other than those educed from the instrument in the act of performing, or simply wait for the performance to start. When it becomes obvious that what is going on is the performance, it becomes obvious that one is being presented with some alternative to conventional music, but it is not clear what the alternative is or should be.[31] Perhaps, since there is no sound, we should be concentrating on the appearance of the performer. Perhaps we should be relishing the joys of anticipation. Perhaps the composer is trying to annoy us, or teach us to control our tempers. Perhaps it is the uncertainty itself that is the performance. Or perhaps it is the silence that a perfect performance might offer us. If people start whispering in the row behind, should they be shushed for interrupting the performance, or encouraged for being the performance? Or is it perhaps the precise length of the performance that is significant, the experience of just that length of time? It is, after all, that which the title of the work specifies—but it can hardly be that, because then one could compose a wholly new work, *4'35"*, without plagiarism, whereas in fact the works could not be distinguished, because one cannot determine the precise instant at which the pianist begins to play.[32] Perhaps the intention is rather that we are to wonder about the institution of public performance itself; or perhaps, again, the appropriate response is precisely this wondering about the composer's intentions. What is presented in the concert hall does not suffice to determine any particular answer to these questions; and to say that all answers are equally good or valid is itself to impose one particular intrepretation on the work, that of artistic ambiguity.

A new art form may well afford an alternative to existing art, an alternative that one hopes will be purer or otherwise better. But the notion that such a new art can *in itself* constitute a rejection or condemnation of some or all other art is incoherent. Either one simply produces an alternative set of art objects or practices, or else one accompanies those objects and practices with (or replaces them by) a program note or manifesto containing the denunciation desired.[33] But then it is the statement and not the object that is the rejection; the object accompanying the statement may lend the rejection some plausibility by showing that one has an alternative ready, but the acceptability of the alternative does nothing of itself to undercut the other art, which is what it always was. It comes down to a rivalry of styles, a battle for attention and markets. If Harold Rosenberg denounces Clement Greenberg as a purveyor of debased academic values and a traitor to the revolution that has transformed the profession of painting, this means no more than that Rosenberg prefers abstract expressionism and Greenberg prefers hard-edged abstractions, and that this preference extends to the stories they tell themselves about their favorite painters—

Strange! that such high dispute shou'd be
'Twixt Tweedledum and Tweedledee.[34]

An antiart purism that rejects all art is obviously absurd if it is a protest from within, in the name of art however conceived. And to reject all art from a standpoint avowedly outside art itself, as by saying that all art is trivial or obsolete, is hardly a form of purism. The nearest one could come would be to reject all art forms and activities in the name of the spirit of art itself, as idols are rejected in the name of a transcendent deity. Such a stance is indeed possible, but is hard to maintain. Just as Buddhism becomes just another religion, and the Quakers' plainness of dress and speech become quaint peculiarities, so the spirit of art must be somehow made evident, and the evidence becomes convention. Antiart once more becomes art. More significantly, an antiart protest can prove its relevance as purism only if it shows that the values pursued by the institutions against which the protest is directed are not merely false in general but are surrogates for the true values it ought to have held, which the protesting movement does possess. But that is to say either that the attacked institution uses the wrong means to pursue the true end or that it adapts to the wrong end means that should have been devoted to the right. But then, after all, a perverted art is being attacked in the name of a true art, and the antiart stance degenerates yet once more to a war of styles.

The sad fatality whereby antiart becomes art is akin to that familiar process whereby prophetic movements in religions become as priestly as what they began by attacking. Antiinstitutionalism, if it persists, must suffer the absurdity of becoming institutionalized. If true art is to be viewed as a protest against the values of society and the false "art" it loves, it becomes either (as on the Marxist view) a counterinstitution representing a different social class or a noninstitutional possibility that may be realized at any time (and is realized at most times) in the interstices of established art. It seems less reasonable to think of this opposition between priestly art and prophetic art as a split between nonart and art (taking "art" as a term of praise) or between art and antiart (taking "art" as a term of abuse) than as a split within art itself—a split, moreover, of a kind that is inevitable in any organization that exists for a purpose, in which a tension may always arise between the primary standards upheld by those who, in the name of the initial end, devalue conventional means and the secondary standards maintained by those who, in systematically perfecting reliable means, lose sight of the end, and in which, as we saw long ago, such a tension may develop into disagreements about what is primary and what is secondary, which is end and which is means.

Problems of the Purist Line

The difficulties that face the antiart versions of purism, namely, that such wholesale criticism cannot dissociate itself from what it attacks without becoming irrelevant, are somewhat analogous to a problem that confronts the more sweeping of those versions of the purist line that attack accepted values in the name of art. One cannot dissociate oneself from *all* the established values of society, and there is really no possible alternative set of values in the name of which the established set can be attacked. The attempt makes the posture of attack itself theatrical and false. What one actually does is to pick out certain values and call them the values by which most men live, or today's values, without any attention to the complexity of the values really embedded in the structure of one's own life and the lives of others. Artists live in society: the role of artist is a social role, and so are the roles of the solitary and the rebel, for solitude is defined by the absence of the company with which one might have been mixing and rebellion by that which is rebelled against.[35] The values and assumptions by which artists, rebels, and solitaries lead most of their lives are those by which their fellows live, though their ideologies and rationalizations may be different. To pretend that whatever one sets up against what one picks out for denunciation has been developed from one's own inner resources shows a lack of self-knowledge that amounts to stupid insensitivity, and someone who sets up as a champion of higher values cannot afford to be found stupidly insensitive.

If it makes no sense to attack the actual value structure of a society, or to oppose onself to society as a whole, no such absurdity attaches to attack on a particular ideology or hierarchy of values, and a commoner version of purism than the extreme one I have just stigmatized singles out for attack the bourgeoisie: bourgeois society epitomizes that subset of social values, value orderings, and so forth which is commercial, brutal, inhuman, and obsolete. But the antibourgeois line turns out to be very hard to work. The bourgeoisie as it figures in the scriptures of the left is nowadays almost as hard to find as the classical proletariat; and if the purist line means by "bourgeoisie" no more than the urban middle class, it is in trouble. Art as an institution and as an idea certainly seems to be a middle-class notion and one characteristic of the bourgeois era; artists themselves tend to be middle class by affiliation if not by origin, and the middle class offers their only effective market.[36] In particular, as Marxists derisively point out, purist art is bourgeois to the core, in its economic assumptions as well as the conditions of its production and consumption. Things are especially difficult for those aspects and sects of the purist line that make it their policy to attack bourgeois values by shocking the bourgeois. They have to keep a sharp eye on bourgeois values to make sure that the shocks keep coming, and of course (it is a standard gibe) it turns out that the bourgeoisie like to be shocked.[37] There appears to be a deep complicity between the artists and their public, who are not really to be offended, but are to be given a refreshing and possibly salutary thrill. And it is all too easy to say that the "bourgeoisie" are conceived on the model of one's parents and grandparents, who are to be made to sit up and take notice of their overtalented and underestimated progeny, and can hardly react otherwise than by an annoying "oppressive tolerance." For to be shocked, scandalized, affronted, insulted by an artist, is not really challenging— I can only be challenged by something that seriously engages my actual life. It is merely amusing. Perhaps the only choice the aggressive purist has is what kind of joke he is going to be.[38]

Not only is every individual artist a social being and thus a bearer and sharer of more social values than he knows how to repudiate, and purist art a bourgeois phenomenon whose protests are for the elegant sophisticate something like a bird's anting, but purist art itself, like every art, is recognizable only as an institution, and as an institution of its society. Thus, like every movement of reform and protest, it is in perpetual danger of being taken over by whatever the dominant institutions of the society are, to the vain fury of its commentators. In our time, the Museum of Modern Art in New York marks the conversion of sackcloth and issues into haute couture by officialdom. It is quite generally true that even successful revolutions are swallowed up by the continuing impetus of the institutions they transform: France after its revolution is no less French than before, and Russia sixty years after the Bolshevik takeover is more Russian than ever. Just so, art after the triumph of purism is artier than it was before. Like Huckleberry Finn, the purist rebel can only maintain his position by constantly moving to keep ahead of the encroaching forces that will civilize him if he stands still.

What I have just written does not in any way rule out a purist theory of art; it only means that one must state one's position carefully. It is quite possible, and not obviously foolish, to maintain that the true value and significance of art in any age is that it makes perceptible some or all of those values by which its society stands ready to be judged but which in its daily concerns it inevitably neglects, and that art today has as its chief meaning that it is an available form of activity that can be kept conspicuously free of commercial dominance and thus, in a stiflingly commercial society, preserves freedom against exploitation, standardization, and vulgarity. But since in every age most of what passes for art is captured by the system and connives at or even celebrates its ruling values, the purist must here mean by "art" only those persons and works whose use of fine-art and similar or related means and institutions is anarchic or deviant—Blake, not Reynolds; Van Gogh, not Bouguereau; Rothko, not Rockwell. The true work of art is a symbolic protest against false values. But what comes of such works when they are produced? If they survive, they become part of the great tradition, as the names just cited attest. If they retain their value as symbolic protest, they do so by combining to constitute an alternative convention, a standing critique directed against the "mainstream" tradition. In hindsight, such a critique is no less traditional, no less established, than what it criticizes.

It is to avoid the inconvenient result that the works of deviant art make up an alternative tradition, and presently become commodities no less than their initially more respectable rivals, that careful purists insist that the work is nothing in itself: what has the redeeming value is the artistic act whereby the work is produced, of which the work is merely the sign. But aside from the standard objection that we seldom have any good evidence about the act of production—we have to deduce its quality from the quality of the product, so that the proposed devaluation of that product is revealed as mere pretense—transferring our attention from product to act (or activity) lands us in a net of new problems. First, once more, the act tends to assume the status of performance, so that we are back where we started. But if we resist this transformation, how is the act to be identified as related to art? The most obvious way is by some evident relation to the established institutions of art—art schools, galleries, art magazines, the art market, or what not. But it is precisely these institutions that the purist attacks in the name of the inner meaning of art. But, then, what remains? The connection between act and art must be established by an inner meaning that cannot be identified by any overt characteristic of act or outcome. The only remaining possibility is that the act should be accompanied by a "story that goes with it."[39] That is, its significance should be that claimed for it by the artist or by some accredited spokesman or critic. But then, yet again, we face the danger that the story itself, with or without the work, should assume the status of a performance in the fine-arts understanding; and, if that danger is avoided, the required valuelessness of the act can be maintained only if the story that goes with it is one that can be told without reliance on the specific qualities of the act or its outcome—

in fact, that the story be one that could be told of many other acts and artists, and thus has no specific relevance to the act in question.[40]

In the last resort, the relevant part of the story that goes with the purist act is always the same: it amounts to saying that the artist is serious and sincere. But now the purist's predicament is worse than ever. Sincerity and seriousness require specific values and beliefs to be serious about—one cannot really be like that legendary young disciple of Heidegger who said "I am committed, but I don't know what to." And the values about which the artist is serious must either be specifically artistic values or not. If they are, one hardly sees why his seriousness does not show itself in some specific quality of his work; but if they are not, the artist becomes a moralist or a politician, distinguished from other moralists and politicians only, if at all, by being less responsible and less well informed, in the way chronicled with justifiable scorn by Hilton Kramer (1973). The alternative to a seriousness that has some positive commitment, however, is mere solemnity; and one of the prevailing tones in writing about the arts in the last few decades has been one of a compulsive and ungrounded earnestness.[41]

The combination of solemnity in attitude with frivolity or emptiness in content has the result that the proart of the purists, with its journalistic posturings and pronunciamentos, is proving a more effective antiart movement than antiart ever did. The merely solemn is the opposite of the serious, and the will to be holier-than-thou usually succeeds only in being sillier-than-thou. Much recent art in the latest modes is thrilling, despite its laudatory press; but the thrill is aesthetic, and the claims to moral significance evident hokum. The notion, sometimes proposed, that the entire practice of art has changed lately, and that art must be redefined to accommodate those changes, is groundless, not because such a change is inherently impossible, but because no more lies behind the claims than a desperate manipulation of the means of publicity. Once more, purism suffers a reversal—the stricter its purity, the more evidently it relapses into an empty posturing.

The last paragraph says only that the purist line, like other movements of art and thought, may have its lunatic fringe, and sometimes that fringe seems to dominate the scene. A subtler and more tenacious difficulty confronts some of its American exponents when they promote purism as the rationale of contemporary art. Contemporary radical art has a complex heritage. Behind this or that aspect of contemporary practice lie, first, the progressive tendencies of strict traditions, whereby (for instance) abstraction in painting emerges from the problems of serious painters without any revolutionary animus; second, revolutions that oppose traditions in the name of the inner tendencies of those traditions themselves, as dodecaphonic music appeared to Schoenberg (sometimes at least) as the only rational continuation from extreme chromaticism; third, futurism, the invocation of a theatrical and dynamic art to symbolize the mechanized and process-oriented aspects of modern civilization, which were pitted against the opulent monumentality of conservatism; fourth, surrealism, opposed like futurism to the monumentality of conservative civilization, but opposing it not in the name of technocracy but in the name of the newly discovered unconscious of significantly free association and serendipitous automatism; and, fifth, Dadaism, opposed to the same aspects of civilization as the others, but not in the name of anything more specific than simple humanity, a value it was not felt necessary to make explicit. All of these movements were reformist or revolutionary, and all were opposed to an officially conservative civilization epitomized in the supposed fixation of the bourgeois on a more luxurious version of what he was used to. But the purport of their diverse radicalisms was various, and their enemies did not by any means coincide. And for the American purist there has been the special difficulty that all these movements had their native settings elsewhere, and the monolithic "bourgeois" culture they united in opposing never had a firm grip on America (to hear two cultured Frenchmen conversing can be a revelation, even now, of what makes avant-gardist varieties of purism seem necessary). The result is that the immediate past of art can seem to be, not a texture of warring movements each with its own alliances and its own rationale, but an undifferentiated mass of "modern art," any part of which may be invoked at any time to justify any procedure that bears a superficial analogy to it.[42] There is accordingly a tendency to lavish on one kind of phenomenon a kind of rhetoric developed to fit something quite different, which adds to the air of unreality that pervades the eloquence surrounding recent art.

To conclude this section on the difficulties of the purist line: the line suffers from one crippling weakness. If purism is to be kept really pure from the aesthetic values that would return it to the classical line, it must sever connections between its procedures and the established procedures of the fine arts. It thus inevitably resorts to arbitrary action. Either the artist exploits his role (like a professor who uses a scheduled mathematics seminar to conduct a political meeting), or his actions acquire an unfocused irrelevance. So the prognosis for purism is rather poor, though one can live with a crippling weakness for a long time.[43]

Purism and the Arts

The fact that for the purist line the work of art has only symbolic value does not, obviously, mean that that line has no place for works of art. On the contrary, the work of art remains that on which interest is usually focused, though it is not that in which the interest is taken. What the relegation of the work to a symbolic function seems bound to eliminate is any interest in the arts—much more so than in the expressive line, whose rejection of determinate forms and practices is, as we saw, somewhat hypocritical. Certainly the concept of a fine art that was fundamental to the classical line, an organized body of knowledge and skills governed by the requirement of producing specific changes in a specific matter, appears flatly incompatible with purism, which rejects the specific positive values by which such an art must be defined.[44] If there were an art of (or in) purism, it would be, not a fine art, but an art of living, a skilled cultivation of purity. But the preferred image of the artist as "holy fool" purified by suffering militates against the recognition of such an art.

The purist line need not, however, abjure the names of arts or of kinds of artists, insofar as such names can be taken to stand for commitment to a way of life rather than for the actual practice of producing objects of a certain sort. In fact, a more specific name is better, as testifying to the genuineness of the commitment. An artist who is no particular sort of artist but merely testifies by his existence to the nobility of the artist's calling has after all some difficulty in establishing that he is indeed an artist and not just a common bum; but if he can say he is a musician or a painter, he can (if his claim be allowed) muster institutional support. In fact, there are two ways by which the names of specific arts can find a place in purism. On the one hand, if "art" is to stand merely for whatever exemplary way of life celebrates uselessness, the words of "music" and "painting" are hardly less appropriate than "art" itself; on the other hand, if it is the practices of art as traditionally understood in the guise of the "fine arts" that afford a repertory of suitably useless activities, that repertory will in fact be divided among the traditional arts, to which the suitability will extend. In practice, the names and activities of the different arts lend themselves differentially to this purpose. The words "artist," "poet," "painter," seem to be symbolically available, "architect," "sculptor," "playwright," and "novelist" less so, while "musician" occupies a middle ground. Why is this so, if it is so? Perhaps it is because one can set up as a poet or an artist or (if one chooses small forms) a painter with small expense and training. Nothing stands in the way of a person performing actions that will symbolize his attachment to these occupations. But a sculptor's traditional materials are bulky and dear, and his techniques more forbidding in their initial stages; and dramatists and architects can hardly operate without a more positive interaction with the public than the purist line encourages. As for "novelist," the term is used to differentiate one writer from another, not by depth of artistic intent, but by the form and dimensions of what is written: it is habitually restricted to those who have actually undertaken the long labor of producing a novel, and thus proved that they were not short-story writers after all. The case of music is more complex. On the one hand, there is still a musical technique of instrumental mastery and compositional skill that is hard to master and must be practiced before an exacting public; on the other hand, there does exist a sort of paramusic that requires no more than an earnestness with regard to sound, or indeed a generalized earnestness of purism so long as that is displayed within the context of the established institutions of music. If I put a butterfly in a box and release it among my friends, that is nothing much; if I manage to assemble the artistic press before doing so, it is art; if I am in a position to persuade the manager of a concert hall to let me do it on his stage before a paying audience, it is music.[45] The title "musician," however, is not bestowed on those whose music takes such forms—perhaps because those musicians who have mastered their instruments have a strong union.

The foregoing paragraphs apply to that variety of the purist line which finds the value of conspicuous inutility only in a reformed art, freed from the commercial and cultural worth ascribed to its products. But we saw that there was another way open to the purist line, in which it was the fine arts themselves, in their consecration to aesthetic as opposed to utilitarian values, that performed the exemplary function. And on this version of the line, the fine arts in their specific difference are precisely the means whereby the value in question is realized, although the specific end by which the arts are defined is, as it were, placed in brackets. One might push this a little further, perhaps, and say that the unworldliness of the artistic vocation is shown by its cultivation of difficult, useless, and obsolete techniques—much in the way that the Japanese have taken obsolete techniques of warfare, archery, and swordsmanship and made a spiritual exercise out of cultivating those techniques in a vacuum by the most indirect and difficult methods.[46] Marshall McLuhan has taken a step in this direction by his insistence that the essense of art is anachronism, that the arts consist of means of communication that have ceased to be habitual and come to be practiced and fostered for their own sakes. In the terms of our third chapter, this amounts to saying that there are arts of disengaged communication because history has divested certain forms of communication of their engagement. But this version of the purist line has not been developed, presumably because it requires one to deny that works of art have the kind of value they evidently have, and their producers the kind of interest they often have. It is more sensible to find conspicuous uselessness in lives and works about whose significance it is less easy to be mistaken.

The Work of Art as Symbol of Purity

The purist line requires that a work of art have no other value than that of a symbol. We are to divert our attention from the work produced to the act of producing it: if the activities of art issue in objects to which value is attached, the whole of art becomes infected with teleology and hence with utility. And in attending to the activity, one must presumably not attend to the performing of the performance as such (to use the terminology of the classical line), because that is action conceived strictly as issuing in an isolable end. Rather, one must attend to that performing in its capacity of activity, mere operation, a slice of living. But this requirement lands us in difficulties.[47] If the requirement of conspicuousness is retained, the work as performance is reinstated in a changed form, for any activity that is isolated for attention is thereby constituted a performance (if only in the attenuated sense that it is a sample of style) and a potential object of criticism: since anything can be an aesthetic object, any performance can be a work of art, and the artist finds himself once more in a form of the trap that, as Danto argued, makes it impossible to scramble out of the art world once one has fallen in. If, on the other hand, the requirement of conspicuousness is rejected, art and artist become unidentifiable, and instead of the purist line we have merely a repudiation or neglect of art, a neglect already amply exemplified by the rest of us in our round of labor, recreation, and slumber. The operations of art inevitably generate works of art, it seems, and these works cannot be dismissed as mere byproducts, because it is by them that the operations of art are differentiated from other operations (the classical line makes this a mere tautology, because whatever there is about an operation that makes it an operation of art ipso facto either is or includes a work of art).

If the purist line cannot eliminate the work of art without eliminating art and therewith itself, one would think it a sounder strategy to grasp the nettle and embrace a purism of the object. If the value of art is that of conspicuous inutility, it should issue in works that are both conspicuous and useless, or conspicuously useless.

How is the combination of conspicuousness and inutility to be effected? There are at least four modes. First, an object can be both useless in itself and conspicuous in its properties. Such are most traditional works of art, which use the devices of fine art to attract attention and are useless precisely because this attractiveness is their function. But the most direct exploitation of this mode is no doubt that of "minimal art" and related forms that systematically simplify the means of their appeal. The extreme case of this would be the exhibition of a plain primed canvas, differing from an empty frame only because an empty frame would reveal through it a surface of undesired and uncontrolled complexity, or the exhibition of sculptures made up of brightly colored, simple forms that hold the attention while discouraging the held attention from active employment, or the performance of music that approximates to white sound.[48]

The second mode of combining uselessness with conspicuousness is that which makes a useful thing conspicuous insofar as it is not useful. Such would be any form of decoration that denies or conceals function (it will be observed that these first two modes between them cover most of the output of the fine and decorative arts, so that the purist line can account for most of what generally counts as art). The habit, common a few years ago among the arty young, of painting flower shapes on cars, and the concomitant resuscitation of the outmoded scripts and stylizations of art nouveau, appear to have been a quite conscious employment of this mode to deride the blatant utility of the machines and commercial announcements to which they were applied. Excluded from this mode and from all others, it seems, is the form that follows function; if anyone were to wish to bring such forms under the rubric of the purist line, which would be a strange thing to do indeed (but strangeness has never inhibited theorists), he could no doubt do so by saying that the curse of utility is neutralized far more effectively by an elegance that drags the useful object itself into the realm of fruition than by an applied decoration that leaves the brutal use unredeemed.

The third mode in which the utility of a thing, or more generally its relation to social or economic ends, is conspicuously denied is a more recent discovery. One takes a useful object, or the unalleviated form of such an object, and thrusts it into the condition of art either by subjecting it to fine-arts technology or more simply by setting it in a fine-arts context. Thus one might make a bronze cast of a beer can by the lost wax process, or carefully paint a United States flag with a vibrant painterly surface, or blow up to giant size a colored strip cartoon, screen dots and all.[49] Or one may more simply sign one's name on a can of soup, which thereby ceases to be a can of soup and becomes a signed soup can (which happens to have soup in), much as the paper used by Samuel Alexander in writing *Space Time and Deity* ceased to be examination papers and became a philosophical manuscript (which happened to have examination answers on the back).[50]

The fourth mode of combining uselessness and conspicuousness is to construct and display something whose uselessness and pointlessness is what is conspicuous. Kurt Schwitters' *Merz* approximated to this mode. A more straightforward exemplification is Tinguely's self-destroying contraptions (especially, one would say, those that did not destroy themselves very efficiently [cf. Canaday 1962, 80-85]) or such devices as a machine that does nothing but turn itself off. But the paradigms of such a mode are "happenings," elaborately pointless activities that exist to be described and photographed, or simply to lack purpose in a communal and dramatic sort of way. On the individual scale, artists will have themselves photographed pacing aimlessly around empty lots or fiddling with bits of cardboard. Such proceedings differ in two ways from mere ways of killing time.[51] First, the performers take them seriously, in the rather special sense that they affect a solemn attitude toward them.[52] Second, they think of them as art and of themselves as artists (or artists' helpers).[53] And in thinking of them as art they think of them as, precisely, nonutilitarian goings-on to be solemn about.

The four modes of achieving conspicuous inutility are not on a par, for a reason that we have already touched on and the full effect of which we must now consider.

On the face of it, perhaps the most practical and common-sensical way to celebrate inutility and put to shame the values of commerce and the workaday world is to devote limitless time and energy to producing objects too precious to use. This is in fact one traditional view of art and perhaps the earliest and most familiar version of the purist line, associated with the name of Ruskin: the true artist is the laborious craftsman who perfects his work to the greater glory of God, beyond the demands of any other possible client. "Art for art's sake" is the paradigm of this attitude.

The weakness of the purism that celebrates inutility by making things too precious to buy and use is that the resulting products, in the very act of losing their utility value, take on an enhanced commodity value, which differs from utility only by being (in the eyes at least of anyone likely to espouse the purist line) yet more debased. And, as Thorstein Veblen (1899) pointed out shortly after the heyday of the "art for art's sake" movement, commodity value when pushed to the extreme of extravagance and uselessness takes on a new significance, that of "conspicuous consumption." People with more purchasing power than they have real occasion for like to own objects on which a great deal of labor has obviously been spent to no good purpose, just to show that they can command such labor resources. One of Veblen's examples is hand-stitched shoes: machine stitching is stronger and looks neater (or so Veblen believes), but has the disadvantage that it costs less. And it is obvious that original works of fine art, especially old and fragile ones, fill the bill even better. If this is so, the more useless labor the artist expended on his product, the greater its services to the basest appetites of a capitalist economy. In this spirit, Roger Fry (1939) came to describe all highly finished works of art as "luxury objects." The use of such language was not quite honest if it implied that the tradition whereby a workman's self-respect was shown in his devotion to detail, in the belief that art demanded such devotion, was never more than a mere front for the love of possessions; but it is true that the artist's work can be put to such use whatever his motives may have been, and this fact is now so well known that an artist can hardly ignore it and is hard put to it to circumvent it.

To rid his work of commodity value, the artist must either bring about a condition of society in which commodity values no longer exist (a task that is, to say the least, beyond his unaided powers) or make his work undesirable. A first step is to ensure that it has no

444

obvious aesthetic value; but this is not enough, for the requirement of conspicuous consumption (as the example of the shoes demonstrates) is not any inherent preciousness in the object but only that it demonstrate its owner's capacity to command the fruits of labor. So the work of art must be not only unattractive but also free from signs of protracted, skilled, or intensive work. It should not attract attention to itself as artifact at all. The care expended on its production, if any, will be devoted largely to producing the appearance of minimal thought. A natural object or piece of industrial or domestic waste picked up and signed by the artist will serve this purpose as well as anything.[54] The signature testifies to the artist's serious concern, without risking the embarrassment of laboring to produce an article of commerce.[55] A similar solution is to make the work of art a disposable or perishable object, a piece of recognizable garbage. Marshall McLuhan, according to the newspapers, once equated all art with garbage, presumably because just as an environment submitted to attention ceases to function as an environment and becomes an art form, so an object of utility that has become useless and been discarded becomes a possible object for attention.[56] But the immediately relevant point was made by an art exhibition that was going the rounds a few years ago, which consisted of transparent plastic bags containing the fragments of works of art torn into shreds for the purpose by the artists—of none of whom, in my ignorance, had I heard, or expected (far less hoped) to hear again.[57]

A device akin to the displaying of found objects or refuse is to use randomizing techniques to ensure that one's work will either lack inherent value or possess it only by unlikely chance. This device appears to be most usual in music and film, where a powerful technical or presentational ambiance suffices to identify the work and a mere will to abstain from sense cannot be relied on to achieve its end. For instance, one may specify that a musical work shall consist of whatever a dozen radio stations shall be broadcasting at an arbitrary time, or set up a film camera at an arbitrary location and let it run for an arbitrary length of time.[58] With such performances we run yet again into the apparent difficulty that one cannot reliably tell from what one sees and hears what its point was meant to be, and one has to choose between a number of alternatives as to how to take it.[59] Some will see it as calculated to produce the effect of massive boredom and a consequent quasi-mystical experience, some as affording random experience from which the audience may construct their own works, some as inculcating by exemplification that old and overvalued truth that anything whatever *can* be an aesthetic object.[60] But the difficulty is only apparent, because from the purist point of view the pure ambiguity of the situation is (or should be, for the point is seldom made) its essence: here is a work of art produced with minimal effort for no reason, and here are you watching or listening to it, you cannot tell why—is this not the triumphantly successful celebration of complete and conspicuous inutility?

Unless he is associated with one of the performing arts that yield no artifact, it is not enough for the artist to keep his work free from aesthetic value and the evidence of labor. So long as the requirement of conspicuousness is retained (and we have seen that it can hardly be dispensed with), his work will still have association value. For if the conspicuousness does not pertain to the evident qualities of the work itself, it can only belong to the circumstances of its production or presentation, and must ultimately depend on its association with a known artist or impresario—and, if the latter, of the impresario in his capacity as artist of the art of presentation. The value that the work thus acquires is comparable to that of a saint's relics: like a lump of dried gristle in a jeweled reliquary is a piece of antiart in a collector's gallery.

In the pursuit of the conspicuously useless, then, one is driven to the uncollectable. Two varieties attracted attention a few years ago. One was a twentieth-century version of the eighteenth-century architectural "folly": the earth work. One dug a ditch and filled it in again, or plowed a pattern in a field, or whatever. The other was "concept art." Here, the idea for a work of art did duty for the work itself.[61] Eventually, the idea *was* the work, for (as the expressive line had demonstrated) nothing is more contemplable than an incorporeal mental content. Association value is lampooned when an artist declares of a hunk of steel that it is a work of art only when accompanied by the artist's certificate declaring it to be so; and this lampoon is shown up as a gesture of desperation when another artist, or the same artist, signs an affidavit solemnly withdrawing from one of his own works all aesthetic value and significance.[62] In these cases, though, it is all too evident that it is not the steel or the repudiated performance that is the work of art, if anything is, but in the former case the whole act of production and authentication and in the latter case the whole act of production and repudiation.[63] As with concept art involving no artifacts at all ("my exhibition consists of closing the gallery down for a week"), the requirement of conspicuousness ensures once more that a quixotic championing of purity cannot be distinguished from a manipulation of the means of publicity. The appearance, at least, is that of a juggling with reputations in an atmosphere of agonizing selfconsciousness,[64] a capitulation to the marketplace more abject than the one it would replace.

Nothing that is recognizable as art, it seems, can be relied on to fulfill the function of conspicuous inutility. Whatever can be noticed can be traded on or traded in. The more desperate the attempts to evade this predicament, the funnier the results. Two ways seem open to the purist line here. One alternative is to ignore the difficulty. What has been shown is not that purism is impossible but that purism is always vulnerable to exploitation or confusion, and it is always open to a bold spirit to accept the vulnerability and take the risk. The other alternative is to accept the absurdity of the situation and the consequent ridiculousness of those who are in it: the ridicule only accentuates the pathos of the earnest artist. Since the value of the work in terms of the purist line can be no more than symbolic, it is really a matter of indifference how other lines of thought and conduct may exploit it: it is after all, as we said at the beginning, not on the work or the operations of art that the purist line must concentrate, but on the figure of the artist. The values of the purist line are spiritual values, of such a sort that it is in the symbolic qualities of a life that we most naturally seek them.

The Artist as Holy Fool

We have seen that to the purist line the work of art is something of an embarrassment: even if it does not become a commodity, its status as outcome of a performing process is bound to endow it with some sort of product value, to drag it into the chains of means and ends in which the pure worth of being is falsified and dissipated. Similarly, the concept of an art is at best irrelevant and at worst anathema not only because it brings in the fine arts and their association with venal official culture but because the very idea of an art as organized skill belongs to goal-seeking and organized society, which is society in just that aspect which cannot be purified from economic taint. The purist line is therefore obliged to fix its attention on art in general, as a spiritual level of attainment; and the only embodiment left for this abstract entity is the artist. The artist appears as an exemplary figure, not because of his works or because of his art, but because of the quality of his activity while being an artist, the kind of person he exemplifies (or at least symbolizes) in his working life. But, once more, this life cannot be identified by expertise or productivity: it must then be irrelevant whether the artist actually does practice his art. What is important is his commitment (or apparent commitment) to the pure values held to be inherent in art. In this, the purist line is the exact opposite of the expressive line, for which the artist is nothing over and above his accomplished works. Hitherto, the artist who never actually painted or composed but exhausted his art in *being an artist* was a butt for easy satire, but now (though purists seldom face this implication of what they are saying) he becomes the central figure in art.

As exemplary figure, the artist must stand for the negation of all utility values, and to make this clear he is usually required to stand for the negation of all respectable values. He must bypass, ignore, or defy convention, and must be in practical matters either a simpleton or outrageously devoid of such prudent honesty as might be mistaken for the best policy. Such bypassing, ignoring, and defying in fact generate three alternative models for the exemplary artist. There is the saintly, Fra Angelico type who is protected from the world of which he is ignorant; there is the untamed innocent, who lives only for art and does not even notice the scandal he causes and the damage he does to the lives and properties of his conventional neighbors;[65] and there is the defiant rebel, consciously and self-consciously repudiating and flouting all conventions and laws other than those of his calling. The most popular image is the second, the bohemian popularized by Murger and his successors. Ideally, such an artist is either starved (like Chatterton) by the bourgeois world or unable (like Beethoven) to retain the money that the bourgeois world lavishly but unfeelingly heaps on him. The positive side of his repudiation or neglect of the values that the bourgeois world espouses is that he either promotes or unself-consciously embodies values that the bourgeois world ignores (though it is a common gibe that the defiance of respectability is sometimes the sole and sufficient evidence that these other values are present). The artist is, in a word, unworldly. Of course, he cannot be effectively exemplary for the society he rejects unless that society can recognize his goals as ones it acknowledges—or, more precisely, unless what a suitable apologist can claim that the artist is doing is recognizable as a possible interpretation of a role that the society thinks of as ideal. But this is no real restriction, since, as we observed before, the artist as a member of the society will inevitably define his role by ideals current in that society even if not effectively dominant there. The figure of the artist thus takes on a familiar ambivalence. The bohemian life is at once squalid and romantic, depraved and ideal, despised and respected. Such ambivalence fits well with the general sacredness of art as a secluded enclave in life, that aspect of the mystic line in which we found affinities to the purist line. The artist is *sacer* in the exact sense of that term to which students of comparative religion call our attention: he is at once accursed and holy, the precious outcast.

One manifestation of the *sacer* is the scapegoat, the innocent creature thrust out of the city to expiate the sins of the fat cats within the walls. And the artist is indeed sometimes spoken of in terms suitable to this role, though it is not clear exactly what the alleged sufferings of the artist in his cold garret have to do with the comfortable guilt of the respectable burgher. Perhaps their Philistinism robs him of his proper public, or he is driven by their vulgarity to produce an anguished and unpopular art. If he is a scapegoat, his agonized vision must somehow be the condition of their comfortable blindness, or something like that. However hard it is to spell out a convincing relationship of this sort, the notion has a plausible ring to it, and it was not surprising to find Harold Rosenberg among the furriers' advertisements in the *New Yorker* representing the painter as bearer of the sins of his age. By the sensitivity of his vision and the eloquence of his pathos Rosenberg almost single-handedly created the myth of the New York painter as culture hero: it was in his version that the purist line seemed to dominate the sixties. "Painting," he wrote, "became the means of confronting in daily practice the problematic nature of modern individuality" (1964, 40); and again, "Expressionist painting also reminds him [sc. the art enthusiast] of the distance between the artist and the art appreciator—a distance of pathos, since the creator of the work has suffered, or even invited upon himself, the injuries of the epoch" (ibid., 49).[66] (Those who naively supposed that the difference was that painters painted, and appreciators did not, stand thus corrected.) The context offered no explanation of these portentous remarks. The former perhaps means that the general problem of how to conduct oneself in a rapidly changing society is uniquely, or at least conspicuously, symbolized by the plight of the creative artist with neither determinate public demand nor consistent professional tradition to channel his creativity; but the latter seems only to express the conviction that expressionist painters have a rougher time than other artists and indeed than all other men, and this conviction seems inexplicable otherwise than as a demand that it shall be so.

The purist line as a general approach to the significance of works of art is a product of this century; the stereotype of the artist as a figure of exemplary inutility is much older. It is an aspect of the romantic cult of genius. To demand radical originality as sole and sufficient mark of a true artistic vocation is enough to establish for artists a special and socially ambivalent role as savior and threat, whether their innovations be social or merely perceptual or technical; for to be thus original is necessarily to appeal to standards other than those by which successful conformity can be appraised. One would also expect the social niche occupied by an original genius to be in some unusual location, for we must somehow explain how the artist has either escaped contamination by conventional notions or been inoculated against them.[67] Such expectations, and a stereotype of the artist that conforms to them, should not surprise us even if actual artists seldom or never fulfill them.

To think of artists as bohemians and at the same time to place a high value on their works is in effect to reduce the value of a work of art to that of a commodity: every social function that might ground a different sort of value is repudiated. But the artist's purity is thus hopelessly compromised, for it is hardly realistic to think of him as a sort of bee producing honey of whose destination at market he is totally unaware. One must therefore either deny any value to works of art or define the scapegoat role, not as the only possibility for a true artist, but as an alternative role. There are in any case good reasons for viewing it thus, since artists do in fact often assume the role of *choragus*, expressing and celebrating the values their society avows. There are various ways of thinking about the relations between these alternative roles. One way is to say that in a healthy society the artist's task is to celebrate its values, in a sick society to express alternatives (it being understood that most if not all actual societies are sick). Another way is to say that every society needs two sorts of artist, one to celebrate what it recognizes and the other to express what it denies or hides. A third way is simply to say that the *choragus* is the lost leader who has sold out. But it is hard to elevate this third way of thinking into a principle: the original lost leader, after all, was Wordsworth,[68] and the roll of patriotic and generally affirmative artists includes most of the great names in the arts, whose stature it would require more fortitude than sense to deny. Besides, conformity and noncomformity, orthodoxy and heresy, are relative terms. In some quarters, where a society defines itself in opposition to some larger group, protest is orthodox and conformity is rebellion. It is possible to make the mere adoption of an adversary stance one's criterion of artistic propriety, without regard to the merits or even the existence of the supposed adversary; but one may then find oneself, in the name of purism, endorsing the denunciation of noncomformity by the conformist, at which point one's purism has reduced itself to a mere preference for satire and kindred genres, and the role of exemplary fool is abandoned.

An artist can hardly assume that role of exemplary fool if he has achieved wordly success. For that reason, it can only function as an alternative role, for a painter can hardly be judged a failure by himself or by anyone else simply because he manages to sell his paintings.[69] Unless one assumes the public discernment and taste to be infallible, one cannot be certain that a good artist will not be favored—by mistake. Those writers who contrive to give the impression that no great artist can be popular usually stop short of actually saying so. On the other hand, if lack of success can hardly be necessary for artistic excellence, it cannot be sufficient either. The unsuccessful artist may be a genius beyond the comprehension of his contemporaries, and thus eligible for the role of exemplary fool, but he may also be unproductive, incompetent, a tedious academician, or merely a beginner who has yet to make his name, and one can hardly make an antihero out of someone merely because he has not made his mark in a profession in which success is possible and desired. Let us suppose, however, that we stick to our purist line and insist that the true artist is an exemplary figure because the values that guide him are such that to succeed (in incomprehensible originality) entails failure in worldly terms, and brings on him inevitable contempt and, thus, loneliness and anguish. This has the consequence, extremely awkward for the purist, that the only true artist is the artist no one, not even the purist, has ever heard of—unless, perhaps, the purist is himself a singularly unsuccessful critic. One can hardly help noticing that most of the suffering artists of whom Harold Rosenberg wrote had become professionally successful and personally prosperous.[70]

Faced with the awkward predicament that if he points to recognizable examples he refutes himself, the purist has two strategies available. One, the more popular, is to rely on the past, and interpret the history of art as showing that the true artists were all misunderstood and unsuccessful because they were "before their time." There is accordingly a branch of popular art history that amounts to the manufacture of posthumous failure for artists. Mozart, Beethoven, even Bach, have suffered from this sort of attention.[71]

> Seven wealthy Towns contend for HOMER Dead
> Through which the Living HOMER begged his Bread,[72]

says Anonymous, though there is no evidence whatever to support the second line. But this strategy works only while we attend to the favorable cases, like Van Gogh; the celebrity of Michelangelo and the prosperity of Shakespeare in their lifetimes, together with many other examples, rob it of plausibility. The alternative strategy, suggested by the failure of this one, is to say that the appearance of success makes no difference. Despite his fame, the melancholy Michelangelo goes on suffering; and who is to say that Shakespeare did not suffer from despair after he retired to Stratford?

This second strategy, securing the artist's unsuccess by making it subjective, looks promising for two reasons. First, if an artist is what he is through renouncing worldly values and committing himself to a struggle in which there can be no victory, then so long as he retains this commitment it can make no difference to him what his financial status or worldly reputation may be (except insofar as gross poverty makes one unable to work), for there will always be another vision to achieve and another problem to solve no less taxing than the last.[73] But the second reason is of a different kind: it is that such a strategy can never be proved in error. A critic who adopts it can always claim to *know* that every artist has, indeed must have, the kind of grimness he postulates: an apparently happy artist must just be very good at hiding the fox under his cloak.[74]

Such easy successes as the second strategy seeks to gain always have their price, and in this case the price is high. In the first place, a claim that can never be refuted can always be challenged: one who appeals to the fact that despair can always be hidden invites the retort that it can always be simulated; and if a struggle admits of no success because it can never end, the same endlessness also precludes final failure. In sports, the claim that victory and defeat are unimportant because "the game's the thing" is not usually thought of as evincing anguish and despair; and the cases of sport and art, different as they are, are sufficiently alike that we may suspect that it is not so much the logic of the situation as the pathos of convinced purism that draws the inference here.

In the end, the effect of the second strategy, with its reliance on untestable assertions about an artist's state of mind, is once more to turn art over to the public relations industry. What is significant is not the work done but how long the artist is said to have spent on it, how difficult he is thought to have found it, the intensity of the spiritual struggles believed to have gone into it.[75] And the saying, thinking, and believing are the work, not of the artist as artist, but of the public relations man, whether this be the artist himself or his employee, dupe, or patron. It makes no difference whether there is truth in the handout or not: what matters is the copywriter's prose style. To serve as an exemplary figure, a symbolic sufferer, all one needs to provide is a peg around which the image can be built.

It is not enough that the exemplary artist of the purist line be useless and unsuccessful. He must be devoted to uselessness. But how can he be? There must be something that he is trying to do. And the object of his endeavors can hardly be fixed by the requirements of the work to be done, however little that work conforms to the preconceived notions of his contemporaries: our devotion to anything surely bestows value on it, and there is no way in which the artist can prevent that value from being expropriated. One solution to the problem is to say that such expropriation merely highlights the condition of the artist as exemplary sufferer by exploiting it, like the Roman epicure reveling in the changing colors of the dying mullet. But other solutions are possible. Harold Rosenberg offers two alternatives. One is that the artist's effort is to discover himself—to discover, that is, the "self" that his painting is to express.[76] But this does not solve the problem. In one sense, whatever the artist does is an expression of himself: even in plagiarism one expresses onself as plagiarist. There is no difference between discovering oneself and discovering what is required to perfect the painting one is working on. And if one seeks to avoid this conclusion by specifying certain characteristics that the discovered self and its expression must have, one is once more simply specifying qualities that the painting must have. In either case, then, talk of self-discovery fails as a way of locating the value of the artist's endeavor somewhere other than in the work produced. Rosenberg's other solution is more ingenious: the object of the artist's endeavor is to get into the history of art, this history being understood, not as a mere record of what critics and public have valued, but as a record of those creations that have in the end proved fruitful in stimulating other creations.[77] Such fruitfulness is beyond the reach of the public relations industry, and immediate success and popularity are irrelevant to it. The judgment of history is unknowable and, in a sense, indeterminate since fruitfulness can be denied and lost.[78] But it is also absolute in that there are no permanent values other than that of contributing to tradition. On this interpretation, the value of a work cannot be appropriated because it is not intrinsic to the particular work but lies in its historical relationships, and the ultimate value lies in the tradition as a whole, which cannot be possessed. This is really a brilliant solution to the most awkward problem of the purist line, whether or not Rosenberg proposed it for that reason: the value that is necessary to save the artist's uselessness from futility exists, but it is imponderable in his own day and is a value that depends for its realization not on the market or the forum but on what may be made of it by other holy fools in their folly.

The thesis that the object of the artist's efforts is to take his place in history has something of the ridiculous about it. One is reminded of the couturier agonizing over whether he has guessed correctly about what length skirts are going to be this season, and some journalists certainly give the impression that the major artists in New York spend half their lives nosing around each others' studios to find out where art history is going to be this week. Surely this cannot be what we meant. We meant, rather, that the artist should be wrestling for something worthwhile, something that the accolade of history might recognize but could not determine. Would he not then do better to get on with his work, not bothering his head about history? *Habent sua fata libelli*, " 'Tis not in mortals to command success," and so forth. But the source of the ridiculousness is not that the end of the artist's endeavor should be to take a place in history, but that he should be self-conscious about it while being at the same time cynical about history. If he believes, as Hegel in first promoting this deification of history believed, that the real is rational, and that history works cunningly through the agency of people who are not thinking about history at all, his only recourse is to work honestly on, hoping but never knowing that what he does will be validated as the course of history becomes in retrospect clearer and more determinate.

The integrity of the purist line can be maintained by confining the value of the artist's work to its contribution to art history thus conceived as a rigidly self-contained system. The artist's value is then strictly that of exemplary person, purveyor of values and bearer of agonies that the public cannot share. But this has the little-noticed though rather obvious consequence that the general public, however devoted to culture, cannot appreciate art and need not bother itself about it. This seems reasonable; one who keeps a dog does not himself bark, and the main advantage of having a scapegoat is to save one from the duty of agonizing over one's sins.[79] Rosenberg (1964, 257) was inclined to upbraid the public for not sharing the artist's agonies, and the public at large is often castigated as backward and Philistine for not appreciating contemporary art.[80] But on this version of the purist line such complaints are absurd.[81]

In conclusion, then, if the intent of the purist line is to establish that the true significance of art in human life is to celebrate inutility, a necessary alternative to the values enshrined in and espoused by our everyday lives, it is singularly difficult to find a version that will preserve the identity of art without compromising the purity of its supposed ideals. It is one thing to say that the artist as such, like other selfless workers and idealists, rebukes the marketplace by his indifference to the price of his work and time, and that this is one of the reasons we respect him; it is quite another thing to make of this indifference the differentia of art. An artist who believes that his duty is to celebrate indifference to the values of society is in a sad quandary, because a paraded neglect is the very opposite of a failure to notice, and few motions are more ungainly than a self-conscious dance of indifference.

XV

CONCLUSION

I have contended that if we wish to think sensibly about that area of human concern toward which the word "art" gestures, it is futile to take our start from the properties of works of art conceived as objects that confront us as alien. Our theorizing will indeed center on works of art, which are the focus of our practical concern and for which, in most views, everything else in art exists—for though the artist is better than his works, it is for their sake that he is an artist—but our thinking becomes incoherent unless we think of those works as, typically, the proper outcome of human endeavor, taking their nature from a context of human action no less certainly than words take their meaning from a language to which they essentially belong. We read them immediately as embedded in that human world to which we ourselves belong, as enmeshed in the web of actual and possible intentions. And if we set works of art apart from other human makings and doings, it will most probably be because they relate to a system of intentions that grounds a recognized practice or set of practices. When we discover that such practices exist and afford the context in which the concept of a work of art first took form, we are encouraged to ground our thinking about art and its works in the notion of an art, an organized body of skill and knowledge directed to such outcomes, and specifically in the notion of that kind of art whose presupposition is that it is to issue in works of art, that is, a fine art. The notion of the fine arts is indeed obsolete in that it has an intolerably musty odor, and bright people nowadays do not use it; but that is not because the phenomena of art are to be otherwise explained, but only because the phrase "fine arts" has become associated with certain specific and historically determined practices from which some of us are still trying to extricate ourselves. To avoid this association, theorists have tried to do without the notion of a fine art, and have dropped the concept of an art from their effective repertory; the result has been that most theorizing on the arts has descended to the level of trivial rubbish or profound incoherence.

For works of art to hold a special place or places in the economy of our shared understanding of human intentions, it is not necessary that they should be united by a common practice or set of practices. It would be enough if they were united by an unmistakable common aspiration or function or other irreducible factor in what is necessary to make human life meaningful. But we would then have to know which factor to fasten on, and its identification would not likely be possible (the history of thought shows indeed that it is not possible) without a unified practice to guide our attention. We did have to recognize, however, that the concepts of an art and of a fine art, even if essential, were not enough to articulate our theorizing about art. Reflection on what a fine art would have to be sufficed to force us to introduce the general concept of art, not in its ancient sense of the method of organizing thought for production, but in its distinctively modern sense of a pure creativity, creation not disciplined but spontaneously achieving an effect as of discipline, one of the most distinctively human capacities and one that could by no means be confined to the domain of the fine arts however far that domain was extended. Next, by considering what the "effect as of discipline" must be in the context of the arts, we were forced to think of that creative spontaneity as a repeated achievement of clear and coherent vision and thus as laying an ever self-renewing foundation for language and culture, the blind forces of life becoming the fabric of mind. So we had to qualify and complicate our theoretical structure centered on the arts and their associated works by adding an alternative view of what was at stake in art, which we called the expressive line.

Nor could we stop there, for to have done so would commit us to a solipsism of the species, the assumption that for all practical and serious theoretical purposes we can proceed as if the minds of men were the only minds to be reckoned with. We can hardly rule out the possibility that this assumption is mistaken; and, if it is mistaken, we can no longer ignore the possibility that the significance of what we call art is centered, not on ourselves, but on our relations to the other mind or minds in the world. The possibility is forced on our attention by the plausibility of the thesis that only an interest in such relations could have accounted for the origin of the practices we know as art, and only such an interest could justify the kind of importance we attach to the arts nowadays. Thus, we had to pursue what we called the mystic line, though that pursuit yielded little that could help rather than hinder the sober theorist. And finally we had to contend with art in crisis. If there are no gods to sustain the mystic line, and if the culture that the expressed intuitions of the expressive line were to underpin disgusts us with its corruption, and if the fine arts are taken over by bureaucrats and admen, and if whatever we freely create is at once degraded to become merchandise, then, all else having failed, the spontaneous imagination of art may become the individual's only recourse against the crass manipulations of mass society, and it may be that that is art's irreducibly essential and inalienable meaning.

Although we thus had to admit alongside our preferred way of thinking about art three others—four if the poetic line be allowed a separate identity—I insisted that these others depended for their possibility and intelligibility on the first: they were not really ways of thinking about a range of phenomena akin to but not coincident with the fine arts and their associated works, nor were they alternative ways of articulating the same field, but derived their apparent force from their being parasitic on the familiar phenomenon of art as already articulated in our classical line. Though an irreducible and indispensable part of what we nowadays find we must say and think about art, they lapse into incoherence as soon as we take them as what they purport to be, the whole truth or the essential truth about any range of phenomena or any distinct part or aspect of the human enterprise. The very concept of art not only (as we all know) arises historically out of that of the fine arts but is parasitic upon that concept or one like it: it depends on the analogies found between separate practices, practices that can be practices only because they are identifiable (and thus practicable fields of endeavor) and hence separable. That is not to say (as some have said) that the fine arts in their traditional identities are sacrosanct—that for all time poetry is poetry and dance is dance—but it is to say that the concept of art is essentially the concept of what is common (as shared significance or animating force) to a set of practices and has no inner resources of its own. The search for an independent theory of art fails, not because (as it has been fashionable to hold) the concept is an irremediably open one, nor because its logic has been misunderstood, but because it derives all the determinacy it has from that of its context of practice. Our preferred classical line offers our best hope, if not our only hope, for a down-to-earth mapping of the territory, a straightforward account of what goes on and what we are all up to, into which the other lines can then feed their chosen significances. Their job is to put the profundity in. But premature profundity is philosophy's bane.

It does not follow that the alternative lines are illegitimate or that the significances they find are unreal or unnecessary. The concept of art has indeed broken free from its links with organized practice, and the repudiation of the classical line with its fine-arts associations is not reversible. But a repudiation must remain aware of what it repudiates, and my argument has to be that the alternative lines appear viable only because the practices on which the classical line relies are so familiar that we do not need to admit to ourselves or to others that they are present to our minds at all.

Are the lines of thought deployed in this book the only ones we need, or the only ones there are, or the only ones there could be—or, at least, the only ones that matter? One could hardly prove that there could be no others. Any argument I produced to show that my scheme was comprehensive (which could only be because it was logically exhaustive) would hold only so long as we stuck to the *principium divisionis* it implied, and one sees no hope whatever of justifying any such sticking by appealing to any higher ground. I am inclined to think, however, that there are no others to be reckoned with, though I sometimes wonder if I have not used the purist line as a ragbag for an assortment of inchoate tendencies of thought any of which might one day start going somewhere.

Certainly, art can be placed in wider contexts, some of which I mentioned in my Introduction—in that of semiotics, for instance, among all the ways in which meanings can be expressed and communicated, or in that of structuralism, among the ways in which the world we live in is articulated and humanized, or in that of existence philosophy, as entering into our self-choice. But it is not art or arts or the fine arts as such that figure in these contexts; it is specific doings and makings that find themselves ranged, for the purposes of these disciplines, alongside other specific phenomena that have nothing to do with art. In these settings, if they are true to themselves, art dissolves.

The suggestion that, if semiotics and the rest are true to themselves, they do not provide a setting for art but an alternative setting for phenomena that thus newly placed are not to be considered as art at all raises a new question. How important are the concept and institutions of art? For it might be that whatever in art is important is so, not because it is art, but always because of something in it that is not art. The answer seems to be that they are not very important, and certainly not nearly so important as they have often been made out to be. What unites the fine arts, and what works of art have in common, is something, but what divides them is more.

459

Those who have been most conscious of the diversity of arts and works have often urged us not to think and speak of "art" at all, because the concept of art is not merely useless but misleading. But no reason other than the diversity in question is given for this veto, which is merely silly. One level of generality or specificity does not invalidate another. Nor does any one classification or context rule out any other. Art, certainly, is not a sort of biological family in which the fine arts are genera, art forms are species, and works individuals. The status and organization of art have no such natural priority over other organizations, and answer to no real essence. Artists and theorists alike may think of a work as *essentially* a work of art—some of the time; but the only context in which it is uniquely appropriate to think of it in that light is the context of art as such. And there is nothing to be said for the view that, for any object, that is the sole context that must override all others. When I say "painting" I do not say art: I say "painting"; and it is mere effrontery to say that in saying that I must have somehow meant "art" too.

Some aspects of the purist line suggest, if not a debunking of the concept of art, a radical revaluation of it. What matters in the world is not ideas but events, including those events that embody ideas. The modern artist as imagined or recognized by Harold Rosenberg may be seen as recognizing this: his art is what he does, and he and his works are important as objects of gossip, as entering into the story of our times. This story is the history of art that replaces the general or abstract idea of art, and is history not now seen in the Hegelian fashion we were expounding, as a developing form of thought, but simply as an interesting chronicle.[1] The events in this chronicle form part of the same story simply because we— agents, reporters, and public alike—have decided to treat them so. What the artists and critics involved have decided to do is precisely to become part of that story: it is not a role they have assumed, a part they are acting out, but a social transaction in which they will be seen to participate.[2] Art, then, we say, looking back, is in itself nothing: the history of art is constituted only by certain people and their doings that make a good story together. And what makes a good story may be a matter of theme, imagery, believable characters, strong incidents, ingenious plot, or mere picaresque whimsy.[3]

The skepticism of the last paragraph is somewhat extreme, not to say paradoxical. But it is hard to find solid reasons for rejecting it. No one has yet worked out the ground rules for dealing with such concepts as art or for dealing with the kind of discourse that the philosophy of art represents—or rather, no body of collective wisdom has been established, and philosophers generally are at sea. Weitz (1956), for instance, wrote as though the only alternative to "Platonism" (that is, the notion that we can only make mutually comprehensible sense when we talk about art if the term "art" is definable) is a particularism entailing that any such term covers an open-ended range of phenomena loosely joined by sharing in a pool of "features" to which items may be added from time to time. But surely this is quite mistaken. In conversational practice, as Wittgenstein's use of his own concept of a language game hinted, it is rather the case that the meaning of such terms is unstable, not because it changes with time, but because it changes from context to context. It is characteristic of the gestural use of language, which I sketched in my Introduction, that consistency and intelligibility are preserved because we understand each other—we respond to the ways in which the meanings of terms are governed by the needs of the point presently at issue. Our terminology has a kind of plastic generality that we all control in practice but no one has aptly captured in theory.

Those philosophers who concern themselves with such matters have a general grasp of how this vagueness and lability of meaning affects our use of words like "red": such words are used as if we said "redder than somewhat" or "less unred than most of the things around here," so that the precise point of calling something red varies from context to context, and on any particular occasion is precisely clear only if the full context has made it so.[4] Weitz and others appear to suppose that "art" functions like "red" (though the analogy they overtly rely on is with the word "game," which Wittgenstein is supposed to have used). But the analogy does not work, because with art we have to do with a *Lebensform*, a form of life, and an associated set of practices, so that the use of the word "art" is connected with the strategies we use to conduct our lives. That is why Collingwood was right to say that the relevant question is not what we mean by the word but what we are trying to mean. Some of the relevant considerations I have dealt with elsewhere (Sparshott 1975a and 1975b), suggesting that our reflective use of such terms as "art" and "philosophy" is partly historical and partly deliberative, as we seek to understand where we are by how we got here and where we can get to from here.

Elsewhere in this book I have said something about the ways in which such talk, and the tacit agreements our talk invokes, fluctuate. I must now repeat that to seek to impose consistency or precision upon such talk, or to demand precision of it, would be lunacy. What possible purpose could be served by a clear and precise answer to such questions as have been discussed in this book? The irreverent might answer that he knew of none, but that if any purpose were served by a vague and equivocal answer, a clear and precise one would have served that purpose better. But I doubt if that is true. Probably the best way to handle such questions is to talk loosely about them until we feel at home in the area, confident that we will not lose ourselves and will not be taken by surprise or put at a disadvantage up some intellectual blind alley by any rogue phenomenon.

In everyday talk, then, the word "art" has an elusiveness of meaning that is not quite that ascribed to it in Weitz's classic discussion of "open concepts," and which tends to assume a definite character of its own insofar as it is animated by theoretical concern or programmatic animus. A theorist, even a theorist of theories like me, cannot (otherwise than on suitable and suitably limited occasion) permit himself such slipperiness, which in a theorist amounts to evasion; though he must be most scrupulous to respect the slipperiness of others. But considerations like those I have been touching on may help to explain what seems to me a curious fact about theories of art. The books propounding those theories are often extremely precise, incisive, and devastating in their criticisms of rival theories and in their accounts of what art is not and aesthetics should not be. But their positive statements of their central tenets are often vague, inexplicit, allusive, reticent, even coy. It is, I think, this almost universal incompleteness and inexplicitness on the crucial issues that makes students mutter about the "wasteland of aesthetics." The explanation is not far to seek. It is that in any transaction with art, creative, critical, or appreciative, total cultural engagement is strictly required. It is not that (as is sometimes said) in aesthetics one has to start by considering great masterpieces rather than simpler and humbler doings; it is that in even the simplest engagements with art we allow no holding back.[5] The full complexities of complicity and understanding are already involved.[6] Just as, in Isenberg's classical argument (1949), a critic's statements and arguments are likely to be unintelligible in themselves because they rely on the reader's willingness and ability to flesh out their meaning from his knowledge of what in the criticized work is too densely textured to be relevantly captured in any finite discourse, so the aesthetic theorist may rely on his reader's intimate knowledge of the way reason is engaged with art, the familiar dynamics of which cannot be captured in a slogan. It is not that he is purporting to say the unsayable; it is that he is, as a matter of obvious necessity, relying on his reader to understand what is said by understanding what it is said about. This is not to say that aestheticians may not be confused or culpably imprecise, for they often are; it is to say that many of those who incautiously accuse them of such faults thereby reveal their own inexperience, stupidity, and lack of logical finesse.

In teaching elementary courses in aesthetics to philosophically naive undergraduates, I have sometimes followed the practice of confronting them from time to time with equivocal objects and inviting them to say whether, in their opinion, the object in question was a work of art; and if so, why they thought so, and if not, why not. To the instructor it was very obvious that the kinds of distinctions made between what was a work of art and what was not, the kinds of considerations invoked, varied with the type of object presented. Different things raised different issues, though all the issues could be and were comfortably debated under the heading "Is this a work of art or not?" Yet no student has ever pointed out that this was happening, that quite different sorts of things had been said last week. On the contrary, many students voiced the expectation that the various discussions would somehow sum up to a single definitive answer to the question "What is a work of art?" asked without other context than, for instance, an examination paper might provide. One might then reasonably ask, Should this tendency to use the expression "work of art" in different ways in different contexts be resisted in the name of consistency and intellectual integrity, or should it be acknowledged in such a way that we always hedge our words and thoughts with such provisos as "for purposes of the present discussion" or "if one means by 'work of art' the following"? Except for classroom purposes, neither seems appropriate; the students' instincts did not mislead them. Every such distinction takes its force from its preemptiveness, from its being the only thing that matters just now. Tomorrow, something else will be at stake, and we will do tomorrow's thinking when tomorrow comes.

The Protagorean relativism of the last few sentences invites the standard refutation that tomorrow's thinking may contradict it. But it will, I hope, be evident that my statement of the position was such as to incorporate a rebuttal of that standard refutation. All I have upheld is the propriety in suitable contexts of unequivocal affirmations couched in terms that might in other circumstances have been used for different purposes in quite different senses.

What holds for everyday talk, and for the relatively naive exercises of my hapless students, holds also for the formal proposals of professed theorists. As Weitz himself was at pains to emphasize, to claim for some resounding statement about the nature of art that it will answer all questions anyone might ask about art, and that the word "art" should henceforth be used only in the way that statement implies, is no doubt a piece of foolishness; but it by no means follows that to make such a statement unequivocally, without any second-order claims about the scope of its applicability, is equally foolish. Nor does it follow that the context of "context-free" theorizing, to which the present discussion belongs, is an illegitimate one. The thesis, all too familiar from the philosophizing of the last quarter of a century, that to propose a "general theory of art" is the act of an imbecile can thus be conceded, but its sting drawn.

What this book has put forward is not itself such a general theory of art but a theory of theories, a metatheory. But, as such, it makes as arrogant and preemptive a claim as any of the theories that fall within its scope. It claims that anyone who wants to think about art in the most general terms, and to find a pattern of thought in which whatever anyone intelligibly says when theorizing about art will find a determinate and appropriate place (or, if he is confused, a set of places), will find the considerations marshaled here helpful in respects in which other ways of talking and thinking will hinder. And it claims further that this way of marshaling them is the one best way. What it provides is a map on which monuments, places, and routes are shown; it does not seek to direct traffic. But, conformably to the foregoing argument, it is a definite map, and carries with it the cartographer's claim that it will guide where others misguide, will help you to your journey's end rather than up the creek. It is compiled in the secret knowledge that there could be other maps. Within that knowledge is concealed the faith that there are none.

APPENDIXES

APPENDIX A

AESTHETIC THIS AND AESTHETIC THAT

I said in the text that the word "aesthetic" most commonly occurs in set phrases: "aesthetic judgment," "aesthetic perception," and the like. Its meaning varies somewhat from one of these phrases to another, and most of the phrases themselves are equivocal. There is indeed, or should be, a maximally extensive and innocuous use for all. The term "aesthetic" marks out a large and vague domain, covering (roughly) whatever pertains to art, the beautiful, and human dispositions and responses akin to those typical of responses to art, the beautiful, or the like. The extreme shadowiness of this domain at its margins does not render it a source of ambiguity: one can use the word "aesthetic" as a gesture in that general direction without being misunderstood. If the word were always used in that vague and unrestrictive way, there would be less trouble than there is. But even that use by itself harbors one problem. Such a phrase as "aesthetic engineering" (to use a phrase that is not, to my knowledge, current) might still mean either "engineering as found in, or pertaining to, the domain of the aesthetic," or it might mean "engineering as *characteristic of*" that domain. And these are very different: the former is neutral, implying only that there is or might be some engineering that has something to do with that domain; but the latter carries the very strong and tendentious implication that there is some distinctive kind or application of engineering that has to do with that domain. In fact, the currency of a set phrase of the form "aesthetic engineering" is almost conclusive evidence that those who habitually use it agree that aesthetic engineering (or whatever) is a special and interesting sort of engineering. Thus, the use of such a phrase virtually testifies to the conviction (or, in careless thinkers, the assumption, or, in idle talkers, the unwitting admission) that there is a sort of engineering, characteristically related to the aesthetic domain, that has a distinctive character of its own. Then, as I said in the main text, we may use the phrase either to *mean* engineering having that character (it being supposed as a contingent *fact* that such engineering is uniquely relevant to the aesthetic) or to *mean* engineering characteristic of the domain (it being acknowledged as a contingent *fact* that such engineering has the specific characteristics we assign it)—and, since our use of the phrase indicates that we find it perfectly obvious that only that sort of engineering could possibly be specific to the domain, it is highly unlikely that we know or could easily decide which we mean, or which we would start to mean if forced to a decision.

Phrases like "aesthetic engineering" become ambiguous, rather than vague and slippery, in the first instance because the domain of the aesthetic has two main provinces: art and beauty—or "sensory contemplation" or whatever. Such phrases are sometimes used with specific reference to art, sometimes with specific reference to sensory contemplation and its appropriate objects: only attention to the actual uses of the specific phrases can establish which. In addition, these set phrases are often, perhaps most often, used with specific meanings that are well understood by their users: those among whom the phrase is current will know, for instance, that "aesthetic engineering" refers to a plan developed at Unterlaken in the 1920s for imposing a single module on street furniture, cigarette cartons, and primary-school textbooks in order to reduce alienation in the urban environment. And it may or may not (in the present case, obviously not) be insinuated that this is *also* a kind of engineering specially appropriate to one or the other province of the domain.

To track down all the recognizably current phrases of the same form as "aesthetic engineering," and to catalog all their discernible ambiguities, would require an encyclopedia. All we need to do here is choose a handful of the best-known phrases and list some of their most notorious uses. What follows is a mere sketch, claiming no scholarly or philosophical distinction, but merely illustrating what I take to be a general truth.

For each of the phrases that follow, the senses distinguished will be numbered according to a single scheme. Uses in which the word "aesthetic" means something like "pertaining to sensory contemplation and its objects" will be designated by the number 1, and if there is more than one such sense, they will be designated as 1a, 1b . . . 1z; senses in which "aesthetic" takes a meaning akin to "pertaining to art" will be designated by the number 2, and if necessary 2a, 2b . . . 2z; senses in which the word "aesthetic" means something specific within the general domain will be designated by the number 3, and if necessary 3a, 3b . . . 3z. Senses or classes of senses, if such there be, that fall outside these categories will be designated by capital letters A, B . . . Z.

The Aesthetic Attitude

The phrase "the aesthetic attitude" is perhaps the commonest of those in which the word "aesthetic" is used, no doubt because the facts that lead people to say that "anything whatever can be an aesthetic object" are most easily met by saying that what makes a situation aesthetic is the frame of mind in which one selects objects for attention and attends to them.[1] The phrase can mean (1a) that attitude to things in which they are subjected to sensory contemplation, that is, looked at or listened to (etc.) attentively and without regard to immediate practical purpose; it may also mean (1b) the attitude in which things are thought of as appropriately subjected to such contemplation. The former of these is an attitude supposedly taken by a contemplator in his contemplating; the latter is rather an attitude toward contemplation itself, and bespeaks a strategy of making the world an object for contemplation. One may then wonder whether "attitude" means quite the same in 1a as it does in 1b. It is hard to say, because the word "attitude" is extraordinarily vague, and one often does not even know whether it is an epistemological term or a psychological one.

"Aesthetic attitude" may also mean (2a) that attitude taken to works of fine art or art objects in which they are regarded as works of art and not in any other capacity (such as that of an article of commerce); or (2b) that attitude, whatever it may be, which is commonly taken (or commonly taken in our society or in the relevant circles thereof) to works of art, whether it ought to be or not; or (2c) the attitude that ought to be taken to works of art, whether it actually is or not. It seems doubtful, and has often been doubted, whether 2b exists and whether 2c can be identified. One might well think, however, that 2a must exist, if the distinction between what is and what is not a work of art can be made in any systematic way. But that proviso need not be granted; and, if it is, one might still argue that "attitude" is not the appropriate term, that to regard something as a work of art is not a matter of attitude at all. Once again, the vagueness of the term "attitude" makes the question undecidable otherwise than in a specific context.

Two special senses of the phrase "aesthetic attitude" are current. One of these (3a) takes the aesthetic attitude to be one of disinterestedness in contemplation. The term "disinterestedness," which is all that distinguishes 3a from 1a, may be thought nugatory, but it is often thought to stand for a recognizable psychical characteristic of certain perceptual attitudes.[2] It is notoriously difficult, however, to say what the disinterestedness in question amounts to. If it is meant that the contemplation yields no satisfaction or is uninterested, one wants to reply that this is incompatible with taking any interest in the object and hence with finding it beautiful, so that the epithet "aesthetic" seems misapplied; but if all that is meant is that in contemplating one is not thinking of gain or advantage, then virtually all contemplation will be disinterested. Yet the notion of disinterested contemplation as the aesthetic attitude remains popular among older writers.[3]

Even more popular until recently, and perhaps the most popular of all candidates for the title "aesthetic attitude," is (3b) an attitude that maintains "psychical distance." Much effort has been given to elaborating descriptions of this sort of attitude since Edward Bullough identified and christened it in 1912. The general idea seems to be that one is neither uninterested in the phenomenon in question nor involved with it as agent or patient would be, but rather directs to it or derives from it a cognitive excitement, a surrogate emotion somehow disconnected from practical concerns. It is then maintained that such an attitude is common to, and to some degree explanatory of, our delighting in such dangerous experiences as storms, our following the actions of stage plays without wanting to interrupt the action, and our enjoyment of works of art and beauty generally.[4]

Aside from the question whether Bullough's account is intelligible, critics doubt that all the cases he cites are cases of the same attitude or sort of attitude, and a fortiori whether he and those who seek to qualify or amplify his account are all talking about the same thing, and hence whether such accounts can be usefully compared with each other.[5] If this doubt could be cleared up, other objections would remain. First, it is not clear that what is described is a sort of attitude rather than an aspect of various attitudes whose differences might be for all relevant purposes more important than their likenesses. Once again, the obscurity of the term "attitude" makes such questions hard to settle. Second, assuming that there is indeed such an attitude, it is objected that there is no evidence that all qualified observers detect such an attitude in themselves, and some who are to all appearance qualified certainly disclaim it. If some noted critic or aesthete denies that he ever "distances" works in the relevant way, are we to call him a liar, or should we impugn his credentials as an appreciator of art? And, third, even if all qualified observers did detect this attitude in themselves (or sincerely avowed it), could it be a *necessary* truth that such an attitude always accompanied the skill in discrimination and discernment in discourse that are the more direct and more clearly relevant mark of the qualified observer? And, even if it were, why should it be the less relevant "psychical distance" that is honored with the name "aesthetic attitude," thus insinuating that it is a person's mental set, rather than his capacities, that counts in matters of art? Moved by such considerations, some critics argue that one should either give up the phrase "aesthetic attitude" altogether or construe it in some way within the scope of the first two groups of senses.[6]

The objections sketched above are powerful, but in the last resort what they tell against is not the attempt to provide a phenomenology of the aesthetic attitude on the lines in question but rather the claim that any attitude can play a strategic role in aesthetic theory—and especially the supposition that calling an attitude "the aesthetic attitude" constitutes any sort of argument for its significance.

In general, the objections leveled against the notion of the aesthetic attitude being one of psychical distance can be brought with appropriate changes against other special uses of phrases of the form "aesthetic *x*." We will not burden our account with repetitions of them. Let it be understood once for all that such uses tend to be open to objections of this sort, which any reader can readily formulate.[7]

Aesthetic Pleasure

The concept of an attitude, like that of a skill, seems indeterminately epistemological or psychological. In adopting an attitude to something, I am deciding how to think as well as feel about it; I am assuming a system of interpretation, not merely registering a complex of feeling. The phrases we have to deal with next fall into a psychological group (pleasure, experience, emotion) and an epistemological group. The epistemological items (perception, quality, object) are distinct but interconnected: each may be defined in terms of the others. But the psychological phrases tend to be used loosely as roughly equivalent to each other or, if used with greater precision, to be tied in meaning to the specific theories of those who use them. This difference arises because the epistemological terms are typically used to clarify (or to obfuscate) the actual subject matter of aesthetics or the philosophy of art; the psychological phrases are more often used in the extraphilosophical justification of accounts of their phenomena. Thus, although great complexities arise, they arise outside the specific area of our concern, in the domain of general psychological or phenomenological speculation or within the specific contexts of a special theory. So we can keep our accounts short.

The concept of aesthetic pleasure is susceptible of great elaboration. There could be a sense of the phrase meaning "delight *taken in*" any specified range of artistic or aesthetic object or activity, and a sense meaning "pleasurable feeling tone *occasioned by*" any such range. We would thus have distinguished an intensional from a causative set of senses. And we could add a set of senses answering to *voluptuous reveling in* each of them, and one answering to a *keenly heightened awareness of* each. But to elaborate such an account would be to write a general treatise on the concept of pleasure and kindred concepts, juxtaposed to an articulation of the range of aesthetic and artistic phenomena to which it would remain purely external. All we need to say here is that, in addition to the range of ambiguities that the word "pleasure" carries everywhere it goes, the phrase "aesthetic pleasure" has its expected ambiguity: it sometimes means (1) enjoyment of sensory contemplation and sometimes (2) delight in works of art. I use the phrases "enjoyment of" and "delight in" to indicate that emphasis shifts slightly toward the objective as we move from one region to the other.

"Aesthetic pleasure" has one special sense, given to it by Santayana. He defines it as "objectified self-enjoyment." There is, he claims, a state of mind in which people interpret as a quality of objects what is really only a reaction in themselves; this state of mind is to be called "aesthetic pleasure"; beauty is the name of the phantom quality thus imputed; and works of art are beautiful artifacts (1896, 37ff.). The objections leveled against the notion of psychical distance as the aesthetic attitude seem eminently applicable to Santayana's construction.

Aesthetic Experience

The term "experience" has a clear common meaning as what distinguishes an experienced per·on from a novice or tyro; but that is not what "aesthetic experience" ever means. Aside from that irrelevant use, the concept of experience is a mass of question-begging confusions. For one thing, the term runs together the different and unclear notions of life-as-one-lives-it and of the-world-as-it-comes-to-one; for another, it tends to enshrine one or another form of the dogmatic reductions of empiricism, whereby life is drained of activity and reduced to a series of awarenesses. These confusions slop over into the phrase "aesthetic experience," where they are augmented by ambiguities and muddles indigenous to the context. Some of the resulting complexities I have dealt with elsewhere (Sparshott 1976a). For present purposes, a rough tentative grouping of the main senses in which the phrase is used will suffice.

First, and least important, since *aisthesis* is the Greek for sense experience and empiricism reduces all experience to sense experience and its simulacra, "aesthetic experience" can be used almost pleonastically (A) for experience as understood by empiricism when attention is paid to its inward and passive aspect. Second, and more important, the same considerations lead to the phrase being used (B) as an equivalent of "aesthetic perception" in any of its senses. Third, "experience" is used as the typical collective term from "experiences" (in the same way that "art" is the collective from "arts"), meaning something like "the inner aspect of episodes": whatever happens to a person seen as an episode in that person's private biography as opposed to public history. For instance, my experience of or in a hurricane is what happened in the hurricane, or what happened to me in the hurricane, from my point of view alone: not that I kept falling, but that I *could not* keep upright. Thus, aesthetic experience may be (C) the inner aspect of experiences involving (C1) sensory contemplation or (C2) works of art. And sometimes, though not usually, an artist's "aesthetic experience" is taken to be (C3) that part of his life which has been taken up into his artistic production. Fourth, "experience" is used as a collective for a special sort of experiences as thus conceived, namely ecstasies, so that "aesthetic experience" may mean (D) ecstasies occasioned by (D1) sensory contemplation or (D2) works of art.[8] Note that I write "occasioned by," indicating that the link between the ecstasy and its correlate is thought of as external and causal: the word "experience" always carries strong suggestions of subjectivity and passivity, which in this context become stronger.

Finally, we must add a catchall. The phrase "aesthetic experience" may be used specifically to designate some special sort of inner happening triggered by sensory contemplation or by works of art.[9]

Some of these phenomena are as commonly, or more commonly, called aesthetic emotion; others include such special manifestations as A. E. Housman's goose bumps (Housman 1933) or Miss Anstruther-Thompson's asthma (Lee 1911). Nothing is to be gained by plunging into that jungle.

It will be evident from the foregoing discussion that looking at a picture in an art gallery (or at a sunset) is, for some authors, invariably and necessarily an aesthetic experience; for others, only if you notice its aesthetic qualities; for others, only if you appreciate it; for others, only if it excites or inspires you; for others again, only if it has this or that specific effect on you.

Aesthetic Emotion

The concept of aesthetic emotion has been called on to do a lot of heavy work in aesthetic theory. On the ground that art is a matter for contemplation rather than argument, it has been supposed that art must achieve its effect by arousing emotion rather than challenging understanding, so that the question what emotions are aroused and how becomes a crucial one for many kinds of theory.[10] If art is primarily a matter of arousing emotions, it must be distinguished either by the kind of emotions aroused or by the way it arouses them. Thus, "aesthetic emotion" may mean either (2a) characteristic emotions aroused by works of art or (2b) emotions of an ordinary sort occurring in a way characteristic of the context of art. And, corresponding to these, we have also (1a) characteristic emotions specific to sensory contemplation and (1b) ordinary emotions occurring in a special way characteristic of sensory contemplation.

The foregoing is grossly oversimplified, because it assumes that "emotion" has a clear meaning to begin with. But in fact the term is even fuller of ambiguities than "experience" was, having been one of the chief victims of theory mongering in the speculative childhood of psychology. The ambiguities are of two sorts. The first arises from effecting divisions in various places and on various principles between thought and feeling; the other arises from splitting up the territory along various lines and on various principles among such terms as "emotion," "feeling," "passion," and "mood." It would be unprofitable to discuss those issues here.

Because "aesthetic emotion" is the kind of term people build into the foundations of their theories, the third set of senses is well populated and consists of a set of opinions, issuing in definitions, about sorts of emotions deemed important enough in themselves to motivate the entire domain of the aesthetic. Here are five of them. First, "aesthetic emotion" may be used (3a) as synonymous with "aesthetic experience" in sense D (especially D2), as a special sort of ecstasy—the "oceanic feeling" is a favorite. Second, a variant of 2b with some admixture of 3a, aesthetic emotion has been (3b) identified with an especially pure emotion supposedly aroused by "significant form," which is the sum of those nonrepresentational properties of just those works of art that do arouse it (the circularity of this theory is notorious).[11] Third, aesthetic emotion may be (3c) identified with a clarified complex of thought and feeling answering to the reconstitution of an intuition—or whatever holds an analogous place in some other version of the expressive line. In this case, it is especially obvious that to accept the definition is to assent to a complex theory with profound epistemological, and probably metaphysical, implications.[12] Fourth, aesthetic emotion may be (3d) equated with empathy, the alleged state of mind in which one feels in one's body a complex of inchoate movements answering to formal properties of what one perceives, and then attributes these movements together with the associated feelings to the perceived object itself.[13] And fifth, aesthetic emotion may be (3e) identified with synesthesia, a postulated state of mind in which a complex of psychological causes, involving the whole of one's sensory apparatus, combine in producing a single harmonious feeling tone.[14]

It is evident that most of the five senses in our third set have at least the appearance of postulating the occurrence of certain events in the perceiver, and thus of being empirical hypotheses that can be falsified. But perhaps they should be taken as saying no more than that, in the typical transaction of a qualified observer with an adequate object to which he feelingly responds, the emotional side of the transaction proceeds as if feelings occurred such as the account stipulates.[15] But in any case these special senses raise in a very urgent way one of the questions mooted in connection with the phrase "aesthetic attitude." Are all the writers who describe these complex states and events and postulate their occurrence giving rival descriptions of what can be independently identified as a single phenomenon? Or are they rather giving alternative explanations of a single identifiable phenomenon, to a single common description of which they might be got to agree? Or are they describing and explaining different sorts of phenomena, all of which are equally real and enter into experiences of art and beauty in different fashions, to different extents, on different occasions? Or are they postulating different phenomena, some of which might be chimerical, but any one of which, if it did occur, would have an indisputable claim to enter into the description of any authentic transaction with art or beauty? Or are they postulating different phenomena, some perhaps chimerical and others misdescribed, of which even those that do occur and are correctly described might or might not be causally necessary to some other important features of the experience, and might or might not be a logically necessary condition of the experience's being one of sensory contemplation or one of a work of art as such? Or what? The possibilities are endless. It is seldom clear which of such claims an author wishes to make, much less which of such claims is inherently the most plausible. Accordingly, use of the phrase "aesthetic emotion" is a quite reliable sign of philosophical naiveté.

Aesthetic Perception

Since the Greek word *aisthesis* can mean "perception," one might expect the phrase "aesthetic perception" to be pleonastic. But pleonasm can be emphatic, and in fact the first meaning of the phrase is (1) the perception characteristic of sensory contemplation—attentive and enjoying perception, perception that dwells on what is perceived and is not incidental to a practical purpose. This might be thought of as perception having to an eminent degree the character of perception (perception *kat'exochên*; perception in spades, doubled). But it may also be thought of as perception notable, not for its properties (all perception is perception equally, it is argued), but for its aim and circumstances: perception in the aesthetic attitude, in fact.[16] One might then expect to find a duality of senses like that of "aesthetic attitude," between perception actually in the service of sensory contemplation and perception appropriate to such contemplation, between perception that might or might not discern the relevant features of an aesthetic object and perception that was called aesthetic because it succeeded in doing so. In fact, however, no one uses "aesthetic perception" for a scrutiny that fails to discern its target and the appropriate features thereof: "perception" is what the Oxford analysts used to call an achievement word, whereas "attitude" is not. On the other hand, this split between two senses does seem to occur in the second family of senses: "aesthetic perception" may mean (2a) the perception of art objects or works of art as such or (2b) the perception of the relevant features of art objects or works of art. The implication would be that (2a) to become aware of a work of art as such, in its characteristic organization, we must and do see it in a special way, becoming aware of qualities and relations of which we remain unaware when looking at (or listening to, etc.) things of other kinds; or it might be that (2b) when looking at (or listening to, etc.) a work of art, we should, to get the best out of it, sensitize ourselves in some special fashion. The details are filled in in various ways, in both versions.[17]

Meanings of the third kind make "aesthetic perception" designate one or another variety of perception that isolates or reveals objects or qualities held to be of special importance to the understanding of art or the enjoyment of beauty. Most basic of these is (3a) that perception which ignores content, substance, reference, iconography, and such and sees only form. What the word "form" includes varies from theory to theory.[18] More specifically, the phrase is used for (3b) the perception of *Gestalten*, a perception that edits what it sees into meaningful wholes. To these we should add the sense given to the phrase by Virgil Aldrich (1963), a sense that he illustrates rather than defines: it is (3c) perception correlated with an aesthetic rather than a physical object, one in which one is not concerned with what is really there, but one manipulates one's perceptual machinery to obtain pleasing or striking sensory effects. Whatever exactly Aldrich means, it is something strikingly different from 3a and 3b. *Gestalt* vision is part of the automatism of perception, whereas Aldrich's ways of seeing are generated by deliberate ways of looking, and while what these ways of looking reveal are in some sense "form," they are not the forms correlated to something else that would be called the content (etc.) of the same object.

I note in conclusion that one well-known textbook by an erudite author appears to use "aesthetic perception," "aesthetic attitude," and "aesthetic experience" as synonyms, substituting one for another without notice (Stolnitz 1959). Such laxity may be excusable when the phrases are on the margin of one's immediate topic (readers will have noted that I do not maintain precision in my use of "art object" and related terms, where precision would require either a string of alternatives or an umbrella term stipulated ad hoc), but not when, as here, their referents are the very subject of discussion. Someone who cannot or will not differentiate between perceptions, attitudes, and experiences is not likely to have anything very interesting to say about any of them.

Aesthetic Qualities

The Greek derivation of "aesthetic" might lead one to expect "aesthetic qualities" to be perceptible qualities, perhaps qualities available only to perception—what are usually called secondary qualities. But this usage is not found. Instead, our first sense is that whereby "aesthetic qualities" are (1a) peculiarly suited to sensory contemplation, that is, can enter into, and be perceived to enter into, and contribute to complex orders and formal arrangements (cf. Prall 1936). There are two significant variants. The notes of suitability and contribution that figure in 1a may be so interpreted that (1b) aesthetic qualities are those that contribute to aesthetic excellence and are by definition good-making characteristics.[19] And (1c) the qualification of "sensory" may be dropped, as it may less often be in the corresponding sense of "aesthetic attitude" and may never be in "aesthetic perception."

The second sense of "aesthetic quality" answers to that of "aesthetic perception," and approximates to (2) "the qualities of works of art as such." We do not find a bifurcation corresponding to the one we found there, which would differentiate between qualities that are ascribed to works of art and qualities that ought to be ascribed to them: the implication of the language of "qualities" is that a thing has them, ascribed or not. But the bifurcation appears in a different guise, between (2a) qualities that works of art do have and (2b) qualities they ought to have (a sense corresponding to 1b). We may also differentiate (2c) qualities the possession of which is always relevant to a thing's being a work of art, in that they are necessary or sufficient conditions of its having that status,[20] from (2d) qualities that a work of art may or may not have, but which may be relevant to its characterization as being just the kind of work it is. No one, of course, uses the phrase to mean "qualities that a work of art has" in the sense that they are qualities of something that is also a work of art, but which are irrelevant to its being one or to its being the kind of work it is. That would be a sort of bad joke, like using "aesthetic perception" to mean something like "seeing or hearing something that is also incidentally a work of art"—although some writers use the phrase "aesthetic experience" in a way that comes perilously close to that absurdity.

Senses of the third sort are many. The senses 3a to 3c are provided by the correlates of the correspondingly numbered senses of "aesthetic perception": formal qualities, *Gestalt* qualities, and whatever qualities Aldrich's percepts have. The phrase is also sometimes used to pick out (3d) the qualities that make up what may be termed the panaesthetic vocabulary, terms that may be meaningfully used of works of any art, such as "balance," "symmetry," "rhythm," "expressiveness," "coherence." The reason for using the phrase in this restricted sense is that such terms seem peculiarly significant for aesthetic theory: the fact that they apply to works of all arts itself suggests a certain unity of the aesthetic domain, to establish which has often been thought an important preliminary task for aesthetics. But others tend to use the phrase for (3e) qualities picked out by the specialized terminology of the fine arts, such as "impasted," "rubato," "ballon," or "euphuistic." This use of the phrase is programmatic, usually evidencing the conviction that such terms as those enumerated under 3d can only be meaningfully used of one art.[21] If used of another art, they are used metaphorically, and if used of more than one art without evident metaphor, they are equivocal; their status as the special vocabulary of the theory of the arts is then taken over by these more special terms. There is, finally, some tendency to use the expression "aesthetic qualities" when one means (3f) those value qualities deemed especially appropriate to works of art, and perhaps to other aesthetic objects as well. These qualities differ from those picked out by 1b and 2b in that some of them denominate special virtues (or vices): as well as "fine" and "beautiful" (which in fact do usually denominate special qualities, but whose status in this regard is somewhat ambivalent), we have terms like "sublime," "masterly," "obscene," and "well made."

Aesthetic Object

With the phrase "aesthetic object" the ambiguities get quite out of hand. There are two reasons for this. The first is that anything can be contemplated, and any perceptible thing can be an object for sensory contemplation. This complicates our first set of senses, because different thinkers differ in the kind and degree of initial suitability they demand of anything they are prepared to call an aesthetic object and in the amount and kind of relativism, subjectivism, and occasionalism they admit. The second reason is that contemplation as such regards appearances and not realities. This complicates the third set of senses, because it means that aesthetic objects are more properly thought of as constructs from qualities than as selected substances, and different thinkers differ widely in what they think about constructs and their construction.

The first thing that may be meant by "an aesthetic object," then, is (1a) anything that may be an object of sensory contemplation, when considered from the point of view of that potentiality—the proviso is necessary, because otherwise the phrase designates all perceptibles. But more often it means (1b) anything that lends itself to, is a fit object for, sensory contemplation (whether because it rewards such contemplation, or because it is contextually or otherwise marked out for such attention). And very often it means (1c) what is actually so contemplated—either in general or on a particular occasion.[22]

By happy contrast, the second set of senses has only one member. Some people (e.g. Beardsley 1958) use the phrase "aesthetic object" to mean (2) "work of art." This rather odd restriction is part of the campaign to equate aesthetics with the philosophy of criticism, and often goes with the dogma that things other than works of art are found to be beautiful or aesthetically interesting only insofar as they resemble works of art or exploit responses that have become habitual in relation to such works. The simplicity this restriction introduces is more than made up for by the plethora of senses in the third category. Numerous as they are, however, they can be succinctly described. First, (3a . . . f) the phrase "aesthetic object" may be used to designate objects insofar as they possess aesthetic qualities in the senses bearing the corresponding number. Second, (3g . . . k) it may be used to designate objects not merely possessing but constituted by aesthetic qualities in any of the senses numbered 3a to 3e. This set of senses arises because, since anything can be an aesthetic object in sense 1a, there are powerful reasons for using the phrase to mean a congeries of relevant qualities rather than a thing—that is, for using "object" as correlative of "subject" rather than as synonymous with "substance"; but, on the other hand, the less careful and painstaking thinking of most of us has such strong reifying tendencies that even those who theoretically eschew the "substance" interpretation of objects tend to slip into it from time to time, and many people opt for it despite its difficulties. In this last set of senses, there is nothing to correspond to "aesthetic qualities" in sense 3f. It makes no sense to speak of objects as *constituted by* beauty, sublimity, and the like: these, if qualities at all, are tertiary or resultant qualities that things have only by virtue of other qualities that they have, and one would rather say that the qualities that constituted an object's beauty also by the same token constituted it an aesthetic object. What answers to the missing sense (3f) of "aesthetic quality" is (3l) that sense of "aesthetic object" in which it picks out whatever has the favorable members of "aesthetic qualities" in that sense. This sense of the phrase is very common and is sharply distinguished from all the others. In this sense, to call something an aesthetic object is to praise it, and much confusion has arisen from the failure to notice that some people use the phrase in that way and others do not.

I have just claimed that the phrase "aesthetic object" is used in at least twelve distinct senses, in addition to those that derive from the fundamental meanings of the term "aesthetic." The claim seems quite preposterous. But it is also quite true, and its truth shows that the phrase "aesthetic object" plays a peculiarly strategic role in the construction of aesthetic theories.

Aesthetic Concepts

With perceptions, qualities, and objects we were in the classical domain of elementary cognition. We now pass to a group of terms pertaining to a field of more elaborate and constructive mental operation: "concept," "judgment," "education," and "theory." Some terms are uncertainly located in these areas: "emotion," for instance, looks like a psychological term, but some thinkers give it a cognitive significance; "education" is sometimes stipulated to be a cognitive matter, but is sometimes used to cover a variety of quite unintellectual processes that produce changes in behavior deemed to be improvements either by those who cause them or by those who suffer them—and sometimes by both. The fact is that these grand strategic terms for categorizing human behavior, such as "intellectual" or "cognitive" or "affective," have no clearly established meaning and answer to no precise or intelligible distinctions, but serve as counters in obscure theoretic games: we use them rather as a token for our uneasy awareness that some distinctions and contrasts need to be made, though we have no settled way of deciding what they might be.

The term "aesthetic concepts" can be disposed of briefly, though it is one that played a leading part in aesthetic theory a few years ago. The concept of a concept parallels that of a quality, if one reflects that every predicate answers either to a concept or a complex of concepts, and vice versa, and that we have no rules for picking out predicates that are not qualities. The important differences are that the term "quality" has objectivist implications (as really being the quality of something) from which "concept" openly prescinds. The phrase "aesthetic concept" opts for the formal rather than the material mode of speech, declaring that the focus of interest is not the way the world is but the way the world is said to be and otherwise talked about. And the phrase always carries the insidious implication that in the kind of discourse to which it refers the distinctive character is imparted by the concepts, the terminology, and not by the rhetorical context.

The insidious implication just referred to is not always intended by the users of the phrase. Thus we may distinguish those who use "aesthetic concepts" to mean (1a) concepts characteristically used in, or even peculiar to, the description of sensory contemplation and its subjects and objects from those who use the phrase to mean (1b) concepts of any sort as used in such description. Correspondingly, we may distinguish those who use it to mean (2a) concepts peculiar to talk about the arts, or having their primary use in such discourse, from those who use it to mean (2b) concepts of any kind as they appear in the context of such discourse.

The phrase "aesthetic concepts" is, however, one of those so closely tied to a particular writer and a particular controversy that its use is normally a signal that one is discussing that author's topic in his own terms. In this case, the author is Frank Sibley, and the discussion stems from an article the actual title of which was "Aesthetic Concepts."[23] In the course of the debate, the phrase seems to have taken on two related but distinguishable meanings: (3a) concepts characteristically used in the description and evaluation of works of art or aesthetic objects or both, for which there are no necessary and sufficient conditions, and (3b) concepts whose correct application to works of art requires taste.

Aesthetic Judgment

The phrase "aesthetic judgment" was virtually patented by Kant. Anyone who uses it may be taken as announcing that he is discussing problems of the sort Kant raised, or is otherwise inserting himself into the philosophical heritage of the *Critique of Judgment*. In the title of that book, "judgment" translates *Urteilskraft*, the faculty of forming judgments, and it is the faculty that primarily concerns Kant; but nowadays "judgment" is almost always used in this context to translate *Urteil*, as a rough synonym of "proposition."

Outside of its Kantian context, philosophers sometimes use the word "judgment" as an exact equivalent to "proposition" and sometimes as referring only to propositions in which something is literally judged, ranked, assessed, evaluated. The basic senses of the phrase "aesthetic judgment" bifurcate accordingly. Thus, one finds the phrase used to mean sometimes (1a) any utterance in the declarative mood relating to sensory contemplation or its objects and sometimes (1b) an evaluative utterance with such reference, and similarly with (2a) declarative and (2b) evaluative utterances relating to works of art.

Among special uses of the phrase, pride of place obviously goes to (3a) the kind of judgment Kant was talking about. There is some ambiguity here, since Kant ascribed to those judgments a set of notes that one might think would not necessarily go together, so that it is unclear how much of what he says is to be counted as true by definition. Perhaps what is basic is that they are judgments typified by "That is beautiful," in which it is understood that the judgment claims universal validity, although its sole basis is a subjective feeling of pleasure.[24]

As a foil to Kant's special sense, I will just mention (3b) a use of the phrase as synonymous with "perception of beauty." This is a solecism, since whatever a judgment is it is not a perception, and perception does not suffice for judgment. Such solecisms, however, abounded in the epistemology of the seventeenth and eighteenth centuries, in which too few philosophers made a clear distinction between having an idea and asserting a proposition.[25] It was left for Santayana (1896, 37ff.) to revive this ancient incompetence and apply it to aesthetics.

For reasons connected with Santayana's solecism, the phrase "aesthetic judgment" has indefinitely many other special senses. Although a perception is not a judgment, one can usually say what one perceives, so that we would expect someone who uses "aesthetic perception" in a special sense to give a corresponding sense to the phrase "aesthetic judgment." Similarly, a writer who uses any phrase of the form "aesthetic *x*" is likely to use "aesthetic judgment" in a corresponding sense: an aesthetic judgment may be one about aesthetic qualities or about aesthetic objects or containing aesthetic concepts and so on indefinitely for any combination of such phrases in any preferred sense. It would be pointless either to enumerate the possibilities or to ascertain which are actually exemplified in any preferred corpus. The Kantian sense is the only one that has established itself.

Aesthetic Education

The concept of education has not usually been worked into general theories of cognition, and the phrase "aesthetic education" plays little part in aesthetics generally. There is, however, a *Journal of Aesthetic Education*, so the phrase has enough currency to earn a small place here. I have considered the ambiguities of the phrase at some length elsewhere (Sparshott 1968). It will be enough for present purposes to note that any phrase of the form "*x* education" is likely to be ambiguous as between education in *x*, education for *x*, and education by means of *x*: that is, training in doing *x* or whatever actions pertain to *x*, learning preparatory to undertaking *x* or the actions pertaining thereto, and training that consists of doing *x* or *x*-related actions for some ulterior end. In addition, "education in *x*" may take the form, not of training in doing *x*, but of learning about *x*: theoretical education of which *x* forms the subject matter. Learning that is merely propaedeutic to *x* but in which *x* is not actually confronted is not likely to be called "*x* education." So this multiplicity of senses in effect reduces to three: learning *x*, learning by means of *x*, and learning about *x*. Another dimension of complication is added by the contested character of the concept of education itself: some people use the term in a very restricted and value-laden sense, so that only practices that impart a critical attitude and a broad intellectual context can be counted; others extend the term to any form of indoctrination or socialization. And perhaps the commonest sense is that which extends the term to cover whatever is taught in colleges of education, the institutionalized procedures of schools.[26]

Setting aside those ambiguities that simply reflect positions taken in the quasi-political discussions just mentioned, we actually find two senses of the phrase "aesthetic education" that belong to our first set, neither of them at all common except in programmatic statements: (1a) a training in sensory contemplation, in which directed practice in that activity is supposed to help one to do it better, and (1b) education in which sensory contemplation is used as a means to whatever intellectual, spiritual, moral, or other end may be proposed for the educational process—to make the learner a better person, in short.

The second group of senses has more members, because the fine arts as a developed social institution obviously lend themselves to a variety of pedagogical ventures that may be treated as complementary or as alternatives, whereas it might not occur to anyone that anything that could be included in our first set was worth doing or even possible. The fine arts offer two avenues of approach: they may be regarded either as activities to be carried on or as activities whose products are to be appreciated; writers use "aesthetic education" without qualification to mean either of these.[27] Aesthetic education may then be (2a) training in the practices of art or (2b) training in which the practices of art are inculcated as a means to some further end such as improving dexterity, cultivating taste, or softening the manners. But the phrase may also mean (2c) learning about the practices of art without actually engaging in those practices. On the appreciative side, the phrase may mean (2d) learning to appreciate art, cultivating taste through practice in appreciating it; or (2e) learning art appreciation for some ulterior end (perhaps as a social accomplishment); or even (2f) learning about art without confronting it, as by studying the history of art, learning the jargons of criticism and expertise, and so forth. No doubt the phrase "aesthetic education" would always be used, in a conceptually cleaner world, as a blanket term to cover all of the foregoing senses, but in fact it is seldom so used.[28]

Our third set of senses has only one member. Friedrich Schiller (1795) used the German equivalent of the phrase to mean, approximately, the cultivation of the faculty of imagination to liberate men from their moral prejudices and appetitive routines. This should really fall within the scope of 1a or 1b, depending on whether one thinks of such liberation as an end in itself or as a means to moral recuperation. Schiller himself vacillates somewhat between the two interpretations. But in fact Schiller thinks of his education as essentially involving the arts, and his sense of the term, which has had some currency, cannot be effectively rendered otherwise than by "what Schiller meant by the phrase."

Aesthetic Theory

The ambiguities of the phrase "aesthetic theory" are fairly straightforward, since it is usually used as a blanket term. Some people use it to mean (1) a theory pertaining to sensory contemplation, its objects, its significance in human life, and the logic of discourse related thereto. Of these, some (1a) restrict the term to philosophical theories; others (1b) accept that the term may be extended to theories in other disciplines (notably psychology) covering the same area. Those who use the term in a more restricted way in this general area usually do so, not because they assign a restricted sense to the phrase itself, but because they accept prior restraints on the proper scope of theorizing in philosophy, psychology, or whatever. Correspondingly, other people use the phrase to mean (2a) a philosophical or (2b) any sort of theory about the fine arts, their significance in human life, and the logic of discourse related thereto.

The third set of senses has at least two significant members. Some people use "aesthetic theory" to mean (3a) "a theory about the aesthetic," one based on the concept of the aesthetic itself (cf. Aldrich 1966). In this context, "the aesthetic" is usually used as a device for marking a specific domain off from other domains, and how this is done depends on what other domains are admitted and what sort of theory is being proposed; no one such sense has achieved general currency. Alternatively, a famous controversy arises from what appears to be a stipulation by Morris Weitz (1956) that "aesthetic theory" shall mean a theory that seeks a definition that will state the necessary and sufficient conditions of art.[29] But these restricted and programmatic uses are somewhat aberrant: "aesthetic theory" is most naturally used, and generally is used, as an unrestricted term covering any sort of theory within the domain of aesthetics and the aesthetic conceived in the broadest possible way.

APPENDIX B
KINDS OF ART

I said in the main text that the most obvious way to classify works of art is by the actual fine-arts and subsidiary traditions of artistic practice to which they relate. Such a classification avoids abstraction and answers to the relation between each work and the vital context from which it issues. In so doing, it both restores the work to the life of history and reflects the actual choices open to artists in exploiting the possibilities of their medium. At the same time, we noted Lukács' protest against conceiving the divisions of the arts and their subordinate practices as *classifications*: they answer rather to *ways of doing*, and the return to the vital context of ways of life makes the concept of classification inappropriate.

Despite the strength of the position sketched above, the equation of fine-arts traditions with the historical life forms of artistic expression could be over hasty. Our second chapter already noted that the practices of arts were grouped by affinities of techniques and markets, as well as by whatever functions determine for the time being their primary standards. And it is notorious (as we have had several occasions to remark) that, in recent decades especially, the technical affinities defining the fine arts have been cut across by unities of expressive practice issuing in "mixed media" or indeterminate-medium works whose institutional affinities seem almost a matter of accident. Only those arts retain stable design traditions in which stubborn technical requirements impose the inertia of craft, as in mosaic, stained glass, and to some extent tapestry, or in which inescapable social demand sets limits, as with architecture.

Failure to cope with the instability of the traditions of fine art is the besetting weakness of all systems of the arts, such as that of Langer (1953), in which systematic significance is assigned to a body of work or practice purportedly identified with one of the fine arts. It is inconceivable that the class of works apt to fulfill the assigned function will coincide precisely with the accredited output of the recognized practitioners of a named art. The systematizer, were he scrupulous, would then be obliged to argue that, on the one hand, all works of the art in question that failed to fulfill the assigned function were merely vestigial, existing for the sake of the others or a byproduct of their making, and, on the other hand, all works of other arts that could be related to the assigned function were either disguised works of the art to which the function properly belonged or else wrongful usurpers of that function. Theorists use these expedients freely, but one would rather not have to.

To compile a plausible system of the arts, then, one would either resort to a purely external taxonomy, like that of Thomas Munro (1949),[1] or reconstruct a system of possible and actual forms and functions, like Alain (1926).[2] And what Alain produces is in essence a new vision of the social world, which I can neither reproduce nor rival.

The aim of this Appendix is neither to furnish a revised taxonomy nor to undertake an imaginary reshaping of social reality. It is merely to propose a classification of fine arts and their objects into five basic kinds, not by traditions of skill, not by design types, not by matters and forms, and not historically either, but in terms of the kinds of relation their order bears to a human being's life in the world. The classification is put forward merely as a way of thinking that may have some interest, and that has not to my knowledge been tried yet. It draws on many familiar sources and lacks the underpinning of a sociology or a metaphysic, so neither originality nor system confers on it any further merit than what may be found on its surface. But it necessarily carries with it the claim that it answers to something in human affairs that cannot be altered: that it could be worked into a phenomenology. What it presupposes is, roughly, that we are active and thinking beings; that in being active we are necessarily embodied in a world in which we act; that the world in which we act is our dwelling place; that as thinking beings the idea of the world is present to us, the world itself vicariously present as our past; and that as active and thinking beings we must project futures as possible alternative realities, so that the projection of alternative realities is familiar to us. All this sounds very much like a vulgarized extract from Sartre, who is himself said to be a vulgarizer of Heidegger. The extra vulgarity, at least, is my own.

I have called the classification one of arts, and so it is if we bear in mind that the individuation of arts is never fixed. In the first instance, it is one of acts and works; but it is perhaps most aptly to be thought of as one of practices. It is not the organization of knowledge and skill that is in question here, but (since we have to do with constant relationships between men and their world) constancies in practice, ways things are steadily done. But, for convenience, I will speak of "arts."

First we have choric arts, arts in which a person puts himself in ordered motion, alone or with others (whether alongside them or in interaction with them). These are arts of gesture, and their culmination is the organization of a ceremony, the "total work of art" embracing the community of which Wagner dreamed—I say their culmination, not their cancellation, because the solitary dancer will continue to dance for himself alone. Most forms of dance, music, song, and theater will partake largely of the nature of choric arts, though they may have other aspects too.

Next, there are scenic arts, arts in which we give order and meaning to the environment in which we live by reshaping it or by adorning it or simply by changing the way we see it or think about it (as some conceptual artists sometimes do). The environment so ordered or adorned is the natural world in the first instance, but the physical world we live in is largely shaped by farmers and engineers who had no thought for the perceptible order of the world (cf. Hoskins 1955). For purposes of this discussion the world as they have left it is nature too, and so also may be the structures of trade and commerce and political power, perceptible in their effects but in themselves objects of awareness only as intelligible presences and pressures. The arts that mostly fall within the scope of the scenic are such as architecture, town and regional planning, landscaping, gardening, and much sculpture and painting, especially such sculpture and painting as is physically or notionally fixed to a set location: the end is an ordered habitat culminating in points of focused attention, alone or in conjunction with ceremony.

Scenic and choric arts alike enhance the activities of life, by changing their quality or by changing the surroundings in which they are carried forward.

A third kind of art is the alethic. In alethic arts, instead of the environment being embellished or transformed, a reminder of another reality is substituted for it, a fragment inserted into the fabric of a life that it does not immediately change. These are arts of recapture and record; they include nostalgia pieces, landscapes and portraits, and whatever yields information that is dwelt on for its own sake. Under this head we would include revelations of being, openers of windows on the transcendent, revealers to the imagination of social or spiritual realities: whatever art is understood and appreciated as a revelation of truth or what might be truth.

489

Parallel to the alethic are the oneiric arts, arts of narrative as fancy, which are enjoyed and appreciated, not as revelations or reminders of a reality other than the present reality, but as alternatives to reality: escapist and fantasy art, the arts of "as if," surrealist and cartoon art, narrative and presentation as pure fiction.

Scenic and choric arts are both modes of ordering everyday life and ordering it around focal points, imparting significance through structure and brightness; alethic and oneiric arts enhance our lives rather by interpolating elements into the shaped or unshaped sequences of that everyday life. But that way of putting it may be misleading. The cinema as Kracauer (1960) conceives it is an alethic art; the animated film of Max Fleischer is certainly, and the surreal film of Dali or Buñuel is presumably, an oneiric art. Alethic and oneiric cinema celebrate, respectively, the weight of physical reality and the lightness of fancy. But whichever kind of film he sees, the man at the cinema is still living, living that part of his life which is going on at the time: the cinema is his real environment, and he is really imagining. So our distinction collapses, or can be made to collapse. Moreover, choric art in ritual allies itself with myth and passes over into the alethic, as one dances the original and always renewed truth; and the focal points of the scenic may well be alethic or oneiric, since nothing marks a place or occasion out for attention more than its being where one passes over into a different mode of being. Perhaps the cynosures that hold the attention most firmly have to be laden with the contemplable content of the alethic or oneiric. The effect of these alliances and transitions may be to make a work of art ambiguous in a number of ways. Consider, for instance, the frescoes of the Sistine Chapel or the mosaics of Daphni. In their content and arrangement their alethic nature is such as to define in their different ways a holy place, one oriented in the world taken by believers to be real; to the tourist they are rather nostalgia pieces, or high points in the scenic world woven by the bus routes of international tourism. Nor should we forget the common argument that art in its specialness, even the most purely scenic art of ornamentation, creates a spiritually segregated and hence sacred or quasi-sacred overlay for the perceptible world, so that all art, by drawing attention to itself in its capacity of mind-dependent beauty, imposes a new dimension of meaning on the world to which it refers and thereby becomes alethic.[3]

Under the skeptical theorist's analytical prism, everything turns into everything else, and the most significant classifications can be so juggled as to destroy their power to sort. But despite the truths that were uttered in the last paragraph, one could insist that what distinguishes the scenic and choric from the alethic and oneiric is fundamental. On the one hand, we have practices that remain within what is perceptually present, even if their status as art demands that we regard them as mere appearance and hence as "nonreal." On the other hand, we have practices that invoke and evoke an elsewhere or elsewhen, other worlds or other dimensions.[4] The former are arts deployed and enjoyed in real time and real space, the here and now of their contemplation; the latter are arts whose abode is the ideal time or imputed timelessness of contemplation, and they deploy a space that has to be otherwise structured than, or discontinuous with, the time and space of our actual lives.

A given practice need not belong definitively or exclusively to one of the four kinds we have named. Faced with this tendency of distinctions to become blurred, or at least not to coincide with differences, one line we could take is to say that indeed most art has a many-sided ambiguity, and this ambiguity is characteristic of all practical life—whatever anyone does has multiple meanings derived from the multiple roles and contexts in which we simultaneously live.[5] To take that line would be to opt for a cheerful view of life, implying that the richness or degradation of one's life is within wide limits a matter of one's choosing to be enriched or to be degraded. Another line, somewhat gloomier, would be to urge that what I have distinguished are not kinds of art but dimensions or levels, and that ideally a work of art has all these dimensions, but in our sad times can only have, or can only be taken to have, one or two of them. This is a pattern of thought that is familiar in many contexts, invoking an ideally integrated humanity in which all values are fully realized all the time (or, since one cannot effectively design buildings while water-skiing, successively within a single integrated lifetime).[6] But too devoted an attachment to this way of thinking breeds illusion. An impoverished art and a mean and monotonous life are certainly to be deplored. But the ideal of a life or a work in which all possible values are realized is not a recreation of human integrity, whether primitive or millennial; it is a neurosis of an acquisitive society, an envious intolerance of goods not one's own.

However that may be, someone inclined to preserve our two contrasted pairs of kinds of art in some other capacity than that of aspects of all art might wish to set beside them a fifth and rather special kind: the calligraphic. If he did so, he would probably assign to such arts a pivotal place, such as one understands was traditionally assigned to them in China.[7] The writing gesture that accompanies thought and word may dance out their meaning, or as it were mime a second thought around them. Dream becomes scene; record becomes environment. In the mosques of Isfahan, the pattern of tile that heads the wall freezes the calligraphic gesture in a text that relates to another environment than that which it dignifies and adorns with its intricate grace.[8]

The arts of writing are the most private of the arts, calling for little or no outlay of apparatus and in their practice scarcely visible or audible. But language is social, and the meanings articulated in it are social property. Analogously (though the analogy is faint), the calligraphic art unites the other pairs. The choric and scenic relate primarily to the life of the community or to one's life within the community: they are done in the open. The alethic and oneiric relate more essentially to the private person, who cannot be *seen* to dream or understand. That is not the less true because our private experiences may be shared and may have a public source, and because our share in a communal life must be our own private share. In the calligraphic gesture the private otherness of thought and dream becomes a public object and its trail of ink takes form and place as scene. Earlier in this Appendix, I pointed out that what we think of as nature is in part the work of farmers and engineers. In the same vein, we could regard every trace of a community's habitation as an inscription, too often a mess of scribbles and coarse graffiti, that a more harmonious life might transform into a calligraphic script in which the order of our intelligence became visible. Briefly, in the eighteenth century, the central art was that of the landscape gardener, incorporating the demesne into a vista, a metaphor for an infinite paradise.[9] Just so, the pure arabesque of a written line stands as analogue for the rational significance it embodies. And between the individual embodiments of gardener and calligrapher stands the anonymous grace of a land shaped by the ordered lives of people living together harmoniously.

The praise of calligraphy, and its elevation to the place of keystone in artistic practice, are characteristic of dilettantist societies in all ages, upper-class *Schwärmerei*. But people who insist on being hardheaded can make little sense of artistic practices. Yet one may well ask, With or without the calligraphic supplement, what is all this about anyway? The suggested division of arts neither reports nor recommends a practical method of organizing activities. It is no more than suggestive—but suggestive of what? The answer must be that the division presented is based on ways in which artistic activities fit into the ordinary ongoing lives of societies, not in relation to social and economic classes, a matter that calls for specific historical studies, but at the same prepolitical and preeconomic level at which the fundamental structures and uses of languages are to be made out.[10] To accept the validity and importance of the classification would be to endorse one possible sort of view as to why there is art and why there are fine arts. The view that lies beneath it is that, although no doubt the daily round and common task of any life that is not indecently painful, alienated, or oppressed will furnish not only all we ought to ask but all the value that could be found anywhere (as a man of perfect spiritual force could extract the last refinement of gustatory delight from an unchanging diet of cold boiled potato), human beings in fact embellish all aspects of their lives in all the ways they could be embellished: by relating part to part, by enriching each part, by hierarchically relating parts in unifying wholes, by summoning to their presence all they can recall or imagine. Our proposed division then corresponds to a simple articulation, on an admittedly unexpressed basis, of actually familiar forms of art in terms of basic ways of living in the world. Its warrant would lie in its suggestion that other relationships and their associated systems of classifications were less fundamental or less comprehensive.[11] Its significance would be that it remains determinedly within the compass of the classical line and the view of human life that it enshrines is Aristotelian, civil, and humane. Not a view for our times, evidently.

APPENDIX C

"GOOD"

Works on aesthetic theory sometimes say what is meant, or what ought to be meant, by calling a work of art good. Unless carefully circumscribed and qualified, such pronouncements should be mistrusted. It is safer to describe types of judgment or types of claims that may be made about works of art, without appropriating the word "good" to any one of them—just as Kant's critique of aesthetic judgment is more readily defensible as isolating a possible kind of judgment that has epistemic importance than as describing what is meant, or stipulating what should be meant, by calling something beautiful. One can indeed say something in general terms about what "good" means: to say that something is "good" is always to relate it positively to wanting or liking or commending, one's own or that of someone else, or to relate it positively to standards that are assumed to hold in the context of the judgment, those standards themselves being relatable to wants or likings or commendations.[1] But within this large area the specific meaning that the word bears on a given occasion will be established by context and by intonation. If the *Oxford English Dictionary* describes the word "good" as "the most general adjective of commendation,"[2] its justification could be, not that the adjective is the vaguest and least tied to specific criteria, but that it is used in the greatest variety of ways. I will briefly mention some of these ways in which simple sentences like "That's good," "This is good," or simply "Good!" may be used, especially when talking about works of art.[3]

"That's good" may be tantamount to (1a) "Wow!" an expression of delight, asserting nothing and hence immune to logical criticism—but not immune to assent or dissent, praise or censure, as expressing a laudable or execrable taste.[4] Alternatively, "That's good" may be tantamount to (1b) "I approve of that!" Like 1a, this is to be understood here not as an assertion but as a mere expression of attitude, such as the logical positivists used to say all value judgments had to be. But whereas in 1a what was expressed was a mere reaction of delight, so that one might almost say that the delight was evinced rather than expressed and belonged among grunts and moans rather than in the domain of articulate language,[5] here in 1b there is a strong commitment of oneself: the use of "good" is performatory of the act of approving, a verbal laying on of hands. This in turn slides into (1c) "I commend that," performatory of the act of commending. Here again one is asserting nothing. But now one is not merely expressing a pleased reaction, or committing oneself to a personal approval; one is thrusting one's taste into the public domain. This is the kind of value judgment that C. L. Stevenson (1944) took as typical, and construed as combining an expression of approval with an elicitation of the approval of others, as though one had said "I approve of that—do so as well."

Someone who means one of the foregoing when he calls something good is not saying anything about the thing he calls good, but he is not saying anything about himself either: to express approval is not to assert as a fact about oneself that one is approving. But asserting such facts about oneself is something one can certainly do, and no doubt it is possible to use the apparently impersonal expression "That's good" as the verbal vehicle of one's doing so,[6] although it would surely be more usual for someone to use such supposed facts as support or explanation, should such be called for, for one of the expressive uses just outlined. It is possible, then, for someone to say "This is good" and mean no more than (2a) "I am enjoying this," simply making a report on his present experiential condition that could be in error only if he was mistaken about his feelings or mistaken in associating them with the object alleged to arouse them.[7] It is less likely, though perhaps still possible, that someone who says "This is good" should mean something like (2b) "I like this," reporting now, not on his immediate feelings at the moment, but on his favorable and appreciative attitude to the object (not "This is pleasing me now" but "This pleases me"). Contrary to some recent philosophical dogma, such a report seems less open to error than 2a, which, though more immediate, is less reflective and hence more open to incautious blunders of self-ignorance and misattribution. But it could still be erroneous through faulty memory or self-deception, or simply by failing to separate an object from its adventitious associations.

Should we add here the possibility that someone who says "This is good" might mean (2c) "Most people like this" or "This is generally approved of"? Hardly; that would rather represent an armchair sociologist's speculation on what lies behind most judgments in the sense 1a. The suggestion that some kind of statistical survey would bear out one's judgment is hardly the sort of thing that enters deeply into one's thought processes when one is calling things good. If they do occur, judgments of the form 2c may be suspected of involving a covert circle or regress. Beneath their ascription of popularity seems to lurk 2b's initial avowal of liking, so that it is as if we were interpreting "This is good" as "This is what most people would call good." But if the word "good" can always be replaced by "what most people would call good," then "This is good" unfolds into "This is what most people would call what most people would call . . . (repeated ad infinitum) good." But the alleged quasi circularity or regress does not obtain, since "good" does not mean the same in the *interpretans* as it does in the *interpretandum*: what the equation would mean would be that one does not use the word "good" in expressing one's individual likings, but only in reference to shared likings—or, at least, that one of the many meanings of "good" is just that. My reason for introducing what might therefore seem a red herring is that a comparable maneuver of interpretation can be worked on virtually any noun or adjective in respect to which the user's command of his own experience, and his confidence in its authority, is imperfect. Thus it makes quite good sense to say that many people, when they say "That's a lion," mean "That's what people call a lion." The reality sustaining the identification is not the world order but the linguistic community, and one's authority as speaker of one's own language is much stronger than one's authority as knower of the world. So too in calling something good a person is likely to be much less in command of his own authentic attitudes and judgments than he is of those of the evaluating community of which he forms a part.[8] But then we should perhaps reinterpret 2c as "This is what *we* like" rather than as "This is what most people like." And now I think it is clear that people very often do mean just that when they call something good.

Under the general heading of "This is what *we* like" there are a number of nuances, which could be treated equally well as separate senses or as subdivisions of 2c. These have in common that they invoke the preferences of different preferred groups, with whom one allies oneself in an approving sort of way. One can thus ally oneself with a group to which one belongs or to a group that one endorses; it seems suitable to treat the former kind of alignment, but not the latter, as special cases of 2c. We then have (2c1) the rather common kind of case in which when one calls something good one means something like "This pleases people like me," a body of like-minded evaluators, as though one were qualifying 2b by adding "and I am not alone in my taste." In the arts, such judgments are called for by the realities of connoisseurship: the differential development of appreciative skills and their associated biases generates relatively fixed sets of preferences, each of which is acknowledged to be the perquisite of a restricted group, not justifiable and not needing justification otherwise than in terms of that developed taste. Alternatively, in calling something good one may be making a quasi-Kantian appeal to the supposed requirements of the shaping imagination, as though one were to say (2c2) "This is what normal people like," with the implication that a pejorative explanation could be found for any deviation: the dissenter was badly schooled or mentally sick or subnormal.[9] Such judgments might be supportable by sociological studies of preferences, supported by statistical correlations of aberrant preferences with defects otherwise determined, together with a suitable causal hypothesis linking the two; but what lies behind them is more likely to be the feeling that whoever does not share an important set of our preferences is *not one of us* and therefore not fully a real human person.

To be differentiated from the foregoing are those common judgments in which "This is good" refers to the system of preferences, not of the speaker's own group, but of those whom he accepts as setting appropriate standards to which he does not himself claim privileged access: (2d) "This pleases the best people" or "This is what the best people like." "Best" reduplicates all the ambiguities of "good," so that one might here expect a plethora of senses corresponding to the ways in which people can be positively related to likings and so on. But of course "best" has not actually been *said* here, and what I want to bring out is something much less bewildering. I am thinking of two kinds of judgment, snobbish and specialist. In the latter case (2d1), what is assumed is the possibility of learning a set of standards whose relevance is not open to question, although one is not implying that one is oneself conversant with them; in the former case (2d2), what is assumed is an actual correlation of social classes with preference groups and an accepted ranking of the former. Good music is simply upper-class music.[10]

The second group of things that are often meant by calling something good is shadowed by a third group, similarly subdivided (3a through 3d2), in which one means, not "This pleases (whomever)" or "This is what (whoever) likes," but "This is *the sort of thing* that pleases (whomever)" or "This is *such as to* please (them)," with definite and strong reference to the presence of steadily good-making characteristics or membership in a steadily satisfactory kind. As the *Oxford English Dictionary* (as cited in n. 2) suggests, there is some reason for thinking of these as the standard meanings of the word, with 3d1 ("This is the kind of thing the best judges like") as the paradigm case. The further one gets away from this sort of meaning, the less appropriate it becomes to engage in discussion of whether things are *really* good or not; and, since attributions of goodness can always be challenged and are expected to be defensible, a sense like 3d1 exercises a sort of gravitational pull over the others. Because of this, it is often argued that this is what "good" always really means: the challengeability and defensibility of judgments of goodness, and the ways in which different kinds of defense are weighed and can be challenged, are matters of logical propriety rather than linguistic decorum or social convention, so that anyone who uses "good" in a way that evades these proprieties is using the word irresponsibly or improperly or in some secondary or derivative sense. But such arguments are hazardous.[11]

That last thing that is sometimes meant by calling something good passes over into a fourth meaning. Sometimes when one says "This is good," it is as if one had said (4) "This *meets the standards* for things of this kind." The implications here are, first, that there are fixed standards, which are beyond challenge in the context and recognized by everyone with the appropriate kind of interest in the thing under discussion, and, second, that there is no question as to what kind the thing should be assigned to. The last assumption is often risky, and many overconfident and confidently wrong judgments come from mistakes in that regard. If one says (as one indeed most often does) not "This is good" but "This is a good so-and-so," the naming of the so-and-so makes that mistake impossible by taking the assigning of a kind out of the area of assumption and making it an explicit part of the judgment. In so doing it imposes a restriction on the scope of the judgment itself, for to call something a good so-and-so is not to imply that it is a good such-and-such.[12]

Corresponding to the would-be factual fourth meaning is a revisionist fifth. Sometimes saying "This is good" is as it were saying (5) "The standards this meets are (should be accepted as) the standards for this kind of thing." The emphasis here is on the "this": "*This* is good." Such a judgment may represent a critical breakthrough, at once recognizing a new kind of performance and setting up by implication a new set of criteria for it. Since it purports to set up new standards by establishing a new paradigm, such a judgment cannot be judged correct, and it cannot exactly be incorrect either: rather, if accepted, it serves as a measure of correctness for other judgments. But removal from the domain of correctness does not make it irresponsible: it may be backed by coherence with a large set of other related judgments, by the introduction of new discriminations, by a reinterpretation of history to provide the new paradigm with a strategic place, and even by the identification of a hitherto unrecognized or undervalued kind of intention that the thing in question may be thought to satisfy.

Very different from the didactic tone of such reformist judgments is the tone of voice—perhaps one of more or less surprised realization—in which one says "This is *good*" meaning (6) that, after all, this kind of thing *can* be liked, *can* be very satisfactory, can have standards that it meets—the sort of thing one means when identifying for oneself or others a viewpoint from which unsuspected virtues can be seen. We have another kind of judgment again when one means something more complex: that (7) one approves or commends a thing (this being performative or expressive as in type 1), specifically because (and then some reason from numbers 2 through 6). And then there are more schematic, ramified judgments: in saying "This is good" one may mean something like (8) "I approve of or commend this for having the qualities for which I or most people or normal people commend or approve of such things." It sounds like a lot to mean, but all that the cumbrous paraphrase does is point to a situation in which, in a single linguistic move, a speaker recognizes an object's character and its compliance with accepted standards, and expresses his adherence to those standards. And all that is essentially a simple thing, a celebration of conformity.

The foregoing account of the multiple ambiguity of the word "good," which obviously could have been extended considerably on the lines laid down, seems absurdly fine-drawn, as well as objectionable on the grounds that a word so ambiguous would be useless: one must have misdescribed a situation that would have been more properly depicted by a much simpler or vaguer "core meaning" for the word, with everything else being relegated to "use" or "contextual implication." But I think that would be a mistake. Other accounts of the same material have had in the end to acknowledge and incorporate comparable complexities, or have avoided the appearance of doing so only by relegating many meanings of the word "good" to the status of "inverted-commas" or "derivative" uses, moves that tend to involve tendentious assimilations. But once these complexities are admitted, generalizations about the objectivity, nonobjectivity, subjectivity, relativity, or absoluteness of all value judgments are shown up as merely absurd. If all the judgments I have described are value judgments, it is evident that they are most various and may be attacked and supported in most various ways. If the generalizer seeks to save his generalization by limiting the scope of his remarks to some subset of the judgments I have surveyed, his remarks lose much of their interest. Assimilations of "value judgments" to a common logical type are stupid and exclusions of types of judgments from one's account are absurd, unless one begins with the logical categorization and then stipulates that "value judgment" shall be used merely as a label for the preferred category. And such stipulations solve nothing. What one has thus excluded will still remain to be dealt with.

From the listing of eight kinds of things one may mean by calling something good, one can extract material that, when combined with distinctions other theorists of criticism have drawn, will justify our grouping judgments of goodness in aesthetic matters into at least the following seven categories:

(1) mere expressions of taste, making no claim to truth, which cannot be argued about but may be censured, ridiculed, applauded, etc.;

(2) judgments on taste, claims about taste, one's own or others', which are in principle open to verification but in practice can seldom be proved or disproved;

(3) appreciative judgments, relating to well-established possibilities of enjoyment and the like, which cannot be proved but may be securely based on experience;

(4) evaluations, assessments of how well things meet requirements, which may in fact be based on (someone's) taste but do not refer to taste and purport to be objective;

(5) appraisals, much the same as evaluations in application to performances, using criteria of success and achievement that do not necessarily invoke "requirements," but purporting to be objective just as evaluations do;

(6) verdictives, performative pronouncements establishing and registering decisions for oneself and others, pragmatically requiring support (as a judge's decision must be supported by a reasoned judgment) but logically independent of it because they are exercises of the absolute judicial function and as such can be set aside but not disproved;

(7) rankings, arranging things in order of merit, which may be done in terms of evaluation or authoritatively by way of verdictive. It is to the former of these that the notion of ranking is generally confined. Once the dimension of ordering has been established, rankings are the easiest of all "value judgments" to confirm, because the presupposition of a ranking is that a coherent set of standards is available, and the ranking itself will usually show what that is. But among things that cannot be readily assigned to the same class, evaluative rankings are impossible or, when possible, ludicrous.[13]

The seven types of judgment are distinct, as were the eight meanings of "good." But that does not mean that on any particular occasion it may be evident either to the speaker or to his audience which is being produced. In fact, in many discussions a large part of what is going on is that the participants are making up their minds what the statements to which they have committed themselves are going to have meant and what logical character their pronouncements will turn out to have had.[14] In this regard, judgments of the goodness of things (or, for that matter, of their beauty) may have a free-floating quality that belongs much more obviously to what people say about their likings. A person who says that he "likes" something may very well not know whether he means that he enjoys it or that he approves of it, not because he has not stopped to reflect, or lacks the terminology necessary to make such a distinction, but because his attitude is floating and indeterminate. If he goes on to say that he likes it "because of" this or that, he may be similarly unclear as to whether he is adducing the causal occasion of his psychological state, the logical ground of his judgment, or the aspect of the object toward which his favor is directed. It seems quite reasonable to suppose that a person often begins by saying he likes something because of something, meaning perhaps that he thinks well of it as well as enjoys it *by virtue of* the features he names. If his gambit is received with derision, he reconstrues it as having only claimed that he happened to find himself pleased by it, the *causal explanation* of this happening being the presence of the features in question. If, on the other hand, the company supports his judgment, he may move forward and take himself in retrospect to have been recognizing its objective worth and naming the *real grounds* of that excellence. There seems to be no compelling reason for saying that his initial move must really have had one or the other character, or that it was originally equivocal, rather than that it proposed a position that was unexplored and unclarified and hence indeterminate because the utterer had not yet reached the point of articulating it. And there is no good reason either for saying that this lack of explicitness was only the psychological, not the logical, character of the utterance.

It may be rather seldom that we reach the point of distinguishing between our being pleased and our recognition of quality.

NOTES

Preface

1. For the "incredible confusion of tongues, the veritable Tower of Babel which seems to me one of the most ominous features of our civilization," see Wellek (1963, 2 and passim). But has anything worth reading ever been written in Esperanto?

2. Intellectual work carried out within a framework that it never calls into question is hack work. T. S. Kuhn (1970) has popularized the phrase "normal science" as a name for hack work in that field, and some have suggested taking over an expression of the same form ("normal philosophy") for hack work in the philosophical field. But Kuhn envisaged a situation in which revolutions were rare and science usually progressed in a stable framework; that situation seldom obtains in philosophy, for which the existence of a stable framework would be something of a scandal. That there is no such thing as "normal art" is argued by Adorno (1970, 250).

Chapter I. Introduction

1. It is *possible* to deny that one of them is a work of art: anyone can say anything, and his saying proves only that he has mastered the relevant part of the grammar of the language. Could such a denial be taken seriously? It ought not to be: it would be a mark of ignorance. One might utter such a denial in defense of a thesis one had espoused, but to espouse a thesis that entailed such a denial would merely be a mark of a more profound ignorance. The status of each of these objects is far more securely established than any theory on the basis of which it could be denied. In any case, such a denial would leave the present argument unaffected, if the ground for it were that the standards mentioned were simply not met in any way, or were inappropriate. If the denial rested on other grounds, we would have to consider what those grounds were: they are probably taken into consideration somewhere or other in the body of this book.

2. T. W. Adorno (1970, 164) points out that the enigmatic character of art appears only *from the outside*. What I am saying in these opening remarks is essentially that there is no need to look at a human activity *from the outside*, and if one chooses to do so, one can claim no privilege for one's view.

3. "Aesthetics as a science or a philosophical inquiry . . . is the outgrowth of an interest in the aesthetic interest. No further justification is needed. Having aesthetic experience is good. To understand it is also good. The first proof for either is that men find it so" (Rader and Jessup 1976, 8).

4. The fact is noted, and some of the reasons for the messiness of the results are unwittingly revealed in the following quotation from a sculptor:

Sculptors, like other people, sometimes try to express their experiences in words and to seek philosophical understanding of them. . . . They try to match the importance and excitement of their experiences with important and exciting-sounding ideas. The dry sandy wastes of fashionable British philosophy have little to offer them. At least the metaphysicians recognized these experiences; they were not frightened by them or seduced by a passion for clarity into denying them and spending their lives inside a linguistic goldfish-bowl. What they wrote may not in fact have been an explanation, but it did have the virtue of at least seeming like one (Rogers 1968, 220-221).

One notes that what the author requires of a theory is not that it be true, clear, or even intelligible but that it sound exciting; he is indifferent to whether or not it explains anything so long as it *seems like* an explanation. Such a "theory" would be the precise theoretical counterpart of *Kitsch*, which seeks to give the impression of being art without actually being so (see below, chap. 2, n. 16). Serious people do not traffic in such wares.

5. A point of view opposite to that represented in the preceding note is stated by Charles Biederman:

It is certainly true that when words or logic have too little relation to the actualities with which they deal, they can become a serious danger to the artist's work. But since no artist can avoid the use of words in connection with his art, then it seems more reasonable to assume that the dangers of words and logic can be best avoided by the artist's becoming as conscious as possible of the manner in which he employs them. Therefore, we cannot take seriously the contention that it is futile to talk or talk too extensively about "art," if for no other reason than that artists and others, including those who make the contention, are continually talking about art anyway (1949, 485).

The disorder and unclarity of aesthetic theory are notorious, but should not be overstated. Morawski (1974) remarks with little exaggeration that the basic positions in aesthetics are few and were all formulated by Socrates' time: changes and apparent novelties usually come from reworking and elaborating old theories to fit new data and new social situations. The appearance of extreme disorder in the field is partly due to the prevalence of enthusiastic amateurism on the part of eminent artists and dilettantes, but also owes something to a certain lack of standardization on the part of more careful thinkers. Fundamental distinctions of method and substance will be made by different authors in different ways, or in ways that do not quite coincide; and the significance of these shared distinctions is not agreed on. With practice, it is easy enough to correlate the different ways of proceeding with each other, but it requires both familiarity with the field and enough sophistication and disengagement not to be the slave of any one of the rivals. The reason for this nonstandardization is that the field of aesthetics and of its subject matter is unstable, and it is not clear what reasons there could be for stabilizing them in any one way rather than any other, or indeed for wishing them to be stabilized at all. In ethics, there are strong reasons for holding that a consensus on what is right and wrong exists and must be maintained (or at least that one must pretend that it exists and pretend to uphold it), and this imparts a stability to ethical theory, which operates under a tacit agreement to define itself by its orientation to that consensus. But aesthetics and art lie under no such obligation.

6. Peter Jones writes: "It is also impossible for a single theory to account for all

the aesthetic problems at any one time, because these problems reflect different stages of constantly changing thought about art and criticism. Some problems, therefore, will be legacies of views already being superseded, others will be harbingers of as yet half-developed views" (1975, 204-205). It is not clear just what this means. Certainly no theory can *solve* all problems, but it might "account for" them by sufficiently characterizing their various theoretical presuppositions. The fact that thought changes does not make it impossible to deal rationally with whatever thought may be fashionable at this time or that, though of course one cannot be sure that anything one says may not be put into a strange light by some change that is yet to take place.

7. There may be some tension between art as a practice and art as a concept. Thus, Adorno writes that art is most vividly present when it destroys the concept of art (1970, 242); and Morris Weitz's seminal essay "The Role of Theory in Aesthetics" (1956) essentially relies on the same insight for its seemingly paradoxical contention that the revolutionary impetus of art renders art forever undefinable.

8. I have written elsewhere on the problems of saying in general terms what this or that form of intellectual or artistic activity is (Sparshott 1975a and 1975b).

9. Such a formalist account of types of actual and possible theory as I offer here is not meant to *replace* a historical account of who actually said what when. On the contrary, it is only in their historical context that theories come to life: actual thinking is always essentially related to its personal, cultural, social, economic, and historical context and legitimately engages our deepest concern. On the other hand, a historical account does not displace or invalidate such formalism as ours: without the permanent possibility of refutation and confirmation, the theory loses its essential character and is reduced to political conversation, and the account of that theory to anecdote.

10. It is not dull at all, really. But Mr. Rogers (n. 4, above) might find it rather sandy.

11. There are three levels on which art can be discussed. One can consider individual works and how they enter into actual experiences of individuals. One can also consider careers, styles, movements, and epochs. On the second level, the general study of art must take into account economic and social determinants, but on the first level they are mostly out of place. And neither level can be considered in abstraction from the other. (It is this relationship between the personal and the historical that J.-P. Sartre works at in his *Questions de méthode* [1957].) But there is also a third level, yet more general, that is concerned with teasing out *what it is* that is socially and economically determined and yet can be recognized as art, and what *sort* of distinction it is that one is making in differentiating what is art from what is not. It is on the third level that my book will be moving, and in doing so it will be much occupied with the first level but hardly at all with the second level.

12. Not every theory that assigns a function to art makes art subservient to another aspect of human life, and not every theory that does so will admit to doing so: one may claim that *whatever* fulfills the assigned function is art. This is characteristic of the expressive line, discussed in chapters 11 and 12. An instructive case is that of Iredell Jenkins (1958), who argues vigorously against the contention that art contributes to any other human good than that proper to it, but then makes art the sole or principle means of "adaptation" according to a theory of evolution somewhat fancifully conceived.

13. Consider, for instance, Anthony Blunt's survey *Artistic Theory in Italy 1450-1600* (1940). It never occurs to the reader even to ask whether any of these theories are true. They are historically explicable and occasionally illuminating, perhaps, but

the question of truth does not even arise. And yet their proponents, not fools but the leading minds of their place and time, held them to be true.

14. Many theorists, of course, are not in their senses. Leaving aside the enthusiastic amateurs, even professional philosophers are selected for their special skills and intellectual capacities, none of which either is or involves wisdom or common sense; nor is there any academic pressure toward collective wisdom or common sense. It follows that the conclusions of philosophers warrant no respect whatever. Their arguments indeed compel respect, as do their analyses, but their selection of what to argue about, and of what premises to argue from, is often merely silly. Of course, common sense is not everything. William Warburton wrote to Hurd: "I don't know whether you have seen Dr. Young's *Conjectures on Original Composition.* He is the finest writer of nonsense, of any of this age. And, had he known that *original composition* consisted in the manner, and not in the matter, he had wrote with common sense, and perhaps very dully under so insufferable a burthen" (Warburton 1809, 213). Since references to common sense are usually met by the remark that in 1491 common sense held that the earth was flat, I had better point out that by the phrase "common sense" I do not mean what the majority of contemporary opinion holds to be the case concerning this or that matter of fact. I mean the sense of the way things go on in life that everyone acquires in the course of his life, provided that he attends honestly to the full measure and weight of his own experience, and the refusal to be shaken out of that sense. That some theorists speak as if they did not know what it would be like to have such a sense is a measure of their craziness.

15. For argument to this effect, see Sparshott (1975a and 1972 esp. "Speculation and Reflection").

16. In the interests of simplicity, I say nothing about debates as to the nature of meaning or the meaning of "meaning," though those debates classify philosophies no less clearly than do those about the scope of what may properly be deemed meaningful.

A shrewd reader will have observed that insofar as the scope of philosophy depends on what the word "meaning" means, the question can only arise for speakers of the English language, since it is unlikely that any word in any other language will translate "meaning" in all contexts. That is quite true. It is also true that opinions and debates in the English-speaking world about the nature of philosophy are notably unlike such opinions and debates elsewhere.

17. Some philosophers would argue that what art is can only be discovered from how the word "art" is used, and the range of uses to be examined could only be restricted by some prior and hence illegitimate decision about what art is. Every use of the word must therefore be taken into account. This is untenable, for many reasons. Not every use of the word is recorded in an available form; if it were, the data would be unwieldy. Nor could a mere accumulation of data disclose the occasions on which the word was used by mistake. More significantly, when such words as "art" are used attentively and deliberately to make theoretical points, they are typically used with the intention of extending or restricting the concept or of emphasizing some one aspect of it. Not all uses of a word are equally normal. Again, one could argue that what the word means is different each time it is used, its precise meaning being a function of its unique context. And certainly each person's use of any word is unique—no two persons would use it in all and only the same contexts. Words may be common currency, but their use is not like that of the coin of the realm. The dictionary takes one only so far, and beyond that point one's understanding

depends on one's comprehension of what in general is under discussion. "How people use the word" is not something we can know, or could use if we did. Our concern here is with the connections and distinctions people use the word "art" to make when they are trying to think clearly in general terms about a certain range of phenomena.

18. This sense of the term does, however, seem to be implied in some works (e.g. Bell 1914; Burnham 1971). More precisely, Burnham equates art with whatever now goes on in those galleries and journals that used to be devoted to painting and sculpture.

19. Richard Wollheim seems to equate a form of life, a complex of thoughts and practices having its own conscious integrity, such as he takes art to be, with what is thought and done in the light of the general *concept* of art (presumably in the sense of the term we are now discussing) (Wollheim 1968, §§50 et seq.). But there may be a certain difficulty, even circularity, in defining a form of life by reference to a concept, for the relevant concept can only be that of the form of life itself. Otherwise we may run into the difficulties posed by Adorno, Weitz, and others (see n. 7, above).

20. An outstanding example of a thinker whose utterances must usually be taken in this way, as contributions to an ideal chat rather than as theorems, is Marshall McLuhan; it was in fact reflection on his work that made me realize the importance of discourse of this kind (Sparshott 1969). But it is not only such dubiously respectable thinkers as McLuhan who use language in this way. It is largely because he insists on drawing definite conclusions from statements containing terms used in this vague manner that Plato's epistemology and ontology evade precise understanding. The "ideas" can neither be perfect particulars, nor classes, nor summed members of classes, nor anything else that a developed logic can locate. The term "idea" and its equivalents point vaguely toward various aspects of the universalizing and abstractive tendency of thought about perceptible objects. Locke's use of the word "idea" has a similar quality: we are seldom puzzled as to what he means—if only he would not keep pretending that he has a theory!

21. Monroe C. Beardsley ascribes to James E. McClellan the contention that, in Beardsley's words, "what properly fits into the blank in 'philosophy of———' is always . . . the name of a practice, which is a form of activity defined by a system of rules or canons governing the actions of those engaged in the practice," its purpose being "to discover the distinctive form which human reason takes in that practice." He quotes McClellan as saying "neither art nor the criticism of art is clearly a practice," from which it follows that there can be no philosophy of art (McClellan 1976, 2; Beardsley 1977, 317-318). As a piece of definitional games-manship, this is merely amusing. But it has a serious point. The philosophy of law and the philosophy of mathematics, which serve McClellan as paradigms, approach the status of well-defined fields of study to the extent that they can and do treat law and mathematics as something like practices in the sense laid down. And we may suspect that there will be a constant tendency in the philosophy of art to *treat art as a practice* in this sense, although it is evidently not one.

22. The word is often extended to experimental psychology, and less often to sociological investigations, in the field of art and "the aesthetic" generally. I have no quarrel with this usage and no reservations about the legitimacy and value of such studies, and I ignore it and them only because they have no bearing on what I want to say.

23. I have used this definition before: "that part of philosophy which deals with

problems arising mainly out of the existence of beautiful things, and men's response to their beauty; out of artistic activities and men's responses to them; and out of the intellectual activities connected therewith" (*SA* 3).

24. In the opening words of his *Aesthetics*, Hegel describes and deplores this tendency to equate aesthetics with the philosophy of art, but he considers the confusion too deeply entrenched to be resisted (Hegel 1835, 1).

25. The word is first used by A. G. Baumgarten (1735), whose principal doctrine these sentences are meant to capture.

It is easy to see how the word "aesthetics" becomes ambiguous. In the original application to poetry, the parallel with logic is attractive: logic deals with the rational effectiveness of argumentative language, aesthetics with the emotional effectiveness of nonargumentative language. The trouble begins when one treats the "images" of poetry as analogous to the images of its "sister art," painting, and generalizes one's study (as Baumgarten already did) to become the study of the conditions of effectiveness of the fine arts in general. For now one's thought is no longer bound by the limitation of its subject matter to a use of language, and it merges with an earlier tendency (exemplified by Addison's "pleasures of the imagination," and continued by such diverse thinkers as Kant and Francis Jeffrey [1816]) which takes the beauties of art not to differ essentially from those of nature. The basic attitude of the *philotheamôn*, the impassioned contemplator of appearances, is after all common to both, whereas part of the initial impulse of Baumgarten's idea, which operates entirely within the scope of human discourse, is that captured by Hegel's insistence that the beauty of art is essentially an *expressive* beauty, "born of the spirit, and born again," and as such to be *contrasted* with the external beauties of nature (Hegel 1835, 2).

26. The way of thinking that makes this equation its starting point is that discussed as the expressive line in chapters 11 and 12.

27. The word "callology" mostly figures in translations from Romance languages and has yet to win the hearts of lexicographers. True English speakers prefer not to admit that they are thinking about beauty. See below, chapter 4, note 2.

28. For the analogy between taste and the moral sense, compare David Hume's essay *Of the Standard of Taste* with book 3 of his *Treatise on Human Nature*. The originator of this line of thought seems to have been Francis Hutcheson (1725); an admirable selection of illustrative texts may be found in Aschenbrenner and Isenberg (1965).

29. In "Is Psychology Relevant to Aesthetics?" George Dickie writes: "Psychological information which relates to the problem of why men create works of art is ruled out as irrelevant because aesthetics (at least philosophical aesthetics) is concerned only with the language and concepts which are used to describe and evaluate works of art. Aesthetics is not concerned with how works of art have come to be but only with the finished consumer product" (1962, 324). This statement is noteworthy, from our present point of view, for three things. First, it tacitly equates aesthetics with the philosophy of art by equating works of art with aesthetic objects whose origin is irrelevant. Second, it equates aesthetics with the philosophy of criticism. And finally, it justifies the forebodings of Tolstoy and Gadamer by treating works of art as "consumer products," the merchandise of the culture industry, as Adorno might say.

30. See Eco (1976), according to whom general semiotic theory should be able to explain every case of sign-function in terms of underlying systems of elements mutually correlated by one or more codes.

31. Since a sign is defined by Eco as "everything which can be taken as significantly substitutable for something else" (1976, 7), one might think that semiotics (as "in principle the discipline of studying everything which can be used in order to lie" [ibid.]) can deal only with representational art. Eco, whose methods are occasionally impressionistic, does not really meet this difficulty. He claims that the "non-semiotic aspects of art" can be "dealt with from a semiotic point of view as soon as it is recognized . . . that every code allows for an *aesthetic use* of its elements" (ibid., 13). But this carries the point only if *everything* aesthetic in art can be reduced to the aesthetic use of elements of a code and then only if all the codes of art codify the uses of substitutive signs.

32. Saussure (1916, 16). The difference between the two notions is discussed by Eco (1976, 14-16 and 30, n. 1). Philip Pettit observes that the arts on which semiology focuses are those that "involve cultural constructions in the way that speech arts involve sentences," and that the requisite sentencelike constructions are mostly found in three areas: the literary arts, nonliterary arts, and such "customary arts" as cuisine and fashion (1975, 33-42).

33. Thus Peter Wollen writes: "Any definition of art must be made as part of a theory of semiology. . . . The whole drift of modern thought about the arts has been to submerge them in general theories of communication" and to deny works of art "any specific aesthetic qualities by which they may be distinguished, except of the most banal kind, like primacy of the expressive over the instrumental or simply institutionalization as art" (1969, 17). One might retort that the most fundamental distinctions are almost always banal, but the banality is not necessarily transferred to discussions carried on in their terms; on the contrary, the banal discussions are those that refuse to take note of elementary differences. I do not know how carefully Wollen chose the word "drift."

Pettit says that the linguistic model should be extensible to nonliterary arts because "a work of non-literary art produces its meaning precisely by the mechanical articulation of its parts" (1975, 55). On the face of it, that would confine its applicability to notational arts such as music and exclude those whose works cannot be broken down into discrete elements.

34. Eco admits that semiotics is a field of study that has yet to become a discipline and explains the difference between the two, though of course he claims to be beginning the transformation (1976, 8).

35. Pettit goes so far as to say that "structuralism is the movement of thought which presses and formulates the case for semiology" (1975, 33).

36. In this sense, structuralism derives from and approximates to the formalism of Russian and Czechoslovakian critical theory (cf. Scholes 1975).

37. If works of art are to be looked at in this way, a work of art from an alien culture should be *no less* unintelligible than an utterance in its language. But that is not the case; the opacities of alien iconography, often appealed to, are absurdly far from carrying the point. Nor will it do to point out that a word in one language may by accident make sense—a different sense—in another. The appropriate analogue is not a word but an entire utterance, and it is rare indeed that a whole sentence makes sense in two languages. The linguistic parallel certainly affords nothing like the familiar case of a whole style or sequence of styles from one civilization being relished by another.

38. In this respect, there is a clear affinity with Freud's approach to art. He too dismissed the overt content of a work as distraction (like the dream work with which unconscious urges cloak themselves in sleep), and its aesthetic patterning as mere

enticement. The likeness is no coincidence. Thinkers in the structuralist and hermeneutic camps rely heavily on Marx and Freud, for both of whom cultural phenomena have real hidden meanings from which appearances distract the common man.

39. Readers trained in English-language critical theory will feel that Barthes is attacking a straw man. His insistence that the expository portion of what he is doing in *S/Z* is not *explication de texte*, because not devoted to bringing out a single hierarchically ordered reading, and is therefore revolutionary reads strangely to us who were reared on Empson's *Seven Types of Ambiguity*. One must suppose that the academicism Barthes attacks lives on somewhere in the French educational system. Certainly Poe's chimerical theories of poetical composition have held generations of French theorists in thrall to his dream of authorial omnipotence (cf. Gibson 1961).

40. It is this dissolution of the work or text into an indeterminate nexus of meanings and definitions that is developed by Derrida's "grammatology." To paraphrase Derrida is to violate his mind, but I read him as rethinking Saussure's distinction between "language" (the impersonal apparatus) and "speech" (the personal act) in terms of Martin Buber's distinction between two "primary words" or ways of relating, I/it (subject to object) and I/thou (person to person), and equating the former in each pair with writing and the latter with talking. Writing and talking thus turn out to be coeval and coequal (the written word does not refer to the spoken word, as theorists since Aristotle had supposed). Writing takes on a life of its own: a system of signs, over which speakers and writers have little control. What a speaker turns out to have said has little to do with what he meant. And the system of signs cannot be escaped by reference to any external reality: there is nothing "beyond the text." Names and descriptions violate the reality of what they name and describe by conferring identity (the only identity there is) only in terms of the system of signs itself. The extratextual reference is forever *elsewhere*. Determinate meaning, authorial intention, and specific form all vanish.

41. The interpretation of artistic meaning as a pattern of aroused, deferred, and eventually gratified expectations was worked out and applied to music by Leonard B. Meyer (1956), who went on to suggest an evaluation of music in terms of the extent to which gratification was delayed (1967). In this later work he acknowledges that his "psychological" account of musical meaning in terms of expectations is vulnerable to the objection that music may be more effective on a second hearing than on the first, though there can now be no question of unexpectedness; accordingly, he rewrites his theory in terms of logical implications and relative probabilities.

42. Culler attributes to Barthesian structuralism the view that "the discovery of structures is an infinite process and must, if it is to be fruitful, be grounded on a theory of how the literary text functions. A work has a structure only in terms of a theory which specifies the ways in which it functions" (1975, 109). A difficulty in this view is that it implies that the codes by which the work is analyzed are artifacts of the critic's ingenuity. It is indeed obvious that some of what Barthes calls codes in *S/Z* are vaguely structured and loosely organized areas of concern, such as art, which Barthes identifies only in a very sketchy way and which do not function in social understanding in anything like the required sense. This is fatal to Barthes' central contention, which is that codes not only structure but actually constitute the social behavior they articulate. Moreover, if they actually did that, there would be no *a priori* reason to deny that literary understanding as such depends on a specific code that incorporates hierarchical principles. Analogies from language and lin-

guistics are a perpetual temptation to critics and aestheticians, and a constant danger.

From the point of view of practical criticism, the fact that the codes to which the critic appeals have no determinate being is no defect. Rather, to multiply them freely is an enriching device of the critic's art.

43. The idea that the "unity in plurality" of the work of art need not be a single unified structure but may be a unity of texture (and hence that a work need have no "beginning," "middle," and "ending") is proposed as a description of a prevailing modern manner by Meyer (1967). This and related issues are suggestively explored by M. Schapiro and his commentators in Hook (1966).

44. The continuity of the most destructured avant-garde works with classical art, and the concomitant continuity of their theoretical implications with the traditional preoccupations of the philosophy of art, are demonstrated in the seminal work of Umberto Eco (1962). He points out that to lack unique structure in the sense of being "open" to multiple perspectives may almost be used as a defining characteristic of works of art. The importance of openness is not a new idea: it had been stressed by Valéry ("The richness of a work of art consists in the number of meanings and values it can assume, while still remaining itself" [1964, 196]) and by Wellek and Warren (1949). What Eco emphasizes is the diversity of aesthetic openness as well as its continuity. Works in "classical" styles strike one as self-contained objects that are open to different perspectives; in baroque styles, the work takes on a character that itself strikes us as indefinite and mysterious; and romantic works are constructed to be fragmentary and suggestive to the point where the spectator as interpreter is relied on to provide such definiteness as the work may have. The next step is to the "open" work of today, in which the spectator is drawn into the actual operation of making the work, the audience drawn into the stage action. Barthes' flat contrast of the classical prefabricated text with the "new novelist's" provision of an indeterminate mass of textuality from which the reader may construct his own structured work misses all these distinctions, as well as being a merely fanciful account of what "new novels" contain. On the narrative voice in the novel, Barthes writes: "The more indeterminate the origin of the statement, the more plural the text. In modern texts, the voices are so treated that any reference is impossible: the discourse, or better, the language, speaks: nothing more" (1970, 41). But the limit of such indeterminacy is not so much plurality as blankness; the reader would be no better off than someone seeing pictures in the fire. In fact, Barthes gives no examples of such modern texts, and it is hard to see how he could. All "readerly" texts (texts that guide a reading) are classical, and there are no "writerly" texts. The "writerly" text, leaving the reader entirely free to construct his own interpretation, would be something like "the novelistic without the novel" (ibid., 4-5). So there is nothing left for the modern text to be.

Chapter II. The Classical Line 1: Arts

1. Merleau-Ponty points out that this likeness of many situations that makes learning possible is inseparable from its converse, a multiplicity in each situation that makes the world a world, both unified and various:

> This power of choosing and varying points of view permits man to create instruments, not under the pressure of a *de facto* situation, but for a virtual use and

especially in order to fabricate others. The meaning of human work therefore is the recognition, beyond the present milieu, of a world of things visible for each "I" under a plurality of aspects, the taking possession of an indefinite time and space (1942, 175).

2. Jerome Bruner (1968) thinks that the distinction between subject and predicate basic to most grammars reflects the experience of grasping something in one hand and operating on it with the other—an experience that is yet more clearly and directly relevant to my distinction between matter and change in an art.

It is tempting to assimilate the distinction between matter and change to the traditional distinction between content and form in a work of art, but it would be a mistake to do so. Both form and content, however they are distinguished, are present in the completed work, as neither matter nor change is present as such. The most one could say is that there is a sort of rough likelihood that we should look to the content to see what remains of the matter and to the form to see what has been made of it.

Gotshalk offers an alternative definition of an art in the classical sense: "In its broadest sense, art is the skilful use of instruments and materials to produce objects of value" (1947, 29). If the word "materials" here means actual *stuffs*, if the word "instruments" is taken literally, and if the word "objects" means *things*, then Gotshalk's definition seems rather better suited to handicraft than to art in general. For materials and valued objects, we should substitute given situation and desired outcome; and skillful use of instruments, though essential to arts in which instruments themselves are necessary, cannot be used to define art as such unless the word "instrument" is used so broadly as to include, for example, a writer's use of his language.

3. The interconnection of techniques generates the development of multipurpose instruments (see the two preceding notes), which then become powerful agents in the unification of arts. A person adept in the use of a complex machine will be called on to do whatever can be done with that machine.

4. The text suggests that the extrinsic organization of an art is normally the work of the practitioners themselves, seeking to make the complexities of their mystery manageable. But (following Hobbes's distinction between commonwealths by covenant and commonwealths by conquest) we can imagine that an art might be institutionally unified by external pressure—by the insistence of a totalitarian government, for instance, on treating a given collection of heterogenous trades as constituting a single administrative unit. In such cases, the exoskeleton of the art would begin as a mere container, though one that in time might coerce or cajole its contents into cohering as a single organism. (I owe this thought to Mr. Robert Bregman).

5. See Plato, *Republic* I, 332 and 340ff. The reference in the formula to *changes* and *matters* affords a special case of Plato's and Aristotle's behavioristic doctrine, according to which mental faculties are to be differentiated by observing their *effects* and the *fields* in which they operate, not by introspection (*Republic* V, 477, and Aristotle, *Nicomachean Ethics* IV.2, 1122b1-2).

6. Sartre writes that "a novel is a *thing*, like a painting or an architectural structure. . . . A novel is made with time and free minds, as a picture is painted with oil and pigment" (1939b, 23). There is no way of telling how exact Sartre thinks the analogy is, and the quotation illustrates the general truth that the "matter" and "change" chosen to define an art will vary according to the argumentative context—in this

case, a polemic designed to reach the conclusion that Mauriac is not really a novelist at all.

Burnham (1971) and others have argued that in much contemporary art the situation about which something has to be done is the state of the art itself, so that the overt transformations performed by the artist become symbolic of transformations of history which the uninitiated cannot perceive—or which the unindoctrinated will not believe in.

7. In identifying a stuff or a situation as that with which, or about which, something is to be done on a given occasion, we have already assimilated it into the context of art, just as the beginning of an action in Aristotle's analysis is already detached from the continuum of time and put into the controlling context of that action. On the other hand, when giving a general definition of an art ("the art of producing health in human bodies" or whatever), we speak of the matter as preexisting. Considerations of this sort led L. A. Reid to differentiate in the fine arts between primary subject matter, conceived as unqualified by aesthetic interest, though such as to arouse that interest, secondary subject matter that is already qualified by aesthetic interest, and tertiary subject matter, which is the content of a formed work and intrinsic to that work (1929, 41-45). Examples would be (1) the person about whom Wordsworth wrote one of his "Lucy" poems, (2) the same person considered by Wordsworth as the topic of that poem, (3) the "Lucy" projected by the completed poem.

8. Working *in* something, using it as a medium susceptible of infinite modification, differs not only from working *on* something, taking something with a definite form of its own and changing that form or developing it further (as when one works *on* a play one is writing), but also from working *with* something, using it as a tool or other resource with definite properties capable of shaping forms in determinate ways. Doing something *with* a thing, using it as a mere tool to manipulate with or as a stuff to be manipulated, is not the same as doing something *to* a thing, accepting it as having a definite form to be modified, or as doing something *about* a thing, taking it as an occasion for action. The use of such prepositional phrases is rich and subtle—more so than these brief indications can suggest.

9. Plato's avoidance of the concept of creation is not surprising. It reflects the general conviction of the Greek philosophers that there is no novelty in the universe: forms can only be rediscovered, not invented (cf. Jäger 1967, 139-140).

10. Note the formulation. What matters is who is taking responsibility for the changes, not who or what is their cause. But the requirement of correction and control still raises the problem of the status of "chance" techniques in the fine arts. Are works that use such methods excluded from the domain of art, or are they exempted from the requirement of control, or do they show that our definition is either faulty or inapplicable to the fine arts? The problem becomes simpler if one distinguishes three things that writers on this topic sometimes confuse. Chance, in the traditional sense of lucky accidents that an artist exploits, is not at all the same as randomization, the use of technical devices to avoid recognizable pattern or merely to disrupt pattern. In fact, it is the precise opposite: it incorporates what was originally unintended into an integral design, whereas randomization intentionally disintegrates design. (The experiments of Iannis Xenakis, which are often mentioned in this connection, really belong to neither class. His procedure, as he describes it, is to use mathematical formulas to generate masses of "sound-points" that will conform to distributions of a certain probability. His works are, in fact, audible exemplifications of statistical formulas. This exemplification is determinate:

what is left indeterminate is only what is indifferent from the point of view of the exemplification. It is worth noting that he justifies his procedure historically as a reaction to a situation in which polyphony has been reduced to absurdity by the lack of audible difference between totally serialized polyphony and complete randomization. Those who think of total serialization as total idiocy will prefer to dispense with this justification. See Xenakis 1971, 8 and passim.) Neither chance nor randomization is the same as the merely adventitious, that which merely happens to happen and is neither produced by deliberate disordering nor rescued from disorder by an ordering technique. Of the three, the first clearly involves the operation of a controlling critical faculty. The second is used in a way that is contextually controlled: disorder and disruption of various specified sorts are introduced at specified places in a work whose overall structure is controlled. And the necessary control is a normal use of technical skill. The place of the merely adventitious is more equivocal. Generally, the effects of weathering or similar natural causes on a work are thought of as part of the work only insofar as one thinks of them as intended by the artist. Descriptions of Marcel Duchamp's *Large Glass* do not usually include the cracks in the glass as part of the work, presumably because critics think (mistakenly, I suspect) that the careless handling that caused them was not invited by the artist. But certainly an artist may provide for the adventitious in his work. This is most evidently the case in the performing arts, where the artist necessarily leaves for a second occasion, and often for other hands, the realization of the work for which he provides script or score. Paul Beaud thinks that the most important difference among composers who use "aleatory" or chance procedures is one that separates those who control them in such a way that they can envisage what the probable outcomes will be like from those who confine themselves to providing a scenario for events they do not foresee, who might therefore better be called "program designers" rather than composers (1974, 214-215).

At every stage in the production of a work, an artist may exploit chance, introduce randomness, and open his work to the unforeseen, in any way or to any extent that he finds proper. The ideal of total control and absolute determinacy in human affairs is an illusory one anyway, and we have seen (see chap. 1, n. 44) how Eco (1962) has explored the ways in which works have been "open" throughout the history of art. Even to provide an occasion may be an exercise of art: providing occasions is not a thing everyone can do. The limit has been nicely located by Allan Kaprow: an artist may leave everything to chance including whether or not a work shall be produced, who shall produce it, and whether if produced it shall be called art, but "others must be made aware of the artist's disavowal of authorship if its meaning is not to be lost," and "in any case, using Chance is a personal act no matter how much it attempts to be otherwise, for *a priori*, it is used, not simply given in to" (1966, 180-181). One may add that to make others aware of one's disavowal of authorship requires skills and personal gifts of no ordinary kind—one can only back into the limelight if the limelight is switched on and focused. All three sorts of chance effect as employed or permitted in the production of works of art must be distinguished from the use of chance as a spiritual discipline, in which an audience is thought of as exposed to merely random experiences that themselves constitute the whole of the work (if "work" is the right word). Of such exercises one is tempted to say that the art employed is that of the impresario, whose skill lies in getting audiences to come to the right place and adopt the right attitude—which, again be it said without irony, is no mean feat. But the temptation is to be resisted. If the description I gave is appropriate, what is undergone is a spiritual exercise, not a work of art in any sense the classical line can encompass. At this point, we must avail ourselves of the very different standpoint that the purist line affords. But it may well be unclear, to the artist as well as to the audience, which is the more appropriate way to think of what is being done—and this unclarity may be construed either as the obliteration of unreal distinctions or as ordinary muddle-headedness.

In sum, it seems best to say that to the limited extent that "chance" techniques do evade the notion of organized skill they do indeed lie outside the boundaries of arts, but their ordinary use is well within those bounds. Above all, one must not lose one's head in such discussions and, through cowardice, admit any and every claim by any and every practitioner of an art as to the status of his practice. He will almost certainly have thought very carefully about what he is doing and should be listened to with respectful attention; but he is extremely unlikely to have thought with equal care about what other people are doing, so that what he says about how his practice relates to theirs need not be believed.

11. See Aristotle, *Nicomachean Ethics* VI.iv and *Poetics* xxv.

12. See Plato, *Gorgias* 462-466. Note that it is only a contingent fact, so far as the argument goes, that arts are ordered to objective values; its truth depends on certain very strong claims about axiology, epistemology, and metaphysics. See note 20, below.

13. *Technê esti systêma ek katalêpseôn syngegymnasmenôn pros ti telos euchrêston tôn en tôi biôi* (H. Von Arnim, *Stoicorum Veterum Fragmenta* II, 93). I have examined the implications of this definition elsewhere (Sparshott 1978). In addition to the point for which I cite it here, the definition makes the point that the knowledge constituting an art is not a mere encyclopedic compilation, but is a functioning organic unity. There is an underlying military metaphor: the bits of knowledge that make up an art are organized in the way that recruits are "welded into an efficient fighting machine."

14. This thesis is put into the mouth of Thrasymachus (*Republic* I, 340 D-342 B), but nothing Plato says elsewhere contradicts it.

15. The concept of perfection applies to the fine arts in an atypical way. Because the unrepeatable ("unique") factors are so important, the perfection to be attained cannot be conceived as the fulfillment of a norm that was clearly envisaged, much less formulated, in advance. But the relevance of some sort of perfection can be seen by considering that artists (and even their more sympathetic critics) are more concerned with getting their work *right* than with making it *good*. It is never a serious question for a painter whether the canvas on which he is working is any good; what is serious is whether he has got it right yet. Whether it is good or not will become important later, but it is irrelevant in the context of creation.

16. It is easy to argue that an unthinking reliance on formulas is no less objectionable than resourceless bungling, but the use of "academic" as a term of abuse is not free from problems. Condemnation of the abuses of academies becomes mixed with a condemnation of academies as such, which requires a different sort of justification. An academy as such is an institution that teaches and maintains traditions of practice, and these are not necessarily evils even in the fine arts. The bad name of "academic" is not automatically applied to conservatories of music or even to the Royal Academy of Dramatic Art.

Part of the bad name of academies comes from the prominence that normal teaching practices give to *techniques*. A technique, as Sartre points out (1943, 520-525), is an item of skill *as seen by others*, something that in mature practice is not only unconscious but strictly has no separate existence as such. An expert practitioner's "technique" is absorbed into the task. A technique is something isolated and acquired by a learner, who has to think about what he is doing while he is doing it. It is only so that he can transmit some of his expertness to such a learner that the expert will "think what he is doing" and break it down into items that can be described, demonstrated, and practiced. The place for techniques as such is in learning and teaching, just as R. M. Hare pointed out that the proper place for moralizing and for the verbalizing of moral principles is in the teaching of children (1952, 60ff). The protest against academicism as the fetishizing of techniques and the associated secondary standards is then a protest not merely against the substitution of means for ends (which could well be a good thing, representing the discovery of a higher and more immediate value) but against the application to experts of a way of thinking suited only to beginners, a requirement that one think of one's own work in an external manner. The protest is finely expressed in some sentences by the sculptor David Smith: "*Define technique*—technique is what others call it when you have become successful at it—technique as far as you are concerned is the way others have done it—technique is nothing you can speak about when you are doing it—it is the expectancy of others: they do not share a *respect for themselves* or for what they are doing" (1968, 59 [my punctuation]).

The crucial complication is introduced into the notion of academicism when one considers that the preserved tradition may be, not one of accepted means (techniques), but one of accepted effects and appearances, including a range of uncritically accepted genres. In this understanding, the concept blends into the no less equivocal concept of *Kitsch*: "Self-evidently," says Clement Greenberg, "all kitsch is academic; and conversely, all that is academic is kitsch" (1939, 11). But what exactly is *Kitsch*? In Greenberg's understanding, it is an imitation of the effects of art, reducing the devices of high art to gimmicks; it is a product of the universal literacy that has entitled the man in the street to claim a place among the public for art without endowing him with the leisure to appreciate it.

The concept of *Kitsch* has been much in fashion, especially among younger devotees of the fine arts, because it seems to pick out a familiar and threatening evil. Cheap and easy substitutes for art prevent people from seeking out the real (and difficult and expensive) thing. *Kitsch* in this understanding is whatever works by being recognized as like prestigious art in its superficial characteristics, but offers immediate gratification and is totally bland, having no distinct character other than its being reminiscent of art. We are all familiar with kinds of objects that we would wish to condemn under this head. But that leads to a difficulty. People come to apply the label to whatever they wish to abuse as a spurious imitation of the appearance of art, and any art at all may be abused on that score, as Greenberg's equation of *Kitsch* with the academic already begins to suggest. As Frye has urged, no one could possibly engage in the practice of one of the fine arts otherwise than in the light of a notion of what art and the particular art in question could be, and that notion could only rest on an understanding of what the art had been and already was (1957, 97ff.). In other words, all art necessarily rests on the imitation of art; consequently all art can be condemned as *Kitsch*, with the abusive imputation that its imitation is superficial and facile. Greenberg, for instance, distinguishes the avant-garde from *Kitsch* on the ground that the former imitates the processes of art, the latter its appearances; but one has only to retort that the avant-garde converts procedures into appearances to obliterate the distinction and open up a rich vein of avant-garde *Kitsch*.

Another difficulty with the concept of *Kitsch* is that some of its most obvious exemplifications do not easily fit its definition. Paintings in fluorescent paint on black velvet, for instance, are a genre that most people who use the term would assign to *Kitsch* without question, but it seems impossible to ascribe their appeal to any systematic resemblance to any more respected genre. The difficulty is exemplified in Gillo Dorfles' anthology on *Kitsch* (1969), in which the term seems to be extended *ad hoc* to any nonrespectable manifestation of the plastic arts that appalls the writers' taste: Italian grave decorations, chic advertising, "tasteful" pornography, or anything the enjoyment of which differentiates the uneducated from the educated townsman. Like "camp," *Kitsch* seems to be a word best abandoned to smart journalism, for which it exercises a deadly attraction.

In conclusion, we may say that to equate academicism with an excessive reliance on secondary standards is not to condemn academies, for an academy need not commit that excess. And we can concede that there is an academicism of genres and of effects as well as one of techniques without equating the former with *Kitsch*, however narrowly we define that, for the superficiality, immediacy of effect, and appeal to the uncultivated that define *Kitsch* are not what is condemned in the academicism of effects and do not properly belong to it.

17. That the ends an institution was originally designed to serve cannot be inferred from those it serves at any subsequent time was forcibly urged by Nietzsche (1887, II, §12).

18. John Shearman writes of Mannerist criticism: "One reads . . . with surprise that artifice is a quality to be nurtured; yet there is clearly no reason why it should not be" (1967, 21). It is not at all clear to me that there is no reason, and for all I know there may be a reason that would convince me, though against my will; what is clear is that no such reason is universally acknowledged.

19. Zeno's definition seems not to make this stipulation. The "insights" (*katalêpseis*) that constitute the art may as well be tricks of the hand as general truths (a *katalêpsis* in the general epistemology of the Stoics is most commonly a singular proposition: what distinguishes it is its degree of assuredness, not its scope), and an art could be such a habit of combining skills as an apprentice acquires. On this view, though not on the Aristotelian view, the "units" of which the art is made up might on further reflection be found to have a somewhat shadowy existence, isolated by an imperfectly justifiable analysis of practice rather than standing as general axioms in a truly systematic whole.

20. Aristotle, *Metaphysics* A, 1-3. Aristotle is here developing Plato's thesis that certain practices do not qualify as arts because they do not rest on any reasoned account of the nature of the material they work in, and consequently they cannot explain why their procedures succeed (*Gorgias* 465 A). It is in this passage that Plato anticipates the Stoics by stipulating that an art must aim at producing (objective) good rather than (subjective) pleasure. But whereas the Stoics' definition may be presumed to rest on their faith that the universe is a rational system, Plato's immediate point is rather that an art cannot qualify as knowledge unless it can guarantee success, and no one can guarantee success in satisfying anything so fickle as popular taste—as indeed the television networks demonstrate afresh every September.

21. Aristotle himself emphasizes this point, both in the *Metaphysics* and in the *Nicomachean Ethics*. The result is a curious cross-evaluation of principles and insights, which is brought into the open in the sphere of morals (where everything is said to depend on one's insight into the situation one acts in, but a grasp of general principles somehow retains its superior status) but not resolved.

22. One cannot say that skill is merely the application of knowledge. All the knowledge in an art must be skillfully applied, but it is possible to construe all its skills as applying principles only by arbitrarily and emptily postulating for every skillful procedure a principle one cannot in fact identify.

23. Plato, *Apology* 22 C-D. But the passage fogs the issue by combining it with others. Plato makes Socrates start by talking about handicrafts and then bring poetry in; and he identifies the craftsman's error as the belief that his expertise extends to matters beyond his professional ken. This charge is confusing, because it means something quite different when leveled against poets, whose lack of general knowledge may be apparent in what their poems say, from what it does when leveled against cobblers. Besides, Plato elsewhere urges that poetry is not a pure craft, but depends largely on uncontrollable inspiration (*Phaedrus* 245 A), so that a poet's inability to explain his meaning need have no bearing on the nature of art as such.

The importance of the arts in Plato's thought is partly explained by the fact that in his day they stood alongside mathematical astronomy (to which in his later years he gave more and more attention) as almost the only structured forms of rational activity and the only ones whose success was demonstrable. The reliable excellence of the craftsman's products proves the validity of his skill. More specifically, by providing indubitable examples of physical objects manifesting rational activity, they offer some clue as to how the physical world itself might be explained as a manifestation of intelligent action. Two factors that account for the later decline in philosophical interest in the arts are the loss of interest in a Platonic world-model and the growth of the pure sciences, which afford intelligible structures that are inherently more spectacular than the arts and to which (through technology) the intelligible structure of the arts may be reduced.

24. The point is made by Aristotle throughout his *Nicomachean Ethics* in connection with moral action as well as with the arts, but a residual intellectualism leads him to imply that in all rational practice there must be implicit general laws (cf. n. 21, above). The necessity of these has been eloquently denied by Gilbert Ryle (1949). The debate continues, rather tediously.

The reference in my text to "manual" operations serves as a handy reminder that the physiological "wisdom of the body" is continuous with the unconscious grace with which we perform unconsidered movements and that in turn with the ineffable cunning of an artist's or artisan's trained muscles. For the sake of these important continuities, I let it stand. But, strictly speaking, it introduces an imprecision, because the contrast relevant at this point is not between head and hand but between that for which one can fully explain one's reasons and that which one does only because in one's trained wisdom one knows it for the right thing to do. And that status of inexplicability may belong to the verbal and intellectual skills of poetizing and theory spinning no less than to handicrafts. An experienced thinker's mind *knows where to go.*

We may as well note here (it should certainly be noted somewhere) that, as a matter of English usage, we tend nowadays to use the word "crafts" where non-verbalized skills are devoted to achieving verbally specified objectives, reserving the word "arts" for cases where ends are incompletely specified or means are incompletely determined.

25. This too is Platonic—*Gorgias* 450. The arts singled out as requiring no use of language, oddly enough, are painting and sculpture.

26. See Plato's *Meno*, especially the insufficiently regarded passage in which Soc-

rates asserts that if teaching is transmitting knowledge from one person to another, there is no such thing as teaching—or learning, either (*Meno* 81-82).

27. Perhaps one should be cautious in identifying what cannot be put into words. The apparent impossibility may simply reflect insufficient motivation, or represent lack of skill in verbalizing.

28. The fact that the distinction between doing and making (which has often been thought important both in defining art and elsewhere) proves on inspection to be neither sharp nor systematic and is made in different places in different languages is important. It suggests that the notion of an artifact or made thing will itself prove more elusive than it seems, and thus cannot be conveniently built into the definition of a work of art. If that is so, it clears the way for our own preferred concept of performance, which will now lack the stigma of ousting the clear, familiar, and unproblematic concept of an artifact.

29. Differences are not only made, they are created ex nihilo: forms may be eternal and matter indestructible, but the difference made when a matter is informed is something new. In this sense, and to this extent, using the word "creation" in connection with the fine arts is innocuous.

30. According to the most obvious interpretation of this analysis, the artisan's intention is a sort of ghostly anticipation of the end product: insofar as an operation is fully technically controlled, what is produced must be simply an embodiment of the form that the artisan had in his mind. Aristotle speaks as if this were literally true, for he says that "the things that come to be by art are those whose form is in the producer's soul" (*Metaphysics* Z, 7); and Karl Marx seems to agree with him: "What distinguishes the worst architect from the best of bees is this, that the architect raises his structure in imagination before he erects it in reality. At the end of every labour-process, we get a result that already existed in the imagination of the labourer at its commencement" (1867, 108). That may well be true of most architects, if we understand "in imagination" to mean "on paper"; but as a generalization it will hardly do. Artists commonly do less and more, and sometimes quite other, than they had in mind. Did Marx himself foresee just how *Das Kapital* would turn out?

31. A common objection to treating what we nowadays call art under the rubric of the fine arts is that in doing so one reduces art to a more or less sophisticated form of *fabrication*. But if what is made is always essentially a difference, and the object of an art is always to produce a certain sort of change, arts as such have nothing essentially to do with fabrication. Anyone who wishes to maintain that the fine arts (or any of the fine arts) have to do with fabrication must have some special reason. An artist does not have to be a handicraftsman just because he is an artist. The difference that an artist makes could merely be putting something in a new light. Those avant-garde artists who spend much of their energy putting things in unfamiliar contexts are operating well within the bounds of art as conceived here. All that is necessary is that their procedures should be the focus of knowledge and skill. That knowledge and skill are in fact involved should be conceded even by persons of conservative taste when they reflect that some, but only a few, artists have contrived to acquire reputations in this way.

32. The considerations touched on in this paragraph and the next are discussed by A. I. Melden (1961), whose account I am for the most part following. The individuation of actions has been more formally and elaborately treated by such writers as Donald Davidson and Alvin I. Goldman, but they add nothing to my purpose. According to Goldman, what I have called the single action of crooking

the finger, firing the gun, and so forth is many actions, the set of all acts on a single "act-tree" (1970, 37). In the taxonomy of actions, as in that of plants, some experts are lumpers and some are splitters—Davidson is something of a lumper, Goldman a splitter. As in botany, there are obvious arguments on both sides. When I say "Hello!" cheerfully, my saying "Hello!" is obviously the same act as my doing so cheerfully, because I only say it once; but it is equally obviously a different act, because it has different causes, in that whatever it was that made me say "Hello!" was not what made me say it cheerfully (Goldman, be it said in passing, builds his whole account on the differentiation of causes, but says nothing at all about the concept of cause, so that the whole thing is rather up in the air). In letting the latter consideration wholly outweigh the former, Goldman firmly opts in favor of saying that "a person performs indefinitely many acts at one time" (ibid., 33), rather than that indefinitely many true answers can be given at any one time to the question "What is he doing?"

Discussions of the individuation of actions, like those of the individuation of arts, are of interest and value insofar as they elucidate the principles that underlie the endlessly shifting identifications and differentiations people make from time to time for this or that purpose, but lose all interest when they propound correct solutions to the alleged problem of what constitutes a single action, irrespective of any particular context of inquiry or practice.

33. The question what someone is *making* does not seem to admit of the same variety of answer. Jokes aside, one can only answer by describing in one way or another the artifact one is working on. The only legitimate variability corresponds to that between wider and narrower scope of action: a man is engaged in making an artifact of which the object he is working on is a component, provided that he is primarily responsible for the whole. A man who is making a piston is making a car if, and only if, he and not someone else is assembling the car.

34. Note that he summoned the brigade neither *while* pushing the button nor *in* pushing the button but *by* pushing the button. The connection is strictly one of efficient causation: by doing one thing he did *something else*, though *all* he did was push the button.

35. The status of such concepts as that of intention has been much discussed in recent philosophy (e.g. Peters 1958; Anscombe 1958). The point of view sketched in the text is one I have elaborated elsewhere (Sparshott 1962). A. I. Goldman reverts to the old Aristotelian tradition by subsuming intentions under antecedent causes—we invoke strategies and states of affairs only insofar as the agent's conception of them caused him to do what he did (1970, 50ff.).

36. Imaginatively or sympathetically, I can conceive of the continuous stream of another's conscious living, and I can think of my own life "objectively" in terms of descriptions that anyone could apply. In fact, however, whether I conceive of my own life in terms of its continuity or in terms of discontinuous acts and events, I am conceiving of *it* and hence thinking of it (in the most literal sense of the term) objectively. The most penetrating treatment of this theme is that by Sartre, who, for example, in a person's having a headache distinguishes three grades of objectivization: his actual (awareness of his) pain at a given moment, his awareness of it as belonging to the headache he has had and will continue to have, and his awareness of it as "a headache" (such as anyone might have and for which, in a sense, the medical profession assumes responsibility) (Sartre 1943, pt. 3, chap. 2, 331-337 and 355-357). If we pursue these issues in an Anglophone rather than a Francophone direction, we find ourselves embroiled in such questions as: Could anyone have a

private language that no one else was capable of learning? Can there be any perception without interpretation, so that one's seeing is entirely a matter of "visual sensation"? When I know I am hearing something, is my knowledge distinguishable from my hearing?

37. Students of literature are fond of quoting W. B. Yeats's line "How can we know the dancer from the dance?" They become angry if you explain, as follows. Pavlova is the dancer, *The Dying Swan* is the dance. If *The Dying Swan* is danced by Pavlova on Monday and Danilova on Tuesday, the dance is the same and the dancer is different. If Pavlova dances *The Dying Swan* on Monday and *Giselle* on Tuesday, the dancer is the same, but the dance is different. If Pavlova dances *The Dying Swan* on Monday, Wednesday, and Saturday matinee, one dancer has danced the same dance three times.

38. The distinction between his *making the journey* and his *riding* is precisely that between what Aristotle calls a movement (*kinêsis*) and an activity (*energeia*). Critics of Aristotle's distinction commonly show themselves incapable, not of understanding his words, but of having the thought necessary to understand the words.

39. Eco somewhat similarly abstracts from Dewey's *Art as Experience* (1934) the concept of an *experience* as a segment of action unified by an established end (Eco 1962, 153-154).

40. Notoriously, the selectivity of technical descriptions easily leads to error if the idealization omits something that was causally relevant but not provided for in current theory. When one suspects such error, one tries to return to "what actually happened"; but one's account of "what actually happened" is still necessarily selective, governed by canons of relevance still determined by what one takes to be the requirements of the art in question, though not by the conventions established in accordance with its secondary standards.

41. Important as it is to exclude the irrelevant from our consideration of art, it is equally important to remember that the exclusion has been achieved by an abstraction. The producer is a man, the product is a thing, his production is an event. On reflection, one realizes that man, thing, and event as such are themselves not given in reality antecedent to all experience, but are themselves identified by a process of selection whereby certain organizations or collections of phenomena are abstracted from the flux of experience or of material reality, even though the selection and abstraction are ones an organism could not but make. This "selection" and "abstraction" are presupposed by all our talk about the world and all our action in it; the further abstraction whereby a man is conceived merely as a producer is presupposed only by that special kind of thought which constitutes technical and critical discourse. But perhaps the analogy is close enough to justify us in saying that just as there really are men doing things in the world, so there really are artists. Abstraction does not abolish reality.

42. The concept of a performance is not far removed from that of an act, conceived as something *done* and distinguished from other acts done (or performed, as we say) even by the same person at the same time. But acts are not as such conceived in abstraction from their consequences, as performances are; and an ongoing activity may be construed as a performance, though not as an act.

43. Our special concept of a performance is by no means remote from the senses established for the word "performance" in common usage. In the performing arts, "performance" is usually used as a relative term: what is performed is a work, which is understood to provide the primary standards by which the performance is judged. A performance in this sense is a realization of what was implicit and partially

specified in a score or script (if there was one) and adumbrated in a series of rehearsals (if there were any). The performance of a work is taken to be a full compliance with those specifications and a full fleshing out of those adumbrations.

The relativity of the concept of performance in its common understanding is not invariable. It is idiomatic to say of a musician's playing on a particular occasion that he gave a fine performance, without implying any reference to an antecedent work— the musician may even have been improvising. What one means is that he played well, as for a discriminating audience (for it would not be appropriate to speak thus of someone playing in private), and that his playing had the character of a complete realization of an artistic intention. Just so, one can say of a painting that "it is a magnificent performance," meaning not that it achieves any formerly adumbrated ends but that it is a bravura piece, painted as if it were intended for a discerning public. Similarly, someone is said to "put on a performance" in everyday life when he does something as though it were directed to an audience, as though displaying his actions for criticism and applause.

It is a commonplace of aesthetics to describe this or that phase in the realization of a work of art as "performance," in explicit analogy to the performance of a play or a musical work: one may so describe a painting in relation to its preparatory sketches, or the experiencing of a work in relation to its unperceived hanging on an unregarded wall (waiting in the wings of experience). My own use of the word differs from these metaphorical uses as it does from those connected with the performing arts, in attending only to the outcome of the making and doing as such and in implying nothing about any previous adumbrations, rehearsals, or intentions and nothing about any relation to an audience.

44. "The central question for the interpreter is how a given work is to be taken, and this includes deciding what has been done" (Jones 1975, 184). On "the interpretive function" in criticism, see chapter 8.

45. Using the word "performance" in an idiosyncratic way quite different from mine, Donald Brook writes:

> A sculpture student . . . might make a clay egg, and his teacher might judge the performance. He might also judge the object, and it is important to distinguish these situations since they are easily conflated by the single approval formula "That's a good egg." But suppose the student had been trying to model a sphere; what should the teacher say? That the student had made a good sculpture *by accident?* . . .
>
> If there is one thing which emerges clearly from any thorough and protracted study of human artefacts it is that sculptures are *all kinds of performances.* . . . They were made to frighten bad spirits, to weigh gold (1968, 209-210).

Brook does not explain what he means by "object" or by "performance," but it seems from the context as quoted that he means the fulfillment of a preset task posed in general terms, and that he does not think it relevant to his pluralist concerns to differentiate between tasks that have artistic significance (e.g. to make a sculpture of a given generic form) and those that have none. Matters are further confused by introducing the pedagogical judgments of a teacher (apparently at a very elementary level). Such judgments are a very special case, often being made relative to a set of standards strictly internal to the particular bit of instruction that is going on. Perhaps what bothers Brook is that a teacher would hardly praise a student for making by accident something that would have been good if only he had been told to model an egg rather than a sphere, for one sees no reason why the teacher should not say that the student's accidental egg was a good *sculpture*, if it really was, by way of incidentally boosting his aesthetic sense and so on.

46. The introduction of the concept of success here may be compared with our earlier contention that the changes effected by art ideally amount to perfections. What is the relation between perfection and success? Roughly, perfection relates to the performance, the *opus operatum*, and success to the performing of it, the *operatio*. A work called perfect is alleged to lack nothing as judged by some ideal that is assumed in the context to be unquestionable; a successful work is one in which the artificer is judged to have attained some goal that he is assumed to have set himself— in formal contexts, that his way of proceeding (e.g. his entering a competition) shows that he has set himself. A critic who calls a work successful is claiming to have understood the workman as well as the work; one who calls a work perfect is implying that understanding was never a problem. Hence, the concept of perfection tends to cling to that of an art, in which the criteria and standards for judgment are assumed to be fixed, rather than to that of performance, in which the relevant standard is the attainment of a particular objective.

Other differences between the concepts of perfection and success are less useful to us. Only actions and attempts can succeed or fail, but anything for which a normal condition can be postulated can be perfect or imperfect. Again, success applies to definite but limited objectives, but perfection is an absolute beyond which one cannot go—even a limited perfection represents an ultimate within its limited sphere. By the same token, there can be degrees of approximation to perfection, whereas, although one can be more or less successful, success tends to be a hit-or-miss affair: either one succeeds or one fails. One might indeed argue that this either/or aspect of the concept of success bears on an important feature of critical practice: that one identifies and interprets a performance for one of two reasons, either to explain what has been succeeded in or to show what has gone wrong.

I will consider in another context (chap. 8) the contention that the concept of success has no proper application to the fine arts on the ground that success requires a more definite preset task than any the artists as such can be held to.

47. The irrelevance of an agent's intention to the nature of his performance is most explicitly recognized in legal contexts, where what the law is has to be fixed without deference to the lawgiver's belief about what law he was giving. Lon Fuller quotes in this connection from Campbell's *Lives of the Lord Chancellors of England:* "If Lord Nottingham drew it, he was the less qualified to construe it, the author of an act considering more what he privately intended than the meaning he has expressed" (Fuller 1969, 86n.).

48. The feeling may mislead: what we will see when we look along the pointing finger, and how we will conceptualize what we see, cannot always be predicted (see Sparshott 1974a). All the same, a person invited to look at Gaudí's *Sagrada Familia* can seldom be in much doubt as to what he is being shown.

49. The inevitability of such distinctions as these is one of the things that encourages exponents of the expressive line to speak of works of art as essentially mental constructs, the embodiment of which in a physical form is a relatively insignificant incident. But in fact the distinctions have no bearing on the special character of works of the fine arts, since they are equally germane to any critical practice.

50. Similarly, existentialists argue that in making his own life a human being assumes responsibility for his physical and psychological equipment and the social setting into which he finds himself born and grown (cf. Sartre 1943). What the artist

seeks is what a human being cannot avoid: that no recalcitrant element should remain unabsorbed into the domain of his freedom.

51. Compare his article "Arts" in the *Encyclopédie*. The subject of his article is not the fine arts but arts in general as the classical line understands them. His primary interest, in fact, is in technology.

52. An important difference among ends is that between those determined by an independent interest and those determined by a technique. If there is an art of medicine, it is because health (and longevity through health) is desired, however it may be achieved; if there is an art of welding, it is because welding is a complex skill the appropriate end of which is simply *having things welded*, an end that could not even be thought of before the technique of welding was developed.

53. Etienne Souriau urges that the appropriate matters of the fine arts are gamuts of sensible qualia (1947, 80-81), so that there can be as many such arts as there can be such gamuts. His argument requires what he indeed asserts: that, as the title of his book implies, the ends of all such arts are essentially the same, so that the changes introduced in the various gamuts are also analogous. "L'art consiste à nous conduire vers une impression de transcendance par rapport à un monde d'êtres et de choses qu'il pose par le seul moyen d'un jeu concertant de *qualia* sensibles, soutenu par un corps physique aménagé en vue de produire ces effets" (ibid., 71).

Maurice Grosser objects against Souriau's notion (though with direct reference to D. W. Prall rather than to Souriau) that the actual pigments a painter works with lack the regular order implied by his theory and supposedly exemplified in a "color solid": what will seem to be one given color in one light may be produced by several alternative blends of pigments that will not necessarily match under different lighting (Grosser 1951, 95-101). And, of course, it is obvious that any change in lighting will change color relationships. Such facts, and analogous facts about the acoustically anomalous properties of human voices and musical instruments, obviously affect the tasks of painters and musicians, but I do not see that they undermine Souriau's analysis. They only show that an artist's use of a gamut is complex.

54. When applied to the fine arts, the statement in the text has a controversial look: Michael Fried, for example, in the course of a polemic against what he regards as a tendency to substitute theater for art proper, attacks "the illusion that the barriers between the arts are in the process of crumbling. . . . Whereas in fact the individual arts have never been more explicitly concerned with the conventions that constitute their respective essences. . . . Within the modernist arts nothing short of *conviction*—specifically, the conviction that a particular painting or sculpture or poem or piece of music can or cannot support comparison with past work within that art whose quality is not in doubt—matters at all" (1967, 457). The statement is especially interesting in view of the common contention that the fine arts are not strictly speaking arts at all, because it suggests that the fine arts manifest the character of individuated arts in an exceptionally high degree (just as Souriau, as we will see in chapter 6, confronts the common claim that works of art are quasi objects with the contention that they are paradigms of objecthood). But what is really at issue here is not the determinacy of an art but the identifiability of a *tradition of work* to which the new work can be related and in terms of which alone it can be understood (compare chapter 8 on the generic function in criticism); and this tradition, even when question-beggingly called the mainstream, is not to be equated with the whole body of practice that pertains to the art in question.

55. The effect of private and public galleries is more equivocal. To some extent, the gallery acts as an accrediting institution: the purchaser goes to a fashionable gallery for a prestige object. To the artist, the gallery represents demand; to the

purchaser, it represents the institution by which art is authenticated and hence may merely transmit the artist's own conception of art. Public galleries complicate the question by sometimes following the baleful example of Diaghilev's request to Cocteau: "Amaze me!" Because they cater to transients, they tend to convert the demand for organized visual space (if that is what painters and sculptors fulfill) into the demand for *an experience*. In general, customers can use public galleries to support private galleries in their authenticating function, and artists can use them to symbolize demand. In both capacities, they are the institutions that play the greatest part in extrinsically organizing the art called "art."

56. For an analogous point about action, see note 32, above. That the identification of arts may have important practical consequences is argued by Thomas Munro (1949, 11ff.), who obviously does not share my view on the futility of enumerations.

57. Institutions are themselves abstractions, existing only in the form of understandings, rules, and conventions whose formulation becomes actual in the things that people say to establish them and do in compliance with them. Reality confronts us with people doing things that they justify with reference to classes of texts or utterances; to refer these actions to "arts" is to postulate the existence of connections, amounting to "organization," the recognition of which calls for an act of the teleological judgment, which can be verified only if one concedes in advance that such connections exist. The existence of an art, like the existence of a nation, represents a collective act of faith.

58. That arts exist in artists is recognized in a definition of an art given in Averroes' commentary on Aristotle's *Metaphysics*—quoted by Benedetto Varchi, who is quoted by Ces. Guesti, who is quoted by Erwin Panofsky in *Idea* (1968, 120), where I found it, and now pass on the torch—*Ars nihil aliud est, quam forma rei artificialis, existens in anima artificis: quae est principium factivum formae artificialis in materia,* "an art is nothing other than the form of an artificial thing as it exists in the maker's mind; this form is the principle that produces the artificial form as it exists in the matter." This looks at first like a confusion: surely the form of the individual work that preexists in the maker's mind is both more determinate and less far-reaching than the set of principles that go to make up the art. But Averroes could be thinking that what exists beforehand in the maker's mind is not the determinate form of the thing to be made but the knowledge and skills that determine the formal principles of all the things the artificer will make: the "artificial form" of the individual work is created, as is the work itself, when this general skill is actually exercised on the particular work. And this is no doubt Aristotle's own doctrine, for shortly after the passage quoted in note 30 he remarks that "the art of medicine and the art of building are the form respectively of health and of a house"; and he reminds us a little later that "a form indicates being of such and such a kind, it is not an individual" (*Metaphysics* Z, 8). After all, we may reflect, a doctor who administers thyroid extract to a cretin cannot know what his patient will be like when the treatment has succeeded.

59. A person who practices an art is not ordinarily called an artist, as I have called him here. That term is reserved for those who practice special arts (the fine arts in general, or the plastic arts in particular), or as a term of praise for those showing prowess and finesse in any art, or for those who fulfill a peculiar social role allied to that of the bohemian, or for those deemed worthy of a peculiar spiritual status. English has no special word for one who practices an art, but according to circumstances or whim may call him an artisan, a craftsman, a workman, an expert, a practitioner, or a professional. Of these, only the word "practitioner" seems to have a definite conceptual relationship with "art," and that word is restricted to a narrow

range of arts, notably medicine. For purely stylistic reasons, and *faute de mieux*, I sometimes use the term "artist" in this section to mean the practitioner of an art, as well as occasionally in its more ordinary significations.

As the term is most commonly used in English, an artist is a very special sort of person—by no means everyone is an artist. But practically everyone is an artist as I am using the term here, an accomplished practitioner of one or more arts, even if of arts not highly esteemed or generally recognized. That is, there will be matters in which he is an expert (he will do them with appropriate knowledge and skill) and on which he is an authority (he will be a good person to turn to for advice not only on how to perform the operations in question but on how to evaluate their products or outcomes).

60. Conversely, Aristotle insists (*Poetics* xxv) that a mistake in anatomy or zoology, though certainly a mistake, is not a mistake in the painter's art as such. One may protest that a novelist who makes a mistake in dialect or manners is the worse novelist for it; but perhaps if that is the case, it shows that the (Balzacian) novelist's art is not one of pure fiction, but calls for him to be a chronicler of his time—as Gilson argues and excludes novel writing from the fine arts accordingly (1964, 37). One might mount a similar argument about animal painting, in which the art is to make it appear that precision was not sought for its own sake but came about of itself in the pursuit of aesthetic values.

61. Any extraneous body of knowledge that an artist brings to his work will be analyzable, just as his art is, into a codifiable and an uncodifiable aspect: the general principles plus the store of information, and the individual understanding with which those principles and facts are put to work on particular occasions. In both aspects it will function as material to be ordered, not as part of the order intrinsic to the art.

62. I said before that a critic abstracts and constructs a performer as agent for the performance he criticizes. The "artist's life" that interests critic and public may be something like the sum of these abstractions, insofar as they cohere into an agency that strikes us as personlike. But there are several possibilities. What I have just mentioned is a constructed or imputed personality correlative with a recognizable style. But it is also possible to take an interest in works as expressions of a real agency. The "artist's life" that answers to such an interest consists of episodes that did indeed take place (or are believed to have done so), but are selected and interpreted for the light they shed on the quality of that agency, whether by congruence or by contrast—and that is something very different from the life as it must have seemed in the living of it to the artist or his personal associates. Neither of these is the same as the "persona" or fictitious personality that an artist assumes as a mask to give order and remoteness to his work (and which, being part of the fiction, belongs to what is performed rather than to the performer), or as the "artistic personality" that an artist such as Salvador Dali assumes as a foil to his oeuvre, of which one hardly knows whether it is to be numbered among his works or construed as a sort of guide to their correct interpretation.

63. All of Sartre's criticism seems committed to this view of art and literature: Genet's work, for example, is construed as a sort of reification of orphaned criminality (Sartre 1952). This is because Sartre thinks of any man's personality and character as fictions of the same order as literary works: since a man's character does not exist, it cannot cause anything.

64. The distinction between what is personal and what belongs to an art can be made to seem more doubtful by such an argument as the following. To understand

anything is to relate it to a context. A painting by de Kooning may make an immediate appeal to an unprepared observer. But it makes more sense when placed in the context of other paintings done by the same man at about the same time, more yet in the context of de Kooning's whole oeuvre. Understanding grows still more as the painting is related successively to the whole painting activity of his place and time, to his whole cultural background, to the entire history of modern painting, to the history of painting as a whole, to the history of civilization. The better one understands the fabric of artifice of which the painting is a fragment and from which it issues, the more one will understand of what de Kooning has done here. But is it not equally true that the painting issues from the life of the man de Kooning, and that the more one knows of the artist, the better one will understand the painting? Is it not likely that his personal friends see things in his work that everyone else misses? George Moore at least professed to understand Manet's painting better because he could recognize in the man the same personal habits that the paintings revealed in the painter. Technical context and personal background, it is argued, contribute to the understanding of a work of art in the same way and in similar degree. To this argument several counters are possible. The first is that the contention is false: there are few cases in which one who knows a painter *otherwise than in his character as a painter* gains much insight into his work. Painters' friends usually know more of their paintings, are exposed to them for longer, than other folk. A man who knows the painter only socially is not likely to acquire more than a feeling of acclimatization: what he takes to be comprehension of the work is really no more than a socially engendered receptivity. The second counter to the argument is that knowing the man may help to understand the painting because one knows something of its subject matter, just as it may be easier to see what a painter has done in a portrait if his subject is someone one knows. The third counter is that if knowledge of a man's personal life did help in the understanding of his work in some other manner than this, it would only be because paintings (like other complex and novel experiences and situations) are not easy to read at first sight and *anything at all* may help; but the help remains extrinsic and catalytic unless it can in the end be grounded in the perceptible quality of the work. The relevant quality of the artist then becomes that of the performer as reconstructed from his performance, and the painting is the-work-of-a-complex-man rather than a piece of work done by a man whose complexities one knows. The cultural and technical context, on the other hand, remains intrinsic to the work: every painting is, more or less consciously, a variation on other paintings.

To the third counter, the only important one, one can rejoin that every painting issues from a real person's hand no less certainly than it does from a tradition of painting, though not everyone will share the easy confidence expressed in the following advertisement placed by Dominion Stores Ltd. in the Scarborough *Mirror* of March 8, 1978, on page 25:

UNDERSTANDING ART IS EASY
IF YOU KNOW HOW TO LOOK AT IT

Learning to tell a Picasso painting from a five year
old's isn't as complicated as you might think.
Because most artists were simple people. And all
you need to understand their work is to understand
their lives.

65. This choice of ways of taking a work of art *as such* is not to be confused with the possibility, explored by Peter Gay (1976), of referring the origin of any work of art, like any other human event, to any or all of three independent systems of causes: cultural, technical, and psychological. None of these systems can be related to a work of art *as such*, because each is defined by its relation to the event *as a whole* (as it really happened). Gay's analyses, though full of interesting information, lack the conceptual penetration necessary to clarify the theoretical issues that perplex us here.

Chapter III. The Classical Line
2. Arts of Disengaged Communication

1. The transition in the text from painter to portraitist is deliberate. The Greek word for a painter of Giotto's sort was *zôgraphos*, which specifically means a limner of living things; similarly, a sculptor was *andriantopoios*, a figure maker. The concept of *zôgraphos* is neatly laid out in Plato's *Protagoras* (312 C-D): "If someone were to ask us 'Of what expertise are painters masters?' we would say something like 'Of that which pertains to the achievement of likenesses' (*tên apergasian tôn eikonôn*), and so on" (my translation). In the *Oxford English Dictionary*, a painter is still *by definition* one who uses colors to produce likenesses on flat surfaces—but not any more.

2. Less real in the sense that the painter is a real person and the people in his painting are only paint, though the painting is a perfectly real painting (and the people in his painting are real people, not stuffed dummies or cardboard cutouts, even though they are only painted people and not real people).

3. The definition appears in the *Epinomis*, usually ascribed to Philip of Opus, though it appears in the Platonic corpus as a posthumous work. In a general taxonomy of the arts, those necessary to sustain life are followed by "a sort of play, mostly mimetic but never serious" (975 D, my translation), using all sorts of instruments and parts of the body, divided into (a) arts using words and music and (b) drawing and the arts derived therefrom, using various liquid and solid media. The elements in this classification are not obscure, but the articulation of the whole is quite garbled, and one cannot determine precisely the principles on which it is based.

The source of Philip's definition is transparently Plato's *Republic* (597 E), where poetry and painting are described as *mimêsis* (glossed as imitation of appearances) through hearing and sight, respectively, though Plato does not there envisage a general classification of "arts of imitation." In the same context Plato also dismisses both sorts of *mimêsis* as play and not "serious" (*spoudê*), as part of a dishonest move that equivocates on the double sense of the latter word as meaning "respectable" as well as "serious," so that the imitative arts, not being *spoudaia*, are said to be for that reason *phaula* "degraded." That *all* "musical creations" (*poiêmata peri tên mousikên* are imitation and likeness making (*mimêsis te kai apeikasia*) is insisted on again in his *Laws* (668 B-C); but there again there is no allusion to any general class of arts of imitation or of likeness making, even though the latter phrase is one more naturally applied to painting than to drama.

4. Rader and Jessup write: "Like other fundamental interests, art becomes a specialized pursuit, aiming to serve a common need. The result is the professional

artist and *fine* art-works which express in a higher degree and with conscious purpose and trained skill the beauty of harmony and appearance which is otherwise sought more or less by the way in practical living. The artist is one of our specialists" (1976, 121). However accurately it defines the artist's function, this puts the development the wrong way round. There is no such specialist as "the artist." Rather, specialists in this or that art of communication, or fabrication, or whatever, come to be grouped together as serving in their different ways a need that is generically the same.

5. The *Epinomis* passage cited in note 3 explicitly denies that all the recreational arts it speaks of are representational. From the *Symposium* one may infer a reason for Plato's lack of interest: the love of beauty is best exercised on things other than artifacts. In the *Republic* (475 D-E) the love of seeing and hearing is recognized as a widespread interest and disparaged.

6. Note that the poetry in question is explicitly restricted to *so much of it as is representational,* a restriction corresponding to that implied for painting by the concept *zôgraphia* itself.

7. Language is not always used to give information: one may also ask questions, make suggestions, give orders, and so on. But, in those cases, I am telling you what I want to know, what I want you to do, and so on. And I use the same linguistic skill (in most languages the very same form of words) whether or not I really want you to do it, really want to know it, and so on.

8. Fictionality (which applies in exactly the same way to what is shown as it does to what is said) is not the same as falsehood—a point that has escaped many theorists and bedeviled many discussions. What is put forward as fictional is not put forward *as untrue,* nor is it (falsely) put forward *as true*: it is put forward *otherwise than as* factually true, whether it is in fact true or not. Fictionality belongs properly to narratives, depictions, and so on as wholes, not to their component parts (such as sentences), and does not directly affect the truth value of those parts. The parts may be asserted, denied, or entertained, as true, or false, or undetermined, in terms of the narrative or presentational framework or of real life; and their value in the one framework may, or may not, be relevant in the other. In a story I am telling, it may be asserted or denied that in 1878 there was a brothel at 17 Jarvis Street, and in the story the assertion or denial may be true or untrue (a mistake or a lie): and *in any case* it may be important to my fiction that there really was a brothel where my story puts it, or that there really was not—or it may be a matter of indifference. But none of those possibilities, all of which are important resources for me as a storyteller, affects in any way the fact that the status of what I am telling is *fictional.*

The contention of the last paragraph, as it stands, requires clarification if not correction. What is the scope of the expression "parts (such as sentences)"? For a chapter of a novel is a part of the novel and is obviously as fictional as the novel itself, and so is any episode within the chapter; but a paragraph is a string of sentences, and so is a whole chapter. It is primarily for this reason that most authorities have insisted that every sentence in a work of fiction is fictional. But simply to say that is to deny an important resource of the storyteller, if not to falsify altogether the nature of what he does. What we should say is something like the following. Fictionality is a property of the whole and of its rhetorically proper parts— its chapters and episodes and whatever else the analysis of fictions as such may come up with or down to. But the component sentences operate in two fields of force: that of the fiction and that of the world in which the writer and the reader both live. A story may exist as told by a pure authorial voice to an abstract audiential ear, but is enclosed within a context in which voice and ear alike are maintained by speaker and hearer. Every sentence of the story belongs to both contexts. Part of understanding the story is understanding for each sentence the extent to which each context properly prevails over it. In his careful study of the logic of fictionality, John Woods (1974) makes an analogous point about statements relating fictional to real-life characters: that Sherlock Holmes was a patient of Sigmund Freud is, as part of Freud's biography, false; as part of Holmes's biography, true (or, rather, since *The Seven-Per-Cent Solution* belongs to the apocrypha, apocryphal).

It may be worthwhile to distinguish between fictionality and auctoriality: what is auctorial is put forward with emphasis on its being *a work of* an author or artist; what is fictional is put forward otherwise than as factually true. A biography or history may have auctoriality but not fictionality. On pure auctoriality, see chapter 9, note 11.

9. Plato in *Republic* X is discussing fictional values exclusively, so it often escapes notice that, in that very passage (cf. 607 C-D), he explicitly acknowledges the reality and power of formal values, though he does not discuss them.

10. See also W. M. Ivins's seminal work (1953) for testimony that the original and prevailing use of prints was to instruct and inform, not to give aesthetic pleasure.

11. The two definitions answer, respectively, to the presentational and fictional development of cognitive skills in disengaged communication. That in itself would afford a reason for looking first at the definition in terms of imitations.

12. The phrase "common bond" (*commune vinculum*, actually) is from Cicero, who applied it to what he vaguely called "all the arts that pertain to humanity" (*Pro Archia Poeta* I.2 [my translation]), including rhetoric and poetry. But that phrase suggests a grouping of arts different from any likely ancestor of the fine arts.

13. Souriau neatly accommodates and defuses this possibility by urging that every gamut of sensible qualia (of which, by the by, he identifies seven: line, color, relief, luminosity, body movement, vocal articulation, and pure sound—a list in which I, for one, would have more confidence if the number of items were less Biblical) generates not one art but two: a single art organized directly and a double art in which part of the organization is carried out indirectly through representation (1947, 88). I wish I could think of things like that—but I'm glad I don't believe them.

14. Karl Aschenbrenner, for instance, summarizes the import of his magisterial collection and analysis of critical utterances in the following words: "One can see immediately, in the classes into which the critiques fall, that the unity of the arts, from the standpoint of criticism, is an accomplished fact. From various a priori standpoints this has often been contested for various insufficient reasons. Here we see that critics offering basic appraisals in visual, auditory and literary art use fundamentally the same body of appraisive concepts, and we can see also where the necessary, particular differences lie" (1974, x). No one has yet cast serious doubt on Aschenbrenner's evidence or his reading of it, and until that is done his view must hold the field.

That the affinity of the fine arts is not recognized only by the modern West is shown by the following extract from the sixth-century Sanskrit text *Vishnudharmottara*, presuming that text to be authentic and correctly rendered:

A King once approached a Sage and asked to be taught the craft of image-making. The following dialogue ensued:

KING: O Sinless One! Be good enough to teach me the methods of image-making.
SAGE: One who does not know the laws of painting can never understand the laws of image-making.

KING: Be then good enough, O Sage, to teach me the laws of painting.

SAGE: But it is difficult to understand the laws of painting without any knowledge of the technique of dancing.

KING: Kindly instruct me then in the art of dancing.

SAGE: This is difficult to understand without a thorough knowledge of instrumental music.

KING: Teach me then, O Sage, the laws of instrumental music.

SAGE: But the laws of instrumental music cannot be learned without a deep knowledge of the arts of vocal music.

KING: If vocal music be the source of all arts, reveal to me, then, O Sage, the laws of vocal music (Gosvami 1961, xv).

If the King, reflecting that a sinless one is likely to be a gormless one, had asked a sculptor instead of a sage, he might have got a different response. Indian theorists belonged to castes for which sculpture was not a possible occupation and for which a theoretical affinity would outweigh a practical divergence.

15. A fine example of Art by Institutionalization is offered by Dr. Reyner Banham: "writers on California pop-art who try to explain that Von Dutch 'is a professional painter of custom cars and not an artist' have got it wrong. Von Dutch is an artist *because* he is a customiser, and because he is accepted as an artist by many members of the Los Angeles art community like Billy Al Bengston" (1978, 330). Mr. Bengston, himself a respected painter, got to be a member of the Los Angeles art community in a rather different way; nor are we told whether *his* reason for accepting Von Dutch as an artist was that he is a customizer.

16. For a lot more about the concept of play in its relation to aesthetics, see Sparshott (1970c) and references there cited.

17. Plato calls his own dialogues play—perhaps in depreciation, perhaps in irony, perhaps simply in recognition of their nature (*Phaedrus* 276 E).

18. This is perhaps the underlying perception of Alain's *Système des beaux arts* (1926).

19. See Schiller (1795). Schiller, like many writers on the topic, could not decide whether the "play" of art was mainly valuable for its contribution to everyday life or because it was itself a superior form of life.

20. See Wittgenstein (1953). Bernard Suits (1978) has produced and defended a definition of a game (not of play) that would not apply to art, though much of what he says sheds light on much in the arts; but it is not certain that Wittgenstein stands refuted, since Suits does not allow usage to be decisive and actually uses his definition to determine what is and what is not properly called a game (Suits 1978, 92). Besides, his argument rests on a verbal separation between "play" and "game" that does not exist in German (the language in which Wittgenstein wrote and thought) or in French.

21. R. F. Dearden protests against the habit of talking as if children spent all their time playing. Much of what they do is work (e.g. drying dishes) or routine (dressing, excreting) or social involvement (visiting), even among the present-day bourgeoisie—a fact that also shows, as he suggests, that the supposed dichotomy of "play" and "work" is absurdly simple-minded (Dearden 1967, 76-77).

22. Aristotle (*Metaphysics* A, 1) distinguishes the arts that provide necessities (and are undertaken from necessity) from those arts that are freely undertaken because they contribute to the quality of life (*pros diagôgên*). Hannah Arendt (1958) elaborates an ancient tradition to distinguish four ways of life: the contemplative, the creative, the active, and the laboring. She assigns the concept of play to the context

of labor, for which value is exhausted in providing the day's consumables. In the active and creative lives, what is valued is what lasts and is remembered. For further discussion, see chapter 10.

23. The pairing of painting and poetry was a commonplace in antiquity and the Renaissance. Here is one of innumerable instances: "*Poetry*, and *Picture*, are Arts of a like nature; and both are busie about imitation. It was excellently said of *Plutarch*, *Poetry* was a speaking Picture, and *Picture* a mute Poesie. For they both invent, faine, and devise many things, and accommodate all they invent to the use, and service of nature" (Jonson 1641, lines 1509ff.).

24. Plato's own word was *mimêsis*, which in its original use comes close to "imitation"—the impersonation of another through the voice. The unnatural extension of the word in Plato's usage seems to come about through insistence, first, on the triviality of the distinction between indirect and direct speech and, second, on the closeness of the analogy between verbal narrative and depiction. A further extension to subjective lyric comes about through the easy transition from impersonating another actual person in grief, through giving an impression of a person in grief (the sort of *mimêsis* actors actually do), through singing as if I were in grief, to singing my grief out—so that a song that expresses my feelings can be said to imitate my inner grieving self.

25. The doctrine in question is taken to be the conventional wisdom and subjected to critical discussion by Zemach (1975), though he does not accept it. The most sustained attack on the idea of likeness and its relevance to depiction is that of Nelson Goodman, who writes: "Similarity cannot be equated with, or measured in terms of, possession of common characteristics," because "any two things have exactly as many properties in common as any other two." Nor can it be equated with the sharing of important properties, because "importance is a highly volatile matter, varying with every shift of context and interest, and quite incapable of supporting the fixed distinctions that philosophers so often seek to rest upon it. . . . Clear enough when loosely confined by contexts and circumstances in ordinary discussion, it is hopelessly ambiguous when torn loose" (Goodman 1972, 443-444). Goodman seems to infer that likeness, since it resists any precise explanation, has itself no explanatory value; and he seems then to infer from that that depiction, if it is to figure in any theory of symbolism, must be explained in terms that bypass the notion of likeness altogether (I say "seems" because Goodman omits crucial steps in the argument he requires). Neither inference is legitimate, because some irreducible terms must figure in any explanation ("denotation" figures as an unexplained term in Goodman's own exposition [1968] and is at least as hard to explain as "likeness"), and because symbol systems are used for communication between sentient beings and therefore require what is psychologically workable rather than what is logically explicable though psychologically null.

Goodman's mistake, if he makes one, is to suppose that context-free analyses have an overriding importance, presumably on the ground that contexts have no stability (are "volatile," to borrow a term from the passage quoted above). But as Walton (1978) and many others have observed, we do know how to look at paintings, what to take into account and (especially) what to leave out of account: the point is that such knowledge and learning *are possible*, that context *can be specified* and may remain stable for long times, and this could not be the case in a world in which "any two things have exactly as many properties in common as any other two" in any interesting way. Goodman's treatment of properties is reminiscent of (is indeed perhaps modeled on) Hume's treatment of relations: any two things are related (since "having nothing to do with" is, technically speaking, as much a relation as any other), and related in an indefinitely large number of ways: when we say in ordinary life that two things are or are not related, we are working with a socially accepted and psychologically effective but logically inexplicable notion of "having to do with." But on a crucial point Goodman's treatment departs from Hume's: whereas Hume, in the tradition of ancient skepticism, inferred that in all practical matters we are necessarily guided by considerations that have no foundation in reason, so that the claims of reason are at least as badly damaged by the requirements of practice as practical justification is undermined by the failure of reason to support it, Goodman appears to accept without irony the priority of reason.

What is the "reason" whose priority Goodman seems to accept so solemnly? In what context of thought does it make sense to say that "any two things have exactly as many properties in common as any other two"? It is on this proposition that Goodman's whole argument turns, but it seems quite crazy. Does he seriously mean that identical twins have no more in common with each other than either has with the polestar? To make sense of the claim, we have to go back to his metaphysical work, where we find that to share a property with something is to belong to the same set as it does, and sets are defined purely extensionally as the sums of their members: in *any* universe of four entities, for instance, *any* two of them will have in common that they belong to one two-member set, two three-member sets, and one four-member set (Goodman 1951). The same considerations apply to any universe of however many members, so that what Goodman says is perfectly true. What most discussions of Goodman's arguments about likeness ignore is that it is *only* on the basis of this quite extraordinary way of thinking about characteristics that what he says has any plausibility. That the way of thinking is truly extraordinary becomes evident as soon as one realizes that it absolutely requires that the "things" said to share characteristics with each other are themselves construed as being *entirely featureless*. (It works like this: in formalized language, we put all characteristics and features into the predicate; if we take that language as describing the world, the world it describes is one consisting of [initially or basically] featureless things that have features. If we then construe predicate terms as assigning things to sets of things, the sets to which they are assigned are sets of things that have no features other than that of forming part of this or that set, the sets themselves being differentiated only by including or excluding members that other sets do not.) And why should anyone adopt so extraordinary a view? Goodman (1951) is quite explicit on the point. Contemporary formal logic works best when construed extensionally, and that logic is the only well-articulated tool of thought we have; consequently, the careful philosopher will think in patterns that conform to that logic. Goodman's way of thinking is in fact Parmenidean: one insists that serious thought be based on the accidental conveniences of the preferred logic of one's day, without stopping to consider whether any effective thinking can be done in those terms.

Despite the foregoing strictures, Goodman's principal contention remains untouched: what is ordinarily meant by likeness must be understood in terms of something like *recognizability*, not in terms of shared characteristics otherwise specifiable.

26. In the very work that contains his "Seven Strictures on Similarity," we find Goodman writing: "Too little regard for system can lead us to run in circles or to overlook important likenesses while we are busy cataloguing subtle distinctions" (1972, 44). There is something odd in writing as if a more scientifically reputable language would be one in which such points *coud not be made*.

27. There is an ambiguity in "intended properties." Goodman points out that one can make a true copy of a diagram, but not of a painting: one can specify exhaustively what features of a diagram are relevant, but in a painting anything that may ever become detectable may be relevant, so that no copyist can guarantee that his copy has copied everything that would ever prove to be relevant (1968, 230). Even the painter cannot specify beforehand exactly what will be discoverable in his painting, though the draftsman of a diagram can. In one sense, only what can be prescribed beforehand can be intended; in another sense, it is enough that something in a message (or whatever) be accepted and endorsed by the author when specified by others. In the latter sense, I can legitimately say yes when asked if I meant something I did not actually think of at the time, but now recognize as part of the overall strategy of my action.

28. Thus, James J. Gibson defines a picture as "a surface so treated that a delimited optical array to a point of observation is made available that contains the same kind of information that is found in the ambient optic arrays of an ordinary environment," it being understood that "information consists of invariants, in the mathematical sense, of the structure of an optic array" (1971, 31). But what constitutes sameness of kind of information remains to be determined. Presumably the argument is that the *same* ability that enables us to recognize something when we see it from an angle we never saw it from before enables us to recognize "it" when we see "it" in a painting.

29. I take it that it is not possible for painting to achieve perfect likeness. The pigment cannot match the range of luminosity of reflected daylight, let alone the phenomena of translucency and depth. It seems unlikely that perfect likeness can be achieved by sculpture.

30. Morawski says of waxwork figures that "a moment's reflection is enough to make us wonder whether even these are the examples of replicas that they appear to be. After all, the whole point of a dummy is to create the illusion of something being what it cannot be" (1974, 206). We are meant to marvel at the likeness, not to be taken in by it—our marveling being expressed in the thought that we *could* be taken in by it, we can imagine ourselves being deceived.

31. Certain anecdotes retailed by the elder Pliny, about birds pecking painted grapes and what not, suggest (despite heroic efforts to interpret them as testifying to the Orpheus-like magic power exercised by art over the animal kingdom) that at one time the function of painting was to produce successful imitations. But the point of those stories seems to be rather that such momentary deceptions served, after they were seen through, as irrefutable testimony to skilled craftsmanship. Similarly, a trompe l'oeil still life by Peto does not succeed by substitution and deception; if one did not know it was a painting, one would not marvel at the likeness, and exposition of the deception would rob the painting of all interest instead of (as is actually the case) being the precondition of its having *any* of the value we find in it. Similarly again, a baroque ceiling in which one cannot tell just where the architecture stops and the painting begins is not a way of saving money by substituting cheap paint for expensive stone, and is not meant to deceive the beholder: it is *the fact that* one cannot tell the difference that enters into the complex experience of make-believe and speculation.

32. I gather from Francis Hare (in a communication to the Toronto Aesthetics Study Group) that in certain experiments judgments of *undefined* "similarity" show a high agreement; but I do not understand enough of what is going on to comment intelligently. For some further information see Berlyne (1976).

534

33. Such a manifest essence is implied in H.-G. Gadamer's observation that, since to recognize something is to see it *as* what was seen before, and hence in abstraction both from its context then and from its context now, what is recognized, and hence what is represented in art, is always the abiding form of a thing (*die bleibende Gestalt*), or in other words its essence (Gadamer 1967, 22-23).

34. The possibility of visual stereotyping reminds us that there is an important difference between modes of likeness that cuts across the distinction between being like and looking like: one thing may be like another because they share specific criteria of identity, whether these criteria pertain to appearance, to function, or to sort; or one thing may be like another because they are associated by conventions and habits of recognition. In the latter case, the learned skill in recognizing is exercised on things or situations as wholes, in the former case, on specific characteristics.

35. Thus, Gombrich writes that "all artistic discoveries are discoveries not of likenesses but of equivalences which enable us to see reality in terms of an image and an image in terms of reality. . . . These identities do not depend on the imitation of individual features so much as on configurations of clues" (1960, 345). In other words, a likeness is produced by a likeness-making method, not by the mechanical combination of discovered likenesses; but it is still true that the resultant likeness is seen, not believed in.

36 It may be possible to arrange painting styles in more than one hierarchy of increasing naturalism, increasing realism, or increasing lifelikeness in this or that respect, and there may be no one overall hierarchy of verisimilitude; but that need not shed any doubt on the relevance of the hierarchies themselves to likeness, or on rankings within the hierarchies, any more than similar considerations in cartography prevent fidelity from being a firm desideratum in maps.

37. If he is an imported dog, he may only be able to recognize *gavagais*, but that will do just as well (for us, not for the dog—he may never be able to catch the *gavagai* he chases). Cf Quine (1960, 51-52).

38. We perform this inspection in confidence that we will find likeness if likeness is there. That we may not "know the convention" does not strike us as a possible hazard. Anecdotes about tribesmen who cannot recognize photographs, if they can be relied on at all, concern tribes who lack any practice of depiction. If there is any difficulty in discerning likenesses in an unfamiliar convention, it is no greater than that of discerning the formal principles by which the picture is organized; it is in no way comparable to the difficulty of understanding what is being said in an unfamiliar language, and there are no techniques of likeness learning comparable to the techniques of language learning. It seems that all civilizations produce likenesses immediately recognizable to members of any other civilization, however variously different their pictorial conventions may be, whereas their languages retain great mutual opacity. Perhaps this is because we in effect confine the word "civilization" to societal organizations in which people who do not know each other have to communicate on matters not already familiar to both of them, so that they have to work out generalizable schemata of depiction, and our text already makes it likely that any such schema will be akin to any other such schemata. What Trobrianders say and show to Trobianders, on the other hand, is all in the family.

Since the subject of convention has come up, it may be worthwhile to glance at the systematic treatment of the topic by Lewis (1969). His definition of a convention requires that it be common knowledge (i.e. everyone knows that everyone knows) that everyone conforms to the practice in question, and everyone prefers to do so provided everyone else does, because in that way a desired coordination can be achieved. It must also be common knowledge that an alternative practice would have achieved the same end (Lewis 1969, 56-58 and 70-74). Is a way of likeness making conventional in this sense? Well, there is (as the end of the preceding paragraph suggests) a coordination problem: everyone should be able to recognize what anyone draws, and (since anything can be mapped onto anything) that requirement does not suffice to determine a precise method of representation. On the other hand, it is by no means clear that those who share a way of drawing think of it as one way of drawing among others rather than as the one right way to show things as they are; and it is not clear that it is typically the case that only one method of representation prevails in a given population, or that anything would be gained if it did. The criterion is never conformity, always recognizability. It would seem to follow that the element of conventionality in general schemes of likeness making is attenuated at best: the topic of quasi conventions or degrees of conventionality is one that Lewis does not broach. On the other hand, schematic and emblematic ways of drawing particular things and kinds of things are conventional in Lewis's sense, unless those who draw in that way believe that their method has moral or magical properties that rival symbolizations would lack.

Even less than representational methods do artistic practices generally conform to Lewis's definition. The "convention" of ending a musical piece with a dominant tonic cadence may prevail as an imperative or serve as a bench mark to organize expectation, and we will have occasion to observe that such organization may well be a necessary resource of the fine arts; but it does not seem to be the case that conformity *as such* is an overriding value, as Lewis requires of a convention.

39. The relationships here can be made to seem mildly paradoxical. As Wollheim says, what looks like the man depicted by a painting is not the painting but the man in the painting (and what looks like the man portrayed by a sculpture is not the sculpture but the sculpted man, or the man-in-the-sculpture) (1968, 16). But the depicted man and the painting are alike in being in the real world, to which the man-in-the-painting does not belong.

W. V. Quine speaks of "the conniving mode of speech: the mode in which we knowingly speak of Olivier as Macbeth, of a statue of a horse as a horse, of a false nickel as a nickel" (1960, 50). It is rather the horse-in-the-statue that we speak of as a horse, because, after all, that is what it is: what does Quine think it is, a camel? To connive, we note, is to acquiesce in and thus facilitate a known evil; but what does Quine take the evil to be? The evil would be the inability to see the horse in the statue and admit that one saw it.

40. The theme here touched on has been made his own by Richard Wollheim in a number of subtle writings. For the immediate point, compare the following: "We could not imagine a man forming any intention at all to represent something, unless he could also anticipate how the drawing would look. . . . The intention . . . looks forward to the representational seeing" (Wollheim 1968, 18).

41. One standard formulation states that in representation the reference is carried by iconicity: it is because the picture is taken to look like such and such that it is taken to refer to such and such, if it refers to anything. Like the notion of likeness, that of iconicity has been attacked. Umberto Eco, for instance, points out that in an outline drawing of a horse "the sole property that my horse possesses (one continuous black line) is precisely the property that a real horse does not possess" (1976, 193-194) and that likeness explains nothing because different cultures have different recognition codes (ibid., 206-207). But one does not see how either of

these truths undermines the distinction between signs that function by being *recognized as* like their originals and those that function (as words do) by being *known to* stand for them. Again, Goodman claims that his analysis reveals that the distinction between iconic and other signs is trivial: the significant distinction is that between dense (depicting) and articulate (linguistic) symbolic schemes (1968, 231). From the point of view of a systematic classification of symbolic schemes, he is quite right; but one does not see how the distinction between reference through recognition and reference through language learning is thereby made anything less than fundamental. It is, I think, only a partly intended consequence of Goodman's position that *any* picture represents Churchill if it denotes Churchill and is a dense and relatively replete symbol—though it does not represent Churchill *as Churchill* unless it is a Churchill picture as well as representing Churchill (Goodman 1972, 123). It is partly intentional, because he wants to allow for the possibility that a picture of a bulldog might represent Churchill (as a bulldog), being a bulldog picture denoting Churchill. But it is perhaps partly unintentional, since the conditions of denotation (and indeed the meaning of "denote") are left entirely open, so that a picture denoting Churchill will be *no more* likely to look like him (be a Churchill picture) than like anything else. Perhaps one can resolve that difficulty by considering that a picture must be a something picture, and, if it represents Churchill, it must represent him as something; and if it represents him as something other than Churchill, one would need a reason. But to say that is to allow a privilege to Churchill pictures that we only allow them because they are, in fact, recognizably pictures of Churchill. And so we go round the mulberry bush.

42. I have in effect been constructing a sort of porphyrian tree of makings-like. Some things are made to be like in function, some in appearance; of the former, some are duplicates (having the same functional properties), some substitutes (fulfilling the same function but not necessarily by the same properties). Of things made to be like in appearance, some have all the relevantly same dimensions and proportions, some merely look similar from a certain standpoint. Of the former, some preserve the same proportions (replicas, some of which are copies), some only the same system of relations (maps). Of those that look similar from a certain standpoint (depictions), some depict actual individuals (portraits), and others depict beings (not necessarily actual) recognizably of a certain kind. Note that I do not incorporate Goodman's classification of symbol systems, not from disrespect or in disparagement, but because it is not necessary to my argument.

43. For some suggestions about what makes a picture a representation of one thing rather than another, see Beardsley (1966b); his position is that portrayal is reference (a portrait denotes someone), but representation is sense (a depiction does not denote anything) (1966b, 77).

44. The cautious wording is deliberate: Goodman's treatment combines intricacy, subtlety, elegance, and puckishness in a way that precludes confident interpretation.

45. The first systematic attempt to show how the fine arts can really all be doing the same thing (viz. imitating) is that of the Abbé Batteux (1746). His point is not that the imitative arts all imitate, an obvious tautology, but that they all have the same function or principle, to imitate *la belle nature*; and *la belle nature*, like Sidney's "golden" world, can be interpreted alternatively as a projected idealized world and as the ideal archetypal world of essences of which our visible world is a poor imitation.

46. Most writers on the question of what it is to be a picture of something fail to take account of the full range of possibilities. Taking into account only pictorial

representation that uses a dense and replete symbol system and works entirely through recognized likeness and assigned denotation (i.e. labels and such), and leaving out of account such alternatives as mapping and diagraming, we still have to reckon with at least the following. Let A be an artist, P his proper public (those for whom he works and on whose complicity in understanding he relies), O an observer from another place and time who has A's work before him and may or may not be cognizant of or interested in A or P, and let M be what A's picture is *of*.

The first thing we have to note is that M may be designated in at least five ways: (1) by a "logically proper name," some appellation or gesture that picks it out, but does not characterize or classify it in any way; (2) by a definite description that identifies and correctly describes it and only it (e.g. "George's favorite horse"—and it *was* his favorite)—obviously, many such descriptions may be used to identify M; (3) by an *incorrect* definite description (e.g. "George's favorite horse"—but really he hated it)—obviously, an infinite number of such descriptions can be used to identify M, and what was "the painter and his wife" yesterday may be "Jan Arnolfini's wedding" tomorrow; (4) by an applicable general description (e.g. "a stallion," and it is one); and (5) an inapplicable general description (e.g. "a stallion," but it is or was a gelding; the artist used his imagination to supply the defects of his model, or the critic overinterpreted, or whatever).

Now, when we say that A has made a drawing of M (designating M in one or more of the above ways), one thing we may mean is that A has set out to make (and has succeeded in making) a drawing of M (thinking of it in one or more of the above ways, not necessarily the one *we* have in mind). And by "making a drawing of M" in this second occurrence (I could have said "drawing M," but did not wish to suggest that such a difference in usage prevails), we may mean (a) a drawing for which M served as model or motif; (b) a drawing referring back to M, denoting M; (c) a drawing apt to serve as a likeness of M (recognizable as M, with or without hints, with or without prior schooling in the style employed, with or without prior acquaintance with drawings of any kind, whether or not the likeness is naturalistic, realistic, or lifelike); (d) a drawing for P to recognize as M; (e) a drawing for P to recognize as meant to represent or portray M; (f) a drawing for P to recognize as meant to be recognized as M. If A is very ambitious, or if we who speak of him are absolutists in our beliefs about likeness, we may add three more possibilities, corresponding to (d), (e), and (f), but with O substituted for P. A's intentions, and our assessment of them, are not confined to only one of (a) through (f): when we say that A draws M, what we have in mind may be any logically possible combination of those, and we probably do not know beforehand just which interpretations we would accept and which we would reject if we had to make up our minds.

A second thing we might mean is that A, whatever he set out to do, drew something that he *now endorses and presents* in one or more of the capacities (a) through (f), though a retrospective endorsement of (a) is perhaps a bit dishonest.

A third thing we might mean is that A has drawn something that P takes in one or more of the capacities (a) through (f); either (1) accepting A's claim for what he has done, or (2) without regard to any claim A may have made, or (3) in defiance of such a claim. If we mean that, it makes a difference whether we are ourselves speaking as P or as O.

There is a fourth possibility: that A has drawn something that P judges A to have meant in one or more of the ways (a) through (f). That sounds a bit far-fetched, but actually something rather like that is what we mean when we talk about drawings children do in nursery school.

Another set of possibilities can be generated simply by substituting projection for reference in the foregoing and making omissions and modifications, eliminating (a), for instance, where necessary. Yet another set can be generated by introducing *O*, who can see *M* in *A*'s picture, recognizes that it may have been meant by *A* in one way and taken by *P* perhaps in another, but nonetheless says that *A* has drawn what he, *O*, sees in *A*'s drawing.

All of the above are real possibilities, and most of them are familiar; and references to "*A*'s drawing of *M*" do not discriminate between them other than contextually. And how would one know when such a list of possibilities was complete? There seems to be a vast, indeterminate range of intertwined relationships.

47. The most famous and outrageous of such simplifications is that whereby Plato in *Republic* X identifies the likeness the painter produces with the kind of image one sees in a mirror. Plato's sleight of hand here is to *assume* the important point, that the painter's likeness refers back to an antecedent reality, and to *assert*, what it would be folly to deny, that the painter's training fits him to reproduce only appearances and not realities. (Even on his own terms, as Suits (1978) makes clear for the first time, suggesting that the painter could save time by using a mirror instead of pigments is like suggesting that one could win a chess game more quickly by forcibly sweeping all one's opponent's pieces off the board.)

Frank Newfeld's illustration to chapter 8 of Suits's book incidentally affords an extreme example of the perplexities of "being a picture of." The drawing is explicitly identified as illustrating a passage in which Suits imagines Sir Edmund Hillary climbing Everest, only to be met on the summit by "an immaculately groomed Londoner, complete with bowler hat and furled unbrella." What Newfeld's drawing shows is a handsome youth in a late Victorian boy's costume, bouquet in hand, scaling a crag on the top of which reclines a lady of the same epoch, carrying an open parasol. What is that a picture of, exactly? One might at a pinch say that it depicted Everest as a ferny crag; but can we really bring ourselves to say that it depicts a bowler-hatted Londoner with furled umbrella as a lady with a parasol? And yet, if we do not say that, how can we say what Newfeld is up to? We can conjecture a set of motives: someone called Sir Edmund Hillary certainly ought to look like that, and the composition works better with a horizontal rather than a vertical figure on the summit, and horizontality becomes the young lady better than it would have the bowler-hatted Londoner. And the drawing has after all *something* in common with Suits's text—a person is climbing a cliff on top of which someone already is. But what are we to say of the relationship? What we in fact say is what I already said: Newfeld has illustrated a passage in which *p* by a drawing that shows *q* (or, to preserve the symmetry, "a drawing in which *q*")—the word "illustrate" is redolent of resignation. And we go on to specify the relationship by saying that the artist has depicted *X* as *Y* or has replaced *X* by *Y*, depending on whether *X* is a named individual or a representative of a type and on whether or not we accept that there is a possible world in which *X* could be *Y*.

48. It is because there need be no perceptible difference between someone saying something seriously and his saying it as part of a play that there are so many plays in which the players represent actors whose real-life situation duplicates or contradicts the situation in the play within the play.

49. Play action and play speech are (unless one is very unlucky) more economical

and pointed than ordinary speech, and a stage actor does not (unless one is extraordinarily unlucky) speak or move as he would in real life: a naturalistic style of acting is one in which we are enabled to imagine that we are watching people going about their business, as a naturalistic painting was one in which we were able to imagine that we were looking at a scene in nature, or that, if we were looking at such a scene, what we saw might be no different from what we were seeing now. An actor's speech must have an element of elocution, and his motion an element of mime. Pure mime can never be naturalistic: to make silent action recognizable, it creates for actions a characteristic look, counterpointed by a nonnaturalistic alternation of expressiveness and inexpressiveness of countenance designed to make impossible even a momentary lapse into the illusion that we are watching someone doing something (other than miming). At the other extreme from the mime is the "double"—someone who, for reasons of economy or security, impersonates a personage, imitating him in looks, speech, and action. He does not act the part of his model and does not do an imitation of him, for his object is, not to move and convince by likeness, nor to amuse by likeness-in-difference, but simply to be like his model and be mistaken for him: his aim really is that which is mistakenly attributed to waxwork effigies and trompe l'oeil paintings. His contrived likeness to his model does not make him a work of fine art, and his impersonation would fail if it were to be one, for it could be one only by being theatrical and convincing rather than mundane and deceptive.

If the dictator's double is not and does not create a work of fine art, and a waxwork figure is not one either, what of the attendant at the waxwork show who traditionally stands near the entrance impersonating one of the waxworks (giving an imitation of a waxwork, perhaps, though he is not an imitation waxwork)? His impersonation may be a work of art, because it fails of its effect if it quite succeeds (as the bogus dictator and the imitation flower should succeed) in deceiving: the aim of his skill is to be found out, though not immediately and not at first with certainty, in such a way that, once penetrated, the disguise can no longer convince. Such a skill might, though it need not, be brought within the domain of the fine arts by a theorist of the classical line.

˙ 50. Plato's objection to acting as a pastime was that one could not in fact do the former of these without doing the latter as well, which he thought fatal to one's integrity (*Republic* IV). It is not clear why he thought it impossible: whether it was psychologically impossible to maintain distance in the first mode, or impossible functionally to give a convincing performance without internalizing the role, or whether it was simply that even in the first mode one must disconnect one's motivation from one's actions and words and thus become insincere.

51. This fundamental ambiguity in the notion of imitation, between imitating a person in action and manufacturing an imitation flower (or whatever), haunts the theory of the fine arts from its beginnings in Plato, who, as I observed before, uses the Greek word *mimeisthai* to mean "depict," although its ordinary meaning was "mimic" or "enact."

52. The view that the fine arts relate to perceptible reality as a whole rather than to particular perceptible things can be held without invoking the idea of nature as process, for one may think of reality as a spatiotemporally organized system. This way of looking at things is expressed, for example, by Charles Biederman: " 'Art,' like 'Science,' is the history of man's evolving penetration into the structure and potentialities of 'reality' " (1949, 443).

53. Central to Aristotle's notion of nature is the concept of a substance, a thing

that has its own identity because it is organized upon some single principle. But the view that nature is essentially made up of substances is not that of modern science, which prefers to think (if at all) in terms of energies and forces. If ancient theorists restricted the term "natural" to organized things, it was because they in fact conceived of nature on the model of the arts—Aristotle's principle that art and nature operate in similar ways was supposed to explain the former as derived from the latter, but really worked the other way round. We might then expect contemporary theorists to think of art as producing processes rather than objects; and sometimes they do, though seldom very coherently (e.g. Burnham 1968, 363ff.). Gadamer makes the related point that in the content of modern art, as in the world of modern science, the thing as abiding object has vanished. In Pythagorean terms, modern art imitates numbers; it is an order that represents an order (1967, 25-26).

54. The notion that the artist produces a world in his work is taken with startling literalness by Etienne Souriau: "Every work of art creates its own universe. And whoever speaks of a universe speaks of a whole built upon a space-time net-work" (1949, 122-123). Souriau introduces this contention as a link in an argument to demonstrate the importance of time in the plastic arts. The argument is odd, for, even if the implication holds, the status of the work as universe making can hardly be *better known* than the presence of temporal relations. Not but what Souriau's immediate point, that in such a painting as Poussin's *Peasants in Arcadia* past and future, memory, regret, fear, and foreboding are an essential part of the overt content of what we see, is a point well taken.

55. A classical expression is that of Zuccaro (1607) as quoted by Panofsky:

I say, therefore, that God, all-bountiful and almighty, and first cause of everything, in order to act externally necessarily looks at and regards the internal Design in which He perceives all things that He has made, is making, will make, and can make with a single glance. . . . He wished to grant him [man] the ability to form in himself an inner intellectual Design, so that by means of it he could know all the creatures and could form in himself a new world. . . . So that with this Design, almost imitating God and vying with Nature, he could produce an infinite number of artificial things resembling natural ones, and by means of painting and sculpture make new Paradises visible on Earth. But in forming this internal Design man is very different from God: God has one simple Design, most perfect in substance, containing all things, which is not different from Him, because all that which is in God is God; man, however, forms within himself various designs corresponding to the different things he conceives (Panofsky 1968, 88).

The whole of Panofsky's work is germane to our theme here.

56. Roman Ingarden's analysis (1931) of the multilevel structure of literary works includes several layers of projected realities.

57. I have explored the implications of this aspect of literary projection elsewhere (Sparshott 1967b). In a rejoinder to my paper, which would apply equally to what I write in this passage, Joseph Margolis (1969) claimed that I was writing about the psychology of imagination, not the logic of fictionality, but I don't think that is quite correct. Nothing I wrote there or write here affects the status of fictionality as here conceived, certainly; but the way in which a system of representation functions is not a psychological matter in any ordinary sense.

A pictorial representation depends on our knowledge of the world and our experience of perception no less than a description does, but in a different way. It is only because we have seen animals in movement that we can see the unicorn in the painting as a real, solid animal prancing along. But we do see the unicorn for all that, and in a naturalistic painting we see as much of it as we would see of any unicorn we only glimpsed for a moment. But we do not see Pickwick or any part of him: we are told enough about him that we can imagine more or less what it would be like to see him if we already know what it would be like to see an early Victorian retired English businessman. Let me illustrate the point from the opposite direction: I have just read in a short story by W. S. Maugham about a man who wore a dirty white stengah-shifter unbuttoned at the neck. But since I know of a stengah-shifter only what the passage tells me, viz. that it is some kind of garment once worn by Europeans in Asia, having buttons, coming up to the neck, and sometimes but not always white, I am left quite in the dark as to what a stengah-shifter is.

58. Arthur Berndtson writes that "the final criticism of the representational theory is perhaps the most elementary: that it cannot be applied generally among the arts, since music, architecture, and certain minor arts have no representative content. Either the theory leads to pluralism in aesthetics, or it must be strained into the view that these arts do indeed represent. Pluralism should not be embraced at the first hypothesis, but only when the field has been surveyed and no alternative remains" (1969, 118). Notice the artless assumption that the unity of the fine arts is so self-evident that the failure to give a single account embracing all of them would constitute pluralism in treating a single topic. Berndtson nowhere explains or defends this assumption.

59. The relation of abstract dance to mime, and thus indirectly to drama, is obviously close, and these are the arts in which the artist uses his body to communicate with. But the place of dance among the fine arts, and indeed the theory of dance in general, remain curiously undeveloped. Perhaps one reason for this is that, historically and prehistorically, a form of dance lies at the basis of all art, and we expect to find that any preliterate society will have elaborate dance rituals; but as the fine arts become sophisticated and articulate, dance is relegated to a marginal place. The theoretical development of the mystic line, in which dance retains its central place, is, as we shall see, comparatively sketchy. A more immediate reason for the neglect of the dance may be that when the concept of the fine arts was being developed, no form of dance played any important part in high culture.

60. Since the author of the text, the composer of the tune, its singer, and the accompanist may be four different people, it is obvious that the plain meaning of the text could be coated with four expressive layers: the author builds into his text (by its rhythm, onomatopoeia, and what not, not to mention the choice of words and syntax) one "way of taking" the plain meaning of what the text says. (Please do not mutter about the "heresy of paraphrase": when I speak of the speech in which Mark Antony apologizes to the dead Caesar for being polite to his assassins and you say that you don't know which one I mean because poetry cannot be paraphrased, you are not showing yourself to be a finely sensitive fellow but a plain fool—the heresy of paraphrase is not the assumption that one can make true statements about the content of a work but the supposition that such statements could afford the basis for a valid critique of the work itself.) The composer of the tune may add another, the singer by the way he sings the tune can add a third, and the accompanist can add a comment of his own. And if artists know each other and their work well, things really can be at least as complicated as that.

61. It is necessary to our argument that the words "feeling" and "emotion" have this wide scope. Many writers have written as if what music did was necessarily to

evince or evoke some such grandly passionate condition as rage, despair, or love. Eduard Hanslick (1854) argued that this must be the case: finely attuned attitudinal states can only be differentiated by, and experienced in relation to, specific states of affairs, so that the precise form of a piece of music, in which its value must lie, cannot be related to its emotional meaning, which accordingly has no musical interest. Gilson shrewdly says of this argument that even those who agree with it do not believe it (1964, 174n.).

62. A musical score is precise only in some respects and with certain qualifications (see Goodman 1968, chap. 5); and the language of "series of notes" really pertains only to notated music. But one can achieve any required measure of precision by specifying a particular performance as heard by an ideally attentive and sharp-eared listener from a specified seat in the hall or whatever else we please.

63. J. W. N. Sullivan offers this finely nuanced formulation: "What art does do is to communicate to us an attitude, an attitude taken up by the artist consequent upon his perceptions, which perceptions may be perceptions of factors in reality. It is characteristic of the greatest art that the attitude it communicates to us is felt by us to be valid, to be the reaction to a more subtle and comprehensive contact with reality than we can normally make" (1927, 22-23). Two things worth noting in this quotation are, first, that Sullivan speaks generally of "the artist," though his actual subject is the musician Beethoven and, second, that the validity we are alleged to feel has nothing to do with the artist's sincerity, but depends on the quality of his experience.

64. Bruce Pattison (1970, 109-110) cites an exceptionally splendid illustration from Daniel's *Songs*:

> Can doleful notes to measured accents set
> Express unmeasured griefs that time forget?
> No, let chromatic tunes, harsh without ground,
>   Be sullen music for a tuneless heart;
> Chromatic tunes most like my passions sound,
>   As if combined to bear their falling part.

But comparable sentiments abound in all ages.

65. One could draw an elaborate parallel in this regard between expression and depiction as I described it. The artist need not express an emotion he feels in his own person, but *projects* an emotion, first, for himself ("Art is the critically controlled purposive activity which aims to create an object having the capacity to reflect to its creator, when he contemplates it with interest in its emotional import, the feeling images that had dictated the specific form and content he gave the object" [Ducasse 1964, 52]) and then for others; but such projection would be inconceivable unless there were such a thing as expressing an emotion one actually felt, so that the connection could be established. Works of art are said to express emotion because they are perceived as having an inherent expressive character, but it is inconceivable that there could be such a character unless the connection between inner feeling and outward and audible (or visible) expression of that feeling were familiar and evident in standard cases of expression. Expression is mediated through conventions as to what expresses what, but such conventions are unthinkable otherwise than on the basis of some immediately sensed affinity between what is expressed and what expresses it, because the music is *heard as* affective (just as the picture is *seen as* like).

66. The demand for sincerity is most familiar from the work of R. G. Collingwood (1938), in which it forms part of a complex (if not confused) argument. In a similar

form, it is a requirement imposed on artists, most often on poets, at many times and places. Yuan Mei (1716-1797), for instance, wrote:

> I like best Chou Li-yuen's remark on poetry: Poetry is what expresses my emotions. Therefore, if I want to write, I do; if not, I don't. There has never been anyone forcing and exhorting me to write poetry. . . . Everywhere he [Wang Shih-chen] went, he must write a poem, and in every poem there must be allusions. From this we can gather that his emotions are not genuine (Liu 1962, 76).

67. Nelson Goodman's account of expression seems to make the nameability of the feeling (or of whatever is expressed) essential. To express a quality is to *exemplify* the quality, that is, to have the quality and to refer to it by having it (as a swatch of tweed exemplifies the cloth it is); and to say that it *has* it is to say that labels meaning the same as our name for the quality denote it. Expression differs from straightforward exemplification in that the denotation is metaphorical. It seems to follow from this that expression is impossible unless there is a vocabulary to mediate it (Goodman 1968, chap. 2). That this rather odd-looking account of expression is not only compatible with but also illuminates a good deal that has been traditionally thought about expression I have argued elsewhere (Sparshott 1974b).

68. Specifically, to play *espressivo* or "expressively" is to play music (any music) in a special kind of way, and one that (as Tormey remarks, 1971, 110ff.) does not express anything in particular: it is to vary the dynamics of a piece, not so as to bring out what it expresses, but rather so as to simulate the tones of a sentimental voice. Theorists who say that all music expresses something or other, or is essentially expressive, do not have this particular means of expressiveness in mind at all, though individuals doubtless exist who think everything should be played *con espressione* in honor of the inherently expressive nature of music.

69. Just as, on Goodman's analysis, a rabbit picture may or may not have the function of denoting a rabbit (being a picture of a rabbit), and this can be determined only contextually by discovering whether rabbits exist and whether the picture has been assigned the function of referring to one or more of them if they do, so it is doubtless to be established contextually whether or not the attitude manifest in a picture is properly to be taken as denoting an attitude of the person who painted it. Practices and proprieties in this area are complex.

70. Otto Baensch points out that people, professions, classes, eras, and cultural units of all sorts are charged with a definite emotional atmosphere, so that history strikes us as "a battle of various emotional worlds and powers" (1924, 20). These affective charges are what I. A. Richards called stock responses and thought peculiar to *Kitsch* rather than to art proper; but Baensch is surely right to urge that they are integral to our awareness of the world, so that the real question is not whether to succumb to them (as Richards thought) but what use to make of them.

71. Guy Sircello (1972) groups together the affective character of materials and subject matter and the manifest attitude as three modes of expression. For a critique of his analysis, see Robinson (1977).

72. For example, Wang Fu-chih (1619-1692) writes (if his translator can be trusted; presumably the Chinese vocabulary has rather different implications from those of the English terms employed):

> "Emotion" and "scene" are called by two different names, but in fact they cannot be separated. Those who can work wonders in poetry can unite the two naturally and leave no boundary line; those who are skilful, can reveal an emotion in a

scene and a scene in an emotion. . . . Though emotion and scene differ in that one lies in the heart and the other in things, they actually engender each other. . . . If one cherishes emotions and can convey them; if one appreciates a scene and is moved in the heart; if one understands the nature of things and can capture their spirit; then one will naturally find inspired and lively lines, and reach the state of natural marvel that shows no signs of technical skill (Liu 1962, 83).

73. Actually this does not follow at all, unless it is construed merely as a rewording of the original version. Otherwise, if I represent *my idea of* an object, I represent something that no one else can represent except by quoting or paraphrasing me; but if I represent the world, but represent it as I see it, then anyone else can represent the very same world, but do so, of course, as he or she sees it.

74. Once more we find an admirable illustration of this attitude in Liu's collection, this time from the sixth-century *Dragon Carvings of a Literary Mind* by Liu Hsieh:

The Book of Poetry was inspired by the dictates of the heart and long pent-up indignation; it expressed the emotions and nature of the poets, in order to satirize their rulers. This is what I call "creating literature for the sake of emotion." On the other hand, the followers of the various schools, who bore no great sorrow in their heart, displayed their talents and adorned their writings with extravagance, in order to acquire reputation and fish for compliments. This is what I call "manufacturing emotion for the sake of literature." Therefore, what is written for the sake of expressing emotion is concise and true to life; what is written for the sake of literature is over-decorative and extravagant (Liu 1962, 71-72).

75. The argument here indicated for the unique significance of expression is essentially that developed by Arthur Berndtson (1969). An elaborate account of various kinds of expression theory is given in *SA*, and I will not repeat it here. I will only add that art can be made out to be a cure for whatever ails your feelings. If they are coarse, it will purify them; if they are inchoate and obscure, it will clarify them; if they are painful, it will neutralize them; if they are too strong, it will drain them off and assuage them; if they are too weak, it will vivify them; if they are scattered, it will integrate them.

76. An elegant statement of the view that makes expression and representation coordinate species of imitation is provided by Claude Lévi-Strauss, who like many cultured Frenchmen despises abstract expressionism (perhaps because it is an American specialty) and advances, perhaps unawares, the surprising thesis that one and the same work cannot be both expressive and representational. In naming something,

one always signifies, either oneself or someone else. It is only here that there is a choice, rather like that open to a painter between representational and non-representational art, which amounts to no more than a choice between assigning a class to an identifiable object or, by putting it outside a class, making the object a means of classing himself by expressing himself through it (Lévi-Strauss 1962, 182).

77. Vitruvius, *De Architectura* I.3, 2: *firmitas, utilitas, venustas*. The English equivalents are those of Sir Henry Wotton (cf. Scott 1914, 1). The two things required of a building are convenience in its disposition of space and strength in its fabric; each of these generates an aesthetic value, in the relation of spaces and the disposition of solids, to which a decorative treatment of façades is added as a third.

What Isidore (*Etymologiarum* XIX, ix-xi) actually says is that buildings have three parts: *dispositio* (laying out the foundations), *constructio* (setting up the walls), and *venustas* (putting on the decoration).

78. The only relevant difference seems to be that one is more accustomed, by long critical tradition, to discussing architectural designs in three contexts: as sturdy and serviceable buildings for use, as elegant solutions to tricky problems in fulfilling function gracefully (Kant's "attached beauty"), and as designs that are pleasing in themselves (Kant's "free beauty").

79. The best and most familiar version is Kant's: roughly, that the mind is whatever is necessary for the existence of an apprehensible world, and what it imposes is the conditions of unified appearance. Transferred to an aesthetic context, these conditions become the requirement that a thing appear to be meant to be the way it is. See the remarks on aesthetic judgment in Appendix A.

80. L. B. Alberti (*De Re Aedificatoria* IX, 5) asserts that the ancient architects "rightly maintained that nature, the greatest of all artists in the invention of forms, was always their model. Therefore they collected the laws according to which she works in her productions, as far as was humanly possible, and introduced them into their methods of building" (cited from Blunt 1940, 19). Natural principles are used, not because nature is divine, but because nature is the most formally inventive of artists.

81. According to one established tradition, literature is divided into lyric, which is primarily expressive, and epic (with tragedy and the novel), which is primarily representational. The formal demand is played down because verbal structures, being articulated by grammar, are not susceptible of *measure*, even in principle. No one thinks that metrical properties and word counts are of primary importance.

82. The reference to "the fine arts" here is no slip of the ballpoint. Though Plato does not distinguish these as a group of arts, he does speak generally of well-proportioned artifacts as a means of moral education (*Republic* III, 400 E-402 C)— though not, be it noted, in the passage where the parallel between painting and poetry is developed. Specific mention is made of poetry, drawing, painting, building, and weaving.

83. Compare Rousseau: "Music is no more the art of combining sounds to please the ear than painting is the art of combining colours to please the eye. If there were no more to it than that, they would both be natural sciences rather than fine arts. Imitation alone raises them to this level" (1761, 55). Since the natural sciences in question would have to be the psychology of color perception and sound perception, Rousseau's argument holds, if at all, only if (as in my treatment) the formal properties of works of art are assigned to imitation.

84. One could go on to argue that the great ages of art have been among those in which the fine arts were exercised in pursuit of some social or religious interest, or under some religious and social control, and not cultivated as ends in themselves. But that would prove little, since a measure of such subordination has been the normal condition of the fine arts. Paintings are painted for people to look at, and someone who wants something to look at will usually want to look at it in a certain specific context and perhaps for a certain purpose. An artist may resist the terms of his commission, but not usually to the point where he is unable to make a sale.

85. A depiction of something may be useful, interesting, or delightful (1) for the interest of the object or person it depicts, (2) for the special information it gives about what it depicts, (3) for its revelation of some social or metaphysical aspect or relation of what it depicts, (4) for some excellence in the way the depiction is carried out (vividly, ingeniously, meticulously, faithfully), (5) for its beauty or interest as a

disposition of forms on a surface, (6) for the relation between the depiction and what is depicted (perspective, distortion, reconstitution), (7) for its revelation of a viewpoint on or attitude to what is depicted, (8) for its revelation of the artist's humanity, (9) for its revelation of an aspect of human subjectivity, and doubtless for other things, too. And all these can be done in relation to imaginary objects or imaginary artists projected by the depiction itself; in that case, the possibility of anecdotal interest is lost, but a new interest in inventiveness becomes possible. In addition, every work is presented and is perceived as in some specific relation of continuity or discontinuity with its surroundings, a relation that itself may be the object of a manifold interest. (None of these interests, not even the first, is compatible with mistaking the depiction for what is depicted; for if it were mistaken for its original, it could give no information about it. The fact that such a mistake has been made, or that one believes it might be made, might give rise to an interest of the fourth or the sixth kind.)

Both proponents and opponents of representational art have often written as if one of these kinds of interest should be preferred to all the others, or as if the possibility of one of them might discredit the others. Both suppositions are entirely irrational. Nor, on the other hand, does the existence of this wide range of possible sources of interest discredit or invalidate a practice of limiting oneself to some part of the range, whether that limitation be individual choice or social convention.

86. The analysis I have presented is in an important respect artificial. In real life we should expect to find complicated relations of inhibition and reinforcement among any motivating factors that we might analyze and a similar complexity of relationship among the imitative modes we have named. Mechanical devices tend to use a single means to a single end, because they are invented to conform to a means-end analysis; organic processes tend to resist such analysis. The fine arts and their works, being institutions and artifacts in which spontaneity and conscious control are in perpetual tension, are partly susceptible to a means-end analysis, but partly resist it.

87. See, for example, Heidegger (1960, 75). The converse of this position is curiously argued by W. Grey Walter, who points out that looking at the painting of a scene rather than the scene itself "represents an economy of a hundredfold in the effort of perception. How much of the value and satisfaction of a painting is attributable to this easement of physiological strain, to the lighter loading of a battery of hard-pressed intra-cranial servo-mechanisms?" (Walter 1951, 187). I suspect that the answer is "practically none"; the fact that the description of a process is complex does not mean that the action embodying it is difficult or unpleasant. My servo-mechanisms may be having a terrible time, but so long as they don't complain to me about it, my heart does not bleed for them.

88. This theme has been explored and developed by Conrad Fiedler, who writes: "Artistic activity begins when man finds himself face to face with the visible world as with something immensely enigmatical; when, driven by an inner necessity and applying the powers of his mind, he grapples with the twisted mass of the visible which presses in upon him and gives it creative form. In the creation of a work of art, man engages in a struggle not for his physical but for his mental existence" (1876, 48).

89. A view of this sort is expressed by Max Scheler in *The Nature of Sympathy* (1954, 252-253). To this category also belongs the most recent attempt to construe all art as imitative, that of Georg Lukács (1963), according to whom every true work of art creates an intensive totality, an effective embodiment of a particular

historical predicament that exemplifies and thus illuminates a class, a historical era, and the nature of the historical process (and thus of man and his world) as a whole. According to Lukács, the importance of this "mimesis" (that term being defined as the transposition of the reflection of a phenomenon of reality into one's own activity [1963, I, 352]) is that its reference, though infinite in the way outlined, is "this-worldly" (*diesseitig*): it is a secular substitute for, and deliverance from, the magical relation of "representation" by which a transcendent force is made to be present in an icon. In music, the mimesis is doubled: a musical work is related to a historical situation in the same way as a novel or a painting, but through the medium of an individual's feelings about that specific situation. Architecture expresses social reality directly, in much the way made familiar by Langer (1953). All the major fine arts are thus taken care of; but what of nonrepresentational works? Lukács chooses not to assimilate them to this or that mode of mimesis, but denounces any nonrealistic use of an art in which realism is possible as a betrayal of the original impulse of art—a denunciation that, as Morawski (1968, 35) observes, begs the question, since we have only Lukács' word for it that the original impulse was one of secularization. Adorno dismisses Lukács' basic idea of "specialness" (*Besonderheit*), a peculiar embodiment of the universal in the particular, as sheer dogmatism, a vague offshoot of the theological doctrine of the symbol (Adorno 1970, 132). One does not see why anyone would propose a theory at once so narrow in scope and so extravagant in interpretation unless one were determined to excuse the grosser policies of the Soviet Union—a possibility that recalls Bertolt Brecht's comment on Lukács and those like him:

> They are, to put it bluntly, enemies of production. Production makes them uncomfortable. You never know where you are with production. Production is the unforeseeable. You never know what's going to come out. And they themselves don't want to produce. They want to play the apparatchik and exercise control over other people. Every one of their criticisms contains a threat (Laing 1978, 55-56).

For an exposition of Lukács' position, see Parkinson (1970) and compare chapter 7, note 28, below.

What looks like an aspect of Lukács' position, but is probably derived from a common Hegelian ancestry, appears in Sartre's "The Artist and His Conscience":

> I would say that an object has a meaning when it incarnates a reality which transcends it but which cannot be apprehended outside of it and which its infiniteness does not allow to be expressed adequately by any system of signs: it is always a matter of a totality, totality of a person, milieu, time or human condition. I would say that the Mona Lisa's smile does not "mean" anything, but that it has a meaning. Through it, that strange fusion of mysticism and naturalism, evidence and mystery which characterize the Renaissance is materialized (1950, 217).

90. I have cited a view of this sort from Gadamer (n. 33, above), and the position is usually associated with the name of Bergson (cf. *SA* 397-399); but it is most at home in Sino-Japanese and Indian aesthetics. Thus Motoori Norinaga (1730-1801) writes:

> Living in this world, a person sees, hears, and meets all kinds of events. If he takes them into his heart and feels the hearts of the events within it, then one

may see that the person knows the hearts of the events, the cores of the facts—he knows *mono no aware* (Ueda 1967, 203).

He adds that it is through literature that the rest of us learn *mono no aware*, "the 'ah'-ness of things" (ibid., 203-205). (Ueda explains that the Japanese word *aware* is a compound of "two interjections, *a* and *hare*, both of which are used when one's heart is greatly moved" [ibid., 199].) This "ah"-ness of things is one opposite of the external truth that moved Gleizes and Metzinger to write:

> Among so-called academic painters some may be gifted; but how could we know it? Their painting is so truthful that it founders in truth, in that negative truth, the mother of morals and everything insipid which, true for the many, is false for the individual (1912, 14).

But along another dimension, the opposite extreme from this external veracity is, as the later history of the movements that Gleizes and Metzinger represented shows, a purely formalist art; and, as Gosvami (1961, 183) shrewdly observes, in reacting from a concern with problems of representation to a concern with problems of design, there is a risk that art will remain on the superficial, problem-solving level and miss the depth of significance that is possible when an artist's subconscious intuitions and conscious experience combine in bringing out *mono no aware*.

A devastating critique of this sort of thinking can be derived from the theory of the proper name in Derrida (1967). Such a name, a unique sign establishing a classification that could not exist without it, draws what is named into the system of absent meanings that Derrida calls writing: what the name means is the person named, who transcends our knowledge as well as our naming; but what the person named *is*, is what the name means, which transcends his life and experience and purports to thrust him into the system of opinions and attitudes and of linguistic and social structures. Thus, if a picture captures my essence or "ah"-ness, what is "ah" about me is out there on the canvas; but the "me" whose "ah"-ness it is supposed to be is not there on the canvas but here where I am. This critique is identical with Aristotle's objection to Plato's theory of "Ideas." To avoid it one might prefer to go back to Lukács' theory cited in note 89, according to which what is illuminated is a totality or system of relationships, and to say that where no such totality can be found, the "ah"-ness is that of the picture (or novel) itself. In the latter case, we seem to be landed with a sort of vestigial theory of representation, which in fact many have espoused, according to which an image symbolizes itself: it is a "suisign," something that has meaning or is meaningful, but whose meaning cannot be conveyed otherwise than by perusal of itself: there is nothing that one cay say it means. Using such terminology of a work seems a pointless maneuver, but at least presents it as something to be made sense of and not merely gaped at. Understanding a work might be like understanding a person: if we complain that someone does not make sense, we do not mean that we cannot translate him or paraphrase him. The converse of this supposed relationship in which an image is itself what it "stands for" would be the relationship explored at the end of Sartre's *Psychology of Imagination*, whereby a thing is reduced to an image of itself:

> We do assume the attitude of esthetic contemplation towards real events or objects. But in such cases everyone of us can feel in himself a sort of recoil in relation to the object contemplated which slips into nothingness so that, from this moment on, it is no longer *perceived*; it functions as an *analogue* of itself, that is, that an unreal image of what it is appears to us through its actual presence. This image

can be purely and simply the object "itself" neutralized, annihilated . . . it can also be the imperfect and confused appearance of *what it could be* through what it is (1940, 253).

91. Thus, Susan Sontag writes: "Art today is a new kind of instrument, an instrument for modifying consciousness and organizing new modes of sensibility" (1966, 296). Biederman (1949) had maintained that all art did this at all times; that contemporary art does it more than other art is also implied by Jack Burnham (1968).

92. Thus Nelson Goodman insists that in art "the drive is curiosity and the end enlightenment. Use of symbols beyond immediate need is for the sake of understanding, not practice; what compels is the urge to know, what delights is discovery, and communication is secondary to the apprehension and formulation of what is to be communicated. The primary purpose is cognition in and for itself; the practicability, pleasure, compulsion, and communicative utility all depend upon this" (1972, 114-115). The rhetoric is irresistible (and reminds us that all our nine alternatives are customarily elaborated with plangent rhetoric and corroborative detail, not nakedly set out as I have stated them). The doctrine is also that of Aristotle's *Poetics*, but Goodman merely asserts it without evidence or argument and without stating why the other eight possibilities (and other varieties of the ninth) are to be ruled out.

The fourth, sixth, and seventh possibilities, which I have not dignified with illustrative notes, are exemplified, respectively, by Richard Bernheimer (1961), Plato's *Republic*, and numerous works by C. G. Jung.

93. Speculations in the schools of Marx and Freud are paradigms of theories that (as explained in the Introduction) are interesting where mine is dull. What is interesting in them is that they offer a secret: what seems to be going on, something that would need to be painstakingly examined, is not at all what is *really* going on, which is something easily accessible to the merest idiot—*provided that he has the right key*, which the theorist is about to give him. It is the conspiracy theory of culture, analogous to the conspiracy theory of history or to a salvationist religion; it seems to be gaining ground everywhere and is a form of pure escapism. Instead of making one's slow way through the hazards and perplexities of life, art, and thought, one is to be *let in on the secret*.

Chapter IV. The Classical Line 3: Arts of Beauty

1. Dubos observes that, out of school, poetry is read only for pleasure (1719, I, 239). Should this be dismissed as frivolous aestheticism, on the ground that the arts should really be valued for their contribution to one's moral and intellectual well-being or to the cause of the revolution? Not really. In the last resort, values are realized nowhere but in experience. What contributes to intellectual advancement is schooling. Marxists make all the world a school (or a prison); Christians make all the world a school for heaven.

2. Perhaps more important, the common terms in which philosophical problems have been traditionally discussed in the West are those used by the Greek philosophers and their Latin translations; the idiosyncrasies of vernaculars have only occasionally disturbed this consensus, which the disruption of Christendom and the

collapse of classical culture are only now beginning to destroy. In Greek, as in German and French, the word for beauty is a common, short word that trips easily off the tongue, is colloquially applicable to a wide range of things, and forms part of many idioms. "Beautiful," by contrast, is a ceremonious trisyllable that covers only a small part of the range of its foreign counterparts. The rest of the range is covered by two short and common words, "fair" and "fine." But (to limit the comparison to Greek) "fair" also means "equitable" (*ison*) and "blonde" (*xanthon*), as well as "beautiful" (*kalon*); and "fine," though equivalent to *kalon* or the adverb *kalôs* in its reference to situations and actions, fails to correspond to it over just that part of its range where "beautiful" is the natural rendering. English, we might say, is peculiar in having no word for "beautiful"; in aesthetic discourse, it is the odd man out. Latin, however, is in a fix similar to that of English. *Pulcher, suavis,* and *formosus* split the ranks of beauty, and *bonum* and *bene* (for which compare "good" and contrast the Greek *agathon*) do the meaner chores for *kalôs*. Britain and Rome, of course, were imperial powers and did not need to think too much about beauty: *excudent alii. . . .* Tolstoy boasts of the fact that the Russians also have no word for beauty: "In Russian, by the word *Krasotá* we mean only that which pleases the sight. And though latterly people have begun to speak of 'an ugly deed' or of 'beautiful music,' it is not good Russian" (1898, 89).

For some discussion of the ambiguities of the word "beauty" and the ways in which those ambiguities affect aesthetic discussion, see *SA* (chap. 3).

3. Only ignorant people, says Adorno, *enjoy* art—the bourgeoisie would like art to be voluptuous and life ascetic, but it would be better the other way round (1970, 24-25). One can see that it is vulgar to use art as an occasion for merely having a good time, but Adorno is almost inclined to think that one should use the fine arts as a means of self-discipline; it is more usual to follow Hanslick, Goodman, Schoenberg, Xenakis, and many others in the tradition of Plato and Aristotle in contrasting an "enjoyment" that is a mere wallowing with an austere and exacting but enthralling exercise of perception and thought. The word *placet* would cover that, but not Adorno's use of art as a means to salvation.

4. Morse Peckham exclaims that "aesthetics lies in ruins not only because of logical faults but also because modern perception theory has destroyed its entire psychological foundation" (1965, 217), that foundation being the thesis that the mind is passive in perception. Why that thesis should be thought fundamental to aesthetics I do not know, unless by "aesthetics" Peckham means the aestheticism of the aesthetes of the 1890s. For one among many diatribes against the passivist implications of "contemplation," see Berleant (1970).

5. Leo Stein points out that the fine arts cannot be primarily sources of pleasure because they do not preempt our attention: we are easily distracted from them, and they require an effort of concentration (1927, 34).

6. It might be thought that the same theoretical purpose could be served by saying that the fine arts are those whose products are preeminently *performances* in our special sense of that term. For to view something as a performance is to view it critically, to size it up in abstraction from its context and, hence, to view it as appearance only. But that is not so. A performance may be the performance of a practical task, and such a performance does not exist to be appreciated. It may be criticized from a practical or moral point of view as fitting or failing to fit the relevant requirement, or according to how well it fits any legal or conceptual requirement. To perform such critical scrutiny may be rewarding, but the point of the performance is presumed not to be to reward critics.

7. The concept of sensory contemplation is not free from awkwardness. No quality can be apprehended and defined as the quality it is by the senses alone, even if we knew where to divide the senses from the rest of us. The restriction to sensory contemplation can be taken as following from the proposition that the fine arts are concerned to present determinate appearances, hence organizations mediated by sensible qualities. But then, since it is the appearance that is contemplated, one may feel justified in stipulating (as the text does here) that part of one's relevant interest in the work be taken in the way it looks or sounds or smells or feels or tastes—as opposed to whatever contrasting kinds of interest there may be. And there is a temptation to follow the "logic" of the same argument further and suppose that in a work of the fine arts the qualities of the proper objects of the senses as such should be sources of gratification. We thus make a transition from the sensory to the sensuous. There is a sense in which "sensuous" qualities are such as opulence of color, richness of sonority, softness to the touch; it is not really clear what these have in common, except that they are conventionally associated with sensuality. Despite the curious arguments of Adrian Stokes (1965), these qualities are of no special interest to the fine arts as such, though particular works and styles exploit them; the supposition to the contrary is probably the outcome of an unthinking mind/body or intellect/sense dualism.

8. It should, however, be noted that poets whose work exploits subtleties of colloquial rhythm are often not appreciated by those whose dialect differs widely from their own. Few Britons can hear the music of W. C. Williams; few Americans that of Stevie Smith.

9. Much of the entrenching is due to Plato's spadework in his *Symposium*. In the following passage, Adam Smith curiously seems to divide the pleasure of music into an intellectual and a sensual aspect:

> In the contemplation of that immense variety of agreeable and melodious sounds, arranged and digested, both in their coincidence and their succession, into so complete and regular a system, the mind in reality enjoys not only a very great sensual, but a very high intellectual pleasure, not unlike that which it derives from the contemplation of a great system in any other science (1795, 246-247).

Smith here seems to confuse the harmonic and melodic system in which music is composed with the audible order in a particular work.

10. The inference, however easy, is mistaken insofar as what we are normally said to see and hear are things and people, not colors and sounds ("see" and "hear" being what Ryle called "achievement words"); but we need not here contest the old argument that *strictly speaking* we hear only audibilia, see only visibilia (roughly to be equated with sounds and colors, respectively). The argument in favor of this analyzability is in fact a double one: as a matter of logic ("what counts as seeing"), only what meets the eye can be seen; as a matter of fact, it is physically impossible that we should see more than the optic nerves transmit. Both arguments can be reversed: as a matter of logic, "see" is a verb whose proper objects are colored and contoured things, not colors and contours; as a matter of fact, it is psychologically impossible to effect the reduction (and neurological explanations of the impossibility can be essayed).

11. Sooner or later, everyone has to quote Maurice Denis's dictum: "Se rappeler qu'un tableau—avant d'être un cheval de bataille, une femme nue, ou une quelconque anecdote—est essentiellement une surface plane recouverte de couleurs en un certain ordre assemblées" (Denis 1890, 1). This is so obviously right that no one

remembers to ask what "before" means here. "Before" in time? No, as soon as it is one it is the other. Valuationally? Not necessarily. Epistemologically, in terms of the artist's preoccupations? Hardly; his attention had better be focused on the horse at least as much as on the picture plane. In terms of the spectator's interpretation? Not likely. In terms of physics? No, physics would speak of lumps of clay, not colors. Logically, in terms of dependence? No; the colors constitute the nude, but it is the nude that defines the "order" in which the colors are assembled. The only believable priority is one in terms of a functional analysis: the painter has rendered the nipple *by* a swirl of sepia, he has laid in a swirl of sepia *to* do the nipple. But this priority of means over ends cannot possibly be what Denis had in mind, for its implications work against what he obviously wants to imply about the art of painting.

Few of those who invoke the authority of Denis's dictum, by the way, think to mention that it is the work of a nineteen-year-old art student and formed the opening paragraph of a manifesto for Symbolism.

12. The point is made rather intemperately by John Berger:

> Formalists are those who use the conventions of their medium (conventions that originally came into being for the purpose of translating aspects of life into art) to keep out or pass over new aspects. Thus, the Tachists use the technical conventions of Impressionism to keep out all observation of the relationship between actual objects. Thus, the more violent Action painters use the technical conventions of expressionism to keep out all social emotions. And, of course, what they keep out is what inspired those who created their conventions (1960, 208).

Berger being a professed Marxist, one does not know whether the ludicrous attribution of motive to the "formalists" is meant literally, or is simply meant to recognize their "objective" tendency.

The demand that painters produce constructions of pure visibilia is not always due to a misinterpretation of the nature of human vision. It may rest on the assumption that all interpretation is interpretation in the interests of utility, that whatever is seen *as* anything is already caught up out of the realm of pure contemplation into that of the workaday world. This was notoriously the position of Roger Fry at one time, not to mention Bergson.

13. The vocabulary of "seeing as" is full of treacherous ambiguities, another set of which will be considered in chapter 8. If I say of a woman that I see her as a witch, I may mean that I think of her as a witch, interpret her behavior as that of a witch; or that I (visually) imagine or picture her as a witch; or that I merely allow my visual impressions to be dominated by witchlike features of her appearance. Seeing my mother as a patch of color is most like the last of these three.

14. To say "He sees a tree as a birch" or vice versa would be an ornamental way of saying that his vision, his capacities for recognizing the relevant components of his surroundings, were unusually precise or unusually vague, respectively. Some philosophers argue that, because to see anything *as* anything is to relate it to other things, whereas it in itself is only what it is, all vision is metaphorical, just as all classificatory or descriptive speech is metaphorical. The assumption of this curious doctrine seems to be that all propositions aspire to the condition of statements of identity; the notion seems worthless. See Turbayne (1962).

I have dealt at length, though not in earnest, with the complexities of "seeing as" in Sparshott (1974a); see also *CC* (131-132). There is an extended treatment of the topic in Tilghman (1970).

Hasty readers of Wittgenstein are cautioned against taking the duck/rabbit as

553

typical of anything discussed here. It is a very special case: a clearly identified and characterized *sign* with two distinct aspects. Usually one sees this *as* a duck-rabbit, that is, as a poor rendering of Jastrow's rendering of what one hopes was a drawing in *Fliegende Blätter* that really could be seen as a duck or as a rabbit—neither Wittgenstein's version nor Jastrow's looks in the least as if it were meant as a drawing of either. Supposing it did, one would still need to distinguish between (a) seeing it as a duck and *not noticing* that it could also be seen as a rabbit; (b) seeing it as a duck, knowing but disregarding the fact that it also had a rabbit aspect; (c) seeing it as a duck while not being blind to its rabbit aspect; (d) seeing it as meant-for-a-duck but accidentally a rabbit—and so on for quite a long time.

15. Most, that is, of those among whom one lives and whom one accepts as normal—or most of those among whom the people who are talking about one live and whom *they* accept as normal.

16. The distinction is very clearly recognized by Saint Augustine: in works of visual and verbal art, the power of reason is perceptible to the senses, and what thus conforms with reason in the visual arts (specifically architecture) is called beautiful (*pulchrum*). This beauty depends on proportion (or, in representational art, on suitability) and appeals to the mind, and is to be distinguished from the mere visual attractiveness that appeals to the eye. And "in things that are made, unequal size in the parts, unless compelled by some necessity, seems as it were to inflict a kind of injury upon one's very gaze" (Augustine, *De Ordine* II, 32-34, my translation). Augustine here plays significantly on words: "unequal" (*iniqua*) can also mean "unfair" or "unjust," and "injury" (*injuria*) means a legal offense as well as a hurt. Disproportion offends against the rights of the mind.

17. Kant himself does seem to keep falling into the trap of supposing that the claims implicit in current types of judgment must be warranted. But the heart of his position is only that anyone who makes such judgments is logically committed to what they imply. If you can abstain from making moral judgments or judgments of taste, good luck to you. Santayana attributes the habit of making such judgments to uncertainty in one's own taste (1896, 39): I suspect that Kant would have attributed a failure to make them to weakness of moral fiber. But, in any case, the thrust of Kant's argument is logical and conceptual, whereas Santayana's concerns are psychological. For further discussion, see Appendix A.

18. Aristotle (*Physics* B 2) adopts from Plato (*Republic* X) the idea that arts tend to be symbiotically related. Rudders, for instance, are the concern of two arts, the user's (the helmsman's) and the maker's (the carpenter's). The user knows what properties a rudder must have to do the job it has to do, but has no idea how to give it those properties. The carpenter knows what sort of wood must be shaped in what manner to give the right weight and tensile strength, but as a carpenter he knows nothing about why rudders have to be the shape the helmsman says. He takes the user's word for that. A similar relation could well obtain in the fine arts. The patron specifies the qualities he requires in a picture (dimensions, subject, prevailing coloration, durability, emotive quality, decorousness, or what not); the painter has no idea why the patron wants all this, and may even be mystified as to why anyone should want pictures at all rather than the nice even coat of interior latex he is equally able to supply, but he knows how to comply with such requirements and does so. This is not a fashionable view, but perhaps only because most patrons nowadays only want something that will either be newsworthy now or prove a good investment later.

19. "All men by nature desire to know. An indication of this is the delight we

take in our senses; for even apart from their usefulness they are loved for themselves; and above all others the sense of sight. For not only with a view to action, but even when we are not going to do anything, we prefer seeing (one might say) to everything else. The reason is that this, most of all the senses, makes us know and brings to light many differences between things" (Aristotle, *Metaphysics*, the opening words in Ross's translation).

20. It could be objected that views are not truly natural beauties, since those who delight in them are unconsciously organizing their visual field on principles derived from some tradition of landscape art. But we are concerned here with what one sees, not how one learns to see it.

21. Rainbows seem to be a borderline case between the second and third kinds: though constituted by a viewpoint, their configuration is invariant. Perhaps partly for this reason, rainbows seem to be preferred objects for looking at chiefly as constituents of views: in themselves, rainbows are a bit tedious. Objects produced by natural forces modifying artifacts (such as ruins) or by artificial modification and control of natural objects (such as gardens) are borderline cases between the fourth or fifth and the second kinds. If we were to add, as a sixth kind of visible, arbitrary stretches of surfaces, we should find recognized beauties among these also: children collect pebbles for the attractiveness of their surface markings and textures.

22. Schafer (1977) expounds the idea of a soundscape and has illustrated it with phonograph records: specific locations at specific times yield characteristic combinations of sounds, which may be delightful as well as interesting.

23. One could formulate—and rebut—a similar specious argument to show that medicine is superfluous. Nature provides enough healthy people—in fact, too many. But sometimes it fails to provide health in those individuals for whom health is specially wanted (by themselves or others); sometimes it provides health too slowly (many doctors use antibiotics to cure conditions that time would heal); sometimes it makes people healthy, but not healthy enough. The absurdity of the objection is obvious in the case of medicine because no one supposes that medicine exists to provide health in the abstract rather than to alleviate the specific condition of this or that individual.

24. People used to *complain* of paintings by such artists as Picasso that they were not realistic, that they were like nothing in nature. This, we should say, is why they were not superfluous.

25. What is logically exhaustive is the following tree:

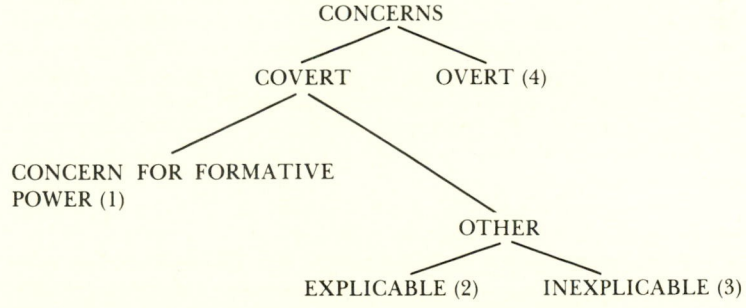

26. Under these first two heads we encounter once more the "form" that answers to a need of the mind as discussed in the previous chapter.

27. This project does not preclude arguments to the effect that the appreciation of all or some works of art serves this or that ulterior end, *provided* that the end is wrought by contemplation and the immediate objective of artist and public is a contemplation enjoyed for itself and not merely valued as a means to the ulterior end. To observe this proviso requires one to walk a tightrope, one on which Marxist aestheticians, such as Morawski (1974), become expert in balancing—unless, as many do, they plunge with solemn deliberation to their intellectual deaths on the rocks of Zhdanovism, to the bewilderment, horror, or derision of their colleagues safe in the West.

28. Paul Valéry eloquently expounds this theme in "Man and the Seashell" (1964).

29. Compare Kaprow (1966) as quoted above (chap. 2, n. 10). From the fact that a work of fine art embodies a system of choices, Arthur Danto (1964) has drawn another, startling consequence: once a person is recognized as "an artist," everything he makes or conspicuously does risks becoming a work of art in which one sees the rejection of all the skills he has chosen not to exercise.

30. Francis J. Kovach (1974, chap. 10) generates immensely elaborate schemata of kinds of beauty from a variety of ontological categorial systems that were worked out without beauty in mind. He argues that only thus can one obtain an objective and nonarbitrary system, escaping the ad hoc, arbitrary, and heterogeneous nature of such traditional categorizations as the sublime, the graceful, and the dumpy. Since the categories he relies on were worked out to meet requirements that were quite other than those of a theory of beauty, however, the result is neither interesting nor relevant.

31. For expositions of this theme, see Maritain (1930, 24) and Kovach (1974, 242).

The thesis that "anything can be found beautiful" or "anything can be an aesthetic object" will play so prominent a part in later discussions that it may be worthwhile citing a version of it that comes with a different metaphysics:

> Since, on the one hand, every given thing may be observed in a purely objective manner and apart from all relations; and since, on the other hand, the will manifests itself in everything at some grade of its objectivity, so that everything is the expression of an Idea; it follows that everything is also *beautiful.* . . . But one thing is more beautiful than another, because it makes this pure objective contemplation easier, it lends itself to it, and, so to speak, even compels it, and then we call it very beautiful (Schopenhauer 1818, §41).

Note that there is an important difference between making perfect beauty the fully appropriate satisfaction of a particular interest or viewpoint and making it a matter of the degree to which a readiness to be captivated is gratified. There is also a difference between the degree of satisfaction that may be found and the ease of finding it.

32. One is tempted to write "every bit as real"—but that would be a mistake, because it appears to invoke the category of *substance*. We must not allow our borrowing of scholastic formulas and arguments to commit us to a metaphysics of substance, from which they may be readily detached.

33. The converse of beauty is sometimes called ugliness; but in fact the concept of the ugly is a complex one with a good deal of positive content (see Read 1962), and the converse of the beautiful as required by our argument is a plain failure to reward attention in any way.

34. It is only if the fine arts are regarded as we are regarding them here that the

restrictions artists observe must be supposed arbitrary. If the arts are regarded as imitative, social reasons for preferences in what is represented are easily adduced; and in Lukács' view (1963), according to which the differentia of art is a specialness that loads individuals with universal significance, different genres become, not preferred forms of expression, but the different ways in which a historical experience manifests itself and as such are not arbitrary in any way at all (see chap. 7, n. 28).

35. This answer is derived from the most elementary considerations of information theory as developed in the context of speech: according to Colin Cherry, "neither the totally unrelated signal nor the totally expected one can be said to communicate" (Gombrich 1963, 97). Attempts have been made to apply the results of information theory to the fine arts, notably by Moles (1966) and Bense (1969), but with inconclusive and disappointing results. The idea is attractive, because a general theory of communicability must somehow include the fine arts in its scope—Goodman's work (1968) testifies to the richness of this approach. But the theory, insofar as it is more than a branch of statistics, in fact deals with the communication of established and intelligible messages somewhat as follows: someone figures out what he wants to say or show; this formulated message is then coded into a form suitable for transmission; the transmission is disentangled from its vehicle and decoded; and the recipient, if all this has been done successfully, has a true copy of the original message. It is up to the recipient to make sense of the message, interpret it, decide how to take it. In other words, information theory has to do *only* with what comes after the formulation of the original message and before its interpretation, and has no application to whatever may lie beyond; but it is precisely what lies outside that domain that concerns artists and their publics and critics. Perhaps all that is directly useful to the theory of art is a crude colloquial analogue of the mathematical theory, such as was already mooted in his homespun way by S. C. Pepper (1949) when he observed that every work must have enough design not to be boring and enough pattern not to be confusing.

The concept of redundancy (a measure of the repetition that adds no new information but is necessary to make sure that no information slips by) is particularly troublesome in the theory of art, because in a piece of music it is seldom quite clear whether a repetition is merely "the same again," and, if it is, whether the quality of recognized sameness does not itself make a difference (the kind of difference no doubt varying with context). Philip Pettit has accordingly found it worthwhile to introduce the notion of satisfaction, which he defines as "the repetition in a work . . . which ensures that the aesthetic subject is given 'enough,' that he is satisfied and not just tantalized. It is a point of the most common experience that the human being enjoys having his expectations fulfilled—as rhyme fulfils expectations in poetry for instance" (1975, 61).

36. In the extreme case, the spectator or auditor himself provides the necessary variation from the expected by changing his expectations. This possibility is further discussed below. One wonders whether it is theoretically possible for someone to imagine a melody to himself by humming on a monotone and imagining a succession of different tonics. I think not.

37. The point has been explored in its relation to music by Meyer (1956) and Rosen (1971). Pierre Boulez (1964) and other advanced thinkers have envisaged the possibility that each work should establish the norm from which its departures establish its meaning—a recipe for guaranteed unintelligibility in macabre parody of the older observation that "every artist creates the taste by which he is enjoyed." As Rosen and Meyer both observe, every notable work in fact modifies the norm

that governs the public's expectations; and thinkers as various as Adorno (1948), Burnham (1971), and Danto (1964) have pushed this to the point where every new work is supposed to transform the norm totally, so that, on the one hand, at any moment in any art the artist must know everything that has been done so that he knows what the relevant norm is from which he must depart (a requirement made to look a little less silly than it is by equating "everything" with what is done in Vienna or in New York or wherever is chic this afternoon) and, on the other hand, the public must acquire a comparable omniscience to appreciate his departures.

Even without going to these self-defeating extremes, the decision that a norm has been exhausted may reflect merely the nervous ennui of an elite more prone to recognize an effect than to appreciate it. The reflex "It's been done" may precede and so preclude any discrimination of what precisely has been done.

38. The distinction is Aristotle's, in the *Poetics*; Frye (1957) works out an analysis of literary genres on this basis.

39. Collocation of the terms "medium" and "message" calls for some mention of H. M. McLuhan. His assertion that "the medium is the message" amounts to this: the set of possibilities, variations within which constitute messages, is not itself any one of those messages, but in relation to the range of possible sets of possibilities is a message of a very powerful sort. He argues that, if any set of possibilities is so pervasive that we cannot become conscious of it as an isolated set and thus cannot identify variations within it, no work of art can be formulated in its terms. Thus, if television so saturates our consciousness as to become our usual way of taking in information, there can be no works of art in television, no one can prefer any TV program to any other, and TV can only affect its audience by modifying their means of sensibility. The argument lacks cogency. Fish may not know they are in water, but this should not prevent them from taking variations in water as guides to behavior: it is just the person to whom water is a rarity who is likely to confuse one kind of water with another. What the immersed fish fails to do is to conceptualize as *changes in the water* the changes to which he responds.

40. The contrast drawn in the text does not, and was not meant to, capture either the history or the essence of the classical and the romantic as they have been variously identified, defined, and explored. Neither term is the other's sole antonym, and each is associated with a number of polymorphous historical movements. A classical style may be thought of as one that emphasizes the whole, as against the fragmentary; the actual shape, as opposed to effect and appearance; isolated form, rather than organic continuity; and self-contained reality, as contrasted with symbolic significance. Romanticism, on the other hand, may stand for the night world of dreams and visions rather than the day world of waking actualities; for the extreme and perverse versus the central and normal (cf. Praz 1933); for the natural and spontaneous, as against artifice; and for freedom and the will as opposed to reason and judgment (cf. Collins 1965, 40). Even in terms of the restricted contrast drawn in the text, the words "classical" and "romantic" wander in meaning, because the terms "form" and "content" are correlative and thus do not in isolation designate anything in particular. The distinction I want is close to that made by Ernst Curtius between classical and mannerist art, that is, between the direct expression of content and an emphasis on expertise and technical elaboration. This in turn reflects Schiller's distinction between naive and sentimental poetry—in which, however, what is contrasted with direct expression is not consciousness of technique but consciousness of self. Schiller makes the distinction a matter of the personality expressed and so takes it out of the domain of the fine arts as such: if transposed into technical terms,

it collapses into that made by Curtius, for a work that betrays consciousness of the artist as artist is precisely one in which the how is emphasized at the expense of the what. For an earlier and more straightforward version of the contrast, one might compare David Hume's essay "Of Simplicity and Refinement in Writing," which treats simplicity and sophisticated elaboration merely as two extremes to be avoided, as in the classical contrast between Attic and Asiatic rhetoric, rather than as distinct styles.

Our contrast between the classical and the romantic can be recognized in Friedländer's contrast between the original and the bizarre, beneath a thick layer of heavy evaluation that confuses bizarrerie with *Kitsch*:

> Something original is strange when first seen, shocking and unpleasant; something bizarre is striking and entertaining. The former is something enduring and permanent and only gains in impressiveness; the latter is a thing of fashion, is ephemeral, causes satiety and vanishes before long. . . . Whoever is creative in a truly original sense—especially if he be a man of genius—aims at being self-sufficient; whoever indulges in the bizarre, endeavours to impress his contemporaries or to amaze them (Friedländer 1942, 242-243).

41. The contrast we make here has affinities with, but is not quite the same as, Isaiah Berlin's opposition of "the hedgehog and the fox," a unified organizing vision and a dispersed awareness of multiple fact. For what an organizing vision organizes may be strange, and plain facts may be plainly observed.

42. Such procedures have always been normal for landscape gardening, which at one time was accounted one of the most important of the fine arts. The gardener is a modifier of landscape, which is essentially the physical world as setting for a human life; his task is, accordingly, to adjust the immediate setting to the wider horizon and to guide the walker's steps and gaze from view to view, from surprise to reassurance. Doxiadis (1937) has argued that Greek architecture similarly was conceived in terms of setups, relations between building and landscape as seen from specific viewpoints.

43. Fried (1967) regards the equation of art with the creation of setups as a perversion, substituting the immediate values of theatricality for the more serious relational values proper to the fine arts. He argues that the higher achievements of such an art as painting nowadays can be understood only in terms of the problems posed by the specific state of that art. But perhaps theatricality, as he conceives it, is generating a tradition of its own; and, in any case, it is idle to expect that the resources of immediacy will rest unexploited, even if we deplore the popular neglect that unsurprisingly overtakes difficult and esoteric work in all the arts.

44. This is certainly true of the bicycle wheel and the *pissoir, Fountain*, which exemplify types of artifact long extolled in the artistic circles haunted by Duchamp as fertile in unnoticed elegance (Banham 1967). I have a lot more to say about Duchamp and his *pissoir* in chapter 14.

45. Presenting a familiar object in a context that invites the spectator to attend to it as a work of art may be intended to incite him, not to look at or listen to the object as such, but rather to meditate on some supposed aspect of the human condition or of contemporary civilization. Just what, if anything, should be identified as the work of art in such cases may be problematic. Some of the perplexities are considered later in connection with the purist line.

46. Evidently the slogan "unity in variety" presents us with another version of two of the three conditions of beauty specified by scholasticism. For an exploration

of the resources of critical discourse in praising and disparaging unities and varieties, see Aschenbrenner (1974, 141-153).

47. Somewhat similarly, insofar as art is unified and unifies, it may be thought to celebrate society and the unity of men; insofar as it makes for the variety it exemplifies, it may be thought to promote anarchy and unbridled individuality—though in both cases the alleged tendency rests on nothing stronger than an apparent affinity. One who believes in these tendencies may then go on to maintain that the highest art is at once reconciliatory and subversive, holding in extreme tension the forces of reconciliation and disruption.

48. I. A. Richards at one time made it fashionable to dismiss all such beloved simplicities as dependent on "stock responses," leaving a cool irony as the only mode appropriate to artistic creation and appreciation. But the reference to "stock responses," by failing to differentiate boring routine from delighted recognition, simply evades the issue. Compare, also, Pettit's remarks on "satisfaction," quoted in note 35, above.

49. This line is worked out by Wellek and Warren (1949). It is never hard to determine what one should say about classics. Since a classic is a work already conceded to have whatever complexity is most aesthetically relevant, one simply says of it whatever is required by whatever aesthetic is either fashionable or one's own favorite—unless one wishes to be daring, in which case one attributes to it whatever qualities are demanded by the aesthetic one most hates. One might define a classic as a work that is critically foolproof, were it not notorious that classics have a way of making fools of their critics.

50. Part of the function of such commonplaces may be like that fulfilled by current slang phrases and by fashions in hobbies and clothes; like phatic communion, they simply celebrate and intensify the sense of community. To some extent and in some contexts, the initial popularity of a catch phrase or a hit tune may be arbitrary or accidental, but once it has gained currency, the very fact of its currency gives it an interest: it becomes the object of a second-order reflection.

51. The analogy between games and art forms breaks down at the point where rules are called in question. Conventions in art change without notice because not only is there no game, and hence no rules constituting the game, but there are no rules to govern it: there is only a system of systems of regularities, whose function is to make meaningful variation possible. There are also second-order conventions, similarly nebulous, about how much change in the first-order conventions can be introduced without scandal; but these in turn can be violated or changed by anyone who is prepared to buck the system for a while. The player of a game, on the other hand, cannot change the rules of a game while he is playing it: he can only abide by them or break them.

L. B. Meyer (1967; cf. chap. 1, n. 41, above) has pointed out that the regularities of artistic conventions and forms cannot function as psychological systems of expectation, since artistic effects seldom rely on ignorance or fail on repetition; nor can they, as I have just said, be rules establishing proprieties. They are, rather, inference systems, establishing procedures as usual or unusual in various respects.

52. This distinction is of the kind previously introduced and discussed under the rubric of kinds of beauty.

53. As before, the qualifier "sensory" is introduced with reservations. Perhaps it is time we admitted that the word is primarily used in this context, not to rule out mathematical systems and such, but to prevent anyone from claiming that one has defined the Beatific Vision as an aesthetic experience—even though Beauty is one of the Names of God.

54. I should here give substance to my general remarks by going through some of the phrases in which the word "aesthetic" is used and pointing out some of the things they are used to mean. But since that discussion would not further my main argument I relegate it to Appendix A.

55. It is because excited people cannot scrutinize things effectively and enjoyably that the fine arts are thought to need calm and detachment and that "contemplation" has been thought an apt word for the cognitive mode uniquely suitable to them.

56. An artificial beauty, for purposes of this argument, is one the production of which requires skill, not necessarily one that displays skill. A display of skill pertains to the secondary standards of an art and, as such, is a vacuous use of a technique subservient to what is still presumed the art's primary end. But in the fine arts the distinction between primary and secondary standards is necessarily unstable, since a display of technique is inherently appreciable. In fact, one way of thinking of the fine arts is as arts generated when the secondary standards of certain other arts become primary to an art of their own. Presumably any identifiable and entrenched set of secondary standards may become primary to.another set of standards, which in turn, when identifiable and entrenched, may become the primary standards of a new fine art. In principle, this could continue ad infinitum; in practice, probably not for more than three or four steps.

57. Various aspects of this theme are explored in *SA* (343ff.); in the last pages of Sartre (1940); and, after Sartre, in Lévi-Strauss (1962) as cited above.

58. There are, in fact, two major possibilities here: one, that all artificial beauties should be construed as in some manner second-order; the other, that only those arts whose beauties are of the second order should be classified together as fine arts, the others presumably being classed as decoration.

59. C. I. Lewis (1946) reduces value to experiences found valuable (that is, enjoyable), analyzing other values in terms of propensity to produce those; but the equation of the initially prized instantaneous experiences with pleasures is rather insinuated than argued. Similarly, Von Wright (1963) insists that only momentary experiences can ultimately be prized, and must be prized as pleasant; but this is an arbitrary dogma on which nothing in his main argument depends (cf. Sparshott 1964). These dogmas go back to Greek philosophy, in which the springs of action are divided into appetite and aversion, and objects of experience are divided into the attractive and the repellent, which could have no other source within experience itself than pleasure and "pain" (the negative counterpart of pleasure). This dualism in the affective qualities of experience and the experienceable is part and parcel of a general dualistic mythology that pervades Greek thought (cf. Tracy 1969).

Chapter V. The Classical Line
4: Arts of Imagination

1. If the ringing sound persists, however, one is not "imagining it," but suffering from a ringing in the ears. To say "It is only my imagination" is to suggest that one has misconstrued or overconstrued a sensible cue, or supposed oneself to have heard a faint sound where there was none to hear: when an unfounded appearance persists or survives close attention, one no longer speaks of imagination because one is not so much quasi hearing or quasi seeing as actually hearing or seeing without real occasion.

2. Aristotle, *De Anima* III.10; Sartre (1943, pt. 1, chap. 1 §§1-2).

3. Not all literature furnishes us with imaginary worlds, or not all in the same way. Epic, novel, story, and all narrative and dramatic forms necessarily evoke the setting, more or less extensive or shadowy, in which the story unfolds, and even a lyric may imply a singer and his world; but literary modes in which the words are connected otherwise than in the grammar of a language, by failing to supply the ordinary connections of concepts, may fail to imply the ordinary connections of persons and objects, and thus may evoke a world only in some remote and metaphorical sense.

4. The alternative views and meanings I discuss here do not necessarily answer to different uses of the word "imagine" and its cognates in everyday speech. For instance, to ask someone to "imagine doing" something or other is to invite him to envision what it would feel like to be doing that thing; to invite him to "imagine himself doing it" asks only that he envision the scene in which he figures as doing so; while to ask him to "imagine that" something is the case need ask no more than that he entertain the hypothesis that it is so. But theorists of the imagination have not usually found it rewarding to take account of these differences of usage (pointed out by Zeno Vendler in an address to the American Society for Aesthetics in 1978).

5. An illusion is not, of course, a hallucination or any kind of error: in an "optical illusion" one is not deceived and does not perceive what is not there; one simply finds oneself perceiving things otherwise than as one knows them to be. In the Muller-Lyer illusion, the lines that one knows to be equal in length persist in looking different in length. People who apply the word "illusion" to art might defend their usage by saying that, in looking at the picture of a horse, one sees what persists in looking like a horse running, although one knows that it is literally neither a horse nor running.

6. People seem to differ greatly in the amount and kind of imagery that runs through their heads when they are imagining things and at other times, but these differences seem to make very little difference to the way the people in question think—the differences are discoverable only by questioning (or by appropriate electroencephalography, no doubt), and cannot be inferred from any consequential difference in the way people carry out any activity calling for intelligence or imagination. Of course, I can never compare directly the pictures I see in my head with the pictures you see in yours, but certain differences are easily inferred from the different things we say about them; in any case, such pictures have nothing to do with what I mean when I say that the reader recreates in imagination the novelist's world. I mean only that, if they fully share the author's language and knowledge, the readers will readily reconstruct the scenes, events, and persons the author creates and the relations between them that his narrative and their created nature entail—a capacity that cannot be equated with the propensity to affirm as "true in the book" any finite or even infinite set of sentences derivable from the sentences he penned, but has to be thought of as the capacity to follow out continuities.

Chapter VI. The Classical Line
5: What Works of Art Are

1. According to Robert Henri, "The object of painting a picture is not to make a picture—however unreasonable this may sound. The picture, if a picture results,

is a' *by-product* and may be useful, valuable, interesting as a sign of what has past. The object, which is back of every true work of art, is *the attainment of a state of being*, a state of high functioning, a more than ordinary moment of existence" (1923, 159). This is sometimes quoted as summing up that great teacher's thought on the art of painting. As such a summary, it would be absurd. A "state of high functioning" that is only contingently and coincidentally connected with the production of paintings has little relevance to the art of painting as that art is practiced; and if the alleged state is more closely connected with the production of paintings, it is improper to call the latter its byproducts. But in fact Henri's dictum was not a pronouncement ex cathedra, but part of a communication to a student whom Henri thought unsuitably preoccupied with winning competitions and so forth. In that context it is sound advice. In other contexts, Henri was equally ready to say such things as "Painting is the expression of ideas in their permanent form" and "one should know as far as possible all the *possibilities* of a medium" (ibid., 116 and 134).

A rhetoric like Henri's is used by Harold Rosenberg when he claims that in "action painting" the canvas was an "arena in which to act," and "what was to go on the canvas was not a picture but an event," so that "the artist gets away from art through his act of painting; the critic can't get away from it" (1959, 25ff.). There is little here beyond a tiresome confusion. What got on the canvas was in the end certainly a picture, whether its getting there was an event or not. And if the canvas was really the arena of the action, the action was that of the brush (or other pigment bearer) *on the canvas*, not the waving of the artist's arm or whatever beforehand. Rosenberg's romantic imagination may have been fired by the aesthetic of Sung landscape painting or other Sino-Japanese art forms influenced by Buddhism, according to which the quick gesture of the spiritually trained artist transfers to the paper a spiritual essence that it captures. But the point is that the gesture is entirely directed (by whatever means) to the brush stroke: in Rosenberg's terms, the action of which it records the trace is precisely the action of making that very brush stroke. If, for instance, Jackson Pollock were to prize one of his paintings for the sake (in part) of the drippings and pourings that produced the loops and skeins of paint now buried far beneath the surface of the final version, that is his right (artists in all ages may value their works for what went into them, not what has come out of them); but the final painting does not preserve their trace and cannot be valued as a record of them. If the painting does bear the trace of those vanished loops and their making, it must be because the inherent dynamic of the painting as it now is points back to them. As for the artist getting away from art through his act of painting, one may concede that in some cases the artist never got as far as art, but one hardly sees in what sense his act of painting can be said to have got him away from it: just what has removed him from what, and by what means? And why should the critic be supposed to *want* to get away from art, but to be unable to do so? If he wanted to get away from art, he could go and play golf. Presumably, what Rosenberg wants to say is that the sole value of the work is as a reminder to the artist of the agony he underwent in painting it (though why he should agonize to produce something merely to remind him of his agony, and what form such agonizing could conceivably take, are not easy questions to answer). Considerations of that sort belong to the purist line and are discussed in chapter 14.

2. An exception might be made in favor of those works that exist to display skill. Interest in a piece of trick Chinese ivory carving would be extinguished if one discovered that it was machine made. If it were so, our interest might be transferred to the machine; with the hand-carved piece, we know what the "machine" is, and

we marvel that it can do what it has. But in our terms we would say that the performance as such is a manifestation of skill, that the secondary standards of sculpture have here become primary standards of the art of virtuoso carving.

3. This distinction between the evaluative and the judgmental is an important one, but not one usually recognized. What I here call the *evaluative* judgment expresses a generalized commendation in respect of a skill and care that has issued in aesthetic excellence, an excellence appropriate to the fine arts. The *judgmental* use of the phrase attributes success in the specific objectives of the fine arts, it being assumed that those objectives are those by which the object under discussion is appropriately assessed.

4. The line between the descriptive and the sortal is a fine one, in that describing anything assigns it to the class of things so describable, and assigning a thing to a class ascribes to it the common character of the members of the class (even if, in the limiting case, that common character be restricted to the fact of membership). But in the next chapter we will have occasion to distinguish between classification and characterization of works of art. Meanwhile, there is an obvious difference between saying that something is a sculpture and, therefore, a work of art and saying that it exemplifies aesthetic qualities and is *therefore* a work of art. It doesn't do to lose sight of the obvious.

5. Morawski writes that the question "What is the work of art?" is the same as the question "What is artistic value?" (1974, 3). It may on occasion be the same, but it depends who is asking and what he wants to know.

6. The straightforward distinction between descriptive and evaluative uses of expressions, popular some years ago, quite obscures this threefold division. In this regard, it is worth noting that some recent writers use the word "artwork," a straightforward sortal for which no evaluative use has been established, instead of "work of art." For further discussion, see note 50, below.

7. The concept of vagueness is itself vague. Morris Weitz distinguishes "perennially flexible" from "irreducibly vague" concepts in aesthetics (1973, 480): the latter, including such style concepts as mannerism, are used to pick out from time to time various sets of phenomena according to various principles from a loosely demarcated historical area; the former, including such "art" concepts as drama, are such that there are always certain features whose relevance to the concept cannot intelligibly be denied. (There are also "perennially debatable" concepts like "tragedy," which function as weapons used by theorists and take their meanings from the theories in which they are functioning for the time being.) Weitz's argument is hardly transparent, but I take it that he would argue that the concept of a work of art as it functions in such a context as ours is flexible rather than vague: for instance, a work of art need not be an artifact, but being or not being an artifact is something that can never be *irrelevant* to something's being a work of art.

8. Ziff (1953) urges that what counts as a work of art changes from time to time, being definable only as what fulfills a certain sort of social role—but this role cannot be defined, since it changes as social structures change. I understand him to be implying that in any society one should be able to identify the role and hence identify what is a work of art in that context—by continuity or analogy or some such means.

9. "A work of art in the classificatory sense is (1) an artifact (2) a set of the aspects of which has had conferred upon it the status of candidate for appreciation by some person or persons acting on behalf of a certain institution (the artworld)" (Dickie 1974, 34). He adds that artifactuality is itself a status that can be conferred at the same time as the status of candidacy, though not by the same act (ibid., 44-45).

564

What this means has not been made clear by those of Dickie's explanations I have read or heard, but the idea seems to be that it is one thing to draw an object into the orbit of human making and doing and another thing to draw it into the narrower orbit of appreciability.

The commoner objections to Dickie's position include the following. It is not clear what counts as conferring the alleged status, nor how anyone is to know that it has been conferred; nor is it clear what difference the alleged conferring would make, since presumably things can be appreciated, if they can be appreciated at all, just as well whether anyone has conferred candidacy on them or not. Again, it is hard to believe that being a work of art should depend on people's doing things "on behalf of" an institution most people have never heard of, and might not believe in (much less be able to identify) if they had. One might also object that if the "artworld" is anything, it is most likely to be that suspect coterie of gallery directors, magazine editors, dealers, and collectors, so that the apparent tendency of Dickie's definition is to take art away from the artist and give it to the manipulators. Presumably, though his writings do not make this clear, what Dickie had in mind was something like the following. The chief denizens of the artworld are artists, presenters of art (gallery directors, dealers, editors, etc.), and the interested public (1974, 36). Artists make things works of art by (usually creating them and then) putting them forward as their own work; presenters make things works of art by displaying them, advertising them, criticizing them, offering them for sale, and so on; the public makes things works of art by treating them (cherishing them, seeking them out, etc.) in the same way that they do those works that artists and presenters have set before them. Artists can do what they do only because presenters and public are there to receive what they do; presenters can do what they do only because artists have furnished the paradigms for such presentation, and because there is a public to present them to; the public can do what they do only because the style of cherishing, seeking, and so on has been defined by artists and presenters. Thus, all three groups of people do what they do in the light of the acknowledged existence of the practice in which they are all involved. And what artists and presenters do is plainly, in their different ways, to present what they present as candidates for appreciation. As for the public, they appreciate what they appreciate; but in establishing by their collective choice new classes of appreciables, they bestow on members of those classes the status of recognized candidate for appreciation, a status that the other members of the artworld can (and in the long run probably *must*) take into account. Now, all these modes of behavior are entirely serious, calling for skill, devotion, and enterprise: there is nothing here to trivialize art. The seriousness, however, cannot be built into our definition without absurdity: it being understood that the kind of thing we have just described is what goes to making things works of art, we cannot lay down a priori just how much or how little of it is required. But, in any case, effectively to confer a status is to do something, to make a difference or to risk a commitment: there must be some way in which one's relation to the multifarious practices of the arts makes one able to affect the status of an object. And one may suspect that, although that ability may be misused on occasion, even frivolously used, it is not in general easily come by.

If the foregoing understanding is correct, Dickie's account of what a work is has great merit and is not harmed by the objections commonly urged against it. As he states it, however, it is a metaphor and relies on the good will of the reader to give it a literal interpretation that he will find benign.

10. The concept of disinterestedness, a staple of eighteenth-century views and

their descendants, has fallen into disrepute. One argues that it is neither sufficient for aesthetic contemplation, in that *any* absorbed interest or activity is disinterested in the required sense, nor necessary, in that the delight one takes in a work of art need not be divorced from the lust of acquisition or the pride of ownership; and, if the disinterestedness required is such that one's interest in a painting should be sharply marked off from one's real-life interest in what it depicts, it is ludicrous to suppose that the aesthetic pleasure males take in paintings of the female nude has *nothing whatever* to do with sexual reverie. To which it may be replied that, insofar as the sexual reverie is a sexual reverie, it is not an element in the contemplation, however sexually tinged the latter may be (otherwise, people would either be incapable of appreciating paintings of sexual objects of the wrong sex or else incapable of recognizing their sexual power), and the same goes (mutatis mutandis) for the pride of ownership, and that is precisely why it is not otiose to mention the disinterestedness of contemplation. It is, however, obvious that a satisfactory treatment of this theme would need great care in stating exactly what was meant by "disinterestedness" in this context, and that such care is not usually taken. For a historical treatment of "disinterestedness" in early aesthetics, see Stolnitz (1961).

In saying that the attention has no end beyond the attending itself, I am not differentiating between attending and any enjoyment or satisfaction found or taken in the attending as such, any pleasure got from it as such. If there is a distinction to be made between attending and finding pleasure in attending, or between setting a value on attending and setting a value on the pleasure of attending, I am content to leave it for others to make.

11. One must not go too far here. The excitements of engagement and involvement, and the engrossed interest of participation in a complex and fascinating activity, are very real; but they do not fall under the head of contemplation, as I intend it, unless they spring from the nature of what one is aware of in one's awareness of that in which one is taking part. If, for instance, one is caught up in an *o altitudo* of oceanic feeling (if I may thus confound the elements), one is not contemplating unless there is some object for one's contemplation; the sheer excitement of being part of a crowd gripped by a common passion is not, in itself, contemplation.

12. Marshall Cohen writes that those who propose to use "contemplation" in the way I have adopted effectively beg the question "whether there is any feature common to the bewildering variety of psychological states, and even physical activities, that may be required for obtaining the varieties of aesthetic experience. . . . If one ought to contemplate a Redon or a Rothko, one ought to scrutinize the Westminster Psalter, survey a Tiepolo ceiling, regard a Watteau, and peer at a scene of Breughel. If we attend to these distinctions we shall be in a position to deny that we must contemplate these works to have a proper aesthetic experience of them" (1962, 490). But this is totally confused. Those who use the term "contemplation" "simply to comprehend *whatever* conditions they suppose necessary for obtaining aesthetic experience" (his phrase, my italics) are thereby explicitly not begging the question of which Cohen speaks, but leaving it open, or, rather, presupposing that there will be a variety of states and actions, whether or not they are bewildered by it. Obviously the sense in which "contemplate" is contrasted with "scrutinize" and "peer at" is not the sense they have in mind. What Cohen is describing is the error of those who suppose that the ordinary use of the word "contemplate" is especially fitted to what one has to do to get the most out of any aesthetic object (cf. chap. 4, n. 55), which is by no means the same as the position he set out to describe.

13. Note that George Dickie's definition of a work of art, cited in note 9, above, risks circularity if "appreciation" is understood as it is taken here. For what kind of appreciation is the object made a candidate? Aesthetic appreciation, presumably; but this is not said, and Dickie has not in general shown himself in favor of defining art or works of art in terms of the aesthetic, preferring to eliminate "the aesthetic" in favor of overt reference to works of art. But if that elimination is performed in the present case, or if we say instead that the candidate is to be appreciated *as a work of art*, the definition becomes overtly circular. Circularity can perhaps be avoided by saying that the appreciation is to be of any kind the artworld traffics in.

14. For an analogous set of interdefinable terms that pose irritating problems of priority in the order of understanding, see the discussion of "aesthetic judgment" and related terms in *SA* (109-112).

15. They may be its keeper's artifacts or joint works. If the keeper prepares the palette, loads the brushes, and deftly removes the paper as soon as it looks right, leaving the ape to exercise his taste in where he puts the brush down on the paper, no doubt ape and keeper jointly constitute an agent, like a rock group and its studio technicians.

16. The question of what can, and what usually does, count as a single thing is a general question for ontology. So far as our requirements go, anything or any collection of things that can be identified is admissible. Logicians can evolve strange candidates. But in practice people identify as things (units, entities, items) only what it is either useful or agreeable or advisable to think about or use in a unified way. Logically, one could identify as an individual the trio consisting of the smell of overripe tomatoes, the square root of two, and the meaning of this sentence; one might call it "George." But there is not much to say about George, and few natural opportunities for saying it.

17. The concept of a performance as I have developed it here and elsewhere seems to me to be free from difficulties and to answer well to a range of our common understandings of what it is to do or make something. But no doubt it would gain in respectability if it could be related to kindred concepts in an ontological framework. I have elsewhere sketched a way of approaching the task of building such a framework and arranging within it much of the material presented in this chapter (Sparshott 1980). The ontology I envisage there diverges from idealist, empiricist, and phenomenological ontologies in not being egocentric. Not that I ignore the egocentric predicament as a possible problem, but the approach is perhaps exhausted by this time and, in any case, cannot have the preemptive status so often claimed for it. It can never be brought to accommodate interpersonal transactions in the real world. The *ego/alter* relation can never generate either the *I/Thou* or the *I/It*, because the *ego* always claims preeminence. After all, it was there first. But who is it? Which of us is to be relegated to the external world, reader: you, or me?

18. "Everything about the painting" is an indeterminate expression, because, since paintings do not consist of determinate sets of discrete parts, and since they take part of their meaning as paintings from their relations to a world that itself undergoes constant change, we cannot enumerate the relationships that will be found aesthetically relevant.

19. It appears that abstract expressionist and action paintings, as these critical labels suggest, are most readily construed as expression designs, hard-edged abstractions as pattern designs, and representational paintings as either message designs or pattern designs, depending on the kind and degree of stylization employed—that is, the degree of obliquity to whatever conventions are currently taken

as rendering likeness realistically. The simplified and hard-outlined paintings recently exported from China are plainly message designs, having the style of information givers, though it would be crass to equate them with posters; and posters themselves when viewed aesthetically are still to be seen as message designs. But obviously any viewpoint *can* be taken to any work, given suitable training or perversity; and my later discussion of the "dimensions" of the work of art will suggest that every work must at least have an expressive and a pattern *aspect* to its design, even though that aspect may not be such as to give the design its character.

20. The idea of a design act may come in handy when one is trying to come to terms with conceptual art and systems-oriented art within the confines of the classical line. A systems-oriented work would be one in which the actual movements of the spectator (or whatever he should be called) enter into the design of the work, of which the artist is as it were the impresario (cf. Burnham 1968, 363ff.). However one identifies the work and its design in such a case, the subjective counterpart of it will surely be less easily thought of as a performer of precisely that work as performance-with-design than as the agent who set up the conditions in which the work came to be achieved. Similarly, in a work of conceptual art in which the idea of the work is for all practical purposes identical with the work itself, the performer corresponding to the performance is unlikely to be of much significance: more significant will be the historical fact of agency, the *having* of the thought. But perhaps that only shows that the classical line is not perfectly equipped to deal with works of this kind, or that I have not found the right way to handle them in terms of that line.

21. The quoted phrase is from Margolis (1965, 44). My reasons for adopting the definition are largely his, and in this chapter and the next I have used the definition in a way inspired by his practice, though in a crude and simple-minded way for which he is not to blame. I differ from Margolis in writing "performance" where he writes "artifact," and in everything that follows from that, and in defining "design" in terms of being an aesthetic object. Margolis offers "as a set of materials organized in a certain way" as an equivalent phrase to "with respect to its design," so that in the end my adaptation turns out to be very different from its original. It is worth noting, by the way, that his gloss on "design" is couched in terms suitable to the classical definition of an art as I outlined it in chapter 2.

22. D. W. Harding argues that, because an author may put into his work things he is unaware of, and a reader may think he finds in a work features it cannot be shown to possess, one might be tempted to make it a first principle of criticism that "the reader is concerned only with two things: the piece of writing as it is and his own mental processes in the face of it." But that, he says, would be a mistake: "If what he enjoys in a work of art is unconnected with the artist's satisfaction, the work becomes an unintended feature of the world, non-social, like a sunset or a canyon, beautiful perhaps but not mediating contact with a human maker." There is an implicit social link between writer and reader, even when the writer's identity is unknown. "We cannot ignore what we suppose to have been someone's satisfaction in having made the object," and the possibility of mistaking the nature of this satisfaction is no different in principle from the possibility of any social misunderstanding (Harding 1963, 163-165). That is, our *sense* of sharing the author's satisfaction is essential to our taking something to be a work of art, whether or not we are mistaken in that sense.

23. We must not lose sight of the fact that someone who calls a bit of driftwood a fine piece of sculpture may have something quite different in mind—see note 30, below.

24. Nelson Goodman falters on this point. Because in his system to be a work of art is to be a character in a symbol system, and to be a symbol is to function in a certain way, he writes: "An object may be a work of art at some times and not at others. Indeed, just by virtue of functioning as a symbol in a certain way does an object become, while so functioning, a work of art. The stone is normally no work of art while in the driveway, but may be so while on display in an art museum. In the driveway it usually performs no symbolic function; in the art museum it exemplifies certain of its properties—e.g., shape, color, texture. . . . On the other hand, a Rembrandt painting may cease to function as a work of art when used to replace a broken window or as a blanket" (1977, 17). But on the next page he very sensibly takes this back: "The Rembrandt painting remains a work of art, as it remains a painting, while functioning only as a blanket; and the stone from the driveway may not strictly become art by functioning as art." The reasons for thus withdrawing the initial gambit are sufficiently obvious, but it is by no means clear that the withdrawal is warranted by the general strategies of Goodman's system.

25. Can one really be said to perform a clearing of tables? Only if that clearing is a single performance, made so by being construed as a unitary task ("Sue Ann! Clear those tables!"—"Yes, Mrs. Armbruster") or carried out in a unified fashion (as might be done by the waiter who in Sartre's *Being and Nothingness* acts out the part of "a waiter"—and, in this instance, does his clearing-the-tables shtick). Otherwise, his activity breaks down into the sequence of the particular things he does, or else becomes a sample of his table-clearing activity; and the "dance" we read into what he does will answer either to some limited and coherent set of his table-clearing motions or to the style of his motion. It does follow from my definition that unless we *either* construe his motion as a sample of style, a continuous fulfillment of an ideal of grace or elegance or something like that, *or* fasten our attention on some set of his actions on which he has himself conferred in his agency a coherent unity of action, we do wrong to attribute to him any performance and hence do wrong to speak of a work of art.

26. This rhetorical question, like many rhetorical questions, probably has a good answer. Pragmatists define truth as that on which all serious investigators will ultimately reach agreement (for where no such agreement is forthcoming, truth is not ascertained; and if no such agreement can ever be relied on, the concept of truth has no application). So we might say that anything is a work of art that will ultimately be accepted by the art world as a whole; for the status of any object on which there is no consensus of elites must always remain equivocal; and if there is never to be a consensus of elites, the concept of a work of art has no clear application. But the parallel is not clear enough to constrain us. It makes a common-sense point to say that in some cases we *don't know* what the truth is, but may find out some day; in other cases, we really do know, because we can be sure that no future investigation will be so serious, or will have such good opportunities, as what has been done already; and in yet other cases we cannot conceive that any investigation will ever establish the truth (since, for instance, all witnesses are dead and all evidence destroyed). This is because we know what it is like to investigate and establish or fail to establish truth in simple cases. But do we really want to say that we *don't know* that something is a work of art except in those cases where too many critics and art historians have been at work to be ignored? Do we know what it is like to *investigate* the claims of something to be a work of art?

27. Considering what would actually have to happen before we really did consider the pipe layer's trench to be a work of art sheds light on the ways George Dickie (1974) and Arthur Danto (1964 and 1981) have set about explaining what art is.

Someone would have to persuade us that the thing was really worth looking at (Dickie), and this could only be because they had discovered a new way of looking at trenches (Danto)—either a way in which trenches could be seen to have properties of a kind already deemed aesthetically relevant, or, more likely, a new set of properties that trenches had, which could be seen to contribute to a new kind of design. In this case, as Danto remarks, it would instantly become potentially relevant to ask of all other works of art whether they had or lacked properties of this newly recognized kind. Both of these would surely be necessary: the new way of seeing would not suffice unless promulgated, and promulgation would not suffice unless the new way of seeing could actually be learned with profit.

E. J. Bond (1975) has argued that it is a necessary and sufficient condition of a thing's being a work of art that it instantiate an art form. It can easily be seen that this interesting and provocative idea fits in with what I have just been saying. If one had really succeeded in seeing a design in the trench, one would necessarily have thereby equipped onself with the capacity to see designs in other trenches and to look at all trenches as potential design bearers. Anything less than that would come to no more than identifying aesthetic properties that were only incidentally those of a trench.

28. If it is possible for a performance to be a work of art by virtue of the design a critique establishes for it, it must in principle be possible for indefinitely many critiques to establish separate designs for one performance. What should we say then? We would have to say that it was a separate work of art when considered with respect to each of those designs severally. This should not worry us. Some theorists do in fact say that different critical interpretations establish different works of art, even in cases where they agree on the essentials of the design. I see no reason to go that far: the cases I envisage are those in which one performance has two or more radically different and unconnected designs, as though a Beethoven symphony were to prove to be a pornographic novel in some language spoken on a planet of Alpha Centauri. Now, someone who claims that a performance is a work of art claims that it has but one design, and he must therefore implicitly claim that to attribute another design to it is to make a mistake. In the case of the pornographic symphonic novel, we shall say that (unless Beethoven was in fact, as I rather suspect, an Alpha Centaurian in disguise) if we and the aliens were to confront each other, it is they who would have to climb down, because they have in an obvious and important way got Beethoven wrong. But so long as no confrontation occurs, there is nothing to prevent them from seeing things their way, just as we can cheerfully identify an African mask as a work of art by virtue of a design that may be quite inaccessible to the carver's compatriots, who are more conversant than we are with the syntax of its symbolism and therefore put its forms together in a way we have yet to learn. Although it is in principle possible for such multiple attributions to occur, however, and the possibility should not faze us, we are surely entitled to rely on our knowledge of the way things go in the world and insist that in practice there aren't going to be any very spectacular cases.

It is always possible, of course, that two divergent critiques may both be mistaken in that each critic attributes to different observable concatenations of features an excitement the real ground of which is some unconscious appeal of features that neither critic dare notice, much as different patients will give widely divergent but equally innocuous readings of the grosser Rorschach blots.

29. It is on this point that I have qualms about the argumentation Danto (1981) uses to establish the connection between being a work of art ("artwork" in his usage)

and being susceptible of interpretation. He relies heavily on extreme and imaginary examples of objects that owe their status as artworks to extravagant interpretations, and apparently seeks thus to lend credibility to the furthest-out manifestations of postwar art. But since the works in question do not exist, there can be no question of anyone actually succeeding in finding authentic interpretations for them. Danto seems unaware of the importance of this omission, with the upshot that much of his book reads less like an explanation of art than like a satire on pseudoart. His philosophy of art incorporates, apparently by inadvertence, a philosophy of chichi.

30. I do not believe that it does. Since Weitz, it has become a commonplace of aesthetics that "someone might say" of a piece of driftwood that it was "a fine piece of sculpture" and, hence, by implication a work of art. He might, indeed. But it is not clear what he would mean. He might be using a metaphor, thinking of waves as sculptors. He might mistakenly suppose that someone had really carved it. He might mean that it was *like* a sculpture, in general or of some particular kind. He might mean that it was just as good to look at as a sculpture. He is more likely to be using that trope whereby the point of using a word is that it does not literally apply, as when we speak of the prime minister as a cretin: there would be no point in calling him one if he really was one (we would then be diagnosing, not abusing or characterizing), and there would be no point in calling the driftwood a piece of sculpture if it really was one. No one calls Michelangelo's *David* a piece of sculpture; and, if one called it a fine piece of sculpture, "fine" would be the only operative word. But it is even more likely that the person who called the driftwood a fine piece of sculpture would have nothing definite in mind. What is the point of deferring to his supposed vagaries? Why should we speculate on what an imaginary person *might* mean by something he *might* say in unspecified circumstances for no stated purpose?

31. Not necessarily to be by artists they are not by: if Chirico in later life forged early Chiricos, painting them over late Chiricos, the results are forgeries.

32. For some remarks on the concept of *Kitsch* and the difficulty of interpreting and applying it, see chapter 2, note 16.

33. Thus, Donald Karshan writes: "Inevitably . . . it is the young artists, and the young artists alone, who define what art is, and will be. Because art is man-made, its existence and the nature of its existence is dependent on its capacity to be continually redefined and made 'real' again and again in each generation" (1970, 549). The significance of this formulation is its recognition that the *same* force that is needed to work with conviction within an established tradition leads inevitably to change if the conditions are suitable. One must demur, incidentally, to the sentimental reference to "young" artists; historically, significant changes are usually the fruit of maturity. Young artists don't know enough about what has to be changed.

34. Do not underrate the deep wisdom in that cliché, usually quoted or parodied in derision. The system of artistic achievement and tradition, and the system of one's own established values, offer equally secure and quite separate contexts for one's trafficking with the arts.

35. Unless the joke is on the bourgeoisie, who (supposedly) lack such appreciation and treat the painting as a mere fetish.

36. "A work of art must be born of conscious intention and deliberate striving: and the spectator, although he may not immediately and fully understand the work, must be able to infer this. This is the fundamental difference (in terms of one's reaction) between discovering a natural object and a man-made one. . . . The reason why young children's paintings are invariably pleasing but are never works of art

571

is that they lack this sense of outward intention and striving. A child paints simply in order to grow up; and his pictures are therefore almost natural objects, almost (and I don't mean this sentimentally) like flowers. The adult artist paints in order to create something outside himself, in order to add to—and to that extent alter—life" (Berger 1960, 64-65). Actually, he does mean it sentimentally—there is more than one way of being sentimental.

37. "Seeing something as a painting in the sense that one sees the tacked-up canvas as a painting, and being convinced that a particular work can stand comparison with the paintings of the past whose quality is not in doubt, are altogether different experiences; it is, I want to say, as though unless something compels conviction as to its quality it is no more than trivially or nominally a painting" (Fried 1967, 444, n. 4).

38. An "art object" is not the same as an *objet d'art*, which tends to be something small and precious, a bijou. But the way of thinking that has in many quarters insinuated the art object into the territory that is properly that of the work of art reflects the sensibility that reduces art to bijouterie.

39. This definition of an art object comes close to Dickie's definition of a work of art, as outlined in note 9, above—though it was reached independently. Dickie's reference to the "artworld" is rendered otiose by my reference to a "work of art" previously defined, but its purport is preserved by my reference to a community and to the intention that an object be "taken" in a certain way. Taken by whom? Why, by the artworld, one may say.

40. His "doing something about them" corresponds to Dickie's conferring of artifactuality. The vagueness in both of our accounts reflects what is surely the case, that in the matter of artistic status there is an immense range of marginal cases, objects and performances that are equivocal in that they have been singled out, attended to, or treated in the ways that works of art and art objects are, but only locally or casually or temporarily or absent-mindedly.

41. Compare Max Beerbohm's caricature "Almost Like Simony," in which we see "Mr Harold Begbie loth to receive, even from Sir William Robertson Nicoll, payment for such work as his" (Beerbohm 1913, no. 30).

42. Conversely, it is not enough that a person should have undergone training; it is necessary that his work embody the skill that training was meant to impart—or perhaps we should even say, *should* have been meant to impart.

43. It would have been simpler to define "a work of fine art" as the product of a practitioner of one of the fine arts in the practice of that art. But that definition would have had only an ideal reference, since it presupposes in the institutions of the fine arts a hard-and-fast quality they have seldom if ever had. The definition in the text is designed to preserve a perspective on reality that people do wish, and rightly wish, to preserve.

44. It is not for the dealer to decide, we say; but that is not for us to decide. Notoriously, the symbiosis between painter and dealer is as close and variable as that between rock group and manager, or between author and editor. Human nature being what it is, it would be as absurd to expect the dealer to refrain from getting in on the painting as to expect the painter to refrain from getting in on the selling. What concerns us here is, not the separation of persons, but the division of functions.

45. Daniel Bell (1976) points to this presumed autonomy of the artist, and the consequent divorce of the cultural realm from the social realm, as a serious weakness in Western industrialized nations. But in real life the claim to autonomy is often no more than a bargaining counter or a debating point or a sop to the ego. Many

artists—those who like to eat or to be known—are to varying degrees in thrall to dealers, editors, funding agencies, network executives, and a host of other representatives of the social realm. All the lamented divorce amounts to is that an artist may go his own way at his own risk, without being jailed or hospitalized. Would Bell really prefer it otherwise?

46. Monroe Beardsley, coinventor of "the intentional fallacy," now says that, whereas it is fallacious to think that a text can be understood as meaning what its author meant it to mean as opposed to what it can mean by what it says, there is no fallacy in assigning to a text the public status the author publicly claims for it—as fiction, as literary biography, or what not (Beardsley 1977). Surely if someone claims, in a context where such a claim has the appropriate illocutionary force, ex cathedra rather than *in poculis*, that what he has produced is meant to be a work of art, then that legitimately affects the way we look at it—especially if we know what *he* means by "work of art."

47. Morse Peckham observes that a work of art is "what the perceiver observes in what has been culturally established as a perceiver's space," and that a work of art may accordingly be defined as "an occasion for a human being to perform the art-perceiving role in the artistic situation, that is, on the artistic stage," or alternatively as "any perceptual field which an individual uses as an occasion for performing the role of art perceiver" (1965, 65-68). In a similar vein, but at least acknowledging that the fine arts and their practitioners do exist, Kendall Walton thinks of the artist as providing the props for a game of make-believe (Walton 1973 and 1978).

48. Horace, in *De Arte Poetica* 416-418, remarks on the inadequacy of the poet's intentions as establishing his credentials, and suggests that a poet who claims bardic authority is to be taken as explaining away his incompetence.

49. The invocation of Plato in this connection is rather risky. Plato observed (*Republic* X) that a manufacturer is an expert only on how to supply the user's requirements: what those requirements are the user knows and must specify. On the other hand, in the *Theaetetus*, he insists that there is a real difference between what is approved now and what will turn out to be desirable in the long run, and suggests that it is the expert's province to know this. Is the expert practitioner of a fine art in the position of one who only knows the means to supply his public's ends, or is he in the position of one who knows better than the public what the public will prove to have wanted? The answer virtually supplies itself. The public cannot judge at first sight what will eventually come to seem good, and the artist is no authority on what will please at first sight; the artist ought to have a fair chance of knowing whether or not his work will stand up, and the public are final authority on what they like here and now. Everything, therefore, turns on whether long-term or short-term use is in question. Beyond that, there is a real tension between actual demand and ideal demand. Even someone who knows what he likes may wish he liked better things and, if he is in the process of educating himself, will try to reach beyond his present capacity for appreciation.

50. The word "artwork" is in current use among aestheticians as a substitute for "work of art." The substitution, apart from pandering to the irritating fad of coining compounds with "art-" as the first member ("artworld," "artscanada" and what have you), serves the purpose of getting away from the everyday vaguenesses of the vernacular expression. In partcular, as I said in note 6, above, "artwork," unlike "work of art," has no evaluative use, being a pure sortal. But for that very reason it is cut off from the functional uses that form the core of the actual meaning of

"work of art": "artwork" comes close in meaning to what my "art object" would mean if that were taken as a pure sortal. Artworks are museum fodder, the merchandise of the artworld.

51. A still sharper identification of the normal case is provided by the intersection of the three definitions of "an artwork," "a work of art," and "a work of fine art," and sharper yet if "work of fine art" is defined in the strict way suggested and rejected in note 43.

52. It is not, of course, a contingent fact that a painting is embodied in an artifact that is nothing other than the painting itself. C. I. Lewis writes that "the direct object of contemplation is an aesthetic essence; an abstraction which theoretically could be identically presented by another physical thing" (1946, 476). But this formulation seems questionable: I would insist that we contemplate *the painting itself*, which is a physical object, even though what we contemplate it *for* is the design that theoretically could be shared with another physical thing, which we might have been contemplating instead.

53. In *SA* I suggested that a work of art was, or was like, a species. If many of them had only one member, it was because of the difficulties of reproduction. Works of art differ from species (or from other species) in that they have a definite origin in time. But animal species have indefinite origins in time, and perhaps animal species and works of art can be assigned or denied temporal origins under the same conditions, as follows. There was a time when there were no human beings and no such thing as man; and if humanity is a timeless essence because it is a potentiality that could always be realized when conditions became right, then so is a work of art. We deny this only because we wish to pay the artist an idle metaphysical compliment by insisting that he creates forms and does not discover them. In fact, works of art are more specieslike than natural species have turned out to be, because their bounds are more readily determined. The fixity of species has proved false of nature, but continues to be plausible of art. The notion of species, however, is little more than a name for the problem: it means a class defined by the formal properties of its members, or the system of properties that defines such a class, but that is not very helpful.

54. Note that the variations here are innumerable: same subject with different lenses, same camera setup with different exposures, same exposures with different development times, same negative with different kinds of variation in printing materials, times, and methods—all leading to slightly or grossly different results, but in a sense all versions of "the same." It is the intricacy of variation that makes the identification and differentiation of works of art in the end a matter of judgment for which practical principles cannot be specified.

55. Remember that works of art can actually be traced to design acts only on the basis of a firm (even if illusory) grasp of what kinds of designs can be and actually are made and how they may be modified. No account of how individuations are performed can be both generally true and informatively detailed, because one can only perform them in the light of one's assumed knowledge of practice. This knowledge includes a lot of information about controversies that are not solvable because they amount to arguments about what is practicable given limitations of material, competence, time, and cash; and people differ widely both in their tolerance of all such limitations and in the particular kinds of limitations they most resist.

56. I mean "performance" here in my own quasi-technical sense, but it coincides with a sense in common use, as Geoffrey Payzant reminds me (in a private communication), in which "old Dr Prouty's performance of the *Messiah*" may be, from

the point of view of the participants even more than the audience, a total experience that can be recalled and reconstructed.

57. Canterbury offers less difficulty to the layman in this regard than Rochester (a poor cathedral, but my own), where the new work stops abruptly, in midarch, just west of the crossing. But what one will accept as unified or harmonious depends on what one's demands are: the demand that a work should show a coherent organization to which everything is subordinated is one that few large-scale works can fulfill. Aesthetic unity is often a matter of unified tone and easy transitions (cf. Schapiro 1966).

58. The motions of the hand in engraving are not those of drawing. In rendering in his own medium what he perceives as the character of his original, the engraver must choose some method and style. In doing so he cannot avoid giving his work a character that the original lacked, as well as missing some of the character that the original had. In addition to these inevitable changes, he may be led to introduce additional modifications of the design to make it more suitable to the new medium (or simply to gratify his own taste). See Ivins (1943) for the inevitable stylization of engravings and Lamb (1962) for the general problem of transposition from drawing to mechanical reproduction.

59. This runs sharply counter to the celebrated thesis of Walter Benjamin (1936), according to whom the original painting or statue, especially in its original setting, has an "aura" that is lost when it is thought of as reproducible, or even as something that is an exhibit in a "museum without walls." The work of art, on this showing, is a sort of genius loci, or perhaps even an oracle to which one makes pilgrimage and which one silently consults as to the destiny of one's soul. So far from all art aspiring to the condition of music, it aspires to the condition of a shrine: only at Bayreuth does music really become art, though for reasons that are not precisely Wagner's. This view of the work of art, however, is entirely incompatible with any possible version of the classical line: it has more to do with the mystic line.

60. The defining properties are not, of course, a handful such as might figure in a dictionary definition: as Aristotle observes, the definition of the *Iliad* would be the *Iliad* (*Metaphysics* Z, 4).

61. The fashion may be over, due to the introduction of a new terminology in a more appropriate theoretical setting by Nelson Goodman. According to Goodman, a work of art is a character in a symbol system (the type), together with its compliance class of marks. The advantage of the new terminology is that the type (the character) is defined syntactically, by its potential relation to other potential characters, and can thus in principle be precisely specified by describing the system to which it belongs in terms of Goodman's precise classification of symbol schemes and systems—unlike the type, which remains disquietingly indeterminate as an abstraction from the tokens. The disadvantage of Goodman's terminology is the same as its advantage: characters are identified syntactically by their relation to other characters in a scheme. When we get down to it, we discover that in the interesting cases there is no scheme and no syntax. The character, incidentally, is not something separate from the class of marks that complies with it, nor is it to be identified with that class itself, for Goodman does not believe in classes. Rather, marks are to be thought of as replicas of each other (Goodman 1968, 131n.). It is a curiously inert formalization, and some theorists feel (even more strongly than they believe, and will argue) that Goodman systematically undermines the notion of a work of art. His symbol systems are conceived without regard to the dynamics of work, and especially without regard to the dynamics of work in the fine arts, and his descriptions and analyses designedly

exclude those problems of loose compliance, of observing the spirit rather than the letter and so on, that are essential to the arts (and toward which my concept of a design act gestured). In Goodman's scheme of things, notoriously, a brilliant rendition of a sonata in which there is *one* wrong note is not a performance of that sonata at all (which makes it likely that some difficult works have never been performed, however often you think you have heard them). Goodman is unabashed when this is pointed out—he knows it very well; he is not trying to account for ordinary usage, but to define identity, which must be transitive (cf. Goodman 1972, 83). If you allow any wrong notes in a performance, a performance that follows a score prepared by transcribing the first performance will be complying with the wrong thing, and after a few such alterations of performance and transcription the work is likely to be unrecognizable. That is true and important. But the conditions of successful performance as generally recognized in music, which allow for all kinds of wrong notes but insist on fidelity to the character of the work, are not vagaries of ordinary language: they are at the center of the practice of the art, and a logical model that denies them is the wrong model.

Any realistic account of the relation between score and performance will need to be cast in much more dynamic terms, such as those used by Roger Sessions:

> The music is not totally present, the idea of the composer is not fully expressed, in any single performance, actual or even conceivable, but rather in the sum of all possible performances. But . . . the number of possible performances is limited by the composer's text and by the musical intentions which that text embodies. . . . We hear many "impossible" performances—impossible sometimes through distortion of the composer's idea, but sometimes also through lack of the vitalizing energy of a genuine impulse (1950, 82).

This will hardly do as it stands, since it implies that the composer knows in advance the limits of what he will accept as a possible performance, but its two essential points are important: that the score does not determine the *idea* of the music, which a musician can recognize in it and to which he must be faithful if he is to be held to have performed the piece properly (and not converted Bach into Brahms), this idea being defined ostensively by the totality of all performances that prove acceptable, whether or not they contain wrong notes; and that no performance of any work can be acceptable unless it has a musical coherence that only the performer can impart. Glenn Gould seems to have shown that musical coherence has nothing to do with a psychologically unified impulse, as Sessions suggests, because an acceptable performance can be patched together out of tapes from performances of disparate character (cf. Payzant 1978, 38-39); but that does not affect the contention that the rendition of the work rather than the composer's architectonic is the locus of the unity of the performance.

While on the subject of scores, one should note that there is a greater difference between a score and the transcription of a performance than Goodman's account allows for. Using a notation to determine a compliance class of marks is quite different from using it to record a particular performance. In fact, the same notation will hardly serve both purposes satisfactorily without modification. The two functions are certainly quite different: reading instructions for playing something is quite different from reading a description of what something sounded like.

62. There are two ways of considering my Golden Cockerel *Iliad*: as a piece of bookmaking, in which the text is treated merely as the occasion for producing patterns of black marks on white, and as an integral work in which the printed

words enter as meaningful text into a design of which they are one set of components. From the former point of view, the book is not a token (and its type not a type) of the megatype *Iliad* at all; I call it the *Iliad* only to distinguish it from other Golden Cockerel productions. The reverse abstraction is therefore equally possible: I can take my copy to be a token not of the Golden Cockerel edition but, attending to the text alone, a token of the type "Pope's *Iliad*." Such intricacies can neither be eliminated nor methodically accommodated in advance by any means that dispenses with a knowledge of what sorts of designs there may be and are, how they are produced, and how they are related. One must know what it is like to be a poet, a translator, a book designer, and a printer.

63. Andrew Harrison (1968) argues that the way the type/token schematism applies to works of art is typical of the way it applies to cultural objects in general—that is, objects that are essentially defined by the role they play in organized human life, including items of money, car models, numbers, and doctrines. But of course he is not speaking of the elaborations and perversions of the schematism that I have perpetrated.

64. In working on an artifact, in performing an action, or in carrying on an activity I am at the same time and in the same process, insofar as my performance is a work of art, developing a design; and if I am thinking of what I am doing as producing a work of art, I am elaborating or excogitating a design. This duality of aspect (for which see also below, note 69) answers to the duality of token and type and to that of token and megatype, depending on just how my activity is conceived and described.

Roger Scruton argues that not all works of art can be *types*: a building, for instance, is essentially a *physical object*, inherently incapable of being reproduced (1974, 24). His argument, so far as I understand it (it is not fully elaborated), is inadequate. If he means that its *physicality* makes it such that it cannot be conceived as a type, this is a familiar argument against an idealism I am not espousing and is easily met by saying that *physicality* is a property like other properties: all that follows is that the tokens of a building-type are all buildings, not plans, photographs, and so on. If he means that a building is what it is because of its relation to its setting in a landscape, then all that follows is that there can be only one token at a time, because room for others can be made only by dismantling the first. If he means that buildings are what they are because of their history, that is no doubt true, but to think of them from that point of view is precisely to think of them not as works of the art of architecture but as hallowed relics.

65. Bernheimer notes that a theatrical producer creates a prototype through rehearsals, which are its *antecedent* replicas (1961, 86). I remark below that no theatrical performance is truly prototypical: one attends a first night for social rather than aesthetic reasons. Indeed, in recent years it has become customary to insert a class of "previews" between rehearsals and full-price performances. What Bernheimer says is strictly true only of shows that are put on for a single occasion, like weddings.

66. I say "normally" because tokens are sometimes derived from templates and the like by other than the standard procedures referred to. One can photograph an engraved plate or take a squeeze from it.

67. The word "in" is placed between quotation marks in these two sentences for different reasons. The waterfall is "in" the picture in a rather special sense of "in," to which attention is thus drawn; but, though special, it is the usual sense of "in" when applied to pictures. No other word is more usual in this sense and context,

and the sense in question is no more special than many of the senses of "in," which only a positivist prejudice makes some philosophers think of as primarily applicable to spatial inclusion. On the other hand, in the phrase "the picture 'in' my reproduction," the use of "in" is distinctly odd, although the meaning is made perfectly clear by the context. It is in fact a telling argument against the objection presented in the text that this use of "in" violates usage whereas the other does not.

68. The authority of the original cannot of course be denied, so long as we know that it has not been tampered with. But it is absurd to suppose that if you or I wanted to make a close study of the composition and iconography of Michelangelo's Sistine Chapel ceiling, the best way to do so would be to go and look at it. We would work from photographs mostly, as in an earlier age artists knew the work of other artists from prints. Consider the words of J.-D. Ingres from *Pensées d'Ingres*:

> It is through prints that we can judge paintings and their merit. Since we can examine them more easily and more readily than we can the originals, we come to realize any weaknesses of style or of composition. At greater leisure, we grasp each meaning more firmly. So the painter must be very particular about his work when he is thinking of reproduction (Lamb 1962, v).

69. J. O. Urmson remarks that in producing a score a composer should not be thought of as creating a type (or megatype) of which the performances will be tokens, because "it is hard to see how there can be a type or a megatype before there are any tokens" (1977, 335). We should go further and say that there can't be. But since the composer has *ex hypothesi* provided what in the context of musical practice is a sufficient set of instructions for generating tokens of the work, and *thereby* of the corresponding type, he has certainly created the type.

It is possible to argue that merely to produce a score is not to compose a musical work, since one can make the appropriate marks on paper without knowing how anything answering to those marks would sound, or even whether it could be sounded at all (one could write a flute part beyond the compass of any flute, for instance). Some (e.g. Brelet 1951) urge that the musical work exists only as and when performed, so that the composer does not as such create a complete work of art; others say that it is only necessary that he know "what it would sound like" in at least one legitimate performance. In my terms, the question is: What, if anything, can the composer be legitimately said to have done or made, to which a design can be intelligibly attributed? That no determinate answer imposes itself a priori reflects the reality of the issues in these continuing controversies.

Goodman, as I remarked above, does not think of scores as sets of instructions but as *definitions* of works, such that from any performance that complies with the score the score itself could be precisely reconstructed—for a "score" is defined as belonging to a notational system, and a criterion of notationality is this mode of transitivity of identity. But he suggests that, "where . . . a composer provides prescriptions in a non-notational system rather than scores, the classes of performances called for do not constitute either autographic or allographic works" (cf. n. 78, below) and thus, if I understand him, do not constitute single works at all, because they can be assigned to the alleged work only with the aid of the contingent historical fact that the performer was understood by himself and others to be performing the work in question (Goodman 1972, 83).

70. A. B. Lord (1960) has many instances of how in an oral culture a singer will count as an exact repetition what to someone used to written texts seems to be a variant. Transcription involves making a kind of decision between alternatives that

was hitherto regarded as insignificant because made spontaneously by the singer as he sang. Folk tunes generally have this character of being made up of phrases each of which admits of variation in ways that singers know but which cannot be definitively described. "The singer," says Bertrand H. Bronson, " 'knows the tune,' and thinks he is singing it all the time. Actually, he is singing variations on a musical idea" (1959, xxvii). The composer in such a tradition can complete a tune in his head by making all the decisions that could not be left to the feeling of the moment. But in transcribing, he could not rely on "the feeling of the moment" to make the requisite supplementary decisions, because he would not be singing (cf. Lloyd 1967, 23).

71. In a similar vein, we have been invited to consider the case of the discovery of what purports to be a fifth symphony by Brahms, consistent in style and quality with the other four and established as such in the world repertoire, which is then discovered to be a pastiche by a contemporary composer named Shmarb and is at once dropped from the repertoire and despised *even though* it still sounds to everyone like an authentic Brahms symphony (Cahn and Griffel 1975). For some time after the article appeared, aestheticians would say "as the case of Shmarb shows," *even though* there was no such case and no case of detected forgery resembles it in the essential points.

72. The phrase "logically possible" here appears in disclaiming quotes, not because I think logical possibility a nonsensical or undefinable notion, but because it is not clear what is logically possible in cases of this sort. There is no evident self-contradiction in the sentence "This twentieth-century writer used a seventeenth-century text to express a twentieth-century sensibility," but the use of the phrase "twentieth-century sensibility" may beg the question: the phrase has no precise meaning, and it seems entirely open to question whether a satisfactory sense could be explicated for it that did not stipulate that such a sensibility could express itself only in characteristically twentieth-century modes of speech. Pierre Menard's task may be like that of squaring the circle, one that seems possible only if one refrains from thinking carefully about the procedures it requires.

73. The legal position would probably be that the second author would not be guilty of plagiarism if he could prove that he indeed had no access to the original work, but could claim no copyright in his work; and the original author could probably secure an injunction forbidding the second author to claim authorship of the work or to circulate it. What an artist has copyright in is, very precisely, the design; and the case law of copyright constitutes an extended study in the identity conditions of designs.

74. The case is in practice complicated by the fact that the phrase "an original work" is ambiguous: it may mean a work that is not a copy, or one that has a quality of novelty or inventiveness. The stipulation that the production of a work of art should amount to creation, in that it brings into the world something the like of which there has never been before, introduces considerations that cannot really be assimilated by the classical line. They are considered in part 2 of this work.

75. Etienne Gilson distinguishes between the "physical existence" of a painting as a solid object made out of clay on canvas, the "artistic existence" it has as carrier of a design that the painter has made once and for all, and its discontinuous and fragmentary "aesthetic existence" as a thing actually seen in different ways at different times (1957, 14-16). Various alternative terminologies have been formulated to handle the relations between these modes of existence (or whatever); it is not necessary, and certainly is not helpful, to say that the work of art *is* one of such

things to the exclusion of the others. In any case, the "aesthetic existence" of the work is presumably that of the work as from time to time perceived, not as on some occasion understood and (in this sense) "interpreted." There is no doubt a continuity between perception and comprehension—between poor lighting and the effects of colorblindness, between colorblindness and a pathological inability to become aware of certain design features, between such inabilities and sheer misunderstanding, between misunderstanding and speculation. But somewhere or other one has crossed a line or zone that divides perception from interpretation.

76. For an attempt to make the truism that Shakespeare's *Othello* is Shakespeare's play, not Jan Kott's or Dover Wilson's, available to the practical critic as a norm, see Hirsch (1967). He seems to me to show that the familiar objections to conceding the artist's authority over his own work can be overcome in principle, but not in practice: there is a method, but there is no way to follow it. For further discussion, see note 85, below.

77. There is a sense in which the statement in the text is exactly wrong. A score does not command, it permits. Its imperatives are hypothetical. Like recipes and other sets of instructions, it enables you to do something by telling you what to do in order to do it. The point seems worth making because John Cage has spoken of the composer's tyranny, and suggested that it may be alleviated by the composer allowing the musicians to play (or the audience to hear) what they like. But the way to do that is for the conductor to let them go home early: Haydn's "Farewell" Symphony is a more effective liberating device.

78. The distinction answers to Goodman's distinction between autographic arts, in which the quality of the work is imparted by the artist's hand so that the origin of the work is essential to its identity, and allographic arts, in which the artist gives instructions with which other executants comply, so that whatever conforms to those instructions must be presumed to comply with the character that the work is, and, hence, the origin of the work is not essential to its identity.

79. Except, of course, that metal is too expensive. The cost of materials is an important factor in art, and so is the cost of time, though young enthusiasts sometimes despise their elders who have discovered the fact.

80. This is likely to happen when a work composed in one frame of mind is revised in a mood of aesthetic or moral repentance. One might suggest the later versions of FitzGerald's *Rubáiyát* and Wordsworth's *Prelude* as possible examples.

81. This distinction between "time" and "space" arts is often attacked on two grounds: it is false to the facts of perception, and it is metaphysically false. It is false to the facts of perception, because the eye leaps over a painting from point to point in a way that is far from random, and a reader's eye does not follow the text across and down the page, but performs a spatial dance upon it (Kolers 1977). It is metaphysically false, because whatever exists must exist in both space and time: musicians must sit somewhere, paintings endure through time. The points are well taken, but do not affect the distinction as made in the text, which is the only relevant one, and which opponents of the distinction are careful not to mention. There is an important complication: a temporal sequence cannot as such be grasped sequentially, because to judge at any time that it is a sequence one must in some fashion have the sequence all in mind at one time; but that does not mysteriously transform it into a *spatial* pattern, as some muddle-headed post-Kantians sometimes say.

82. A matrix or other archetype can be used as a means to a performance of other than the kind its maker intended by changing (as it were) the projection used

in mapping. But the possibility of changing the mechanism does not affect the fact that a mechanism is relied on. The statement in the text is imprecise in the sense that different machines have different sound-making characteristics. I have ignored these in the same spirit that one ignores, when discussing music, the make of piano or the acoustic qualities of a hall; but I may have been wrong to do so, for the fussiness of electronic composers about the qualities of loudspeakers varies inversely with the interest of the sounds the loudspeakers are to reproduce.

83. Before the days of tape, the perforated roll of a player piano had much the same character. But rolls were made from prototypical performances.

84. There are commonly two stages. First, a song is written and can then be variously arranged and performed. Then the song is made the basis of a recording, which becomes the definitive performance. Popular singers on TV shows often do not sing their songs, but mouth and gesticulate in time to their records.

85. Bear in mind here that a performance may be defined by such an interpretive critique, which constitutes it the performance it is. It must be so, for there is no other procedure than reliance on a convincing judgment by which one could ascertain or decide what the "actual" performance is. This is not to say that all such critiques will pass muster, or that works of a familiar kind are problematic or equivocal before they are criticized; nor can it be allowed to undermine the absolute priority of Shakespeare in determining what *Othello* is by making it what he makes it (cf. n. 76). But it is to say that the consensus arising from familiarity can always be questioned and that Shakespeare, in doing what he did, may have done more or less than he knew. The scope of a critic's freedom to create a performance by interpreting obviously varies with the kind of performance criticized. See chapter 8 on "the critical function."

86. An example of this (alluded to before) would be Ezra Pound's *Homage to Sextus Propertius* in which Propertius' lines are sometimes translated and sometimes commented on. Notoriously (for Robert Graves made a big thing of it) Pound "renders" *Cimbrorumque minas, auxiliumque Mari* as "the Welsh mines, and what Marus made out of them." If that is a translation, every word except "and" is wrong. Either Pound merely glanced at the Latin and allowed it to suggest English words to his mind by resemblance and contiguity, or (more likely, for one could hardly be so wrong by accident) he is making a rather pointless joke. Yet the work as a whole does, and is clearly meant to, bear some imprint of the Propertian mind. Is there a sharp line between very free translation and original composition under the influence of an original?

87. D. W. Gotshalk, using a schema like the one I adopted in *SA*, attributes to the work an additional, social dimension (1947, 38). His dimensions are material, formal, expressive, and functional. This looks more like the analysis sketched in the text than it really is. The account taken as standard in my text belongs to a phenomenology of *contemplanda*: that is, it has to do with the different ways in which works of art as such are encountered, or the different elements in such an encounter. But Gotshalk is giving an account of the possible types of art theory, and hence is describing the different ways in which things that are primarily works of art can be thought of. The difference, though subtle, is important. Gotshalk's fourth dimension is a natural companion of his other three, but cannot be set alongside the three in my text.

88. If we consider an artifact as the typical incarnation of a performance that is a work of art, we see that the artifact as outcome of, and hence as projecting, a making and doing has itself three dimensions or levels (which metaphor we use is

immaterial here). As artifact, it projects the action of giving it its characteristic form, the shaping activity; as performance, it projects the achievement of realizing that in it which is realized and achieved; as work of art, it projects the performance that answers more narrowly to the design act, the performance precisely of achieving its design. The last two may coincide, but need not. In any complex case, the object projects a triple agency of artificer, performer, and designer (strictly, overall performer and design performer). Our awareness of the object may, and I would say does and should, as it were shimmer, as we become simultaneously or differentially aware of the various aspects of the complex human meaning of what is before us—much as various theorists of the drama in the late nineteenth century attributed to the spectator's normal and proper mode of attention a "pendulum movement," a shifting of attention between stage reality and auditorium reality that itself was the essential character of theatrical experience.

89. Iredell Jenkins identifies three kinds of aesthetic material: sensuous and emotional elements, formal properties, and symbolic meanings (1958, 195-196). In our terms, what he has done is split the expression dimension into an immediate (emotional) and a mediated (social) aspect. But he also introduces another close analogue of our three dimensions by identifying three factors in any adaptive situation: the self (import), the particular objects one interacts with (particularity), and the world (connectedness) (ibid., 15-16). Obviously, his particularity answers to our presence, his connectedness to our formal/representational structure, his import to our expressiveness. He himself associates the aesthetic with particularity, the affective with import, and the cognitive with connectedness (ibid., 18); and that is legitimate, so long as one does not identify art with the aesthetic. Jenkins' own view appears to be that it is indeed the special function of art to emphasize particularity, but specifically to do so by returning import and connectedness, which tend to get out of hand and lead fantasy lives of their own, to their proper intimate relationship to particularity.

Another version of three-dimensionality lies beneath Stefan Morawski's definition of a work of art:

> We call that object a work of art which possesses at least a minimal expressive structure of qualities and qualitative patterns, given sensorily and imaginatively in a direct or an indirectly evocative (semanticized) way. These qualitative patterns and the definite structure enhance each other, building up an autotelic, relatively autonomous whole, set off more or less from reality while it remains nonetheless a part of reality. This object, I must add, is an artifact, in the sense that it is either directly produced owing to a given techne or it is the result of some idea of arrangement. Finally, this object is somehow related to the artist's creative individuality (1974, 115).

This definition, even in the context of the long explanations that lead up to it, has its vaguenesses. But with rough justice we can say that it combines the external condition of artifactuality with three dimensions of appearance: autonomy answers to our presence, the expressive structure of patterns is our formal/representational dimension, and the relation to creative individuality is our expression.

Two trinities that answer less closely to our paradigm are the classical three aspects of beauty and Alberti's three sources of beauty. In the classical trinity, *claritas* or brightness is what we call presence, *unitas* or integration of form is what we include in our formal dimension—but then *integritas* or wholeness, lack of defect, is left to answer to our expressive dimension, which of course (since what is beautiful need not be expressive at all) it fails to do. In Alberti's threefold division (*De Re Aedificatoria* VI, 4; cited from Blunt 1940, 16), we read that "what pleases us in the most beautiful and lovely things springs either from a rational inspiration of the mind, or from the hand of the artist, or is produced by nature from materials," to which he adds that and how it is the hand that gives grace and the mind that gives dignity to the work. This in effect reflects the Platonic association of personality with the body and impersonal order with the mind, so that what nature supplies corresponds to our presence, what the mind supplies is the formal dimension, and what the hand contributes is expression; but to read Alberti's text thus requires a certain willful license of interpretation.

A different way of handling the kind of multidimensionality we are exploring was tried by such American pragmatists of the thirties and forties as S. C. Pepper, according to whom, in the actual contemplation of a work of art, we find nothing but presence; but this presence changes its character when it becomes "funded" by a more analytic examination of the work and by critical discourse itself. But one might urge that if the renewed contemplation is indeed changed in explicable ways by the activities that fund it, the change can only be that the dimensions of possible experience revealed by the analysis are in fact present, though of course not talked about, in the contemplation itself: in a unified experience, what had to be unified must be present in the final unity. But it is not clear whether the issue here is one of phenomenology or one of rhetoric.

90. Roman Ingarden (1931) constructs a work of (literary) art out of a polyphony in which all the voices are in effect on our second level: our "presence" becomes a system of word-sounds, which combine the properties of auditory quality and association; and our "expression" becomes part of the world of objects subtended by the words as meaningful, being explicitly reinterpreted as "metaphysical qualities" such as those perceived in the tragic view of life. Ingarden denies that the authorial voice is present in the work unless there is a specific narrator. This is all deliberate policy to preserve the integrity of the work as a complex structured object: it is not so much that Ingarden reinterprets the first and third dimensions as that he chooses to ignore them.

91. It is perhaps necessary to emphasize that the world of representation to which the work belongs is not one whose details depend on the real world. When we look at a Canaletto, those of us who know Venice know what is around the next corner; but that is part of our world (and Canaletto's, too), not of the world of the particular picture we look at. Similarly, the expressive world to which a work belongs is not to be confused with the actual corpus of an artist's work, which may or may not have that sort of consistency.

The notion of a world of representation that a given work generates and to which it thereby belongs is not one that can be made precise, and probably not one that can be made good against objections. A work in fact suggests a number of kinds of continuation on this or that hypothesis, the hypotheses themselves acquiring this or that measure of plausibility from one's background understanding (or prejudice) as to what is possible as a design. For instance (as Lee Brown pointed out while commenting on a paper at a conference in Cincinnati in 1978), Goya's portrait of the duchess of Alba projects a world in which we might expect a horse-drawn carriage down the road—but why not a Chevrolet? On one way of thinking, a series of concentric colored rectangles by Albers could be continued by yet one more rectangle—but why not a painting of an entirely different sort in which it serves as a foil or a contrasting episode? The question of just what aspect of a painting affords

583

the basis for just what kind of "continuation" is so wide open that the notion of a single subtended world begins to seem quite vacuous. One should rather speak of sets of possible worlds, each corresponding to the identification of a pictorial or painting procedure and a specific mode of continuation or iteration. Still and all, we know what would count in these and most other cases as "more of the same" or "another of the same," and someone who didn't know that would be some sort of imbecile.

92. What Dufrenne does with his notion of a world of representation fills the place taken by Nelson Goodman's notion of a symbol system in which the individual work is a character. Dufrenne's way of doing it seems to have the disadvantages of being vague and metaphorical where Goodman's is precise and literal and devoid of the "metaphysical" overtones that make some hardheaded philosophers queasy at the thought of "worlds." But this is illusion. Goodman's notion is metaphorical, too: there is no system in which individual works are characters; all we actually have is the work that we understand and the confidence in our comprehension of it. Dufrenne's vague sense of a possibility of continuing, without one's being able to specify any continuation, is much closer to reality. The concept of a world, of an indefinite continuation providing a horizon, seems exactly right; all the points at which Goodman differs from it are points where Goodman is exactly wrong. Nor is Goodman's claim in fact precise. Since there is no system, we cannot specify what it would be for two pictures to be characters of the same system. Yet Goodman writes as though there were a system in which a picture was a character, not that a picture projects the idea of a system. It is illuminating to compare a remark of Max Black which comes close to what Goodman was to say:

> Since a given picture represents what it does by virtue of *conventions* (however natural these may seem in some cases), every representational picture belongs to an enveloping series of pictures governed by the same principles of representation: I cannot understand a picture of a dwarf without knowing what it would be like to have a picture of him shown taller, scowling instead of smiling, and so on (Black 1964, 79).

One readily sees what is meant, and concurs. To understand a picture is to grasp what difference would be made by any variation the artist might have introduced. And yet, what is meant by saying that there are conventions by virtue of which the picture represents? Realistic styles are as individualized as styles of abstraction, and in no sense are new styles introduced by agreement. What is meant by saying that a convention may "seem natural"? And how does what comes after the parenthesis follow from what comes before it? Is there really one enveloping series of pictures, or are there a multiplicity of series? In fact, Black's talk of conventions and series, like Goodman's talk of symbol systems, is almost purely decorative. Black would have lost nothing by starting with "I cannot understand the picture of a dwarf . . ." other than the sense that there is *some* general truth about the meaningfulness of representational pictures that the example illustrates.

93. Dufrenne himself confuses the stylistic unity that a work projects as its expressive world with the actual unified style of the historical artist. My account of Dufrenne has not been too faithful to his exposition: his abundant subtleties often leave out the straightforward statement of his plain meaning, which has to be reconstructed to provide an underpinning for his elaborations. In addition, his account of the three dimensions is heavily and perhaps unnecessarily Kantianized: the level of representation is said to be that of space, the level or dimension of

expression that of time, and the dimension of presence is assigned to a prespatio-temporal level of awareness. The importation of Kant will add interest and value in the eyes of some, but a repudiation of Kantian categories does not undermine the dimensional analysis itself.

94. The apparent necessity of three dimensions may be partly a matter of superstition: not only does Euclidean space have three dimensions, but the Christian God has three Persons and the Platonic soul has three Parts. What can hardly be denied is that a work of art has the three dimensions of presence, structure, and expression—once the question has been formulated in such terms. Emphasis on a different mode of analysis might have made four or five dimensions equally "inevitable." It might. But it hasn't yet.

95. Plotinus attacks the then popular idea that beauty consists in a proper proportion of parts by pointing out that we must then deny beauty to a cloudless blue sky, whereas the very paradigm of beauty would be an undifferentiated effulgence of luminosity (a bright white light). But he is not talking about works of art. One might argue, following Arthur Danto, that an undifferentiated black or white or even unpainted canvas could be a work of art by implicitly conveying the abstention from all the differentiations that might have been made—just as the undifferentiated divine reality contains implicitly all the beauties and perfections of the essences on which it might confer essentiality and existence. But I think the analogy fails. In Plotinus, the One is that from which all possible entities ultimately emanate, but a human being can be meaningfully said to abstain from action only when there is some specific action from which he abstains. Otherwise, he just isn't doing anything, and a painter whose painting was a purely general abstention just wouldn't be painting anything.

Chapter VII. The Classical Line
6: What Works of Art Are Like

1. Thus Kant (1790, §46) argued that the original invention of a creative genius generates a rule that his successors can follow; the thesis has been developed by Vincent Tomas (1958). A similar thought lies behind E. J. Bond's contention (1975, 182) that it is a necessary condition of a work of art that it either belong to an existing art form or be the origin of a new one (cf. chap. 6, n. 27, above).

2. Artistic change, in which art form succeeds art form in prevailing practice, might give way to artistic acceleration, in which what succeeded each other would be styles of artistic variation. But a tradition of continuous revolution might to a later age seem as homogeneous as any other historical style.

3. "Boundaries" is not in every respect an appropriate word, for we saw in chapter 2 that arts might be defined by focuses rather than by bounded areas. One feels a need here for the undeveloped science that someone has called botryology, the study of clumping. How many ways are there of classifying things? One way is by paradigm cases: things are classified according to which of a number of ideal specimens they come closest to. This gives internally ordered classes, with large dim boundary areas. Another way is by use of defining properties: anything to which the properties that define a class can be assigned belongs to the class. This gives some sharpness along the boundaries and equality of status within the class. Another way is by "family likenesses," by which membership in a class depends on having

enough of a set of traits no one of which is necessary or sufficient. This may explain how some existing classifications seem to work, but will hardly do to set up new ones unless one knows how to decide what is "enough." Another way is by historical lineages and lines of development. This depends on being able to decide what is a transition and what is a discontinuity. Another way is by felt congruities, which is fine if all concerned feel the same congruities. And who knows how many more there might be? Someone should certainly work on it.

4. One is aware that Noam Chomsky has argued that a child could not acquire a language unless it had an innate knowledge of the scope of possible grammars: otherwise, the scanty and degenerate data available to it would not suffice for it to detect the appropriate formal patterns among the infinite possibilities compatible with that data. One might then wonder whether children also have an innate knowledge of possible forms, since a picture presents data that could in principle be organized in infinitely many ways. Gestalt psychology cannot provide the answer, because Gestalt principles impose a certain type of form that is not always the one most relevant from the artistic point of view (cf. Ehrenzweig 1967).

5. One might insert before this last residual category one defined by Van Meter Ames at the 1969 meeting of the American Society for Aesthetics: a work of art is anything personally presented and vouched for by anyone. This was greeted with great applause from the assembled avant-gardists, who appreciated its openness. But Ames did not specify what the thing must be vouched for *as*: if as a work of art, there must be a prior understanding as to what a work of art is for the vouching to be possible; if as something else, the vouching would be irrelevant. Perhaps the tone of voice used in the vouching shows what is meant? But in our terms we could say that a work of art is any performance presented and personally vouched for as an aesthetic object, that is, picked out and declared a fit object for contemplation. In fact, this would be a compromise between our proposed definitions of a work of art and of an art object.

In the published version of his paper, Ames followed a dithyrambic enumeration of artistic extremes (mostly familiar by repute, and mostly described in the terms that made them familiar) by the following very different formulation: "What any man makes, which deserves attention, can qualify as art, along with what is only selected, perhaps signed to signify that something has been found especially worth attending to" (Ames 1971, 47). This sounds quite close to the formulation I have used in this book, and even closer to Dickie's, until one reflects that the atom bomb certainly deserved attention and a cholera epidemic is especially worth attending to.

6. It is often argued that the applicability to any work of such words as "informative," "emotive," "hortatory," or "interrogative" must exclude it altogether from the domain of art, because contemplation is replaced by some practical response. This seems to be a mistake. Obviously if one takes a work literally as an instruction one is to follow, an inquisition one must reply to or the like, one is not responding to its aesthetic qualities; but one may well respond to its quality as a performance having the characteristics of a communication aimed at eliciting such responses. It may well be true that some people cannot enjoy anything that they have formally identified as propaganda, unless perhaps they can confine their attention to its pattern aspects and filter out whatever pertains to its character as message. But this seems to me a weakness of the aesthetic digestion. Why could not one observe how well someone wheedles?

7. Classifications answering roughly to the three dimensions of the work of art

are not unknown. For instance, Khatchadourian distinguished four criteria of artistic excellence: that it stimulate to reflection, or arouse to imagination, or show expressive force, or simply give pleasure, through what in this work I have called its design (1971, 54); and in a shadowy way the first two of these answer to the representational level, the third to expression, the fourth to presence. The match is, of course, by no means exact, but that would not be expected since Khatchadourian is traveling his own road; it is enough that the kinds of criteria he invokes belong to the same general sort as those whereby our three dimensions are distinguished. And, since there are four kinds of criteria, answering in fact to four functions that Khatchadourian finds assigned to art, it would be reasonable to distinguish four kinds of art related to the four functions and associated criteria.

Another related classification is sketched by Schafer. He traces all music theory back to two Greek myths, that of Athena's invention of the *aulos* to mimic the lament of Euryale (Pindar, Pythian 12) and that of Hermes' discovery of the sonic properties of the shell and dried tendons of a turtle (Homer, *Hymn to Hermes*): "In the first of these myths music arises as a subjective emotion; in the second it arises with the discovery of the sonic properties in the materials of the universe" (Schafer 1977, 6). And he goes on to approximate the contrast between Athena and Hermes to that between Apollo and Dionysus: "In the Dionysian myth, music is conceived as internal sound breaking forth from the human breast; in the Apollonian it is external sound, God-sent to remind us of the harmony of the universe" (ibid.). Schafer claims as his objective the return of music from personal expression to the "search for the harmonizing influence of sounds in the world about us," as in a diagram from Robert Fludd's *Utriusque Cosmi Historia* (1617), "in which the earth forms the body of an instrument across which strings are stretched and tuned by a divine hand" (ibid.). But in fact what is shown in Fludd's diagram is not the earth: it is a circle showing the superterrestrial regions, the heavens, and the supercelestial domains of revealed truth, and diagramming their proportions. The error (or willful reinterpretation) is significant, for Schafer's whole book was meant to put the organization of untuned sound in the place assigned by the classical theorists he cites to the mathematical proportions of musical scales: he conflates acoustic mass with audible structure. Once this conflation is undone, we find our threefold classification: the music of emotion (now denounced), the music of (representative and inherent) structure, and the music of sheer sound.

8. Mathematical proofs, scientific experiments, and philosophical systems are never art objects, because although their status as aesthetic objects may be widely recognized, it is never institutionalized. But there seems no good reason why it should not be.

9. Collections of chess problems, and even more evidently collections of chess games, suggest by their manner that the objects they present are to be taken as works of art, so there is a sense in which they are elevated to the rank of art objects. But since the constituency of those who appreciate chess does not coincide with any of the publics who appreciate the arts conventionally dubbed "art" or "the fine arts," the institutional status of chess remains equivocal.

10. Some contemporary musical works (including some by Iannis Xenakis) represent the more or less arbitrary audible representation of sets of mathematical formulas, in which the real interest of the piece is supposed to lie. I would think that the interest of such a piece could be musical only to the extent that the choice of the audible embodiment was not arbitrary but was justified by its heard effect; in such a case, however, the interest would to that extent no longer be that of the

equations. Of course, it might happen that arbitrary auditory embodiment of an interesting mathematical expression would be an interesting sound, but one does not see why this should be more than a coincidence. Some philosophers have thought otherwise. The Pythagoreans maintained that all important characteristics of anything could be analyzed numerically, and that the analysis would somehow yield a numerological explanation of the importance. And Leibniz told Christian Goldbach, in a famous but elusive letter, that pleasure taken in music was really pleasure taken unconsciously in the mathematical operations that the music enshrined (cf. Haase 1960, 499). But these theses rest on nothing more than assertion. Musical relationships, like other relationships, can be expressed in numerical terms, but musical interest and mathematical interest are not the same.

Xenakis' own position is different from that of Pythagoras or Leibniz. So far from arguing that the beauty of music derives from its intelligible structure, he holds that beauty is irrelevant. Sound and music are to be considered "a vast potential reservoir in which a knowledge of the laws of thought and the structured creations of thought may find a completely new medium of materialization," and "the quantity of information carried by the sounds must be the true criterion of the validity of a particular music" (Xenakis 1971, ix). What difference it makes that the laws of thought are embodied in the medium of sound is something Xenakis nowhere explains.

11. One might argue that musical form is shown to be intellectual rather than sensuous in its appeal by the fact that a musical piece can be very variously orchestrated without losing its essential form. This is supposed to show that it is the intelligible relationships, not the sound patterns, that constitute the musical interest. But that is at best a half-truth: all the alternative structures yielded by such rearrangements are structures of audible sound, and, although the sounds produced are different, the more important relations between the sounds are the same and are what make the piece of music the same piece. And a relation between sounds is no less an audible phenomenon than is the quality of a particular sound. In any case, it is not true of *all* musical works that instrumental timbre is of secondary importance. Change of timbre can be used as a structural principle.

In literary works, however, the essential order is not perceptible at all. One can see or hear a word, but one cannot see or hear what it means, and the significant relations are those that hold between words as bearers of meaning. In poetry the sound of the words matters more than it usually does in prose, which is one of the reasons why it is said more often of poetry than of prose that it cannot be translated. Even so, that untranslatability is due to the impossibility of finding sufficiently precise equivalents for meanings as much as to the impossibility of finding equivalences of sound to match the equivalences of sense. Poetry characteristically differs from prose in exploiting simultaneously all possible meanings of a word, whereas prose sticks to one meaning determined by context; context-bound complexes of meaning can usually be reproduced in other languages, but the configurations of potential meaning associated with particular words usually cannot.

An analogy for the differences between perceptible and intelligible beauties can be found in the realm of personal appeal. There is a sensuous beauty of form and feature; there is also a beauty of personality that is intelligible, something to think about and dwell on, which is not tied to any *particular* sequence of manifestations, though there is a sort of way in which it is shown. But there is also a mixed form of beauty, that of a way or form of life realized in the art of living, in which the components (or the elements revealed by analysis, for one does not live by fits and starts) are deeds in which the perceptible and the intelligible enjoy an equal status. One does the handsome thing.

12. See especially McLuhan and Parker (1968). The essential point here is less the sheer qualitative difference between sensibilia than the different ways in which the senses relate us to the world and the different parts they consequently play in our lives. For instance, Ong remarks that hearing differs from the other senses in that sound results from the present exercise of force, which makes it suitable as the preeminent sense for social communication (Ong 1967, 112 and 123).

13. Note that we speak here of the relevant relations presented or specified, not of the extension in space and time of what is experienced or the experiencing of it. The confusion is widespread. Thus we find Northrop Frye objecting that

> McLuhan . . . has expanded the two unresolved factors of explication into a portentous historical contrast between the "linear" demands of the old printed media and the "simultaneous" impact of the new electronic ones. The real distinction however is not between different kinds of media, but between two operations of the mind which are employed in every contact with every medium. There is a "simultaneous" response to print; there is a "linear" response to a painting, for there is a preliminary dance of the eye before we take in the whole picture; music, at the opposite end of experience, has its score, the spatial presentation symbolizing a simultaneous understanding of it (Frye 1971, 26).

What Frye says here is that every adequate experience of a complex object requires a moment of analysis, which must take time, and a moment of synthesis, which requires simultaneity—the same insight that lies beneath the pragmatist account of the experience of art outlined in our section on the "dimensions" of the work of art. But the musical score, insinuating a connection between simultaneity and spatiality, is a red herring; and nothing in what Frye says tells against McLuhan's claim that media differ in the relative emphasis they place on analysis and synthesis. Neither author draws the essential distinction between the order according to which an object is organized and the sequence of the processes whereby we apprise ourselves of that order.

14. This does not mean that there is only one point in space from which a picture (even a picture drawn according to a strict system of perspective) can be seen properly—that is true only of trick pictures, like the skull in Holbein's *Ambassadors*: it means just what it says, so that anyone not standing at the postulated point places himself "to one side" or "close up" or "far away."

15. By "impermeable" here I mean only that one does not actually (unless one is a scrambling child) go through it: Henry Moore's and Barbara Hepworth's sculptures are often to be *seen as* permeable, and some of David Smith's are to be *seen through*, and so on; but to go through these complexities, like those mentioned in the text, would enrich my analysis rather than undermine it.

16. Martin Heidegger and Susanne Langer both take architectural space to symbolize a community's sense of its own structure as dwelling in its land.

17. In one way musical structures depend on ideal rather than actual durations. This is obviously true of the typical structure as determined by a score. But even in an actual performance, the durations enter into the musical structure, not just by being what they are, but by being interpreted as variants on such regularities as a score determines. Again, interrupting a musical piece to turn a phonograph record over does not destroy the order of the piece, although our awareness of that order may be impaired; and if we have to interrupt our playing of a piece and start afresh,

the start of our second attempt is not musically "after" where we broke off. On the other hand, there is an obvious way in which musical structures depend on actual durations as structures in English prosody do not. Regularly metrical verses, when properly spoken, have no regularity: the ideal regularity of the meter does not in any way govern what is to be heard—it is *possible* to chant English verse to a regular beat, as Scottish children do when they learn their psalms, but this method is not artistically sound. And considerations of actual duration do not in any way enter into the structures of normal prose works in nonquantitative languages (whatever may be true of Ciceronian *clausulae*). Clearly there is work to be done in sorting out the part played by ideal and actual durations in music and literature, but it is at least true that the order in both alike is structured in terms of temporal succession and sequence, however that succession is patterned or arranged.

18. Among primarily temporal works involving spatial elements in their order one would number works calling for antiphonal choirs and offstage instruments; among primarily spatial works with temporal aspects are gardens and buildings in which the perceiver's movements are required to follow a certain sequence. But in the latter case it may be enough that the sequence be understood, not actually experienced, just as a detective story is not necessarily spoiled if one looks at the end first to see how it all comes out. In fact, one cannot really appreciate a surprise effect while one is actually being surprised.

It may be worthwhile here to enumerate some of the temporal aspects of spatial works and vice versa. In spatial works, pictures and sculptures have temporal origins and histories; any visual work must last long enough to be adequately observed; pictorial arts may present episodes with implicit pasts and futures, and in nonrepresentational works the tensions generated may be such as to imply past and future movement; three-dimensional arts rely on sequences of changing aspects and views; processional ways, gardens, and such may impose a programmed series of experiences; and in any case, if we are to say the artist has created a world in any sense at all, it is true a priori that such a world must have a temporal as well as a spatial aspect. On the other side, sounds must have sources located in space; stereophony, or any effective part separation, requires spatial separation of sound sources; particular works may require that the performers bear specific relations to each other or to the audience; in opera, sound expresses action in space; there is a metaphorical space generated by the composer's use of wide and narrow intervals, high and low notes; and again, if the artist creates a world in any sense at all, that world must a priori have spatial as well as temporal extension in whatever the appropriate sense is.

19. Nelson Goodman's classification by types of symbol system, though exhaustive and internally coherent, classifies arts rather than works. His system does indeed deny the distinction, since works are equated with characters in symbol systems; but that equation is the measure of his failure to provide a theory of art.

20. Ivan Vitányi observes that

The punctum saliens of all public cultural and educational programmes is that the vast majority of people need two kinds of music. One type is for the more festive occasions and is received as autonomous art, separated from everyday life, the other is consumed for entertainment and relaxation and is closely connected with everyday life.

The criterium for the first is *value*, for the second *applicability*. The separation of the two and the development of autonomous art is the result of historical processes (namely the development of industrial commodity production, i.e. early capitalism). This fact also determines the nature of their relationship: the one cannot replace the other. Society as a whole cannot do without autonomous art, but in a sociological sense it is more expendable than "Gebrauchsmusik." Significant groups of society are lacking higher-level artistic experiences, but they need artistic experience as such on the everyday level (Bontinck 1974, 74-75).

Vitányi here seems to fuse three distinctions: music for special occasions versus everyday music; music for the elite versus music for the masses; and listening music versus dancing or working music. They are all summed up in the one distinction between the special and the nonspecial, which is identified with that between the autonomous and the heteronomous.

21. In Nietzsche's original exposition (1872), the Dionysian is the ecstatic dance in which a people celebrates its triumph over agony, and the Apollonian is the vision of the God, the dream that disguises that pain and makes it endurable; both alike are contrasted with the Socratic or self-critical mode of art that produces an object for appreciation, and are a transvaluation of Schopenhauer's contrast between music, which embodies the Will, and the other arts, which generate reconciling ideas. This is far from the vulgar use of the terms that equates "Dionysian" with a mood of ecstasy and "Apollonian" with one of serenity.

22. One used to hear much of "systems art" in which the spectator was "programmed into" the work. All systems art belongs to what Fried calls theater. One suspects, incidentally, that those who extol the "systems approach" have never served in the army, in which they would have learned that elaborate schemes based on predictions of what people will do result in the condition known as snafu.

23. Fried's special use of the term "theater" and his denial that theater can be art change the accepted reference of the word "art" to exploit its emotive connotations; but he would argue that to call such things art, inserting them into the institutions of art, is an abuse of those institutions and a pretense that "art" means less than it always has. The "family resemblance" theory of concept formation encourages the debasement of thought and would seat false claimants at the family table.

24. The idea of facilitating a response supposes that the response is already prepared, needing only a trigger to set it off. If that is the right way to look at it, the essential structure is provided by the spectator, not by the work that serves as stimulus, so that the "facilitating" work does not lie between the work that structures and the work that provokes, but should be contrasted with both.

25. It makes no difference if someone just happens to be present and observes, or comes along afterward and discovers; or, if it makes a difference, the difference is not of a kind that concerns us here. The point here is the relation of artistic appreciation to a vital involvement in a personal relationship: whether a work is performed *for* or *with* people, or *as in their presence*, not whether there are people around.

26. The account admits of further complication. In cases where audience and performers are not the same, for instance, we could distinguish those works where the two are intermingled from those where they are separated in space or time or both.

27. Thus Roger Sessions writes:

Listening to music, as we understand it, is a relatively late, relatively sophisticated, and even a rather artificial means of access to it, and . . . even until fairly recent times composers presumably did not think of their music primarily as being listened to, but rather as being played and sung, or at most as being heard incidentally as part of an occasion (1950, 4).

Aristotle in his *Politics*, however, already distinguishes between the kind of music a person plays for himself and his friends and the kind a professional plays for his clients.

28. Some influential classifications of works of art cover only a relatively small part of the range of what usually passes for art. They depend on assigning to all art a single function, everything that does not contribute to this function being dismissed as nonart, as art by courtesy or by institutional association, as vestigial, as art so called in an inverted-commas sense, or at best as nonexemplary and subsidiary art, which passes in the ranks and swells the numbers but cannot be allowed a speaking part. The primary distinction then becomes whether a claimant to the status of art fulfills the assigned function; the secondary distinctions are, among rejects, the ways in which the function rests unfulfilled (through inadequacy, evasion, fraudulent substitution, or simple irrelevance) and, among successful claimants, the ways in which the function is fulfilled. Such classifications (for which the treatment of the functions in *SA* would afford one possible groundwork) are tendentious, but are more exciting than the sort of thing sketched in the text. What I have done is external and schematic and hence inert and incapable of engaging active concern: works of art are obviously *for* something, and the most vital classifications will obviously be in terms of how they relate to urgent practical interests. Our reason for excluding such classifications here is that the proposed functions are extraneous to art as such in the sense that, in order to fulfill them without falling outside the domain of art, a work must already be a work of art (or artwork, etc.) as here defined and characterized. Functional classifications of art find that they either have to gloss over this fact or (as is usually the case) assume it in their procedures while ignoring or denying it in their formal statements.

A simple and notorious example of such a functional classification of art is that of Tolstoy. The function of art is to communicate feelings. A purported work of art is then admitted or rejected into the fold according to whether it fulfills this function or not, those that do not being casually assigned to such categories as sources of aesthetic pleasure, occasions for display, showcases for ingenuity, and so on. Those that do perform the assigned function are then simply sorted into the good, which communicate good feelings, and the bad, which communicate bad feelings; and the good are further sorted into the specifically Christian, promoting specifically the brotherhood of man and the fatherhood of God (and, I dare say, the motherhood of Russia, though this is not spelled out), and the good but secular. A more elaborate example (which in its careful elaboration I described in *SA* as the model of what a functional aesthetic theory should be) is that of Langer, in which art is the articulate presentation of modes of sentience and the kinds of art answer to the principal categories of human affective life that call for such expression. But the most important examples for our own time are to be found in Marxism, for which art, like everything else, is not only assigned a place within the overall concerns of practical life but is indeed constituted by that place. I am not referring to the idiot Marxism of your neighborhood agitator, for whom art is either a byproduct of economic relationships or a mere tool to societal ends, but to serious theorists who take dialectic seriously. Among Marxists we may mention particularly Lukács, whose enormous *Eigenart des Aesthetischen* (1963) reduced most commentators to years of stunned silence. Lukács assigns art a double function: that of representing the true nature of reality (the inner workings of the natural-historical process) and that of supplanting its predecessor, magic (which substitutes for those workings mythical entities with which art proper has nothing to do). Music, he concedes, does not represent reality directly, but does so indirectly by expressing the specific feelings with which reality is experienced. What, then, of the classification of art? Obviously the main distinction is between what performs the function and what does not, whether by aborting it (magic) or by evading it (abstract art). Within what is accepted as art, the classification is by what the reality is that is expressed, and that reduces to the social-historical origin of the work (which constitutes the reality represented) and the specific aspect of it that is singled out: a genre that attains currency in any age will answer to a crucial way in which reality impinges. But in all this what makes art art is the specificity of what is expressed, the way the general nature of reality is embodied in a unique and uniquely illuminating experience. Having said that, though, we go on to deny that the idea of classification is applicable: a historical, vital relationship is not a generic one. A work is not an *example* of a genre, but inheres in it, and in the same way genres are not subdivisions of arts and arts are not subdivisions of art, but each inheres as a totality within the wider historical totality that it specifies. In short, a thoroughly historical theory of art substitutes specification for classification.

A Marxist who manages to maintain a functional classification is Stefan Morawski, who does so by confining himself to a particular historical situation, that in which alienation prevails: in which, that is, all or most people have lost control of the meanings of their lives because the determinants of their larger patterns of actions and the contexts in which those patterns make sense are in the hands of others or are so widely diffused as to be in effect wholly alien. Morawski then operates with a general notion of what art is that is more like that developed in our classical line than it is like Lukács' notion. He might have said, but does not, that it is only in an alienated world that the concept of art has any true applicability, as it is certainly only in the world that a Marxist would so describe that the notions of the fine arts and of art as such have arisen. In any case, we are in a position to see what the functions of art in an alienated world must be by considering what ways there can be of coping with alienation. Morawski thus distinguishes three kinds of art: Orphic, Promethean, and Philoctetean. Orphic art effects, through its own integration and the synesthesia it thus induces, a certain wholeness of feeling and restores a kind of unifying balance to the disoriented and self-estranged person. Promethean art inspires one through a forward-looking promise of restored unity to courageous striving for improvement of self and society. Philoctetean art consoles and strengthens the individual by awakening in him the sources of his lost emotional unity. In inferior forms of art (which we should classify as *Kitsch*, though they do not quite coincide with what that name usually denotes), these functions are inverted or as it were parodied. The Orphic art of restored balance is paralleled by the merely aesthetic arts of amusement, decoration, and academicism generally. Promethean heroism is paralleled by idyllic arts that sunder the ideal from practice and by amoral arts that deny the present but not in the name of any better time to be brought about. Philoctetean consolation is accompanied by nihilistic or escapist refusals to admit the reality of value. And on the margins of art altogether are two different functions that are fulfilled not so much by art as by what sometimes replaces art or purports to do so: works that are purely informative or straightforwardly life or-ganizing (like town planning) are not art because they lie outside the domain peculiar to art, which is that of a fused enrichment of cognition and feeling (Morawski 1974,

316-321). What gives Morawski's scheme its peculiar interest is the care with which it locates a multiplicity of related functions at the center, at the periphery, and outside the borders of art conceived in a unified functional manner. It suffers, however, from the defect of arbitrariness, in the sense that it rests on the contestable judgment that all men, or all men to the extent that art is relevant to their lives, are essentially self-estranged—that is, that self-estrangement is not an aspect of their lives but the whole of their lives, so that to be alive is simply to be self-estranged in this way or that.

29. Karl Aschenbrenner (1974) pertinently observes that to characterize a thing, to ascribe a certain character to the thing as a whole, is not the same as to describe it, to enumerate its regional properties, and so on. It is the former that comes close to classification. Even so, I do not think anything in the present context requires us to take note of this important point.

30. The obvious exceptions to this generalization are those predicates that amount to affirmations that something is a performance or is one that can be contemplated or has a design. Other exceptions will be mentioned later.

31. This suggestion is vindicated in the layout as well as the substance of Aschenbrenner's *Concepts of Criticism* (1974).

32. Note how often the phrase "it seems to follow" occurs in these pages. Its recurrence is not a mere nervous tic: it is to indicate that the plausible reasonings cited are no more than plausible, though this is not the proper occasion for investigating their merits.

33. For the term "Janus-word," see Nowell-Smith (1954), p. 100 and passim; for the doctrine see also Hare (1952, chap. 7).

34. For a survey of its heyday, see Margolis (1965, chap. 8).

35. This doctrine is consistent with C. I. Lewis's definition of "aesthetic value" as "a quality which solicits contemplative regard and affords a relatively enduring enjoyment for such contemplation" (1946, 468).

36. This point should not be confused with a different point that often used to be made, namely, that the words used to convey design properties must be such that rules for using them successfully could not be specified in general terms for all users of a language. That is true, but primarily because rules for applying a term successfully can never be specified: such rules for application would need further rules for *their* application, and so on to infinity. Successful linguistic performance requires skills that go beyond logical and linguistic competence.

Peter Kivy, in a singularly rich examination of the thesis that aesthetic terms cannot be condition governed, points out that one such term applicable to music is "unified." A musical work is truly unified if and only if it has a monothematic structure, and the presence or absence of monothematic structure can be verified and falsified by close analysis (Kivy 1973, 5-18 and passim). He concedes, however, that one cannot compile a complete list of monothematic-making features, and he does not effectively allay suspicions that such quasi-demonstrable unity is, as such, of interest to musicologists rather than to music lovers; so the question is not conclusively closed. On the other hand, perhaps what counts as a monothematic quality is determined by the appreciability of the unity it specifies.

37. Michael Tanner writes that "the concept of evaluation would have an uneasy and equivocal role to play in aesthetics" if people's evaluations of works of art diverged largely from their affection for them, though particular discrepancies are not uncommon (1968, 68). The divergence between evaluation—that is, estimation

of merit by the most relevant standard—and affection is not to be confused with either of two other divergences: that between one's *knowledge* of a thing's worth and one's ability to *recognize* that worth (cf. Fry 1939, chap. 1) and that between one's appreciation of something (that is, one's getting from it what it has to offer) and one's personal liking for it or overall approval of it. It is the last named kind (more strictly, pair of kinds) of divergence that we are considering at this point in the text.

38. In the paper to which Tanner (n. 37) is replying, F. N. Sibley remarks that it is absurd to cite the necessity of mental preconditions as evidence that aesthetic properties cannot be objective: it would be absurd, for example, to expect a child to be able to recognize that certain passages in *King Lear* are exceptionally moving, and absurd to cite his inability as tending to show that they are not in fact moving (Sibley 1968, 40); and he reminds us that "we often know on evidence we cannot ignore what we and our friends are insensitive to, where we make finer discriminations than they, that we discern things now that we could not see when we were younger; we allow we may be wrong, we try again, and we seek help, often successfully, from critics and friends" (ibid., 44). Everything, in fact, happens as if there were objective properties we were trying to be able to get to see; so why should we assert that there are no such properties? (ibid., 44-45). One hardly sees how Tanner's rejoinder that there could be different sets of people making just as many and just as fine discriminations, but different ones, tells against the argument; and his claim that it is no mark of a qualified judge to be able to make discriminations "in the nether regions of art" ignores the basic point that one is a qualified judge only of that which one has qualified oneself to judge, and a qualified judge of the nether regions must settle the point of precedence between a louse and a flea (Tanner 1968, 58-59). The point that an ability to make fine discriminations depends on prolonged practice in the precise field within which the discriminations are to be made was already central to David Hume's argument in his essay "Of the Standard of Taste" (1757).

39. The uneasiness need not reflect an insecurity in one's values, as Santayana insinuates (1896, 41-42); it could be a logical unease. There can be no real evidence for the sameness or difference in the ways of reading the design, other than the sameness or difference of the responses to it, so the claim in the text seems for ever unjustifiable. It is not clear, however, that there could not be a case in which each of two viewers agreed with everything the other said by way of describing the design, and in fact said *just what the other would have said*, and yet differed in that one liked it and the other did not.

40. For the lack of cohesion of today's public, see Meyer (1967, pt. 2).

41. Although I shall expect you to understand me and recognize what I am talking about when I describe the man's brave actions, it is not always possible to get agreement on what a person may most appropriately be said to have done or (granted agreement there) on which of his actions count most toward a description of his behavioral tendencies (see Melden 1961). It is a mistake to suppose, as many do, that such difficulties are distinctive of aesthetic as opposed to moral criticism.

42. This is not to say that one cannot relate to people otherwise than in communion: one may deal with them by technique (making friends and influencing people), by gross classifications (as in relations of authority), by observation and generalization (as in the social sciences). And so one can with works of art. But in the same sense in which personal relations are primary in human intercourse, so a direct involvement is primary in our commerce with works of art. And just as some

people feel it is wicked to deal with people other than in an I-Thou communion, so some people feel it is wrong to talk about works of art, classify them, buy them, and so on.

43. This seems to be the position adopted by Adam Smith: "Instrumental Music is said sometimes to imitate motion; but in reality it only either imitates the particular sounds which accompany certain motions, or it produces sounds of which the time and measure bear some correspondence to the variations, to the pauses and interruptions, to the successive accelerations and retardations of the motion which it means to imitate." Music does not imitate grave or gay incidents, he continues, but by variation of speed and pitch "soothes us into each of these dispositions: it becomes itself a gay, a sedate, or a melancholy object; and the mind naturally assumes the mood or disposition which at the time corresponds to the object which engages its attention. Whatever we feel from Instrumental Music is an original, and not a sympathetic feeling" (1795, 241-242). The precise meaning of this is not quite clear; but since the aroused feeling is not sympathetic, presumably the sedateness that qualifies the object is to be construed as a recognized propensity to induce sedateness, much as a hilarious incident is one with a recognized propensity to induce hilarity. If Smith is not understood in this way, it is hard to see in what sense the gaiety of the object could correspond to the gaiety of the mood it induces, or why it should induce it.

44. Tilghman (1970, 13-14) forcibly reminds us that the experience of art is a matter of perceiving, not of feeling, and that to recognize the emotional character of a work is precisely that, to *recognize* the character *of the work*, not to have any particular kind of feeling.

45. I could right now, if you asked me, compose for you a mournful or a perky or a gay or a portentous piece of music. My only problems would be technical. There simply is no such problem as that of putting myself into the appropriate frame of mind, other than the frame of mind in which I am disposed to compose music.

46. A subtle exposition of this view by O. K. Bouwsma (1950) was for several years the accepted doctrine of English-speaking philosophers of art. Appropriate articulations are provided by Langer (1953) and Meyer (1956).

47. It is essentially this view of the matter that is elaborated in the *Affektenlehre* of Mattheson and Marpurg in the early eighteenth century: an elaborate anatomy of the passions, derived from Descartes, is correlated with a comparable anatomy of musical forms and effects, but it is almost a matter of indifference whether the correlations are merely symbolic relations or causal relations or what.

48. According to Cooke this language, though conventional, has become second nature to us and is based on a natural congruity. Not all conventions are equally workable: "Colonel Bogey" *could not* be a wistful tune in any system (though it may be wistfully used). Attempts to demonstrate a natural language of tonality go back in the European tradition to Pythagoras, and were first systematized by Damon at Athens in the age of Pericles (cf. Lasserre 1954). We are sometimes invited to consider the paradoxicalness of using physical and mathematical arguments (as is still commonly done) to prove the *intuitive* priority of a tonal system; but there is no paradox if one thinks of man as part of nature and takes mathematics to enshrine the principles on which nature is built.

Setting aside the mathematicizing impetus, Damon's system rests on an association of instrumental music with the singing voice, of the singing voice with the speaking voice at its most affective, and of affective speech with the feeling it expresses; and these associations do seem hard to get away from.

49. The view in the text, though still generally held by English-speaking philosophers, is contestable. Suppose we were to discover that the beings we call cats were, and had always been, not animals but robot spies from Mars; would that discovery show that we had been wrong to call them cats? According to my text, no, because "cat" is what we call that familiar kind of being, whatever it is; according to the other view, though, yes, because what we *always meant* by "cat" was a certain kind of animal, and the functioning of the word in our language (and thought) depended on that meaning. So it may be argued that, though the word "cheerful" is consistently used to designate a certain recognizable kind of music and may be correctly or incorrectly applied on that basis, still by calling the music cheerful we *have always meant* that it had something to do with the cheerfulness of persons; and, if the place of the word in the semantic structure of the language is governed by that meaning, then, if the connection is found not to obtain in fact, it may be that we will have to say that everyone was using the word wrongly. The issue really depends on the relative closeness of the relation between semantics and linguistic structure, on the one hand, and ostension, on the other.

50. The contrast between expressing gloom and expressing one's own gloom, as sketched in the text, is so sharp that the word "express" can hardly be said to mean the same thing in the two cases; and yet it is evident that they are closely allied. This almost paradoxical relation between two senses of "express" goes far to account for the fact that what I discuss in later chapters as the expressive line of art theory differs radically from the "expression" aspect of the theory of the fine arts as imitative arts, and yet is almost invariably confused therewith by its exponents as well as its critics.

The contrast between the two senses of "express" bedevils Nelson Goodman's (admittedly idiosyncratic) treatment of the concept (see chap. 3, n. 67). He takes "A expresses X" to mean "A metaphorically exemplifies X," where to exemplify a quality is to have it and to refer to a label equivalent to the name of the quality: if a sad tune expresses sadness, it is metaphorically sad in such a way that the metaphorical sadness is part of its meaning, i.e. our attention is called to the fact that a word like "sad" could be applied to the work. In this view, *any* quality that is metaphorically exemplified is expressed: the fact that the vocabulary of feeling is often metaphorically applied to works of art has nothing whatever to do with the concept of expression. Goodman's theory is ingenious and illuminating, so far; but then he goes on to say that a work may also express its artist's feelings, and makes no attempt to show how the revised concept of expression can be adapted to this context.

51. We should be wary of the insidious suggestion that mood words differ from the feeling-related dynamic characters of which Hanslick and Langer speak only by being more vague. Osborne makes the valuable observation that "when we use emotional language about works of art we attribute to them the qualities of moods not the feeling tones of concrete emotions. . . . But the moods are not highly structured as works of art are structured. [A mood] . . . has duration, but no internal structure" (1963, 114), and thus has nothing in common with those dynamic patterns in which Langer and Hanslick see (wrongly, in Osborne's view) analogues of emotive life.

As for the mood words themselves, the apparent fact that people show no marked agreement in the mood words they apply to pieces of music may show that they find the expressiveness of the music indefinite, or that their use of language is imprecise or idiosyncratic (one's choice of shadings in vocabulary is surely part of one's personal style), or often that no particular word is especially appropriate, because our mood vocabulary is spotty as well as vague.

C. C. Pratt found (1931) that anyone offered a choice of two contrasted mood words will easily be able to apply one to a given piece of music, and that people with similar cultural backgrounds show almost complete unanimity in the way they make such attributions. The force of this observation is diminished by Gombrich's celebrated observation that the same ease of application and a comparable agreement is found when the imposed choice is between two phonetically contrasted nonsense syllables, "pong" and "ping," and, moreover, that this holds true when the syllables are applied, not to works of art, but to almost any pair of objects or persons that can be brought into any kind of contrastive relation (1962, 370). This observation seems to show that the existence of such agreement in the application of mood words to musical and other works of art does not suffice to prove that that application is especially appropriate; the appropriateness must be separately established. Gombrich's observation squares with Goodman's hunch that any well-ordered and well-grounded set of terms can be applied metaphorically to any similarly well-structured field, without its use having to be relearned.

52. It could be argued that "anything that is said of any complex situation" is always criticism: what makes something a situation is that people, with their actions and reactions, are involved in it—a situation is an involvement of people or the involvement of a single person, as in Sartre's usage (1943, pt. 4, chap. 1); and what makes a situation complex is that he or they are involved in ways that defy simple description or evaluation.

53. Such terms as "graceful," with its reference to body movement and deportment, and "delicate," with its evocation of the fastidious, verge on being expressive terms. There is no sharp line to be drawn between what is characteristic of free mammalian movement, what is expressive of vitality in freedom, and what is delighted in as free of awkwardness and constraint: we are thus free to treat "graceful" as a Janus-word combining a descriptive with an evaluative aspect, as an aesthetic term requiring taste for its appropriate use or reflecting connoisseurship in the specific way it is used, or merely as a term with complex but purely descriptive applications. Our responses to works of art, as to situations, are always whole responses, and our terminology reflects this holism. Consequently, our analyses of this terminology can only pick out prevailing tendencies, or describe relationships that usage does not unequivocally illustrate.

54. The concept of a notation to which I appeal here is that established by Goodman (1968). The term "element," meaning the final term arrived at by some form of analysis, implies some such relation as that of a letter of the alphabet (Latin *elementum*) to written language. To speak of an element is always either to invoke some particular mode of analysis, whose possibility and relevance is thereby assumed, or to imply yet more strongly that only one mode of analysis is legitimate or possible.

55. One word that deserves special attention from this point of view is "modern." In one of its uses this word is contrasted with "traditional" and should mean something like "contemporary" or "related to present times," and thus have some of the connotations of "fashionable." But the "present times" involved in its application

seem to have become frozen at various dates. Thus, modern music begins somewhere from Debussy to Schoenberg and means approximately music not relying on tonality, whereas modern jazz begins about 1940 and means self-conscious jazz. Meanwhile, modern painting begins with the Impressionists and means any painting whose procedures are not plausibly described as the representation of objects. Thus "modern" comes to be almost a period term like "baroque," but with a yet more incoherent temporal base. What is implied by its use is suggested by its being contrasted with "traditional": in the civilization whose death throes we are currently witnessing, the arts, for all their reactions and revolutions, worked within traditions of design: the public could understand and enjoy them because their style was continuous with the vernacular styles that everyone employed for whatever artistic expression they might undertake. The modern artist, by contrast, uses an idiom that his public never uses and does not understand, so that his work is comprehensible only by an elite that is defined solely by its having learned the idiom. Consequently, many people contrast "modern" art or poetry, not with "traditional" art or poetry, but simply with art or poetry. Meanwhile, on the one hand, "modern" is also still used in contrast to "ancient" to designate whatever in artistic practice does not subscribe to the principles ascribed to the Greeks and Romans; and, on the other hand, as the "modern" periods in the other sense become protracted and accordingly appear in developing hindsight not as antitraditional but as themselves incarnating traditions that do no more than continue the tradition of changing traditions, the "modern" becomes contrasted with the "contemporary" or with the "hypermodern" or with the "postmodern," depending on the context. (Roughly, if the public at large catches up with the "modern," as has happened in the visual arts, one uses "contemporary" for what is still ahead of them; if the public has not caught up with the "modern," as has happened in music and to some extent in literature, one may use the term "postmodern" for that with which the elite public of the "modern" has yet to come to terms. But that is so rough as to be downright false, and it is better to admit that the use of compounds starting with "post-" is a fad of self-consciously advanced literary theory: a friend of mine once counted thirty-one such terms at a single conference in Minneapolis. "Hypermodern" was actually just a chess term invented by Paul Keres and soon forgotten; it meant *never* opening with P-K4.)

A term that belongs in the same box with "modern" is "avant-garde." Just as "modern" sounds as if it ought to mean whatever at any time is distinctively contemporary, so "avant-garde" sounds as if it ought to mean whatever at any time is in the forefront of artistic progress, the cowcatcher of the *Zeitgeist*. But in the mouths of many it too is becoming the name of a set of styles. As "modern" art in the sense we chiefly considered is defined by its isolation from its putative public, so "avant-garde" art was to be defined by its reversal of the conventions and transmitted skills of the fine-arts traditions. But since the presupposition of the concept is that those skills and traditions are essentially static, no one should be surprised that the "avant-garde" works produced today embody the same reversals as, and thus differ in no important respect from, the "avant-garde" works of sixty years ago.

56. Northrop Frye thus stipulates that "romanticism" refers to the period 1790-1830; primarily to the arts, and within them to the literature, of that period, and only derivatively to other cultural phenomena; in the arts, only to some artists and works, and those not self-chosen but identified in retrospect (1963, 1-2). The first of these stipulations he regards as avoiding "the fallacy of timeless characterization,"

hitherto (and I trust henceforth) unknown to logic. Without such stipulations, one would be reduced to the nominalist abjuration of historical understanding that Wellek attributes to Lovejoy and rightly deplores (Frye 1963, 107).

57. If a style concept is grounded in the shared practice of a small, self-aware group of artists, what unites them and thus grounds the concept could be anything that can be shared in a practice, subject to two important restrictions. First, what is shared must be something they deem central to their own practice, defining the essential quality of their own work and setting it off from that of others; second, the shared quality must be sufficiently perceptible and important to the critical public for the concept to become established. What a critic can admit to be central to the work of a group he admires (or at least takes seriously enough to discuss) must be something that he himself can take seriously as defining the essence of a shared practice. And this may be something that did not and could not seem central to the artists themselves.

58. What could such an independent reason be? Is *Zeitgeist* not just a name for the perceived coherence itself, as palpable and indefinable as the personality of an individual? Possibly. But one might have metaphysical reasons, such as a supposition that intelligible coherence was the ground of any reality, or anthropological reasons, such as the belief that, since lives are not led in watertight compartments, what people bring to one context will have much in common with what the same people or their associates bring to another context.

59. This notion achieved wide currency a few decades ago under the influence of Ruth Benedict (1934).

60. This denial is associated with the school of Croce. Croce's own position was, or became, finely nuanced. In his 1935 essay, "The Baroque," he urged that the term "baroque" be used, not as a generic concept, but in its original sense, "to denote the form of artistic bad taste which characterized a great part of the architecture and also of the sculpture and painting of the eighteenth century," which "substitutes for poetic truth and the charm which it inspires, the shock of the unexpected, the astounding, which excites, amazes and pleases in virtue of the thrill which it communicates"; and he pleads that such terms should be restricted to their historical contexts, not applied analogously to similar faults in the work of other periods (Croce 1966, 409-420). The urge to astound, one would have thought, is an urge to astound whenever and wherever it urges anyone, and one fails to see why it should retain a special name just because it happens to occur at a certain place and time. But if the special name is justified because this bad taste then took a special *form*, one does not see why the name of the form is not a generic term. Perhaps the argument is that such a form should be called baroque only to abuse it; but if one is abusing it for a specific reason and by virtue of specific qualities, one must be able to identify those qualities and supply that reason. In the end one is led to conclude that Croce is one of those people who can maintain the ineffability and inexplicability of certain classes of experience only by carefully preserving a logical and epistemological incompetence that absolves them from responsibility for the logical consequences of what they choose to assert.

61. A classical example is the Group of Seven, an affiliation of Toronto-based landscape painters of changing membership, whose artistic impulses were very different and whose common style is popularly identified with that of another painter who had died before the group was formed.

62. These remarks are largely prompted by Morris Weitz's profound and penetrating, but in my view wrongheaded, study of the way the term "Mannerism"

functions in art history (Weitz 1970). He takes his evidence to show that statements to the effect that Mannerism *really is* this or that can never be supported and, in fact, involve conceptual error. But it is less clear what he thinks follows from this. Sometimes it appears that he thinks such claims should never be made, but he does not dispute the value of the critical works that are built around such claims. He does not in fact consider what value they might have if they are taken to be not literally true in the way that "Napoleon fought at Waterloo in 1815" is literally true. Why should they not be taken as proposals that art historians should cease to think about "Mannerism" in the way former historians did, but should instead adopt new paradigms, boundary dates, and so on? The merits of these proposals could then be seriously discussed, as they in fact are, in terms of whether the proposed rewriting of history leads to better comprehension. Weitz either fails to see, or does not think it important to emphasize, that such a refurbishing of historical tools is at stake: he treats the matter as if it were a mere squabble, forever undecidable and hence futile, over the metaphysical status of the entity "Mannerism." and the identification of the Platonic idea of which "Mannerism" should be the proper name. Of course, the use of such locutions as "Mannerism *really is*" thus and such might be thought to have such implications; but perhaps it need not. And it is probably true, however disreputable, that one can only do history creatively if one adopts a standpoint and sticks to it. If there are a dozen standpoints and perspectives, all equally good, it does not follow that it is the part of wisdom, or even that it is possible, to take them all at once: it is a condition of vision that whatever is seen can only be seen from this position or that, and that perspectives can only be combined after they have been separately established in individual clarity.

Chapter VIII. The Classical Line
7: The Critical Function

1. *CC* assumed that this concept of criticism was not only the most general but also (being etymologically warranted by *krites* "judge") original or basic. But it is not so, as Wellek (1963) sufficiently shows: no earlier sense is attested for the word than that of general literary competence. I have considered matters from this angle in a more recent study (Sparshott 1981b).

2. This is implicit in the assimilation of critical judgments to legal verdicts in Margaret Macdonald (1949). The explicit argument of this justly celebrated article is that the logical relation of critical reasons to summary judgments is like that of legal argumentation to a judicial verdict, which does not constitute an inference from it so much as pronounce in the light of it. But what explains the looseness of fit is the fact that the pronouncement is authoritative.

3. Critical discourse may be addressed from expert to expert, a sharing of insights and expertise; from inexpert to inexpert, a joint celebration; from expert to inexpert (taken as the norm in most of the literature), instruction and edification; or from inexpert to expert, as so often in academic exercises. What is relevant in making these distinctions is not the actual measure of skill and knowledge of the participants but the basis on which the discussion proceeds: how much expertness the participant supposes in himself and in his interlocutors, and the condition on which he and they consequently participate in the conversation—the terms of the communicative contract.

4. I take this to be a cardinal principle in understanding any social institution in a pluralistic society: that all possible uses of it will be made by someone, every demand made on it will be somewhere fulfilled. Otherwise, there will be an opportunity going begging, and this can only be until someone notices the opportunity and takes it. This self-evident principle disposes at once of a great deal of high-minded cant and a great deal of low-minded evidence gathering.

5. Note that this evaporation takes place only if we carry our inductivism to some such length as counting as criticism whatever is contained in a book of which the primary concern is criticism in some functional sense, or which is written by someone chiefly known as a critic. On any other interpretation, its force may be mitigated by such considerations as I adduce in Sparshott (1981b).

6. The object of a critique need not be a single performance: it may be a set of performances conceived either as having a common character or as constituting an oeuvre, a sort of superperformance or an articulated style in which what is principally criticized may be analogous to the way in which an activity is performed. If it be thought that the use of the term "performance" in this context makes the discussion viciously circular, such a phrase as "books or works" may be substituted without serious loss (see once more Sparshott 1981b).

7. Wallace Stevens is often quoted as saying that a poem should resist comprehension almost successfully. This could hardly be a general rule, unless understood in some very special manner: it is absurd to say that a poem must be difficult (even Eliot only said that poetry must be difficult *nowadays*), and hardly less absurd to say that there must be some mental achievement in relation to it that counts as total comprehension. But the considerations brought to bear in the text do suggest that a sense of difficulty overcome must be an element in the appreciation of at least some poems and perhaps, for some readers, of most of the poems they are able to appreciate at all. Stevens as an insurance executive, and Eliot as a Harvard graduate student, might be suspected of a bias against intelligibility.

The insight expressed in Stevens's dictum can be seen as affording the basis for a recent poetics, according to which the reader tries and fails to interpret a poem as having reference in the ordinary way, until its resistance of his understanding forces him to take it as a nonreferential interplay of texts and codes (Riffaterre 1978). But I am convinced by Margolis's demonstration (1980b) that the resulting poetics, though heuristically valuable, lacks general validity.

8. This was the position taken up by Croce, and after him by Collingwood, with regard to art and intuition: only a perfectly integrated intuition could really be an intuition at all, and only an intuition can be a work of art. It follows that there can be no such thing as a bad or unsuccessful work of art, since an intuition is simply what it is, antecedent to any discourse.

9. It is of this facile negative carping that it is said that criticism is easy, art is hard—or, as Samuel Johnson put it,

> Criticism is a study by which men grow important and formidable at a very small expense. The power of invention has been conferred by nature upon few, and the labour of learning those sciences, which may by mere labour be obtained, is too great to be willingly endured; but every man can exert such judgment as he has upon the works of others; and he whom nature has made weak, and idleness keeps ignorant, may yet support his vanity by the name of a Critick (Johnson 1759, 325).

But Johnson might have reflected that it is not hard to practice any art incompetently, and not easy to practice criticism competently.

10. Bernard Harrison (1960, 211-214) appears to argue that, because no such standards are available to criticism, the concept of success has no application to works of art: to succeed is to comply with the specific requirements of a preestablished task, and with any such requirements an indifferent work may comply as well as a masterpiece. But he gives no reason for this curious restriction on the notion of success, exemplified by the claim that in "Dove Sono" Mozart was "trying to write a sad, nostalgic tune." He asserts indeed that "to be able to say of a thing that it was achieved well or ill, we must be dealing with something which is fairly concrete, and has more than one instance" (ibid., 213-214). But "achieved well or ill" is not quite the same as success, and his assertion that the specific quality of Jane Austen's wit is not the sort of thing that one might unsuccessfully attempt to bring off is neither argued for nor plausible. Cases where a very specific project just fails to come off are surely not uncommon. But perhaps the best way to understand his argument is as denying that the concept of success plays any crucial role in criticism, as opposed to the discipline of creation: he is concerned lest overall judgments of success or failure preempt the place of complex judgments of greater or less excellence in this or that respect and context, such judgments being best construed as advice to have greater or less confidence in one's attempt to find something that will reward appreciation in the respect and context in question.

11. This is not to say that no layman can keep up with any trend. One can keep oneself *au fait* with selected objects of one's enthusiasm: notoriously, adolescents make very fine discriminations in the field of popular music where all is noise to their elders. It is rather that no one can bestow the necessary energy on more than one or two selected fields without making such discrimination his primary preoccupation and thus, in effect, becoming a critic.

12. The culturally conscientious reader may feel inclined to exclaim at this point that such a state of society, though possible indeed (as the Egyptian experience showed), is a bad state of society, and its products cannot rank as art. But nothing in our previous discussion warrants this conclusion; and such a reader may be asked to shuck his scruples for a while, at least while he is theorizing, and consider that the fine spirits of such a tradition bound society would sneer at him with as much confidence as he sneers at them. When he puts this book down, he may resume his prejudices.

13. David Hume pointed out a relevant ambiguity in the notion of relation (referred to in another connection in chap. 3, n. 25). Things often strike us as *unrelated*, though theoretically any two things are related to each other in an indefinite number of ways (*Treatise on Human Nature* I.i.5). What I have referred to in the text as significant relation is what Hume called natural relation; but my argument is that significant relationships are not natural but learned (Hume's own use of the term "natural" implies not that perceived relationships are unlearned but that in them one idea actually does call up another).

14. The argument supposes that what is or used to be experienced as "distortion" is a departure from a scheme of representation experienced or posited as "lifelike" or "naturalistic," not from the way things *really look*. This does not rule out the possibility, mooted above (chap. 3 on "imitative play"), that some representational schemes correspond to simpler, more intuitively accessible, hence more "natural," ways of mapping than others.

15. This position is vigorously denied by Dufrenne (1953). He argues that the design of an aesthetic object is *perceived*, not imposed, and must therefore be really there to be perceived: the work of art, the vehicle of the aesthetic object, must therefore be such as to *call forth* its appropriate realization in perception. To achieve

this perception is indeed a task, but it is a task to which education can, in principle, contribute nothing. The effect of education can only be to hinder perception by inculcating irrelevant expectations and perceptual distortions. This thesis seems to me quite incredible. Of course there are occasions when a pattern suddenly emerges, when one comes to grasp what was previously obscure simply by continued exposure to the object in question. But to suggest an invariable sharp or absolute contrast between perception and failure of perception, or to deny that exposure to other related works may be a practically necessary condition of vision, seems to me so far from reality that I cannot comprehend how one could bring oneself to it.

16. This appears to be Prall's position (1936, 185ff.). An extreme attempt to separate the new from the old is attributed to Dubuffet by Roger Cardinal:

> The basic confusion springs from the word *culture* itself. It has two meanings: (1) knowledge of and deference to works from the past (or at least those works whose survival has been engineered by the histories of Art); (2) the active development of individual thinking. What has happened is that the first meaning has come to asphyxiate the second. This dictatorship of the past over the present is something that Dubuffet cannot stomach. He even rages over the necessity to use an inherited language, French, to express himself (1972, 126-127).

One notes here the equation of knowledge with subservience as opposed to mastery, the conspiracy theory of art history, and the question-begging notion of "individual thinking," brought out in the odd notion that one expresses one's thoughts *against* a language rather than *in* a language. Does Dubuffet mean that he has determinate thoughts that he cannot express in French, but could express in some other language (presumably some language from which one could not translate into French), or that he has thoughts that are determinate, but could not be put into any language? Or is it only that he fastidiously objects to using a language that others have sullied, as one might object to using someone else's bathwater? Presumably, since he admits the necessity, it is only the last. One wonders mildly whether Dubuffet knows, and if he knows whether it pains him to know, that he and his collection of *art brut* are typical phenomena of the art world.

The opposite position to the one attributed to Dubuffet is well stated by Valéry. Because of the insistence on literary "values,"

> each newcomer feels obliged to try to *do something else*, forgetting that if he himself is *someone*, he will necessarily do that *something else*. This demand for novelty leads to ruin, since, to begin with, it creates a kind of automatism. *Counterimitation* has become a very real reflex. Works are made subject not to the state of mind of their author but to that of his surroundings. . . . The rapid succession of quests for the new at all costs leads to a real exhaustion of the resources of art. Boldness of ideas, of language, even of forms is valuable . . . it is the *rule of being bold* that is detestable. It has a dangerous effect on the public, in whom it inculcates first the need for shock and then boredom with it, while giving birth to facile amateurs who admire everything put before them so long as they can be sure they are the first to admire (1958, 127-128).

But he goes on to embrace the absurdity antithetical to Dubuffet's, observing that "not the least of the pleasures of rhyme is the rage it inspires in those poor people who think they know something more important than a *convention*. They hold the naïve belief that a thought *can* be more profound, more organic . . . than any mere convention" (ibid., 179 [ellipses in the original]). The antithesis is absurd because, just as a language does not say anything but is that in which one says what is said, so a convention can hardly have or lack profundity in the sense in which a thought can lack or have profundity. "In what," Valéry goes on to ask, "would the artist's special position consist if he did not consider certain details inviolable? For example, the alternation of masculine and feminine rhymes. No inspiration must be allowed to ignore them. *This* is irritating, *this* is nonsense, but without *this*, everything falls apart, and the poet corrupts the artist, and the arbitrariness of the moment overcomes the arbitrariness of an order superior to the moment" (ibid., 181). That is finely said, but the antithesis between binding convention and the inspiration of the moment is not exhaustive: the conventional order could be revoked or suspended in the name of an alternative order. In fact, such a convention as the alternation of masculine and feminine rhymes could function in at least four different ways. First, it could be an absolute condition of acceptability, a strict taboo, as Valéry seems to suggest; second, it could be a strong but not absolute rule, to be violated at grave artistic risk (it is common for artistic conventions to function thus); third, it could serve as a strict rule defining a style or manner of writing that was itself voluntary, one alternative among others (which seems to be the case in French poetry at the time when Valéry was writing); and fourth, it could function as a resource, a differentiation of rhymes and relation between them, which a poem might or might not rely on.

17. A yet more conservative notion of originality than that extracted from Paul Valéry in note 16 may be found in Hegel, whose "originality" comes close to what has more recently been dubbed "authenticity": true originality means drawing on the central originating creative force of reason, which, because reason in the world is one, will manifest itself on different occasions in ways marked by deep affinities rather than by superficial divergences. Education initiates one into the inevitable rightness of tradition, saves one from the slavery of having to do one's own thing because one does not know what to do—as children babble nonsense because they want to express themselves and communicate with others, but cannot do so because they have not yet learned a language to talk in (as poor Dubuffet has had to do):

> By educated men, we may prima facie understand those who without the obtrusion of personal idiosyncrasy can do what others do. It is precisely the idiosyncrasy, however, which uneducated men display, since their behavior is not governed by the universal characteristics of a situation. . . . Thus education rubs edges off particular characteristics until a man conducts himself in accordance with the nature of the thing. Genuine originality, which produces the real thing, demands genuine education, while bastard originality adopts eccentricities which only enter the heads of the uneducated (Hegel 1821, 268).

Hegel's remark is of special interest because the contrast between deep originality and surface eccentricity, and their correlation, respectively, with profound knowledge and superficial or defective knowledge, have familiar application to the arts; but the general concept of education, with its normalizing and generalizing tendencies, is less evidently applicable, nor does Hegel himself think of the arts in this way. Hegel seems to be identifying two phenomena, but it is not easy to see how they are to be separated. In Hegel's terms, the artist does not "do what others do," because every work of art is the fusion of an idea with its proper formal embodiment (but, then, so should every fine action be). The solution of the conundrum, however, is a simple one and has been given in our description of Lukács' (1963) theory: what is universal is not general but historically diversified, and what each artist does is to give unique expression to this or that aspect in which the whole is manifest.

18. C. I. Lewis cites three factors in judgmental competence in any field: "a greater

breadth of pertinent experience, and perhaps some higher degree of the requisite powers of discernment, as well as their special place in the continuity of a tradition which represents the social working of a human critical capacity" (1946, 460). This goes for teatasters as well as scientists. The third factor seems harder to evaluate as we get further from such highly institutionalized areas as the connoisseurship of liqueur brandies, but Lewis may be right in thinking it indispensable, though it is commonly overlooked. Lewis's triad overlaps that cited with equal generality of reference by Plato in *Republic* IX: experience, intuition, and logic. Tradition supplies the place of logic, it seems. And perhaps it should. Sheer argumentation has no place in a judgment of quality; its place is properly supplied by familiarity with the way such judgments are articulated and interrelated in the context of an established critical practice of judgment.

19. One could argue that even to be hidebound is to be effectively ignorant of alternative traditions.

20. This might not be the case in Dickie's (1974) institutional view of art, according to which a work of art is any artifact for which someone has claimed the status of candidate for appreciation. But, of course, such a claim would be merely foolish unless it rested on a firm understanding of what there was to be appreciated—and modes of appreciability could hardly be specified otherwise than in relation to the appreciable properties of some extant works.

21. Harold Bloom (1973) goes so far as to urge that a poet can only be "strong" by wrestling with and overcoming some great poet of the past. But this doctrine seems to be a gratuitous display of the sentimental machismo so common among literary Americans.

22. This should not be taken to imply that at any moment of time there is *one* definitive "state of the art" that defines *the* situation for all artists or for all practitioners of a given art (cf. chap. 4, n. 37). This naive and ahistoric view was espoused, largely for polemic reasons, by T. W. Adorno (1948): the immediate purpose was to confer unique legitimacy on the compositions of Adorno's musical circle; the deeper purpose was the Kantian one of defining a single musically determined *duty* for composers as the only way to emancipate them from the smothering blandishments of a society ready and able to convert any indulgence in any pleasure into a means of Circean bewitchment and enslavement. The enterprise fails because Adorno was not able to find any way as convincing as Kant's to establish the uniqueness of the categorical imperative. For the reasons why Adorno's basic presumption of a single "state of the art" cannot be maintained—Vienna in 1900 is not the universe— see Abraham (1974).

23. The best exploration of this theme known to me is that of Sartre (1943, pt. 4, chap. 1), though his rhetoric belies his analysis. An important consideration is that one's situation, though objective, is constituted as what it is only in terms of envisaged possibilities for action.

24. This theme forms the basis of a powerful critique of what was then modern architecture, in Frankl (1914).

25. In the moral case, the dialectic of freedom and reason has a dual aspect. Morally, one is not justified in ignoring either demand; practically, one cannot do so entirely, for, on the one hand, no code suffices to determine fully the conditions of its own application, and, on the other hand, when one ignores or transgresses prevailing codes, they remain inescapably that which one is ignoring or transgressing. For some further considerations, see Sparshott (1970b). In the aesthetic case, the tension between originality and tradition, between freedom and reason, need

have no moral implications, though many writers adopt a moralistic tone; it is primarily a practical matter of the requirements—both logical and psychological—of intelligibility and effectiveness, of interpretation and appreciation.

26. Berel Lang (1975, 198ff.) develops a position that comes perhaps as close as one can to this absurd position without absurdity. That is, it is essential to art that the order a work presents should be open, and a critic's presentation of a work has the character of a performative: his critique *makes* the work to be such as he proclaims it to be, and his declaration pertains to his own selfhood. But Lang does not forget that such a constitutive utterance may, like other performatives, be infelicitous if the openness it purports to exploit is not such that others can follow him in what he makes of the work.

27. I referred in an earlier chapter to Gilson's distinction (1957) between the aesthetic mode of existence of a work (the work-as-perceived on this or that occasion) and its artistic existence, what the artist has wrought in it. These can be determinate and different only if we introduce some such step as equating the latter with physical changes in a medium—with an artifact, in effect; and this, in the case of painting, Gilson is happy to do, since he attributes agency to the painter's hand. Gilson's distinction is valuable, but the point at issue in our text is precisely that of giving an adequately precise, relevant, and informative sense to the phrase "what the artist has done."

28. This is not meant to rule out or invalidate the use of chance, indeterminate or random techniques, or even second-order indeterminacies (as when a composer leaves it to the performers when to introduce what sort of indeterminacy); it requires only that for critical purposes the work be such that control be exercised over the lack of control. See chapter 2, note 10.

29. When we speak of "inevitability" in a work, or say that "not one note could be changed," I take it that we are paying a rhetorical compliment to the power of a work's design—it might in fact be changed into something quite different that would strike us as equally "inevitable" (this must be true, because by changing *enough* notes one could change any work into any other work).

30. I have not forgotten that Susan Sontag has written a book called *Against Interpretation*. But her effective arguments are against what Cleanth Brooks calls the heresy of paraphrase—against supposing that an interpretation of a work is to be substituted for the work, that the work exists for the sake of its paraphrase, that what cannot be paraphrased is of no interest, and so on; and that is a heresy for which few will go to the stake. Sure, it's a catchy title.

31. Two classic sources for palpable errors in interpretation are the protocols in I. A. Richards' *Practical Criticism* (1929) and, at a higher level, Panofsky's (1955) study of palpable misconstructions of the "death in Arcady" theme in painting.

32. An analogue might be found in the disagreements of philosophers in, for instance, ethical theory. They seem to differ about everything; yet in fact they agree in what can be argued, what must be taken into account, what follows from what—in fact, in all that differentiates them from the beginning student in philosophy, who complains that in philosophy there is nothing to learn and will not be told that what unites the warring sects is precisely the sum of what he has to learn.

33. The difference between "not incorrect" and "correct" here is somewhat like that between "not proven" and "not guilty" in a Scottish court—but, indeed, whatever we may think about double negatives, we all know the difference between being right and merely not being wrong.

A follower of Stevenson, were any to have survived to the present day, would argue that a phrase such as "cannot be traced" is question begging because covertly evaluative: it registers a decision to declare any purported "tracing" to be unconvincing or unfounded, which in the last resort means no more than that we do not approve of it. For further attempts on my part to establish a connection between relevance and the possibility of tracing connections, see Sparshott (1970a and 1973a).

34. Stevenson's emotivism does not work very well when applied to objects and actions related to a determinate task or function, and he himself does not apply it directly in such cases.

35. Most works of art, as we have seen, are thought of as such only by being assignable to kinds; and we suggested that perhaps this is true of all works, if one concedes that a work may be the first of its kind. Insofar as the kind in question is a familiar one, which it must usually be, what is prima facie relevant is thereby determined: the words in a book, the visible marks on a canvas, what happens on stage in a play, mark out areas wherein whatever is discernible is prima facie relevant. More precisely, knowledgeability in art (such as a critic must possess) consists largely in understanding the complex conventions (and human factors) governing what one should have to take into account and what one may leave aside for this or that specific critical or appreciative purpose.

In the text I have used the phrase "as many as possible of its elements." My discussion of the characterization of works of art purported to show that such a phrase must be misleading, in that what the elements of a work were could not be established independently of a mode of analysis of which those elements appeared as the end product. I do not intend to repudiate that argument: the "elements" referred to in the text here may be construed as those elements established by any plausibly relevant mode of analysis. I do not wish to argue for the thesis that modes of analysis should themselves be multiplied to the limit.

36. The distinction between the normal and the aberrant, the traditional and the innovative, is a treacherous one. In Mahler's words, *Tradition ist Schlamperei*, "tradition is slovenliness." What passes for the normal and time-tested presentation is simply a habit that it would be too much trouble (both for performers and for audiences) to change; and, to take a different sort of case, the traditional presentations of Gilbert and Sullivan by the D'Oyly Carte Opera Company are clutched tenaciously to the public's bosom, neither because they serve as a classical norm nor because it saves trouble, but in that fetishistic frame of mind that impels small children to reject every change of wording and of intonation in a familiar bedtime story. But did Mahler's scorn for *Schlamperei* justify his practice of playing the *Leonora 3* Overture in the middle of *Fidelio*, to beef up the music, *as a regular thing*? (Actually, I gather from Kurt Blaukopf [1974, 170-171] that this, despite what we were all taught at school, was not Mahler's reason at all: it was a desperate measure to cover what would otherwise have been an intolerably long scene change, due to the technical inadequacies of the Vienna stage. I further gather from Blaukopf that Mahler's remark about *Schlamperei* was not a generalization: what he said was, "What you theatre people call tradition is really just complacency and slackness" [ibid.]. He was referring specifically to an absurd staging of the Prisoners' Chorus in the same opera, which had been defended as "the tradition." Rather than delete the libels outside this parenthesis, I correct them thus, so that you too, reader, if you had believed them before, may now cease to believe them.)

Perhaps we can rule out what is deliberately done for fun, for a change, as a gimmick, because it seems like a good idea at the time, "anything to prevent it being done straight" (Flanders and Swann); but what about innovations produced by a visionary artist who "sees it like that," for whom the work seems to demand what to everyone else seems eccentric? For maybe what he sees now everyone else will come to see, or should see even if they don't; and it is of course possible that even what an irresponsible undergraduate director does as a joke or a gimmick will be what the next generation will see as the only proper and responsible way to do it. But this is nothing more than that tiresome and unconvincing platitude that insanity is only an abusive term for a minority view. We can safeguard ourselves by confining our consideration to what is quite enough for our purposes, to a distinction between what is recognized as normal or abnormal within the relevant cultural community.

37. Curiously, Leavis always takes this as the limit of a proper *negative* response to criticism, whereas I am claiming that it is the limit of assent. Surely one can sometimes say to a critic not "Yes, but . . ." but "No, because . . ."

38. One feels rather a spoilsport to point this out, but Hamlet's killing of his uncle, whatever dramatic sympathy it may evoke, is murder, just as his killing of Polonius is. It is not even tyrannicide: Claudius may be a tyrant, though the audience is given no reason to take him for one, but that is not the reason for Hamlet's act.

39. The score of Luciano Berio's *Sequenza 5* for trombone solo includes the following instructions:

> On the stage a very low stand and a chair. Walking on stage and during the performance of section A the performer (white tie, spot from above etc.) strikes the pose of a variety showman about to sing an old favourite. . . . Just before section B he utters a bewildered "Why?" and sits down without pausing. He must perform section B as though rehearsing in an empty hall (Berio 1968).

In this case, some of the concomitants usually excluded from a musical performance are, retrospectively at least, included in it by the "bewildered" question. But, unless it is to draw attention to a difference between the A and the B music, which I confess escapes my ear, the purport of this charade is obscure. Can I not play this piece for a friend, on a rainy Sunday afternoon, without dressing up for it? If a member of the audience replies "Because it's in the score!" should he be thrown out or given a percentage of the fee? The interesting question raised is, Do we need, or do we feel the need of, a determinate answer to the question just *how much* of the performer's comportment is thus brought into the music's field of gravity? Would it be wrong to take the "Why?" as calling into question, not the conventions of platform presentation, but the whole vanguard caper to which the question pertained? It is surely a besetting weakness of works in this genre that they tend to leave the performers unprepared for any response to the "unconventional" material that is equally unconventional: they hope to God the audience will just sit there and not try to get into the act.

40. The skill of construing such improvised works, which is also called on for the construing of any work whose scale is such that it eludes the artist's perfect conscious formal control, seems to be very close to the divinatory and form-restoring skill we bring to understanding *talk*. In any protracted discourse, both syntactical patterns and trains of thought are likely to become tangled. The hearer's task is not to decipher the grammar but to understand both the person and what he is saying, which includes an estimate of the degree of coherence the person is achieving. Insofar as such procedures are appropriate to understanding an improvisation, it cannot strictly be called a performance, and hence is not exactly a work of art.

41. This quality of amplitude is akin to, but not the same as, Kant's mathematical sublime: an overwhelming object produces in one way the idea of an infinite ordering power; an inexhaustible world produces it in another way.

42. Anton Ehrenzweig (1967) suggests a different sort of relationship between indeterminate forms and *Gestalten*. The indefiniteness of the sketch, and the minute forms of the painter's brushwork and line, generate a form that can be scanned and appreciated but not understood: *Gestalten* and geometrical or symmetrical forms that the artist consciously imposes and the spectator knowingly reconstructs are of secondary import, distracting attention from the subversive gratifications of the vital textures. The interpreter can, of course, indicate the presence of these textures, but his interpretation can go no further. The thesis seems hazardous. That nervous vitality in the handling of a surface is a supreme artistic value has been attested by others—for example, by Roger Fry in his *Last Lectures* (1939)—and what seems to be it is recognized in the "rhythmic vitality" of the Chinese aesthetics of painting and in the *rasa* of Indian poetics. That the value is independent of other formal values and of representational considerations seems evident. That the critic can deal with it, not by anything we should want to call interpretation, but only by evocative description seems reasonably certain. That it has the psychological connection with infantile experience that Ehrenzweig ascribes to it, and that it plays the role of the good guy in the Neo-Freudian psychodrama in which the overt content and organized form of the work stand for the repressive bad guy, there seems no particular reason to believe; but people inclined to psychoanalytic interpretations of the appropriate school will incline to believe it. It seems to me like a suitable impossible thing to believe before breakfast.

43. Thus, to some modern readers the interest of *The Tempest* focuses on the "colonial" relations between Prospero and Caliban (and Ariel), relations clearly intended by the playwright, but of which the significance in his day cannot have been at all like what it is in ours.

44. This would be one interchange in the "dialogue indefeasible by time," which a masterpiece, according to Malraux (1953, 69), maintains with successive generations.

45. See William Empson (1935) and compare Margolis's discussion (1965). Margolis curiously writes as if such interpretation in the light of a myth were the only kind of interpretation there is. He does not say why; it may be because all other activities called interpretation should, in the interests of clarity and precision, be called aspecting, seeing as, reading, or something else, and the word "interpretation" is to be reserved for the deliberate application of an independently comprehensible system to a form that one is capable of understanding in its own terms without it. If that is the reason, one takes the point; criticism would then have a fourfold function, descriptive, generic, interpretive, and evaluative. But to adopt so restrictive a usage leaves one at a disadvantage in dealing with the already well-established controversies mooted in our text.

46. In this, they differ from the alternative readings supposed by modern romantics to have been brought to every text by medieval literary method: those yielding literal, allegorical, moral, and anagogical meanings. These would be mutually supplementary, and would presumably need to be established in sequence. That medieval critics knew the difference between talking literally and talking figuratively is clear enough; that they actually developed and used a multilevel scheme, as opposed to sometimes talking about one (Dante, *Convito* II, 1, is the favorite reference; Beardsley [1966a, 109] cites an application of it from John Cassian [A.D.

360-435]; Augustine's *De Doctrina Christiana* seems to have been the fountainhead), is not so clear. I have heard the suggestion derided by Etienne Gilson, a man whose derision one would rather not incur. Whether widely practiced or not, the method seems to have been a successor to the Stoic method of allegorical exegesis, given its final form by Crates of Mallos in the second century B.C., which found literal, ethical, and metaphysical meanings for selected passages (cf. Dillon 1977, 142).

47. The prints of M. C. Escher are often exploitations of such ambiguities with little else in the design to interest, but Escher himself says, "I often seem to have more in common with mathematicians than with my fellow artists" (1971, 8).

48. One may also use the "seeing as" trope to cover the case of interpretive myths—one sees *Alice in Wonderland* as a Freudian allegory. But as Margolis points out (1965, 106), it is misleading to use the same language for cases in which one succeeds in getting, or can't help getting, one of two alternative readings of an ambiguous pattern, as one does for cases in which one *decides* to accept a mythology as relevant.

49. A similar, and similarly mild, interest attaches to the notorious fact that in Indo-European languages a large part of the vocabulary for understanding is borrowed from the vocabulary for vision. It is equally interesting, in view of the complete lack of any evidence, that one habitually says this, rather than that the vocabulary of vision is borrowed from the vocabulary for understanding, or that the two vocabularies are cognate.

50. I have heard this (or what sounded like this) vehemently argued by Professor Ralph Cohen. I am not sure that injustice is the issue; the works themselves are not altered by our interpretations, but, *herrlich wie am ersten Tag*, await any later interpreter and any later recoverer of pristine significance with equal placidity. Of course, if I impute my latter-day meaning to the author personally, I am unjust to him; but to do that is not to interpret, but to claim a status for one's interpretation.

51. This problem of attractive interest was widely discussed in early Greek philosophy under the name of friendship (*philia*) and has since been lost sight of. It was diversely argued that attraction was between opposites or of like for like or based on more complex relations of congeniality or reinforced understanding. See Plato's *Lysis*.

52. As we observed in discussing the "conditions of beauty" in chapter 4, to say that subtlety and complexity are the grounds of sustained appreciation runs the risk of being self-confirming. That a work attracts many interpreters proves that it is susceptible of multifarious interpretations, hence complex; if it arouses sustained interest through the ages, it follows that it is capable of being the occasion of very various aesthetic experiences and the target of varied interests, so that, again, it must be complex. If, despite that, the work is evidently *not* complex, we say it is "subtle"—that is to say, it has a complexity that gives the impression of simplicity. We have in fact already seen that a measure of complexity cannot be found; a measure of subtlety is even less likely to be attainable.

53. George Boas (1950), showing that the sustained celebrity of the *Mona Lisa* has been explained at different times in utterly different ways, infers that its reputation is self-sustaining. This position would have to be modified if it were ever found that, of two equally well established notorieties, one succeeded in maintaining itself while the other fizzled out. We might then say that because the Parthenon is still esteemed, the *Apollo Belvedere* somewhat blown upon, the *Laocoön* making a modest comeback after going through a bad patch consequent upon excessive boosting, and the Portland Vase quite neglected and forgotten, the true worth of the first had seen it through, while a meretricious element in the fame of the others

had tended to drag them down from their former eminence. Of course, these changes might be fortuitous, and the changing fashions they reflect might be reversed. A future age might degrade the Parthenon and exalt the Portland Vase, as a byproduct of who can say what casual redirection of the attention? It may seem unthinkable now, but no more than the present widespread indifference to Virgil and Raphael would have seemed a century ago. Nonetheless, such shifts make it impossible to agree that the magnitude of a reputation *suffices* to sustain it. Of course, reputations tend to sustain themselves—who could doubt that? But the position becomes nugatory as soon as it is thus modified: what in the world could a reputation be if it had no tendency to self-perpetuation? It is no less true, and no more startling, that puffs tend to defeat themselves. All that is interesting is the relative strength of these factors, and Boas has nothing to say on this that is both true and interesting. He ignores, incidentally, the obvious and familiar argument that the diversity of the grounds alleged for the excellence of such a work as the *Mona Lisa* tends to show that it has a diverse *and thoroughly integrated* excellence and that the works whose reputations survive are precisely those in which "everything works together" in this way, even if at any given time only certain currently fashionable features are noticed or singled out for mention.

54. It is because of this neglect of the artist's evaluation and understanding in favor of the critic's that Valéry consistently argued that the poet only furnishes the materials for a poem, the reader being the true poet. Structuralist theorists have recently pushed this position to the point where paradox tips over into silliness by implying that the text is a blank, a void, which the critic must fill. If that were true, what a critic finds to say about any two works would be interchangeable. One is inclined to retort that such critics do exist, but are not commonly esteemed. The retort falls flat, because, if the theory is true, the critical texts will themselves also be blanks for a metacritic to fill. But, then, the structuralist texts that expound these startling-sounding doctrines will be mere blanks too, and we may fill them in as we please.

55. The problematic situation is not unique to the arts, but is common to all serious intellectual work in philosophy and the sciences. Knowledge must be culturally conditioned, but is not relativized: we see what there is to see in the direction we look from where we stand through the glasses we have in the light there is (cf. Fackenheim 1961). Again, the divergence of any two minds raises the same questions as the most extreme cultural separation.

56. The best known work in this field is that of Hans-Georg Gadamer (1960). He levels a devastating critique against the aestheticism that would treat the work of art as isolated object of a special sort of experience, but it is not clear what he has to offer instead, beyond an enumeration of ideals: the factuality of the work is to be respected, but it is also to be seen as expressing the life of its time, as affecting that life in many aspects, and, in both of these capacities, entering into the lives of its successive publics as a mediation of the continuing life of the people.

An analogue for the kind of renewal in variety that Gadamer points toward may be found in the encounter of two persons. Each person has his own continuing life as an individual, but is a "different person" to different people because he enters into their lives in different ways, in different contexts and for different purposes, and may behave differently toward them, too. Nor is his individuality incompatible with his being in many ways typical of his place and time and expressive of it, as well as being influential in it because he acts in and on it. There is one respect in which the analogy fails: a person is different to different people partly because he does in fact adapt his behavior to his role and his company. This source of variation is lacking in the work of art, except to the extent that plays may be produced, books edited and printed, pictures cleaned and hung, in ways that reflect the way each successive age thinks about such works in general and about the work in particular. For the rest, the variations in the work must be contributed by those who encounter it and by the impersonal tooth of time.

57. Man, the argument goes, is a "political animal," that is, one whose nature is realized (his capacities fulfilled) only in a political community. And a political community is defined by its sharing a common conception of what is a good life for its members to lead together. The basic function of speech is to enable men to share these common conceptions—hence, no doubt, the diversity of tongues (Aristotle, *Politics* I).

58. It was once fashionable to deny that this is so, on the grounds that some cultures do not think in terms of means and ends at all. The evidence favoring this thesis included nonsequentiality in narrative techniques and a structuring of life in terms of repetition of ritual rather than purposive organization. But the Trobrianders, whose peculiarities as described by Malinowski were the main source of the doctrine, do in fact *do* things as we do; and we lack the required information on the supposed nonevaluative discourse about things to be done that are ritually determined. It is no doubt partly true that Western civilization is obsessed with evaluation, as an expression, first, of the Enlightenment, then of the doctrines of progress, and finally of consumerism. But even that cannot be the whole truth, or it would not be evident to people like us that it is an obsession.

59. It is these cases that lend support to C. L. Stevenson's (1944) contention that to call something good is in the first instance no more than to express a favorable attitude to it and to seek to evoke such an attitude in others. For a reconciliation of such a view with the relevance of bill filling, see Hare (1952).

60. It sounds odd to say that Carlo Dolcis are defined in terms of a set of purposes, rather than by their provenance. For it is plainly not Dolci's purposes that are in question here. Yet, odd as it is, that is what I want to say. To speak of "Carlo Dolcis" in this way is already to acknowledge his name as defining a style and hence a possible taste: good Carlo Dolcis are the kind of Carlo Dolcis that people who like Carlo Dolcis like.

61. It is habitual among philosophers to write as though "good," and corresponding terms in other tongues, were always used to evaluate. It is a useful convention, but can be misleading, since the other uses to which the word is in fact put may distract one from the process of evaluation itself. For some thoughts on the variety of uses of "good," and some implications of that variety, see Appendix C.

62. Students in aesthetics courses seem to find it natural to use it, so perhaps its rarity reflects only the infrequency with which everyday conversation reaches the appropriate level of reflective abstraction. The phrase "bad work of art" (and hence by inference "good work of art") is not completely unknown. Here is an example: "You can say it is fundamentally so boring that it has made no difference at all, in which case it is a bad work of art" (Carroll and Lucie-Smith 1973, 107).

Whatever the frequency of this particular phrase itself, one does often say that one work is better than another, and one often uses other expressions that have the same force of generally praising something as a work of art; so the unusualness of the phrase is of no likely consequence. It might be objected that the expression is pleonastic, in that to call anything a work of art is to invoke those aspects of it that fit it for contemplation, and whatever so fits it qualifies it as good in that respect.

But we saw that there could be a poor work of art: one that, when examined for such properties, failed to show them. And something with meager aesthetic properties might be a work of art indeed, but not a good one.

63. The Carlo Dolci example is borrowed from R. M. Hare's *Language of Morals* (1952). Hare's treatment is such as to suggest that, unless one thinks that good Carlo Dolcis are good paintings (and, indeed, good things), one's use of "good" in speaking of them is, as it were, in quotation marks of horror or of attribution. But I do not see why one cannot seriously assess the merits of things of a sort one has no relish for (see Sparshott 1958).

64. See, for instance, Carroll and Lucie-Smith on this: "I've always felt that the chief duty of criticism, like it or not, is evaluation. . . . And you must admit that on the bottom line of the calculation one has to come up with either 'This is good' or 'This is bad,' or at least 'This is better or worse than . . .' " (1973, 106). I suppose it is true that if there is to be a calculation it must have a bottom line, but why must there always be a calculation? Only, I would have thought, if one were jurying a show (in which case one would act as selector, not as critic), or if one were considering a purchase (in which case excellence as a work of art would surely never be the sole deciding factor). Otherwise, such blunt bottom lines seem rather to serve certain limited special purposes, such as saying whether a young Turk's rivalry with a master of his genre has been successful, or whether a second novel has maintained the promise of a first. So far from it being a natural conclusion to a critique, it provokes one always to seek the special reason for its inclusion.

65. On Aschenbrenner's principle, then, if ambiguity is a possible excellence, so also must definiteness of meaning be. See chapter 7, above.

66. Compare Edmund Wilson's foreword to *The Triple Thinkers* (1962, 7-8), where he thinks it necessary to defend his essays from the expected charge that what they discuss is not always relevant to central evaluative issues.

67. Harold Osborne writes: "In essence all critical writing is an amplification of one of two elementary types of statement: either the critic says 'I like this' or he says 'This is good' " (1955, 2). This requires that evaluations cannot be supported or explained, but only repeated at greater length; and it further supposes that the critic has no exegetical labor to perform—or, if he does, it is lost labor. Not surprisingly he concludes that, "until the theory of beauty is considerably more advanced, such criticism as is not purely autobiographical is likely, therefore, to remain indeterminate, unmeaning gibberish" (ibid., 3). We note that Osborne here calls in evidence the supposedly observed fact, or universally held opinion, that all criticism hitherto written is either autobiography or gibberish. Lukács, Frye, Leavis, Coleridge, Johnson—gibberers all. Dear me.

68. Micha Namenwirth reported to the 1964 meeting of the American Society for Aesthetics the results of his examination of the critical reception of Schoenberg's works. Unfamiliar works, he found, tended to be praised or decried without qualification or supporting descriptions, and their reception showed wider discrepancies in evaluation. Critiques of works became more specific as the works became more familiar. I am not aware that his findings have been published.

69. Mill's modification is important: not the amount of pleasure alone but the "quality" of the pleasure (its congruence with the main values endorsed by the person pleased) is important. Thus, we may construe F. R. Leavis's demand that literature show a sensitivity to the quality of life that becomes at its highest pitch religious as a demand that literature yield a higher pleasure than that of mere

entertainment or formal gratification. If the demand is not construed thus, literature is reduced to a vehicle of moralizing and a means of moral improvement.

70. One should not, however, go overboard on this theme. Roger Fry, reporting more in sorrow than in anger on Roger de Piles' ranking of painters on the basis of a numerical grading scheme, observes that the first place is assigned to a nonentity (Albano), ahead of those we now recognize as the great masters (1939, 21). But on looking at what de Piles wrote, we find that the only reason Albano comes first is that the list is in alphabetical order (1708, 397). Actually, de Piles does not rank the painters at all: he assigns his marks in each of four categories (*composition, dessein, coloris, expression*), each of which he says could be further subdivided. So far from summing these (he does not even say whether they *could be* summed, something that, of course, could be done only if each of the four factors were weighted the same for all painters), he says that the main point of the exercise is to warn people against reacting to painters on the basis of *one* factor only—which, as it happens, is what Fry did in his disparagement of the wretched Albano, whom he considers only under the head of *expression*. If we do tot up the totals, we find that Rubens and Raphael come out on top, and Giovanni Francesco is at the bottom; Albano comes fairly low on the list. In fact, the rankings we get, though not likely to conform to the critical judgment of anyone alive today, are far from outrageous.

71. Richard Wollheim (1968) thus pointedly remarks that he is deliberately abstaining from discussing questions of value. But he does not say for which of many equally probable reasons he is abstaining—because they are boring, or irrelevant, or too much discussed already, or beyond his competence, or would make his book longer than his publisher would pay for. There is an implicit suggestion that the right people in the best circles know all that sort of thing without it being explained to them; but out here in the colonies. . . .

Kovach (1974) has a characteristically thorough survey of the factors that make the fluctuation of taste explicable, if not predictable.

72. The advantages of spelling out the implications of the metaphor of "taste" seem to have been realized first by Thomas Reid in his *Essays on the Intellectual Powers of Man* (1785).

73. This admittedly contradicts W. C. Williams's unexplained and undefended claim that people die every day for lack of what is found in poems (1962, 161-162). But Dr. Williams was presumably not speaking there in his capacity as pediatrician.

74. It is characteristic of this that one of Wittgenstein's paradigms of aesthetic discussion is discussion with one's tailor on the cut of a coat. A clear light is shed on the peculiarity of the circumstances that Wittgenstein takes as typical by the introduction to Leitner (1973).

75. For complaints about the complacency of the Viennese public, see Adorno and Krenek (1974, 203).

Chapter IX. The Classical Line
8: The Artist

1. See Blunt (1940, chap. 4). We recall that it was precisely this claim that Plato challenged in *Republic* X, on the ground that it was knowledge of fine-arts techniques that artists labored to acquire and displayed in their works, while knowledge of the

subject matter of their art formed no part either of their training and professional competence or of that in which their success or failure was perceptible.

2. See Fischer (1963, chap. 3). Fischer adds that the apparent freedom of the artist, on which he prided himself, was illusory: emancipation from patron and public in fact meant slavery to the market or to the whims of critics and coteries whose irresponsibility did not mitigate their tyranny.

3. Vitruvius, in *De Architectura* I.1, made this claim on behalf of architecture— reasonably enough, for a town planner must know about the conditions of infection, and architects must know how to fit things to the scale of the human body (cf. Gutman 1972). Renaissance painters took over the claim, without of course being able to claim the same justification (see Blunt 1940, chap. 4).

4. The relation between divine and human creation has been subtly explored, and its historical importance for aesthetics demonstrated, by Milton C. Nahm (1956).

5. Compare Gilson (1957). One important difference between the fine arts as arts of imitation and as arts of beauty is that the former seem to call rather for applicable knowledge and the latter for reproducible skill. On the face of it, one cannot say what someone must know in order to make a beautiful thing, for beauty in itself is not something one knows about separately from one's knowledge of particular sorts of beautiful things (a point Aristotle makes against Plato about goodness, in *Nicomachean Ethics* I. vi); one must simply make what one makes in a certain fashion, that is, beautifully. But if the fine arts are arts of imitation, one must presumably know about whatever it is one is imitating, whether that be a structure or a system of appearances or a generative process (cf. n. 1, above).

6. From "Lord Finchley" in Belloc (1970, 210). I have commented adversely, both in *SA* and when quoting Rader and Jessup in an earlier chapter, on the practice of saying that art (or the concern for the aesthetic) "gets specialized" in the fine arts, as though an undifferentiated "art impulse" came first. But that is not at all the same thing as saying, as is obviously true, that such diffused practices as modeling and versifying get specialized in the corresponding fine arts.

7. Plato, *Phaedrus* 245 A: "The person who comes to the doors of poetry without madness from the Muses, convinced that technique will have made him an adequate poet, gets nowhere; the poetry of the self-controlled is annihilated by that of the crazed" (my translation).

8. Milton C. Nahm finds the first serious theoretical consideration of the implications of this phrase in Fray Benito Jerónimo Feijoo's essay on "The 'I Know Not What,' " which he prints (Nahm 1975, 336-344). Feijoo's main point is much the same as that of Isenberg (1949): because a work is an individual, not a congeries, its precise character and effect are necessarily something that cannot be precisely stated.

9. "I hate, and I love. Perhaps you wonder why I should do that. I don't know, but I feel that it is so, and I am tormented."—Catullus.

10. The phrase forms the title of the study of the image of the artist by Wittkower and Wittkower (1969).

11. The pieces I have in mind have a curiously equivocal character. From one point of view, the true artist, the performer of what is effectively performed, is not so much the artist who gains the auctorial status as the team (however organized or conned) from the fine-arts institutions that displays and publicizes the artist's act of authorship. In fact, it may be that the same purpose would be served if the same engines of publicity were put into motion on behalf of some random action of a person himself taken at random, or a fictitious act of a fictitious person, although,

in that case, my principles oblige me to say that an error has been committed, in that there would not have been even a minimal performance other than the performance of publicizing. From another point of view, it is necessary for the effective conveying of the status of auctoriality that the agents of publicity (and presumably the artist himself) identify and emphasize the random slice of life or stuff or whatever of which authorship is claimed, even though the point of the exercise is that what is thus singled out and celebrated continues to have no significance whatever. It therefore requires the most delicate judgment (or the most irresponsible effrontery) to determine whether the significance of the "piece" lies in the acts of creative publicizing, in the occult qualities of whatever it is of which authorship is claimed, or (as in the case that alone concerns us now) in the pure act of authoring itself.

Chapter X. *The Idea of Art*

1. What is called oriental philosophy is a miscellaneous lot of practices and texts stemming from various concerns, none of them identical with the critical concern for which the term *philosophia* was originally coined and then reserved. The origin and development of that concern are integral to the Western civilization it did much to shape. In stretching the word "philosophy" to cover other forms of intellectual activity no less integral to other civilizations, one is acknowledging a certain analogical likeness among the roles they all play in their different contexts; but to be impressed by that analogy is, precisely, to be insensitive to the concern that philosophy expresses and shapes. One could say the same sort of thing about science and even art, as modes of activity only possible in a civilization that has taken the singular shape ours has. To use a phrase like "oriental philosophy" without qualms is to show oneself excluded from the conceptual scheme by which one's civilization is defined and thus to be uneducated, for to lack education is precisely to lack access to that scheme. As concepts like those of philosophy, science, and art lose their specific shape, civilization disintegrates, and the idea of education becomes empty. All this may well be happening, and none of us any the worse for it, for an outworn civilization may be no great loss: we are simply ridding ourselves of what Twyla Tharp has called "that European bullshit."

2. The agreement of Hegel is regarded in some circles as the kiss of death. But wrongly. The only way to differ from Hegel on the topics to which he most attended is by being stupider than he, and not to attend to such topics at all is stupider yet. What is amiss with Hegel is the tendency to suppose that the problems to which his methods do not lend themselves are not important problems.

3. That is, if he speaks German and is in the habit of quoting Goethe's *Faust*.

4. A curious illustration of this pervasive demand for symbolic grandeur is the great reputation among sophisticated philosophers in the 1950s of an article by John Passmore (1951), himself a sophisticated philosopher, on "The Dreariness of Aesthetics." This was an attack on all general theories of art, not on the ground that the term was too vague and various in its use to support a general theory, but on the grounds that art is such an adventurous and exciting thing that its works are much too special for there to be a general theory about them. That is to say, the attack was launched in the name of a theory of art of the most extreme generality—and also of the utmost poverty and banality. It often happens in philosophy that widely acclaimed debunkings turn out to be ignorant and inconsistent, the

acclaim being based, not on their efficacy, but on the desire of the acclaimers to be excused from studying the object of the attack.

5. Timothy Binkley (1977) argues that art is a practice, not to be defined by defining the work of art, which is whatever the artist does in pursuit of whatever the practice of art may be at the time. His account is based entirely on the work of Marcel Duchamp, who is surely a dangerous paradigm, his procedures being parasitic on the institutions devised to sustain the work of others and often plainly designed either as a comment on existing art or even as an attack on it. If his work has become "normal" art by adoption, that can hardly be because of the nature of his own activity: his example might support Dickie's institutional view of art, but not the one Binkley proposes (see the incisive argument in Diffey 1979). When one asks, with special reference to Duchamp, what kind of practice art could possibly be, the only coherent answers are those that fall within the scope of the purist line. The arts may be "practices," if that term is suitably understood; but the point of saying "art" is to go beyond the arts and, hence, to go beyond specific practices.

6. According to Preston McClanahan, "the Balinese have a saying: 'We have no art, we do everything the best way we can' " (1971, 37). This dictum is widely quoted with respectful solemnity, but should not be. In what language do they say this? What word is translated "art"? And what precisely does that word (in whatever language it is) mean? What is it that they are denying of their practice? And is their denial true? No hint is given as to the answer to any of these questions. If the dictum means that the Balinese think that the English word "art" means "something to the doing or making of which special care has been devoted," which is the only interpretation on which the dictum makes literal sense, it only shows that the Balinese in question do not speak English very well. The only condition on which it could make some sort of sense (as opposed to being a mere mistranslation) would be if art were taken as it is at this point in the text, as activity manifesting some especially significant capacity of mankind. It could then be taken to mean that the Balinese do not allow that any human activities are the outcome of more significant capacities than any others (worshiping or excreting, it's all one), all have equal dignity and deserve equal care. That would be a tenable position and not out of keeping with Balinese values as described by Gregory Bateson. "Actions which are culturally correct (*patoet*)," he writes, "are acceptable and aesthetically valued. Actions which are permissible (*dadi*) are of more or less neutral value" (1949, 119). What this suggests is a situation like that represented by the Greek concept of the *kalon* before the fine arts were recognized as a single grouping, and much before the concept of art as we know it arose: one in which actions of any culturally valued sort could be distinguished as noble/fine/beautiful. Bateson characterizes Balinese society as one in which "neither the individual nor the village is concerned to maximize any single variable" (ibid., 124), a noncompetitive, hierarchical, and strongly formalized society in which one would expect that any such categorization of practices as "the fine arts" represents would go against the social grain. The saying reported by McClanahan could then be taken to mean that, among the social practices and rituals in which it is possible to be *patoet*, none is allowed any distinctive inner meaning and none has any special affinity with any other. But that is far from what it says.

7. That art as we think of it belongs to the contemplative rather than to the practical or productive life, and hence has the thought forms appropriate to theology and metaphysics rather than to art in the classical sense, was stated by Jacques Maritain (1930).

8. See Peckham (1965). His argument, to the limited extent that it makes consistent sense, is that the function of art is to provide alternative orders to those that have become habitual, and that the order it provides is usually at first identified merely as absence of order (because traditional orders are absent); and indeed that one might say that it is the denial or undermining of the old order rather than the provision of an alternative that is art's *primary* function.

9. It is supposed to be very wicked to talk about faculties, as involving commitment to obsolete psychology. It is not usually made clear what error is involved: "the old faculty psychology" is supposed to be an evil too familiar and fearsome to need description or for its description to be endurable—like "the sin against the holy spirit" or "neocolonialism." What I intend is, I think, harmless; I sketched it at the beginning of chapter 5. If there is a sort of thing that people do, and people learn to do, it seems obvious enough that people can learn to do that sort of thing, and the fact that people who haven't (yet) done it could learn to do so may be a fact we want to talk about. If the sort of behavior we have in mind is one that we think very important, and one that is very complex and various, we may want to express our sense of this by saying that "mankind" has a capacity or a faculty for such and such. We then say that the broadest and most important divisions of intelligent behavior represent the *faculties* of the mind. An old man who has "lost the use of his faculties" is one who can no longer count, talk coherently, perceive, and so on: we enumerate the faculties he has lost by enumerating the important sorts of things he can't do any more. I suppose the objection to this way of talking is that it presupposes that the groupings of behavior are *determined* by the antecedent organization of mind or brain *in all cases*, rather than being arrived at ad hoc or socially determined and then mapped back onto the mind. It presupposes no such thing, however, and no such thing is required by anything I want to say here. All I want to maintain is that, if it makes plain sense to speak of a certain sort of thing that people do, it makes equally plain sense to speak of their ability to do so; and sometimes it is the latter we want to talk about and not the former.

10. This argument, which played so large a part in eighteenth-century speculation, is undermined by a recent trend of speculation typified by Fodor (1975). According to this thesis, one could not learn a language unless one already knew a language: to learn what a word means, one must frame and test hypotheses about its meaning, and these hypotheses must themselves be cast in some "language" or other. Presumably, therefore, human beings (and other animals) have languages built into their cerebral cortices. It is not clear, however, that the kind of language Fodor postulates affects the issue. The concepts of natural languages are probably at the top of immensely complex hierarchies of abbreviations, the "language" at the cortical base being about as neutral as the language constituted by a TV screen's capacity for having its dots activated or inactivated. The implications of this whole line of argument are very obscure, much depending on systematic equivocation in the jargons of epistemology and data processing. It is quite unclear what is claimed for the innate system of representation by calling it a language; but it seems clear that the leap from whatever level of organization the innate system represents to the actual concepts and intuitions involved in the languages people overtly use is great enough to preserve whatever force the eighteenth-century argument may have had.

11. Germain Bazin, whose history of museums sheds much light on the development of the idea of the fine arts, remarks that in the nineteenth century the idea of the museum split to embrace two forms: a treasury of high art and a repository to encompass "all the creations of human life, even the most humble" (Bazin 1967,

195). Museum people certainly have a tendency to suppose that what they choose to display must for that very reason be art, or be just as good as art.

12. The very use of the term "art" testifies to a fact on which we will have occasion to remark later, namely, that the nonclassical lines transparently link their preferred practices and significances to the preferred practices, the most admired products, and even the sustaining institutions of the fine arts, with which they assume that their adepts are thoroughly familiar. In fact, these other lines avow their secondary status by this dependence on the establishment of the classical line: in no case does the rejection of the classical line, however vehement, go to the length of thinking in terms independent of it.

13. This doctrine could be extracted from Plato's distinction between the "arts" that seek to do good and the mere "knacks" that are content to give pleasure (Plato, *Gorgias* 462 Bff.), if we added the premise that it is never nice to be done good to.

14. Notoriously, this possibility is illustrated by the fate of Dadaism and other gestures of disgust from the early years of this century. The original intention was to express horror at the state of civilization that issued in the First World War by inserting insulting or absurd objects into the context of the fine arts. But in the course of years these things not only acquired a nostalgic appeal but also took on a period charm as expressive of the sensibility of their age and milieu; they also (because their makers were men of taste and feeling) had a certain inescapable charm of their own: they ceased to offend and became art. Some people then said that it was *because* they were art that they had given offense in the first place; whether this was a great discovery, an intellectual breakthrough, or rather a stupid confusion, an intellectual breakdown, we need not consider here. I return to this topic in discussing the purist line.

15. Three sorts of sparrow visit our bird feeder in spring: chipping sparrows, white-crowned sparrows, and house sparrows. English ornithologists tell me that only the last are *true* sparrows; the others are only American sparrows and belong to a different family. American ornithologists say that these others are *true* sparrows, and that the house sparrows (or *English* sparrows), nasty pushy things, are really not sparrows at all but weaver finches. The Americans have economy on their side (a weaver finch doesn't need to be a sparrow *as well*), the English have history (English sparrows were sparrows when Leif the Lucky was in knee pants); both sets of scientists are resigned to the fact that people like me will go on calling them all sparrows anyway.

16. I would insist on two points here. First, the sense and reference of a word as used in conversation are fixed, insofar as they are fixed at all, by the whole context, not the context as it has developed up to that point. Second, our understanding of how someone is using such a term does not take the form of framing a definite hypothesis or hypotheses but rather of a certain wary vigilance, in which our knowledge of the range of meaning the word has, the idiosyncrasies of our respondent, the vagaries of linguistic practice generally, and the perversity of the human heart, enable us to keep certain ranges of possibilities in mind and to exclude others. We must bear in mind, too, that people are not always consistent in the meaning they assign to a word throughout a conversational context, and often we have no way of knowing whether someone is being vague or inconsistent or merely inexplicit. We contrive to catch drifts—see the end of Appendix C.

17. There are of course jackasses who would do just that, being too high-minded to turn their attention to such things. They are not to be confused with those who,

having taken such phenomena into account, give themselves and others reason to think that what finally concerns a philosophy of art should be what differentiates high art from them, not what unites them; nor with those who deliberately ignore them because they think it more profitable to produce an anatomy, or a phenomenology, of the paradigms of art, and let the marginal or undeveloped manifestations go by the board. What makes a person a jackass is that he simply does not make up his mind what to do or think about them at all.

18. My use of Hall's distinction does not mean that I endorse it with a whole heart. On its empirical side, I am not competent to offer an opinion; as a theoretical structure, it strikes me as inadequately thought out. But in broad terms the threefold distinction among modes of social control is convincing and useful.

19. The reasoning is approximately that of the legendary official of the Chinese imperial court who refused to look up to see (what he had never seen) an airplane fly by. He understood (he said) that this was a machine made for the purpose of flying; it was therefore to be expected that it would fly. What was there to look at? The surprising thing would be if it did *not* fly. There is something specious about the reasoning, as one may see from an analogy: one might say that there is no point in performing the sexual act, since it is essentially always the same. True. But what is always the same in it is just what continues to please.

20. According to René Wellek, the decisive changes, all belonging to the eighteenth century, are "the rise of an emotional concept of poetry, the establishment of the historical point of view, and the implied rejection of the imitation theory, of the rules and genres": in short, "the general rejection of the neoclassical creed" (1955, 2). But this heterogeneous set of developments in literary theory cannot be separated from the development of the concept of the fine arts. Bazin ascribes the notion that works of art are of a mysterious and transcendent excellence, appropriate to a golden age of vanished splendor, to the postrevolutionary admission of the general public into the art museums that had hitherto been the preserve of connoisseurs (1967, 160).

21. A purely innovative thought, one may suppose, would not be discursive but would be something like an instantaneous vision or an image, which could appear all at once like a lightning-lit landscape. Gaston Bachelard, if I understand him, thought that the philosophy of art would then have to be similarly spasmodic, presumably because a completely novel vision would be falsified if it were related to anything else instead of being made the occasion for a totally unprecedented commentary. "If there be a philosophy of poetry, it must appear and reappear through a significant verse, in total adherence to an isolated image. . . . The philosophy of poetry must acknowledge that the poetic act has no past, at least no recent past, in which its preparation and appearance could be followed" (Bachelard 1958, xi). The qualification about the recent past is necessary because the poetic image will prove to be a transformation of some earlier experience or experiences of the poet (cf. SA 227-229 and 408-413).

22. It is conceivable that this notion appears already in the irresistibly arcane lines of Pindar's Olympian 2, 94f.: "Wise is he who knows many things by nature: facile learners who can say anything gabble uncontrollably, like grackles, before the holy eagle of Zeus" (my attempt to translate).

23. The key text is by Edward Young: "An *Original* may be said to be of a *Vegetable* nature; it rises spontaneously from the vital root of genius; it *grows*, it is not *made*: *Imitations* are often a sort of *manufacture* wrought up by those *mechanics*, *art*, and

labour, out of pre-existent materials not their own" (1759, 7). (I have already cited Warburton's sniffy dismissal of this position.) A subtle and suggestive version of the image of vegetable growth is that of Paul Klee:

> Nobody would affirm that the tree grows its crown in the image of its root. Between above and below can be no mirrored reflection. It is obvious that different functions expanding in different elements must produce vital divergences.
>
> But it is just the artist who at times is denied those departures from nature which his art demands. He has even been charged with incompetence and deliberate distortion.
>
> And yet, standing at his appointed place, the trunk of the tree, he does nothing other than gather and pass on what comes to him from the depths. He neither serves nor rules—he transmits.
>
> His position is humble. And the beauty at the crown is not his own. He is merely a channel (1924, 77).

There is a study of the idea of organic form in Wimsatt (1976, 205-223).

24. This account of what creativity in art must be is based on Tomas (1958). His account is developed by Beardsley (1965), who goes on to denounce the result as irrelevant to aesthetics. The denunciation is made from a standpoint incompatible with the poetic line, and therefore irrelevant to most of those who have thought artistic creation worth discussing; but the legitimacy of the poetic line is what is chiefly at issue. I animadverted briefly on the "creative process" in *SA* (227-229), and have discussed it so extensively elsewhere (Sparshott 1966a, 1974a ["Xanthippe"], 1977) that I hold myself excused from going into it again.

25. Compare Coleridge's 1808 lectures on Shakespeare: ". . . imagination, or the power by which one image or feeling is made to modify many others and by a sort of *fusion to force many into one*" (Coleridge 1930, I.188). But the force of Coleridge's argument is weakened by his examples, which are cases of the "pathetic fallacy," or of such a homogeneity of imagery as might surely be produced by systematic labor no less than by a unifying and vivifying power (cf. chap. 13, n. 64).

26. Thus Boccioni: "The sculptor must not shrink from any means in order to obtain a *reality*. Nothing is more stupid than to fear to deviate from the art we practise. There is neither painting, nor sculpture, nor music, nor poetry. The only truth is creation" (1913, 55). The statement is a little puzzling, since Boccioni's sculptures are not easily mistaken for sonnets or for sonatas.

The scandal of separate arts has to some extent died away, in that to be only a painter or only a sculptor nowadays is in some circles taken as assigning one to a backwater of the art world, the main current (or *cloaca maxima*) of art history passing through those artists who are only artists—or, as others would say, through sculptors who are *not even* sculptors. At its worst, the scandal was not gravely embarrassing: specialism was easily explained away by considerations of institutional convenience, as we have seen. Theorists who, like Michael Fried, insist that serious works of art must be firmly related to specific arts are evidently adherents of the classical line and opponents of the poetic line, whatever terminology they may use.

27. It is unclear whether Brighton wishes to make the transition from the excellence of the performer as such to the excellence of the person who performs. If the distinction were present to his mind (as it probably is not), it seems unlikely that he would want to make the transition; but, if he does not, his position is rather hard to make out.

28. In case it is not obvious, consider that if his works are absolutely novel, they

must be novel *to him*, issuing from him therefore inexplicably. Others may conjecture, but he knows for certain, that they have no recognizable antecedents.

Chapter XI. The Expressive Line
1: Art as Expression

1. One of the basic theses of the expressive line is that the artist cannot know beforehand what his work of art will be, because the knowledge of what it is is the work itself. Conception cannot precede execution, says Merleau-Ponty, because only thoughts already uttered are clear: "There is nothing but a vague fever before the act of artistic expression, and only the work itself, completed and understood, is proof that there was *something* rather than *nothing* to be said" (Merleau-Ponty 1964, 19). Note that the "act of artistic expression" is spoken of here as though it were instantaneous and indivisible. Obviously a composer who has finished a movement for a symphony (one thinks of Walton's first, of which the first three movements were performed some years before the finale was composed) knows that there was *something* to be said; and so must Milton have known halfway through *Paradise Lost*, even if no one book had been perfected beyond the need of revision. Similarly, Beethoven's notebooks suggest that the point at which one knows there was something to be said is not the point at which the work is completed. Even an *uncompletable* work, as Schubert's "Unfinished" Symphony may have been, may not be one in which there was nothing to be said, but only one in which closure was precluded. Like many exponents of the expressive line, Merleau-Ponty is for the moment equating works of art with lyric fragments, gestures, lightning sketches—I say "for the moment," because he has just been discussing that slow and laborious worker, Cézanne, of whom it would be strange to say that his inability to resolve his canvases left open the possibility that there was "nothing to be said."

2. The average man, says Naum Gabo, "is convinced that on his judgment depend the value and the existence of the work of art. He does not suspect that through the mere fact of its existence a work of art has already performed the function for which it has been made and has affected his concept of the world regardless of whether he wants it to or not. The creative processes in the domain of Art are as sovereign as the creative processes in Science" (1937, 105). Someone who thought the fine arts imitated nature in its processes of creation might say that, except that on that view the new creation would not affect everyman's concept of the world. It is on the expressive line that the new work represents a new possibility of thought that as such affects the whole structure of thought and perception as a new scientific theory affects science as a whole. Gabo is, of course, coming on rather strong.

3. Note that Tormey is concerned with the English word, which is scarcely relevant to the expressive line, in which "expression" functions as a translation of the German *Ausdruck* and Italian and French texts have played a larger part than English.

4. According to Tormey, the core of the "expression theory" of art is the thesis that "if art object O has expressive quality Q, then there was a prior activity C of the artist A such that in doing C, A expressed his F for X by imparting Q to O (where F is a feeling state and Q is the qualitative analogue of F)" (1971, 103). No doubt such views have been held, but the thesis as stated is neither any version of the expressive line nor anything we found it necessary to explore in the classical line: it is a causal theory about the genesis of aesthetic properties. (The closest we

623

came to it was in saying that one interpretation of the expression or feeling vocabulary was to hold that the attribution of such a property to a work of art was to postulate the corresponding feeling in the artist.) It is, however, questionable whether the expressive line can actually avoid adopting this thesis, despite its repudiation of it: the avoidance depends on finding either substitutes for or suitably nonreductive interpretations of Tormey's "expressive quality," "prior activity," "expressing one's F for X," "imparting Q to O," "feeling state," and "qualitative analogue," all of which insinuate a sturdy Lockian metaphysics that no adherent of the expressive line would espouse.

5. Croce writes: "If one examines some poetical work with the intent of arriving at what it is that makes us describe it as poetical, two elements are immediately recognized as being constant and necessary in a poem: a complex of images, and a feeling which inspires this. . . . But they are not to be thought of as two strands, not even as two closely interwoven strands, because in effect the feeling has been wholly converted into images, the complex of images which we have recalled; it is a feeling which has been contemplated and therewith resolved and surpassed. Poetry, then, is neither feeling, nor image, nor the sum of these two, but is 'contemplation of feeling,' 'lyrical intuition,' or, what comes to the same, 'pure intuition' " (1928, 215-216). And he goes on to say that a work of any other art must in the same way be either "lyrical intuition" or something other than art. At first it looks as if this formulation must be a version of Tormey's formula cited in note 4, because he says the feeling has been converted, which suggests that the artist first had the feeling and then produced its qualitative analogue in the form of imagery. But then it appears that both the feeling and the imagery are accessible (inseparably) in the poem. On further reflection, it proves impossible to say what precisely is being asserted. I would like to think it was something like what stands in my text, that the image and the feeling are inseparable in that they are achieved in one and the same act.

6. O. K. Bouwsma's famous article, "The Expression Theory of Art" (1950), does not claim to deal with the specific doctrines of expression theorists, and operates solely within the ambit of the classical line; he is therefore subject to our strictures only because he evidently supposes there is no other line. John Hospers' masterly and magisterial article (1955), on the other hand, does purport to be relevant to such thinkers as Collingwood, and shows complete lack of understanding.

7. S. K. Langer's theory belongs to the classical line: it is indeed a singularly pertinacious attempt to develop a theory of art in terms of expression-as-imitation. But Langer does not use the word "expression"—wisely, one would have said, except that her preference for the word "symbol" ended by causing her at least as much trouble from critics as "expression" would have caused.

8. It is not only in aesthetics that philosophers support sophisticated positions by crude arguments and illustrations that, if taken seriously, would undermine them. An example is Leibniz's attempt to convey the sense of his thesis of the identity of indiscernibles by inviting someone to see for himself that no two blades of grass on a lawn were exactly alike.

9. This impulse is represented in a very pure form by the seventeenth-century writer Chin Sheng-t'an: "Poetry is nothing extraordinary; it is only the words which rise from the heart and lie at the tip of the tongue, and which everyone cannot help longing to utter. The scholars, making use of the ten thousand volumes they have studied thoroughly in their lifetime, cut such words into form and embellish them with elegance. . . . How can the number of words and lines in a poem be

limited? Poetry is a sudden cry from the heart, which comes to everyone, even a woman or a child, in the morning or at mid-night. . . . If every piece must have eight lines and every line must have five or seven syllables, how can that be called poetry?" (Liu 1962, 73-75).

10. I say "in a sense" because in another way the meaning of a word in a context depends on the context: our general understanding of what the words and constructions in a passage mean and can mean establishes a sense for the passage as a whole, which then reciprocally determines a more precise meaning for each word. If it were not for this "hermeneutic circle," poems could not have the character the expressive line assigns to art.

11. The notion of a "unitary complex" sounds perverse, even contradictory, but the notion is necessary and not difficult. What is grasped or intuited is grasped as a single whole, not reducible to parts in relation; but it cannot be such that no distinctions can be discerned in it, no structure ascribed to it.

12. How "language use" has to be defined for this to be true is a nice question. Syntactical variability, the use of symbols in no fixed causal relation with the environment, the distinction between sense and reference, and making the symbol system itself an object of conscious thought and manipulation might be necessary features. Since we are not ourselves trying to develop a theory in the expressive line, we may leave the issue undetermined: all that is required is that one take as a criterion of humanity language use as *somehow* defined, and then argue that language use as thus defined requires language creation.

13. The original formulation of the line, as of so much else, may be the work of Vico: "Men at first feel without perceiving, then they perceive with a troubled and agitated spirit, finally they reflect with a clear mind. This axiom is the principle of poetic sentences, which are formed by feelings of passion and emotion, whereas philosophic sentences are formed by reflection and reasoning. The more the latter rise toward uniformity, the closer they approach the truth; the more the former descend to particulars, the more certain they become" (1744, §§218-219). We note that Vico here espouses the Platonic (and anti-Aristotelian) equation of particularity and sensuality. A basic impulse of the expressive line in its mature form is to reverse this equation, and affirm that the universal and general must always be blurred (like a composite photograph) and only the individual can be clearly cognized. Then, since one cannot after all equate emotion and intellect in joint opposition to perception and intuition of individuals, one says that general truths have as their natural concomitant diffuse feelings, and precise feelings are correlated with sharp vision.

14. One's personal language, as thus conceived, is a combination of an idiolect with an individual manner of using the common language. One's own language is a modification of the common language in precisely the same way that one's way of life is an individual version of the way of life shared by one's community: in learning the folkways, one learns to be an individual and could not learn either without learning the other.

15. We have here the makings of a paradox. If a symbol is merely routine, it will not draw attention to itself, but will leave our attention free to attend to what it symbolizes. Conversely, a symbol that is novel, such as the expressive symbols we are here concerned with, will draw attention to itself and thus be opaque: "A man that looks on glasse, on it may stay his eye; or, if he pleaseth, through it passe, and then the heav'n espie." So the new, expressive symbol, so far from capturing the experience it was meant to symbolize, becomes a substitute for it; it is clichés that leave us free to dwell on the quality of the experience itself.

The paradox fails to come off, because it supposes that symbol and symbolized are separable, which is what the expressive line denies: in drawing attention to itself, the symbol *is* revealing its meaning. Whether the cost of thus avoiding the paradox is intellectually acceptable is one of the key questions to be faced in accepting or rejecting the expressive line.

16. This thesis may be dismissed as a piece of mystification. But if one thus dismisses it, one is committed to saying that my understanding of something someone says to me is normally reducible without remainder to the separate meanings of the identifiable constituents of the utterance and the statable relationships in which they stand, and presumably also to saying that, in speaking or painting or composing a piece of music, the proper focus of my attention is the individual notes, words, brush strokes, and so on, which I combine. This is not mystification but sheer idiocy. However, though not a mystification, the statement in the text is not illuminating.

17. One implication of this thesis is that art and language are in some way *opposed* to any experience that is not expressed in them. Thus, Conrad Fiedler writes: "Artistic activity begins when man . . . grapples with the twisted mass of the visible which presses in upon him and gives it creative form" (1876, 46; cf. chap. 3, n.88). The true artist, he adds, cannot acquiesce in this phenomenal chaos: "He does not release his perceptual experiences until they are developed into a visual conception, clear in all its parts, something that has attained a complete, necessary existence" (ibid., 58).

18. The history and bibliography of these interwoven themes far exceeds my ability, as well as my intent; but perhaps the nearest thing to an exploitation of the Aristotelian insight in the expressive line is that of Humboldt: language in general supplies the a priori framework of cognition; a given language articulates the cultural experience of its speakers, so that a given utterance is meaningful by its relation to the whole of experience (cf. Steiner 1975, chap. 2, esp. 81-82). The unity of interlocking meaning and value that Aristotle ascribes to a human life is here ascribed to the totality of the users of a language (the thought is already inherent in Aristotle's relation, stated in the *Politics*, of the individual to a society [*polis*] in which alone he can live, and in which language serves as the integrator of values). It is characteristic of the expressive line that it refuses to distinguish between language in general and art in general (cf. n. 22, below). It may be inferred from Humboldt's position that the individuality of any performance or utterance or intuition or work of art is illusory, and the inference is often drawn. But it is not legitimate. In Lukács' terms, the individual is a special focus for the universal; an utterance says just what it says in the language it uses—it does not *affirm* the whole structure in terms of which it is articulated. Difficulties arise only when expressions like "absolute origin" are used and insisted on without qualification, so that the claim of uniqueness, just because it is unqualified, becomes empty.

19. Baumgarten (1735, §15) used Leibniz's distinction of three grades of perception: distinct (logically articulated), obscure (unformed), and, between them, clear perceptions that have definite form but lack logical articulation (cf. Croce 1932, 435-438).

20. The appellation "confused" is question begging because that word definitely implies some mixing of one entity or quality with another, and there is no a priori reason to suppose that logical distinctions are prerequisite to the separation of the separate. Plato's familiar argument from the *Republic*, from which all this line of thought ultimately stems, relies wholly on the fact that what one calls something

depends on what language one uses and the context in which one is speaking: a particular person, though just the size he is, will be "tall" in one population and "short" in another, so that the distinction between the short and the tall depends on one's conceptual scheme and is systematically confused by perception. The reference to "confusion" is to be justified by the consideration that "just the size he is" is not given to perception, for one would never notice if his height increased by .01 millimeter.

The supposition that intuitions can be distinct because they have *some* quality of being just-this-and-not-anything-else (though not one capturable by the intellectual stipulations of a notational scheme) that is different from the "clarity" (nothing obscure, hidden, not-worked-out) that intuitions were already conceded to have may be hard to make good. Perhaps one could develop an argument that an intuition as such, being a mental content, can be distinct, though an external form in which it is embodied cannot. But I would not myself care to undertake that assignment.

21. It is often argued that psychological hypotheses of this sort are irrelevant to philosophy. But that need not be so: the status of such hypotheses is obscure. It may be that they stand for a convergence of conceptual reformation, hermeneutic congruence, and observation. Infatuated with a programmatically falsified view of the physical sciences, many thinkers were led to a premature insistence on an experimental testing of specific hypotheses that only becomes relevant at an advanced stage in the general ordering of a field of thought. Until that stage is reached, intellectual progress may depend on an informal reordering of views in the light of observations and objections adduced on no other system than a sense of ease or constraint. Fortunately, the heyday of premature experimentalism seems to have waned.

22. Some of Croce's later writings have been thought to move in the direction of psychologism and expressivism, though this may be an illusion—it is not clear whether one has to do with a change of mind or only a change of topic or a modification of rhetoric. In any case, I shall assign to those writings a secondary position, as I will to R. G. Collingwood (1938). Collingwood's is by far the subtlest, richest, and philosophically most profound version of the expressive line, but for that very reason does not lend itself well to generalizing expositions. Collingwood wrote to Croce about *Principles of Art* as follows:

> If you should read the book, you will find that the doctrine taught in it is in all essentials your own, as I have learned it from you and reconstructed it in my own mind, in terms of my own experience, over a period of many years: for my central theme is the identity of art and language, and my book is nothing but an exposition of that theme and some of its implications. In a few particulars I have modified or even controverted doctrines maintained in your original *Estetica*, but always in the belief that my modifications are true to the spirit of your own work and to the principles of which you have given us the classical exposition (Donagan 1962, 315-316).

Collingwood's estimation of the relationship is so generally accepted that it is almost usual to refer to "the Croce-Collingwood theory of art"; but it is doubtful whether it is correct. I will remark on some points at which Collingwood's modifications seem crucial.

23. Theoretically, it is doubtful whether this learning should be necessary. On one view, it is merely a short cut: it is irrelevant that the Greek painters of El Greco's youth painted thus; we are misled into thinking it relevant by the equally irrelevant

historical fact that the Venetian painters and their successors did not. On another view, it is like learning the language a poem is written in, a task that is continuous with learning just how the poet's contemporaries used that language. But it becomes hard to see how such historical reconstruction (which Croce himself thought of as the critic's prime function) is compatible with the rigors of the expressive line.

24. The world may be experienced as beautiful in moments when its total order seems evident or its disorder is envisaged in a context of order. To see the world as beautiful is a necessary condition of honest deism, as to feel it as good is a necessary condition of honest theism; but it is not a sufficient condition, for the perceived beauty may reflect a Faustian triumph of egoistic will.

25. Trevor-Roper's study (1970) of the effects of defective vision on art argues persuasively that many artists' styles depend on mechanical defects in their eyes that impose on their vision a precise dimming or clouding, so that if the defect is removed (as by the removal of a cataract), the artist becomes unable to paint.

26. H. M. Sheffer used to urge his students, "Never say 'in some sense,' say in what sense" (*teste* T. A. Goudge). The sense in which our perception of the world has the status of intuition is that it is clear as a whole and in its parts and distinct in its parts (it is of course trivially distinct as a whole, or it would not be a world). The hedging "in some sense" is inserted because the notion of distinctness invoked is at best controversial and, further, it is by no means clear what is meant by speaking of perception of the world. A lot of work would have to be done before the relation between "awareness of the world" and intuition was clarified to the point where one could ask people to take it seriously; as yet, it remains little more than a rhetorical trope.

27. Collingwood says of consciousness that, "in attending to a present feeling, it perpetuates that feeling, though at the cost of turning it into something new, no longer sheer or crude feeling (impression) but domesticated feeling or imagination (idea)" (1938, 223). His use of the terms "impression" and "idea" is in conscious homage to Hume.

28. Croce wrote in a late paper: "Poetry cannot copy or imitate feeling, because feeling, which in its own sphere has form, is in the presence of art formless, indeterminate, chaos, and so on, since chaos is a mere negative moment, nothingness. Like every other spiritual activity, poetry, which creates the solution, creates therewith the problem, creates along with the form also the content as not formless but formed matter" (1935a, 277). The assertion that feeling in its own sphere has form but is nothingness in relation to art names the problem at the cost of making it apparently insoluble. Two alternative models are suggested: that of a formed something that becomes matter for a further form, like I-beams as material for a skyscraper, and that of formed somethings that sacrifice their form for another, like toy soldiers being melted down to make bullets. Neither seems apposite. If feelings are matter for art, they retain their form and their identity as feelings and are not nothingness. If they become formless and nothingness, what is meant by calling them feeling? One should rather speak of an indeterminately potential "life." A common-sense solution is: out of his diffuse mass of knowledge of many specific feelings and situations, the poet can imagine new specific feelings and situations; it is his knowledge of *indefinitely* multiple specificities that enables the artist to envisage new ones. But the trouble with that solution is that it reduces intuitions to the exact epistemic level of the impressions from which they rise, and thus reduces to a commonplace form of the classical line. I don't know what Croce meant.

29. According to Matthew Lipman, art is an ordering process (he defines a process

as "a spatio-temporal context in which so profound a qualitative transformation occurs that the whole can be discriminated against the background of other natural events") that produces "an order which is unified and harmonious. It proceeds, that is to say, from a state which is felt as somehow unsatisfactory to one which is eminently enjoyable" (1967, 14-15).

30. I have developed this theme further in "Speculation and Reflection" (Sparshott 1972).

31. The fact that Socrates does not see the problem does not mean that Plato has no solutions to offer. Fundamentally, Plato (in *Protagoras, Phaedo,* and *Republic*) offers a hierarchy of rationales for behavior that roughly complies with current moral standards: social conditioning, hedonistic calculation of one's long-term interests as an individual, concern for mental health (moral deviance being associated with mental imbalance), prudent calculation of long-term advantage in a social context, "justice" or objective calculation of the ad hoc requirements of a situation, ascetic indifference to personal advantage, and a vision of the entire structure of the world as a fact-value system. Since most people have a sound practical grasp of what is right and wrong to do (otherwise human societies could not have survived), all these rationales support approximately the same behavior in most cases. This remote harmony, however, does not solve the Socratic problem, which is based on the assumption of ignorance, and it has no bearing at all on the analogous problem that is our concern, because a main tenet of the expressive line is that art neither justifies nor is justified.

32. Langer's theory *as a whole* cannot be pressed into the service of the expressive line. In making specific arts and art forms symbolic of designated modes of feeling, she commits herself to the classical line, and incidentally gives her critics the opening they require.

33. One might argue that the very use of the word "perceive" constitutes a claim that the object is independently there to be perceived and, in some way, *as* perceived. But whether such a claim is really implied, and just what the claim would amount to, are difficult issues that do not affect our argument here.

34. One may, and often does, have strong hunches that this or that episode reflects something in the artist's personal life, and unwary exponents of the expressive line may adduce these in evidence. But it is unwise to do so. You and I and everyone who isn't a congenital idiot may know perfectly well, from the suddenly rancorous tone, the out-of-key vividness, the out-of-character remark, the overindulgent narration, that for the nonce the person has taken over from the artist; but we can't prove it, and what we observe is the defect or oddity in the work, the rancor, the indulgence, the discrepancy. I think it is, as my examples suggest, in failures that our hunches are strongest: in a success there should be nothing to notice. And perhaps one should concede that, with failures, the expressive liner can make his hunches true *ex hypothesi.* What sticks out is what is not integrated into the work; and since the author of the work did write it, what is not integrated pertains to him, not as one who intuits, but, necessarily, as a person, the liver of a personal life.

35. For a critique of "covering law" explanations in history, see Dray (1957). For "narrative connection," see Gallie (1964).

36. Collingwood's work in fact suggests not two but three models. First, there is the passage from crude feeling as psychological disturbance to the expressed (cognitively saturated) form of that feeling; then there is the development from inchoate expression to fulfilled expression, with no suggestion that the initial stage is a

significant event in the artist's life; and finally there is the psychological transition from arbitrary impression to an epistemologically original intuition and its expression.

37. The third level, with its emotional charge, is important for two reasons. First, it allows for genuine works of art with a discursive content (like the *Divine Comedy*). Second, it allows for a vertical integration of meaningful life: any kind of thinking, at any level of reference or self-reference, may have the unitary significance of conscious experience, just as it may enter into the diffuse background of the psychic. Unless we adduce some such considerations, the expressive line risks relapsing into the romantic taste for the simple gesture and the lyric cry. (I assume that it is a risk; obviously for those who endorse it, it is no relapse but a recovery of truth.)

38. A role for the impression turns up, in a central but much misunderstood passage of Collingwood's book, at the level of reimpression (see n. 54, below).

39. Collingwood's most impressive treatment of this theme is that of the posthumous *Idea of Nature* (1945). In his earlier work, he wrote that a philosopher

> trying to determine the general nature of knowledge . . . might assume that anything which could be called knowledge at all, however humble or elementary a kind of knowledge, could be relied upon to exhibit that general nature as well as any other. Philosophers as it were instinctively avoid this way of approaching a question, because they feel that the full nature of anything is exemplified only in the highest forms of it. . . . And because the lower in a scale of forms is in some sense opposed to the higher, they realize that a theory proceeding on this assumption is likely to find itself maintaining that the highest forms of knowledge, morality, art, and so forth are not forms of knowledge and the like at all (1933, 113-114).

Applying this pattern, we see that an impression as first phase of a developing intuition could be contrasted with the developed intuition it becomes: identity and opposition are identified as well as opposed. Although it is conceivable that Collingwood would have wished to apply his version of dynamic development in this way, it is not clear that he did so, or how he thought the application would be carried out if he did.

40. Although Heidegger is customarily related to his master Husserl in the phenomenological movement, his later thought may with equal justice be regarded as an eddy in the mainstream of German romanticism: his sentimental antiquarianism and his fascination with Hölderlin are central to his thinking. "Language is the primordial poetry (*Urdichtung*) in which a people speaks being," he says (1961, 146), and "The thinker utters Being. The poet names what is Holy" (1943, 391). But when it comes to clarifying such gnomes, he maintains a passionate reticence. If the end of authentic existence is *poetic dwelling*, in which one preserves the earth, receives heaven, and waits on the divine (cf. Langan 1959, 125ff.), art (all of which is an original poetizing) preserves a true relation to an underlying established reality; but of course the "dwelling" might be related to that reality as a house to bricks, rather than as an inhabited cave to the same cave when vacant. No doubt Heidegger would say that to press for clarity or a choice between options betrays a preference for artificial systems and an estrangement from Being: philosophical *thinking (Denken)* is to be a form of incantation. The closing paragraphs of this section acknowledge that, even in terms of the expressive line in general, his strategy could be right.

41. In effect, one is arguing here that Collingwood's "psychic level" does not exist

or has no resources or has no systematic significance. One should bear in mind that not all layering theories of the human mind support the expressive line: for instance, the thesis that conscious mental processes are a superficial layer over an unconscious mass do not do so, if conscious determinants are judged superficial, as they usually are. One can hold, too, that the ability to invent language is the crucial distinction between man and other animals, or is one aspect of the cortical development that marks that distinction, without committing onself to anything that looks like the expressive line.

On the evolutionary scale, Jacques Monod argues that language may literally have made man: a comparatively small development of the brain would make rudimentary language possible, and, once such language was in use, it would confer an immense selective advantage on linguistic skill and thus lead rapidly to the development of strains with increased capacities for language—in other words, homo sapiens (Monod 1969, 15-16; cited from Steiner 1975, 128).

42. Practically the same distinction as that between success and failure of attention is unexceptionable in slightly different theoretical frameworks: for instance, between the "everyday" and "authentic" existence. There we do indeed have alternative modes of living in the world.

43. "I cannot define my perception of a thing without *virtually* drawing it, and I cannot draw it without a willed intention which *strikingly transforms what I thought I had seen and knew well already*. It dawns on me that I did not know what I knew: even my best friend's nose" (Valéry 1960, 36).

44. Lynton Lamb observes:

Visual imagination not only differs between individuals, it differs fundamentally in kind between writers and artists. Writers can suggest through words mental images that remain with us *as* mental images. For artists, the "ability" to draw is not merely an extra manual skill: it is a creative ability to see and analyse *those things that the hand can finally materialize*; so that this final act becomes much more than "transference" of an idea to paper. It is its creation in a visible form, rather than an echo of something already existing in the mind. The visual imagination of an artist and his ability to draw are thus interlocked: it is the knowledge of what he *can* draw that prompts a vision of what he should.

Even for those who write and illustrate their own books, the two kinds of visualization are different. . . . Drawing evokes a visual image from my *paper* by the cross-tension of lines and dots and touches; writing forms an image in my *head* through the associations of the words I set down (Lamb 1962, 44).

Lamb's position (he writes novels as well as drawing) is subtle and complex. It combines two separate points: an artist sees analytically in terms of his capacity to draw in general and in terms of his future drawing, and the image as it will be drawn is not itself produced by this analysis, but is created on paper by the interaction of marks as they are made. That is, one can know what one will draw and what one's drawing will be like, but cannot know just what it will be. No one, to my knowledge, has yet produced a version of the expressive line the spirit of which does not violate this duality.

45. Collingwood (1938, 300-302). His critics almost always neglect this explicit repudiation, presumably because they only read part 1 of his book in which the significance of the repudiation does not become apparent.

46. In his *Autobiography*, Collingwood congratulates himself on having learned

from his early acquaintance with painters what many philosophers of art never learn: no work is ever finished; the artist simply runs out of time (1939, 2). So far is the achievement of an intuition from being the artist's personal transition from painful darkness to the certainty of peace and light.

There is a close parallel between the artist whose friends must drag him away from the easel to prevent his spoiling a work that everyone except himself can see is finished and the chimpanzee artist whose keeper must snatch its brushes away at the crucial moment when its aesthetic sense is about to give way to its delight in motor activity (cf. Gombrich 1979, 13)—a situation of which I was first apprised by the late Sir Herbert Read, and to which I have alluded above (chap. 6, n. 15).

47. Can we apply the analogy to literature and say that a poet has not completed his poem until he has actually recited it or written it down? It seems not, for at least three reasons. First, words as such are not visibilia or audibilia—if they were, a written word could not be the same as the "same" word spoken, and it would be impossible to read a written text aloud. Second, it may be argued that the object of the literary artist's work is not the token but the type; and, third, if the former two fail to convince, it is alleged that running through words in one's mind is often if not always accompanied by subliminal movements of the speech organs, so that in this sense the poem that has been thought through has already been spoken though not uttered.

48. If Goodman is right in saying that the nature of pictorial symbolization is such that there can be no theoretical limit to the visual aspects of a painting that may prove relevant to its interpretation and appreciation, so that not even the artist can be certain that two apparently identical versions of his painting do not have differences that later connoisseurs will see and find significant (1968, chap. 3), externalization cannot be indifferent even to the limited extent that the text here implies. If a painter necessarily paints more than he knows he paints (though he may be subliminally aware of more than he knows), it follows that it is logically impossible for him to know in advance exactly what he will paint. But Goodman's whole approach is radically incompatible with any version of the expressive line.

49. I cannot imagine what the different ways that affect its nature as clear and distinct idea would be. In fact, it seems to be logically impossible that I should be able to imagine them—the impossibility is like that incurred by TV commercials that purport to show that the color of the advertised set is better than the color of the viewer's own set. But that does not matter. The formal possibility is all that concerns us here.

50. For some artists, the same may be true in allographic arts: in *SA* I cited Stravinsky (1942, 54) on the importance of the experience of working with musical materials. But with "psychological necessity" it is hard to get beyond the beliefs of individuals about themselves.

51. My colleague Geoffrey Payzant (1970) reports that string players hear music, as it were, through their hands, in terms of the positions their hands would adopt to produce the notes they hear. Mechanical tinkering with the sounds they hear can produce acute mental discomfort, since their ears and their hands in fact report different notes. Are we to say that it is only psychologically, not logically necessary that only a string player could be affected in this way? And can we really believe that someone who experiences music in this way will not inevitably write for strings otherwise than someone who does not? Well, but if that is so, a sufficiently informed person should be able to tell from any piece of music for strings whether the

composer was himself a string player or not; and this, so far as I am aware, has never been seriously made out. (Perhaps it follows only that any string-playing composer for strings composes for strings otherwise than he himself would were he not such a player, but not in any way that can be generalized.) What does seem to follow from such data is that, though the structure of a piece of music may be the same for all informed listeners, its precise musical character cannot be the same for all. One must then either say that intuitions for strings are only accessible to string players (or, alternatively, only to those who are not string players), or concede to musical designs an ambiguity of a sort peculiarly hard for the expressive line to assimilate (because the ambiguity cannot itself be an aesthetic feature).

In any case, the phenomena to which Payzant refers do not quite meet the case, for the physical involvement is not direct: it is enough that one know what it is to play a stringed instrument, and thus feel in one's hand what one hears; it is not necessary that one be playing at the time. And then one is inclined to retort to Bosanquet in Dewey's words: "Whether a musician, a painter, or architect works out his original emotional idea in terms of auditory or visual imagery or in the actual medium as he works is of relatively minor importance. For the imagery is of the objective medium undergoing development" (1934, 75). And indeed Bosanquet can only say what he does because he is *imagining* the difference between painting and imagining.

It seems that all we have here is a very special case of the contention (see Wollheim 1968, 37) that an artist's intuitions depend on knowledge of his actual medium, so that Crocean intuitions in the area of fine art are parasitic on physical works of art. That is no skin off Croce's nose.

52. This point has a strong family resemblance to the kind of argument Wittgenstein (1953) used to establish the impossibility of a language that would be (in some sense) private. It is, accordingly, highly controversial. If one can be deluded about the completeness of an intuition, can one not be equally deluded about the evidence of one's eyes, or the evidence of one's ears, when one hears one's friends congratulating one on another completed work? What kind of *serious* doubt would an externalization be needed to allay? It is not altogether easy to say.

53. The essential point, to my mind, is that of risk. The artist is, in a way that his critic is not, responsible for his achievement. The artist courts, as the critic does not, despair, disaster, and humiliation.

54. The chance becomes less improbable if the artist lives as a full member of a closely knit community. Collingwood, contrary to popular opinions about him, maintains that it is an artist's prime duty to share the life of his time, so that the emotions he expresses will be those of the community of which he is the voice; it is the perversion of art for artists to live in esoteric cliques, so that the experience to which their intuitions relate is one remote from most people's lives (1938, 311ff.). In assigning a public duty to the artist, Collingwood is sometimes thought to be whimsically contradicting his essential distinction between art (which knows no distinction between means and end, and allows the artist no purpose other than that of pure expression) and craft. But that is not at all the case. Collingwood is not saying that an artist must set about saying what people want to hear, or make verses about what he reads in the papers. He is saying that, in taking on the vocation of artist, an artist must make himself such that his pure expression will spontaneously relate to the life of his place and time. It is not that he must strive or pretend to see this or that; it is that he must place himself where what he sees will most aid the hampered

vision of others. And why must he? Is this a moral imperative? That is not clearly explained. I think it is partly a matter of social duty, partly a matter of the epistemological function of clarifications.

55. Croce's position stems from a critical reflection on Hegel in almost as direct a fashion as Collingwood's does from a critical reflection on Croce. See Croce (1906).

Chapter XII. The Expressive Line
2: Arts, Works, Artists

1. Hume's own argument is tricky. The status of the concession that an experienced enjoyment is grounded on a principle is dubious. When it is pointed out that the principle in question should guarantee the appreciation of the work whose credentials are in dispute, what is to prevent one from saying that one's experienced lack of appreciation in this case proves that the grounding principle cannot after all be what explained one's enjoyment of the first work? If someone tells me that what explains my liking of honey is its stickiness, so I ought to like castor oil because that is sticky, too, I shall reply that my dislike of castor oil suffices to prove that the stickiness of honey cannot explain my liking it.

2. Parker (1939) makes a public dimension one of three criteria of a work of art: his intention is to set art off from daydreams. He leaves the nature of this social or public requirement entirely open; his instinct for vagueness here annoys some readers, but I think he is right.

3. Lord Clark's television series on *Civilization* shows at once how it is tempting and possible to dismiss the weight of culture as a confidence trick, and how difficult it is. How all too obvious, and how all too impressive, those well-worn images were! With what genial hospitality our host showed us round the mansion of culture where people like him dwell and people like us only visit! And what a relief to reflect that simply by *not being educated* one could escape all that lumber and be born again into the life of authentic urban squalor. But all the time I was actually looking, I was convinced beyond argument and moved beyond resistance.

A more single-minded reaction, and one that incidentally sheds some light on Michael Fried's distinction between "art" and "theater" to which I so often refer, is displayed in Jeff Nuttall's *Bomb Culture*:

> One knew that, say, the Belvedere *Apollo* was "Art," and one knew that the part one had to play was "Awestruck." This prevented any enjoyment. Shatter the *Apollo*, and the pieces, being no longer "Art," were as wonderful and enjoyable as pebbles on a beach (1968, 97).

Well, one might say, that's what you get for letting the public into museums (see chap. 10, n. 20). Certainly, it is proverbially reassuring to know that there are "plenty more pebbles on the beach." But one might wonder if, supposing one had not been told about having to play the part of "Awestruck," something might not have been lost rather than gained by shattering the Apollo, or if Nuttall really thinks a nice piece of marble was ruined when someone carved an Apollo out of it. . . . Suppose one were to write as follows:

> One knew that, say, Jeff Nuttall was "Human," and one knew that the part one had to play was "Polite." This prevented any enjoyment. Cut Jeff up, and the

pieces, being no longer "Human," were as wonderful and appetizing as joints in a butcher's showcase.

The analogy is not, admittedly, exact.

4. Presumably what Collingwood means by different degrees of embodiment is the kind of complex hierarchy of arts in terms of adequacy of matter to form that Hegel (1835) elaborated, most recently manifested in Lévi-Strauss's resuscitation of the argument that music is the supreme art because, instead of superimposing a cultural code on a natural one, its coding is cultural at both levels (Lévi-Strauss 1964, 15-30).

5. See chapter 2, note 15. A more superficial distinction between internalized technique and applied craftsmanship, involving our distinction between primary and secondary standards, is drawn in the following statement by Avner Zis:

> It would be wrong to confuse technique and mere craftsmanship: the artist's technique indicates the degree to which he has mastered the expressive means of his art, while mere craftsmanship, implying the demonstration of an artist's technical resources, is found where true art is lacking. . . . When Alexander Blok came to the conclusion that he was able to write poetry too well, he started wondering if he ought not to stop writing poetry altogether for a time. He was frightened that skilled craftsmanship might be the death of his poetry. . . . While skill lends a work superficial character, true mastery is essential for it to achieve depth. Craftsmanship is by no means the same thing as true mastery, just as the means of expression and representation in art should not be identified with artistic form. The means of expression and representation used by the artist are only ingredients of form (1977, 142-143).

6. Misunderstanding of the nature of recursive originality, in which assimilated expressions serve as impressions from which new expressions may spring, seems to be one of the origins of the thesis that art in every age but the earliest becomes its own subject. One may argue, as Northrop Frye does, that every beginning poet derives from existing poems the realization that there are such things as poems, and what they are, and what they could now be, without going on to assert that every poem is in fact about other poems. The fatal further step seems to be taken by Harold Bloom in *The Anxiety of Influence* (1973), according to which every "strong" poet (hardly a neutral qualification, though a very obscure one) defines himself by his difference from some great predecessor, exactly (and damagingly) like the mythical newcomer in an American schoolyard who is expected to make himself at home by punching up the reigning bully. And, as we have observed before, Jack Burnham points out that excessive consciousness of the history of art leads the artist to the realization that the only true works are original works, and originality is defined by the uniqueness of one's place in the history of art, so that at any moment there can be but one true and necessary work, that which takes the next step in that history—and this is at least enough for any mortal artist to think of, so that artistic energy exhausts itself in defining a relation to "the history of art so far," which thus becomes the sole content of the work.

7. Croce, as we have seen, acknowledges this point in saying that feeling is fully formed in its own realm. But it is not easy to see what he thinks follows, and what he thinks does not follow, from this.

8. I do not think this position can be satisfactorily worked out. But there is no harm in trying.

9. Adorno (1970, 65) is among those who have pointed to the utility of traditions and genres as making art possible by limiting the range of necessary choice. Note that in the expressive line, as opposed to the classical line, the distinctness of "this and not that" must be, not "this *as opposed to* that," but an emphatic "this and nothing else" that battens on a learned sharpness of focus.

10. It is tempting to invoke a Hegelian dialectic and say that the identity of the feeling is given up only to be regained at a higher level. But that won't work. The dialectic will not permit just *anything*. In this case, the transformation will not work either way. If the inner feeling is on a higher level than the outward expression, then the expression was not an expression at all but a symptom. If it is at a lower level, criticism has nothing to gain by reconstructing it; it belongs to the "impression."

11. To put forward such a thesis one needs a certain courage in eccentricity. Elijah Jordan had the right qualifications (1952, 48; quoted at *SA* 416n.). So does Frances A. Yates, who writes of Giordano Bruno:

> He creates inwardly the vast forms of his cosmic imagination, and when he externalizes these forms in literary creation, works of genius spring to life, the dialogues which he wrote in England. Had he externalized in art the statues which he moulds in memory, or the magnificent fresco of the images of the constellations which he paints in the *Spaccio della bestia trionfante*, a great artist would have appeared. But it was Bruno's mission to paint and mould within, to teach that the artist, the poet, and the philosopher, are all one, for the Mother of the Muses is Memory. Nothing comes out but what has first been formed within, and it therefore is within that the significant work is done (1966, 305).

One is reminded of the mother who was convinced her little son would be good at languages, because he spoke such good broken English.

12. Arnold Schoenberg, when asked if he was the notorious composer, replied: "Somebody had to be, and nobody else wanted to, so I took on the job myself" (1964, 290). In a more solemn mood, he wrote to the American Academy of Arts and Letters in 1947 that "my own feeling was that I had fallen into an ocean of boiling water; and, as I couldn't swim and knew no other way out, I struggled with my arms and legs as best I could" (Stuckenschmidt 1959, 140).

13. On the most intractable of these difficult cases, that of the musical performer giving his own rendering of a work, Croce's followers at least took a hard line: they insisted that such a performer was a mere channel for the composer's intuition. See Fubini (1968, 216) and his references.

14. Relevant here is Isenberg's thesis, developed in his "Critical Communication" (1949), that a critic's descriptions are logically incomplete without the work described. The critic's words suggest that he is drawing inferences from the presence in the work of certain named or described features, the relevant nature of which could be inferred from what he says; but in fact what supports the inference is a perceived aspect of the work, which the critic's words help us to locate and make the ground of an appreciative judgment comparable to his own.

15. One suppressed difficulty of the expressive line in its pure form is that in fact only public art is exposed to criticism. Not only does the expressivist, as we have observed, organize his thinking around the approach accepted as proper to masterpieces of art, but his serious critical activity is carried out entirely within the public domain of art. Of course, expressions not in this domain are occasionally made the object of critical discourse, both within the thought-world of expressivism

and without; but such démarches have, transparently and without exception, the character of self-conscious journalistic ploys.

16. There are, certainly, writers, and quite eminent writers at that, of whom it is true. An egregious example is Lionello Venturi, who writes as follows:

> Artistic expression is not of concepts, since the formulation of concepts is the work of logic, but of sentiments—practical feeling, desire and will. Outside artistic activity beauty does not exist, because nothing exists outside spiritual activity. What is called beauty, when it is not an object of the senses, is only the perfection of art. Since the category of the beautiful does not exist, all the other categories of the laws of art, of kinds, of types fall to the ground; and the only reality of art is in the personality of the artist, as it is manifested in his works of art (1964, 325).

What is one to make of this argument? Obviously the words "logic" and "concept" are not used in the ways philosophers use them. Presumably what is meant by "concepts" is something like "propositions." But then the contrast between concepts and sentiments (as that word is used here) is absurd: desire and will (and presumably other "practical feelings," if they are to be of the same sort) are propositional attitudes: to desire or will is to desire or will that something take place, and the specification of what is to take place is no less a proposition than is an assertion of what has occurred or will occur. If all that is meant is that works of art are not as such records of the past or present or prophecies of the future, why should we go on to say that they must therefore express wishes and the like? Why should they not simply express intuitions, set forth visions and thoughts without any necessary commitment as to whether what is intuited answers to something to be feared, to be desired, or corresponding to some historical event? The contrast of concept and sentiment is factitious and the inference as unwarranted as what is inferred is inherently implausible.

Again, the reason for saying that beauty does not exist outside art is absurd. The thesis that nothing exists outside spiritual activity is one of metaphysical idealism; and, just because it applies to everything, it can have no specific consequences as applied to any one thing. (If all the suspects are left-handed, the fact that the murderer used his left hand cannot cast more suspicion on any one of them that it does on each of the others.) If nothing exists outside spiritual activity, then "what is called beauty" and is an "object of the senses" does not exist outside spiritual activity, though Venturi seems to concede that it exists outside artistic activity (as why should it not?). One does not see what is meant by saying that "the category of the beautiful does not exist" (Venturi has nothing to say about categories and their existence). If all he means is that the word "beauty" as applied to the objects of the senses (among which most people would include many works of art) and the same word as applied to the perfection of art are equivocal, in the same way that "bridge" is equivocal as applied to a card game and to a thing for suicides to dive off, then what he says is inherently incredible and quite unsupported by the preceding statement. Again, if Venturi thinks that, because beauty as the perfection of art has nothing to do with beauty as an object of the sense, it follows that one can no longer be justified in speaking of kinds, types, and laws of art (for I suppose that is what he means by saying that the associated "categories fall to the ground," as though their elastic had given way), he is mistaken. All that follows is that if there are such kinds and types, they cannot be kinds and types of the beauty that belongs to an object of the senses, and the laws could not be laws for achieving that beauty: we need a separate argument to show that there cannot be types or kinds of perfection in art and laws for achieving it or them. And finally, if beauty is the perfection of art and as such exists only in artistic activity, it would seem to follow that the reality of art cannot reside in the personality of the artist over and above his works of art. And, if it did, we would have to say that there can indeed be laws, types, and kinds of art, because art is assigned the task of manifesting personality, and this task, like other tasks, can be done well or ill, skillfully or unskillfully, in this way or in that way.

Part of Venturi's intention is by no means obscure. He wishes to find support for the contention that works of art are unique in a way that debars critics from applying preconceived notions or standards and, above all, sets of criteria of "beauty," "formal excellence," and the like. The contention is, as we have seen, popular, and many theorists have sought knockdown arguments in its favor; but it is hard to find a formulation that is free from objection. It looks as if what Venturi, an avowed disciple of Croce, has done is to rely on his mentor's prestige and venture a hastily allusive version of his doctrines without heeding the intellectual difficulties or paying regard to the necessity of avoiding tempting errors. We saw how careful Croce was (despite his vagueness on crucial points) to differentiate the "human roots" of the expressed feeling from the artist's personality, with which Venturi (and this, we may now recall, was the original reason for the citation that has occasioned this long diatribe) has equated it; and there is a celebrated chapter that Croce devotes to the distinction between Shakespeare's personal character and his artistic character (Croce 1920, 117-137; for a terser and blunter statement, see Croce 1935b, 141).

In general, Venturi's *History of Art Criticism*, with its touchingly naive trust in an infallible contemporary consciousness that is forever on his and Croce's side ("The history of aesthetics," Venturi writes, ". . . offers a fundamental and unquestionable critical nucleus. If not by a point, it could be represented by a line from Baumgarten to Croce" [1964, 325]), makes it startlingly evident that he, and probably Croce as well, is merely continuing the seventeenth-century *Querelle des anciens et des modernes*, with its associated rivalry between French and Italian approaches to music making.

17. And what does "really" mean in this connection? For some general remarks, see my "Is Reality Really Real?" (Sparshott 1972). The meaning here would be that everyman is not apparently an artist, because he does not do the things by which artists are recognized; but he is really one, because he does the things that makes artists artistic (like a king incognito who does not wear his crown or feed his corgis, but has state documents brought for his signature by hand of covert but trusty messenger). A closer analogy would be the scholastic thesis according to which everything that exists is, must be, really beautiful, because nothing can exist without beauty—but some things sure don't look like it, so we only call those things beautiful that *even we* can't help seeing beauty in. It is not that they are exceptionally beautiful, but that their beauty is of a kind conspicuous to us. Just so, the people we call artists are not more artists than other folk, but other folks' artistry is of a kind that, because ubiquitous, we don't notice.

18. One specific way in which every person is an artist relates to the public's capacity to frame an intuition from an artist's expression (cf. Collingwood 1938, 118-119). As impression, the externalization of such an expression may afford part of the basis for intuitions of one's own. But a person must also be supposed to have the capacity to penetrate the externalization and recapture (reintuit) the original intuition expressed. If the externalization is successful and undamaged, the pen-

etration required is minimal, and the word is used simply to acknowledge the logical gap between what the eye receives and what one intelligently sees with the eye. But the logical gap is important. The reintuition is presumably independent of any particular experience of contact with the externalization. But it can hardly be independent of such contact in general: the work must have been seen or heard one or more times, even it if makes only a contingently psychological difference what times and what sorts of times they were. But then the intuitive act of reintuition is not the same act as the original act of intuiting, because it is essentially an act of recovery and the other was not. So, logically, the act whereby one intuits another's expression is an original intuitive act, logically on a par with that of the original artist; and in this way the expressive line makes artists of us all. I do after all recompose the Shakespeare sonnet that I read, just as Pierre Menard rewrites *Don Quixote.*

What is wrong with this picture? Better you should ask what is right with this picture. I think the expressive line has no other expedient than to say that, after all, the intuition is the same, but the human achievement is less. It is causally, not epistemically, that the reintuition is linked to the externalization. If I land someone ten feet below the summit of Everest by helicopter, I have facilitated his reaching the summit, but I have not put him there. He has reached the top just as surely as Tenzing did. But it wasn't, in his case, much of an achievement (less, by a long way, than my flying a helicopter up there; but that is another story).

Croce points out that a poet can reexperience his own work years after he has written it, when he is a changed person; and he argues that if this is possible, it must be equally possible for anyone else who is suitably equipped and has the appropriate attitude to recapture the same intuition (1935a, 62). But one might well ask how one knows it is the same intuition that the poet himself recovers, or even what is meant by calling it the same. Like anyone else, the poet can read what he once wrote, and, if he has a good memory, he may recall (what other readers are unlikely to know) any specific associations and images that accompanied the writing and made it personally significant to him; he may also recall the circumstances of the writing and what his life felt like then. But this does not seem to me to add up to recapturing an original intuition.

19. The child, one might suggest, is not old enough to know corn when he sees it.

20. It is often said that the myth of childhood innocence, and of childhood itself, is coeval with romanticism. But Vaughan is earlier than that. Philippe Aries (1962) traces the idea of childhood back to the sixteenth century. But Jesus is earlier than that, and so is Plato.

21. A certain childlikeness is a common characteristic of artists in the English fiction of this century, for example, of John Bidlake in Huxley's *Point Counter Point.* As with Gully Jimson in Joyce Cary's *The Horse's Mouth*, the childlike vision is somewhat arbitrarily associated with (or symbolized by) a childish failure of socialization—the artist has not made the transition from the pleasure principle to the reality principle. In Bidlake, this childishness is connected with an immediate response to sensual impressions, transferring the artist's originality from the sphere of expression to that of impression (this is not true of Jimson)—but no doubt this is part of Huxley's presentation of Bidlake as a painter whose talent has failed him in old age just because he continues to rely on immediate sensation. Bidlake is closely modeled on the real attributes of Augustus John, as Holroyd's biography (1974) shows; but the selection of John as type figure probably owes more to the strength of the

antecedent stereotype than the stereotype owes to John, in view of the shaky nature of John's eventual achievement.

22. This notwithstanding Tennyson's comparison of himself to a child with "no language but a cry" and other eloquent testimonies by poets to their lack of linguistic resource.

23. We have already seen that the expressive line is torn not only between the idea that art is important as the humanizer of mankind and the idea that its significance lies in its representing the level of absolute epistemic origin but also between regarding originality as the achievement of a unified and underived intuition and regarding it as the fruit of unpremeditated lyrical or gestural spontaneity. The latter contrast is reflected in the distinction, and the failure to distinguish, between artistic originality and childish freshness (for this see also Berger, as quoted above, in chap. 6, n. 36). The same contrast may appear as that between expression and self-expression, as at the end of our quotation from Venturi in note 16, which continues: "The only reality of art is in the personality of the artist, as it is manifested in his works of art. There exist the individuality of the artist and the universal idea of art: between the individual and the universal there are no intermediate verities" (1964, 325). (The last point squares with our preferred version of Croce, except that for him the "individual" has to be the individual work, not the person of the artist.)

The nature of the value of "self-expression," often cited as what makes child art precious to the children and to all the pure in heart, is decidedly equivocal. The value cannot in any case be that of the individual self expressed, since the presumption is precisely that the child's self is as yet unformed: the value is that of artlessness; the expression is unforced and comes from inside rather than outside— it goes back to those Crocean roots of manhood (in this case, childhood) and is not contaminated by learned devices. On any other understanding, of course, self-expression bids fair to slip back into the classical line, in which the artist's skill lies (like that of Proust) in exploiting the resources of a subtle and subtly cultivated temperament.

In general terms, the concept of self-expression invites an Aristotelian conundrum. What is it that most truly expresses (reveals, exhibits) a man's character: what he does spontaneously or what he does most deliberately? Obviously the latter, because it embodies his most considered commitments; equally obviously the former, because he has no time to falsify the response that indicates what is now second nature to him. How do we choose between these two? The answer is easy: we do not choose. The spontaneous act reveals the core of his being, the deliberate one reveals his being in its comprehensiveness.

So too with art. We see now why the child's spontaneous output is valued as self-expression: the value is in the first instance therapeutic or recreational. The spontaneous act comes from the core, not from the comprehensiveness, of the child's being. In so coming, it affords relief from the heavy pressures of learning and socialization, which in the schooling process force a child always to live at the extremities of his being.

The psychology, pedagogy, and aesthetics of that position have been strongly attacked by Rudolf Arnheim (1954, 168; see *SA* 225-226): it traps the child, at an age when learning is life, within its own incompetence; and the complaint has been linked by Arendt (1961) with a general indictment of the educational ideologues who have been laboring to confine young people within the restrictive world of childishness. And one might add that the insistence on self-expression is not only bad pedagogy and worse aesthetics but is doubly dishonest. It is dishonest, first, because it is a covertly moral demand, the child's art combining the characters of therapy and confession and liable to be used against him by the hired manipulators of the school system; and, second, the test of whether the demand for spontaneous self-expression has been met is not actually one of directness and sincerity—how could it be? Only the child is judge of that, if anyone is. The test is whether what the child does conforms to the teacher's canons of self-expression as applied to that age group. In other words, the test is the strictly academic one of stylistic compliance, the style being laid down at the teacher's training college. The child has to learn a style, but he is not told that that is what he has to learn, nor can the style itself be justified in stylistic terms. The child has to pick up what he has to do, as best he can, from cues other than the teacher's instructions. (One is given to understand that the same pressure is imposed on students of art at some art schools: in the name of pure creativity, the teachers purport to withhold all guidance, but of course they do not withdraw their influence over the students' future careers, and the latter have to figure out what is expected of them in the absence of all cues. Many quit, or succumb to neurosis.)

Finally, to revert to the general topic of spontaneity and self-expression, if the child has no formed self to express, and certainly no artistic self to express, self-expression is not necessarily the same for him as it is for the mature artist. It is not clear whether the spontaneity demanded of a mature artist calls only for an unpremeditated quality in the expression at the moment of utterance, or whether it is required that no learning should have gone to its making. Both views raise difficulties. The first is open to the objection that the experienced practitioner of an art shows his experience and mastery precisely in the spontaneity of its exercise, in that he does not have to think about how to do what he knows so well how to do. The second is open to the objection that whatever any organism does cannot but be a function of its experience and habituation—no component of "original nature" can be isolated. The only question is what sort of function it will be and what sorts of experience and habituation enter into it in what ways. The difficulty of finding a theoretically satisfactory version of the contrast between the natural and the artificial in behavior, which intuitively seems obvious and easy, is one of the things that drives people to formulate a theory of expression in terms of epistemic primacy rather than psychological originality.

24. *On the Aesthetic Education of Man* (1795) made the aesthetic frame of mind the only one that is truly free and therefore truly human; however, this frame of mind is shown in the enjoyment of art no less than in its creation, so that the art lover would be as much a specialist in humanity as the artist.

25. The boundary that is seldom crossed is that between radically different aesthetic languages—sculptors, painters, and even potters will practice each other's arts on occasion as a sideline, but nothing in their art equips or encourages them to make a transition to verbal or musical expression. Of course, some visual artists write or compose; but so do some insurance salesmen.

Chapter XIII. The Mystic Line

1. It is only when the concept of art is envisaged basically as what is distinctive of the fine arts as such that it points ineluctably in this direction. The concept itself

grows to maturity and flourishes in the historical context of the Romantic movement, and can take on various colors from that protean context. Hermeticism and occultism form a strong strain within the romantic movement. When Heidegger builds his whole theory of art around Hölderlin's vision of the poet as the possessed source of an utterance that is at once wholly innocent and terribly dangerous, intermediary between men and the dead gods, he fastens unerringly on something central to the tradition in which he places himself (see Heidegger 1971).

2. "There is, however, a noticeable narrowing down of the whole field of art to the purely aesthetic, and more often than not, the great ideals of humanity are no longer involved. Art seems thus more and more a reflection of our own age of rigid specialization and of our strictly scientific and technological culture. That this culture is less favorable to an artistic climate and to a high level of quality than previous ones I am inclined to assume" (Rosenberg 1967, 232).

3. The relation of "art for art's sake" to the expressive line is more complex and ambiguous. The most refined versions of that line may be thought of as precisely what comes of applying such purism to the expressive version of the classical line: merely by eliminating every vestige of biographical reference and sanative function we arrive at the idea of a pure expression of intuition, and the rest of the expressive line can be represented as inventing a market for this dubious product.

4. Aristotle in *Poetics* did indeed make the recognition of likeness a source of pleasure in art, and this certainly involves a reference outside the work; so the "debater's trick," it seems, is an assault on no straw man. But Aristotle's further remarks on the unimportance of actual possibility as opposed to probability, coupled with his general metaphysical position whereby the same form can be realized in many kinds of matter, disincline one to take him as referring to actual comparisons with external realities. If we do take him so, we shall dismiss his opinion as one of the many quaint pieces of archaic rubbish in which his works abound.

More recently, Scruton has reiterated Aristotle's point that an interest in lifelikeness is not an interest in literal truth but a demand for convincingness (1976, 274). He insists that a representational work is one in which the specifically artistic interest includes an interest both in the subject and in the thoughts expressed about that subject, and which is misunderstood unless such interest is taken and is recognized to be required (ibid., 273 and 281). But it is clear that he means by "subject" something internal to the work and not its external referent, if any.

5. The appropriate riposte to the position in the text is that it is only through a quibble that the nonformalist speaks of what a work represents as being *presented*— as though to understand what a person tells one were to *put words into his mouth*. Barker Fairley's painting of me is a portrait of *me*, dammit. And a similar painting representing no individual is still an invitation to envisage such a person. It denotes no one; but it is a *denoting gesture*, like pointing to something that is not there (in chapter 3 I referred to this as "projecting"). Goodman's argument, that such paintings are people pictures but not pictures of people, is, as everyone feels it to be, the wrong way round. The issue between these positions seems undecidable in the absence of an argumentative context (such as Goodman provides) that imperatively calls for one or the other.

6. On this showing, the mystic line fulfills the function outlined for such aesthetic theories by Morris Weitz (1956): it recalls attention to, and dramatizes, a neglected function or aspect of art by pretending that it is the chief character by which art is to be defined. But Weitz (writing in the immediate aftermath of the publication of Wittgenstein's *Philosophical Investigations*) took as his unit particular works of art,

which he conceived as identified by a bundle of characteristics, not all of which each work would have, so that a redefinition would promote a shift of relative emphasis among these. The view being sympathetically presented here is concerned, not with isolated objects that are works of art (actually "art objects" in the terminology of chapter 6), but with art as a major form of human activity, to be defined like other such activities by a prevailing purpose or set of purposes, so that a change in this purpose will itself bring about a shift of emphasis among the characteristics of the practice, or may render them pointless. In the present instance, the effect of the reorientation of art would be to restore significance to the characteristics by which the practice is already defined.

7. Similarly, when Dylan Thomas prefaced his poems (1952) with the remark that "these poems . . . are written for the love of Man, and in praise of God, and I'd be a damn' fool if they weren't," citing the example of a shepherd who explained why he took certain superstitious precautions by saying "I'd be a damn' fool if I didn't"— you don't have to take him or Donna Wilshire seriously, but if you want to know why you should, well, you're a damn' fool if you don't. It is an argument at least as good as most arguments in theology.

8. We note that the forces are *to be discovered*, that is, we do not as yet know what they are; and we also note that the discovery is perpetually renewed, so that it must be an existential discovery, not one whose content can be recorded for posterity. These conditions preclude all theological and metaphysical system, although not all cult, except to the extent that they themselves presuppose a world such as makes discoveries of this sort possible—makes it possible, that is, that experiences of the kind envisaged should count as discoveries.

9. The rejection of adulthood (presumably a reaction against the disappearance of intelligible and fulfillable adult roles in a world of perpetual technological crisis) was reflected sartorially as well as in the proliferation of play religions: blue-jeans are preschool play clothes, and Mary Quant's invention of the miniskirt was (as she explained) a protest against having to wear grown-up clothes.

10. An evident power (a power that shows itself) is not the same as an apparent power (that which appears to be a power, whether it is or not), nor as evidence of power (that which shows that there is a power, but is not itself that power). To speak of "evident power" is to make a strong claim.

11. There is a charming fable of an art historian who noticed that certain villagers were in the habit of genuflecting to a certain place in the wall of their parish church. Having the plaster stripped from the wall at that spot, he discovered a long forgotten wall painting of the Virgin and Child.

12. This was preeminently true of the expressive line, which makes of art a formative process so defined as to be a prerequisite to any communication and thus, in effect, the primary characteristic of human as opposed to other animal activity. It may be urged that if expression is thus universal and necessary, it will look after itself, much as breathing does; the reply would have to be that breathing is difficult in foul air and yoga does marvels with deep breath, and that if expression is not carried to the level of art, the quality of life is debased—as it is among us.

13. One might retort that in a nonliterate society the changes are not cumulative and thus cancel each other out, so that the overall effect is as if no change took place. Memory, it will be said, is no substitute for writing, since when no records are kept, the "remembered past" changes with the present, being indeed merely the projected self-image of the present. But this is not certain: Professor T. McFeat reports that in experimental situations small groups preserve information with

astonishingly little distortion. Perhaps one may conjecture that at least the idea of cumulative and directional change is not likely to attract a society that lacks the idea of keeping records.

14. With a naturally social animal such as man, it is very hard to say what "natural" and "connatural" mean. Certainly not innate, one says—but, then, what does "innate" mean? It is natural to learn, and one is born with whatever is necessary to learn how to learn. Let us say that if one can define what flourishing is for a human being and a human society, and if one can specify what conditions are benign for such individuals and societies, then whatever is common to those flourishing in benign conditions is natural. One should also include as natural whatever is invariant in pathology, in the sense that it can be brought under a causal law without invoking cultural conventions; but that would be "natural in the circumstances," not natural without qualification.

15. See Giedion (1964). It has long been customary to cite these cave paintings as evidence for the original magical function of the visual arts. But the evidence lies in the repeated assertions of commentators (whose bellwether was the Abbé Breuil), based on inferences from the preferred subject matter. We should remind ourselves that we know nothing about the circumstances in which, or the ends for which, the paintings were made; that we do not know what other visual arts the paleolithic peoples may have produced, nor what proportion of their artistic energies was spent on the cave paintings (whose survival is an accident of their location); that we do not know what part, large or small, the cave paintings played in the lives of how many or what sort of persons; and that we know nothing of what verbal or musical arts the same people may have practiced. As the sole evidence for the artistic activity of the human race over several millennia, the cave paintings offer a ludicrously tiny sample. The most we can say is that the paintings are such as we would expect to find if they had the function we conjecture for them, except that we have no good explanation for the inaccessibility of their locations.

If paleolithic naturalism demands a magical explanation, so does neolithic non-naturalism:

> The neolithic artist wanted a world of forms illustrating not changeable and transient activities and events . . . but rather the relations of people to one another and to the cosmos within an unchanging system. The intention was not to suppress the content of life but to dominate it, to compel it to surrender its physical ascendancy to the power of creative will—to man's drive to manipulate and refashion his world (Raphael 1947, 76).

Raphael, we observe, writes as positively as if he had been the neolithic artist's private secretary, whereas in reality he is just making it up. Anyway, with the paleolithic and the neolithic accounted for (and, since visual art must be either naturalistic or not, any conceivable future discovery already taken care of), we can sum up: "Art in the dawn of humanity had little to do with beauty and nothing at all to do with any aesthetic desire: it was a magic tool or weapon of the human collective in its struggle for survival" (Fischer 1963, 36). The argument is really very simple. As good Marxists, we know on faith that art belongs to the superstructure and merely reflects the forces in the economic substructure. In dealing with art in historical times, where the facts are known, we have to admit that the relationship is "mediated," that is, does not really obtain; in dealing with prehistory, we can allow our dogma a free rein.

16. To do so would be tantamount to accepting Collingwood's distinction between

art proper and "art falsely so called," but rejecting his encomium on the former. "Art" and "work of art" are indeed laudatory terms, but it does not follow that whatever earns them is good by definition; the laudation is tied to a context of secular appreciation, and a rejection of the world's values may well put such evaluations into parentheses.

17. The congruence in procedures between poetry and theology was already noted by Thomas Aquinas in *Comm. in I Lib. Sent. Petri Lombardi* Prol. Q.1 a.5. The principles of theology, he points out, are ill adapted to human reason, the human condition being such that we are in the habit of filtering our knowledge through the channels of the senses, so we have to be eased into theology by analogies drawn from sensible things. That is, theology relies on metaphors, symbols, parables. To the objection (the third) that poetry, as far as possible from truth, cannot suitably use the same means as theology, which is the highest truth, Aquinas replies: "Poetic knowledge is of those things which, because of their deficiency in truth, cannot be grasped by reason, and that is why it is proper for reason to be seduced, as it were, by certain likenesses. Theology, on the other hand, treats of those things that are beyond reason, and the reason why the symbolic mode is common to both is that neither is commensurate with the reason" (ibid., my translation).

18. Most illuminating in this connection is Picasso's reaction to his first visit to the Trocadéro museum:

> The smell of dampness and rot there stuck in my throat. It depressed me so much I wanted to get out fast, but I stayed and studied. Men had made those masks and other objects for a sacred purpose, a magic purpose, as a kind of mediation between themselves and the unknown, hostile forces that surrounded them, in order to overcome their fear and horror by giving it a form and an image. At that moment I realized that this was what painting was all about. Painting isn't an aesthetic operation; it's a form of magic designed as a mediator between this strange, hostile world and us, a way of seizing the power by giving form to our terrors as well as our desires. When I came to that realization, I knew I had found my way (Gilot and Lake 1965, 248).

The doctrine is that of Max Raphael (n. 16, above); but which way round does Picasso's mind go? Apparently he starts by finding the masks powerful, and powerful in that they express terrifyingness. He interprets this as manifesting fear first felt and then overcome. Since there was fear, it must have had an object, so he first postulates "unknown hostile forces" and then attributes the hostility to the world at large. Instead of starting with dread of a dreadful world and then averting its horrors with art, we start here with a dreadful art and then interpret the world in such a way as to justify the art. But why does Picasso do this in the first place? Apparently because (since he has yet to discover what painting "is all about") his technique and expressive capacities as a painter outrun his convictions about what is to be painted (see Berger 1965 for the view that Picasso suffered from this all his life), but now he has *found his way*: merely in order to enable him to paint better, he will attribute to the world a hostility such that it can be symbolically overcome by painting. That is what I meant by "aesthetic and frivolous for all its ostentatious solemnity."

19. Morawski remarks that a magical object resembles a work of art in having the same formal structure, in being representational, and in expressing a communal (tribal) or even a personal attitude. He goes on to say that "not until the nineteenth century was there ever—in all history, so far as I am aware—the overt declaration

of a break from the subordination of artistic value to utility value or fetish value" (1974, 67). But this is beside the point because he wants to argue that the specific values of art depended on these others, not that (as he says here) they were postponed to them. It is one thing to deny artistic values priority; it is an altogether different thing to deny them autonomy.

20. Most critics would concede that at least the visual arts revived in the nineteenth century, with Manet and Degas if not already with Constable and Delacroix, however deeply one may deplore the absence of big themes from impressionist canvases; but no one would say that this was because painting had returned to a religious context. In fact, the alleged vapidity is restricted to works in those genres that the Renaissance had favored; one should speak of a redirection of energies rather than a decline in strength. In any case, the bulk of the work done in any age must seem vapid to later ages, for whom it lacks immediate relevance: for obvious reasons, most of the work done fulfills the daily routine of one's craft, or is turned out to meet the specifications of the market and make a livelihood—like the tourist souvenirs from Africa. And if one redirects one's gaze from the visual arts to music and literature, it requires some fortitude to regard music between Bach and Wagner as inferior in depth and power to any other music, or to ignore the scope and force that prose fiction acquires for the first time in the nineteenth century (with *Don Quixote* as almost the sole exception).

21. One can, of course, define "religion" so as to include whatever is of deep interest to anyone or whatever is comprehensive in scope, so that the equation of triviality and secularity becomes tautologous. But the more substantive claim that only religious art can be great or good art is a matter of faith, like the traditional argument that a secular morality is impossible, that divine revelation gives that morality its content and the fear of divine retribution its force. All evidence tells against the former thesis, and none supports the latter, though no doubt any vengeful deity makes a good stick to beat dogs with, if one thinks that is a good way to train a dog.

22. The probable efficacy of this method may be gauged (as my parenthesis was meant to suggest) by the evident difficulty people have in refraining from answering their telephones.

23. One would expect the latter belief to be the more generally held, if only out of respect to the power concerned. An example would be an Iroquois mask of the False Face Society, which has no life unless it is carved upside down on a living tree, which then has a ring of bark stripped away below the mask and is thus killed. If an identical-looking mask is not made in this way, it can be freely sold as a souvenir or a work of art. This is not surprising, since the whole point of the enterprise is to bring a power under control; one would expect the process of doing so to be significant in its entirety. Examples to the contrary are more at home in picturesque or sentimental fiction, like Oscar Wilde's *Picture of Dorian Gray* or Adelaide Ann Procter's "A Lost Chord." (Part of the point of that subtle and underestimated song, incidentally, is that to have the effect of a "grand Amen" it would have to be a cadence, not a chord, so the organist will *never* find it—"only in heaven," where eternity supplants time and music is emancipated from the sequential conditions of the music we know, will he strike lucky.)

24. Jalaluddin Rumi says in the *Mathnawi* that "there is a secret in the melody of the flute which if divulged would upset the scheme of things." Since the flute is specified, the secret is presumably not in the melody as a sequence of tones but in some aspect of the playing of something on the flute. But what, precisely? And how

widespread does promulgation have to be before it counts as divulging? Does the scheme of things get more upset the more people are in on the secret, or is there a cutoff point at which *one* more person in the know will suffice to unravel the total fabric? Did Rumi think he knew the answers to such questions? And, if he did, had he good reason to think his answers the right ones? One might as well probe the logic of a deodorant commercial.

25. The concept of the supernatural only makes sense within the context of a reductive theory of nature. It is crucial to the mystic line that if such a theory is adopted, one cannot live by it: one has a choice between accepting the reality of something supernatural, or expanding one's conception of nature, or ignoring the facts of one's own life as one lives it.

26. The language I use here assumes that religious values take precedence over aesthetic values, if the two can be distinguished: "There are things that are important beyond all this fiddle" (Moore 1951, 40). Everyone who admits the distinction does allow the precedence to religion—however one defines religion, one's definition would somehow have to locate within religion whatever the supreme values are. An aesthetic attitude could be defined as one that either allows religious and ethical values no place, or only allows them a place within the framework of aesthetic interests; and such an attitude is certainly possible. I would not, however, take into account here the "aesthetic" as conceived by Kierkegaard in *Either/Or*, which appears to me chimerical. The attitude postulated by Kierkegaard is one that pretends to admit ethical and religious attitudes, but subordinates them to a frivolous eclecticism described initially in terms that preclude such subordination. This is a preacher's daydream.

27. A paradigm of this form of argument is afforded by Tolstoy (1898): the function of art is to effect the contagion of emotion; but if the emotion is a bad one, this function is better unfulfilled. The ultimate *mission* of art is to spread emotions associated with Tolstoy's own version of Christianity.

Van der Leeuw (1963, 328ff.) has an elaborate schema relating the major arts to the names and powers of the Christian Trinity. If this is taken seriously, it implies that non-Christian peoples who practice those arts are unconsciously avowing a Christian theology. This seems a bit steep.

28. One would expect this benevolent-spectator's view of the mystic line to be common, but in fact most of those theorists who disavow religious belief tend to deplore any art that purports to stand in any such relation. At best, the ground for this depreciation is that religious beliefs are psychologically damaging or sociologically mystifying; but a zeal in iconoclasm is really inexplicable unless the iconoclast dreads what he smashes.

29. I have heard a poet, reading a poem on Aphrodite, assure his audience that he really did believe in her divinity. I don't know how he knew whether he believed in her or not.

30. There is a clear exemplification of this pattern of thought in relation to morality in Gabriel Marcel's "The Dangerous Situation of Ethical Values" (1943). The world is (though it cannot be shown to be) the field of a divine providence: society only flourishes when values are preserved in a mutual care based on a faith in this providence. He develops the theme in a way that is of interest for our purposes: originally, values were sustained in a pre-Christian context by a natural piety in which the world provided the divine ambiance; then Catholic piety based on Catholic theology gives the whole pattern a truer form; but when Catholicism falls victim to skepticism, the old natural piety vanishes along with it, and social

values collapse. One can easily imagine someone taking a similar line in relation to art: an understandable reaction against churchly art has led to the unthinking and crippling rejection of the original nonchurchly attitude toward the holy that alone can sustain a significant art. In fact, something very close to this is maintained by Jack Burnham in a recent book: "It is left to the most original artists of our times, an artist like Dennis Oppenheim, to shamanize us into realizing our true condition. Thus, only by artistic means can the originally-sick man, the shaman, mutilate his body, chant prayers in the fields, invert the evils of his tribe, and in doing so draw people away from substitute objects and back toward the ancient memories of life and productivity" (1974, 143). Art today, he urges, can be a means of restoring ritual at the interface of humanity and the inhuman, as in Newton Harrison's celebrations of ecosystems and food chains. In other words, religiosity is to be restored without religion, or piety without dogma: thus art recovers its health and imparts health to society. It has to be said that Burnham may not be entirely serious in what he asserts, since he has functioned as a sort of marriage broker in the ideology of contemporary art, in successive works matching new fads in art with trendy preoccupations in a way that compels admiration rather than arousing conviction. But the viability of an author's ideas is not a function of his sincerity in propounding them.

31. Coomaraswamy's material seems suspect to me: he consistently interprets his texts in a Platonizing sense, and the texts he relies on seem to have been compiled by Brahmans whose theological education was in general sounder than their grasp of artistic practice (cf. chap. 3, n. 14). The prevalence of similarly otherworldly views in the Chinese literature on painting—or at least, in those writers whose works are translated and popularized in the West—can, somewhat similarly, be attributed to the works' being written by gentlemen amateurs. It may be that high-minded views of art prevail throughout the world, not because art as such is associated with exalted states of mind, but because writers on art are more likely to be amateurs than practitioners of the arts they write about. By contrast, one might compare Cennino Cennini's handbook on painting (1437): after a perfunctory page or so saying what a wonderful affair painting is, the rest of the treatise deals with practical methods. How important is the grace before the meat?

32. The text here suggests that doctrine is more important than attitude; we must remind ourselves that this ranking is by no means obvious. Opinions in themselves are of no consequence.

Someone who espoused our fourth possibility might quote the beginning of Augustine's *Confessions*: "Thou has made us for Thyself, and our hearts are restless till they rest in Thee." If the world is really such, one's orientation in it will surely be affected otherwise than in one's beliefs and disbeliefs: the heart turns to God of itself, as the monarch butterfly in autumn flies toward an unknown tree in a Mexican valley.

33. Freud certainly would not postulate any such connection: on his theory, the artist's work suffices to establish that link with reality which religion (as a symbol of patricidal guilt) also affords. Art and religion run parallel and have comparable but not identical functions.

34. The classical expression of this point is that of Marx:

> Greek mythology is not only the arsenal of Greek art, but also its basis. . . . All mythology subdues, controls and fashions the forces of nature in the imagination and through imagination; it disappears therefore when real control over these

forces is established. What becomes of Fama side by side with Printing House Square? (1859, 216).

To which one is inclined to retort, first, that Homer's *Odyssey*, neither the least nor the latest monument of Greek art, has nothing perceptible to do with controlling the forces of nature; and, second, that at least Fama's printers do not go on strike.

35. That not all preliterate art is religious or magical in function, and that even less is formally explicable in terms of such functions, is affirmed by all modern authorities—for example, by Willett, who cites Margaret Trowell's differentiation of three types of art in Africa, "spirit-regarding art," "man-regarding art," and "art of ritual display" (1971, 41).

Part of the reason for the propensity of missionaries to dismiss their clients' values wholesale was that what they had to offer in the guise of Christianity included a large part of their own Western folkways.

36. The American self-image is still curiously dominated, not by the myth of the frontier, but by the myth of that myth: people suppose that *everyone else* holds values appropriate to life in the wilderness.

37. The contention that only one kind of serious context can rescue art from triviality is a puzzling one. (The contention reminds one of those who urge that because serialism represents the main stream in modern music, it follows that diatonic composition, electronic music, and so on are not merely byways but positively vicious, betrayals of the spirit of music if not of the spirit of man. Even when called *The Philosophy of Modern Music*, such utterances manifestly have the character of partisan outcries.) Perhaps the best way to make the contention plausible would be to say that the prevalence of degraded, aesthetic art, or art devoted to other interests (however important in themselves), obscured the all-important mediating function, and that by a sort of Gresham's law of values the facile and the immediate crowd the valuable hard currency out from public circulation. But the reply to that would be that if there is a real need for mediation, only a work that purports to mediate will seem to fulfill it, so that the alleged displacement could not have taken place unless the religious demand had dried up. In that case, the energies of the proselytizers of the mystic line should be devoted, not to the conversion of art, but to the revival of the demand.

An analogy for the mental attitude expressed in the denunciation of all secular art is afforded by the familiar complaint that all the best young artists nowadays have been seduced into going in for the worst style. It seldom occurs to those who complain thus that the alleged state of affairs is such as to cast doubt on their identification either of excellence in young artists or of depravity in style: what attracts the brightest is most likely to be the best. But in fact the dynamics of decadence, degeneration, and deterioration are little explored. In what conditions are high standards abandoned in favor of the perverse or the facile? Why do hard things suddenly cease to seem worth doing? And stone gods founder in the sand.

38. It was for the same sort of reason that Hegel declared that art had been superseded, and religion, too. There are now clearer and more direct and adequate ways for mind to express itself. We understand the world so much better nowadays that our standards of understanding have been raised, and religion can no longer satisfy them; nor can the sort of ideas we have nowadays be given external embodiments in beautiful forms. Hegel had, however, noticed that art was still going on: all sorts of ideas that could be given adequate form had not yet had such forms given them, and the development of art would not be completed until this task

(real, though superseded) was accomplished—just as Bach continued to work out the possibilities of his obsolete manner, and Schoenberg said there was still a lot of good music to be written in C major.

39. The contention that religion is essential to art because it embraces all depth of feeling for reality as such is very different from the opinion Rader and Jessup also express that "the whole range of religious attitudes . . . have found expression in powerful works of the artistic imagination. Throughout the centuries art and religion have been closely intertwined—hence to understand the one it is necessary to understand the other" (1976, 210). What they are saying here is that religious values form one part (even if a very important part) of the content of art. This doctrine leaves no room for a purely or essentially religious art. It is in fact one of the positions with which I contrasted the mystic line at the beginning of this chapter.

40. Stephen C. Pepper consistently held that the value of any work must depend on the tenability of the "world hypothesis" required for its appreciation: insofar as a work depends on "mysticism," it must be an inferior work, since explanations in terms of mysticism are valueless. A supernatural force can always be invoked to explain anything, and the supposed explanation may take any form. But Pepper never explained why the requirements for analyzing a physical process should be the same as those for appreciating a work of imagination. See especially Pepper (1945).

An analogy for the harmless division of labor among mental processes may be found in Mackenzie King's earnest quest for guidance from dead pets and parents. C. P. Stacey's study of the material (1976), though hostile, leads him to the conclusion that the spirits never advised King to do anything his spectacular political intuition would have led him not to do. I suspect that it was just because King's success depended on a developed mental tact that could not be simplified into pros and cons that he needed the support of the spirit world, to render his subtle judgment immune to reductive rebuttal. One knows exactly what kind of art would embody a defensible world hypothesis: simplistic and dull.

41. Euhemerism is one of the ways in which sophisticated people who are determined to remain associated with an orthodoxy contrive to explain its cruder aspects away. As Tiresias says in Euripides' *Bacchae*: Dionysus is really only the chap who invented wine—but dance anyway.

42. In some contexts, everyone takes self-evidence as the criterion of truth: the only question is what contexts those are, and what counts as self-evidence. Heidegger is not being merely silly when he construes truth as Greek *aletheia*, and etymologizes that into *a-letheia*, "unhiddenness"—though, in general, etymology in argument is fool's gold, and one does not show profundity by sticking a hyphen in the middle of an innocent word.

43. This mystery is well expressed in Browning's lines in "Abt Vogler," though the connection between the first two lines and the last two is less than clear:

> But here is the finger of God, a flash of the will that can,
>   Existent behind all laws, that made them and, lo, they are!
> And I know not if, save in this, such gift be allowed to man,
>   That out of three sounds he frame, not a fourth sound, but a star.

Abt Vogler, incidentally, figures here as the man who found the lost chord (cf. n. 23, above).

44. Thomas Aquinas, *Summa Theologica*, pt. 1, q. 2, art. 3 (my translation). Aquinas certainly intends his argument in the latter sense, for the appeal to "all men" takes

us deliberately out of the Judeo-Christian context, and the argument itself is derived from the pagan Aristotle (cf. *Summa Contra Gentiles*, bk. 1 chap. 13).

45. Gervase Mathew (1963, 132) reports that Photius identified three elements in aesthetic perception: joy, wonder, and inner turmoil. He thinks that in the last of these Photius is alluding directly to the angel that troubled the waters of the pool of Bethesda (John 5:4). Certainly the same word (*tarachê*) is used, but the context hardly bears Mathew out: the rhetoric is aesthetic, and the allusions pagan rather than Christian. Photius is extolling the architecture of his new basilica. Whereas Orpheus made trees move, he says, the beholder of the vestibule of the new church suffers the opposite effect—he is rooted to the spot with admiration. But once he manages to get himself inside, he is filled with such joy and inner turmoil and wonder, is so bewildered by the multiplicity of radiant beauties, as by the stars of heaven, that he is, as it were, spun round and becomes altogether beside himself. Photius concludes with a striking anticipation of late nineteenth-century psychological aesthetics: "With his own multifarious revolutions, his continuous movements, which the brilliance of the spectacle coming at him from every side quite compels the spectator to undergo, he imaginatively transfers his own experience to what he sees" (Photius, *Homily III*, *PG* CII 568C-569A, my translation).

46. This, after all, appears to be the purport of the celebrated thesis of Walter Benjamin, to which I have alluded before:

> We know that the earliest art works originated in the service of a ritual—first the magical, then the religious kind. It is significant that the existence of the work of art with reference to its aura is never entirely separated from its ritual function. In other words, the unique value of the "authentic" work of art has its basis in ritual, the location of its original use value. This ritualistic basis, however remote, is still recognizable as secularized ritual even in the most profane forms of the cult of beauty. . . . Art reacted [to photography, which threatens authenticity and hence tends to dissipate the "aura," the sense of immediate presence] with the doctrine of *l'art pour l'art*, that is, with a theology of art. . . . For the first time in world history, mechanical reproduction emancipates the work of art from its parasitic dependence on ritual. . . . The instant the criterion of authenticity ceases to be applicable to artistic production, the total function of art is reversed. Instead of being based on ritual, it begins to be based on another practice—politics (1936, 223-224).

I am sure the tendencies Benjamin points to here are real enough, but one would like to think that Benjamin did not believe that what he was writing was the literal truth. He was the kind of thinker commentators are always making allowances for.

47. That a special domain is not necessarily a sacred domain (as some writers have suggested it is), and can perhaps be mistaken for (or function as) a sacred domain only where no domains are sacred, is suggested by Douglas Fraser's remark about frames:

> Used as a means of separating the artistic from the ordinary world, this drawing of a line around forms to isolate them from the field, creates a special domain that is truly aesthetic rather than magical or religious. The frame has no obvious source other than the will of the artist and his decision to differentiate his vision from ordinary and supernatural experience (1962, 138-139).

48. This appears to assume a separation between musician and audience, which might itself be denounced as a result of the degradation of musical life. But it does

not: the musician should know that he is playing competently, whether or not he is playing successfully; and he should know this in a way unlike that in which he knows he has made his oblations.

49. I have attended a performance of works by Stockhausen at which we were assured by a program note that the performers had fasted in this or that fashion. This remained, for me, on the level of mere information; and, had it not, whatever effect it had on me would have been the effect of the statement itself, a statement that I had no way of knowing to be true or untrue. If they had made the audience fast with them, that would have meant something. Perhaps the musicians feared that, if the Father saw them in secret, the box office would not reward them openly.

50. It is possible that an electric light bulb might suddenly light up without anyone switching it on, or even connecting it to an electrical supply. But the sense in which it is possible is one that most people leave out of their practical reckonings.

51. W. B. Yeats, "A Dialogue of Self and Soul" (1950, 267).

52. See Herrigel (1953). The exercise was to stand broadside to the target, draw the bow in the most painful fashion, and let the arrow release itself and hit the target without one's volition. After months of frustration, Herrigel tried to control the flight of the arrow somewhat. His teacher dismissed him in a huff, and would not take him back without weeks of persuasion. In the end, the arrow found the target, and Herrigel found it most enlightening.

53. Our contemporaries can most readily think of power in its ubiquitous identity in terms of the electrical supply (of which our understanding is in most cases mythological); the metaphor is in many respects excellent. Perhaps we should after all have called this line of argument the power line.

54. Compare Mascall: "The image or the image complex, like the word or the word-complex, is an *objectum quo*, by the entertainment and contemplation of which the mind is able to enter into intimate cognitive union with the reality of which it is a manifestation" (1957, 112); and Kierkegaard: "The Middle Ages are altogether impregnated with the idea of representation, partly conscious, partly unconscious; the total is represented in a single individual, yet in such a way that it is only a single aspect which is determined as totality, and which now appears in a single individual, who is because of this, both more and less than an individual" (1843, I, 86). Both of these authors ascribe to tradition the view that the represented presence is present or accessible in the image, in part at least. But Mathew (1963, chap. 8) denies that the iconodule's image had any magical identity with its prototype, quoting John Damascene's *De Imaginibus* and Julian the Apostate's *Letter to Theodorus* ("He who loves the gods delights to gaze on the images of the gods and their likenesses, and feels reverence and shudders in awe of the gods who look at him from the unseen world" [translated by W. C. Wright, Loeb ed., II, 309]). The image earns *proskynesis*, a ceremonial gesture of respect, but not *latreia*, reverential service. Mathew argues that the prototype of the relation is that of the emperor's image to the emperor (or the United States flag to the American Constitution): disrespect to the former is disrespect to the latter, who or which is present in it by proxy—but only by proxy. Another analogy is the soldier's use of a pinup: no girl is at hand, but her real proxy presence is what gives the soldier solace. One suspects that once more the ascription of some more cognitively literalistic belief to the Ages of Faith or to the heathen is due to the sentimentalist's romanticizing of the former and the missionary's blackguarding of the latter.

Gregory Bateson appears to reinvent the notion of an image as described in the last paragraph, and calls it a sacrament. He suggests that sacramental, as opposed to merely metaphorical, thinking is at the center of "great art and religion and all the rest of it." Sacramentally, the swan figure in *Swan Lake* "is not a real swan but a pretend swan. It is also a pretend-not human being. It is also 'really' a young lady wearing a white dress. And a real swan would resemble a young lady in certain ways. . . . It is not one of these statements but their combination which constitutes a sacrament. The 'pretend' and the 'pretend not' and the 'really' somehow get fused together into a single meaning" (1954, 37).

55. Bernheimer argues that this evident affinity is adventitious, a product of the decay of faith (1961, 218-220). As the social and liturgical framework that sustained the inherent efficacy of the sacred image falls away, the artist seeks to make up the deficit through the evident power he gives to the image. This partly explains the fact (touched on elsewhere in my text) that the most sacred images and locations of power are not works of art but sticks, rocks, locations, and so on, which owe all their importance to the context that gives knowledge of their power; but the generalization seems dubious.

56. The appropriate sense of "expression" here is that articulated by Goodman (1968). A thing exemplifies what it expresses; it does so metaphorically; and it refers to a *label* of what is expressed—that is, for present purposes, the power is in the work; the power that is in the work is only metaphorically the same as the power in itself (it is transposed into another mode); and one knows that this is happening because one knows the power by one of its names (we know that this power is Dionysus).

57. This difficulty in the mystic line seems at first sight analogous to difficulties in the presentation and criticism of certain modes of the fine arts, notably with action painting and pop art. With the former of these, as we have seen, it was alleged that the painting was a byproduct of the act of painting, so that the painting needed the support of a series of photographs of the artist at work; with the latter, the work in a museum had to be accompanied by a long screed explaining that these really were the artist's old socks, and so forth, just as, in one of Damon Runyon's stories, the tipster made his implausible tips more acceptable by saying "A story goes with it." But in the case of action painting and pop art, the practice of telling the tale was acceptable only if one accepted the story *as part of the work*, as the patter is part of the conjurer's act; and that is plainly not what the mystic line claims of the relation between the work of sacred power and its accompanying ritual.

58. The rest of this paragraph is based on notes I find filed without comment among my papers. They are thoughts I do not remember thinking, so it is possible that the sequence of thought belongs to someone else—I don't know who it would be.

59. See Panofsky (1968, 32ff.) for the Neoplatonist dilemma: Plato's theory of ideas must deprive art either of symbolic meaning or of independent value, because if it relates only to visibles, it cannot have the former and in its relation to the ideas it cannot have the latter.

60. Plotinus, *Enneads* I.6. His remarks are not explicit, and it is possible that my gloss on his text is erroneous. John Dillon, adducing *Enneads* V.8.i and citing what seems an antecedent passage from Cicero's *Orator* (8ff.), thinks that "the artist is not making a copy of a copy, but is rather in direct contact with the archetype, and in a way which is, it is suggested, uniquely open to him as an artist" (1977, 94-95). I think this is wrong. Certainly the artist is in direct contact with archetypes, but the archetypes are not those of the objects to be depicted: they are those of beauty and of his art. A close look at the wording of the Cicero passage does not rule out

this interpretation even for Cicero and his source (Antiochus?), though it is certainly ambiguous. Plotinus, as I read him, accepts Plato's argument that a work of art cannot depict, and cannot effectively symbolize, a purely intelligible entity. The intelligible basis of changing appearances cannot be identified with any one appearance—in fact, Plato's whole theory depends on the contrast between a cause and the effects it causes. The reason any beautiful person, even one such as might be portrayed by Phidias' statue of Zeus, will seem ugly in some contexts is not because it is not quite beautiful enough (as though an *extra hard* tug on one's bootstraps might lift one to the ceiling), but because it is a visible beauty, and visibilia as such are necessarily subject to contextuality. Other disciples of Plato have lacked Plotinus' discernment. Sir Joshua Reynolds' Platonism, filtered through the brains of Prebendary Zachariah Mudge (cf. Hilles 1936, 20n.), amounts to a plea for representing idealized stereotypes, which are not less particular than other particulars but only less individualized, so that we end up with a recipe for bad painting. Raphael's famous remark, made in a letter, about using a mental image as a substitute for selecting the prettiest bits from various pretty girls (Goldwater and Treves 1945, 7; cf. Panofsky 1968, 60) strikes one as mild sex talk rather than theory.

61. There is an alternative: that the artist's style imposes unity, symbolizing in its personal choice of perfection that aspect of the world whereby it is the best of all possible worlds (if that is what it is). But what a style thus unifies is not a work but an oeuvre; so this possibility does not really fall within the scope of the present section.

62. The solitary exception among reputable Western cosmogonies is Plato's *Timaeus* 28 Aff., in which a single world is patterned after many eternal exemplars. But thus to place the exemplars outside the divine implies a second-order cosmos within which divine agency is one factor, and that thought pattern does not concern us here.

63. See chapter 10, note 24, above. Beardsley (1965) offers a reasoned repudiation of the notions that either the initial impetus of a work or its final condition can properly be said to determine the quality of the whole. A notorious example of the devolution of a work from a series of determinants is *The Pickwick Papers*: the original idea of a jocular series of sporting mishaps was modified, first, by the fact that Dickens was stronger minded than the illustrator to whose ideas he should have been subordinate, then by the invention of the character of Mr. Pickwick, and then continuously by the inevitable disparity between the character of an elderly man's innocence and that of his youthful companions. The fact that the work was issued in parts as they were written means that it transforms itself before our eyes. (Its transformation does not necessarily detract from its artistic status, since its eventual theme is the journey of innocence into experience, to which transformations of understanding and perspective are appropriate.)

64. A recent attempt to explain this kind of unity through personality (perhaps the only serious attempt ever made to explain it) is Guy Sircello's *Mind and Art* (1972). Coleridge's own thought is not elaborated to a point at which it might enlighten rather than stimulate. His examples of imaginative, as opposed to merely fanciful, imagery suggest that he has little more in mind than a rather heavy use of the pathetic fallacy—that is, the work he calls imaginative is that which *asserts* a unity of cosmic power rather than that which manifests it in its own structure.

Somewhat similarly, the Sino-Japanese paintings commonly cited as capturing whatever powers there may be tend to be those combining rapidity and sketchiness of execution with an expressionistic emphasis on gesture and eyeball.

65. William Blake, Introduction to *Songs of Experience*. Note that in the following stanza it is not clear whether it is the Bard or the Holy Word "That might controll / The starry pole; / And fallen fallen light renew!"

66. Santayana writes that "where poetry . . . comes to the consciousness of its highest function, that of portraying the ideals of experience and destiny, then the poet becomes aware that he is essentially a prophet, and either devotes himself, like Homer or Dante, to the loving expression of the religion that exists, or like Lucretius or Wordsworth, to the heralding of one which he believes to be possible" (1900, 286). We note here that the prophetic function of the poet has nothing to do with insight: it is a mere matter of spokesmanship on behalf of a system of belief to be validated elsewhere. Very different is the view expressed by Descartes in his *Cogitationes Privatae*:

> It may seem strange that the really important pronouncements are found in the works of poets rather than of philosophers. The reason is that poets have written with the ecstasy and power of imagination. There are in us seeds of knowledge as in a flint; philosophers extract them by reason but poets strike them out by imagination, and then they shine more brightly (Beck 1952, 296).

It has to be admitted that Descartes is here saying what in the text I say can only be said by one "innocent of epistemology and ontology." It is in fact very hard to see what kind of knowledge Descartes could have in mind, in which the difference between a poet and a philosopher (which includes what we would nowadays call a scientist) is that of the means of access to innate sources of knowledge. One might, for instance, argue that artists are better than scientists at noticing things in human affairs, being more subtly aware of nuances in behavior and empathetically aware of their significance, but that is not innate knowledge or seeds of knowledge.

67. For the artist's vision, see Engels' notorious letter to Ferdinand Lasalle of May 8, 1859: "That Balzac was thus compelled to go against his own class sympathies and political prejudices, that he *saw* the necessity of the downfall of his favorite nobles and described them as people deserving no better fate; that he *saw* the real men of the future where, for the time being, they alone were to be found—that I consider one of the greatest triumphs of realism, and one of the greatest triumphs of old Balzac" (Lang and Williams 1972, 50 [italics in the original]). Engels says that he has learned more from Balzac "than from all the professional historians, economists and statisticians of the period together" (ibid.). It would, of course, be unfair thus to cite a theorist's correspondence for his opinions were it not that in his theoretical work there is no statement, whether confirming or countervailing, of comparable weight.

One supposes that it was the authority of this pronouncement of Engels, which may have been motivated more by simple honesty than by doctrinal consistency, that made Lukács think that the rather idealistic looking argument of *Die Eigenart des Aesthetischen* could be reconciled with Marxist orthodoxy.

68. There is much to be said for Trotsky's robust assertion that "all through history, mind limps after reality. . . . The traditional identification of poet and prophet is acceptable only in the sense that the poet is about as slow in reflecting his epoch as the prophet" (1923, 19-20).

69. He adds "on whom the pale moon gleams," but the moon gleams alike on all who go out at night, including poachers—unless the latter are skulking in the shadows. Is the meaning rather that poets are lunatic, or that they are nocturnal? Elizabeth Sewell points out that we have no reason to imagine (as we usually do)

that Orpheus with his lute made animate and inanimate nature dance to his tune in bright sunshine, and suggests that we think of him as doing so in almost complete darkness, "in a night which includes ourselves" (1960, 56).

Chapter XIV. The Purist Line

1. Of the rival goods mentioned, thought and research are subjected to the various tyrannies of logic, verification, and cost-benefit analysis, and friendship for people is falsified by love of pleasure, hope for favors, and hero worship.

2. One may compare the existentialist pathos of freedom as developed by Sartre (1943): human freedom cannot be destroyed, but it is as if it were always under threat, for everything conspires to conceal it and to obstruct actions in which it is manifest. Similarly, no intuition as such can be a commodity; but the market in art, and the institutions in which art is displayed, conspire to create the overpowering illusion that it is about to become one. In both cases, there is a sense in which breaking through the illusion is a real service to freedom or to art.

3. Thus war and sickness bring, together with suffering, a relief from routine obligation that may be welcomed with joy.

4. See d'Harnoncourt and McShine:

Duchamp sent instructions from Buenos Aires for a Readymade to be executed by his sister Suzanne and her husband Jean Crotti in Paris: a geometry book was to be hung out on the balcony of their apartment. Duchamp described this work in an interview with Pierre Cabanne: ". . . the wind had to go through the book, choose its own problems, turn and tear out the pages. Suzanne did a small painting of it, 'Marcel's Unhappy Readymade.' That's all that's left, since the wind tore it up. It amused me to bring the idea of happy and unhappy into readymades, and then the rain, the wind, the pages flying, it was an amusing idea" (1973, 288-289).

Note that this is an entry from an exhibition catalog, solemnly headed "130. 'Unhappy Readymade' [Ready-made malheureux], 1919 (Buenos Aires—Paris)." And what corresponds to the entry? Nothing. See notes 6 and 61.

5. Duchamp's work is a mine of endlessly subtle ironies. Nothing is what it seems, except the things that seem to be more than they seem to be—and *especially* those. Observe, in the preceding note, how Duchamp, instead of hanging a book out, sends transatlantic instructions for the "execution of a Readymade" and for the bestowing of a title on it (by means of a painting whose title names the readymade)—and then, in describing it to an interviewer, he says "It was an amusing idea" and describes it just as if he *had* hung the book out himself. Or again, he tells Cabanne: "When I put a bicycle wheel on a stool, the fork down, there was no idea of a 'readymade,' or anything else. It was just a distraction. I didn't have any special reason to do it, or any intention of showing it, or describing anything" (Cabanne 1967, 47). Oh, sure. But we note from the d'Harnoncourt and McShine catalog (1973, 270) that the original (1913) is lost and there have been several later versions, the latest *in an edition of six*—a delightful lampoon on the custom of limiting castings of bronze statues to six (to keep prices up), or *is* it a lampoon, and not just a rip-off? Do the authors see the joke?

Duchamps "Unhappy Readymade," as an exemplary action, stands in direct descent from those anecdotes in the elder Pliny about birds pecking painted grapes, anecdotes that illuminate the state of an art and its aspirations at a certain historical moment. But there is a difference: the stories in Pliny imply as their object paintings that would be excellent paintings (by the standards the stories imply) even without the stories. But the exemplary actions of a Duchamp are exemplary only because they are reported actions. It is then a short step to the discovery that the exemplary act need not even be witty or interesting, since the report of it has to be independently arranged for in any event.

6. Duchamp is not unmindful of this: the preceding notes have drawn attention to his use of retrospective interviews to add extra layers of disingenuousness as a sort of stucco to the edifice of his lifework, and to the analogous appearance of catalogs of his exhibition as yet further accretions. Schwartz's complete catalog (1969) is far from being an ordinary *catalogue raisonné*: in its pretentious opulence and the ludicrous solemnity of its anecdotage it is a cult object of a different order, an act of piety that is also a self-ridiculing rip-off. Similarly, sets of miniaturized reproductions of Duchamp's works are on the market, at a respectable price: here is the Duchamp story, in delightfully preposterous form (a miniature replica of a *ready-made?*), itself a major item in the story—or is it merely an act of cynical effrontery and money spinning? How one hopes there is no ascertainable answer.

Duchamp, it seems, is a central and unavoidable figure in the purist line, but he does not certainly belong to it. The career of Duchamp is exemplary, but as aesthetic object: he figures as ironist, not as scapegoat, unless we read (as we well may) his irony as despair.

7. In considering the case of Duchamp, one should not ignore his position as adviser to rich collectors, a position that would have made him a key figure in the artworld in any case (cf. Tomkins 1965, 61-62). (Similarly, it is a mistake to deplore, as is sometimes done, Bernard Berenson's putting his great scholarship and expertise at the service of the rich; it is plainly on the latter's connection with wealth, not on his undoubted erudition and taste, that his singular reputation depends.)

8. This remark by Levine curiously combines two different theses: first, that certain works require the cooperation of public or critic for their completion (cf. Eco 1962), either by way of actual participation or by way of providing the required interpretation and definition to isolate and identify a performance (in my "classical line" sense); and, second, that certain works require a *graphic record* for their identification and hence for their existence. The points are very tenuously related, and one sees no reason why they should both apply to the same works or kinds of work. Perhaps a sentence or two dropped out of the middle, or failed to get put in.

9. The term "media" may be defined by this practice. When one speaks of "the media," one is thinking, not of channels of communication or even (as Marshall McLuhan would have it) of forms of sentience, but of means of manipulating the responses of a mass audience.

10. "If we extend the meaning of software to cover the entire art information processing cycle, then art books, catalogs, interviews, reviews, advertisements, sales, and contracts are all software extensions of art, and as such legitimately embody the work of art. The art object is, in effect, an information 'trigger' for mobilizing the information cycle" (Burnham 1974, 28). And he interprets Les Levine (with what justice I cannot say) as pushing this line of thought to its "logical" conclusion:

> Every artist of any substance sells his art through shrewd advertising and press agentry. For Levine these are legitimate art forms. . . . Levine, I feel, has set out

to vindicate the art system, namely, that anything can be sold with enough public relations energy behind it. His integrity lies in the fact that he has refused to feed collectors' neuroses with illusions of permanence and quality (ibid., 37).

The last sentence is ambiguous: does Burnham mean that Levine's work is worthless and he honestly refuses to pretend that it is not, or that quality is an illusion and Levine (unlike most artists) has enough integrity not to pretend otherwise? Or does it even mean that Levine could make his work look good if he wanted to, but nobly refuses to do so?

In introducing that quotation, I put "logical" in quotes because the fact that anything can be sold does not mean that everything is worth buying. The appropriate context is supplied by another Burnham: commenting on Messrs. Sotheby's experiments in promoting new classes of collectables in 1958-1959, Bonnie Burnham remarks that "the auction room's proven ability to revive the art market at slack moments has convinced both the general public and the professionals that anything can be promoted as art, so long as the technique of promotion is right" (1975, 204). But the effect of such promotions cannot be expected to be lasting (the inner meaning of the contemporary scorn for "permanence" is undoubtedly to discount this truth): it is axiomatic among advertising men that even the best campaign can have only short-term effectiveness unless it is promoting a good product. If Jack Burnham is going to draw on data-processing jargon for his imagery, he might recall the old adage "Garbage in—garbage out."

11. If the purist art of exemplary incidents is reconstrued or perverted into an art of stuntsmanship, it is open to the strictures of Fried (1967) and others against theatrical art as affording nothing that one can take seriously because it offers nothing to continued, committed, and funded attention. Years before, Paul Valéry had similarly deplored the situation in which the reputations of painters depended on the talents of the writers who promoted or denounced them. "In this fashion, painting has fallen an unhappy prey to the prompt and powerful techniques of politics and the stock exchange" (Valéry 1935, 60). What Valéry deplores is what Burnhams (n. 10) proclaim. But Valéry continues by pointing to the consequence that lasting value is sacrificed to immediate impact, so that "any artist who fails to begin by shocking, by being sufficiently laughed at and insulted, must be third-rate," and "the idea of art is more and more divorced from that of the highest development of one human being, and, through him, of a few others" (ibid., 60). It would be hard to insert a phrase like "the highest development of one human being" into Jack Burnham's apologia for Levine. Valéry explains: "What I call 'Great Art' is simply art that demands the employment of *all* of a man's faculties, to produce works which invoke and bring into play all of another man's faculties for their comprehension" (ibid., 78). Somehow, Burnham has to translate that into "illusions of permanence and quality," and it is obvious that he does so in the first instance by bypassing the question of bringing "faculties into play."

One of the interesting things about the confrontation between Burnham and Valéry is that the latter's stance is precisely that of purism: art is prized just because of the noncommercial values it stands for, whereas Burnham's Levine (by equating the exchange of information with an exchange of goods and then taking the metaphor literally) discounts all values except commercial ones.

12. Adorno claims that even affirmative and celebratory works of art are polemical, because "in separating themselves with emphasis from the world of experience as what is other than they, they bear witness that that world itself should become

something different, unconscious schemas of its transformation" (1970, 235 [my translation]).

13. One should not forget the standard Marxist reply to those who set art up against economically based values. The reply is that nothing is independent of the economic. Independence, whether celebrated or manifested, is one special economic relationship: the inadvertent appropriation of surplus value. Its inadvertence does not exculpate it, but identifies it as an uncontrolled connivance with whatever dominates the means of distribution. The fact of the artist's freedom symbolizes irresponsible privilege, and his use of his freedom is a defense of power because it is not an attack upon it—neutrality is oppression's best friend.

14. The status of the artistic freedom that is only a recognition of necessity is a matter of some controversy. "I believe art is born, not of 'I can,' but of 'I must,' " says Schoenberg (Reich 1971, 57). But Xenakis grumbles that "questions of choice in the category outside-time are disregarded by musicians, as though they were unable to hear, and especially unable to think. In fact, they drift along unconscious, carried away by the agitations of superficial musical fashions which they undergo heedlessly" (1971, 208). From this point of view, Adorno's grim grappling with destiny is essentially no different from the facilities of Tin Pan Alley: both alike represent a refusal to confront the possibility of basic choice.

15. Note the exact parallel with one of the standard arguments against representational art: that representational content is always irrelevant, therefore always a potential distraction, and therefore to be avoided (cf. Bell 1914, 25).

16. "We can search from the Renaissance all the way back to the Altamira and Lascaux cave depictions of pre-class society without finding any objects of art which 'dissented,' " says Morawski (1974, 238). But this judgment requires us to disqualify (for instance) Aristophanic comedy, on the grounds that its nay-saying was institutionalized; and that invites the retort that dissent and subversion are always, at one level or another, part of the pattern of that from which they dissent. So a somewhat weaker claim seems in order.

17. Adorno's statement quoted in note 12 is canceled by another earlier in the book (1970, 10), according to which art is at once the negation of reality (because it offers an alternative organization) and its affirmation (because it provides its elements with a form).

18. One could argue thus by extension from Greenberg's stigmatization of academic art as *Kitsch* (chap. 2, n. 16)—an argument that, as I pointed out at the time, can be extended to any length in any direction.

19. A "comprador" (the word is Portuguese in origin) was a native agent used by an alien merchant; the word is currently used as a term of abuse by Marxists and other ideologists to indicate someone who has treacherously "sold out" to the class enemy, or the imperialist intruder, or some other person with whom cooperation is held to be wicked.

20. "Biologically speaking, art is a blasphemy. We were given our eyes to see things, not to look at them" (Fry 1919, 47). Note that the language is theological, not scientific. The suggestion is that all activities of an animal other than those by which it sustains its existence and propagates its species are somehow improper, as though Darwin had discovered a moral imperative rather than a law of nature, or as though nature were a market economy. There is no good reason for adopting this point of view.

21. See chapter 10, note 14, above. According to Bartel, my discovery of a faded period charm in Duchamp's assembled ready-mades in Philadelphia was inappro-

priate, for he writes: "Duchamp's comment on the glorification of his readymades is terse and bitter: 'I threw the *urinoir* into their faces, and now they come and admire it for its beauty' " (1979, 51, n. 11). Terse and bitter the comment may be, but it is also entirely disingenuous: for something of what really happened, see note 61, below.

22. Harold Rosenberg, in the course of a symposium on antiart at the American Society for Aesthetics on October 28, 1972, referred to what he called the "aesthetics of discomfiture," according to which anything can be a work of art *except* a conventional painting. But this is a two-edged judgment, as may be seen by considering what Hilton Kramer has to say about Duchamp's work in Philadelphia (see preceding note):

> Duchamp's art has nowhere to go except to the museum, where its presence does indeed modify the "existing monuments" in a way Eliot had not foreseen. It deprives them—and us—of their essential seriousness. Duchamp's legendary assault on the work of art as traditionally conceived effectively demonstrates that there is no such thing as an object or a gesture that, within the magical museum context, cannot be experienced as art, and this demonstration has the effect of consigning both the idea of tradition and the museum itself to a limbo of arbitrary choices and gratuitous assertions (1973, 18).

But it is surely obvious that if we and the monuments had any essential seriousness, it would take more than Duchamp to deprive us of it. Either our false pretensions are exploded or irony is defeated (as so often) by reasoned conviction. We are returned once more to Michael Fried's thesis (1967): anything can be experienced as art, but not everything can be taken seriously as art, because seriousness can be acquired only contextually as part of an intelligible transaction with the world. And now back to Rosenberg: if anything can be a work of art except something that can be engaged with seriously, in Fried's terms, art as such and as opposed to conventional painting is consigned to frivolity.

23. J. L. Austin (1962) distinguished in every utterance three aspects: the locutionary, what the utterance means as a matter of lexicon and syntax; the illocutionary force, what the utterance brings about, if correctly uttered, by virtue of its utterance in context; and its perlocutionary force, the effect it has (or is meant to have) as a matter of causality in this or that context. Thus, the words THIN ICE painted on a board at the edge of a frozen lake designate, as a matter of language, a kind of stuff and one of its dimensions; as a matter of the propriety of notice posting, they constitute a warning (whether the person who put the notice up meant to warn anyone or not); and as a matter of perlocutionary force they may have the effect of daring a youth to venture out. Austin died before he could polish the distinction, and there are some doubts as to the best way to work it; but that is near enough. The extension by analogy to works of art has not been thoroughly explored and may turn out to be useless; but I would suppose that a work might as a matter of quasi locution be a silk-screen print portraying a girl gesturing with a rifle, as a matter of illocution be a poster announcing what it announces (as all designs of a given sort displayed in a given fashion may be taken to be), and as a matter of perlocution constitute an offense or an inspiration to its unwilling or willing public. Being a protest is more like being an offense than like being a poster.

24. Jan van der Marck quotes his own catalog statement: "With the whole idea of a modern museum and its usefulness somewhat up for grabs, Christo's packaged monument succeeds in parodying all the associations a museum evokes" (1969, 34).

Elsewhere in his article he provides two other explanations of Christo's activities, compatible neither with each other nor with this one. His mind is somewhat up for grabs, evidently.

In the address cited in note 22, Harold Rosenberg observed that at one time artists set out to make the bourgeoisie uncomfortable; later, they made critics uncomfortable; now, museum directors make artists uncomfortable.

25. One may ask, Just what illusion is dispelled? Who suffered from it? What are we to make of the pie if we did not suffer from the illusion? For similar questions asked about "empty" art, and some answers to them, see Sparshott (1976b) and Danto (1976).

26. Thus, a roadside notice reading BEWARE is no doubt a warning. But a warning of what?

27. Possible readings include: (1) the *Mona Lisa* is just as good in reproduction as in original oil, and just as good with mustaches as without; (2) see me desecrate a sacred object; (3) see me desecrate an object that you think is sacred but I don't; (4) the *Mona Lisa* is so banal that it needs overpainting to revive its interest; (5) by overpainting, however slight, I convert this painting into my own original work; (6) fine art is no more to be taken seriously than a schoolboy's graffito; (7) a schoolboy's graffito is no less to be taken seriously than fine art; (8) the art audience is so gullible I bet they will even be solemn about this piece of nonsense; (9) fine as it is, Leonardo's painting would be even finer with beard and mustaches; (10) in the age of reproduction, works of art lose their magical aura, as W. Benjamin will say; (11) we need something to fill that blank space on the wall, and this is all I have time for.

Some time after compiling the above list, I discovered three alternative meanings for *L.H.O.O.Q.*, offered by Schwartz: first, it may be connected with "a folk practice at Argos, where brides used to put on a false beard on their wedding night"; second, Duchamp himself has said, "The curious thing about that moustache and goatee is that when you look at it the *Mona Lisa* becomes a man. It is not a woman disguised as a man; it is a real man, and that was my discovery, without realizing it at the time"; and "finally, Roché recalls, 'When he drew the elegant moustaches on the *Mona Lisa* he was saying: "Don't let yourself be hypnotized by the smiles of yesterday; rather invent the smiles of tomorrow"'" (Schwartz 1969, 477). The relevance of the alleged folk practice at Argos, which otherwise seems rather far-fetched, is presumably that it establishes a connection between the facial hair and the caption; but that connection is perhaps sufficiently established by the more widely diffused folk practice of scribbling on posters.

If Duchamp was in earnest in suggesting the masculinity of the *Mona Lisa*, his discovery suggests another layer of meaning in *L.H.O.O.Q. Rasée*, which is simply a small reproduction of the *Mona Lisa* pasted on the invitation card to a dinner (in 1965) on the occasion of the preview of the collection in which *L.H.O.O.Q.* now is (Schwartz 1969, 546; Catalog no. 375, classifying it as a "Ready-made").

28. It is worth noting, since it is seldom noted, that conventional piano music is often played by the pianist for himself alone or among his friends. It is hard to imagine *4'33"* played otherwise than as a concert piece. It is also hard to imagine it successfully performed for an audience forwarned of its nature. Listening is always possible, and the opportunity afforded by *4'33"* is no better than any other. One could not be a second time *tricked into* inadvertently listening, if that is the intention.

29. One should bear in mind, however, that Cage has said many different wise and witty things on different occasions, and also that he has been known to become indignant with musicians who resist his own tyranny as composer and conductor.

In his lecture "Indeterminacy" (Folkways recording FT 3704A, 1959) he speaks of his unsuccessful attempts to get orchestral players to perform one of his works correctly, and concludes: "I must find a way to let people be free without their becoming foolish, so that their freedom will make them noble." This sounds fine until one reflects that a musician may not recognize a composer's right to decide whether and how he shall be free and noble, and may have his own ideas about what is foolish and what is responsible.

30. Since the alternative would be another composition *by Cage*, this contention is perhaps not so extravagant as it sounds.

31. One popularizing author has no doubts about the piece's meaning, for she writes: "The work consists of sounds made by the audience as people sit and fidget in their chairs, wondering during the 4 minutes and 33 seconds of silence what is going to happen. The outrage of that!" (De Val 1978, 12). It should be noted that Cage's score does not specify audience sounds rather than ambient sounds, and certainly does not instruct the audience to wonder.

32. Although the title specifies four minutes and thirty-three seconds, the score itself stipulates that the work may be played on any instrument or combination of instruments and may take any amount of time. Since this last fact is not generally known even among those who keep abreast of trends (cf. n. 31), it might be interesting to confront such an audience with a performance that took two hours. Incidentally, it is not obvious why *4'33"* is so much better known than the same composer's *0'00"*, of which my writing this note was a private performance.

33. The irrelevance of manifestoes of rebellion to the manifest qualities of the art to which they are attached, the gratuitousness of the declarations of sincerity and integrity on behalf of artists by their critical champions, and the necessity of the "software" of publicity, all of which are referred to in this section, are part and parcel of the subjugation of art to interpretation, of which much has been made in recent years. "The moment something is considered an artwork," writes Danto, "it becomes subject to an *interpretation*. It owes its existence as an artwork to this, and when its claim to art is defeated, it loses its interpretation and becomes a mere thing. . . . Art exists in an atmosphere of interpretation and an artwork is thus a vehicle of interpretation" (1973, 561). I take it that Danto is here making two points and perhaps implying, but I think not stating, a third. First, when we know an alleged artwork is a fake (this is the context of Danto's discussion at this point), we no longer try to figure out what it means or try to appreciate its artistic meaning, because we know it has no serious meaning—it is a piece of *Kitsch*, simulating the look of an artistic statement without actually being one. Second, to have the status of an artwork is, precisely, to be a legitimate claimant for interpretation of a specific sort. But third (and this is *not* said), the last sentence suggests that the work exists for the sake of the interpretation, which is independent of it, so that any clever talker could make an artwork of anything. But consider the case of Raphael's cartoons for tapestry, which belong to an oeuvre that established a language for European painting. These may be uninterpretable for us because the message is one in which we can no longer take an interest. Still, we know they are in principle interpretable; they make a pictorial statement even if it is one to which we are deaf and blind, and we may even sense their eminent interpretability. In losing their interpretation, they become, in practice, mere things (perhaps art objects in my sense); but they await new interpreters, and the interpreters when they come will have to understand their language. Nothing in what Danto says here or elsewhere

suggests that the statement an artwork makes is one we as interpreters put into its mouth.

A subtle shift takes place when Danto's editors raise what seems to be the same issue (though, to do them justice, they are not discussing Danto's article): "In many ways," they say, "the plastic arts are no longer self-sustaining. These days, artworks require an elaborate philosophical and critical rationale in order to be understood as artworks" (Dickie and Sclafani 1977, 423). The air here is heavy with questions that are never answered. What does "understood as artworks" mean? Understood in relation to the concept of art, or simply understood? Is it some particular rationale that is needed, or is it only that an artwork must be provided with some rationale or other, much as one has to register at a motel under some name or other? And what exactly is the relation of the rationale to the work? And, perhaps most important, when did "these days" start, and how was the date fixed?

What the alleged dependence of contemporary art on criticism may come down to can be seen from Krauss's preface to her monograph on David Smith, where she writes: "My knowledge of modern painting and sculpture was developed largely through the critical essays of, and discussions with, Clement Greenberg and Michael Fried. With their aid I began, in the early sixties, to write criticism" (1971, vii). And the first thing she says about Smith is a paraphrase of Fried on Frank Stella. Whether her knowledge of modern painting and sculpture at any stage required acquaintance with the works themselves is not revealed. For the relation between Fried and Stella, see Rosenberg (1972, 129ff.).

34. John Byrom's epigram on the dispute between the partisans of Handel and those of Bononcini. The names may remind us that it is not the merits of the artists that are to be belittled, but the stature of the generalizations around which the invective is assembled.

35. Like so many things, this truth was most sharply expressed by Hegel: "The entire Cynical mode of life adopted by Diogenes was nothing more or less than a product of Athenian social life, and what determined it was the way of thinking against which his whole manner protested. Hence it was not independent of social conditions but simply their result; it was itself a rude product of luxury" (1821, 269).

36. For one thing, art is expensive: its clientele must be either wealthy individuals or substantial institutions, which are run by well-paid professionals and directed by leaders of society.

There is indeed such a thing as an art of the proletariat, of the uneducated and leisureless urban workers, but it is unsophisticated without being innocent and most often corrupt, and the purist line abhors it. It is corrupt, not because of innate depravity, but because to resist the corruption of taste requires strenuous education followed by some leisure. Education may be a perverting force, as Tolstoy thought, but it is less damaging than a lack of education in a mass society.

37. So standard is the gibe that it has been given classic form by Goscinny and Uderzo (1963).

38. Becoming a joke is not necessarily a disaster for the purist line: the pathos of the ridiculous can be a valuable resource. The potent myth of the sad clown answers to a widespread recognition that knowingly to make oneself ridiculous is one form of martyrdom.

39. For "a story that goes with it" see chapter 13, note 57, and compare Tom Wolfe's rather intemperate article in *Harper's* (1975). It is instructive to compare

663

Wolfe's diatribe with Hilton Kramer's response (1975): Kramer accepts the justice of Wolfe's strictures, but resents that they should be voiced by someone other than an authenticated member of the arts establishment. Philistines, it seems, are not to recognize rubbish and effrontery and call them by their names, but must leave that to their betters. The attitude is one familiar from other walks of intellectual life.

40. Northrop Frye draws attention to a similarly arbitrary pinning of sermons on texts in a field somewhat peripheral to art:

> A new art of divination or augury has developed, in which the underlying trends of the contemporary world are interpreted by vogues and fashions in dress, speech or entertainment. Thus if there appears a vogue for white lipstick among certain groups of young women, that may represent a new impersonality in sexual relationship, a parody of white supremacy, the dramatization of a death-wish, or the social projection of a clown archetype (1967, 21).

The parallel is of some significance, as it suggests that the alleged dependence of contemporary visual art on critics (see n. 33) may owe less to the dumbness of art than to the garrulity of critics.

The looseness of fit between work and commentary was strikingly demonstrated by an art reviewer a few years ago. In April 1971 he wrote of an experimental film on exhibit at the Castelli Gallery:

> The rhythm is quick and repetitive; it has an awkwardness which comes from an easy sort of perfection—exact mechanical redundancy, which is, in effect, the absence of the reflexiveness that characterizes organic cycles with their straying from exactness to indicate that the goal of perfect exactitude is being held, or, rather, entertained (Ratcliff 1971a, 25).

There follows a column or two of discourse on Nietzsche and Merleau-Ponty, after which the reviewer concludes that "Nauman expresses the faulty, damaged quality of his half-determined consciousness, caught in a failed or failing reductionism where it remains only to cling to the reductionist motive: Nauman expresses his expressionism" (ibid., 26). In the following month, however, the same reviewer reported: "I was mistaken in describing Nauman's exhibit there: what I described last month was the interval between the runs of his film, not the film itself" (Ratcliff 1971b, 39)—but he decides to let his critique stand.

41. The groundless earnestness, as well as the desperate attempt to make it appear grounded, is one of the things that contributes to the situation that William Empson attributes to the fact that art critics "have never had an ideological purge" that would inhibit their propensity to talk rubbish (he believes, for some reason, that literary critics have undergone this cleansing). He continues:

> The catalogue of a picture exhibition is often very intimidating; a steady iron-hard jet of absolutely total nonsense, as if under great pressure from a hose and recalling among human utterances only the speech of Lucky in *Waiting for Godot*, is what they play upon the spectator to make sure of keeping him cowed (1968, 341).

But Empson's facetiousness averts attention from a very real and puzzling problem. Why do such critics, who must be presumed to be educated, sensitive, and responsible professionals, think it proper to write absolutely total nonsense? To what situation is it that they are intelligently and appropriately responding?

664

42. Happily, this situation has greatly changed and is still changing, thanks to the devoted labors of our historians of art.

43. My text in this section (and elsewhere) has commented largely on vanguard movements in art and may thus have given the impression that vanguardism is inherently purist, or that purism is essentially vanguardist. Neither of these is the case: the relation between purism and vanguardism is external and contingent. There can, as we have seen, be a purism that relates to the works and operations of the fine arts as conservatively conceived, merely redefining their values. It is true that this position is difficult to maintain, and that it is these difficulties that drive purists to turn to antiart, pop art, and minimalist modes. But the difficulties they find there are just as great, if less obvious, so that the conservative version is not to be ruled out on that account. On the other hand, the very idea of an avant-garde, if taken seriously, requires a strict relation not only to an established fine-arts tradition from which it is to depart but to fine-arts values, which it modifies, transvalues, or reverses. Vanguardism collapses into purism, or takes refuge in purist rhetoric, when it becomes self-conscious and thereby finds its task impossible in terms of the fine-arts tradition, or generally what I have called the classical line. I have repeatedly cited, from Burnham and others, the judgment that as artists in general become self-conscious about their originality and their place in history, they find they have saddled themselves with the self-contradictory situation in which each of them in each work is to revolutionize the total history of art (self-contradictory because the simultaneous revolutions mean that there can be no total). An analogous fatality is implicit in Clement Greenberg's incisive dissection of vanguardism (1971). Since Manet, every significant artist began the significant phase of his career by being shockingly different; since the Italian Futurists, the shocking becomes an end in itself. But that means that the shock can be produced by a move in any direction at all, not necessarily in a direction vitally related to what came before and hence capable of being no less vitally related to a successor. As Octavio Paz tellingly puts it:

> The Futurists, Dadaists, Ultraists, and Surrealists all knew that their rejection of Romanticism was itself a romantic act, in the tradition which Romanticism itself had inaugurated, that tradition which seeks continuity through rejection. But none of them realized the peculiar and truly unique relation of the avant-garde with earlier poetic movements. All were conscious of the paradoxical nature of their rejection, namely, that as they denied the past they prolonged it, and in so doing confirmed it; none of them noticed that, unlike Romanticism, whose rejection initiated this tradition, theirs brought one to a close. The avant-garde is the great breach, and with it the "tradition against itself" comes to an end (1974, 102-103).

The vanguard stance thus becomes a timeless one, a bare assertion of a perfectly abstract value. Purism is the only refuge. But that is not because vanguardism is vanguardism; it is because a vanguard interested only in its distance from the main body is no longer a vanguard, just as someone interested only in the fact of belonging to a tradition or to history cannot add to a tradition or become a significant historical figure.

44. It is not skillfulness as such that is abjured: a purist artist may be adept in all kinds of industrial and postindustrial techniques, sometimes on the principle of spoiling the Egyptians but often for their own sakes. What is objected to is only the organization of such skill for specific purposes of the wrong kind.

665

45. Several of my acquaintances in the musical world have told me about the butterfly; but not one of them has described (much less criticized) the performance, or evinced any interest in it beyond the bare fact itself. This I take to be typical of the purist attitude, as opposed to that of vanguard movements within the classical line, although my informants themselves showed no sign of being aware of the discrepancy.

One professional composer has told me of the despair induced in him by such practices and, more generally, by the extreme diversity of compositional practice: in this situation, one simply does not know how to proceed as a composer. It was evident that he felt no inclination to dismiss any such current practice as improper, irrelevant, absurd, or merely silly. One might ask why a composer who did not know how to proceed would not recognize that he had nothing to say to the world, and simply stop composing; but he was a professional teacher of composition and may have felt that that option was not open to him.

46. Compare Herrigel (1953) and see chapter 13, note 52, above. A haunting image of the purity of art as combining uselessness, difficulty, and obsoleteness is presented in Franz Kafka's story "The Hunger Artist."

47. Harold Rosenberg writes: "The work is identical with the movement, psychological and manual, that creates it; when the movement stops, the work is done" (1964, 99). We have seen already that such pronouncements land one in difficulties. How is this movement to be differentiated, even notionally, from other movements if not by the work in which it issues or the form that unites it? And does Rosenberg seriously mean that the work is identical with the movement? If so, then "work" is clearly taken in the sense of working, operation rather than opus. But if that is what is meant, how can it be said that the work is created? If what he means is that the resulting artifact has no other value than that of a sort of reminder of a spiritual struggle the artist has undergone, what was the struggle about if not to overcome the difficulties in the way of achieving something?

48. Any example adduced here may be questioned: a minimalist work may be, or may be held to be, one that differs from other works of art only in that the variations on which its form relies are of extreme subtlety, or, if it is such that this interpretation is implausible, may in its emptiness be construed as earnest or ironic comment on this or that aspect of the artworld (cf. Danto 1974).

49. I am not unaware that the works alluded to (a) admit of alternative explanations, (b) may be fine works by traditional standards, and (c) are exploitations of objects that already function at least in part as images. An exhibition of chairs mounted at the Art Gallery of Ontario in 1975 might be thought a better example had its organizer not surrounded it with an aura of naughtiness ("How would Toronto and the Art Gallery of Ontario react to the impiety toward high art which this exhibition might suggest to some?"—surely a more suitable question in 1915 than in 1975) and hokum ("Like other such exhibitions its intention is to give pleasure, while hinting at an underlying 'religious' commemoration"—this quotation, like the preceding one, is from the introduction to the catalog of the show by Alvin Balkind). In fact, there are no unequivocal examples of anything to be mentioned in this chapter. Nor can there be, since the purist line emphasizes, not what things are, but what they may be held to stand for.

50. What does one do to such an object, or to any object, by signing it? Well, one signs it, of course. But to sign a statement may be to claim authorship, to express agreement, to assume responsibility, to attest one's presence by a graffito, or to leave a token of oneself by leaving an autograph in a child's album. So signing is

in itself an act of indeterminate meaning; when it has a definite meaning, it takes that meaning from its context. (Things get more complex still when one "signs" a document or object with a false name, like Duchamp putting the quasi name "R. Mutt" (for German *Armut*, "poverty"? R. the mutt?) on his *Fountain* as though it were an artist's signature. See note 61.)

Some writers attribute to the act of signing powers of an indeterminately miraculous nature. Thus, Hugh Kenner writes:

> The signature on the soup can transforms it from a mere item of commerce into a slight but irreducible, complex, somewhat facetious utterance having to do with the status of the artist, the nature of art, the autism of a culture that buys what it eats unseen and then looks at nothing it buys, photolithographed abundance, conspicuous nonconsumption, and the long history of artifact as counterfeit.
>
> For we need not compose our utterances so long as we endorse them (1966, 153).

If Kenner had confined himself to just one of these options, we might have been open to argument supporting the preferred interpretation. But to claim that appending a name to a can is to make an "utterance" on *all* these topics, even or especially a quite unspecified utterance "having to do" with them, is to defy credulity. One hopes that Kenner means that by signing the can and conferring on it the status of an utterance, the artist invites his audience to meditate on all the things that utterance might be, of which his listed messages are specimens. But that is very far from what Kenner says, and one is really not entitled to suppose that he means anything in particular.

51. In addition to spy stories and doctor-nurse romances, "this *genus* comprises as its *species*, gaming, swinging, or swaying on a chair or gate; spitting over a bridge; smoking; snuff-taking; *tête à tête* quarrels after dinner between husband and wife; conning word by word all the advertisements of a daily newspaper in a public house on a rainy day, &c. &c. &c." (Coleridge 1817, chap. 3, n. 1).

52. Misplaced solemnity has, F. B. Randall argues, always been characteristic of high art, and amounts to a conspiracy to ignore absurdities. In fact the power of art may lie in its power to overcome absurdity. He writes of Picasso's *Guernica*: "It is hilarious. . . . The dead baby is particularly funny. . . . Each goofy element is transformed, after our knowledge sinks in, into something terrible" (1971, 338). The point is an important one, though the way Randall puts it implies a tendency to giggle at everything strange.

53. Les Levine writes:

> I've never seen a work of art I didn't like. Good or bad are irrelevant in terms of process. On a process level being totally excited is of no more value than being totally bored. If you run around in your backyard and make a good painting, it's just the same as running around in your backyard and making a bad painting. Running around is running around (1969, 484).

The point made in the second sentence seems to be the one that used to be made by saying that process is irrelevant to artistic worth: running around has nothing to do with whether a painting is good or bad, because it has nothing to do with painting. Presumably the reversal is deliberate and ironic, because otherwise what Levine writes makes no sense at all. As it stands, the connection between the first sentence, a joking variation on a cant phrase of public relations humanitarianism, and the sentences that follow seems to be one of freely facile association: Levine speaks as one with a right and a duty to speak for Art, so when he talks about running around he must be saying something authoritative about art.

54. Just as signing is an ambiguous act (n. 50), "found objects" are not all of the same sort, nor is it always obvious to which of the identifiable sorts a given object belongs. A tourist's driftwood lamp is a picturesque souvenir; Picasso's bull, made from a bicycle saddle and handlebars, is a transformation at once witty and moving; Duchamp's *Fountain* is a recognition of unnoticed elegance or a gesture of contempt or both; Warhol's soup cans and Brillo boxes are perhaps a salute to the practical psychology of the commercial image or perhaps an act of homage to the quotidian.

55. Ambiguous as the act of signing may be, it is always a solemn one: to affix one's signature is always to make some sort of commitment or declaration, even if only one that appropriates by desecration.

56. McLuhan made the equation between art and garbage in a speech to the art critics of the world assembled in Ottawa, according to the Toronto *Globe and Mail* for August 24, 1970. If he gave reasons, the paper did not report them. One cannot be sure, of course, that the reporter divined McLuhan's meaning.

57. One presumes that the art historical significance of the exhibition had something to do with Rauschenberg's *Erased De Kooning Drawing*, but not much. One wonders, incidentally, why Rauschenberg's démarche is supposed to count as a work of art, whereas Clement Greenberg's *Stripped David Smith Sculpture* and Winston Churchill's *Demolished Graham Sutherland Portrait* do not—Greenberg, after all, is a guru of the art world, and Churchill a painter. Or rather, one knows why this is (it is because the first has, and the others lack, an integral relation to other practices of the same place and time), and one wonders why one is supposed to accept the explanation.

58. In such cases the possession of the work of art is not in question. But for the work of art to take on the character of a fetish it is not necessary that it should be an artifact that can be owned: it is enough that its character can be made the object of a cult, and the production of an inherently worthless or uninteresting work might be thought to obviate this.

59. One could ask the artist. But he might lie; or he might not know; and his intentions cannot be thought to determine the actual meaning of what he has done; and his reply might be as ambiguous as his work; and he may have been misled by his own publicity or by officious critics; and he may simply be such an arrant fool or rogue that we should pay no attention to any word he utters.

60. It was reported that at a performance for the New Music Society of Cage's piece for twelve radios (*Imaginary Landscape No. 4*) the work failed because the concert had gone on too long: by the time Cage's work began, almost all radio stations had gone off the air (see Tomkins 1965, 113-114). But how did the reporter know then, and how does one know now, that this "failure" was not part of the performance?—But the story comes from Cage himself.—But how do we know that Cage was not setting the New Music Society up, that their frustration was not the true content of the work?

Similarly, those who frequent "mixed media" concerts observe that they usually start late and that the well-meaning boobies running the show seldom manage to make the equipment work. But who is to say that their incompetence is not assumed or half-consciously preserved? After all, nothing is so useless as incompetence, and nothing so conspicuously useless as a public display of it, in the course of which the inarticulate helplessness of the impresario makes vivid his status as holy fool.

61. The idea of concept art could have been derived from reflection on that

exemplary incident to which I have alluded several times (see especially chap. 4, n. 44): Duchamp's exhibition of a urinal at the Grand Central Gallery, New York, in 1917, in a Society of Independent Artists show, under the title *Fountain* and with the signature "R. Mutt." The work was not in fact displayed. So how does one know it was ever submitted? Because the art press said so. And how did they know? Because Duchamp and his friends told them about it. So far as the public was concerned, exactly the same effect would have been achieved if the story had been told without anyone going to the trouble of taking the urinal into the gallery and taking it out again.

Because so much has been made of this episode, by me and many others, a rather fuller account of it would not be out of place. According to d'Harnoncourt and McShine, commenting on a showing of the "third version in edition of eight, 1964" (the original having been lost),

> The urinal, purchased from "Mott Works" Company in New York and signed "R. Mutt," was submitted to the jury-free Independents exhibition but was suppressed by the hanging committee. The photograph reproduced here was taken by Alfred Stieglitz shortly after *Fountain* was rejected, and it illustrated an anonymous editorial (entitled "The Richard Mutt Case") in the second issue of *The Blind Man* (published in May 1917 by Duchamp, Beatrice Wood and H.-P. Roché) which came to the defense: "Now Mr. Mutt's fountain is not immoral, that is absurd, no more than a bathtub is immoral. It is a fixture that you see every day in plumbers' show windows. Whether Mr. Mutt with his own hands made the fountain or not has no importance. He CHOSE it. He took an ordinary article of life, placed it so that its useful significance disappeared under the new title and point of view—created a new thought for that object" (1973, 283).

We note that this article, in the concoction of which Duchamp obviously took part, not only professes to believe in the existence of an R. Mutt but attributes to "him" an innocently aestheticizing intention, though we have seen that (allegedly) on another occasion Duchamp professed indignation that his attempt to scandalize had not succeeded.

That things are still not quite what they seem we gather from Arturo Schwartz, who, instead of referring bluntly to "rejection," remarks that "the hanging committee *to which he* [Duchamp] *belonged* placed the object where it would be difficult to see, and Duchamp resigned" (1969, 466 [my italics]). *Fountain* could not be rejected, of course, because it was a nonjuried show. And who persuaded the Independents to mount a nonjuried show? Duchamp did, apparently, abetted by his friend and patron Arensberg, who after the show opened went to the gallery in the guise of an intending purchaser and professed indignation when *Fountain* was not in sight (it was in the back room, one gathers, behind a partition). So the sequence of events seems to have been something like this: (1) Duchamp becomes a founding member of Independent Artists, (2) Duchamp founds "little magazine," financed by Arensberg, (3) Duchamp sponsors nonjuried show, (4) Duchamp submits urinal, (5) hanging committee (Duchamp a member) "suppresses" urinal, (6) Arensberg buys urinal, (7) Duchamp's friend Stieglitz photographs urinal, (8) Duchamp writes article defending urinal in the magazine he founded for the purpose, (9) Duchamp lets magazine die after a decent interval, (10) Arensberg "loses" urinal (it can't be easy to lose a urinal) (additional details from Cabanne 1967, 54-55). These people were certainly having themselves a lot of fun, and the full story, whatever it is, seems not to have been much like "Duchamp signed and exhibited a urinal" or

"Duchamp tried to exhibit a urinal but the gallery rejected it," which is what one is usually told. Perhaps Arensberg was chosen for his initials.

62. It would be pointless to record the name of the artist and of the work in question, since it is entirely worthless.

63. Harold Rosenberg writes: "The uncollectable object serves as an advertisement for the showman-artist, whose processes are indeed more interesting than his product and who markets his signature appended to commonplace relics" (1972, 38). Since Rosenberg's earlier writings denounced people who found artists' products more interesting than their processes, one must suppose that either he underwent a change of heart, or he thinks that an uninteresting product cannot issue from an interesting process, or he is indulging in sarcasm without observing that his earlier position lays itself open to similar sarcasm in a similar way.

64. The typical avant-garde artwork of the early seventies was a snapshot of a young man in jeans, looking abstracted or soulful: the artist testifying to his artistry.

65. "The artist must arrive at a new estimate of things, all must go into the melting-pot in the hope that out of the pot may emerge a new consciousness of himself. For this end he must keep himself free from all creed, from all dogma, from all opinion, remembering that as he accepts the opinions of others he loses his talent, all his feelings and ideas must be his own, for Art is a personal rethinking of life from end to end, and for this reason the artist is always eccentric. He is almost unaware of your moral codes, he laughs at them when he thinks of them, which is rarely, and he is unashamed as a little child" (Moore 1914, 103).

66. Arnold Schoenberg wrote in 1910:

Art is the cry of distress uttered by those who experience at first hand the fate of mankind. Who are not reconciled to it, but come to grips with it. Who do not apathetically wait upon the motor called "hidden forces," but hurl themselves in among the moving wheels, to understand how it all works. Who do not turn their eyes away, to shield themselves from emotions, but open them wide, so as to tackle what must be tackled. Who do, however, often close their eyes, in order to perceive things incommunicable by the senses, to envision within themselves the process that only seems to be in the world outside. The world revolves within— inside them: what bursts out is merely the echo—the work of art! (MacDonald 1976, 58).

One hardly knows what to make of this. What has this to do with what specifically that artists (which artists?) suffer and do? Are we meant to *believe* it? Surely not. But what then? Schoenberg writes as an expressionist, a member of a movement committed to strident expression of extreme feeling; and there is some truth at least to Deryck Cooke's contention (1959, xiii) that the twelve-tone procedures that Schoenberg eventually developed to replace his expressionist methods can at present be experienced as expressing only harsh and painful feelings, because we inevitably construe all we hear in terms of the tonal-based emotional "language" of customary music, and that this will continue to be the case until twelve-tone music is familiar enough to be spontaneously heard in its own terms. And that, we may add, seems to be never, for there is no sign that Schoenberg's language will ever be used widely enough to form habits.

67. This issue has not gone unnoticed: Plato devotes several pages of *Republic* VI (see especially 496 C) to its application to philosophy.

68. Just for a handful of silver he left us,
   Just for a riband to stick in his coat

—Robert Browning in *Dramatic Romances and Lyrics*, 1845. The occasion was Words-worth's acceptance of the laureateship in 1843.

69. Athenaeus (*Deipnosophistae* XIV, 631 f) records the opposite view: "In earlier times popularity with the masses was a sign of bad art (*kakotechnia*); hence, when a certain aulos-player once received loud applause, Asopodorus of Phlius, who was himself still waiting in the wings, said 'What's this? Something awful must have happened!' " (my translation). But the assumption here is that "the masses" (*ochloi*) are not the entire public, nor the most relevant one.

70. Rosenberg is sensitive to the challenge that this fact poses for what he calls "the crisis-dynamics of contemporary painting" (1964, 42), but does not say how the challenge is to be met. Instead, he observes that many of those who draw attention to this fact are themselves infected with the profit motive. So they may be, but they are not being set up, by themselves or anyone else, as paragons of suffering purity.

71. Peter Mellen (1970, 99) remarks on how the Group of Seven painters and their historians exaggerate the hostility with which their work was received. In fact, early notices were largely favorable. The misrepresentation looks like part of a campaign to exaggerate both the difference between the group and their Canadian contemporaries and the affinity between their work and that of such advanced painting in Europe as had been derided at the Armory Show.

72. Epilogue to *Aesop at Tunbridge*, 1698; cited from *Oxford Dictionary of Quotations*, 2d ed., p. 9.

73. T. S. Eliot, like a burglar throwing an unusually juicy piece of meat to a dog, observed in "East Coker" that each of his attempts to write a poem was "a different kind of failure," because, having written the poem, he had no further use for the specific verbal skill it embodied—either he no longer wanted to say those things, or he no longer wanted to say them in that way (Eliot 1963, 202-203). But the attempt, while it is an attempt, is not yet a failure; Eliot might have said, with greater truth but less plangency, that every attempt thus far had issued in a (then new) kind of success (such as "East Coker" is usually held to have been), because one *had* got the better of words for what one *then* had to say—the fact that one has not yet mastered the technique for what one has yet to say is only to be expected, and does not show that one will not master it in good time.

74. A version of this case is argued by Reinhard Kuhn (1976): all great art is a product of profound ennui, which is a sign of honesty and profundity because it is the outcome of an encounter with the nothingness of human life. We know that every great artist must find everything in life hollow and worthless, because cheer-fulness and commitment are sure signs of self-deception and shallowness, both of which are obviously incompatible with great art.

75. Rosenberg derides those who think of the works of his favorite painters as paintings rather than as "the signs pointing to the artistic situation and his emotional conclusions about it" (1964, 42). But how is this signifying function performed? Are the paintings effects of the situation and conclusions, or expressions of them, or representations of them, or what? If they are expressions or representations, why are they not paintings like other paintings? If they are effects, how does Ro-senberg claim to have established the causal relation? Through biography, or through interpretation of the painting? If the latter, this is nothing but a singularly naive version of the expression theory of art; if the former, Rosenberg's criticism reduces to his personal belief in the sincerity of his friends. Perhaps there is some third possibility; but what could it be? It can hardly be an inductive generalization to the

effect that every known painting of the relevant kind has proved to be the outcome of the painter's reaching emotional conclusions about the artistic situation.

76. Rosenberg speaks of "the change of art from picture-making to creation and self-creation, into a means, that is, for each individual to define himself through his use of the materials of art" (1964, 104).

77. This view of history was brought into prominence, if not invented, by Hegel for the history of philosophy. A history of art, philosophy, science, or any other such form of spiritual endeavor cannot consist of a mere record of persons and their doings, but must be an account of genuine philosophical (or whatever) actions: and these must be original (since to repeat another's words or thoughts adds nothing to the history of philosophy) and must contribute to later actions (otherwise any arbitrary eccentricity would earn its place in the chronicle). If these requirements are taken seriously, the history of philosophy must become the unfolding of a single constructive development of philosophic thought, always differentiating itself and always returning to unity. And on any other view, no meaningful history of philosophy can be written and there would be no such thing as philosophy to have its history written. The object of the artist's proper ambition, according to the view being considered here, is to be found in the end to have contributed to the single unfolding entity that is art.

In this connection, Rosenberg writes: "The function of art is no longer to satisfy wants, including intellectual wants, but to serve as a stimulus to further creation. . . . Art comes into being through a chain of inspiration" (1964, 111). It seems to follow from this that the stimulus art provides is not wanted by those it stimulates, but that may not be intended. It does follow that art is of interest only to other artists.

It is fair to add that Rosenberg once said (in a discussion at a meeting of the American Society for Aesthetics in Sarasota, Florida, in 1972) that he himself would gladly dissociate himself from history, his own preferences being for the unhistorical. If "historical" art is as hermetically self-enclosed as I have suggested, this attitude is not only comprehensible but inevitable; but it does rather rob the overall view of plausibility.

78. The relevant view of history is that according to which the past is always the past of a particular present, and new developments can always change the historical significance of past events, convert blind alleys into mainstreams and so on. The appropriate foundation for this view is C. S. Peirce's theory of truth, according to which truth is that on which all scientific endeavor ultimately converges.

It is important not to confuse this view of the artist's place in history with the one considered earlier, according to which the condition of an art at any given place and time determines a specific task and an artist contributes to history by discovering and performing that task.

79. This is partly obscured by the peculiar Christian use of the scapegoat figure, whereby the function of the scapegoat figure is not so much to ease the load of past misdeeds as to make us feel doubly guilty about them by brooding on the goat's innocence. Incidentally, there is something peculiar in the idea of a self-conscious scapegoat: someone who insists on suffering on my behalf is suspected of being less interested in my welfare than in his own virtue.

80. Arnold Schoenberg is said to have been puzzled by the unwillingness of American students to accept his music: since they were in general intellectually adventurous, it was surprising that they rejected a music that offered just such an

intellectual adventure. But his puzzlement was irrational, insofar as the problems in question were specifically composers' problems.

T. W. Adorno, surprisingly enough in one who is known as the great champion of Schoenberg's school, offers what may be used as a more general excuse for the hedonistic Americans: the problem solving to which Schoenberg's activities on their strictly intellectual side are analogous is not the serious overcoming of difficulties but the solution of intellectual puzzles, an activity on which the Viennese intelligentia of the late empire were forced to exercise their brains because they were cut off from any serious participation in public affairs (Adorno, 1948, 62, n. 24).

81. It is always silly to grumble about the public. If the value of a work lies entirely in its place in history, it cannot also be a proper object of appreciation or enjoyment. If, on the other hand, its value is one that could be enjoyed, then if the work was meant for enjoyment but failed, the joke is on the artist; and if the work was not meant for enjoyment, the public is not to blame for not enjoying it. The public is, of course, missing *something*. Anyone who fails to enjoy something enjoyable is obviously missing something, and anyone who is totally unresponsive to the significant art of his time is missing a great deal. But in this life everyone is bound to miss a great deal. We must husband our energies and spend them as our judgment and the pattern of our lives dictate. Those many critics who seek to make us feel guilty for not attending to whatever excellent work they would promote deserve no more respect than the advertiser who would make us feel guilty because we do not scent our oxters with his spray.

Chapter XV. Conclusion

1. Since we observed that the purist line risks converting every art into the art of public relations, it is worth noting that this view of history is that appropriate to the mass media, in which events are thought of in terms of immediate impact, as news stories to be used up and succeeded by others.

2. The notion that events have consequences but ideas have none, so that a work of note is of no consequence but its production and publication change the world, is borrowed from the final chapter of Arendt (1959). The idea that art is a series of ongoing transactions among people who understand each other is one of the master themes of Wollheim (1968).

3. The attitude embodied in the idea that art is what makes a certain good story is characteristic of Duchamp as revealed to Cabanne (1967) and of John Cage. It is the transformation into anecdote of the sense of joint discovery necessary to any revolutionary group of artists: if art is what I and my friends are doing, the story of what I and my friends do is the story of art.

4. It is evident that the terms used here invoke a regress: if "red" means "more or less red," then that in turn means "more or less more or less red," and so to infinity. To avoid such a regress is not worth the trouble. If we insist that our descriptions of such mental strategies as are used in the deployment of our concepts be couched in formally unobjectionable terms, then we are deliberately crippling ourselves by subjecting what works through flexibility to what works by being inflexible. The temptation here is to avoid the regress by saying that we call things red by virtue of their approximation, or relative approximation, to standard or

paradigm cases of redness. But the temptation should be resisted. It is true that there are brilliant, pure, very red reds such that anyone who in any context (other than a trick one) denied they were red would be doing something very strange; but it does not follow either that we have such cases in the back of our minds whenever we call other things red, or that the concept of redness is to be explicated in terms of them.

5. This point is sometimes put by saying that art requires the engagement or commitment or involvement of the "complete" or "total" human being. But this language, unless introduced by careful theorizing, risks being meaningless; it is not clear in what sense a person is a totality. The point is rather that an attitude is demanded in which there are no reservations. And this is indeed a matter of demand, not of experience: unreserved commitment is the price of admission, and not to pay it earns scorn. The justification of this demand (or piece of cant) varies according to which line of art-theoretical thought one is engaged in. In the classical line, it has to be that no a priori limits can be imposed on what may be a design; in the expressive line, that conscious reserve precludes intuition; in the purist line, perhaps that reservations represent vested interests; in the poetic line, that imagination and creation are by definition unlimited in scope. The mystic line has no place for the demand: the only unreserved commitment called for is a commitment to what is symbolized, and therefore not to anything in the symbolizing of it.

6. There is an interesting contrast between this commitment to complexity and what was until lately the practice in teaching the philosophy of science, where the actual workings of science were never encountered and one studied only the abstract logic of inductive inference and falsification. This practice went with a systematic falsification of the nature of scientific thought in the teaching of the sciences themselves, in which intensive training in the techniques and findings of "normal science" were (and to a large extent still are) divorced from any systematic study of the relation between those topics and understanding the world. Similarly, ethics can be taught at an elementary level without encountering the perplexities of actually trying to live a life, because it is possible and useful to isolate choices that turn on explicable considerations of general import. In the field of aesthetics, it is argued, no such choice is ever an issue, and no good pedagogical purpose is served by pretending that it is.

Appendix A. Aesthetic This and Aesthetic That

1. "What Makes a Situation Aesthetic?" is the title of a seminal article by J. O. Urmson (1957).

2. The alleged difficulties in specifying an appropriate sense for "disinterested," despite the respect paid them in the text, are largely factitious: what is meant is that attention is paid to the appreciable qualities of the object as object, disregarding any relation the object may have to any purposes of one's own formulated without regard to the object itself. The meaning is hardly obscure, and the difficulty in finding a foolproof formulation is largely that of *anticipating* what sort of verbal quibble one's adversary will come up with. If indeed the outcome of one's explanatory labors is that virtually all contemplation properly so called is disinterested, that will only have shown that all contemplation as such is, in a sense that the

explanation will have clarified, aesthetic. It will be recalled that in developing the classical line we defined works of art as contemplanda.

3. The rise of the "counterculture" and its transformation into the orthodoxy of the 1970s has given renewed currency among the young to the set of ideas and values that the word "disinterested" captured.

4. See Bullough (1912). For an attempted demonstration that Bullough's account and all similar views are incoherent, see Dickie (1964); for a closer and equally destructive (and perverse) analysis, see Price (1977); for a more sympathetic presentation, see Khatchadourian (1971, 164-173).

5. My own opinion is that the notion of distance is eminently useful, and hence popular among those who discuss writing, because there are a lot of different factors that authors use to manipulate the degree and manner of the reader's involvement: framing devices, circumlocutions, and so on—and analogously, to some extent, in other arts. These devices do not all do the same thing, but they are plainly synergic; and readers and spectators accordingly recognize them as affecting in a unified way the manner in which one relates to a work. Bullough's errors include divorcing the "distancing" effects from technique, making them a matter of attitude, and making one particular handling of them a criterion of artistic success. His article retains its classical status nonetheless, because the phenomena he first brought into focus deserved to be discussed seriously, and his foolhardy willingness to bring them all into the same context answers to a practical reality. Neither the term "distance" nor the central notion was his own discovery. D'Alembert observed in his "Preliminary Discourse" to the *Encyclopédie* that "as for the objects which, when real, excite only sad or tumultuous sentiments, imitation of them is more pleasing than the objects themselves, because it places us at precisely that distance where we experience the pleasure of the emotion without feeling its disturbance" (1751, 37). Bullough's contribution was to generalize the observation and bring it into the center of aesthetic debate.

6. See Dickie (1964). Dickie favors "attitude to works of art," if anything, but this is ambiguous. It could be taken in any of the ways specified in our second set of senses. If we take it as tantamount to (2a) "attitude to works of art as such," some critics object that the concept of the aesthetic has to be smuggled in again to explain the significance of the qualification "as such." But that is not necessarily the case, for there are other ways of identifying works of art. Dickie's argument is that the specific conditions of presentation for a given art or art form suffice to do the work the alleged attitude was supposed to do, and control the way the informed public sees and understands. On the substantive issue, he seems to be right: to see a play properly, what we have to do is no more and no less than to follow the complex conventions of the theater in question. But an advocate of the aesthetic attitude might retort that the *willingness* to follow the requisite conventions defines, precisely, the aesthetic attitude: there is, after all, a difference between being ready to follow them and being not ready to do so, and this difference, since it does not depend on the audience's actually doing or perceiving anything, can only be one of mental set. And why should that mental set not be called the aesthetic attitude? It is, after all, almost precisely what Coleridge called a "willing suspension of disbelief"!

7. To save the reader the trouble, here is a start: (1) is the *x* in question recognizable? (2) is it a single phenomenon (are important differences being blurred?)? (3) is it invariably connected with art or beauty, or only sometimes? (4) if the connection is invariable, is it necessary or contingent? (5) if the connection is nec-

essary, is it the *x* that makes the phenomena associated with it aesthetic, or is it they that make the *x* aesthetically significant? In short, can the claim to individuality and unique significance implicit in phrases of the form *"the* aesthetic *x"* be made good? These, of course, are only questions; they acquire the status of objections insofar as they have not been forestalled, which they almost never have.

8. For the equation of experiences with ecstasies, see *Oxford English Dictionary,* s.v. "experience."

9. See, for example, Berleant, who states: Aesthetic experience is "experience that is active-receptive, qualitative, sensuous, immediate, intuitive, non-cognitive, unique, intrinsic and integral. When these features predominate as a group in an experiential situation, that experience takes on a prevailing aesthetic character" (1970, 188). Much of the book goes to explaining what these "features" are. But one is left wondering just what is claimed in the second sentence. Is it that the features are found to correlate with a separately identifiable character, the "aesthetic"? If so, what is that character? Or is it that there is a recognizable kind of experience that in its typical form has all these features and is defined by them, but retains something of its character when only a few of them are lacking? Or what?

10. The supposition is illogical. One can be engrossed and intellectually challenged without having to go through any discursive argument, and contemplation is a cognitive relation rather than primarily an affective one.

11. The theory is that of Bell (1914); the charge of circularity is leveled by Lake (1954) and believed by many. But the circularity is not vicious. Bell's argument is that some people do find a delight in pure form unlike anything they derive from anything else, and that this delight rather than any other mode of satisfaction must be what is specific to art (and hence what art exists to provide), since all other modes of satisfaction (moral uplift, anecdotal interest, etc.) can equally well be taken in what is not art. Even the objection that this "aesthetic emotion" has no demonstrably unique character falls rather flat, because Bell does not suppose that all forms affect us all in the same way: all he says is that there are people who take in forms a delight, and find in them a significance, that they do not take or find elsewhere. Bell is often thought of as a careless and sloppy thinker, but the self-indulgence of his critics far surpasses anything he allowed himself.

12. Note that R. G. Collingwood himself, whose view that art is the expression of emotion is glanced at here, firmly repudiated the notion that there was any specifically "aesthetic" emotion, unless one wished to give that name to the feeling of relief that an emotion had finally been expressed. In a similar vein, Langer (1953) denies that there is any "aesthetic emotion" beyond the artist's satisfaction in having got something right. Collingwood and Langer take this line because they think art has an important function to fulfill in relation to emotion in general, so that to introduce a special "aesthetic emotion" is misleading. Tolstoy (1898), curiously enough, who also thought that it was the business of art to do something important about feeling, namely, to communicate it, maintained that there *was* a specifically aesthetic emotion of some importance, namely, the joy in communication itself.

13. See *SA* (240-245) for a review of this now obsolete literature. The affinity with Santayana's views on "aesthetic pleasure" is evident. At the end of the last century and the beginning of this, there was a vogue for explanations in terms of the projection of subjective states on the outside world.

14. The notion of synesthesia is usually associated with the scientific phase of I. A. Richards (see Ogden, Richards, and Wood 1925—Richards told me circa 1970 that he still endorsed the views expressed there), but the notion is occasionally revived.

15. What does it mean to say that something "proceeds as if" something were the case, in this instance, as if feelings of a certain sort occurred? Either the feelings sometimes do occur or they do not. If they do, there is no need for an "as if"; if they do not, how can we possibly know how things would go if they did? All that can be meant is that when we tell a story involving such suppositious feelings, the story somehow sounds right. But what makes it sound right? Is this metaphor, metaphysics, mythology?

16. "Perception in the aesthetic attitude" sounds like something that could be exemplified by crouching gracefully and peering through a keyhole. This prompts the reflection that talk of "the aesthetic attitude" makes the transaction with art something to be approached through notions of decorum or with a book on etiquette. The nouveau riche learns the aesthetic attitude as he learns which knife to eat his peas off. As Clement Greenberg (1939, 9ff.) points out, the approach to art by way of an attitude thus generates *Kitsch*.

17. The duality between seeing a work of art *as it is* and seeing it *in the right way* or *as one should* is a very shadowy one, since the presumption in dealing with a work of art is always that it exists in order to be dealt with in a certain sort of way.

18. For some of the polarities that "form" and "content" may cover, see *SA* (chap. 13).

19. Throughout this discussion, we speak of "aesthetic qualities," of which the singular is "an aesthetic quality." "Aesthetic quality" in the singular and with a definite article or without an article has an evaluative sense, rather like "aesthetic merit," or it refers to a thing's having the status of an aesthetic object or a work of art.

20. The equation of relevance with being a necessary or sufficient condition in this context is not quite precise. Some writers urge that some possible features of a work of art (artifactuality would be a conspicuous example) are neither necessary nor sufficient for a thing's being a work of art, but are always relevant, because they are such that if a work lacks them its lacking them is significant. If a work of art is not an artifact, some special explanation is called for to show how it can be a work of art *despite that*.

21. This conviction can lead its victims to great lengths: for instance, it is fashionable in some quarters to say that literary works cannot have structure, because structures are necessarily constituted by the spatial relations of physically discrete parts, so that really the concept of structure in the fine arts is confined to architecture.

22. The distinction between what is an object in general, an object *for* perception and cognition, and what is an object only on a given occasion, the object of a particular perception or cognition, affords the opportunity for at least doubling the number of alleged senses. Perhaps the opportunity should have been seized: no split in general epistemology is deeper than that between those who hold that an object is a construct from perceptions, those who think of it as "a permanent possibility of sensation," and those who think of it as a thing in itself that may be the object of perceptions and cognitions, which more or less successfully disclose it. But it seems better to relegate to a footnote in this context the recognition that persons committed to different epistemologies and metaphysics will assign different senses to the term "object" and hence to the phrase "aesthetic object."

23. Sibley (1959). See the devastating critique by Cohen (1973), with additional bibliography, and the survey of the issue in Khatchadourian (1971, chaps. 5 and 6), in which the phrase "aesthetic terms" is preferred, but without change of meaning. Cohen takes the position that whether a term is or is not "aesthetic" in any

interesting sense is determined by context; but he seems inclined to suppose that an acceptable sense for the phrase would in any case have had to belong to the ranges of senses 1 or 2.

In the same vein as Cohen, Jeffrey Olen (1977) observes that qualities are ascribed to works of art in the context of (actual or implied) interpretations, which as such cannot be factually determined. Aesthetic qualities therefore cannot be objective. One may take Olen's arguments as implying that aesthetic concepts (which correlate with aesthetic qualities) are not condition governed (in a stronger sense than that in which the correct and apt use of a concept can never be condition governed), so Sibley was right for a reason not alien to Cohen's mind.

24. It is a characteristic peculiarity of Kant's treatment that aesthetic judgments (judgments of taste) are always positive, based on a subjective pleasure that is assigned a sort of universality, although logically it is hard to see why a subjective displeasure or a subjective indifference could not be assigned a like universality. Presumably the reason for this asymmetry is that, except in rather special circumstances, seeing something is better evidence for its being there than failure to see something is for its not being there. But this argument, which I used above to explain why positive criticism is more secure than negative criticism, seems to lack force when one is speaking of the harmonious interaction of faculties supposed necessary and common to all percipients.

An attempt to explain what Kant is up to may not be out of place. I take him to be answering the question: What does it mean to call something beautiful *as opposed to* perfect and *as opposed to* pleasant? We mean more than calling it pleasant, so we are not simply recording our personal feelings about it; but since we are not calling it good or perfect, we are not assessing it by the standards appropriate to any kind of thing, hence not relating it to any concept. Rather, we are taking the kind of pleasure we find in it as evidence that it must please everyone: we are cognizing it as the object of a necessary pleasure, in which the awareness of the necessity is a part of what pleases. This is only possible if the thing projects, as it were, an ideal concept to which it, and it alone, perfectly conforms and a purpose that is nothing other than purposiveness itself—the thing is as if it existed for the sake of being what it is and appearing as it appears. The only condition on which a judgment of this sort would be other than absurd would be if the objects on which it is rightly passed are uniquely suited to the relevant mental powers, the powers of representation: the ground of the judgment must lie in the free play of the imagination (the manifold of intuition comes together without resistance, as it were) and understanding (just the way the thing is, is pellucidly intelligible without our having to impose any preformed schematism on it). Of course, Kant adds (1790 §19), our judgment that the pleasure we take in what we see is *necessary* is always conditional on our judgment being correct—something we can never know.

Kant is far from claiming that all the judgments we pass on works of art conform to this peculiar pattern, since many such judgments involve the invocation of rules and genres (thus aiming at a "union of taste with reason" [ibid., §16]), and he has no direct interest in art criticism as such. Kant's philosophical interest is exclusively in the curious epistemological nature of judgments that make a universal claim on an avowedly subjective basis, even though historically his discussion arises from the rhetoric of contemporary connoisseurship. It is therefore disconcerting to find a reputable philosopher writing in a reputable journal that

for Kant aesthetic judgments do not come through concentrating on concepts. . . . But some explanation seems required of how this account is consistent with many common kinds of aesthetic judgments. . . . Do we not recognize a sonata because we possess a concept,. "sonata form"? (Carrier 1978, 43).

Obviously Carrier is using "aesthetic judgment" in sense 2a, and simply takes it for granted that Kant must be too.

25. See Keeling (1934, 134, n. 1), who in turn cites Franz Brentano.

26. A variant of this sense seems to confine "education" to what is taught only in colleges of education and found, thank heaven, nowhere else on earth.

27. The institutions of the fine arts afford careers in administration ("museology" and the like), for which training is required; but no one has yet had the gall to call such training aesthetic education.

28. Similarly, in a recent review of the literature on "music education," I discovered that writers had various and arbitrary notions about what the term covered. See Sparshott (1981a).

29. This notion of what aesthetic theory is has been widely accepted, but seems inexplicable: why on earth should an aesthetic theory be a theory that attempts that? I suggested in *SA* that the notion might arise from the practice of textbooks that present theories in the form of slogans extracted from them ("Tolstoy says that art is the communication of feeling"); but this, despite the enormous influence of M. M. Rader's anthology, which employs this sort of rhetoric, is hardly plausible, since similar simplifications in textbooks in other fields have seldom if ever led to comparable idiocies. More recently I have come to suspect that Weitz's attribution of this aim to "traditional aesthetics" is due to his attaching undue weight to an article by a former teacher of his, DeWitt H. Parker (1939). Parker explicitly claimed that the possibility of aesthetics rested on the possibility of finding such necessary and sufficient conditions, the search for which thus became the whole duty of the discipline. But that would not account for the spread of the doctrine among those for whom Parker was just another dotard. Perhaps such intellectual fads are no more to be explained than other epidemics of folly and fashion, like the rapid spread of the use of the word "cohort" to mean "colleague." It cannot be denied, of course, that aesthetic theorists do brandish slogans, and italicize them too, and may well call them definitions; but such a definition out of its context of argument and exegesis has no independent significance.

Appendix B. Kinds of Art

1. Since Munro follows no single principle and does not effectively criticize the principles of others, his work can hardly be called a taxonomy: it is rather a huge heap of data, whose value as such is enhanced rather than diminished by Munro's resolute refusal to admit into his work such subjective factors as intelligence and discrimination.

2. From Alain one learns such things as that the primary art form is the public ceremony, and that architecture as an art is primarily a setting for ceremony; that the main division of arts is between the social and the solitary; and that the primary object of imagination is human action, in the form of the voice (for the ear), gesture (for the eye), and body movement (proprioceptively). In short, the arts are to be referred back to the inherent order of which human life is susceptible. This Appendix embodies a remote and vulgarized echo of some of Alain's notions.

3. The standard exposition of the theme of the segregated and hence sacred

nature of all art is that of J. Huizinga (1955). One way of developing this point of view is Hegel's, in which art figures as the highest level of nature and the lowest level of culture (which is also God). One version of it figured in our treatment both of the mystic line and of the purist line.

4. Because alethic and oneiric art open up other regions and other worlds, while scenic and choric arts modify the realities of this region of this world, one is inclined to point the contrast between them by saying that the latter affect the structure of life and the former operate with fragmented images, torn loose from their vital context. It then appears that the contrast is akin to that previously made between the "classical" arts of structure and the "romantic" arts of surface. But that analogy would not be very helpful; a fragmentary embellishment belongs to the scenic, a fully structured imaginary world (a heterocosm) to the alethic or oneiric. The contrast between affecting the structure of life and merely touching its surface has not figured in our discussion; one suspects that the former is possible only when the scenic or the choric passes over into the alethic in ritual. That view of the matter is certainly implicit in the *Record of Music*, a Confucian treatise on music and ceremonial from the Han Dynasty, which states that "in music of the grandest style there is the same harmony that prevails between heaven and earth; in ceremonies of the grandest form there is the same graduation that exists between heaven and earth. . . . In the visible sphere there are ceremonies and music; in the invisible, the spiritual agencies" (Legge 1885, bk. I, §19). The transition from such an exacting music to a merely superficial music of the scenic appears to be marked in the following anecdote (a Sinologist informs me, however, that the somnolence of the marquis in the anecdote might be a diplomatic reaction to suspected heresy rather than what to the unitiated it seems to be, inability or reluctance to expend the spiritual energy needed to appreciate the heavier manifestations of the alethic):

> The Marquis Wên of Wei asked Tzŭ-hsia, saying "When in my square-cut dark robes and cap I listen to the ancient music, I am only afraid that I shall go to sleep. When I listen to the music of Chêng and Wei, I do not feel tired; let me ask why I should feel so differently under the old and the new music."
>
> Tsŭ-hsia replied, "In the old music, (the performers) advance and retire all together; the music is harmonious, correct, and in large volume. . . . But now, in the new music, (the performers) advance and retire without any regular order; the music is corrupt to excess. . . . What you ask about is music; and what you like is sound" (ibid., III, §§6-9).

5. This insistence on the openness and ambiguity of all our strategies in life, which has been a pervasive theme of this book, might seem more tendentious than it is. Does it not, for instance, run counter to Heidegger's demand for authenticity, or to Sartre's insistence on an existential psychoanalysis that would explain all a person's actions and strategies as variations on a single project or life choice? Does it not describe the other-directed man, whose life is a heteronomous series of responses to others, as opposed to the inner-directed man, who follows the light of his autonomous conscience? No, it does not. A single style may be shown in many roles and in responding to many calls. To be stiff to others and blind to the complexities of one's situation is not to show authenticity and autonomy but merely to be insensitive and stupid.

6. The best-known expression of this utopian ideal is in a few sentences by Marx and Engels (1846, 22), in which the abolition of the alienation inherent in industrial division of labor is imagined to make each individual life complete as including

(because not compelled to exclude) all possible forms of value. This is the pure Hegelian dialectic: the undifferentiated life of primitive communism is replaced by the more clearly articulated ways of life in which tasks are specialized and performed by specialists—but the resulting divisions must be reconciled in a higher unity in which every specialism is a property of the whole, which can only be the individual consciousness. But what in Hegel is the superindividual of the Divine Spirit can in Marx only be each human person. Unfortunately, it takes more than a revolution to cram an infinite ocean into a pint pot.

7. See for instance Lin (1935, 291), quoted in *SA* (126n.). Mario Praz invokes calligraphy in a European context as a key to the often sensed but seldom adequately explained analogy between literary and visual arts: what is in common to the arts of an age is most likely to be something like the *ductus*, the flow of form, the ways of handling and organizing material in such a way as to express personality and sensibility, the purest exemplification of which is, precisely, handwriting (Praz 1970, 26).

8. Arthur Pope writes in terms strongly reminiscent of what Lin says about China: "All the arts of Persia are closely interrelated and.all express a common cultural inspiration. The great Islamic art of calligraphy, with its standards of rhythm, precision and expressive form instructs and disciplines other arts" (1965, 133). One may conjecture that in every civilization in which calligraphy is recognized as a major art, it is assigned this pivotal place among the arts, signifying in itself the will to unify.

9. And, of course, if necessary, dispossessing the local peasantry so as to get an unobstructed view.

10. That the fundamental structures of language and behavior cannot be construed as class phenomena and are not fundamentally affected by changes in the means and relations of productions is argued by no less an authority than Stalin (1951).

11. As with other classifications, what appear here as subdivisions of major kinds may be of major significance. I mentioned in the text that the alethic includes theological and metaphysical as well as anecdotal references to reality, and the difference of kind among these may be thought more important than that between the anecdotally alethic and the analogous forms of oneiric. And Schafer (1977, 117-118) draws attention to modes of musical experience that are radically different in the way they enter into our lives, although they all belong within the scenic as here conceived. There is concert-hall music, requiring close attention, making fine discriminations, evoking class distinctions and the division of labor; there is domestic music as of the old parlor piano and the new phonograph, in which the sound envelops the listener, pervading auditory and social space (an effect Schafer also finds in the music of the ideally classless church, where a resonant stone building is filled with voices of a choir who thereby lose precise location); and there is outdoor music, band-shell music in which the sound engages our peripheral hearing and becomes part of the landscape.

Appendix C. "Good"

1. Definitions of goodness that seem to escape this net can be made out not to have done so. To say that "This is good" means "This ought to exist for its own

sake," as G. E. Moore (1903) said, is merely to remove limitations on the likings involved; to say that whatever is good is rightly placed in a duly ordered whole (or is itself such a whole) is also to generalize, but in another way; to say that whatever is real is good just insofar as it has being is to appeal to a sort of ideal connoisseurship. To elevate these into intrinsic, absolute, or metaphysical goodness does not bypass all interests, but merely attenuates and generalizes them; and lack of specificity is no virtue.

2. The dictionary goes on to say, "implying the existence in a high, or at least satisfactory, degree of characteristic qualities which are either admirable in themselves or useful for some purpose." The reference to "characteristic qualities" is too specific for such kittle cattle as works of art, and in fact seems (*pace* my treatment in Sparshott 1958) proper only to one important set of senses of the word, not to all. The stipulation of qualities is reiterated when the dictionary passes on to substances ("of things: having in adequate degree those properties which a thing of the kind ought to have," thus shoving the responsibility off onto the unexplained fiat in "ought to have"), but is dropped when it deals with nonsubstantial entities, to which a work of art (as performance) belongs. Aristotle (*Nicomachean Ethics* I.vi) warned us all of the complications that follow because "goodness is predicated in all the categories alike." Do good times and good places have characteristic qualities? There is a lot of off-the-shelf philosophy in dictionaries, and sometimes its shelf life has been exceeded.

3. Am I talking about meanings of the word, or about ways in which the word is used? The former, if I have to choose. I am contending that there are no simpler terms to which the meaning of the word "good" in the phrase "This is good" could be reduced in such contexts as I am imagining.

This distinction between meaning and use is, certainly, unclear, and may be thought to have been superseded by more sophisticated distinctions between locutionary, illocutionary, and perlocutionary forces, or between components of propositions and elements in speech acts. And with a word like "good" it is singularly hard to differentiate between what a word means, what it can be used to mean, and what a person means by using it. I do not know that the nature of my undertaking can be better explained than by saying that I am exploring what on this or that occasion would be the least misleading paraphrase of an utterance with the word "good" in it, the least misleading answer to the question "What does 'good' mean here?" Certainly what I am doing here is not meant to be armchair linguistics: what I am talking about is not linguistic competence and the associated grammar but argumentative acceptability and the associated logic. The distinction is admittedly not an easy one to explain—Gilbert Ryle used to infuriate the serious-minded by saying that it was one of "smell." But it seems evident to me that a disquisition on the semantics of the word "good" such as Katz provides (1966, 283-317) neither disqualifies nor is disqualified by anything in this Appendix.

4. Margolis writes, unexceptionably, that "an evaluation is a kind of judgment that places a value upon something; evaluating is scrutinizing with a view to assigning a value; valuing or prizing or enjoying or taking an interest in are simply occurrences, neither activities nor judgments of any sort. We are, therefore, not bound, logically, to justify our tastes, our preferences" (1965, 127). But tastes and preferences, if not acted on at all, are doubtfully real, and if acted on have consequences in the public world; so we may be called on to justify them after all, by justifying ourselves for having them.

5. The distinction here is between making a sound or movement that is caused

by a feeling and may thus be taken as a sign of one's having it (as the dentist interprets my wincing as a sign that he is hurting me), and expressing a feeling by consciously doing something in which the quality of the feeling is made clear to myself and others (as when a poet composes "A Charm against the Toothache")— neither of which is at all the same as informing people of the fact that one is being hurt, or has a toothache. The distinction is not sharp, because I may *let myself* wince in the dentist's chair, or may use an expressive form to explain myself to the world, or may use my announcement expressively. So I say that the crudest uses of "good" are *almost* evincings, not quite: they have not quite fallen out of language. (What it is for a linguistic expression to drop out of language may be seen from Aubrey's anecdote of the lady who, while being embraced by Sir Walter Raleigh, protested "Sweet Sir Walter," but "at last as the danger and the pleasure at the same time grew higher, she cried in the ecstasey, Swisser Swatter Swisser Swatter" [Aubrey 1949, 255-256].)

6. A strong objection to the possibility of such an interpretation, often cited as conclusive, is that to contradict someone who says "That's good" by saying "No, you don't" is not merely grammatically inappropriate but irrelevant to the point of unintelligibility. But it is only the grammatical and linguistic impropriety that is beyond dispute. To contradict someone who says "That's good" by saying "You don't really approve of that" or "So you honestly like that sort of thing?" is not obviously irrelevant or inappropriate, and is certainly not unusual. These language games are very intricate, and their rules are not to be disposed of by a few bluff apothegms. The second of the rejoinders cited, however, can be met with the rebuttal "I didn't say I liked it; I said it was good." If the first rejoinder cannot suitably be met in the same way, that may be because to approve of something is to think that it is good.

7. Note that I have here moved from "That is good" to "This is good." That is there, this is here: what is referred to as "that" is set at a distance, separated from one's experience of it by space or by memory. In the "This is good" that means "I am enjoying this," there is no discrimination between the object that is enjoyed and the enjoyment of it.

8. Compare the title essay in Stanley Cavell's *Must We Mean What We Say?* (1969) for a discussion of a speaker's justified confidence in his knowledge of the language he speaks.

9. It is essentially the basis of this kind of judgment that Hume explores (1757). To call something good can only mean that it pleases the best judges. But who are the best judges? Those who are capable of making the finest relevant discriminations, having made close study of the relevant material, and those who have the best judgment in general, being most apt to assign works to the most suitable reference classes. If we ask why these are the best judges, the answer can only be that the requirements of knowledge, precision, and breadth are not specific to connoisseurship, but are those we make in any field of activity whatever and in the world at large. Then, what is it to please the best judges? It is to be approved by them in circumstances other than those that in every sphere of life we take to disqualify our own judgment, such as haste and prejudice. Thus, Hume can equate goodness with "being approved by the finest taste" without the circularity of which some accuse him.

10. The position that upper-class music is good ex officio, which is what is meant here, is not to be confused with the contention that upper-class music is good de facto. It is arguable that, because only upper classes can be leisured as well as wealthy,

they have more time to listen, better education, more acute perception (because not deafened by factory noise), and more intelligence (having inherited the brains that moved their ancestors up the social ladder), as well as the money to hire the best musicians, and that these benefits are cumulative in that later generations are brought up in an ambiance of good music. Even those who for doctrinaire reasons (or simply from observing the dismal cultural condition of landed gentry) would reject that argument would surely admit, in a less culturally critical area, that even if not all rich people are judges of good wine, virtually all judges of good wine are rich.

11. I used that strategy in Sparshott (1958), though I covered myself to some extent by describing "good" as a "philosopher's dummy." In Sparshott (1970a) I recast the central issue in terms of types of judgment rather than the meanings of words.

12. Although by specifying the class of comparison within which a thing is called good one protects onself formally from the mistake of tacitly assigning a thing to an inappropriate class and judging it by reference to that, the protection is only formal. By calling it a good so-and-so, one is not saying anything about whether it is a good or a bad such-and-such; but by implying that its merits as a so-and-so are the ones worth mentioning, one is implying that a so-and-so is what it most relevantly is. And that implication could be foolish—or, as often, malicious.

13. Although evaluative rankings of disparate things are irrational, verdictive rankings are not. Every well-grounded preference in a complex choice situation implies a verdictive ranking. There is a sense in which such things as an "athlete of the year award" are absurd: how can one establish that the best goalkeeper is better than the best center, or the best football player better than the best jockey? But such awards are made and by no means absurdly, though everyone knows that they would be endlessly contestable if the judges' decision were not final.

14. Some of the ambiguities in judgments of goodness, and the ways they can be exploited, are illustrated in the exchange between a witness (Eugene Thaw) and a lawyer (Martin Gitlin) in a 1963 court case (*United States v. Caswell*). The witness distinguishes between good technique and a good painting, which he says is understood by dealers to be "one that is aesthetically satisfying; one that achieves its intention; one that is of good quality as a work of aesthetics." The lawyer purports to summarize this in the words "A good painting . . . is a painting that appeals to your aesthetic sense." The witness, rather surprisingly, accepts this formulation, after which the lawyer gets him to agree, first, that what appeals to one person's aesthetic sense may not appeal to that of another and, second, "that your personal aesthetic sense *has a lot to do with* the evaluation and appraisal of a painting by you" (Esterow 1973, 53-54 [my italics]). On this basis, the lawyer says in his address to the jury: "Mr. Thaw testified that for him it is a good painting. He likes it, and to some degree, or was it fully—I don't recall—this is what, this liking, this personal aesthetic appreciation is what sets value for him. He is setting this value because he has a business to run and he makes his profit this way" (ibid., 59). We note in this exchange that the lawyer's strategy is to allow no room for the possibility that there is such a thing as a good painting, as appraised by the witness's trained professional judgment, but to insist on the choice between strictly technical criteria and mere personal preference: "quality as a work of aesthetics" and "aesthetically satisfying" are transformed into "appeals to your aesthetic sense," which in the concluding speech becomes simply "he likes it," augmented by the insinuation that a subjective liking is interested and therefore a manifestation of the profit motive.

BIBLIOGRAPHIC KEY TO WORKS CITED

If the date by which a work is keyed here and in the text differs from the edition for which bibliographic data are provided, it is the date of the first edition in the original language unless otherwise specified. The edition for which data are provided is in each case that consulted in the preparation of this book.

Abraham 1974: Gerald Abraham. *The Tradition of Western Music.* London: Oxford University Press, 1974.

Adorno 1948: Theodor W. Adorno. *The Philosophy of Modern Music.* Translated by Anne Mitchell and Wesley V. Bloomster. London: Sheed and Ward, 1973.

Adorno 1956: Theodor W. Adorno. *Dissonanzen: Musik in der verwalteten Welt.* 3d ed. Frankfurt: Suhrkamp, 1963.

Adorno 1970: Theodor W. Adorno. *Théorie esthétique.* Translated by Marc Jimenez. Paris: Klincksieck, 1974.

Adorno and Krenek 1974: Theodor W. Adorno and Ernst Krenek. *Briefwechsel.* Frankfurt: Suhrkamp, 1974.

Alain 1926: Alain. *Système des beaux arts.* 4th ed. Paris: Gallimard, 1926.

Aldrich 1963: Virgil Aldrich. *Philosophy of Art.* Englewood Cliffs: Prentice-Hall, 1963.

Aldrich 1966: Virgil C. Aldrich. "Back to Aesthetic Experience." *JAAC* 24, 1966, 365-372.

Ames 1971: Van Meter Ames. "Is It Art?" *JAAC* 30, 1971, 39-47.

Anscombe 1958: G. E. M. Anscombe. *Intention.* Oxford: Blackwell, 1958.

Arendt 1958: Hannah Arendt. *The Human Condition.* New York: Doubleday, 1959.

Arendt 1961: Hannah Arendt. "The Crisis in Education." In her *Between Past and Future.* 2d. ed. New York: Viking, 1961.

Aries 1962: Philippe Aries. *Centuries of Childhood.* Translated by Robert Baldick. New York: Vintage Books, 1965.

Arnheim 1954: Rudolf Arnheim. *Art and Visual Perception.* Berkeley: University of California Press, 1954.

Arnheim 1969: Rudolf Arnheim. *Visual Thinking*. Berkeley: University of California Press, 1969.

Aschenbrenner 1974: Karl Aschenbrenner. *The Concepts of Criticism*. Dordrecht: Reidel, 1974.

Aschenbrenner and Isenberg 1965: Karl Aschenbrenner and Arnold Isenberg, eds. *Aesthetic Theories*. Englewood Cliffs: Prentice-Hall, 1965.

Aubrey 1949: John Aubrey. *Brief Lives*. Edited by Oliver Lawson Dick. London: Secker and Warburg, 1949.

Austin 1962: J. L. Austin. *How to Do Things with Words*. Cambridge: Harvard University Press, 1962.

Bachelard 1958: Gaston Bachelard. *Poetics of Space*. Translated by Maria Jolas. Boston: Beacon Press, 1969.

Bacon 1734: Francis Bacon. *Valerius Terminus*. In J. Spedding, R. L. Ellis, and D. D. Heath, eds., *Works of Francis Bacon*, vol. 3, 215-252. London: Longmans, 1857.

Baensch 1924: Otto Baensch. "Art and Feeling." In Langer 1961, 10-36.

Banham 1967: Reyner Banham. *Theory and Design in the First Machine Age*. 2d. ed. New York: Praeger, 1967.

Banham 1968: Reyner Banham. "The Art of Doing Your Thing." *The Listener* 80, 12 September 1968, 330-331.

Barrett 1966: Cyril Barrett, S. J., ed. *Collected Papers in Aesthetics*. Oxford: Blackwell, 1966.

Bartel 1979: Timothy W. Bartel. "Appreciation and Dickie's Definition of Art." *BJA* 19, 1979, 44-51.

Barthes 1970: Roland Barthes. *S/Z*. Translated by Richard Miller. New York: Hill and Wang, 1974.

Bateson 1949: Gregory Bateson. "Bali: The Value System of a Steady State." In his *Steps to an Ecology of Mind*, 107-127. San Francisco: Chandler, 1972.

Bateson 1954: Gregory Bateson. "Metalogue: Why a Swan?" In his *Steps to an Ecology of Mind*, 33-37. San Francisco: Chandler, 1972.

Batteux 1746: Charles Batteux. *Les Beaux arts reduits à un même principe*. Paris: Durand, 1746.

Baumgarten 1735: A. G. Baumgarten. *Reflections on Poetry*. Translated by Karl Aschenbrenner and William B. Holther. Berkeley: University of California Press, 1954.

Bazin 1967: Germain Bazin. *The Museum Age*. Translated by Jane van Nuis Cahill. New York: Universe Books, 1967.

Beardsley 1958: Monroe C. Beardsley. *Aesthetics*. New York: Harcourt, Brace, 1958.

Beardsley 1965: Monroe C. Beardsley. "On the Creation of Art." In Jacobus 1968, 53-72.

Beardsley 1966a: Monroe C. Beardsley. *Aesthetics from Classical Greece to the Present*. New York: Macmillan, 1966.

Beardsley 1966b: Monroe C. Beardsley. "The Limits of Critical Interpretation." In Hook 1966, 61-87.

Beardsley 1970: Monroe C. Beardsley. *The Possibility of Criticism*. Detroit: Wayne State University Press, 1970.

Beardsley 1977: Monroe C. Beardsley. "The Philosophy of Literature." In Dickie and Sclafani 1977, 317-333.

Beaud 1974: Paul Beaud. "Musical Sub-Cultures in France." In Bontinck 1974.

Beck 1952: Leslie J. Beck. *The Method of Descartes*. London: Oxford University Press, 1952.

Beerbohm 1913: Max Beerbohm. *Fifty Caricatures*. London: Heinemann, 1913.

Bell 1914: Clive Bell. *Art*. London: Chatto and Windus, 1914.

Bell 1976: Daniel Bell. *The Cultural Contradictions of Capitalism*. New York: Basic Books, 1976.

Belloc 1970: Hilaire Belloc. *Complete Verse*. London: Duckworth, 1970.

Benedict 1934: Ruth Benedict. *Patterns of Culture*. New York: Houghton Mifflin, 1934.

Benjamin 1936: Walter Benjamin. "The Work of Art in the Age of Its Mechanical Reproducibility." In his *Illuminations*, 217-252. Translated by Harry Zohn. New York: Schocken, 1969.

Bense 1969: Max Bense. *Einführung in die informationstheoretische Aesthetik*. Reinbek bei Hamburg: Rowohlt, 1969.

Berger 1960: John Berger. *Permanent Red*. London: Methuen, 1960.

Berger 1965: John Berger. *Success and Failure of Picasso*. Harmondsworth: Penguin Books, 1965.

Berio 1968: Luciano Berio. *Sequenza V for Trombone Solo*. London: Universal Edition, 1968.

Berleant 1970: Arnold Berleant. *The Aesthetic Field*. Springfield: Thomas, 1970.

Berlyne 1976: D. E. Berlyne. "The New Experimental Aesthetics and the Problem of Classifying Works of Art." *Scientific Aesthetics* 1, 1976, 85-106.

Berndtson 1969: Arthur Berndtson. *Art, Expression and Beauty*. New York: Holt, Rinehart, Winston, 1969.

Bernheimer 1961: Richard Bernheimer. *The Nature of Representa-*

tion: A Phenomenological Inquiry. New York: New York University Press, 1961.

Biederman 1949: Charles Biederman. *Art as the Evolution of Visual Knowledge*. Red Wing, Minnesota: Biederman, 1949.

Binkley 1977: Timothy Binkley. "Piece: Contra Aesthetics." *JAAC* 25, 1977, 265-277.

Black 1964: Max Black. *Companion to Wittgenstein's Tractatus*. Cambridge: Cambridge University Press, 1964.

Blaukopf 1974: Kurt Blaukopf. *Mahler*. Translated by Inge Goodwin. London: Futura, 1974.

Bloom 1973: Harold Bloom. *The Anxiety of Influence*. New York: Oxford University Press, 1973.

Blunt 1940: Anthony Blunt. *Artistic Theory in Italy 1450-1600*. Oxford: Clarendon Press, 1940.

Boas 1950: George Boas. *Wingless Pegasus*. Baltimore: Johns Hopkins University Press, 1950.

Boccioni 1913: Umberto Boccioni. "Technical Manifesto of Futurist Sculpture." In Herbert 1964.

Bond 1975: E. J. Bond. "The Essential Nature of Art." *APQ* 12, 1975, 177-183.

Bontinck 1974: Irmgard Bontinck, ed. *New Patterns of Musical Behaviour*. Vienna: Universal Edition, 1974.

Borges 1962: Jorge Luis Borges. "Pierre Menard, Author of Don Quixote." In his *Ficciones*. New York: Grove Press, 1962.

Bosanquet 1915: Bernard Bosanquet. *Three Lectures on Aesthetic*. London: Macmillan, 1915.

Boulez 1964: Pierre Boulez. *Penser la musique d'aujourd'hui*. Geneva: Gonthier, 1964.

Bouwsma 1950: O. K. Bouwsma. "The Expression Theory of Art." In Max Black, ed., *Philosophical Analysis*. Ithaca: Cornell University Press, 1950.

Brelet 1951: Gisèle Brelet. *L'Interprétation créatrice*. Paris: Presses Universitaires de France, 1951.

Brighton 1971: C. R. Brighton. Review of *Avant-Garde Attitudes* and *Flight from the Object*. *BJA* 11, 1971, 105.

Bronson 1959: Bertrand H. Bronson. *The Traditional Tunes of the Child Ballads*. Princeton: Princeton University Press, 1959.

Brook 1968: Donald Brook. "Rogers on Sculptural Thinking." In Osborne 1968.

Bruner 1968: Jerome Bruner. *Processes of Cognitive Growth*. Oxford: Clarendon Press, 1968.

Bullough 1912: Edward Bullough. "Psychical Distance as a Factor in Art and as an Aesthetic Principle." In his *Aesthetics*. London: Bowes and Bowes, 1957.

Burnham 1968. Jack Burnham. *Beyond Modern Sculpture*. New York: Braziller, 1968.

Burnham 1971: Jack Burnham. *The Structure of Art*. New York: Braziller, 1971.

Burnham 1974: Jack Burnham. *Great Western Salt Works: Essays on the Meaning of Post-Formalist Art*. New York: Braziller, 1974.

Burnham 1975: Bonnie Burnham. *The Art Crisis*. London: Collins, 1975.

Cabanne 1967: Pierre Cabanne. *Dialogues with Marcel Duchamp*. Translated by Ron Padgett. London: Thames and Hudson, 1971.

Cage 1966: John Cage. *Silence*. 2d ed. Cambridge: MIT Press, 1966.

Cahn and Griffel 1975: Steven M. Cahn and Michael Griffel. "The Strange Case of John Shmarb: An Aesthetic Puzzle." *JAAC* 34, 1975, 21-22.

Canaday 1962: John Canaday. *Embattled Critic*. New York: Noonday Press, 1962.

Cardinal 1972: Roger Cardinal. *Outsider Art*. London: Studio Vista, 1972.

Carrier 1978: David Carrier. Review of *Imagination*, by Mary Warnock. *JP* 75, January 1978, 40-44.

Carroll and Lucie-Smith 1973: Donald Carroll and Edward Lucie-Smith. *Movements in Modern Art*. New York: Horizon Press, 1973.

Cavell 1969: Stanley Cavell. *Must We Mean What We Say?* New York: Scribners, 1969.

Cennini 1437: Cennino Cennini. *Treatise on Painting*, dated 1437. Translated by Mary P. Merrifield. London: Lumley, 1844.

Cohen 1962: Marshall Cohen. "Aesthetic Essence." In Dickie and Sclafani 1977, 484-499.

Cohen 1973: Ted Cohen. "Aesthetic/Non-Aesthetic and the Concept of Taste." *Theoria* 39, 1973, 113-152.

Coleman 1968: Francis J. Coleman, ed. *Contemporary Studies in Aesthetics*. New York: McGraw-Hill, 1968.

Coleridge 1817: S. T. Coleridge. *Biographia Literaria*. Edited by J. Shawcross. London: Oxford University Press, 1907.

Coleridge 1930: S. T. Coleridge. *Shakespearean Criticism*. Edited by T. M. Raysor. 2d ed. London: Dent, 1960.

Collingwood 1925: R. G. Collingwood. *Outlines of a Philosophy of Art*. London: Oxford University Press, 1925.

Collingwood 1933: R. G. Collingwood. *An Essay on Philosophical Method*. Oxford: Clarendon Press, 1933.

Collingwood 1938: R. G. Collingwood. *Principles of Art.* Oxford: Clarendon Press, 1938

Collingwood 1939: R. G. Collingwood. *An Autobiography.* London: Oxford University Press, 1939.

Collingwood 1942: R. G. Collingwood. *The New Leviathan.* Oxford: Clarendon Press, 1942.

Collingwood 1945: R. G. Collingwood. *The Idea of Nature.* Oxford: Clarendon Press, 1945.

Collingwood 1946: R. G. Collingwood. *The Idea of History.* Oxford: Clarendon Press, 1946.

Collins 1965: Peter Collins. *Changing Ideals in Modern Architecture, 1750-1950.* London: Faber and Faber, 1965.

Cooke 1959: Deryck Cooke. *The Language of Music.* London: Oxford University Press, 1959.

Coomaraswamy 1977: Ananda K. Coomaraswamy. *Selected Essays.* Princeton: Princeton University Press, 1977.

Crittenden 1968: Brian Crittenden. "From Description to Evaluation in Aesthetic Judgments." *JAE* 2, 1968, 37-58.

Croce 1901: Benedetto Croce. *Aesthetic as the Science of General Linguistic.* Translated by Douglas Ainslie. 2d ed. London: Macmillan, 1922.

Croce 1906: Benedetto Croce. *What Is Living and What Is Dead of the Philosophy of Hegel.* Translated by Douglas Ainslie. London: Macmillan, 1915.

Croce 1919: "Criticism and History of the Figurative Arts: The Present Phase." In Croce 1966.

Croce 1920: Benedetto Croce. *Ariosto, Shakespeare, and Corneille.* Translated by Douglas Ainslie. New York: Henry Holt, 1920.

Croce 1928: Benedetto Croce. "Aesthetica in Nuce." In Croce 1966.

Croce 1932: Benedetto Croce. "The Aesthetics of Baumgarten." In Croce 1966.

Croce 1935a: Benedetto Croce. "Expression Pure and Otherwise." In Croce 1966.

Croce 1935b: Benedetto Croce. *La Poésie.* Translated by D. Dreyfus. Paris: Presses Universitaires de France, 1950.

Croce 1966: Benedetto Croce. *Philosophy Poetry History.* Translated by Cecil Sprigge. London: Oxford University Press, 1966.

Culler 1975: Jonathan Culler. *Structuralist Poetics.* London: Routledge and Kegan Paul, 1975.

D'Alembert 1751: Jean Le Rond D'Alembert. *Preliminary Discourse to the Encyclopedia of Diderot.* Translated by Richard Schwab and Walter Rex. Indianapolis: Bobbs-Merrill, 1963.

Danto 1964: Arthur C. Danto. "The Artworld." in Dickie and Sclafani 1977.

Danto 1973: Arthur C. Danto. "Artworks and Real Things." In Dickie and Sclafani 1977.

Danto 1974: Arthur C. Danto. "The Transfiguration of the Commonplace." *JAAC* 33, 1974-75, 139-148.

Danto 1976: Arthur C. Danto. "An Answer or Two for Sparshott." *JAAC* 35, 1976-77, 81-82.

Danto 1981: Arthur C. Danto. *The Transfiguration of the Commonplace: A Philosophy of Art*. Cambridge: Harvard University Press, 1981.

Dearden 1967: R. F. Dearden. "The Concept of Play." In R. S. Peters, ed., *The Concept of Education*, 73-91. London: Routledge and Kegan Paul, 1967.

Denis 1890: Maurice Denis. "Definition du néo-traditionnisme." In his *Theories 1890-1910*. 4th ed. Paris: L. Ronart et J. Watelin, 1920.

Derrida 1967: Jacques Derrida. *Of Grammatology*. Translated by Gayatri Chakravorty Spivak. Baltimore: Johns Hopkins University Press, 1976.

De Val 1978: Dorothy De Val. "The Enfant Terrible Is Now a Senior Citizen." *Music Magazine* 1, January-February 1978, 12-13.

Dewey 1934: John Dewey. *Art as Experience*. New York: Minton, Balch, 1934.

Dickie 1962: George Dickie. "Is Psychology Relevant to Aesthetics?" In Coleman 1968, 321-335.

Dickie 1964: George Dickie. "The Myth of the Aesthetic Attitude." *APQ* 1, 1964, 56-66.

Dickie 1974: George Dickie. *Art and the Aesthetic: An Institutional Analysis*. Ithaca: Cornell University Press, 1974.

Dickie and Sclafani 1977: George Dickie and R. J. Sclafani, eds. *Aesthetics: A Critical Anthology*. New York: St. Martin's Press, 1977.

Diffey 1979: T. J. Diffey. "On Defining Art." *BJA* 19, 1979, 15-23.

Dillon 1977: John Dillon. *The Middle Platonists*. Ithaca: Cornell University Press, 1977.

Donagan 1962: Alan Donagan. *The Later Philosophy of R. G. Collingwood*. London: Oxford University Press, 1962.

Dorfles 1969: Gillo Dorfles, ed. *Kitsch: The World of Bad Taste*. London: Studio Vista, 1969.

Doxiadis 1937: Constantinos A. Doxiadis. *Architectural Space in Ancient Greece*. Translated by Jaqueline Tyrwhitt. Cambridge: MIT Press, 1972.

Dray 1957: W. H. Dray. *Laws and Explanation in History.* Oxford: Oxford University Press, 1957.

Dubos, 1719: J. B. Du Bos (sic), *Critical Reflections on Poetry, Painting and Music.* 5th ed. Translated by Thomas Nugent. London: John Nourse, 1748.

Ducasse 1929: C. J. Ducasse. *The Philosophy of Art.* New York: Dial Press, 1929.

Ducasse 1964: C. J. Ducasse. "Art as the Language of the Emotions." In Jacobus 1968.

Dufrenne 1953: Mikel Dufrenne. *Phenomenology of Aesthetic Experience.* Translated by Edward S. Casey and Albert A. Anderson. Evanston: Northwestern University Press, 1973.

Eco 1962: Umberto Eco. *L'Oeuvre ouverte.* Translated by Chantal Roux de Bézieux. Paris: Editions du Seuil, 1965.

Eco 1976: Umberto Eco. *A Theory of Semiotics.* Bloomington: Indiana University Press, 1976.

Ehrenzweig 1967: Anton Ehrenzweig. *The Hidden Order of Art.* London: Paladin Books, 1970.

Eliade 1964: Mircea Eliade. *Shamanism: Archaic Techniques of Ecstasy.* Translated by Willard R. Trask. Princeton: Princeton University Press, 1964.

Eliot 1963: T. S. Eliot. *Collected Poems 1909-1962.* New York: Harcourt, Brace, and Jovanovich, 1963.

Empson 1935: William Empson. *Some Versions of Pastoral.* London: Chatto and Windus, 1935.

Empson 1968: William Empson. "Rhythm and Imagery in English Poetry." In Osborne 1968.

Escher 1971: M. C. Escher. *The Graphic Work of M. C. Escher.* New York: Ballantine Books, 1971.

Esterow 1973: Milton Esterow. *The Art Stealers.* 2d ed. New York: Macmillan, 1973.

Fackenheim 1961: Emil L. Fackenheim. *Metaphysics and Historicity.* Milwaukee: Marquette University Press, 1961.

Fergusson 1949: Francis Fergusson. *The Idea of a Theater.* Princeton: Princeton University Press, 1949.

Fiedler 1876: Conrad Fiedler. *On Judging Works of Visual Art.* Translated by Henry Schaefer-Simmern and Fulmer Mood. 2d ed. Berkeley: University of California Press, 1957.

Findlay 1968: J. N. Findlay. "The Perspicuous and the Poignant." In Osborne 1968, 124-147.

Fischer 1963: Ernst Fischer. *The Necessity of Art.* Harmondsworth: Penguin Books, 1963.

Focillon 1942: Henri Focillon. *The Life of Forms in Art.* Translated by Charles Beecher Hogan and George Kubler. New Haven: Yale University Press, 1942.

Fodor 1975: J. A. Fodor. *The Language of Thought.* New York: Crowell, 1975.

Frankl 1914: Paul Frankl. *Principles of Architectural History.* Translated by James F. O'Gorman. Cambridge: MIT Press, 1968.

Fraser 1962: Douglas Fraser. *Primitive Art.* London: Thames and Hudson, 1962.

Fried 1967: Michael Fried. "Art and Objecthood." In Dickie and Sclafani 1977, 438-460.

Friedländer 1942: Max J. Friedländer. *On Art and Connoisseurship.* Translated by Tancred Borenius. Boston: Beacon Press, 1960.

Fry 1919: Roger Fry. "The Artist's Vision." In his *Vision and Design.* London: Chatto and Windus, 1920.

Fry 1939: Roger Fry. *Last Lectures.* Cambridge: Cambridge University Press, 1939.

Frye 1957: Northrop Frye. *Anatomy of Criticism.* Princeton: Princeton University Press, 1957.

Frye 1963: Northrop Frye, ed. *Romanticism Reconsidered.* New York: Columbia University Press, 1963.

Frye 1967: Northrop Frye. *The Modern Century.* Toronto: Oxford University Press, 1967.

Frye 1971: Northrop Frye. *The Critical Path.* Bloomington: Indiana University Press, 1971.

Fubini 1968: Enrico Fubini. *L'estetica musicale dal settecento a oggi.* 2d ed. Torino: Einaudi, 1968.

Fuller 1969: Lon Fuller. *Morality and the Law.* 2d ed. New Haven: Yale University Press, 1969.

Gabo 1937: Naum Gabo. "The Constructive Idea in Art." In Herbert 1964.

Gadamer 1960: Hans-Georg Gadamer. *Truth and Method.* London: Sheed and Ward, 1975.

Gadamer 1967: Hans-Georg Gadamer. *Kleine Schriften, II: Interpretationen.* Tübingen: J. C. B. Mohr, 1967.

Gallie 1964: W. B. Gallie. *Philosophy and the Historical Understanding.* London: Chatto and Windus, 1964.

Gay 1976: Peter Gay. *Art and Act.* New York: Harper and Row, 1976.

Gibson 1961: Robert Gibson. *Modern French Poets on Poetry.* Cambridge: Cambridge University Press, 1961.

Gibson 1971: James J. Gibson. "The Information Available in Paintings." *Leonardo* 4, 1971, 27-35.

Giedion 1964: Siegfried Giedion. *The Eternal Present, I: The Beginnings of Art*. Princeton: Princeton University Press, 1964.

Gilot and Lake 1965: Françoise Gilot and Carlton Lake. *Life with Picasso*. New York: Signet Books, 1965.

Gilson 1957: Etienne Gilson. *Painting and Reality*. New York: Pantheon, 1957.

Gilson 1963: Etienne Gilson. *The Arts of the Beautiful*. New York: Scribners, 1965.

Gilson 1964: Etienne Gilson. *Forms and Substances in the Arts*. Translated by Salvator Attanasio. New York: Scribners, 1966.

Gleizes and Metzinger 1912: Albert Gleizes and Jean Metzinger. "Cubism." In Herbert 1964.

Goldman 1970: Alvin I. Goldman. *A Theory of Human Action*. Englewood Cliffs: Prentice-Hall, 1970.

Goldwater and Treves 1945: Robert Goldwater and Marco Treves, eds. *Artists on Art*. New York: Pantheon, 1945.

Gombrich 1960: E. H. Gombrich. *Art and Illusion*. New York: Pantheon, 1960.

Gombrich 1963: E. H. Gombrich. *Meditations on a Hobby Horse*. London: Phaidon, 1963.

Gombrich 1979: E. H. Gombrich. *The Sense of Order*. London: Phaidon, 1979.

Goodman 1951: Nelson Goodman. *The Structure of Appearance*. Cambridge: Harvard University Press, 1951.

Goodman 1968: Nelson Goodman. *Languages of Art*. Indianapolis: Bobbs-Merrill, 1968.

Goodman 1972: Nelson Goodman. *Problems and Projects*. Indianapolis: Bobbs-Merrill, 1972.

Goodman 1977: Nelson Goodman. "When Is Art?" In David Perkins and Barbara Leonidas, eds., *The Arts and Cognition*, 11-19. Baltimore: Johns Hopkins University Press, 1977.

Goscinny and Uderzo 1963: René Goscinny and A. Uderzo. *Astérix et les Goths*. Paris: Dargaud, 1963.

Gosvami 1961: O. Gosvami. *The Story of Indian Music*. 2d ed. Bombay: Asia Publishing House, 1961.

Gotshalk 1947: D. W. Gotshalk. *Art and the Social Order*. Chicago: University of Chicago Press, 1947.

Greenberg 1939: Clement Greenberg. "Avant-Garde and Kitsch." In his *Art and Culture*, 3-21. Boston: Beacon Press, 1971.

Greenberg 1971: Clement Greenberg. "Counter-Avant-Garde." *Art International* 15, May 1971, 16-19.

Greene 1940: T. M. Greene. *The Arts and the Art of Criticism*. Princeton: Princeton University Press, 1940.

Grosser 1951: Maurice Grosser. *The Painter's Eye*. New York: Mentor Books, 1956.

Gutman 1972: Robert Gutman, ed. *People and Buildings*. New York: Basic Books, 1972.

Haase 1960: Rudolf Haase. "Leibniz." In *Die Musik in Geschichte und Gegenwart*, Bd. 8, 498-503. Kassel: Bärenreiter, 1960.

Hall 1959: E. W. Hall. *The Silent Language*. New York: Doubleday, 1959.

Han 1965: Han Suyin. *The Crippled Tree*. London: Cape, 1965.

Hanslick 1854: Eduard Hanslick. *The Beautiful in Music*. Translated by Gustav Cohen. New York: Liberal Arts Press, 1957.

Harding 1963: D. W. Harding. *Experience into Words*. London: Chatto and Windus, 1963.

Hare 1952: Richard M. Hare. *The Language of Morals*. Oxford: Clarendon Press, 1952.

Hare 1963: Richard M. Hare. *Freedom and Reason*. Oxford: Clarendon Press, 1963.

d'Harnoncourt and McShine 1973: Anne d'Harnoncourt and Kynaston McShine, eds. *Marcel Duchamp*. New York: Museum of Modern Art, 1973.

Harrison 1960: Bernard Harrison. "Some Uses of 'Good' in Criticism." *Mind* 69, 1960, 206-222.

Harrison 1968: Andrew Harrison. "Works of Art and Other Cultural Objects." *PAS* 68, 1967-68, 105-128.

Hartman 1967: Robert S. Hartman. *The Structure of Value: Foundations of Scientific Axiology*. Carbondale: Southern Illinois University Press, 1967.

Hegel 1821: G. W. F. Hegel. *Philosophy of Right*. Translated by T. M. Knox. Oxford: Clarendon Press, 1942.

Hegel 1835: G. W. F. Hegel. *Aesthetics*. Translated by T. M. Knox. Oxford: Clarendon Press, 1975.

Heidegger 1943: Martin Heidegger. Postscript to "What Is Metaphysics?" Translated by R. F. C. Hull and Alan Crick. In his *Existence and Being*. London: Vision Press, 1949.

Heidegger 1960: Martin Heidegger. "The Origin of the Work of Art." In Heidegger 1971.

Heidegger 1961: Martin Heidegger. *An Introduction to Metaphysics*. Translated by Ralph Manheim. Garden City: Anchor Books, 1961.

Heidegger 1971: Martin Heidegger. *Poetry, Language and Thought*. Translated by Albert Hofstadter. New York: Harper and Row, 1971.

Henri 1923: Robert Henri. *The Art Spirit*. New York: Lippincott, 1923.

Hepburn 1966: R. W. Hepburn. "Emotions and Emotional Qualities." In Barrett 1966.

Herbert 1964: Robert L. Herbert, ed. *Modern Artists on Art*. Englewood Cliffs: Prentice-Hall, 1964.

Herder 1772: J. G. Herder. "Essay on the Origin of Language." In Moran 1966.

Herrigel 1953: Eugene Herrigel. *Zen in the Art of Archery*. New York: Pantheon, 1953.

Hilles 1936: F. W. Hilles. *The Literary Career of Sir Joshua Reynolds*. Cambridge: Cambridge University Press, 1936.

Hirsch 1967: E. D. Hirsch. *Validity in Interpretation*. New Haven: Yale University Press, 1967.

Holroyd 1974: Michael Holroyd. *Augustus John: A Biography*. London: Heinemann, 1974-75.

Hook 1966: Sidney Hook, ed. *Art and Philosophy*. New York: New York University Press, 1966.

Hoskins 1955: W. G. Hoskins. *The Making of the English Landscape*. London: Hodder and Stoughton, 1955.

Hospers 1955: John Hospers. "The Concept of Artistic Expression." *PAS* 55, 1954-55, 313-344.

Housman 1933: A. E. Housman. *The Name and Nature of Poetry*. Cambridge: Cambridge University Press, 1933.

Huizinga 1955: Johan Huizinga. *Homo Ludens: A Study of the Play Element in Culture*. Translated by R. F. C. Hull. Boston: Beacon Press, 1955.

Hume 1757: David Hume. "Of the Standard of Taste." In his *Four Dissertations*. London: A. Millar, 1757.

Hutcheson 1725: Francis Hutcheson. *Inquiry into the Original of Our Ideas of Beauty and Virtue*. 4th ed. London: D. Midwinter and others, 1738.

Ingarden 1931: Roman Ingarden. *The Literary Work of Art*. Translated by George G. Grabowicz. Evanston: Northwestern University Press, 1973.

Isenberg 1949: Arnold Isenberg. "Critical Communication." In his *Aesthetics and the Theory of Criticism*. Chicago: University of Chicago Press, 1973.

Ivins 1943: W. M. Ivins, Jr. *How Prints Look*. Boston: Beacon Press, 1958.

Ivins 1953: W. M. Ivins, Jr. *Prints and Visual Communication*. Cambridge: Harvard University Press, 1953.

Jacobus 1968: Lee A. Jacobus, ed. *Aesthetics and the Arts*. New York: McGraw-Hill, 1968.

Jäger 1967: Gerhard Jäger. *"Nus" in Platons Dialogen*. Göttingen: Vandenhoeck und Ruprecht, 1967.

Jeffrey 1816: Francis Jeffrey. "Essay on Beauty." In Aschenbrenner and Isenberg 1965, 277-294.

Jenkins 1958: Iredell Jenkins. *Art and the Human Enterprise*. Cambridge: Harvard University Press, 1958.

Johnson 1759: Samuel Johnson. *The Idler*. In his *Collected Works*, vol. 4. Oxford: Talboys and Wheeler, 1825.

Jones 1975: Peter Jones. *Philosophy and the Novel*. Oxford: Clarendon Press, 1975.

Jonson 1641: Ben Jonson. *Timber: or, Discoveries,* in his *Works*, vol. 8. Edited by C. H. Herferd and Percy and Evelyn Simpson. Oxford: Clarendon Press, 1947.

Kant 1790: Immanuel Kant. *Critique of Judgment*. Translated by J. C. Meredith. Oxford: Clarendon Press, 1952.

Kaprow 1966: Allan Kaprow. *Assemblage, Environments and Happenings*. New York: Abrams, 1966.

Karshan 1970: Donald Karshan. "The Seventies: Post-Object Art." In Dickie and Sclafani 1977.

Katz 1966: Jerrold Katz. *The Philosophy of Language*. New York: Harper and Row, 1966.

Keeling 1934: S. V. Keeling. *Descartes*. London: Benn, 1934.

Kenner 1966: Hugh Kenner. "The Counterfeiters." In Jacobus 1968, 148-160.

Khatchadourian 1971: Haig Khatchadourian. *The Concept of Art*. New York: New York University Press, 1971.

Kierkegaard 1843: S. Kierkegaard. *Either/Or*. Translated by W. Lowrie. Garden City: Anchor Books, 1959.

Kingsley 1864: Charles Kingsley. *The Water-Babies*. London: Macmillan, 1864.

Kivy 1973: Peter Kivy. *Speaking of Art*. The Hague: Martinus Nijhoff, 1973.

Klee 1924: Paul Klee. "On Modern Art." In Herbert 1964.

Kolers 1977: Paul A. Kolers. "Reading Pictures and Reading Text." In David Perkins and Barbara Leonidas, eds., *The Arts and Cognition*, 136-164. Baltimore: Johns Hopkins University Press, 1977.

Kovach 1974: Francis J. Kovach. *Philosophy of Beauty*. Norman: University of Oklahoma Press, 1974.

Kracauer 1960: Siegfried Kracauer. *Theory of Film*. New York: Oxford University Press, 1960.

Kramer 1973: Hilton Kramer. *The Age of the Avant-Garde*. New York: Farrar, Strauss and Giroux, 1973.

Kramer 1975: Hilton Kramer. "Revenge of the Philistines." *Commentary* 59, May 1975, 35-40.

Krauss 1971: Rosalind E. Krauss. *Terminal Iron Works*. Cambridge: MIT Press, 1971.

Kris 1952: Ernst Kris. *Psychoanalytic Explorations in Art*. New York: International Universities Press, 1952.

Kuhn 1970: T. S. Kuhn. *The Structure of Scientific Revolutions*. 2d ed. Chicago: University of Chicago Press, 1970.

Kuhn 1976: Reinhard Kuhn. *The Demon of Noontide*. Princeton: Princeton University Press, 1976.

Laing 1978: D. Laing. *The Marxist Theory of Art*. Hassocks: Harvester Press, 1978.

Lake 1954: Beryl Lake. "A Study of the Irrefutability of Two Aesthetic Theories." In W. Elton, ed., *Aesthetics and Language*, 100-113. Oxford: Blackwell, 1954.

Lamb 1962: Lynton Lamb. *Drawing for Illustration*. New York: Oxford University Press, 1962.

Lang 1975: Berel Lang. *Art and Inquiry*. Detroit: Wayne State University Press, 1975.

Lang and Williams 1972: Berel Lang and Forrest Williams, eds. *Marxism and Art*. New York: David McKay, 1972.

Langan 1959: Thomas D. Langan. *The Meaning of Heidegger*. New York: Columbia University Press, 1959.

Langer 1942: S. K. Langer. *Philosophy in a New Key*. Cambridge: Harvard University Press, 1942.

Langer 1953: S. K. Langer. *Feeling and Form*. New York: Scribners, 1953.

Langer 1961: S. K. Langer, ed. *Reflections on Art*. New York: Oxford University Press, 1961.

Lasserre 1954: François Lasserre. Introduction to Pseudo-Plutarch, *De Musica*. Olten: Urs Graf, 1954.

Lee 1911: Vernon Lee. *Beauty and Ugliness*. London: Lane, 1911.

Leeuw 1963: Gerardus van der Leeuw. *Sacred and Profane Beauty: The Holy in Art*. Translated by David E. Green. New York: Holt, Rinehart, Winston, 1963.

Legge 1885: James Legge, trans. *Yo Ki or the Record of Music*. In Max Mueller, ed., *Sacred Books of the East*, vol. 28. London: Oxford University Press, 1885.

Leitner 1973. Bernard Leitner. *The Architecture of Ludwig Wittgenstein: A Documentation*. Halifax: Nova Scotia College of Art and Design, 1973.

Levine 1969: Les Levine. "For Immediate Release." *Art and the Artist*, May 1969, 46-50. Cited from Burnham 1974.

Lévi-Strauss 1962: Claude Lévi-Strauss. *The Savage Mind*. Chicago: University of Chicago Press, 1966.

Lévi-Strauss 1964: Claude Lévi-Strauss. *The Raw and the Cooked*. Translated by John and Doreen Weightman. New York: Harper and Row, 1969.

Lewis 1946: C. I. Lewis. *An Analysis of Knowledge and Valuation*. La Salle: Open Court, 1946.

Lewis 1969: David K. Lewis. *Convention: A Philosophical Study*. Cambridge: Harvard University Press, 1969.

Lewis 1973: David K. Lewis. *Counterfactuals*. Cambridge: Harvard University Press, 1973.

Lin 1935: Lin Yutang. *My Country and My People*. London: Heinemann, 1935.

Lipman 1967: Matthew Lipman. *What Happens in Art*. New York: Appleton Century Crofts, 1967.

Liu 1962: J. J. Y. Liu. *The Art of Chinese Poetry*. London: Routledge and Kegan Paul, 1962.

Lloyd 1967: A. L. Lloyd. *Folksong in England*. New York: International Publishers, 1967.

Locke 1694: John Locke. *An Essay Concerning Human Understanding*. 2d ed. Edited by Alexander Campbell Fraser. London: Oxford University Press, 1894.

Lord 1960: Arthur B. Lord. *The Singer of Tales*. Cambridge: Harvard University Press, 1960.

Lukács 1963: Georg Lukács. *Aesthetik, I: Die Eigenart des Aesthetischen*. Darmstadt: Luchterhand, 1963.

McClanahan 1971: Preston McClanahan. "To Prove the Fact of Existence." *Arts Magazine* 45, no. 8, Summer 1971, 37-39.

McClellan 1976: James E. McClellan. *The Philosophy of Education*. Englewood Cliffs: Prentice-Hall, 1976.

Macdonald 1949: Margaret Macdonald. "Some Distinctive Features of Arguments Used in Criticism of the Arts." *PAS* Supp. vol. 23, 1949, 183-194.

MacDonald 1976: Malcolm MacDonald. *Schoenberg*. London: Dent, 1976.

McLuhan and Parker 1968: Marshall McLuhan and Harley Parker. *Through the Vanishing Point*. New York: Harper and Row, 1968.

Malraux 1953: André Malraux. *The Voices of Silence*. Translated by Stuart Gilbert. Garden City: Doubleday, 1953.

Marcel 1943: Gabriel Marcel. "The Dangerous Situation of Ethical Values." In his *Homo Viator*. Translated by Emma Crauford. Chicago: Regnery, 1957.

Marck 1969: Jan van der Marck. "Why Pack a Museum?" *ArtsCanada* 26, no. 5, October 1969, 34-37.

Margolis 1965: Joseph Margolis. *The Language of Art and Art Criticism*. Detroit: Wayne State University Press, 1965.

Margolis 1969: Joseph Margolis. "Psychological and Logical Distinctions Respecting Fiction." *JAAC* 27, 1969, 257-260.

Margolis 1980a: Joseph Margolis. *Art and Philosophy*. Atlantic Heights: Humanities Press, 1980.

Margolis 1980b: Joseph Margolis. Review of Riffaterre 1978. *JAAC* 39, 1980, 93-97.

Maritain 1930: Jacques Maritain. *Art and Scholasticism*. London: Sheed and Ward, 1930.

Maritain 1953: Jacques Maritain. *Creative Intuition in Art and Poetry*. New York: Pantheon, 1953.

Martin 1978: D. Martin. Letter to the editor. *Scots Magazine*, New Series 108, March 1978, 654-656.

Marx 1859: Karl Marx. *Contribution to the Critique of Political Economy*. Translated by S. W. Ryazanskaya. New York: International Publishers, 1970.

Marx 1867: Karl Marx. *Capital*, vol. 1. Translated by Samuel Morse and Edward Aveling. Chicago: Charles H. Kerr, 1906.

Marx and Engels 1846: Karl Marx and Friedrich Engels. *The German Ideology*. Translated by R. Pascal. New York: International Publishers, 1947.

Mascall 1957: E. L. Mascall. *Words and Images*. London: Longmans, Green, 1957.

Mathew 1963: Gervase Mathew. *Byzantine Aesthetics*. London: John Murray, 1963.

Melden 1961: A. I. Melden. *Free Action*. London: Routledge and Kegan Paul, 1961.

Mellen 1970: Peter Mellen. *The Group of Seven*. Toronto: McClelland and Stewart, 1970.

Merleau-Ponty 1942: Maurice Merleau-Ponty. *The Structure of Behaviour*. Translated by Alden L. Fisher. London: Methuen, 1965.

Merleau-Ponty 1964: Maurice Merleau-Ponty. *Sense and Non-Sense*. Translated by Herbert L. Dreyfus and Patricia A. Dreyfus. Evanston: Northwestern University Press, 1964.

Meyer 1956: Leonard B. Meyer. *Emotion and Meaning in Music*. Chicago: University of Chicago Press, 1956.

Meyer 1967: Leonard B. Meyer. *Music, the Arts, and Ideas*. Chicago: University of Chicago Press, 1967.

Moles 1966: Abraham Moles. *Information Theory and Aesthetic Perception*. Translated by Joel E. Cohen. Urbana: University of Illinois Press, 1966.

Monod 1969: Jacques Monod. *From Biology to Ethics*. San Diego: Salk Institute, 1969.

Moore 1903: G. E. Moore. *Principia Ethica*. Cambridge: Cambridge University Press, 1903.

Moore 1914: George Moore. *Vale*. London: Heinemann, 1947.

Moore 1951: Marianne Moore. *Collected Poems*. London: Faber and Faber, 1951.

Moran 1966: John H. Moran, ed. and trans. *On the Origin of Language*. New York: Ungar, 1966.

Morawski 1968: Stefan Morawski. "Mimesis—Lukacs' Universal Principle." *Science and Society* 32, 1968, 26-36.

Morawski 1974: Stefan Morawski. *Inquiries into the Fundamentals of Aesthetics*. Cambridge: MIT Press, 1974.

Munro 1949: Thomas Munro. *The Arts and Their Interrelations*. New York: Liberal Arts Press, 1949.

Nahm 1956: Milton C. Nahm. *The Artist as Creator*. Baltimore: Johns Hopkins University Press, 1956.

Nahm 1975: Milton C. Nahm, ed. *Readings in Philosophy of Art and Aesthetics*. Englewood Cliffs: Prentice-Hall, 1975.

Namenwirth 1964: Micha Namenwirth. "The Classification of Standards in Music Criticism." Paper read to American Society for Aesthetics, 31 October 1964.

Nietzsche 1872: Friedrich Nietzsche. *The Birth of Tragedy from the Spirit of Music*. Translated by Walter Kaufman. New York: Vintage Books, 1967.

Nietzsche 1887: Friedrich Nietzsche. *On the Genealogy of Morals*. Translated by Walter Kaufman. New York: Vintage Books, 1969.

Nowell-Smith 1954: P. H. Nowell-Smith. *Ethics*. Harmondsworth: Penguin Books, 1954.

Nuttall 1968: Jeff Nuttall. *Bomb Culture*. New York: Delta Books, 1970.

Ogden, Richards, and Wood 1925: C. K. Ogden, I. A. Richards, and James Wood. *The Foundations of Aesthetics*. London: Allen and Unwin, 1925.

Olen 1977: Jeffrey Olen. "Theories, Interpretations and Aesthetic Qualities." *JAAC* 35, 1977, 425-431.

Ong 1967: Walter Ong, S. J. *Presence of the Word*. New Haven: Yale University Press, 1967.

Osborne 1955: Harold Osborne. *Aesthetics and Criticism*. London: Routledge and Kegan Paul, 1955.

Osborne 1963: Harold Osborne. "The Quality of Feeling in Art." In Osborne 1968.

Osborne 1968: Harold Osborne, ed. *Aesthetics in the Modern World*. London: Thames and Hudson, 1968.

O'Shaughnessy 1874: Arthur O'Shaughnessy. "Ode." In his *Music and Moonlight*. London: Chatto and Windus, 1874.

Panofsky 1954: Erwin Panofsky. *Galileo as a Critic of the Arts*. The Hague: Martinus Nijhoff, 1954.

Panofsky 1955: Erwin Panofsky. *Meaning in the Visual Arts*. Garden City: Anchor Books, 1955.

Panofsky 1968: Erwin Panofsky. *Idea*. Translated by Joseph J. S. Peake. Columbia: University of South Carolina Press, 1968.

Parker 1939: DeWitt H. Parker. "The Nature of Art." *Revue internationale de philosophie* 1, 1939, 684-702.

Parkinson 1970: G. H. R. Parkinson. "Lukács on the Central Category of Aesthetics." In his *Georg Lukács*, 109-146. London: Weidenfeld and Nicolson, 1970.

Passmore 1951: J. A. Passmore. "The Dreariness of Aesthetics." *Mind* 60, 1951, 318-335.

Pattison 1970: Bruce Pattison. *Music and Poetry of the English Renaissance*. 2d ed. London: Methuen, 1970.

Payzant 1970: Geoffrey Payzant. *Keys in Musical Perception. Ideas* (CBC broadcast), January 5-9, 1970.

Payzant 1978: Geoffrey Payzant. *Glenn Gould, Music and Mind*. Toronto: Van Nostrand Reinhold, 1978.

Paz 1974: Octavio Paz. *Children of the Mire*. Translated by Rachel Phillips. Cambridge: Harvard University Press, 1974.

Peckham 1965: Morse Peckham. *Man's Rage for Chaos*. New York: Schocken, 1967.

Peirce 1933: Charles S. Peirce. *Collected Papers of Charles Sanders Peirce*, vol. 4. Edited by Charles Hartshorne and Paul Weiss. Cambridge: Harvard University Press, 1933.

Pepper 1945: Stephen C. Pepper. *The Basis of Criticism in the Arts*. Cambridge: Harvard University Press, 1945.

Pepper 1949: Stephen C. Pepper. *Principles of Art Appreciation*. New York: Harcourt, Brace and World, 1949.

Peters 1958: R. S. Peters. *The Concept of Motivation*. London: Routledge and Kegan Paul, 1958.

Pettit 1975: Philip Pettit. *The Concept of Structuralism*. Berkeley: University of California Press, 1975.

Piles 1708: Roger de Piles. *Cours de peinture par principes*. Paris: Barrois l'aîné, 1791.

Podro 1972: Michael Podro. *The Manifold in Perception*. London: Oxford University Press, 1972.

Pope 1965: Arthur Upham Pope. *Persian Architecture*. New York: Braziller, 1965.

Prall 1936: D. W. Prall. *Aesthetic Analysis*. New York: Crowell, 1936.

Pratt 1931: Carroll C. Pratt. *The Meaning of Music*. New York: McGraw-Hill, 1931.

Praz 1933: Mario Praz. *The Romantic Agony*. Translated by Angus Davidson. London: Oxford University Press, 1933.

Praz 1970: Mario Praz. *Mnemosyne: The Parallel between Literature and the Visual Arts*. Princeton: Princeton University Press, 1970.

Price 1977: Kingsley Price. "The Truth about Psychical Distance." *JAAC* 35, 1977, 411-423.

Quine 1960: W. V. Quine. *Word and Object*. Cambridge: Harvard University Press, 1960.

Quinton 1973: Anthony Quinton. *The Nature of Things*. London: Routledge and Kegan Paul, 1973.

Rader and Jessup 1976: Melvin Rader and Bertram Jessup. *Art and Human Values*. Englewood Cliffs: Prentice-Hall, 1976.

Radford 1978: Colin Radford. "Fakes." *Mind* 87, 1978, 66-76.

Randall 1971: Francis B. Randall. "The Goofy in Art." *BJA* 11, 1971, 327-340.

Raphael 1947: Max Raphael. *Prehistoric Pottery and Civilization in Egypt*. Translated by Norbert Guterman. New York: Pantheon, 1947.

Ratcliff 1971a: Carter Ratcliff. "New York Letter." *Art International* 15, no. 4, April 1971, 25ff.

Ratcliff 1971b: Carter Ratcliff. "New York Letter." *Art International* 15, no. 5, May 1971, 32ff.

Rawls 1955: John Rawls. "Two Concepts of Rules." *PR* 64, 1955, 3-32.

Read 1962: Herbert Read. "Beauty and the Beast." In *Eranos-Jahrbuch XXX*, 175-210. Zurich: Rhein-Verlag, 1962.

Reich 1971: Willi Reich. *Schoenberg: A Critical Biography*. Translated by Leo Black. London: Longmans, 1971.

Reid 1785: Thomas Reid. "On Taste." In his *Essays on the Intellectual Powers of Man*. William Hamilton, ed., *The Works of Thomas Reid*. 6th ed. Edinburgh: Maclachlan and Stewart, 1863.

Reid 1929: L. A. Reid. "Beauty and Significance." In Langer 1961.

Richards 1929: I. A. Richards. *Practical Criticism*. London: Kegan Paul, 1929.

Riffaterre 1978: Michael Riffaterre. *Semiotics of Poetry*. Bloomington: Indiana University Press, 1978.

Robinson 1974: Jenefer M. Robinson. "The Individuation of Speech Acts." *PQ* 24, 1974, 316-336.

Robinson 1977: Jenefer M. Robinson. "The Eliminability of Artistic Acts." *JAAC* 36, 1977, 81-89.

Rogers 1968: L. R. Rogers. "Sculptural Thinking—III." In Osborne 1968.

Rosen 1971: Charles Rosen. *The Classical Style*. New York: Viking, 1971.

Rosenberg 1959: Harold Rosenberg. *The Tradition of the New*. New York: Horizon Press, 1959.

Rosenberg 1964: Harold Rosenberg. *The Anxious Object*. New York: Horizon Press, 1964.

Rosenberg 1967: Jakob Rosenberg. *On Quality in Art*. Princeton: Princeton University Press, 1967.

Rosenberg 1972: Harold Rosenberg. *The De-Definition of Art*. New York: Horizon Press, 1972.

Rousseau 1761: Jean-Jacques Rousseau. "Essay on the Origin of Languages." Written in 1761. In Moran 1966.

Ryle 1949: Gilbert Ryle. *The Concept of Mind*. London: Hutchinson, 1949.

Santayana 1896: George Santayana. *The Sense of Beauty*. New York: Collier Books, 1961.

Santayana 1900: George Santayana. *Interpretations of Poetry and Religion*. New York: Harper Torchbooks, 1957.

Sartre 1939a: Jean-Paul Sartre. *The Emotions: Outline of a Theory*. Translated by Bernard Frechtman. New York: Philosophical Library, 1948.

Sartre 1939b: Jean-Paul Sartre. "François Mauriac and Freedom." In his *Literary Essays*. Translated by Annette Michelson. New York: Philosophical Library, 1957.

Sartre 1940: Jean-Paul Sartre. *The Psychology of Imagination*. Translated by Bernard Frechtman. New York: Washington Square Press, 1965.

Sartre 1943: Jean-Paul Sartre. *Being and Nothingness*. Translated by Hazel E. Barnes. New York: Philosophical Library, 1956.

Sartre 1946: Jean-Paul Sartre. *Existentialism and Humanism*. Translated by Philip Mairet. London: Eyre Methuen, 1973.

Sartre 1950: Jean-Paul Sartre. "The Artist and His Conscience." Translated by Benita Eisler. In Lang and Williams 1972, 213-225.

Sartre 1952: Jean-Paul Sartre. *Saint Genet, Actor and Martyr*. Translated by Bernard Frechtman. New York: Braziller, 1962.

Sartre 1957: Jean-Paul Sartre. *Search for a Method*. Translated by Hazel E. Barnes. New York: Knopf, 1963.

Sartre 1965: Jean-Paul Sartre. *Situations*. Translated by Benita Eisler. New York: Braziller, 1965.

Sartre 1973: Jean-Paul Sartre. "A Structure of Language." In his *Politics and Literature*. Translated by J. A. Underwood. London: Calder and Boyars, 1973.

Saussure 1916: F. de Saussure. *Course in General Linguistics*. Translated by Wade Baskin. New York: Philosophical Library, 1959.

Schafer 1977: R. Murray Schafer. *The Tuning of the World*. Toronto: McClelland and Stewart, 1977.

Schapiro 1966: Meyer Schapiro. "On Perfection, Coherence and Unity of Form and Content." In Hook 1966, 3-15.

Scheler 1954: Max Scheler. *The Nature of Sympathy*. Translated by Peter Heath. London: Routledge and Kegan Paul, 1954.

Schiller 1795: J. C. F. Schiller. *On the Aesthetic Education of Man*. Translated by Elizabeth M. Wilkinson and L. A. Willoughby. Oxford: Clarendon Press, 1967.

Schoenberg 1964: Arnold Schoenberg. *Letters*. Edited and translated by Erwin Stein. London: Faber and Faber, 1964.

Scholes 1975: Robert Scholes. *Structuralism in Literature*. New Haven: Yale University Press, 1975.

Schopenhauer 1818: Arthur Schopenhauer. *The World as Will and Representation*. Translated by E. F. Payne. London: Routledge and Kegan Paul, 1883.

Schwartz 1969: Arturo Schwartz. *The Complete Works of Marcel Duchamp*. London: Thames and Hudson, 1969.

Scott 1914: Geoffrey Scott. *The Architecture of Humanism*. London: Constable, 1914.

Scruton 1974: Roger Scruton. *Art and Imagination*. London: Methuen, 1974.

Scruton 1976: Roger Scruton. "Representation in Music." *Philosophy* 51, 1976, 273-287.

Searle 1969: John R. Searle. *Speech Acts: An Essay in the Philosophy of Language*. Cambridge: Cambridge University Press, 1969.

Sessions 1950: Roger Sessions. *The Musical Experience of Composer, Performer, Listener*. New York: Atheneum, 1965.

Sewell 1960: Elizabeth Sewell. *The Orphic Voice*. London: Routledge and Kegan Paul, 1960.

Sharpe 1979: R. A. Sharpe. "Type, Token, Interpretation and Performance." *Mind* 88, 1979, 437-440.

Shearman 1967: John Shearman. *Mannerism*. Harmondsworth: Penguin Books, 1967.

Sibley 1959: Frank N. Sibley. "Aesthetic Concepts." *PR* 68, 1959, 421-450.

Sibley 1968: Frank N. Sibley. "Objectivity in Aesthetics." *PAS* Supp. vol. 42, 1968, 31-54.

Sircello 1972: Guy Sircello. *Mind and Art*. Princeton: Princeton University Press, 1972.

Smith 1795: Adam Smith. "Of the Nature of That Imitation Which Takes Place in What Are Called the Imitative Arts." In Aschenbrenner and Isenberg 1965.

Smith 1968: David Smith. *David Smith By David Smith*. London: Thames and Hudson, 1968.

Sontag 1966: Susan Sontag: *Against Interpretation and Other Essays*. New York: Farrar, Strauss and Giroux, 1966.

Souriau 1947: Etienne Souriau. *La Correspondance des arts*. Paris: Flammarion, 1947.

Souriau 1949: Etienne Souriau. "Time in the Plastic Arts." In Langer 1961, 122-141.

Sparshott 1958: F. E. Sparshott. *An Enquiry into Goodness and Related Concepts*. Toronto: University of Toronto Press, 1958.

Sparshott 1962: F. E. Sparshott. "The Concept of Purpose." *Ethics* 62, 1962, 157-170.

Sparshott 1964: F. E. Sparshott. Review of Von Wright 1963. *Ethics* 74, 1964, 223-225.

Sparshott 1966a: F. E. Sparshott. "Philosophy and the Creative Process." *West Coast Review* 1, 1966, 4-13.

Sparshott 1966b: F. E. Sparshott. "Socrates and Thrasymachus." *Monist* 50, 1966, 421-459.

Sparshott 1967a: F. E. Sparshott. "Art as a Source of Knowledge." *Proceedings of the Seventh Interamerican Philosophy Congress* 1, 231-236.

Sparshott 1967b: F. E. Sparshott. "Truth in Fiction." *JAAC* 26, 1967, 3-7.

Sparshott 1968: F. E. Sparshott. "The Unity of Aesthetic Education." *JAE* 2, 1968, 9-21.

Sparshott 1969: F. E. Sparshott. "The Gutenberg Nebula." *JAE* 3, 1969, 135-155.

Sparshott 1970a: F. E. Sparshott. "Disputed Evaluations." *APQ* 7, 1970, 131-142.

Sparshott 1970b: F. E. Sparshott. "First Steps in the Theory of Practice." In Howard Kiefer and Milton K. Munitz, eds., *Ethics and Social Justice*, 21-44. Albany: State University of New York Press, 1970.

Sparshott 1970c: F. E. Sparshott. "Play." In Ralph A. Smith, ed., *Aesthetic Concepts and Education*, 107-134. Urbana: University of Illinois Press, 1970.

Sparshott 1972: F. E. Sparshott. *Looking for Philosophy*. Montreal: McGill-Queen's University Press, 1972.

Sparshott 1973a: F. E. Sparshott. "Iterations and Explications on Relevance." *Dialogue* 12, 1973, 330-333.

Sparshott 1973b: F. E. Sparshott. "Work—The Concept: Past, Present, and Future." *JAE* 7, 1973, 23-38.

Sparshott 1974a: F. E. Sparshott. "As: or, The Limits of Metaphor." *New Literary History* 6, 1974, 75-94.

Sparshott 1974b: F. E. Sparshott. "Goodman on Expression." *Monist* 58, 1974, 187-202.

Sparshott 1975a: F. E. Sparshott. "On Saying What Philosophy Is." *Philosophy in Context* 4, 1974, 17-27.

Sparshott 1975b: F. E. Sparshott. "On the Possibility of a General Theory of Literature." *Centrum* 3, 1975, 5-22.

Sparshott 1976a: F. E. Sparshott. "Religious Experience and Aesthetic Experience." In John King-Farlow, ed., *The Challenge of Religion Today*, 96-114. New York: Science History Publications, 1976.

Sparshott 1976b: F. E. Sparshott. "Some Questions for Danto." *JAAC* 35, 1976, 79-80.

Sparshott 1977: F. E. Sparshott. "Every Horse Has a Mouth." *Philosophy and Literature* 1, 1977, 147-169.

Sparshott 1978: F. E. Sparshott. "Zeno on Art: Anatomy of a Definition." In J. M. Rist, ed., *The Stoics*, 273-290. Berkeley: University of California Press, 1978.

Sparshott 1979: Francis Sparshott. "Poets as Readers." *Transactions of the Royal Society of Canada*, Series 4, 17, 1979, 147-158.

Sparshott 1980: Francis Sparshott. "What Works of Art Are: Notes Towards a Homespun Ontology." *Pacific Philosophical Quarterly* 61, 1980, 346-367.

Sparshott 1981a: F. E. Sparshott. "Education in Music: Conceptual Aspects." In *New Grove Dictionary of Music and Musicians*, vol. 6, 54-58. London: Macmillan, 1981.

Sparshott 1981b: Francis Sparshott. "The Problem of the Problem of Criticism." In Paul Hernadi, ed., *What Is Criticism?* Bloomington: Indiana University Press, 1981.

Stacey 1976: C. P. Stacey. *A Very Double Life*. Toronto: Macmillan, 1976.

Stalin 1951: Josef Stalin. *Marxism and Linguistics*. Excerpted in Lang and Williams 1972, 80-87.

Stein 1927: Leo Stein. *The ABC of Aesthetics*. New York: Boni and Liveright, 1927.

Steiner 1975: George Steiner. *After Babel*. London: Oxford University Press, 1975.

Stevenson 1938: C. L. Stevenson. "Persuasive Definitions." *Mind* 47, 1938, 331-350.

Stevenson 1944: C. L. Stevenson. *Ethics and Language*. New Haven: Yale University Press, 1944.

Stevenson 1957: C. L. Stevenson. "On 'What Is a Poem?' " *PR* 66, 1957, 329-362.

Stevenson 1962: C. L. Stevenson. "On the Reasons That Can Be Given for the Interpretation of a Poem." In Joseph Margolis, ed., *Philosophy Looks at the Arts*. 121-139. New York: Scribners, 1962.

Stokes 1965: Adrian Stokes. *The Invitation in Art*. London: Tavistock Publications, 1965.

Stolnitz 1959: Jerome Stolnitz. *Aesthetics and the Philosophy of Art Criticism*. Boston: Houghton Mifflin, 1959.

Stolnitz 1961: Jerome Stolnitz. "On the Origins of 'Aesthetic Disinterestedness.' " *JAAC* 20, 1961, 131-143.

Stravinsky 1936: Igor Stravinsky. *Stravinsky: An Autobiography*. New York: Simon and Schuster, 1936.

Stravinsky 1942: Igor Stravinsky. *The Poetics of Music in Six Lessons*. Translated by Arthur Knodel and Ingolf Dahl. New York: Vintage Books, 1956.

Strawson 1959: P. F. Strawson. *Individuals*. London: Methuen, 1959.

Stuckenschmidt 1959: H. H. Stuckenschmidt. *Arnold Schoenberg*. Translated by Edith Temple Roberts and Humphrey Searle. London: Calder, 1959.

Suits 1978: Bernard Suits. *The Grasshopper*. Toronto: University of Toronto Press, 1978.

Sullivan 1927: J. W. N. Sullivan. *Beethoven*. Harmondsworth: Penguin Books, 1949.

Sze 1963: Mai-Mai Sze. *The Tao of Painting*. Princeton: Princeton University Press, 1963.

Tanner 1968: Michael Tanner. "Objectivity in Aesthetics." *PAS* Supp. vol. 42, 1968, 55-72.

Thomas 1952: Dylan Thomas. *Collected Poems 1934-1952*. London: Dent, 1952.

Tilghman 1970: B. R. Tilghman. *The Expression of Emotion in the Visual Arts*. The Hague: Martinus Nijhoff, 1970.

Tolstoy 1898: Leo Tolstoy. *What Is Art?* Translated by Aylmer Maude. London: Oxford University Press, 1930.

Tomas 1958: Vincent Tomas. "Creativity in Art." *PR* 67, 1958, 1-15.

Tomkins 1965: Calvin Tomkins. *The Bride and the Bachelors*. London: Weidenfeld and Nicolson, 1965.

Tormey 1971: Alan Tormey. *The Concept of Expression*. Princeton: Princeton University Press, 1971.

Tracy 1969: Theodore Tracy. *Physiological Theory and the Doctrine of the Mean in Plato and Aristotle*. The Hague: Mouton, 1969.

Trevor-Roper 1970: Patrick Trevor-Roper. *The World through Blunted Sight*. London: Thames and Hudson, 1970.

Trotsky 1923: Leon Trotsky. *Literature and Revolution*. New York: Russell and Russell, n.d.

Turbayne 1962: Colin M. Turbayne. *The Myth of Metaphor*. New Haven: Yale University Press, 1962.

Ueda 1967: Makoto Ueda. *Literary and Art Theories in Japan*. Cleveland: Case Western Reserve Press, 1967.

Urmson 1957: J. O. Urmson. "What Makes a Situation Aesthetic?" *PAS* Supp. vol. 31, 1957, 75-92.

Urmson 1977: J. O. Urmson. "Literature." In Dickie and Sclafani 1977, 334-341.

Valéry 1935: Paul Valéry. "Degas Dance Drawings." In Valéry 1960.

Valéry 1958: Paul Valéry. *The Art of Poetry*. Translated by Denise Folliot. *Collected Works*, vol. 7. New York: Vintage Books, 1961.

Valéry 1960: Paul Valéry. *Degas Manet Morisot*. Translated by David Paul. *Collected Works*, vol. 12. New York: Pantheon, 1960.

Valéry 1964: Paul Valéry. *Aesthetics*. Translated by Ralph Manheim. *Collected Works*, vol. 13. New York: Pantheon, 1964.

Vasari 1550: Giorgio Vasari. *Lives of the Painters, Sculptors and Architects*. Translated by A. B. Hinds. London: Dent, 1963.

Veblen 1899: Thorstein Veblen. *The Theory of the Leisure Class*. New York: Macmillan, 1889.

Venturi 1964: Lionello Venturi. *History of Art Criticism*. Translated by Charles Marriott. 2d ed. New York: Dutton, 1964.

Vico 1744: Giambattista Vico. *New Science*. 3d ed. Translated by Thomas G. Bergin and Max H. Fisch. Ithaca: Cornell University Press, 1948.

Von Wright 1963: G. H. Von Wright. *Varieties of Goodness*. London: Routledge and Kegan Paul, 1963.

Walter 1951: W. Grey Walter. "Activity Patterns in the Human Brain." In L. L. Whyte, ed., *Aspects of Form*, 179-195. Bloomington: Indiana University Press, 1951.

Walton 1973: Kendall Walton. "Pictures and Make-Believe." *PR* 72, 1973, 283-319.

Walton 1978: Kendall Walton. "Fearing Fictions." *JP* 75, 1978, 5-27.

Warburton 1809: [William Warburton]. *Letters from a Late Eminent Prelate to One of His Friends*. New York: E. Sargeant, 1809.

Warnock 1976: Mary Warnock. *Imagination*. Berkeley: University of California Press, 1976.

Weitz 1956: Morris Weitz. "The Role of Theory in Aesthetics." *JAAC* 15, 1956, 27-35.

Weitz 1964: Morris Weitz. *Hamlet and the Philosophy of Literary Criticism*. Chicago: University of Chicago Press, 1964.

Weitz 1970: Morris Weitz. "Genre and Style." In Howard Kiefer and Milton K. Munitz, eds., *Perspectives in Education, Religion, and the Arts*. Albany: State University of New York Press, 1970.

Weitz 1973: Morris Weitz. "Wittgenstein's Aesthetics." In Dickie and Sclafani 1977, 474-483.

Wellek 1955: René Wellek. *History of Modern Criticism*, vol. 2. New Haven: Yale University Press, 1955.

Wellek 1963: René Wellek. *Concepts of Criticism*. New Haven: Yale University Press, 1963.

Wellek and Warren 1949: René Wellek and Austin Warren. *Theory of Literature*. New York: Harvest Books, 1956.

Willett 1971: Frank Willett. *African Art*. New York: Praeger, 1971.

Williams 1962: William Carlos Williams. "Asphodel, That Greeny Flower." In his *Pictures from Brueghel and Other Poems*. Norfolk: New Directions, 1962.

Wilshire 1977: Donna Wilshire. Review of Gloria Orenstein, *The Theater of the Marvellous. JAAC* 35, 1977, 497-499.

Wilson 1962: Edmund Wilson. *The Triple Thinkers*. Harmondsworth: Penguin, 1962.

Wimsatt 1976: W. K. Wimsatt. *The Day of the Leopard*. New Haven: Yale University Press, 1976.

710

Wittgenstein 1953: Ludwig Wittgenstein. *Philosophical Investigations.* Translated by G. E. M. Anscombe. Oxford: Blackwell, 1953.

Wittgenstein 1966: Ludwig Wittgenstein. *Lectures and Conversations on Aesthetics, Psychology and Religious Belief.* Edited by Cyril Barrett. Oxford: Blackwell, 1966.

Wittkower and Wittkower 1969: Rudolf Wittkower and Margot Wittkower. *Born under Saturn: The Character and Conduct of Artists.* New York: Norton, 1969.

Wolfe 1975: Thomas K. Wolfe. "Painted Word." *Harper's* 250, April 1975, 57-92.

Wollen 1969: Peter Wollen. *Signs and Meaning in the Cinema.* London: Secker and Warburg, 1969.

Wollheim 1965: Richard Wollheim. *On Drawing an Object.* London: H. K. Lewis, 1965.

Wollheim 1968: Richard Wollheim. *Art and Its Objects.* New York: Harper and Row, 1968.

Woods 1974: John Woods. *The Logic of Fiction.* Atlantic Heights: Humanities Press, 1974.

Xenakis 1971: Iannis Xenakis. *Formalized Music: Thought and Mathematics in Composition.* Bloomington: Indiana University Press, 1971.

Yates 1966: Frances A. Yates. *The Art of Memory.* London: Routledge and Kegan Paul, 1966.

Yeats 1950: W. B. Yeats. *Collected Poems.* 2d ed. London: Macmillan, 1950.

Young 1759: Edward Young. *Conjectures on Original Composition.* Leeds: Scolar Press, 1966.

Zemach 1975: Eddy M. Zemach. "Description and Depiction." *Mind* 84, 1975, 567-578.

Ziff 1953: Paul Ziff. "The Task of Defining a Work of Art." *PR* 62, 1953, 58-78.

Zis 1977: Avner Zis. *Foundations of Marxist Aesthetics.* Moscow: Progress Publishing House, 1977.

Zuccaro 1607: Federico Zuccaro. *L'Idea de' Pittori, scultori ed architetti.* Torino, 1607. Cited from Panofsky (1968).

INDEX

abilities, 137

Abraham, Gerald, 606

absurdity, 118

academicism, 515-17, 549

act, identity of, 520

acting, 80, 539-40

action, 139

action painting, 563, 653

actions, 35

activities, 37-38

activity as art, 441

Addison, J., 142, 508

Adorno, T. W., 503, 508, 636; on art history, 558, 606, 649, 659; asceticism of, 551, 658-59; on autonomy of art, 201-202, 423-24; on concept of art, 505, 507; on Lukács, 548; on Vienna, 615, 673

Aesop at Tunbridge, 671

aesthetic, 104, 127-30, 244, 467-86; attitude, 469-71; concepts, 481-82; education, 484-85; emotion, 474-76; experience, 472-74; judgment, 208-216, 315, 482-83; object, 150-51, 479-81; perception, 476-77; pleasure, 471-72; qualities, 208-210, 478-79; theory, 485-86

aesthetics, 15-17, 128, 503-504, 507-508

Affektenlehre, 596

agent, 153

"ah"-ness, 549

Alain, 488, 531, 679

Albano, F., 615

Albee, E., 224-25

Alberti, L. B., 546, 582-83

Aldrich, V., 152, 477

alethic arts, 489-92

Alexander, S., 443

Alice in Wonderland, 257

allographic and autographic arts, 578, 580

Ames, V. M., 586

Anscombe, G.E.M., 520

antiart, 426, 428-33, 437

Antiochus, 654

anything can be. beautiful, 120-21, 124

apes as artists, 153, 567, 632

Apollonian art, 203-204, 591

application of skill, 50-51

appraisal, 500

appreciation, 103-104, 151-52, 208-210, 500

archetype, 176

architecture, 91-92, 95, 170, 384, 577

Arendt, H., 288, 531-32, 640, 673

Arensberg, W. C., 669

Aries, P., 639

Aristophanes, 659

Aristotle: on action, 139, 513; on art and form, 302; on art as imitative, 81; on art and prudence, 273; on arts, 26, 28-29, 31-32, 64, 69, 525, 531, 554; behaviorism of, 512; on end of fine arts, 134; on equity, 50, 52; *Ethics* of, 517, 518, 616, 682; on evaluation, 262; on fame, 300; on making, 519; on matter, 107; *Metaphysics* of, 517, 554-55, 575; on movement and activity, 521; on nature, 540-41; on participation, 277; on pleasures, 101, 551; *Poetics* of, 35, 526, 542, 550, 558; *Politics* of, 592, 613, 626; on rationality, 310-11, 330; on verbalization and skill, 32

Arnheim, R., 93, 640

art: and civilization, 284; classical concept of, 10, 25-57; in classical line, 293-96; as conspicuous expression, 348-49; and craft, 518; evident

726

LIBRARY OF CONGRESS CATALOGING IN PUBLICATION DATA

Sparshott, Francis Edward, 1926-
    The theory of the arts.

    Includes bibliographical references and index.
    1. Arts—Philosophy.   2.   Aesthetics.
I.   Title.
BH39.S634   700′.1   82-5333
ISBN 0-691-07266-3   AACR2
ISBN 0-691-10130-2 (lim. pbk. ed.)